QUEEN MARY

James Pope-Hennessy was a writer of unusual range and beguilingly fluent style. He was born in 1916 and educated at Downside and Balliol College, Oxford. From 1947 to 1949 he was literary editor of *The Spectator*. By then, he had already decided that writing was his vocation, and for the rest of his life he earned his living by the pen. He died in 1974.

Also by James Pope-Hennessy

London Fabric

America Is an Atmosphere

Aspects of Provence

Monckton Miles (2 volumes)

Sins of the Fathers (Phoenix Press)

Anthony Trollope

QUEEN MARY
1867–1953

James Pope-Hennessy

PHOENIX
PRESS

5 UPPER SAINT MARTIN'S LANE
LONDON
WC2H 9EA

A PHOENIX PRESS PAPERBACK

First published in Great Britain
by George Allen and Unwin Limited in 1959
This paperback edition published in 2000
by Phoenix Press,
a division of The Orion Publishing Group Ltd,
Orion House, 5 Upper St Martin's Lane,
London WC2H 9EA

Copyright © James Pope-Hennessy, 1959

A CIP catalogue record for this book
is available from the British Library.

Printed in Great Britain by
Clays Ltd, St Ives plc

ISBN 1 84212 032 8

CONTENTS

ILLUSTRATIONS

1. Portraits of H R H Princess Mary Adelaide, Duchess of Teck and of H S H Francis, Duke of Teck, *circa* 1866
(From the paintings by Henry Weigall, Jr., in the possession of the 2nd Marquess of Cambridge)

2. H R H the Duchess of Teck with her daughter Princess May and two elder sons, 1873; two photographs of Princess May of Teck in 1874
(From photographs by W. and D. Downey, by permission of *The Radio Times* Hulton Picture Library)

3. Duke Alexander of Württemberg, father of the Duke of Teck
(From the painting in the possession of the 2nd Marquess of Cambridge)

   Princess Catherine of Württemberg
(From a photograph in the possession of H R H the Princess of Wied, Princess of Württemberg)

4. Schloss Rumpenheim, near Offenbach
(From a gouache drawing in the Royal Library at Windsor Castle)

5. H R H Princess Augusta, Duchess of Cambridge
(From the portrait painted by Heinrich von Angeli in 1877 and now at Windsor Castle. By gracious permission of Her Majesty the Queen)

6. Princess May of Teck with her three brothers, *circa* 1886
(From a photograph in the possession of Mr. T. Baylis)

7. H R H the Duchess of Teck with Princess May in the garden at White Lodge, *circa* 1888
(From a photograph by R. Craigie)

8. Princess May of Teck in 1890
(From a photograph by Russell & Sons in the possession of H H Prince Wolfgang of Hesse)

9. H R H the Duchess of Teck with Princess May, Prince Adolphus, and Prince Alexander of Teck. The fifth member of the group is Princess Louise of Wales
(From a photograph taken at St. Moritz 1887)

   Princess May with her elder brothers Prince Adolphus and Prince Francis of Teck in the garden at White Lodge, June 1891
(From a photograph in Queen Mary's album)

10. Prince Albert Victor, Duke of Clarence, outside Marlborough House in June 1890. The Duke of Clarence is flanked by two members of his staff.
(From a photograph; by permission of *The Radio Times* Hulton Picture Library)

NUMERICAL REFERENCES

The general reader is warned that the frequent numerical references after quotations in the text of this book are solely for the benefit of students. The notes to which these small numerals refer give only sources and dates, and are to be found at the end of the book, on pp. 625–670.

When, in August 1955, I was invited to undertake this work, the private papers of Her Majesty the late Queen Mary had already been removed from Marlborough House to the Royal Archives at Windsor Castle, where they are still being catalogued. By gracious permission of Her Majesty the Queen I have been given unrestricted access to these papers, as well as to all other relevant material in the Royal Archives. These manuscript sources included:

1. Queen Mary's Diaries, kept daily from 1891 until the year of her death, 1953. There is also a solitary volume for the year 1884.

2. The Diaries of King George V.

3. The letters exchanged between King George V and Queen Mary.

4. The Diaries and letters of Queen Victoria; the Journals and letters of Princess Mary Adelaide, Duchess of Teck, and the letters of her husband, Francis, 1st Duke of Teck; the letters of Princess Augusta Caroline, Grand Duchess of Mecklenburg-Strelitz, of King Edward VII, of Queen Alexandra, of the Empress Frederick, of Prince Albert Victor, Duke of Clarence and of other members of the Royal Family.

5. The letters of Queen Mary to her friends, returned to her upon their deaths.

6. The letters and papers of Prince Adolphus, 2nd Duke of Teck and, after 1917, 1st Marquess of Cambridge, deposited in the Royal Archives by his son, the present Marquess.

I have also been kindly allowed to make use of certain material outside the Royal Archives, including:

1. *The Athlone Papers.* These comprise letters of Queen Mary's parents, of Queen Mary herself and of her elder brothers, to Prince Alexander George of Teck, later Earl of Athlone. They are in the possession of Her Royal Highness Princess Alice, Countess of Athlone, who has generously allowed me to have access to them.

2. *The Papers of His Royal Highness the Duke of Windsor.* These papers, which comprise the letters of King George V, of Queen Mary and of other members of the Royal Family to the Duke of Windsor are in His Royal Highness's possession in France, where he has given me every facility to work at them.

3. *The Kronberg Archives.* These consist of the letters of Queen Victoria to the Empress Frederick, as well as the Empress's correspondence with her own children, and are preserved at Schloss Friedrichshof, Kronberg, near Frankfurt-am-Main. For permission to make use of these archives I am indebted to His Royal Highness, Prince Philip, Landgrave of Hesse (Cassel).

These main sources of unpublished manuscript material I have supplemented by reference to further collections in private hands, the most notable being the papers of Mrs Charles Hunt, of the late Sir Dominic Colnaghi, and of the late Lady Bertha Dawkins.

I have also consulted many published works on the history of the period covered by this book, as well as a considerable number of biographies and volumes of memoirs. Of these I should mention in particular the *Memoir* (in two volumes) of Queen Mary's mother, the Duchess of Teck, by C. Kinloch Cooke, published in 1900; the *Personal Memoir* of King George V by Mr John Gore, and the *Life and Reign* of the same monarch by Sir Harold Nicolson; and the *Life and Reign* of King George VI by Sir John Wheeler-Bennett.

The writer of a biography of a personage recently dead has one advantage over those writing about some figure in the remote past: he can consult, and speak with, the surviving relations, friends, and—in the case of Royalty—members of the staff of his subject. If I follow the discreet example of Mr Gore, Sir Harold Nicolson and Sir John Wheeler-Bennett and do not set down the names of all the many, many people who have helped me in this way, it is not for want of gratitude but simply that the list would be too long. I must, however, record the faultless kindness and assistance which I have received from the members of Queen Mary's family, both in this country and abroad.

Only those who have been privileged to work in the Royal Archives at Windsor Castle can realise how much this book owes to the experience and the amiable personal interest of Sir Owen Morshead, now Librarian Emeritus at Windsor, as well as to the patience and co-operation of his successor as Librarian and Deputy-Keeper of the

Royal Archives, Mr Robert Mackworth-Young and his staff, most notably Miss Leta Smith, Miss Hedley, Miss Price Hill, and Mrs Lawrence Morshead. For constructive but unsparing criticism, and for constant encouragement in my work on this book I am also vastly indebted to Sir Alan Lascelles, Private Secretary and Keeper of the Archives to King George VI and to Queen Elizabeth II.

During the three years in which I have been working on this biography I have indeed been lucky to have had the assistance of Mrs Gordon Waterfield. Without the aid of Mrs Waterfield's precision, power of concentration and total understanding of the book's aims, it would never have appeared in its present form. I should also like to thank Mr Rudolf Kandaouroff for the exactitude with which he has prepared the genealogical tables and helped in many other ways during the writing of this book, as well as Miss Jillian Moore, of the Royal Geographical Society, for the skill with which she has drawn the map.

JAMES POPE-HENNESSY

Hagnau-am-Bodensee
Abbey Leix, Ireland
Villa Isolana, Lido-Venezia
Hotel Schwan, Gmunden
9 Ladbroke Grove, London

January 1956–February 1959

GENEALOGICAL TABLES

Table I

DESCENT OF KING GEORGE V AND QUEEN MARY FROM GEORGE III

Table showing the relationship of Queen Victoria to the Cambridge family and the kinship of Princess Victoria Mary Teck – later Queen Mary – to her husband Prince George, Duke of York – later King George V – as descendants of George III.

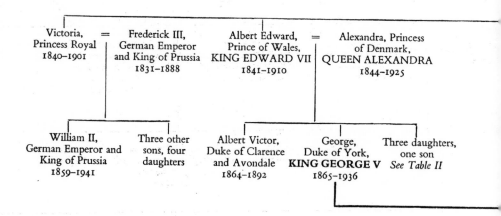

| Victoria, Princess Royal 1840–1901 | = | Frederick III, German Emperor and King of Prussia 1831–1888 | Albert Edward, Prince of Wales, KING EDWARD VII 1841–1910 | = | Alexandra, Princess of Denmark, QUEEN ALEXANDRA 1844–1925 |

| William II, German Emperor and King of Prussia 1859–1941 | Three other sons, four daughters | Albert Victor, Duke of Clarence and Avondale 1864–1892 | George, Duke of York, KING GEORGE V 1865–1936 | Three daughters, one son *See Table II* |

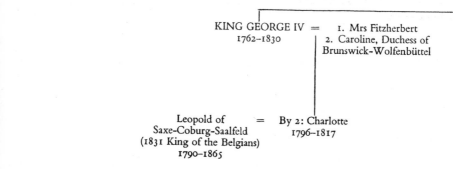

KING GEORGE IV = 1. Mrs Fitzherbert
1762–1830   2. Caroline, Duchess of
                      Brunswick-Wolfenbüttel

Leopold of   = By 2: Charlotte
Saxe-Coburg-Saalfeld   1796–1817
(1831 King of the Belgians)
1790–1865

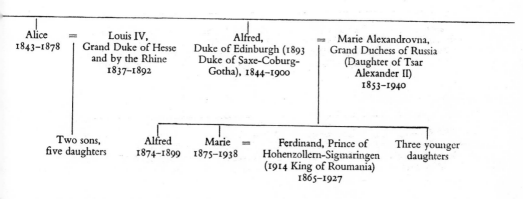

Alice   =   Louis IV,   Alfred,   =   Marie Alexandrovna,
1843–1878   Grand Duke of Hesse   Duke of Edinburgh (1893   Grand Duchess of Russia
             and by the Rhine   Duke of Saxe-Coburg-   (Daughter of Tsar
             1837–1892   Gotha), 1844–1900   Alexander II)
                                                                  1853–1940

Two sons,   Alfred   Marie =   Ferdinand, Prince of   Three younger
five daughters   1874–1899   1875–1938   Hohenzollern-Sigmaringen   daughters
                                          (1914 King of Roumania)
                                          1865–1927

Table I continued

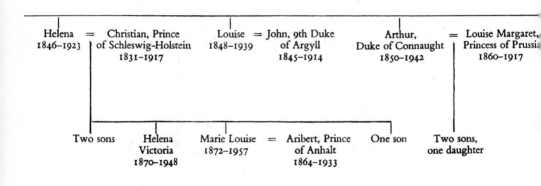

Frederick, = Frederica, KING WILLIAM IV = Adelaide,
Duke of York Princess of 1765–1837 Princess of
1763–1803 Prussia Saxe-Meiningen
1767–1840 1792–1849

Helena = Christian, Prince Louise = John, 9th Duke Arthur, = Louise Margaret,
1846–1923 of Schleswig-Holstein 1848–1939 of Argyll Duke of Connaught Princess of Prussia
1831–1917 1845–1914 1850–1942 1860–1917

Two sons Helena Marie Louise = Aribert, Prince One son Two sons,
Victoria 1872–1957 of Anhalt one daughter
1870–1948 1864–1933

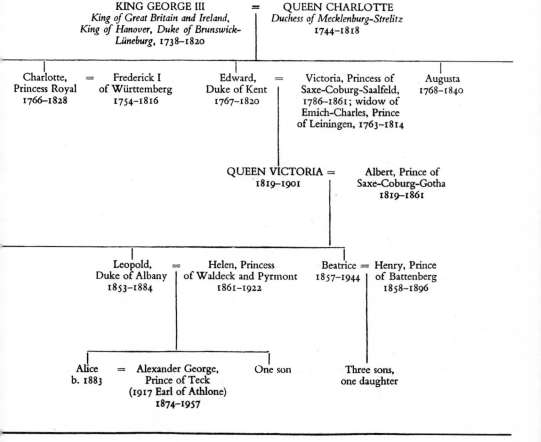

KING GEORGE III = **QUEEN CHARLOTTE**
King of Great Britain and Ireland, *Duchess of Mecklenburg-Strelitz*
King of Hanover, Duke of Brunswick- 1744–1818
Lüneburg, 1738–1820

Charlotte, = Frederick I   Edward, = Victoria, Princess of   Augusta
Princess Royal   of Württemberg   Duke of Kent   Saxe-Coburg-Saalfeld,   1768–1840
1766–1828   1754–1816   1767–1820   1786–1861; widow of
                                         Emich-Charles, Prince
                                         of Leiningen, 1763–1814

QUEEN VICTORIA = Albert, Prince of
1819–1901   Saxe-Coburg-Gotha
               1819–1861

Leopold, = Helen, Princess   Beatrice = Henry, Prince
Duke of Albany   of Waldeck and Pyrmont   1857–1944   of Battenberg
1853–1884   1861–1922   1858–1896

Alice = Alexander George,   One son   Three sons,
b. 1883   Prince of Teck   one daughter
     (1917 Earl of Athlone)
     1874–1957

Table I continued

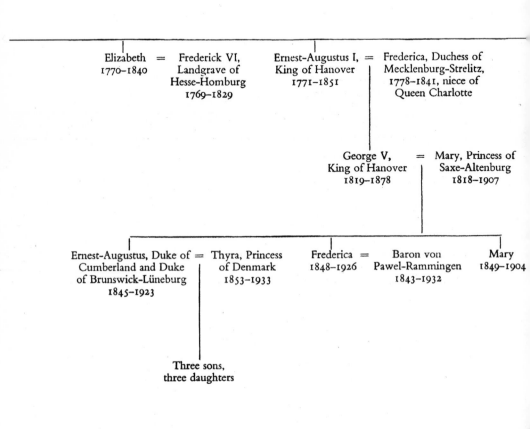

Elizabeth = Frederick VI,
1770–1840   Landgrave of
            Hesse-Homburg
            1769–1829

Ernest-Augustus I, = Frederica, Duchess of
King of Hanover   Mecklenburg-Strelitz,
1771–1851   1778–1841, niece of
                     Queen Charlotte

George V,   = Mary, Princess of
King of Hanover   Saxe-Altenburg
1819–1878   1818–1907

Ernest-Augustus, Duke of = Thyra, Princess
Cumberland and Duke   of Denmark
of Brunswick-Lüneburg   1853–1933
1845–1923

Frederica = Baron von
1848–1926   Pawel-Rammingen
            1843–1932

Mary
1849–1904

Three sons,
three daughters

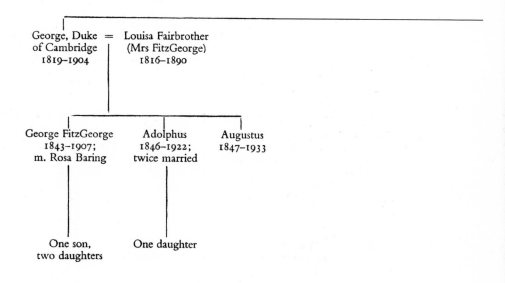

Augustus,   =   1. Lady Augusta Murray
Duke of Sussex   1768–1830
1773–1843   2. Lady Cecilia Gore,
                 Duchess of Inverness
                    1788–1873

George, Duke = Louisa Fairbrother
of Cambridge   (Mrs FitzGeorge)
1819–1904   1816–1890

George FitzGeorge   Adolphus   Augustus
1843–1907;   1846–1922;   1847–1933
m. Rosa Baring   twice married

One son,   One daughter
two daughters

Table I continued

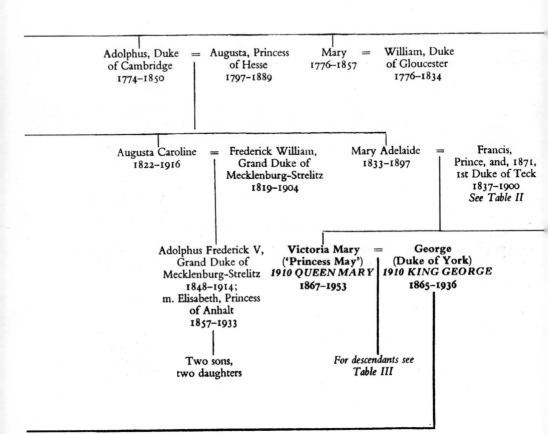

Adolphus, Duke = Augusta, Princess   Mary = William, Duke
of Cambridge   of Hesse   1776–1857   of Gloucester
1774–1850   1797–1889   1776–1834

Augusta Caroline = Frederick William,   Mary Adelaide = Francis,
1822–1916   Grand Duke of   1833–1897   Prince, and, 1871,
Mecklenburg-Strelitz   1st Duke of Teck
1819–1904   1837–1900
See Table II

Adolphus Frederick V,   **Victoria Mary** = **George**
Grand Duke of   **('Princess May')**   **(Duke of York)**
Mecklenburg-Strelitz   *1910 QUEEN MARY*   *1910 KING GEORGE*
1848–1914;   **1867–1953**   **1865–1936**
m. Elisabeth, Princess
of Anhalt
1857–1933

Two sons,   *For descendants see*
two daughters   *Table III*

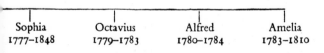

Sophia	Octavius	Alfred	Amelia
1777–1848	1779–1783	1780–1784	1783–1810

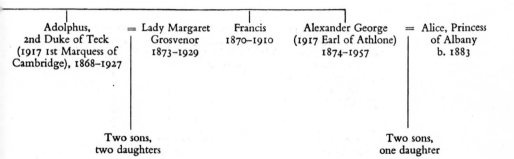

| Adolphus, 2nd Duke of Teck (1917 1st Marquess of Cambridge), 1868–1927 | = Lady Margaret Grosvenor 1873–1929 | Francis 1870–1910 | Alexander George (1917 Earl of Athlone) 1874–1957 | = Alice, Princess of Albany b. 1883 |

Two sons, two daughters

Two sons, one daughter

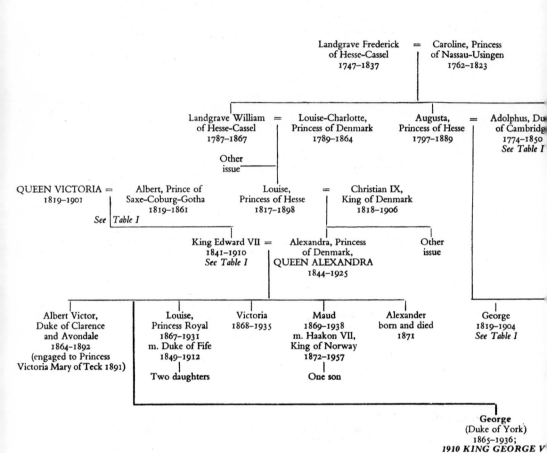

Landgrave Frederick = Caroline, Princess
of Hesse-Cassel   of Nassau-Usingen
1747–1837   1762–1823

Landgrave William = Louise-Charlotte,   Augusta,   = Adolphus, Du
of Hesse-Cassel   Princess of Denmark   Princess of Hesse   of Cambridg
1787–1867   1789–1864   1797–1889   1774–1850
                                                                        See Table I
              Other
              issue

QUEEN VICTORIA =   Albert, Prince of   Louise,   =   Christian IX,   Other
1819–1901   Saxe-Coburg-Gotha   Princess of Hesse   King of Denmark   issue
                       1819–1861   1817–1898   1818–1906
        See Table I

                    King Edward VII =   Alexandra, Princess
                      1841–1910   of Denmark,
                      See Table I   QUEEN ALEXANDRA
                                           1844–1925

Albert Victor,   Louise,   Victoria   Maud   Alexander   George
Duke of Clarence   Princess Royal   1868–1935   1869–1938   born and died   1819–1904
and Avondale   1867–1931   m. Haakon VII,   1871   See Table I
1864–1892   m. Duke of Fife   King of Norway
(engaged to Princess 1849–1912   1872–1957
Victoria Mary of Teck 1891)
                      Two daughters   One son

                                                          George
                                                          (Duke of York)
                                                          1865–1936;
                                                          1910 KING GEORGE V

Table II

THE FURTHER KINSHIP OF KING GEORGE V AND QUEEN MARY

Table showing the ancestry of Queen Alexandria, the descendants, in the first generation, of King Edward VII and Queen Alexandria, and the descendants, in the first generation, of Francis, first Duke of Teck, and of Princess Mary Adelaide, Duchess of Teck. The Table shows also the parentage and sisters of Francis, first Duke of Teck.

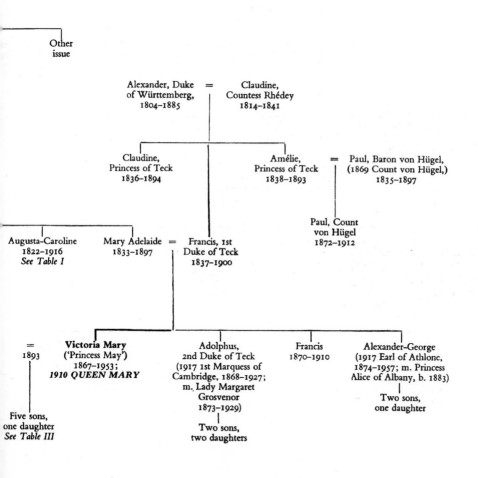

Table III

THE DESCENDANTS OF KING GEORGE V AND QUEEN MARY

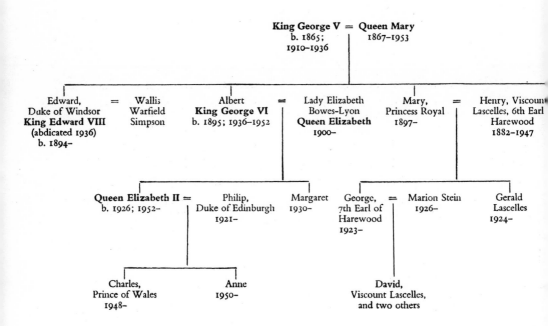

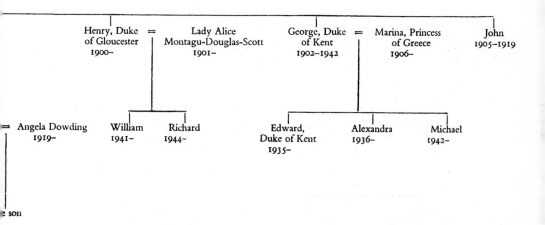

Henry, Duke = Lady Alice   George, Duke = Marina, Princess   John
of Gloucester   Montagu-Douglas-Scott   of Kent   of Greece   1905–1919
1900–   1901–   1902–1942   1906–

= Angela Dowding   William   Richard   Edward,   Alexandra   Michael
1919–   1941–   1944–   Duke of Kent   1936–   1942–
1935–

e son

22°
26°
54°
52°
50°
48°
NORTH SEA
SCHLESWIG
HOLSTEIN
Schw
MECK
HANOVER
Weser
Elbe
HOLLAND
BRUNSWICK
PRU
Rhine
WALDECK
Cassel
HESSE
WEIMAR
BELGIUM
MEININGEN
NASSAU
Homburg
Frankfurt
Hanau
Coburg
Main
Darmstadt
BADEN
Ludwigsburg
Stuttgart
BAV
WÜRTTEMBURG
FRANCE
Mu
Rhine
Friedrichshafen
L. Constance
Rorschach
L. Lucerne
Seelisburg
SWITZERLAND
St. Moritz
L. Geneva

THE GERMAN EMPIRE IN 1867
*Map designed to illustrate
the early travels of
Princess May of Teck*

BOOK ONE

PRINCESS MAY
1867–1893

THE WORLD OF
PRINCESS MAY OF TECK

NOTE: This short list is intended to aid the reader in identifying recurrent figures of Princess May's childhood and youth, particularly those referred to in quotations from letters by their family nicknames. The list covers the period 1867 to 1893, and contains no birth or death dates. For this as for all fuller information about these persons, the reader is recommended to the text, the footnotes, and the genealogical tables at the end of the volume.

———

PRINCESS MAY	*H S H Princess Victoria Mary of Teck*
Dolly, her eldest brother	*H S H Prince Adolphus of Teck*
Frank, her second brother	*H S H Prince Francis of Teck*
Alge, her third brother	*H S H Prince Alexander George of Teck*
Mama, their mother	*H R H Princess Mary Adelaide of Cambridge, Duchess of Teck*
Papa, their father	*H S H Prince Francis, Duke of Teck*
Grandmama	*H R H Princess Augusta of Hesse, Duchess of Cambridge, mother of the Duchess of Teck*
Geraldo	*Lady Geraldine Somerset, lady-in-waiting to the Duchess of Cambridge*
Aunt Augusta	*H R H Princess Augusta Caroline, Grand-Duchess of Mecklenburg-Strelitz, elder sister of the Duchess of Teck*
Uncle Fritz	*Frederick William, Grand Duke of Mecklenburg-Strelitz, the husband of above*
Dolphus	*Adolphus Frederick, Hereditary Grand Duke of Mecklenburg-Strelitz, only child of above*
Uncle George	*H R H Prince George, Duke of Cambridge, only brother of the Duchess of Teck*

Aunt Queen or Grandmama	*Her Majesty Queen Victoria, first cousin of the Duchess of Teck*
Uncle Bertie or Uncle Wales	*HRH Prince Albert Edward, Prince of Wales, eldest son of Queen Victoria*
Aunt Alix or Motherdear	*HRH Princess Alexandra of Denmark, Princess of Wales, wife of above*

'The Wales cousins'

Eddy	*HRH Prince Albert Victor, Duke of Clarence and Avondale, elder son of above*
Georgie	*HRH Prince George, Duke of York, second son of the Prince and Princess of Wales*
Louise	*HRH Princess Louise, eldest daughter of the Prince and Princess of Wales*
Toria	*HRH Princess Victoria, second daughter of the Prince and Princess of Wales*
Harry	*HRH Princess Maud, third daughter of the Prince and Princess of Wales*

Grosspapa	*Duke Alexander of Württemberg, an elderly widower, father of the Duke of Teck*
Aunt Claudine	*Princess Claudine of Teck, elder daughter of above*
Aunt Amélie	*Princess Amélie of Teck, Countess von Hügel, younger daughter of Duke Alexander*
Aunt Catherine	*Princess Frederic of Württemberg, widow of her first cousin, and related to the Duke of Teck*
Uncle Willy	*Prince William, son of above, a widower, and heir to the kingdom of Württemberg*
Affie	*Princess Pauline, only child of Prince William*
Georgiana, Lady Wolverton	*A rich friend and neighbour of the Duchess of Teck*
Peter	*Mr Peter Wells, a rich man-about-town in Florence*

Bianca	*Miss Bianca Light, a Florentine friend of the Duchess of Teck and owner of the Villa I Cedri*
Mr Thaddy	*Mr Thaddeus Jones, a lively young Irish painter*
Little Emily	*Miss Emily Alcock, a 'charming' American girl*
Girdie	*Mrs Mary Girdlestone, the Teck children's nurse*
Gutman	*Fräulein Gutman, Princess May's German governess*
Bricka, or 'good old Hélène'	*Mademoiselle Hélène Bricka, an Alsatian in charge of Princess May's later studies*

CHAPTER ONE

A MAY CHILD
AND HER PARENTS

ONE LATE April day in the year 1867 a letter from England reached Schloss Reinthal, the turreted, ochre-coloured castle of the von Hügel family, hidden in the fir woods of the Styrian hills, within an easy distance of Graz. Written to the châtelaine of Reinthal by her only brother, Prince Teck, this letter told her that his wife, the former Princess Mary Adelaide of Cambridge, was expecting their first child within a few weeks' time. The doctors had predicted 26 May as the date for the birth. 'I am looking over Kensington Palace', wrote Prince Teck, in German, from his mother-in-law's house at Kew, 'as I want to be established there by at least the 6th. . . . Let us hope that a nice baby will be born there in the lovely month of May.'[1]

Sure enough, with a precision that marked her actions throughout the course of her long life, the child did in fact appear in that lovely month and upon the very day the doctors named. The new baby was born just before midnight on 26 May, in the presence of her mother's sister, the Grand Duchess of Mecklenburg-Strelitz (who had driven across the Park from St James's Palace) and of her mother's close friends, the Duchesse d'Aumale and Lady Elizabeth Adeane. As the next day dawned over London, the Duchesse d'Aumale hastened off in her carriage through the flowery lanes of Kensington to Cambridge Cottage, Kew, there to give the first news of the birth to the child's German grandmother, the old Duchess of Cambridge, whilst 'Augusta Strelitz' remained with her sister at Kensington. There had been considerable anxiety about the event, since Princess Mary Adelaide, a personage of unusual girth, was already thirty-three, an age then considered dangerous for the bearing of a first child. 'Poor Mary,' the Crown Princess Frederick had written to Queen Victoria from Berlin in December 1866, 'it seems most alarming —with her size—and at her age—her prospects must fill her with fear.'[2]

So soon as the public announcement was made that morning in London more than one thousand persons flocked towards Kensington Palace to inscribe their names. For though Prince Teck himself was still scarcely known in London, Princess Mary Adelaide (whom he had married in the previous June) had a multitude of friends amongst the limited circle of rich or aristocratic persons who then comprised 'General Society'. She had managed to combine this purely social popularity with a gift for inspiring a wild affectionate enthusiasm amongst the London crowd, which relished 'Fat Mary's' stout, benevolent appearance and her jovial yet imperious manner. It was this gift which had never been entirely welcome to her first cousin, the retiring, six-years' widowed Queen.

By 5 June Princess Mary Adelaide was well enough to write herself to her husband's relatives at Reinthal: 'I have indeed much to be thankful for, lying as I do here with Baby in her cradle by me, Francis with *Yes** on his lap on the other side.'3 Because of the month in which the little girl was born her doting mother would refer to her as 'my May-flower' or, more simply, 'May'. The spring name caught. Long after she had married, in fact until the year in which her husband ascended the throne of England, the girl born on 26 May 1867, at Kensington Palace, was known affectionately to her friends and to the English public as 'Princess May'.

Word of Princess May's birth was immediately telegraphed to Queen Victoria, who was in the midst of her spring seclusion at Balmoral. But, prolific in royal circles, this spring of 1867 had already produced other infant competitors for the Queen's attention. At Marlborough House the Princess of Wales had given birth to a daughter, Louise, on 20 February, while Queen Victoria's own child Helena had just been delivered of a son, 'Christle'. It was this latter, Schleswig-Holstein, boy who was currently absorbing all the Queen's eager attention. Cousin Mary Teck's girl inevitably took second, if not third, place. 'Mary T[eck] is going on perfectly well (to everyone's astonishment) & it is a very fine child', the Queen wrote cursorily to the Crown Princess Frederick on 2 June. 'However nothing can beat Lenchen's Boy—who one really sees grow *daily*— He is a splendid fellow.'†4 In after years, when Princess May had

---

* 'Yes' was Princess Mary Adelaide's small dog.

† Known in the family as 'Lenchen', Helena, Princess of Great Britain and Ireland, was the third daughter and fifth child of Queen Victoria and the Prince Consort. Born in 1846, she married Christian, Prince of Schleswig-Holstein-

married the heir-presumptive to the throne, Queen Victoria would dwell upon the coincidence by which the girl had been born two days after the Queen's own birthday and, as she herself had been, at Kensington. 'I like to feel your birthday is so near mine, that you were born in the same House as I was & that you bear my name. It is very curious that it should be so',5 she wrote to her, for instance, in May 1896. But at the actual time the arrival of the Teck baby made little impact upon Queen Victoria, nor was she struck by its coincidental aspect. She nevertheless wrote to the mother with that genuine kindness that often characterised her behaviour, from Balmoral, on 4 June:

I send you today a quilt wh. Lenchen, Louise & I have worked for you (our names are put into it) with much pleasure and send you today [*sic*] hoping you may use it on your sofa. I need not repeat to you, my dearest Mary how *truly*, really happy I have been at your safe & prosperous confinement & the birth of your little girl. I have known & loved you dearly from your earliest *infancy*—my darling Husband was *very* fond of you—& your happiness has ever been very near my heart—& therefore my joy at this event is *most sincere*. Could my own dearest Husband but have witnessed it & be able to join me in visiting you at my poor old Home!6

The Queen had often had before, and was to have again, occasions to complain of her Cambridge cousin's dilatory habits in answering letters; once Princess Mary Adelaide got going on one of her voluminous 'journal-letters' few, if any, of her contemporaries in England could surpass her talent for amusing description, but it was the effort to begin a letter which daunted her, and the Queen was sometimes chagrined to find that her own missives were never given any special priority over the mass of general correspondence which flooded Princess Mary Adelaide's work-tables at Kensington Palace and at White Lodge. It was thus not until a fortnight later, and with an excuse which was somewhat lame, that Princess Mary sent her thanks for the Queen's present:

With a *rather shaky* hand and my feet under your quilt, [she wrote on 18 June] I take up for the *first* time my pen, to thank you, and that warmly and lovingly, for your charming gift, which I prize more than I can express as the joint work of those very dear to me; as well as for all your kind and tender interest in my safety and well-doing and pleasure at the birth of our dear little girl, whom I quite *long* to present to you. . . . with grateful

---

Sonderburg-Augustenburg (1831–1917) in 1866 and died in 1923. Their first child, Christian Victor, known as 'Christle', died in the South African War in 1900.

messages and love to Helena and Louise for their share in the *couvrepied*, I remain ever, in fond gratitude for all your *sisterly* kindness, Your devoted and most affectionate Cousin Mary Adelaide.7

Back at Windsor in June, Queen Victoria made one of her expeditions to London—rare at that period—to inspect the rival babies at Marlborough House and at Kensington. Princess Louise, the Prince of Wales's first daughter,* was pronounced to be a 'poor little Baby' with a cough, and not to 'look very strong'. At five o'clock on the same day on which she had thus confirmed her private theory that the Wales children were liable to be undersized and 'pigeon-breasted' ('the race will be a puny one which would have distressed darling Papa' she had written on an earlier occasion to her eldest daughter and confidante, the Crown Princess Frederick†8) the Queen set off again from Buckingham Palace, headed this time westwards in an open carriage and four through 'the densely crowded Park to see dear Mary Teck. It seemed so strange', she noted in her Journal 'to drive into the old courtyard and to get out at the door, the very knockers of which were old friends. My dear old home, how many memories it evoked walking through the well-known rooms!' Going up to the top of the house, to the big light bedroom in which she and her mother had slept in the years before her accession to the throne, the Queen there found Princess Mary Adelaide, 'Aunt Cambridge', and the baby. This last proved 'a *very* fine child, with quantities of hair —brushed up into a curl on the top of its head!—& very pretty features & a dark skin'. Seen again nearly a year later 'Mary T's baby' seemed 'a dear merry healthy Child, but not as handsome as she ought to be'.9 For the moment, however, the Kensington Palace infant seemed in every way superior to that lying in its bassinet at Marlborough House.

On this first visit to a child for whom, many years later, she was

* Louise, Princess of Great Britain and Ireland, born 1867, died 1931, married Alexander, Duke of Fife (1849–1912), in 1889. The third child and first daughter of Albert Edward, Prince of Wales, and his wife Alexandra, Princess Louise was created Princess Royal in 1905.

† Victoria, Princess Royal, born 1840, died 1901, was the eldest daughter of Queen Victoria and the Prince Consort. In 1858 she had married Frederick, Crown Prince of Prussia, who succeeded his father Wilhelm I as German Emperor and King of Prussia in 1888 and died ninety-nine days later of cancer of the throat. Queen Victoria's bi-weekly letters to this eldest daughter are preserved at Schloss Friedrichshof, Kronberg, and the Empress Frederick's replies are in the Royal Archives at Windsor Castle.

to develop a high admiration, the Queen was told of the burden of names provisionally selected for the baby to carry through life: Agnes Augusta Victoria Mary Louise Olga Pauline Claudine. 'Agnes after Franz's grandmother', she diligently noted, 'and Claudine after his mother, Augusta after Aunt Cambridge and Augusta Strelitz, and Victoria after me. I am to be one of the godparents.'[10] But when the baby was christened by the Archbishop of Canterbury at Kensington Palace on 27 July, the sequence of names had been for some reason rearranged. The list now read Victoria Mary Augusta Louise Olga Pauline Claudine Agnes. It seems likely that this new dispensation was the result of a determined effort by the old Duchess of Cambridge and her elder daughter the Grand Duchess of Mecklenburg-Strelitz. To both of these ladies the child's direct descent from King George III and her kinship with the reigning sovereign of Great Britain were far more significant than her morganatic Württemberg and Rhèdey ancestry on her father's side. According to this, the official Cambridge view, Prince Teck was indeed fortunate to have been allowed to marry a Princess of Great Britain and Ireland; for after the wedding they chose to forget their secret satisfaction at getting Princess Mary Adelaide married off at all. In any case if the changed order of Christian names was intended to flatter the Queen, it singularly failed to do so:

I must say I am *shocked* that you have been *worried out* of calling the Baby *Agnes*—such a pretty name [she wrote, from Osborne, on the christening day, to Princess Mary Adelaide] and *I* think the *father's* family ought *always* to be considered *first*. However *Mary* is of course dear to us—for your & dear At. Gloucester's sakes.[11]

This was not the first reprimand which Queen Victoria had felt bound to deliver to her younger Cambridge cousin. Nor was it to be, by a long way, the last.

II

We now tend to think of Queen Victoria in matriarchal terms, as head of a numerous family of English and German descendants. Yet when she first came to the throne, and indeed until her children had grown up and married, she had only three collaterals of her own generation in England*—the Cambridge cousins. These cousins were

* Her fourth collateral, George Prince of Cumberland (King of Hanover, 1851), born 1819, died 1878, was the son of Ernest Augustus, Duke of Cumberland

the children of the Queen's uncle, Adolphus, Duke of Cambridge, seventh son of George III. In the near-panic* caused by Princess Charlotte's death in 1817 (an event which suddenly left the English throne with no direct heir in the third generation) the Duke of Cambridge had married Augusta, Princess of Hesse, a daughter of Friedrich, Landgrave of Hesse-Cassel, and his wife Caroline, Princess of Nassau-Usingen. They had lived for many years in Hanover, where the Duke was Viceroy, returning to England at Queen Victoria's accession when Hanover was separated from the English Crown. There had thus been a brief period—between the death of William IV in 1837 and the birth of Queen Victoria's first child, the Princess Royal, in 1840—in which the Cambridge family were very high up in the line of succession to the English throne.

Adolphus, Duke of Cambridge, had died in 1850 and was succeeded in the Dukedom by his only son, George. This, the second and the last Duke of Cambridge, born in 1819, is remembered as having held the position of Commander-in-Chief of the British Army for a span of thirty-nine years, during which he consistently opposed every suggestion for modernisation or reform. In 1847 he had bewildered his mother and his sisters by contracting a private marriage with an actress, Louisa Fairbrother. Miss Fairbrother was subsequently known as Mrs FitzGeorge and bore the Duke three FitzGeorge sons, upon whom their little Teck cousins were taught to look askance. Despite this marriage, Queen Victoria continued on excellent terms with the Duke of Cambridge. His sisters she treated with a certain reserve, whilst their mother, 'Aunt Cambridge', inspired her with no special affection.

The Duchess of Cambridge was a large, stately German lady, with a heavy, rather coarse face, and thick black eyebrows which gave her what her niece Victoria called 'a severity of expression'. She wore shiny black pomatum on her hair, which was turned sleekly in beneath

(1771–1851), who became King of Hanover in 1837 and, as fifth son of George III, was (to the nation's horror) Queen Victoria's heir-presumptive until the birth of her first child, Victoria, Princess Royal.

* Of the seven sons of George III who survived infancy three, at the date of Princess Charlotte's death, were bachelors, and the four who were married were either childless or without lawful issue. Three rapid marriages were arranged: Adolphus, Duke of Cambridge, m. Augusta of Hesse-Cassel, 7 May 1818; Edward, Duke of Kent, m. Victoria of Saxe-Coburg-Saalfeld, widow of Prince Emich-Charles of Leiningen, 29 May 1818; and William, Duke of Clarence (afterwards William IV), m. Adelaide of Saxe-Meiningen, 11 June 1818.

an elaborate cap. Some people thought her proud and haughty, while others judged her 'one of those exceptional people who had the gift of winning hearts'.[12] She spoke English with a strong German accent. She was clever rather than highly educated, and had what was then called 'a sense of fun'. In her own household she was rated to have a perfect temper, to think of herself last, and to be remarkably industrious, since she liked knitting or doing needlework while her lady read to her aloud. Essentially formidable, and, in her latter years, a permanent invalid, the Duchess never succeeded in winning the hearts of her grandchildren, who resented the hours they had to spend in her rooms at St James's Palace, and who remembered to their dying day her 'stingy teas' of buns and rusks. Writing from Frogmore in 1909 to her Aunt Augusta Strelitz, Princess May reflected upon her own fear of her grandmother, the old Duchess of Cambridge:

I still meet older people sometimes who knew dear Grandmama & invariably talk so nicely of her. I wish I had been older to appreciate her properly, but in spite of her great kindness to us we were always rather afraid of her. . . . I know that if ever we had a chance of talking to her alone we loved listening to her interesting reminiscences but these talks were few and far between.[13]

To which her aunt replied that she wished:

You had been able really to know Grandmama; as it was you could not get in real contact with her, besides she looked and could be rather severe, with her firm old notions and principles, though her heart ever was full of love for all her belongings. . . .[14]

In 1843 the Duchess of Cambridge had successfully married off her elder daughter, Princess Augusta Caroline, to the son and heir of the Grand Duke of Mecklenburg-Strelitz, whose wife, the Grand Duchess Marie, had been a Princess of Hesse and was own sister to the Duchess of Cambridge herself. This marriage between first cousins meant that the elder Cambridge sister went to live in Strelitz, and, though she came over to London with her husband almost annually, and was on occasion importunate about having rooms of her own at St James's (which Queen Victoria refused to give her) or about crossing the Channel, as the Queen's daughters did, in a private steamer, she ceased to impinge greatly upon the Queen's consciousness.

In early days Princess Augusta Caroline had indeed caused Queen Victoria annoyance: 'she was altogether very jealous of my position in Society, as being very popular' Princess Augusta recalled in old age, in another letter to her niece Princess May in which she recounted 'a scene I had with the Queen at a small Ball in the Gallery during the Tsarevitch Alexander's stay in London, when he was more attentive to me than to her'. On her side Princess Augusta could not forgive the fact that 'Albert's German influence' had caused the title 'Princess of Great Britain and Ireland' to be changed, in the case of the Cambridge sisters, to 'Princess of Cambridge'—'giving to each the *Fathers* title for a *family* name, which is perfectly wrong'.[15] For Princess Augusta Caroline harboured strong feelings about her status as a granddaughter of George III: 'The Grand Duchess of Mecklenburg', wrote Queen Sophie of Holland in 1867,[16] 'is one of those who keep themselves in hot water about their rank and cannot bear the second place. . . . I always wonder when clever people dwindle away their lives with such petty preoccupations.'

Eight years after Princess Augusta's marriage, her younger sister Mary Adelaide made her debut, at the age of seventeen, at the official opening of the Great Exhibition. Chaperoned by the Queen's mother, the Duchess of Kent, she wore white roses 'with long branches of a lovely feathery kind of flower' on her head.[17] Soon she and her mother were, in Lord Redesdale's word, 'the only members of the Royal Family who were seen in general society' where 'their presence always gave pleasure. They were so gracious and unaffectedly gratified at any attempt to entertain them.'[18] Since she did not marry until 1866 there were fifteen long years—fifteen crowded London seasons—during which Princess Mary Adelaide and her mother ('the stout parties from Kew', as Lord Clarendon irreverently called them[19]) moved freely in Tory society in the metropolis. They themselves gave musical parties, small dances or receptions for the diplomatic corps at St James's Palace or at Cambridge Cottage, a pretty, simple house with handsome rooms for entertaining tacked on to it, on Kew Green. In this way 'the Cambridges' seemed to display a genial aspect of Royalty which was in contrast to the more formal atmosphere of Buckingham Palace and Windsor Castle, where the emphasis lay on the serious and the domestic sides of royal and family life. Theirs was a happy, kindly existence. It was filled with high-spirited gaiety. A large part of it was devoted to various practical charities. It was almost entirely independent of the Court.

This independence sometimes went too far, and was judged to amount to carelessness, if not to disrespect, as on an occasion in February 1863 when Princess Mary Adelaide, by omitting to attend a Drawing-Room, failed to perform her duty as a member of the Royal Family.

Whilst Her Majesty is always anxious to live upon the most friendly terms with the Duchess of Cambridge and Princess Mary [Sir Charles Phipps was told to write to Lord Granville, selected as a go-between in this 'unpleasant matter'] Her Majesty considers it to be a duty, from which She may not shrink, to maintain her own proper position, and to require those marks of proper respect and attention from all the members of the Royal family, which have always been acknowledged to be due, and which were always most Strictly insisted upon by Her Royal Uncles.

Lord Granville was asked to see the Duke of Cambridge and to remonstrate with him over his sister's behaviour; upon which the Duke 'alluded to the little the Duchess of Cambridge had seen of the Queen, and to their not knowing even now whether they were to be invited to the Castle, excepting for the marriage'.*[20]

It is episodes such as this which explain Queen Victoria's attitude of comparative detachment over the birth of her cousin's first child, Princess May.

III

Six months after their baby's birth, Princess Mary Adelaide and her husband were asked to dine and sleep at Windsor Castle one November night. It was thus that, in her long withdrawal from active life after the death of the Prince Consort, the Queen would from time to time summon those relations whom she wished to see. 'She is alas! grown enormous & has never recovered her strength', the Queen reported of her cousin, to Berlin, '—but they are very happy together; the Baby had a cold & cld therefore not come.' A fortnight later they were asked again, this time for two nights. They brought with them 'their little Baby—a dear spritely little thing—but not a *fine* or a remarkably handsome Child; but I am sure she *will* be pretty', wrote the Queen, adding: 'It is a *real* pleasure to see dear Mary now—she is so bright & happy & also her fine qualities come out to such advantage now that she is happy. But her *size* is fearful! It is *really* a misfortune.'[21]

Like most diminutive persons, Queen Victoria found anyone very much larger than herself a trifle oppressive. Yet there was no exag-

* i.e., the marriage of Albert Edward, Prince of Wales, and Princess Alexandra of Denmark, celebrated at St George's Chapel, Windsor, 10 March 1863.

geration in her references to her cousin Mary Adelaide's obesity. This handicap had long rendered Princess Mary Adelaide a problem piece upon the family chessboard: a Princess who had remained so long unmarried as to have begun to seem unmarriageable. When, therefore, in April 1866, Princess Mary Adelaide had accepted Prince Teck's offer of marriage (made in the Rhododendron Walk in Kew Gardens after what her sister called an 'incredibly short' acquaintanceship), the Queen and her whole family had breathed a sigh of relief. For it was supposed that several previous suitors from the Continent had been deterred by their first glimpse of Princess Mary's appearance.

The tragedy about this appearance, for a proud and intelligent girl, had been the sense that had she not been thoroughly stout she might have been distinctly beautiful. She was tall, and had ash-blonde hair with a pretty, natural wave in it, dark blue eyes fringed by dark lashes beneath dark brows, 'a creamy complexion', a sweet expression and beautiful teeth. She would look her best in a mourning dress, cut low at the bosom, with black garnets 'sparkling like black diamonds on her white neck'.[22] In 1857, when she was twenty-four, the American Minister to the Court of St James's estimated that this 'very fat, very thick-set and very proud young lady' must weigh at least two hundred and fifty pounds.[23] Another witness who sat near her in the theatre described her afterwards as 'that mountain of a girl', whilst the flippant world of the aristocracy referred to her as 'our domestic Embonpoint'. Surrey neighbours spoke of the way that the springs of a carriage would 'groan' as she entered it. Young officers were admired for the skill with which they could steer Princess Mary Adelaide through a complicated dance. Once, at a great ball at Orleans House, Twickenham, Princess Mary Adelaide, 'looking splendidly handsome with a wreath of purple grapes round her wavy hair', and dancing the Lancers with the Comte de Paris as partner, had collided with another girl and knocked her 'flat down' on her back.[24]

Princess Mary Adelaide was very fond of clothes and jewellery. Her favourite colour was blue, though as a young girl she often wore white, and went to one of her first Drawing-Rooms at Buckingham Palace in a crinoline trimmed with scarlet poppies and with scarlet poppies 'at the side of her head below the plumes and falling amongst the folds of the gold-spangled white tulle veil'.[25]

Members of Princess Mary Adelaide's family were painfully aware of the problems posed by her size. When the Empress Eugénie had suggested that 'la Princesse Marie de Cambridge' should marry Prince

Oscar of Sweden, Queen Victoria replied that Prince Oscar *'pourrait ne pas être content de se trouver engagé à une jeune Princesse . . . qui, quoique bien belle, spirituelle et bien instruite et possédant un excellent cœur est cependant plus forte que la plûpart des jeunes dames de son âge'.*[26] 'Meyer says that he knows both a horse and saddle which will suit you',[27] the Queen wrote tactfully to her cousin in 1853, when urging her to take riding lessons in Windsor Great Park. When the Duchess of Cambridge (travelling incognita as Lady Culloden) looked in on King Leopold on her way through Brussels in 1852, the old King scribbled off to his niece Queen Victoria: 'I found her extremely well and very curious, as usual, but poor Mary, such a beautiful child, is grown out of all *Compass*, to my great regret. Leopold, who is all longitude, was her neighbour and looked quite alarmed.'[28] Princess Mary Adelaide was at this time seventeen.

Photographs confirm these contemporary judgements, as do the memories of those still living who knew Princess Mary as Duchess of Teck. These eye-witnesses recall the Princess's quick, graceful movements, despite her bulk; the nimble way she stepped down from a carriage, the easy gesture with which she would give her hand to be kissed. It was a part of her charm that she herself made jokes about her weight and would allow small relatives to test it on her velvet-covered scales, or spontaneously demonstrate a tarantella to the dancing-class to which her daughter went. No member of the Royal Family could wave so valiantly from a carriage, and in any royal procession she was certain of the longest and the loudest cheer. Children adored her, for she was easy-going and high-spirited, impulsive and generous, and had no idea of time. This notorious unpunctuality, together with a total lack of any sense for money, were the cause of many of the troubles which her children shared and witnessed in their youth. They may be taken as the direct psychological reason for her daughter's equally notorious punctiliousness about time and for her sense of order. Her own letters, which, once begun, might run on for thirty or more pages, offer the surest evidence of Princess Mary Adelaide's exceptional, and wholly delightful, qualities of head and heart.

Queen Victoria, however, was both more sedate and more care-worn than her younger cousin. High spirits were never the key to the Queen's heart and, at a period when she herself had chosen virtually to disappear from public gaze, Princess Mary's popularity seemed ostentatious and almost deliberately sought. What were in fact a

B

genuine love of human beings, a compassionate reaction to want in any form, and a happy wish to please, were misinterpreted by the Queen and her immediate family. 'Mary is very popular, and justly so,' the Empress Frederick wrote to her mother in 1891, 'still I think she courts popularity perhaps more than sisters would care to do,—but I may be wrong!'[29]

The project for Princess Mary Adelaide to marry Prince Oscar, the second surviving son* of the King of Sweden and Norway, had, as we know, been invented by the Empress Eugénie, who first put it forward in a private letter to Queen Victoria in April 1856: '*J'ai pensé içi dans mon petit coin que la Princesse Marie de Cambridge a vingt-deux ans et que leurs âges et leurs positions réciproques vont bien ensemble et si cette petite combinaison convenait à Votre Majesté je me réjouirais d'avoir eu une idée qui put contribuer au bonheur d'un membre de Votre famille.*'[30] Queen Victoria had thereupon suggested that Prince Oscar and Princess Mary Adelaide had better meet. He came to London, saw her several times, and withdrew to Paris without having proposed. Further discreet enquiries revealed that he had no wish to marry Princess Mary, and in the following year he proposed to, and was accepted by, Sophie, Princess of Nassau.

Five months later, in September 1856, the fashionable Italian sculptor Marochetti, who had been much impressed by Princess Mary when she gave him sittings for a bust, was empowered by Cavour to bring her an official offer of marriage from the King of Sardinia. Passed on, with the Queen's sanction, to Princess Mary, who was then with her mother in Baden, this offer was refused by her on religious grounds: 'how would the announcement of the marriage of an English Princess (a Guelph) with a papist Sovereign be taken by John Bull?' she asked her brother.[31] The Duchess of Cambridge, who shared Lord Clarendon's fear that, to the Piedmontese, Princess Mary Adelaide might appear 'as a sort of Anne Boleyn', supported her daughter in her refusal. The Duchess was convinced that, once in Turin, Princess Mary would be poisoned by the Jesuits. This Sardinian tentative had at least the merit of being a genuine offer of marriage genuinely refused. It thus compensated somewhat for the mortification felt by Princess Mary Adelaide at the failure of Prince Oscar to come up to the mark—a failure known to London Society.

* Prince Oscar (1829–1907) succeeded his elder brother Charles XV as King of Sweden and Norway in 1872. It was as King Oscar II that he renounced the throne of Norway, which then became a separate kingdom, in 1905.

Three years before this, in 1853, the Queen and the Prince Consort, as well as the Duchess of Cambridge herself, had been disturbed at a secret feeler put out by Napoleon III that Princess Mary should marry his profligate cousin Napoleon, son of ex-King Jerome. On this occasion, also, religion had been pleaded as the reason for a refusal. In the light of this and of the Sardinian offer the Queen then decreed that no more Catholics could be considered, even were it the Archduke Leopold, whom the Crown Princess Frederick at one time put forward as a candidate: 'he is popular & bears a good reputation wh. with me goes before the rest'.[32] Other bridegrooms thought of over the years included Prince Edward of Saxe-Weimar, the Duke of Brunswick (strongly favoured by Queen Victoria: 'The Duke of Brunswick is the match for her & I wish we could bring it about'[33]), the Duke of Saxe-Meiningen, Prince William of Baden, Prince Waldemar of Holstein, Prince Nicholas of Nassau and Prince William of Hesse-Philippsthal-Barchfeld. 'Alas!' declared Lord Clarendon, who was personally sympathetic towards Princess Mary Adelaide and was always anxious to help her, 'no German Prince will venture on *so vast an undertaking.*'[34] Another factor was Princess Mary's manner, which stiff German princelings did not like. Recounting for Queen Victoria's benefit a conversation she had with Princess Mary Adelaide's brother in Berlin in September 1858, the Crown Princess of Prussia summed up this feeling:

Uncle George ... said also that when foreign Princes came to your Court, her Behaviour put him out a good deal; that she laughed & talked a gt. deal too much with other gentlemen, which together with her being so very tall & stout rather frightens people, he said a good deal of this was nervousness with her, & as she is no longer a child she cannot help being '*préoccupée*' with the idea of her future, & that makes her manner still less quiet & natural.[35]

Princess Mary herself now expressed 'a horror' of life at small German courts and stated categorically that she had no wish to leave her country. She was once or twice suspected of an emotion about some member of the English peerage, and was even thought to have proposed to Lord Skelmersdale, who was himself in love with his future wife, Lord Clarendon's favourite daughter Alice. But some such practical solution as this was likewise forbidden by the Queen, who considered that in such a union Princess Mary Adelaide 'would hardly have been able for many reasons to maintain her rank'[36]—a remark which offended the Cambridge family, and became still more vexing when the Queen's own daughter, Louise, was allowed to marry Lord Lorne.*

Putting a gallant face on her prolonged spinsterhood, Princess Mary Adelaide would assert, with her infectious laugh, that she was getting reconciled to becoming 'a jolly old maid', although to her brother she rather pathetically confessed to 'having occasionally indulged in gloomy dreams of an old-maidish future, coupled with a homely and dreary position'.[37] The Duke of Cambridge thought that 'some Younger Brother who need not be always in Germany & whom it might suit to live occasionally in England wd be the best husband';[38] but that had been in 1856, and ten years rolled by without Princess Mary Adelaide being any nearer the married state. 'Mary C. is looking old—& not thinner', Queen Victoria wrote in 1866; and again, in February of the same year: 'Mary C. is unaccountable—I always think she will marry some German *Kammerherr* or young officer! It wd really be the best thing.'[39]

Two months after this not very kind comment, Princess Mary Adelaide was engaged. Within another two she was married.

IV

His Serene Highness Prince Franz of Teck had been born in Vienna in 1837. He was thus four years younger than his bride. His father was Duke Alexander of Württemberg, who would have been heir-apparent to the reigning King of Württemberg if he had not made a morganatic marriage and thus forfeited his rights to the succession. It was in 1835 that Duke Alexander had married a beautiful Hungarian, Countess Rhèdey of Kis-Redé, who had then been created Countess Hohenstein. She bore him three children: Claudine, born in 1836; Franz, born in 1837; and Amélie, born in 1838. Three years after the birth of her third child Countess Hohenstein, on horseback, was watching a review of Austrian troops near Vienna. Her horse reared, and ran away with her. She was thrown, and trampled to death by a squadron of cavalry which happened to be passing at the gallop. Her

---

* Louise, Princess of Great Britain and Ireland, b. 1848, d. 1939, was the sixth child and fourth daughter of Queen Victoria and the Prince Consort. In 1871 she married John, Marquess of Lorne (1845–1914) but had no children. Lord Lorne refused the Queen's offer of a dukedom on his marriage, and in 1900 succeeded his father as tenth Duke of Argyll.

coffin was carried up into the mountain fastnesses of Transylvania, from which her family had sprung, and buried in the little rustic church of Erdó Szent-György. Sixty years later a wall-tablet to her memory was put up in the church by her granddaughter Queen Mary, then Princess of Wales.

Perhaps because of this sad and striking story, perhaps because of his own outstanding good looks, Countess Hohenstein's son Franz became, as he grew up in Vienna, a pet of the Emperor and Empress of Austria. He accompanied the ailing Empress Elizabeth to Madeira in 1860, when she travelled on board the *Victoria and Albert*, lent her by the Queen of England. As an officer in the Imperial Gendarmerie Guard, Count Hohenstein—so he was then called—witnessed the Battle of Solferino, in which he acted as an aide-de-camp to the commanding general of the Austrian troops. In 1863 he was made a Serene Highness and given the title of Prince of Teck, a subsidiary name of the Württemberg house.

As King Leopold of the Belgians was quick to point out to Queen Victoria, when sending on a message from the Orleans Queen Dowager of Württemberg about her young nephew's matrimonial aspirations, Prince Teck was not *ebenbürtig* (of equal birth) with Princess Mary Adelaide. This argument carried no weight with the Queen, whose views on morganatic blood were far ahead of those of continental royalties. 'I have always thought it & do think it very wrong & very absurd that because his Mother was not a Princess he is not to succeed in Württemberg just as much as the Battenbergs in Hesse',[40] she wrote once to Princess Mary Adelaide. A more palpable drawback, as the members of the Cambridge family observed to one another, was that Prince Teck was penniless. But the young man had one great, though of its essence, temporary advantage: at twenty-nine he was still exceedingly handsome. While good looks alone are not customarily supposed to form a really stable basis for a marriage, they have often been the cause of swift nuptial decisions and precipitate engagements. It was not for nothing that Prince Teck had been known to Viennese court society as *der schöne Uhlan*.

Princess Mary Adelaide's bridegroom was tall, well-built and elegant. His profile was much admired, he had a fine high forehead, beautiful eyes 'with a very pleasant, kind expression', waxed moustachios and a little tuft of an imperial beneath his lower lip. His hair was of so true a black that a lady in Vienna once said of him: 'his hair is not black it is dark blue'. 'Very nice & amiable, thoroughly unassuming

& very gentlemanlike & certainly very good looking', was Queen
Victoria's verdict on Prince Teck, when he went down to Osborne for
one night in April to be welcomed into the English Royal Family
'as a future cousin'. His dark good looks stirred the Queen to envy,
for in a letter to the Crown Princess of Prussia describing his
Osborne visit she continued:

> I do *wish* one cld find some more black eyed Pces or Pcesses for *our*
> Children!—I can't help thinking what dear Papa said—that it was in fact
> a blessing when there was some little *imperfection* in the *pure Royal* descent
> & that some fresh blood was infused. In Pce Teck's case this is a very good
> thing & so it is in Christian* only I wish his Mother had been dark.—For
> that constant fair hair & blue eyes makes the blood so lymphatic.—Dear
> Alix has added *no* strength to the family. . . . I must end for today, my
> somewhat *odd* letter, but it is *not* as *trivial* as you may think for darling
> Papa—*often* with vehemence said: 'We *must have some strong dark blood.*'

What Queen Victoria forgot, and Princess Mary Adelaide did not yet
know, is that persons with strong, dark blood are sometimes subject
to strong, dark rages. There were many occasions during her thirty-
one years of married life when Princess Mary might well have wished
that her husband had been a little more 'lymphatic'.

At a later period, when Prince Teck came under rather heavy fire
from his wife's family on account of her well-known extravagance,
some of his own friends like Prince Edward of Saxe-Weimar declared
that he had been 'regularly dragged into' the marriage by the Cambridges. He himself, when driven hard, once remarked that, had he
wished, he could have married an English north-country heiress with
eighty thousand pounds a year instead of Princess Mary.[42] It is only
fair to the Cambridge family to remember that, while they welcomed
Teck with open arms, the original initiative had been his, not theirs.
In this he had been abetted by the Prince and Princess of Wales,
who had taken a fancy to him on the Continent early in 1865. 'You
see, they all wanted to find a husband for my Mother', Queen Mary
once explained to someone who asked her how her father had first
come to this country. 'So once when King Edward (then Prince of
Wales) was out in Vienna he met this handsome young officer in the
Austrian Army, liked him, invited him to England on a visit, introduced him to my Mother—and everyone seemed to think it would
do—and it did.'

* Princess Helena's husband, Prince Christian of Schleswig-Holstein: see
footnote on p. 24.

At the moment of Prince Teck's arrival in England on this speculative visit, in March 1866, Princess Mary Adelaide would, in the normal course, still have been disporting herself in her brother-in-law's little northern German capital of Neu Strelitz, where she had been helping her sister the Grand Duchess Augusta to improvise *thé-dansants* and dinner-parties, musical evenings, private theatricals and a highly successful charity bazaar. The Grand Duke and his wife lived in one part of the square old Schloss which stood facing the cobbled central *Platz* of the town; while in another part 'Tante Marie', the Dowager Grand Duchess, at once Princess Augusta's aunt and mother-in-law, held her small, stiff, separate court. Winters in Strelitz were fierce and set in early, with snow knee-deep around the town and great crystal squares cut from the lakes to fill the ice-houses of those who wished to entertain. The linden trees would glitter in the sun, looking, as the Grand Duke said, 'like currants well sugared'. Boar-hunting was in full swing about the countryside; and in the sedate, well-heated houses of the town, with their cheerful, big porcelain stoves, simple and charming gaieties whiled away the long cold months before the spring.

Princess Mary had tried hard to please, this winter at Neu Strelitz. 'She is certainly changed', the Grand Duchess wrote to their brother, the Duke of Cambridge, in the tone of grudging approval usually adopted by elder sisters or brothers about some younger one: 'she nearly worked herself to death for that tiresome bazaar . . . and nothing would stop her'.43 The Cambridges' plan was to keep Princess Mary in ignorance of the 'T' project: 'Mama writes me word that I am to bring her back or send her by the middle of next month (*pour cause*)', the Grand Duchess wrote in another letter to her brother: 'now that is very well but how is it to be managed? without giving her a reason? . . . Do you really think *it* may do? with the difference of years, no money, name or position?' 'May *it* succeed, as our last chance, provided she likes him,' she wrote again, some days later, 'it would indeed be an excellent thing to *settle* her in life; she bears no restraint whatever, & becomes more difficult to manage every day, so both for her & most particularly for Mama it would be of the greatest importance to get her settled down by herself.' 'You must remember', she wrote prophetically, 'that she is more spoilt than either you or me, & that she requires more to live upon than we do, whose tastes and requirements are simpler than hers.'44 In justice to Princess Mary Adelaide it should here be remarked that her sister the

Grand Duchess Augusta was famously parsimonious, a trait inherited from their mother.

On the disingenuous excuse that her mother, the Duchess of Cambridge, could no longer get on without her, Princess Mary Adelaide was despatched to London from Neu Strelitz towards the end of February, in the charge of an apple-cheeked *Hofdame* of the Grand Ducal court, Frau Willichen Schreve. 'The *sample* of Strelitz beauty that is to accompany Mary to England—for indeed she could not travel without a lady—is not what I could have wished to have exhibited *there*, but she is an excellent creature & will not be seen much',45 wrote the Grand Duchess; for to royalties in that bygone era the gift for 'not being seen much' and 'not being really in the way' was a first qualification for the often unrewarding position of lady-in-waiting.

Prince Teck reached London in mid-March. On 10 April he and Princess Mary became engaged. The Duke of Cambridge wrote 'a dear funny letter' describing this event to his Strelitz sister, who replied with alacrity:

Since I have received your different letters, Mary's, Mama's, yours, I feel *perfectly reassured* & *happy* that it should be as it is, and indeed, we can wish *her* & *ourselves* joy that this marriage has been settled! Who would have thought it possible and in so short a time too! To me it is like a dream! I see her as you say, 'rushing about like an emancipated schoolgirl'. . . . We can but be happy & grateful for this *wonderful* & *happy conclusion* of her girlhood!46

No sooner was the engagement announced than the Duchess of Cambridge and Princess Mary Adelaide began, with Prince Teck's connivance, to agitate for a change in his status and title. The Foreign Secretary, Lord Clarendon, was approached and asked whether he could persuade the Queen to write to the King of Württemberg saying that she would like Prince Teck to become a Württemberg Duke. This she refused to do, and it was not until five years later, in September 1871, that King Carl of Württemberg gave his cousin a dukedom. Even then he was not made a Duke of Württemberg but Duke of Teck. The Queen was next asked to give her new relation the English title of 'Highness' and the Order of the Bath. 'The Bath, Prince Teck shall certainly have,' she wrote to Princess Mary in May, 'but the Title of "Highness" I think wld be of little use, and it wld hardly do to let him go *before* Edward Weimar.'*47 These fruitless attempts to inflate Prince Teck's position were made against the sensible advice of Princess Mary's brother-in-law, the Grand Duke of Mecklenburg-Strelitz. The Grand Duchess wrote that 'Fritz' was strongly against their asking the King of Württemberg for a dukedom, since he would not wish to grant it, and that in any case Princess Mary's own title was superior to anything that they could glean from the little court of Württemberg. He also suggested that if they became Duke and Duchess of Württemberg they would need more money, because 'more would be expected' of them. 'As P. of Teck he is the charming & agreeable husband of Princess Mary *et voilà tout*', this wise message ended.48

'*Et voilà tout*'—there was the rub, there the seed of much dissension. Prince Teck had spent his life in the Austrian Army, from which he had just resigned. He was not a brilliant man but he did not care for a life of idleness. Yet, save for a brief and rather inglorious participation in the Egyptian campaign of 1882, he was never allowed, in England, to make himself of any use. Disraeli, who had a wide imaginative grasp of affairs, once put forward the proposal that the Tecks should go as Viceroy and Vicereine to Ireland, on the theory recurrent to Victorian statesmen, but always rejected by the Queen herself, that the presence in Ireland of a member of the Royal Family might help to conciliate that turbulent island. The Queen had refused to consider this proposal: and the Duke of Teck was left to his diurnal pastimes of gardening at White Lodge, choosing wallpapers and brocades, collecting Chinese pottery, moving the furniture around, helping his wife to entertain, and arranging the jewels on her person and the flowers in her hair. This, in spite of his strong and genuine affection for his family, was not a fulfilling life. It was to be predicted that as he became older he would become more restless and more irritable, and that—a minor German royalty who was not even quite a royalty—he should increasingly attach an almost incredible importance to such trivia as precedence and rank. 'There is a dreadful

* Prince Edward of Saxe-Weimar (1823–1902) was the son of Duke Bernard of Saxe-Weimar-Eisenach by his wife Ida, Princess of Saxe-Coburg-Meiningen, a sister of Queen Adelaide. Born at Bushy Park, Prince Edward made his career in the British Army, and, in 1851, made a morganatic marriage with Lady Augusta Gordon-Lennox, who was called Countess of Dornburg in Germany, but, by virtue of a decree of Queen Victoria's, ranked in England as Princess Edward of Saxe-Weimar. Friends of the Tecks, the Weimars had a house in Portland Place. They had no children.

B*

feud going on between [Leiningen] and Teck on the question of precedence', Sir Henry Ponsonby wrote to his wife from Buckingham Palace in 1878, 'and I heard that Teck would go nowhere, where there was a chance of meeting Leiningen.* This has stirred up the pride of Gleichen† who . . . now claims to be called His Serene Highness and to rank before Teck—Teck's fury is redoubled. He declares that in Württemberg he goes into the closet with the whole royal family and asks triumphantly if Leiningen or Gleichen can do as much. Tis said the matter will come before the Queen.'⁴⁹ But these were troubles in the future; and the only apparent threat to perfect happiness, on the June morning on which Princess Mary Adelaide was wedded to Prince Teck at Kew, was the imminent danger of the outbreak of war between Prussia and Austria, a disaster which would involve the bridegroom's rejoining the Imperial Army in Vienna without a moment's delay. At the Duchess of Cambridge's reception at Kew on the eve of the wedding, Prince Teck replied 'almost tearfully' to one guest's congratulations, 'saying that he could not help thinking even on this eventful day of his poor fatherland'.⁵⁰

The outbreak, in June 1866, of the Austro-Prussian War spelt not only the doom of Austria but sounded the death-knell to the freedom and local power of all the little German courts, Württemberger or Strelitzer alike. When the Tecks celebrated their Silver Wedding, in June 1891, the Grand Duchess Augusta wrote to her sister: 'I so remember *that 12th* June, whilst I was putting on my blue Dress with Queen Charlotte's fine Lace, Fritz came in with Bülow's Telegram, that Prussia had upset the Diet at Frankfurt; and asking Fritz what line he would take! this was the beginning of the end of all things.'⁵¹ However, the wedding in the little rustic church on Kew Green passed off happily enough. The village was thronged with well-wishers, both because of the local popularity of Princess

* Ernest, Prince of Leiningen (1830–1904), an Admiral in the British Navy, was the grandson of Queen Victoria's mother, the Duchess of Kent (1786–1861) by her first marriage to Emich-Charles, Prince of Leiningen (1763–1814), and thus was nephew to Queen Victoria's beloved half-sister, Feodora, who married Ernest, Prince of Hohenlohe-Langenburg. Prince Ernest of Leiningen's mother was Marie, Countess Klebelsberg, so that he, like Teck, was of morganatic blood. He married Marie, Princess of Baden (1834–1899).

† Victor, Prince of Hohenlohe-Langenburg (1833–1891) was the third son and fourth child of Queen Victoria's half-sister Feodora of Leiningen (see previous note). In 1861 he contracted a morganatic marriage with Miss Laura Seymour (1832–1912) and took the title of Count Gleichen.

Mary Adelaide and her mother and because it was one of the first functions the Queen had attended since her widowhood. 'Dear Mary looked very handsome & *very happy*', the Queen wrote later.[52] '. . . She was very quiet & self-possessed. *Franz* was very nervous. The Fracas with the China caused by the Bp. of Winchester was *considerable. Such* an absurd thing to happen! . . .'*

The newly-married couple set blithely off for Ashridge, lent them for their honeymoon by Lady Marion Alford. They were accompanied by the good wishes, as well as the doubts, of their relatives. To the worldly-wise of that generation, marriages contracted after the first flush of youth was over took on something of the quality of a potential battleground. Which party, they pondered, would gain the upper hand? Queen Victoria's half-sister, Princess Feodora of Hohenlohe-Langenburg, backed Princess Mary Adelaide:

. . . I cannot deny, that I was much astonished at the suddenness of Mary's *Verlobung* with that very young looking Prince Teck. May they be happy, is all one can say and wish. As for his being *unter dem Pantoffel,* by and by, I have no doubt of, but if so I have no pity on him, for it is always the man's own fault if that is the case. Certainly Mary is *mighty* but I think, if she is fond of a person she may be able of showing great devotion and affection. She is much cleverer than he is.[53]

The Queen, on the other hand, took the opposite view:

. . . I think really she is vy fortunate, for Pce Teck, is not at all wanting, & has a vy firm will & opinion of his own so that Mary who is excessively fond of him, will certainly obey him; her manner is already—quieter & she talks most sensibly of her future.[54]

After a broken honeymoon of only fifteen days Prince Teck started for Vienna, taking his bride with him as far as Stuttgart, where he left her in charge of his Württemberg relations, at their stiff, Teutonic court. Proving too late to take part in the Six Weeks' War, Teck returned to Stuttgart to fetch his wife, settled with her for some weeks in Vienna and then moved on to his sister's, at Schloss Reinthal near Graz. They were home again in September, borrowing a corner house in Prince's Gate for three months, whilst their rooms at Kensington

* History does not record what the Bishop of Winchester (who had been assisting the Archbishop of Canterbury at the wedding service) did to the china. The incident presumably occurred in the library at Cambridge Cottage, where the royal table for the breakfast was laid, the rest of the party sitting down in a gaily decorated tent.

were being got ready. 'I am thankful to say that the Queen has given us the greater portion of the apartment she and Aunt Kent occupied at Kensington Palace in days of yore, which the Board of Works promise to get ready for us by the month of May', Princess Mary Adelaide wrote to a friend, 'and which, if they please to spend a little money upon it may be made a very charming abode, as the rooms are handsome and comfortable.'[55]

It was in this spacious chain of rooms at Kensington Palace that Princess May and her three brothers were born. Although the Tecks' apartment comprised the ground floor, below the vast painted State Rooms of the Palace, a part of these latter were used as nurseries. 'It was quaint and pretty to see the little ones in their cots with allegorical figures hovering above them', wrote one of the Duchess of Cambridge's ladies, Miss Ella Taylor.[56] It was thus literally from the cradle that Princess May began to realise that her circumstances, and so perhaps her destiny, were different from those of all the other children born in the borough of Kensington in May 1867.

CHAPTER TWO

KENSINGTON PALACE
AND MARLBOROUGH HOUSE

THE BIRTH of Princess May in 1867 was followed on 13 August 1868 by that of the Tecks' eldest son, Adolphus. On 9 January 1870, a second son, Prince Francis, appeared upon the scene. These were both fine-looking, large children, but their births were heralded by tiresome, vociferous expressions of anxiety on the part of Princess Mary Adelaide's immediate relations, similar to those which had preceded and accompanied the birth of Princess May. 'Your confinement *really* was a surprise, to me at least', her sister wrote from Strelitz on the birth of Prince 'Frank'. '. . . But now I really hope this charming little Trio will suffice. . . . Tomorrow I suppose your bed will be pushed into the Morning room? not today as it is Friday! I see it all before me, Clarky coming in with Baby, and later with a bottle of Champagne!'[1] The fourth and last child, Alexander George, was born on 14 April 1874. 'Mary Teck was safely confined yesterday with another & *still* bigger boy! That seems hardly possible', was the Queen's comment, in a letter from Osborne to her daughter at Berlin.[2]

Thus was the general ground-plan for Princess May's youth prepared: the only girl in a family of four. Known as 'the Peacemaker' in nursery and, later, schoolboy squabbles, she early learned to exercise her native discretion, firmness and tact. Her eldest brother, Prince Dolly, fair-haired and blue-eyed like herself, was throughout his life the closest to her of the three. Prince Frank and the baby, a plump child called at his Aunt Augusta's suggestion and much to the Duchess of Cambridge's annoyance 'Alge',* as a contraction of Alexander George, were very dark, like their father. Prince Dolly and Prince Frank were startlingly handsome children; in the nursery their sister would refer to them as 'Beauty Boys'. The blonde Prince Dolly especially appealed to Princess May's aesthetic sense: 'dearest Dolly . . .

* Pronounced 'Algy'.

is *so* beautiful that he quite took our breath away', she wrote to her aunt in November 1890, when her brother, then twenty-two, returned from India: 'he has grown very much & is much thinner & has such a smart figure. His face is longer & his nose has become straighter, in fact his profile is lovely & he is more like the pictures of the old Royal Family than ever.'3 All through her life mere physical beauty was greatly enhanced, in the eyes of Princess May, by any element of the family-historical. In the same way a portrait or miniature of some unknown personage might be exquisitely painted and so worthy of wholehearted approval; but if it turned out to be the picture of some member of 'the old Royal Family' it became automatically an object of admiration—and desire.

This potent interest in family history, which became a guiding factor in later years when, as Queen Mary, she was constantly adding to the Royal Collections pictures and objects of family interest bought out of her own private purse, was first imbibed from her mother, who never forgot that she was a granddaughter of George III. It was also richly fed by her aunt, Augusta Strelitz, whose views and recollections, purveyed in long, lively weekly letters, became a strong influence in Princess May's mental development. The Grand Duchess of Mecklenburg-Strelitz outwitted all her contemporaries in the Royal Family by living merrily on until the age of ninety-four. She died during the First World War, in 1916, having for long enjoyed the triumphant position of being the only living English Princess who had taken part in the Coronation of William IV, and, consequently, able to advise Queen Alexandra and after her Queen Mary on the long-forgotten court etiquette of Queen Adelaide's day.

The very fact of living in old Kensington Palace, with its mellow red brickwork, fine rooms designed by Wren and re-decorated by Kent, its smoke-dark panelling and dim, lofty painted ceilings increased Princess May's natural passion for the past. Here William III had conducted affairs of state, here George II had argued with Queen Caroline, who knotted fringe and gossiped to Lord Hervey in the long shallow galleries which smelt of bees-wax. Princess May's night-nursery was, as we have seen, one of the old State Rooms, and when her parents wished to entertain at dinner—which they wished frequently—their guests would eat in the Council Room on the ground-floor of the Palace. The Tecks' apartments had been sumptu-ously re-furnished: 'How handsomely and comfortably the rooms at Kensington are arranged', the Crown Princess, herself a person of taste, wrote to her mother, from St Leonards-on-Sea in November 1868.4 'I am already looking forward so much to pay you frequent little visits at Kensington which I don't know at all yet, and which I heard from all sides is quite lovely', the Princess of Wales wrote prettily, six months after Princess May's birth.5

It was generally recognised that Prince Teck knew all about what would now be called 'interior decoration'. 'He had', wrote a contemporary, 'the art of making his surroundings thoroughly comfortable', and Princess Mary 'submitted her judgement to his' in all matters of carpeting, curtains, upholstery and the disposal of pictures and pieces of furniture about their rooms. He shared with his cousin, Prince William of Württemberg, afterwards King William II, an almost feminine urge to arrange and re-arrange rooms. Like his cousin he was very musical and had the quiet and charming German love of home-life—'never so happy', a member of the household noted, 'as within his own walls'. The Tecks' salon was dominated by the great full-length Lawrence of George IV, now in the Wallace Collection, which had been given to the Duke of Teck by Lord Conyngham. Royal relics, such as Queen Charlotte's sedan chairs, abounded at Kensington Palace; while living survivals of the late Georgian past were near at hand—ranging from the dear little old Duchess of Inverness, whose quarters were in another part of the same building, to Mr Beckham, the Duke of Sussex's venerable page, who 'lived in a little house near the Serpentine, in Kensington Gardens & our nurse used to take us sometimes to see him', as Queen Mary recalled forty years after.6

Protecting the privileged inmates of the Palace from the public sward of Kensington Gardens was the 'pretty and delightful garden of our own' where warm summer's afternoons were spent by Princess May tucked up, in ruched muslin bonnet and pelisse, in her three-wheeled perambulator with its heavy silk-fringed canopy nodding above her head. Here, too, a laden tea-table placed upon a carpet on the lawn would form a focal point for little family gatherings—Prince Teck, his wife, her brother the Duke of Cambridge, her mother the old Duchess, or her sister the Grand Duchess of Mecklenburg-Strelitz. The region immediately outside the purlieus of this private garden was regarded with a certain suspicion, for the Round Pond was thought to give off noxious vapours, harmful to a gently-nurtured child. In July 1868, when she was fourteen months old, Princess May was seized with violent spasms: 'Whether she caught a slight chill, or the effluvia from the pond in Kensington Gardens, which was in a very unhealthy state, and which the nursery windows face, I know not', wrote her anxious mother, describing 'an alarming relapse', after which the baby 'all the next day lay in a state of collapse'. The Duchess of Cambridge intervened and 'very wisely insisted on carrying her off to Kew, to be away from the pond, and out nearly all day in the garden, under the shade of the old chestnut tree'.7

When they ventured farther afield, quite beyond the small world of the Round Pond and Mr Beckham's cottage by the Serpentine, they did so in a manner calculated to impress even more clearly on Princess May's mind her parents' and her own semi-royal status. In 1871 Queen Victoria initiated a frustrating private enquiry into why her cousin Princess Mary Adelaide and Prince Teck were using Royal livery (of scarlet and dark blue) for their own servants and coachmen, and why their carriages were painted, like her own, the Sovereign's colour, chocolate brown. It was also noticed that the Grand Duke and the Grand Duchess of Mecklenburg-Strelitz seemed to be making use of similar liveries and similar carriages. Such a thing had not even been done by Prince Leopold of Saxe-Coburg-Gotha, husband of Princess Charlotte; for both before and after her death he had used his own liveries of green and gold, with green carriages and grey horses— 'very handsome'. It was a delicate matter, and the answer to the question was ambiguous: the Teck servants did indeed wear scarlet coats, but 'the Waistcoats & other part of the Dress, are *Black*, & not *Blue*, as in the Royal Livery—though bound with Gold Lace, the same as The Queen's servants. The undress is the same blue as the Queen's.' It was asserted that the waistcoats were black instead of dark blue because this was the Württemberg livery at the court of Stuttgart. 'Their carriages', it was added, 'are exactly the same as the Queen's with the exception of the difference of the Crowns.'8 There the matter rested, until brought up again by Sir Henry Ponsonby in 1881, when Lord Sydney recapitulated the Württemberg argument, admitting that 'the nuance was very fine' and that 'practically there is little difference from the other Members of the Royal Family'. 'This ought not to be!' minuted the Queen on a summary of the results of this second investigation, 'Livery or undress shd be their own'.9 All that a small child would notice would be the fact that her parents and her brothers lived, in style, in a Royal Palace, and that when they left it on some expedition they did so in equipages apparently identical in every detail with those used by the Queen of England herself.

Apart from the stories and traditions of the Palace in which she was reared in comparative pomp, contemporary family history, in the form of living members of the family, was passing before Princess May's attentive eyes. 'I am the last of the family who has a good memory of what the family in 1874 looked like', Queen Mary wrote to the Librarian of Windsor Castle in 1948. 'I was always interested when members of the family came to see Mama, & had a good stare to take them all in.'[10]

II

So, at the age of seven—for such she was in 1874—Princess May was already sharpening those very exceptional faculties of observation and of photographic memory for which she was famous in after life. However, there was one aspect of the visiting members of 'the Family' which would have made them rather easy to remember: their rarity. At that period British Royalties were few and far between. 'It is not to be wished that the Royal family shd become too large', wrote Queen Victoria, who, as the mother of nine children, might have been thought to have herself done more than anybody else to expand it. 'It is a weakness, rather than strength.'[11] As we have noticed, Queen Victoria had only four first cousins in her own generation. Three of these were Princess May's mother, Princess May's uncle and Princess May's aunt—all figures too closely familiar to be subjects for a child's blue-eyed stare.

Of the officially recognised widows of George III's sons, old aunts who had doted on Princess May's mother as a girl, all but two were dead when Princess May was born. Queen Adelaide had died in 1849, the Duchess of Gloucester in 1857, the Duchess of Kent in 1861. There remained the Duchess of Inverness, the former Lady Cecilia Buggin, who had been the Duke of Sussex's second wife and who had never claimed Royal rank. The Duchess of Inverness was aged, squat and small. She dressed in a bygone mode and had quaint, cosy old ways. She lived in discreet state in a wing of Kensington Palace, entertaining in a dining-room which was 'fitted up like a tent & was very stuffy'. Although her French was feeble, and she made no claims to conversational sparkle, she was a favourite with the diplomatic corps, and was noted for her genial hospitality: 'no-one that called on her ever left her presence without hearing the words—"Come and dine".'[12] It was the Duchess of Inverness who had given Queen

Charlotte's fine sedan chairs to the Duchess of Teck, who subsequently
sold them to Queen Victoria for three hundred pounds. She was also
generous to the Teck children: 'I hope you went to see the Duchess
of Inverness, who always gives you such nice things', Princess May's
father wrote to her, from Sandringham, in the New Year of 1871.[13]
The Duchess of Inverness died in 1873, when Princess May was six.
By 1874 there remained of that old Royal generation in England only
Princess May's own grandmother, the Duchess of Cambridge.
'Grandmama' lived on until 1889, when Princess May was a young
woman; but, after a paralytic stroke at Neu Strelitz in 1873, the
Duchess of Cambridge had become, as the Teck children knew to
their cost, more visited than visiting. Thus there were left, for childish
observation, only Queen Victoria herself and her family of nine.

During Princess May's childhood the Queen came rarely to London
and very seldom indeed to Kensington. From time to time she would
send for the Teck children to have a look at them, as, for instance, in
May 1872, when she wrote to the Duchess of Teck: 'I have so much
to do & have suffered so much from my head lately that I fear I cannot
undertake to see *you* this time—but if *you* will send Girdlestone* with
the children by $\frac{1}{2}$ past 10 on Wednesday I cld find a few minutes to
see them—wh. I long to do'; or, in July 1874: 'Your darling chubby
Boys looked beautiful yesterday & May much better.'[14] Each 26
May the Queen would remember her goddaughter Princess May's
birthday, and send her a gift—a Balmoral album 'with likenesses of
ourselves' in one instance, and she would also take great trouble over
the making, and despatch from Ballater, of Highland kilts, complete
with silver ornaments, for the Teck boys. Princess May and her
brothers would in their turn send the Queen birthday presents—a
box with forget-me-nots 'drawn from nature' on it, a plate painted by
Princess May with gold which had to be 'fired several times', a 'novelty
for flowers' and, once, an ambitious fretwork basket in which they
had all collaborated. 'The Children made the basket for you', wrote the
Duchess of Teck, '(all traced, for cutting out with a saw, and therefore
not quite so difficult as would appear). They are overjoyed at your
kind mention of their work and you cannot think the pleasure they
took, in making the basket for you!—but they are amply rewarded by
your gracious mention of it.'[15] There was at least one further example
of such collaboration: 'My brothers and I have had great pleasure in
working You a pockethandkerchief case, which we lay most respect-

* Mrs Girdlestone, called 'Girdie', head nurse to the three elder Teck children.

fully at Your feet and hope You will kindly use in remembrance of Your dutiful and loving little Niece and Nephews', Princess May wrote to the Queen, in May 1877, in a round childish hand.[16] Such was Queen Victoria's pleasant relationship with her juvenile cousins, the little Tecks.

The Duchess of Teck was friendly with several of the Queen's own children, though not especially intimate with any of them; for here a purely chronological factor intervened. Having been born in 1833, she was fourteen years younger than the Queen, but at the same time twenty-four years older than the Queen's youngest child. To the Queen, Princess Mary Adelaide had always seemed a young cousin, isolated, as it were, in a mezzanine generation of her own; to the Queen's sons and daughters she had seemed in their childhood an older relative, almost an unmarried aunt. 'She was the friend of my youth when we were girls together, and though she was eight years older than I am, I was sincerely attached to her', the Queen's eldest daughter, Princess 'Vicky' wrote, as Empress Frederick, after the Duchess of Teck's death.[17] In 1858 Princess Vicky had married and gone to live in Berlin. The next sister, Princess Alice, was ten years younger than Princess Mary Adelaide, who used at one time to drive her in her pony phaeton through the Park. In 1862 Princess Alice also had married and retired to Germany, going to live in Darmstadt where she died of diphtheria in 1878. The Queen's third daughter, Princess Helena, thirteen years Princess Mary Adelaide's junior, had married in 1866, the same year as herself. They had never been on noticeably warm terms with one another, and Princess Mary Adelaide had indeed earned a sharp reprimand from the Queen for forgetting, in her own nuptial excitement, to write to congratulate her on 'Lenchen's' engagement to Prince Christian of Schleswig-Holstein. Of the Queen's other children, Prince Alfred was often at sea, or in such naval stations as Malta; in 1874 he married the only daughter of the Tsar Alexander II, a devout, dowdy and haughty-seeming woman, who did not trouble to placate Princess Mary Adelaide's strong Russophobia. Princess Louise, who was married to Lord Lorne in 1871, had apartments in Kensington Palace, but lived much in Scotland, and, from 1878 until 1883, was in Canada where her husband was Governor-General. The three youngest members of the family, Arthur, Leopold and Beatrice, were kept at the Queen's side until they, each in turn, married: their children, born during the decade of the eighteen-eighties, were small babies when Princess May was in her 'teens. And so it turned out that of all Queen Victoria's children and their families, those with whom the Tecks were on the best terms were also those into whose intimacy fate was to carry Princess May of Teck: the Wales family, living in fashionable luxury at Marlborough House, and headed by Albert Edward, Prince of Wales, Princess May's future father-in-law and future King.

III

The Duchess of Teck's friendship with the Prince of Wales was of long standing, but it was tinged by fear. He could charm her, as he could, if he wished, charm anyone who came into his orbit for, with the possible exception of Prince Leopold, Duke of Albany, he was by far the most fascinating of Queen Victoria's sons and he had a true kindness of heart. It was his sense of humour that Princess Mary Adelaide found disquieting: 'Wales, who is in very good looks, was most dear and nice, and not in that *odious chaffing* mood I so dislike',[18] she wrote in February 1875, after a luncheon at Marlborough House. Some people, like her mother's lady-in-waiting, Lady Geraldine Somerset, believed this fear to be mutual, and that the Prince of Wales found the Duchess of Teck as unnerving as she found him. In any case her attitude seems likely to have infected Princess May, who was never really at her ease with 'Uncle Wales', either before or after she became his daughter-in-law. She may also, as she grew up, have been influenced by her mother's stalwart views on what she called the 'fast ladies and gamblers' of the Prince of Wales's circle, on the dreadfully Russophile proclivities of the Marlborough House family, and on their signal lack of interest in literature or any other of the arts.

In 1858, when he was just seventeen, the Prince of Wales had been virtually shut up at White Lodge in Richmond Park with a couple of tutors, 'so as to be', in his father the Prince Consort's words, 'away from the world and devote himself exclusively to study'. In this case being away from the world meant being within easy reach of the Duchess of Cambridge's house at Kew, and it was here that he attended his first dinner-party. To relieve the tedium of these cloistral months at White Lodge, the boy would pay visits to his old Aunt Cambridge and her daughter towards sundown, rowing up-river from Richmond or Mortlake and mooring his boat alongside the old landing-stage at Brentford Ferry. He would despatch little letters to Princess Mary Adelaide saying that he intended 'rowing round by

Kew Gardens today as we told you yesterday', or sending her 'some parts of the pheasant which I shot which is arranged for ladies' hats, & will you be so kind as to choose which part you like best'.[19] This amiable, cousinly relationship with the Cambridges was made suddenly more intimate by the Prince's marriage, in March 1863, to Princess Alexandra of Denmark.

Princess Alexandra of Schleswig-Holstein-Sonderburg-Glucksburg was a daughter of the elected heir to the old King of Denmark. In the year of Princess Alexandra's marriage he succeeded to the Danish throne as Christian IX. His wife, Droning Louise, was the daughter of the Landgrave William of Hesse-Cassel, the Duchess of Cambridge's brother. As the old Duchess's great-niece, Princess Alexandra was thus a cousin to Princess Mary Adelaide.

When she first settled in England as the ravishing Princess of Wales—'something exquisite and flowerlike . . . a beautiful rose or a rare orchid or an absolutely faultless carnation . . . , a garden flower that had been grown by a superlative gardener, who knew every trick of his art'[20]—'Alix' had naturally turned to her Cambridge cousin for companionship. At the Wales marriage in St George's Chapel, Windsor, Princess Mary Adelaide had been prominent: 'I never saw a finer piece of acting', wrote an eyewitness, 'than Princess Mary heading the English Royal procession. Morally as well as physically the place was not big enough to hold her.'[21] Ever since she was a small child the bride had known and loved Princess Mary Adelaide, who used to call her 'la petite Alexandrine' and would push her about in a little carriage round the courtyard of Rumpenheim, the quiet summer residence of the Landgrave William of Hesse-Cassel, an old white-washed, green-shuttered Schloss with a cupola'd clock-tower and a terrace walk along the gentle, leafy banks of the Main near Frankfurt. On her side Princess Mary Adelaide responded to the young Princess of Wales's trusting affection with her customary impulsiveness: 'She is a very great darling, and I *just adore her.*'[22]

In the earlier days of the Waleses' marriage, Princess Mary Adelaide would get frequent notes from Marlborough House asking her to drive with them in the Park, to go to their box at a theatre and to dine afterwards, to accompany the Princess of Wales to one of Hallé's afternoon concerts, or to advise her where she could most quickly get a jet diadem made. A random note in 'dear Alix's' indecipherably looped handwriting which resembled a strip of crochet-work or loose knitting, would, for example, read: 'I shall be delighted to dine

with you tomorrow but my little Man unfortunately has for some
time already been engaged to see a *billiard* match played at the
St James Hall and therefore hopes you will excuse him, he regrets so
much it happens to be tomorrow—*Au revoir ma chère* till tomorrow.
I hope your Sister in law enjoyed the ball—How is your poor tooth?
Clarky? and baby?'²³ They would ecstatically exchange Christmas
and birthday presents: 'Many many thanks for your *lovely* Xmas
presents', wrote the Princess of Wales in December 1878, '—the pin
is quite charming so is that delightful tricoloured pencil—but as for
that *darling* puggy—I really have no words to express my admiration
for it—it is simply an *adorable* pug and shall *never* leave my dressing
table—wherever I go—*he* will have to come too and keep guard over
me like a black faced angel that it is—I really am delighted with it—
and never saw one like it.'²⁴ The Duke and Duchess of Teck were
asked regularly to stay at Sandringham, going down in the Prince of
Wales's Special and eating what the Duchess once described as 'a
capital *hot* lunch of chicken & rice & beefsteaks & fried potatoes',²⁵
as the train slipped through the 'flat monotonous' East Anglian
countryside. Another journey to Sandringham, in April 1883, was less
auspicious, as the Duke of Teck told his sons in a letter showing his
not unattractive sense of the absurd:

Here I am—I found Mama & May very well & happy. . . . Muire packed
my Railway-wrapper in the Portmanteau God knows what he thinks a
Wrapper is for & he forgot my Ulster (the thick one) which I specially
mentioned to him, so if we go out driving I have got nothing but my
Walking Overcoat. My Dressingcase Clock stopped & my watch which
I wear in evening Dress was so dirty that in cleaning it I broock the glass.
My flask filled with Cherry Brandy, was not well screwed up, and spoiled
the lining of my waist coat which was in the bag, luckily not very much. . . .
The Hat-Box in which Mamas Bonet & something else was put, was not
properly fastened, and on the Railway Porter taking it out of the Van,
Bonet &c rolled along the Platform, was caught by an other Porter &
thrown back in to the Van, as if some dirty rag.²⁶

   Whenever the Duchess of Teck was separated from her children
in their nursery days, she would sit down late at night and write to
them of her doings. She would describe days at Sandringham for
their benefit—driving, with 'Aunt Alix' in a low basket carriage with
four swift horses, or how the whole party stood on chairs holding
hands to toast the New Year one midnight in a loving-cup of hot
punch, or watching the 'dear little trio' of the Wales girls riding

their ponies to hounds for the first time. She was always a tremendous favourite with the Wales children: 'I have been in the nursery', she wrote to 'her chicks' in February 1873 from Sandringham, '(such a nice large room!) all this afternoon and Looloo, Victoria & sweet tiny Maudie have been showing me all their pretty picturebooks; after which I assisted at their tea. . . . Aunt Alix calls me, so goodbye & God bless you.'[27]

It thus seemed in the natural order of things that Princess May should become familiarly acquainted in childhood with her cousins and contemporaries: the two boys and three girls of the Prince and Princess of Wales.

IV

The two Wales boys, Prince Albert Victor, known as 'Eddy', and Prince George, known as 'Georgie', had been born in 1864 and 1865 respectively. The eldest girl, Princess Louise, three months older than Princess May, was born in February 1867 when her mother was suffering from the attack of rheumatic fever which left her with a stiff leg, cause of the famous 'Alexandra limp'. The two younger girls were near in age to Princess May's elder brothers: Princess Victoria was born in 1868, the same year as Prince Dolly of Teck, and Princess Maud, born in 1869, was only a few months senior to Prince Frank.

In early childhood the members of the two families would play happily together on equal terms. It was only as they grew older that certain tonal differences between the Tecks and the Waleses became evident to each. On the one hand, the Teck children, and notably Princess May, had a wider and sounder educational basis than that of the Wales family; while on the other hand the five Waleses, headed by Prince Eddy, heir-presumptive to the throne, were always conscious that the Tecks were less thoroughly Royal than themselves. They could not overlook the father's morganatic blood. For that mid-Victorian world, which now seems to us as archaic as that of the Tudors, was, for all its subtleties, starkly simple in outline. Things were still what they seemed. The pyramid of class remained unshaken and unchipped. There was the working class, the middle class, the gentry, the aristocracy, and, at the apex, the Royal Family. Enlightened persons might question the absolute validity of these arrangements; but, both in their own eyes and in those of the country at large, the Royal Family shone as a race apart, denizens of a red and gold

Valhalla, however homely, virtuous and unpretentious their habits might be.

'Today is Georgie's birthday, can your little girl come and play with them after luncheon?' the Princess of Wales wrote to Princess Mary Adelaide on 3 June 1870. 'Could not your Children meet mine at Chiswick instead of coming here as I know ours like that better than playing here in the garden.'[28] Chiswick House had been lent to the Prince and Princess of Wales by its owner, the Duke of Devonshire. Here, on long summer afternoons, the Teck and Wales children would frolic together amongst the sphinxes and the obelisks, and in the small temple by the lake. The little girls would play with the Wales girls' 'rickety old dolls' and 'battered toys'—for they were brought up to have the inexpensive tastes their mother had developed during a spartan and impoverished childhood in Copenhagen. The little boys would amuse themselves by the miniature lake's side, pushing about on the water the wooden boats carved for them by one of the Chiswick footmen. As the shadows lengthened they would be called in to tea with their nurses, who 'treated them without ceremony'. Meanwhile the Duchess of Teck, a coloured parasol on her shoulder, would stroll beneath the cedar trees, a voluminous, jovial figure, with the tiny, jewel-like Princess of Wales at her side. Sometimes, in these days before she was incarcerated by paralysis, the old Duchess of Cambridge would come with one of her ladies to sit and watch the children: a stern and very foreign grandmother, before whose guttural vowels the children quailed.*

In her more lugubrious moods Queen Victoria would refer to the Wales children as 'poor frail little *fairies*', and complain of them as being 'puny and pale'[29]—a fact she attributed to their having been born in such swift succession and to the over-active social life she thought the Princess of Wales was leading to please her husband, the Prince. The only really delicate one of the lot was Prince Eddy. Since he was heir-presumptive this delicateness naturally worried the Queen.

Prince Eddy (who flashed into Princess May's later life as her

---

* Queen Mary never forgot these Chiswick afternoons. On 17 June 1937, not long after her seventieth birthday, she went to see an exhibition of pictures in Chiswick House: 'The house', she recorded in her Diary for that day, 'is in a bad state of repair. . . . Walked in the garden & saw the flower beds which G. & Eddy & the sisters had when Papa had the house from 1866–1879.' By 'G.' Queen Mary meant her husband, King George V, then eighteen months dead; 'Papa' was her father-in-law, the Prince of Wales, afterwards King Edward VII.

fiancé, only to leave it six weeks after for the tomb) was a melancholy, wistful-looking child, although when he laughed or smiled he closely resembled his mother. Unlike his brother and his sisters he was not at all boisterous. Quiet and almost apathetic he 'never seemed to mind what he did or what happened to him' and his character was no tougher than his health. The others, as they grew, conceived that passion for practical jokes which distinguished the Danish royal family, forming, as it were, an invisible belt of private, knock-about behaviour linking the Palace in Athens with that at Copenhagen, and both of these with Sandringham and Marlborough House. When they were not at the top of their form in this direction the Wales sisters tended to speak sorrowfully, in a minor key, prefixing the words 'dear little' or 'poor little' to anyone whom they discussed: 'It gave a special quality to all talks with them', one of their young Edinburgh cousins has recorded, 'as though life would have been very wonderful and everything very beautiful, if it had not been so sad.'[30] From childhood on, the three sisters loved to accumulate small objects— bronze, stone or china animals, shells, minute vases, little water-colours of gardens or of daffodil fields, or of Windsor Castle in the mist, miniatures, a myriad velvet-covered photograph frames containing tiny pictures of each other, their horses and their dogs. This taste for collecting the diminutive was one which Princess May shared; but, while quite capable before her marriage of taking part in such fashionable country-house romps as sliding down the staircase on a tea-tray, she lived on a different wave-length from that of her cousins and future sisters-in-law. This psychological fact is essential to any understanding of her life and character. It cannot be ignored by anyone trying to construct a faithful portrait of her, as Queen Mary herself tacitly admitted when passing for publication a lengthy passage on this subject in Mr John Gore's authorised life of her husband, King George V. 'If any of them were alive I could not pass it', she said, 'but it is *true*, and they are all dead.'

In one sense the Wales sisters were never fully liberated from their childhood, and even when they were young women they liked going to or giving children's parties. 'Alge . . . came here on Saty 20th to go up with us to Marlboro' House to a *children's party* for Louise's *19th* birthday!' Princess May wrote to her Aunt Augusta in February 1886. 'Does not that seem too ridiculous? . . . Everybody seemed to enjoy themselves, but I was shy, & bored. . . . Cousins like these juvenile entertainments, we don't relish 'em!'[31]

Yet Princess May was not a prig. It was simply that, under her parents' supervision, she had been provided with a serious educational framework, to which, as she grew older, she had the wisdom and the drive constantly to add. An observer all her life, she was keenly interested in everything that came within her purview. Greatly increased during the years 1883, 1884 and 1885 when her parents withdrew with their family to Florence, this interest was first awakened during the earlier period of their family life at the White Lodge.

CHAPTER THREE

CHILDHOOD INFLUENCES

THE SET of rooms at Kensington Palace which the Queen had granted to Princess Mary Adelaide on her marriage to Prince Teck in 1866 were stately and capacious. The scale of the apartments suggested—nay, in Princess Mary Adelaide's eyes, they demanded—a lavish standard of hospitality; for while Princess Mary's family, from the Queen downwards, had seen her marriage as a quiet and final solution to her problems, she herself regarded it in quite another light: as the long-wished opportunity to blossom forth as a hostess and to show the town that her entertainments could be every bit as fine and as delightful as those at Marlborough House.

Every visiting Royalty in London would come to pay their respects to the Teck couple, and each visitor became the splendid excuse for a grand dinner-party. Before such a festivity, Princess Mary Adelaide, wearing a housemaid's apron, and assisted by Prince Teck, would herself put the finishing touches to the luxurious floral decorations of the table. These dinner-parties were held in the Council Room, and so, indeed, were many other less technically august receptions, when statesmen like Lord Beaconsfield or hostesses like the Tecks' neighbour, Lady Holland, would mingle with all that Princess Mary Adelaide considered choicest in the contemporary London scene.

Such hospitality, with its essential ingredients of the chefs and the pairs of 'match footmen', the superlative wine and food, cost money. Despite a frugal mother and an elder sister whom even the Cambridge family thought stingy, the Duchess of Teck had grown up with a total disregard for the niceties of finance. Debts began to accumulate. Herself of a thoughtless generosity, Princess Mary Adelaide would never deprive others of an occasion to exhibit a similar virtue. Close friends like Baroness Burdett-Coutts could be relied on to come forward in a crisis; there was soon a handsome and impressive overdraft at Coutts's bank. Local tradespeople found their unpaid accounts with Her Royal Highness running into four figures, but with it all the Duchess remained charmingly heedless and unperturbed—for she was embarked on the heady career of a London hostess, and she liked above all things to give pleasure to her guests. So oblivious was she of her actual financial position that on one occasion, when opening a new church hall at Kensington to the building of which one of the Tecks' chief creditors, Mr John Barker, the Kensington grocer, had largely contributed, the Duchess greatly startled the assembled company by turning gracefully towards him on the platform and announcing with a bewitching smile: 'And now I must propose a special vote of thanks to Mr Barker, to whom we all owe so much.'

This was soon the established pattern of life at Kensington Palace: but to Princess Mary Adelaide's ideas Kensington Palace was not really enough. Why should one have to spend the summer staying about in friends' country-houses, or even visiting stiff German relatives in stone-floored *Schlösser* on the Continent? From 'why indeed?' the answer to this question became 'why not a country *pied-à-terre?*' and quickly crystallised into an obsessive craving '*Why not White Lodge?*' Within two years of her daughter's birth, Princess Mary Adelaide had set her heart on White Lodge in Richmond Park. Crown property, it had been the residence of her late aunt, the Duchess of Gloucester, who had been the Ranger of Richmond Park. In 1867 and 1868 the Prince and Princess of Wales had made use of it as a Saturday to Monday retreat. White Lodge, standing just within the Robin Hood Gate into Richmond Park, was only a ten-mile drive from Kensington. It was near the Duchess of Cambridge's cottage at Kew. It was within temptingly easy reach of Windsor Castle, should one happen to be summoned there for any reason. It was also a healthy place, and in this capacity would provide Princess May and her brothers with a refuge from the harmful effluvia of that suspect Kensington Pond.

Princess Mary Adelaide was a wheedler. She never minded asking the Queen a favour, however often or bluntly she was refused. Queen Victoria was one of the kindest-hearted human beings ever born, but she had learned to put up what would now be called 'a sales-resistance' to her stout cousin's sometimes importunate requests. In later years this resistance became even firmer—'The Duchess of Teck may have a carriage tomorrow but Sir Henry* must make it very clear that it must not be asked for again' ran a peremptory message, sent to Ponsonby through one of the Queen's ladies in 1888.[1] Over White Lodge, none the less, the Queen yielded gradually, but against her

---

* Sir Henry Ponsonby (1825–1895), Private Secretary to Queen Victoria from 1870 until his death.

better judgement. 'I thank you for your dear letter recd the day before yesterday', she wrote to Princess Mary Adelaide on 22 March 1869, from Windsor, '& am quite ready to let you *try* the White Lodge for a month as you seem so anxious to do so. There may be arrangements to make respecting the Servants—&c & it wld therefore be well I think if you cld see Sir Thomas Biddulph* yourself.'²

The Queen's reluctance to allow her cousin to install herself and her family at Richmond arose from a bleak knowledge of the income granted by Parliament to Princess Mary Adelaide on her marriage, and a fairly shrewd assessment of what two establishments run on her cousin's principles were liable to cost. When, in 1878, the Duchess of Teck came to plead with her for a private loan of £1,200 to keep the most vociferous of their creditors at bay, the Queen refused it on the sensible grounds that to help a cousin would set a precedent and that 'if once it is done it will be asked for again & again'. These were the reasons she gave on paper to Sir Thomas Biddulph; to her cousin she only remarked that 'it was far too much for her to undertake to keep up *two* Houses'. To this the Duchess of Teck replied that she had 'often feared [it], but did so for the Childrens healths'.³

By August 1870 the family were comfortably and permanently established at White Lodge. It soon became more of a home to them than Kensington Palace, where the apartments (kept, of course, in full running order) began themselves to take on the atmosphere of a *pied-à-terre*; for, if one had plenty of good horses and carriages, it was quite possible to conduct a social London life from Richmond, returning thither in the small hours of the morning after a dinner, a concert or a theatre. Besides the benefit to the children of living at White Lodge, the place provided an occupation for another member of the family—their father, the Duke of Teck.† The Duke became a passionate gardener, turning the wilderness of White Lodge garden into a 'Paradise', and buying lilacs and syringas wholesale. He was even sometimes assisted in his activities by the Duchess of Teck, who would step heavily down in the twilight from her 'brown den' upstairs, or her 'blue boudoir' on the terrace floor, to help 'Francis' snip the withered brown heads of dead roses from the bushes in the old rose

* Sir Thomas Biddulph (1809–1878), Master of Queen Victoria's Household, 1851; Keeper of the Privy Purse, 1867.

† The reader is here reminded that King Carl of Württemberg gave his cousin Prince Teck a dukedom in September 1871. Prince Teck and his wife will therefore henceforward in these pages be described as Duke and Duchess of Teck.

garden. The Duke was driven to make a profession out of a pastime, for he had otherwise sadly little to do.

Der schöne Uhlan had always been happiest in the company of bright young military officers, but his life in England gave him few opportunities of mixing with these. Soon after his marriage he had been gazetted Honorary Colonel of the Post Office Volunteers. He took the unexacting and undistinguished duties of this post seriously, attending the Volunteers' mess dinners at Limmer's Hotel and going into camp with the battalion under canvas at Aldershot. In the brief Egyptian Expedition of 1882* he volunteered for service and was attached with a Major's duties to Lord Wolseley's staff. Owing to what his brother-in-law the Duke of Cambridge, then Commander-in-Chief, called 'Francis' . . . very impaired vision' he proved, if anything, an incubus in the desert, and was not happy there. 'Franz Teck does not look well and seems in very low spirits. I don't think he enjoys himself out here at all',[4] the Duke of Connaught† wrote to his mother Queen Victoria, from the tented desert camp at Tel el Mahuta in September 1882. Soon after this expedition the perennial request that the Duke of Teck be given the English style of 'Royal Highness' turned up once again on Queen Victoria's writing-desk. She minuted to Sir Henry Ponsonby that 'it wld be strange to do it *now*, just after the war in wh he has done nothing—tho' he has been very kind about the wounded'.[5]

The Duke of Teck was left with no work other than that of making the White Lodge garden, and attending his wife, like a thin dark shadow, at the public functions, or Drawing-Rooms or Courts to which she went. The Duke of Cambridge would write of 'giving him occupation & interest, the want of which he feels so acutely',[6] but nothing was done about it. This state of affairs involved, for Teck, a prolonged nagging mental frustration, which naturally found its only outlet in attacks of 'nerves'.

* In support of the Khedive Tewfik. Lord Wolseley's force arrived in the middle of August, and after routing Arabi's army at Tel-el-Kebir, entered Cairo on 14 September. The British Army thereafter remained in Egypt for seventy-four years.

† Arthur, Prince of Great Britain and Ireland, KG (1850–1942), was the third son and seventh child of Queen Victoria and the Prince Consort. Created Duke of Connaught and Strathearn in 1874, he married in 1879 Louise Margaret, Princess of Prussia, daughter of Prince Frederick Charles of Prussia; she was born in 1860 and died in 1917. The Duke of Connaught had a long and distinguished military career.

II

The history of White Lodge previous to its tenancy by Princess May's parents is simple to summarise. It was built by George I as a hunting-box, enlarged by George II (whose Queen, Caroline, used it frequently and in whose memory the avenue leading to the Lodge from the Richmond side is called 'The Queen's Ride') and then inhabited, successively, by Lord Bute and by the younger Pitt's successor in the Premiership, Addington. It was then assigned to Mary, Duchess of Gloucester, twelfth child of George III. After her death in 1857 Queen Victoria occasionally stayed at White Lodge, and ended by lending it to her friend Lady Phipps. As we have seen, the Prince of Wales was sent there to study in 1858, and he and the Princess of Wales made a desultory use of the house in 1867 and 1868. The Duke and Duchess of Teck lived there from 1870 until they departed in temporary exile to Italy in 1883. Returning to England in 1885, they settled at White Lodge, and it was here that they both died. To their daughter Princess May, White Lodge was in childhood her chief home, and later, for eight years more, her only one. She left it to marry the Duke of York in 1893.

The White Lodge stood, as it still stands,* just within the palings of Richmond Park. Although at that time quiet and secluded, it is in fact near the main carriage road, and its grounds consist of five acres of garden only. Facing south, the house seems at first sight to be larger than it actually is. The central block or *corps de logis*, to which entrance is gained through a pillared portico and a glassed-in entrance hall, contains but six rooms on the ground floor, and of these only one, the drawing-room, overlooking the garden and the Queen's Ride, is of any substantial size. On each side of this *corps de logis*, curving corridors—the 'Green Corridor' and the 'Children's Corridor'— connect the main block with the two wings, each of which again contains six rooms only on the principal floor; and they are very small rooms at that. The bedroom floor was a warren of tiny rooms, the only good-sized one being the Duchess of Teck's bedroom which lay, flanked by her dressing-room and the 'den' in which she 'transacted business', directly over the large drawing-room.

White Lodge is a shallow and rather impermanent-feeling house,

* Since 1955 White Lodge has been the junior School of the Royal (formerly Sadler's Wells) Ballet.

its best features being the long corridors and the inner hall which has a fine balustraded staircase winding up to the first floor. From this inner hall you stepped straight into the drawing-room, which had French windows giving on to steps into the garden. On either side of the drawing-room, and accessible by doors opening from it, were two oblong rooms—that on the right as you came in was the Duke of Teck's study, also used as the Library, a room with a pilastered alcove holding bookshelves which could contain at most some eight hundred books; that on the left the Blue Room, which was the Duchess of Teck's boudoir, and had an elegant ironwork balcony. The Duchess's favourite nook was in none of these rooms, but in an embrasure in the Green Corridor, and here she would by preference receive her friends. Princess May slept in what she once described as 'a smallish bedroom top of staircase on right'. As she grew up, she was allotted a sitting-room of her own 'at the end of the long corridor in the right wing, a long way from the bedroom', but with the advantage of having a handsome verandah on which you could sit out.7

The rooms at White Lodge were furnished in the fashion of the day: that is to say that they were loaded with ottomans and sofas draped with shawls, large tables covered with Turkey rugs, small occasional tables as ubiquitous as mushrooms in an October field, elaborate inlaid chairs, ornamental stools with twisted legs, and many palms in pots. Family portraits stood about on varnished easels, while other pictures, small and large, peppered the brocaded walls as thickly as though they had been shot out at them from some gigantic gun. On the floors were strewn eastern carpets. The larger pieces of furniture came brand-new from Maple's emporium. The arrangement of the rooms was the Duke's.

Princess Mary Adelaide had learned wonderingly, at Kensington Palace in 1867, that she had married a man who was not only a handsome Austrian officer but an expert in modern taste. She had let him have his will over the decoration of Kensington, and she now did the same at White Lodge. The results delighted her; beaming and jubilant, she would confide to her journal, or to her sister by letter, just how wonderful the inside of the house was becoming. More exciting still, the Duke kept the furniture in what might be termed a permanent state of flux, preparing surprises for anniversaries and snatching at any opportunity for an almost neurotic rotation and change. On her thirty-seventh birthday, 27 November 1870, the Duchess was led into the drawing-room at White Lodge, on her return from a satisfactory visit to her friend 'Florence Londesborough' at Londesborough Lodge, near Scarborough:

On our return Francis took me into the drawing-room where the bright red cretonne curtains and loose covers were my first pleasant surprise; and then into the blue morning-room, which, had the carpet arrived in time, would have been quite ready for use, thanks to dear Francis. The blue parrots on the buff ground of the cretonne curtains and covers are deliciously pretty.[8]

From now on, they formed the habit of sitting in the Blue Morning-Room after dinner.

In the next few years further re-arrangements were made, until in January 1875 perfection was achieved. In a letter to Strelitz the Duchess described the new look of the Blue Morning-Room, or Boudoir. Into this small and narrow room a good quantity of furniture had now, under the Duke's directions, been compressed:

After dinner I was taken into the blue boudoir to be *agreeably* surprised which I *most certainly* was, for never have I seen a room more improved! The new corner sofa by good luck chanced to be too short for the corner it had been originally ordered for; so Francis put it between the windows (under your & Alix's pictures) for which corner it seems *made*! The cabinet, he removed to the wall under Mamma's picture, where it looks beautiful & its place under the 3 chicks' portraits, is filled by the large sofa. In the corner by the cabinet, stands an easel with Swinton's sketch of Francis on it & in front of this the round blue leather table making a back to the small *chaise-longue*, which is placed cornerwise to the fire, with a small table in front of it. Behind the armchair, which takes up the opposite corner of the fireplace, now stands the little black Japanese *whatnot* from the Green Corridor; to be ultimately replaced by the new black cabinet ordered of Maple for my Christmas by Francis. The high whatnot, which used to be in the corner between the windows, now fills up the space between the sofa & the door into the dining room. The whole effect is *most* perfect & so delighted me ... most snug & *cosy*!

This density of effect in the privileged Blue Boudoir had at first been achieved at the expense of the drawing-room, which the Duke of Teck 'had arranged . . . rather stiffly . . & left it very bare, which I did not at all approve of'.[9] This was soon rectified in the following month: 'the large round table left as it stood at Christmastime, with the Queen's statuette on it; & two small red armchairs & the sofa red

c

velvet table arranged near it, in the large centre window, instead of the former arrangement by which the table quite blocked up the window, & with the red *pâté* covered with books (as at Ashridge!) in front of the low screen, that hides the piano'. To make a little space in the Blue Boudoir two small inlaid cabinets, lined with blue silk, which had belonged to 'dear Aunt Mary' Gloucester and were probably among the best pieces of furniture in the house had been 'transferred' upstairs to the Duchess's 'brown den'.[10]

Such descriptions of Victorian interiors may make stuffy reading today, but we should remember that, by the glow of the oil-lamps—the White Lodge did not then boast gas—these over-furnished rooms must have seemed extraordinarily comfortable and agreeable, for the Duke of Teck had aimed at and achieved that German ideal for which there is no equivalent word in our own language: *Gemütlichkeit*. We should also bear in mind that rooms read of merely, or seen in faded beige photographs, do not resemble rooms in action—animated by parents and children, servants, dogs, kittens. Summer and winter, too, the White Lodge rooms were filled with flowers: 'my blue boudoir gay . . . with tulips, camelias etc. (the *cut* ones from Kew!)', as the Duchess wrote one sleety January morning from her sitting-room overlooking the bare, windswept garden, some eighty-odd winters ago.[11]

III

Princess May's early upbringing at White Lodge and at Kensington was merry but fairly strict. Both parents held firm views on preparing children to face the world, and the little Tecks were not cosseted or spoiled. Speaking of her daughter one day to an old friend of her own, Mrs Dalrymple, the Duchess said: 'A child has quite enough to do, Ellinor, to learn obedience, and attend to her lessons, and to *grow*, without many parties and late hours, which take the freshness of childhood away, and the brightness and beauty from girlhood—and then children become intolerable. There are too many grown-up children in the present day.'[12] This did not mean that the Duchess was a severe parent, for she was far too warmly affectionate and demonstrative for that. She spent what was, for those days, an unusual amount of time with her children, going often into the nursery, playing with them in either the Children's or the Green Corridor, swinging them on the garden swing, organising 'tea-picnics' in neighbouring woods and expeditions to pick primroses or bluebells, or to gather blackberries when in season. There were card games—snap, 'geographical Lotto' and something called 'the Egg game'—and there were occasional treats like a visit to the circus or to Maskelyne and Cook's. The Duke of Teck, who was something of a German martinet to his sons, was indulgent to his daughter, whom he called 'dearest Pussy-cat', and who would send him little notes enclosing pressed violets when he was away from home.

As a very small girl Princess May had been delicate, and had caused her parents some anxiety. She soon grew out of this, and by the age of eight she was healthy and 'alarmingly tall'. By then she had also passed through an awkward stage in looks, which, in 1874, Queen Victoria had been quick to notice: 'Mary's boys are splendid but her little girl is very plain.'[13] 'She is quick and clever and musical', her mother wrote of May.[14] She learned French and was making good headway with German under the Hanoverian nursery-governess Anna Mund, a sufferer from chronic asthma. Summers at White Lodge were spent, when practicable, out-of-doors. 'We have been living as much as possible in the open air', the Duchess wrote in the summer of 1880, 'and for days I was able to make the garden my sitting-room, and write my letters (*innumerable*) out-of-doors. Our life has been a very pleasant one, for we have had weekly visitors from Saturday to Monday or so, have been cultivating our agreeable *voisinage*, had sundry cricket-matches and tea-picnics in Coombe wood.' 'We are *très recherchés* and *much visited*!' she wrote, that same spring, to Lady Aylesford.[15] Birthdays were richly celebrated; Christmas Eve was marked by a galaxy of presents, arranged round the tall Christmas tree in the darkened dining-room. The presents were piled up on tables, each member of the family having his or her own table. The tree was lighted with candles set in wooden hoops encircling it, and one of the footmen had the special duty of extinguishing these as they guttered, using a damp sponge on a long bamboo pole. Princess May also got extra presents, if her mother had been abroad: 'a blue stone heart' from Frankfurt, or little felt hats from Homburg.

The Duchess of Teck liked to record details of their daily lives— the first time the two elder boys put on their 'violet Morgan suits', or an evening in which she herself had 'eaten up nearly all the buttered toast' destined for nursery tea. Food formed an all-important element in their lives. Writing to their parents, the children would describe what they had had for tea—apricot tartelettes or plovers' eggs—at

Clarence House or Marlborough House. The Duchess, who of all persons should have tried to bant, was herself a *gourmet*. 'I was always warning Mary to be careful about what she eats, but she never took my advice. Now she has got the bill for it', her husband had written to his elder sister only one year after marriage. 'I only write you this so that you are not disappointed when you see her next.'[16] At Hopetoun House, whither the family went two years running for a long autumn holiday by the sea, the little Hope boys and girls were astounded at how much the Teck family could eat. They prolonged Hopetoun meals to two or three hours, and one of the Hope girls has never forgotten the peculiar emphasis which the Duchess would put into the two words 'rich cream', rolling her r's lusciously as she spoke. On one of these visits she announced that her London doctor had ordered her to eat dry Abernethy biscuits before, but not (as one might think) instead of, rich cream. There she would sit crumbling the biscuits, her 'frog's eyes' fixed on the next course, while her host's children fidgeted to get down from the table and away to the sea-shore.

It was, by and large, a sunny childhood, but the darker side of life was not neglected. The Duchess of Teck was notoriously charitable, and she was determined that Princess May and her brothers should early learn of the existence and the habits of 'the Poor'. Mr Carr Glyn, the vicar of Kensington, who gave the children their Scripture lessons when they were in London—at White Lodge the Duchess herself undertook this task—was instructed to take the little Tecks to visit the Poor in their tenements and hovels. 'On one of these expeditions, Her Royal Highness sent a dinner to a destitute family, and gave instructions that the children were to stop and see the poor people eat it, showing at once her practical mind and her goodness of heart.'[17] Such golden opportunities to observe the Poor at feeding-time in their natural surroundings were supplemented by hearsay, and by children's story-books designed to shed light on this murky and mystifying subject of poverty. 'In the evening we read Penfold, a very nice book which Miss Gutman lent us', Princess May wrote, when she was almost fifteen, to her mother. 'She says it is very much like it really is among the poor.'[18]

Princess May was also enlisted from her nursery days to take part in her mother's charities, notably the Surrey Needlework Guild, which provided clothing for poor persons, and the Royal Cambridge Asylum. The Needlework Guild will be considered in a subsequent chapter. A few words about the Royal Cambridge Asylum will be apposite here.

IV

The Prince Consort had laid the foundation-stone of the Royal Cambridge Asylum in 1851. It had been built on land given by the Cambridge family and stood on the outskirts of Kingston-on-Thames. Designed to house some seventy old soldiers' widows, it was dedicated to the memory of Princess May's grandfather, Adolphus, Duke of Cambridge, and was the particular care of her mother and of Uncle George Cambridge. Both as Princess, and as Queen Consort, she retained an active interest in the Asylum's affairs. This interest dated from the earliest days at White Lodge.

The old ladies, who were nominated to the Asylum, liked to think of it as 'a little Hampton Court'. Each old woman had a room of her own, with a bed in a curtained alcove, and a small pantry with sink, taps and cupboard space. Their allowance was five shillings a week. The Duchess of Teck presided over the meetings of the female committee which ran the home, her brother the Duke of Cambridge over the committee of men.

On certain specified dates, notably that of the old Duke of Cambridge's death, the Duchess of Teck and her daughter Princess May would repair to the Royal Cambridge Asylum and there distribute packets of sugar and tea, or White Lodge vegetables to the old ladies. 'Tuesday afternoon, we spent at the R. Cambridge Asylum, distributing a whole *cart load* of vegetables & fruit to the 70 Inmates. Both May & I stood till we nearly dropped!' the Duchess of Teck wrote in a chatty letter to her youngest son, at school, in September 1887.[19]

So long as the old Duchess of Cambridge remained mobile she, too, would attend these festivities, as, for example, in mid-May 1870 when the pensioners were, oddly, partaking of 'their postponed annual Christmas dinner'. '... Found all the widows comfortably enjoying roast mutton and plum pudding ... in the presence of dear Mama, several of the Ladies' Committee, and Hampton Court ladies and Sir Edward Cust', we read in the Duchess of Teck's journal for that day. 'After the dinner we visited the infirm widows in their rooms, and then saw Lady Gomm distribute Augusta's bounty (in commemoration of Mama's miraculous escape in the accident of May 8, 1869) to the widows on the terrace.'[20] The accident of 8 May 1869 had occurred on the Kew Road, along which the Duchess of Cambridge, with Colonel Purves in attendance, was peacefully bowling in her brougham. A hansom cab had darted out from behind a market cart and, crashing headlong into the Royal brougham, overturned it. 'HRH was not hurt', Mr Kinloch Cooke assures us. 'Col. Purves was, however, less fortunate; he severely injured his leg, and two months later died of lock-jaw.'[21]

As the years went by, the good old noun 'asylum' took on a new and less pleasing connotation. A movement was started among the inmates to have the name changed to 'Home'. 'Imagine, some old goose declared: she would not enter the "Asylum", unless it was named a "Home"!' Princess May's aunt Augusta Strelitz told her in June 1901, 'the weak Princes giving in to this, when I said "then let her keep out of it, but don't alter the name, given to it 50 years ago by both Duchesses Cambridge and Gloucester", this strengthened their backbone and the "Asylum" is saved. I hope you approve?'[22] Her niece, then Duchess of York, replied most emphatically that she did.

As well as helping her mother in the Cambridge Asylum distributions, Princess May was taught from infancy to think of children less fortunate than herself. Like her brothers she was given money to hand out in charity, and she would annually send a quantity of her discarded toys to the 'Princess Mary's Village Homes for Little Girls', a novel institution at Addlestone for the care of 'convicts' children' during their parents' term of imprisonment.

As the years went by, the Duchess of Teck's philanthropic activities multiplied, and in all of these she was willingly aided by Princess May. But it was small incidents like childish visits to the Royal Cambridge Asylum, or the despatch of used playthings to Addlestone, that first aroused Princess May's intense and well-known concern for housing conditions, for hospitals and for every kind of ameliorative social work.

V

Thus was Princess May of Teck early educated to an interest in social questions and to a consciousness of social need. After 1874 she and her brothers also began a lengthy and, on their side, a most involuntary training in the horrors of incurable sickness and creeping old age. This lesson was learned in their almost daily visits to their grandmother, the old Duchess of Cambridge, who had returned, partially paralysed, from Strelitz when Princess May was seven years old. The Duchess survived her first stroke for fifteen years, kept alive by assiduous medical attention which could not, however, allay her steady and perceptible decline. Instead of being shielded from this terrifying spectacle, Princess May and her brothers were expected to entertain and divert the old lady, to sing *Les Trois Anges* or *God Save the Queen* to her, or, on manifold other occasions, to remain silently in her sitting-room looking at an album while their mother tried to cheer up the querulous invalid. It is highly probable that the constant sight of this once proud old lady seated helpless, bent and bald in her chair, gave Princess May her lifelong distaste for illness and for invalids; just as the destruction of a cottage at Rumpenheim by lightning during a thunderstorm, when she was three years old, gave her a fear of thunder which she never afterwards lost. Such childhood experiences leave an indelible imprint.

It was in November 1873, a few days before the whole Teck family were expected there for Christmas, that the Duchess was stricken, at Neu Strelitz, with paralysis of one arm and one leg. She had been out driving in an open carriage in the crisp winter weather. After getting home and when seated at the dinner-table, she suffered a stroke. At first she could be neither moved from the ground floor to her apartments above, nor could she be dressed; but when the Teck family arrived in December she was carried up on a *chaise-longue* to her rooms 'and bore the move wonderfully well, without any sensation of giddiness', as the Duchess of Teck wrote to Queen Victoria who, always interested in serious illness, had asked for detailed bulletins on Aunt Cambridge. 'Our presence here is evidently a pleasure and relief to her', the Duchess of Teck continued, 'and she delights in having the children in her room for a few minutes at a time every day.'[23]

The Duchess of Cambridge was very much controlled by her lady-in-waiting, Lady Geraldine Somerset, an unpredictable and jealous personage who harboured a hopeless passion for the old Duchess's son George, balanced by an equally strong animosity towards Princess Mary Adelaide, Duchess of Teck. In after years Lady Geraldine succeeded in doing the Duchess of Teck a good deal of harm, in a waspish and mischief-making way. 'Poor Geraldine, she really looked after the boys and me, but May was a thorn in her eye and she had a diabolical hate against Mary', the Duke of Teck wrote in 1889.[24] In June 1874 it was decided to move the Duchess of Cambridge back to England, where she could be in her own house. The journey was accomplished with the help of Lady Geraldine, who described it in a letter as 'an awful undertaking! *forty* unbroken hours of railroad in HRH's state! . . . she suffered terribly and many times I thought she would have to give it up & stop somewhere. Now after a good night and a quiet day, tho' most dreadfully *brisée de membres* and feeling *very* weak, she is most wonderful today, not any *really* the worse'.[25] The arrival of the Royal invalid in England meant that she ceased to be the responsibility of the Mecklenburg-Strelitz family, and became that of her son George, Duke of Cambridge, who was always very busy, and of her younger daughter, the Duchess of Teck, whose leisure allowed her to spend many hours in the sick-room, under Lady Geraldine's vindictive gaze.

Princess Mary Adelaide's letters to her cousin Queen Victoria now became long and even, for a brief period, frequent. They dealt wholly with the 'dear patient's' state, whether she had slept or not, how violent the paroxysms of pain in the arm could be, whether she was 'worn, weak and drowsy', or whether a new régime of turtle soup, fowl and puddings, with an increased 'allowance of champagne and brandy' was likely to answer. In the winter of 1874 the Grand Duchess of Mecklenburg-Strelitz came over to London, and temporarily relieved her sister of some of these duties; but when she left in February 1875, the onus of amusing their mother was once more squarely placed on Princess Mary Adelaide, who would rush backwards and forwards between Kew and White Lodge. She would usually take some of the children with her, and if she found that she herself 'could not be spared from home' she would send 'the chicks' on their own. Sometimes 'the chicks' were driven to take their own childish defensive measures: 'I fear . . . they rather tired & fidgeted their dear Grandmamma, as they were noisy & giggly over their tea & did not mind what they were told', their mother wrote of one long February afternoon when the four of them had been shut up in Cambridge Cottage, Kew.[26]

The Duke of Teck was also enlisted in the fight to help the Duchess of Cambridge forget her ailments, for on these she was already tending gruffly to harp. The old Duchess was very fond of her son-in-law: 'Her love for me was really touching', he wrote, perhaps complacently, after her death. 'Even my voice, she said "was the most pleasant of any of her relations". I have lost my best friend.'[27] One evening, after the invalid had been persuaded to take 'a little *mock* white soup; chicken broth, thickened with vermicelli & made with *asses' milk* instead of cream', she herself suggested that her son-in-law should display his taste and talent by re-arranging her most treasured pictures on her 'ivy screen'. 'On the left leaf of the screen, in order that Mamma may see them from her armchair now hang at the top, Papa in the centre, between you and George on his right', the Duchess of Teck wrote to her sister, '& I, in the swing, on his left & immediately underneath ... a watercoloured picture of a French fisherman's family—On the shelf below this, Francis placed all the *Miniatures*, off the writing table: ... *you, I, Tilla* as children &c. Your gift, the Saviour by Kannengasser, & Tante's Raphael angels have not been moved from the centre panel, but on the right in place of the white group in the centre, now hangs a little Swiss picture (landscape) in a wooden frame, your gift I fancy, & above it a smaller one, that used to stand in a corner of her writing-table. (I give you these details, because in a letter to Mamma, you the other day said, you could now no longer picture to yourself the screen.)'[28]

Another and more ambitious attempt that year to lighten the Duchess of Cambridge's gloom consisted of a visit from her sister, the Dowager Grand Duchess of Mecklenburg-Strelitz, Princess Mary Adelaide's 'Tante Marie'. But Tante Marie wanted to seize this opportunity to go out and about in London, instead of listening all day to her sister's complaints; and the fact that she, several years the Duchess of Cambridge's senior, should be spry and active gave her sister small pleasure. Moreover, the Dowager Grand Duchess could not speak English which made the calls of her sister's English friends awkward and stiff.

The old Duchess of Cambridge had always been sociable and it was natural that she should wish to try to distract herself by seeing her old friends. With this in view she determined to be moved to London, so as to settle permanently into her apartments at St James's Palace. 'Your acct. of your dear Mama is very cheering—but I am *not* pleased at the thought of her going to London', Queen Victoria wrote to the Duchess of Teck in August 1875, 'the gloom & fog of wh. in Sept—Oct.—Nov.—& Dec.—are indescribably depressing & the noise of wh. *at all* times is very bad for an Invalid. But what do you mean by saying you hope to take her up to Town in my pony Chair? That wld be most *dangerous* & I am sure disagreeable thro' streets & thoroughfares & she wd be mobbed & molested in every way. Some low, long carriage, wld be far the best.'[29]

c*

Queen Victoria had given her aunt an invalid chair, designed to be drawn by a small pony. In March 1875 she had visited her at Cambridge Cottage. The Queen reported that she found the old woman 'unaltered as to expression & mind—only so venerable in a little white Cap & even her hair quite white, & the dark eyebrows also very nearly so—so that the severity of expression is all gone. She is quite helpless & one arm all but powerless.'30 Two years later the Queen begged her Aunt Cambridge to give either Rosa Koberwein or the new Court painter von Angeli* some sittings for a portrait. Von Angeli was chosen and the result, now at Windsor Castle, is reproduced in this book.

Towards the end of the year 1875 the Duchess of Cambridge finally got her way. She was transported from Kew to St James's Palace where she lived on in growing decrepitude, inhabiting the dark apartments afterwards given to Princess May and her husband, when this suite of rooms was re-christened York House. The old Duchess became more and more bent as she aged. In her last years such daily visitors as the singer Tosti could only speak to the old lady by kneeling beside her on the floor. One of her habits was to keep her cap and wig on a stand by her chair, and she would clap these on to her head, often crookedly, when anyone came to call. Sometimes she would even dispense with this formality. 'Tea with the old Duchess of Cambridge', we read in a passage from the *Memoirs* of a Battenberg Princess, Marie of Erbach-Schönberg,† describing her first visit to London in May 1882, when she stayed with the Edinburghs

---

* Heinrich von Angeli (1840–1918), the Austrian portrait painter, obtained high favour at the Courts of Austria, England, Russia and Germany. Sent to paint Queen Victoria by her eldest daughter the Crown Princess of Prussia (who had discovered von Angeli in Vienna in 1873), he was often employed by the Queen, who incidentally commissioned him to paint Princess May of Teck during her engagement to the Duke of York in 1893. 'I like him very much,' the Queen wrote of von Angeli, 'and what I like is his honesty, total want of flattery and appreciation of character . . . he catches the likeness at once. . . . He has in fact told me again and again how little he cares for positive beauty or great youth, but rather paints older people with character and expression.' (Letter from Osborne, 3 April 1875, now in the Kronberg Archives.) See plate 5.

† Marie, Princess of Battenberg (1852–1923), was the eldest child and only daughter of Alexander, Prince of Hesse and by the Rhine, by his morganatic marriage with Julie, Countess Hauke. One of her four brothers was Henry, Prince of Battenberg (1858–1896), who married in 1885 Queen Victoria's youngest daughter, Princess Beatrice (1857–1944). In 1871 she had married Gustavus, Count of Erbach-Schönberg (1840–1908), who was created a Prince in 1903.

at 'splendid and simple' Clarence House. '...At first I was quite disconcerted, for she wore no cap, and her absolutely bald head looked like a very big egg.'[31]

The Duchess of Cambridge's move to London did not mean that her Teck grandchildren saw much less of her than when she had been at Kew, for they would often accompany their mother to St James's from White Lodge. Sometimes she might leave them to amuse themselves by the hour in the waiting carriage, while she sat with the invalid; but more usually she would lead one or other of them into the Duchess's presence. Sunday was especially a St James's Palace day: 'It was touching to see the children on a Sunday afternoon gathered round the invalid's chair, and to hear Grandmama and the little ones sing the hymn "Thy Will be done",' writes an eyewitness.[32] The Teck boys were at school for a large part of each year, but their sister was not; so it was Princess May who, of the four of them, was at St James's Palace the most.

A living *memento mori*, the old Duchess of Cambridge scared her granddaughter. 'I think', Princess May wrote conclusively in after years, her theme these visits, 'an invalid rather frightens young people.'[33]

VI

Although it might, in awful moments of gloom or boredom, have seemed so, St James's Palace was not the only London house open to the Teck children. We have seen that they maintained a fairly even friendship with the Wales family at Marlborough House. There were the gardens of Chiswick House and Holland House for them to play in. There were also, more rarely, visits to the little Edinburgh cousins at Clarence House, reigned over by Aunt Marie Edinburgh, a Russian whose haughty manner and eccentricities concealed a kind, religious heart.

The Duchess of Edinburgh's private rooms at Clarence House contained glittering, jewelled ikons and mysterious shrines before which oil-lamps twinkled in the gloom. Wherever she lived she kept a Russian priest and two chanters. She brought up her children in the Anglican faith, but to a stoic view of life. They must never admit to illness, and they were taught to eat up everything that was put before them. It would have done the shy and tongue-tied Princess May good to have seen more of Aunt Marie, one of whose *dicta* was that Royal children must be taught to converse freely: 'Nothing', she would say, 'is more hopeless than a Princess who never opens her mouth.' The Duchess of Edinburgh hated a bracing climate and was the only member of the Royal Family who did not find Osborne too relaxing. She disliked windy places, because she had never been able to put two hat-pins in her hats, and consequently these blew off easily; she said that as a girl at St Petersburg she had not been taught to put in a hat-pin with her left hand, and she did not propose to begin trying to do so now. Her soft leather boots, made in St Petersburg and sent in quantity to London, fitted either foot equally well for she declared it irrational to fancy that you needed a left one and a right. She spoke perfect English, but preferred to speak French as being the only elegant language in Europe.

'Your children are so nice and so immensely grown', the Duchess of Edinburgh wrote to their mother after a Christmas-time tea-party at Clarence House in 1878. 'The boys are too splendid, I would not believe their age. The little girl looks quite well now. They had tea in my room and we held long conversations; they were particularly interested in the description of the Russian winter and I had to relate about it while they were having their tea with great appetites. They are now romping with my children and making a tremendous noise. Thank you for having sent them, they are so very charming and so well behaved.'[34]

Four years after this Christmas of 1878, the first family separation took place: in May 1882 Prince Dolly and Prince Frank went to boarding school. 'Oh dear! how we all choked & gulped down our sobs, as we saw the clarence with our precious boys, turn the corner & disappear', their fond mother wrote to them on the same day this wrench took place. 'Then *very sadly* we all betook ourselves to our rooms & May, Alge, & I indulged, if the truth must be told, in a bit of a cry, from which Papa, who we verily believe, had done the same, roused us very wisely & sent May and Alge into the garden.'[35] The two elder boys were later sent to Wellington, where Prince Dolly was more successful than Prince Frank, whose practical jokes maddened his masters. Prince Frank was later removed and sent to Cheltenham College. The youngest boy, Prince Alge, when his turn came, went to Eton.

The disappearance of Prince Dolly from her life for so many weeks in each year affected Princess May severely, for he was always her favourite brother. She would write to him assiduously, describing her daily doings. She hardly ever wrote to Prince Frank.

Princess May was now fourteen. For some years she had been taken to children's parties and to dancing classes. At all of these she suffered considerably, for, once outside the home circle, she was, and for many, many years remained, infinitely shy. The psychological causes of this major handicap are not far to seek: for the Duchess of Teck's impulsive, entertaining and at times indiscreet conversation was hard for a growing daughter to rival. The girl reacted against it by becoming a silent listener and observer.* The Duchess was a devoted parent, but she could often seem an embarrassing one. It was, to begin with, unorthodox, if not unique, to have a mother who was so very much larger than the ordinary run of parents. At Taglioni's dancing classes at her little house in Connaught Square, the other children would giggle when they saw that Princess May's mother needed two gilt chairs, not one, to sit upon. Princess May was acutely conscious that her mother might at any moment appear in an absurd light to those who did not know her, and she would nervously try to prevent Princess Mary Adelaide being caught, for instance, without the braid of false hair which she wore, like a crown, forward on the top of her head. She was perfectly aware of her own shyness but, like most sensitive children, she did not know how it could best be overcome. The Duchess of Teck only made it worse by applying her own rough-and-ready method for curing shyness to Princess May—which was to refer in company to this shyness in the presence of the wretched girl herself.

The dancing classes of Taglioni and of Mr d'Egville thus became periods of martyrdom for Princess May. Taglioni, who was by then small and wizened, had lost all the money she had saved from her great days, and had been obliged, in old age, to open a dancing school. The lessons normally took place in the Connaught Square house, but sometimes the children would meet at Kensington Palace and have their lessons there. 'Yesterday', wrote Princess May's Aunt Augusta in August 1877, 'I went to Taglioni's lesson, the dear Chicks danced

---

* When once, many years later, discussing her childhood Queen Mary remarked that her own silence was due to her mother's having been so talkative: 'and then in our day', she added, 'children were brought up to be seen and not heard. There's something in it: we learned a lot by listening to our elders—only when we went out into company it was supposed that hey presto! we should at once scintillate in sparkling conversation, whereas we were like that girl in one of Mary Cholmondeley's books, who "hid her burning hands in her lap and talked about bees".'

very nicely, May especially graceful, I had a nice talk with Taglioni who remained on till near 5 o'clock.'³⁶

At fourteen Princess May was rather tall and big for her age, temporarily inclined to gawkiness, and dressed in unyielding, stiff and buttoned-up clothes. Her fair hair, which was of a shade between light brown and gold, was unusually thick. While other girls of her age would have their hair dressed for bed-time in four plaits, Princess May had six. It was artificially curled, and at this moment of her life she wore it 'up' in front and 'down' at the back.

Among the varied tortures devised by Taglioni was a deportment lesson, which involved each girl going alone into the back drawing-room in Connaught Square, draping herself with a chenille tablecloth as a train, and entering the front drawing-room, before the rest of the class. This effort distressed Princess May as much as its variation at Mr d'Egville's classes, where the girls went round the room in turn, dropping curtsies. Hard driven by embarrassment, Princess May would try to evade this exercise by saying: 'Well, thank goodness, curtsying is one thing *I* shall never have to do.' But Mr d'Egville and the Duchess of Teck were adamant, and round the room she had to go. At Lord Hopetoun's coming-of-age party at Hopetoun, where the Teck family was staying when Princess May was thirteen, she tried to hide behind her mother in the procession to the dais in the ballroom, and her teeth were chattering with fright.

The long autumn visit of the whole Teck family to Hopetoun in 1881 had been preceded, the year before, by a sojourn of some weeks there by Prince Dolly, Prince Frank and their tutor. In 1882 the whole family settled there once more for another six weeks, for staying at Hopetoun House was at once a pleasure and an economy. Hopetoun is a great grey Palladian structure, standing above the sea, not far from Edinburgh. Its turfy lawns are a mile long, and it is surrounded by huge beech trees, laurels, rhododendrons, yews and holly. It overhangs the sandy sea-shore, and commands a distant view of mountains. The Teck children would run about the shore collecting crystals and pebbles, or prising giant sea-anemones out of rock-pools. There was a large swimming-bath filled with warm water, and in this 'Princessy' as the Hope children called Princess May, would luxuriate by the hour, ignoring her nurse's constant cry: 'Princess, you must get out, come along, Princess, you must get out.' The old Duchess of Cambridge had called her granddaughter 'self-willed' as a tiny child, and indeed Princess May possessed a streak of obstinacy as strong as that of Queen Victoria herself.

The small Hopes soon noticed that, although 'Princessy' was speechless with shyness before many people, she was high-spirited and even mischievous when she got to know children well. Once, at Henley regatta, she snatched off the new blue silk sash which Dorrie Hope was wearing and hurled it into the Thames.

The Tecks' bright little hosts were quick to notice the Duke of Teck's peculiarities: how he would chain-smoke one pipe after another, shout at his boys and, on occasion, in a fit of temper, even yell in public at the Duchess, who managed to maintain a serene dignity in the face of his guttural outbursts. This was late in 1882, when financial worries were pressing like sharp knives into the Duke's mind, and only some months before the family were asked by Queen Victoria and the Duchess of Cambridge to withdraw to the Continent to economise for several years. Before following them into this Florentine exile, we must glance at another and very important aspect of Princess May's childhood: the various visits she paid with her parents to their German relations at Rumpenheim, Neu Strelitz and Reinthal.

CHAPTER FOUR

RUMPENHEIM, NEU STRELITZ AND REINTHAL

IF, IN ENGLAND, in the 'sixties and 'seventies of the last century, there was a temporary dearth of royalties, the same was never true of Germany. The Prussian victory in the war of 1866 had deprived the German kings, princes, and grand dukes of their political power, and in several cases of their sovereignty as well. The Cambridges' closest relations had been hard hit: 'Alas! all the dearest countries that my heart loved best have been *stolen* (I can't give it another name)', the Duchess of Cambridge had written at this time.[1] '. . . Hanover, which is the cradle of our English family, Hesse is mine, and Nassau was my dearest own mother's; so you may judge of my feelings at this moment.' But, whether in exile in other parts of Germany or in Austria, or allowed to lead a puppet existence in their own small capitals, these minor royal families continued to keep up their accustomed state. They also travelled freely at the appropriate seasons of the year, assembling in such spas as Homburg or Ems or Nauheim, or seeking in summer-time the fresh, chill air of mountain resorts.

To the Duchess of Teck one of the purest pleasures of travel on the Continent had always been the probability of meeting such royal persons, to most of whom she was in some way or another related. A typical encounter, at Seelisberg, is recorded in her journal for July 1884. Walking with her children along the muddy mountain track below the Kenzli she was 'accosted by a lady I did not at first sight recognise—Ada Hohenlohe, Duchess of Augustenberg, who, with her lady, von Krach, had come over from Axenstein . . .; it is years and years since we met in our youthful days, and she has much aged'.[2]

A large portion of Princess Mary Adelaide's youthful days had been spent in annual visits to Germany with her mother, the Duchess of Cambridge. Each visit had involved a series of delightful meetings with German relatives and friends, ecstatic recognitions in some *Platanen-*

Allee or in the shady gardens of Bad Homburg, bright with circular beds of purple and chrome-yellow heartsease in June. There were gay *Geburtstagsschokolade* for royal birthdays, '*grandes embrassades*' on arriving and leaving, innocent gossipings over the Carlsbad water, eager discussions of matrimonial projects. Her journal for these years reads as a positive litany of names: Adelheid of Nassau and Hilda of Baden, Mimi and Frederick of Dessau, Tilla of Lippe with her Charlottchen and her little Bathildis. There was Olga of Württemberg and her sister-in-law Vera Württemberg, otherwise the Duchess Eugène. There were Mecklenburg-Strelitzes and Mecklenburg-Schwerins and Saxe-Meiningens and Oldenburgs, and Hélène of Waldeck and Princess Adalbert (with Elvira and Clara); the Grand Duchess Stephanie, the little Erbprinz of Wied, Hermann Weimar, the King and Queen of Saxony, the 'poor Queen of Hanover' and Sophie of Holland. There were royalties, too, from farther south on the map of Europe: the Infanta Maria de la Paz, who had married a Baden, and the Duke of Parma, and the Duchess of Madrid. About these personages there hovered, like a cloud of moths, the ladies-in-waiting: Countess Ahlefeldt and Countess Reventlow, Countess Bassewitz and her sister Olga Uxküll, Fräulein Heyden, Willichen Schreve, Mademoiselle Molière (known as 'Vivi'), Fräulein Lolhoffel, Fräulein Lohn, Fräulein Bees and Fräulein Trott. Implicit in the presence of these ladies, as in that of their male counterparts the *Kammerherren* and equerries, was the axiom that even minor royalties neither could nor should exist, let alone travel, without constant succour and support.

As a major element in the Duchess of Teck's mythology, these people, or talk about them, became also a part of the climate of Princess May's childhood. Such talk impressed her with the old idea of European royalty as a closed shop.

This childhood familiarity with the calm, doomed world of privilege, epitomised by these personages with royal heraldic achievements on the panels of their carriages, and by their ladies and equerries, their dressers and other attendants, their smartly liveried footmen, their comfortless *Schlösser*, their royal barges on the Bodensee, their special saloon carriages on railway trains, formed an historical object lesson which Princess May never forgot. At the end of her life, a widowed Queen Dowager living in Marlborough House, she alone of all her family could remember the connections of the English Royal House with such persons, and could in a trice explain who was who and which was which in the most complex of continental genealogical trees.

II

Princess May had her first glimpse of this galaxy of German royal relatives before she was old enough to register the experience in her mind, for, at only five months, she was taken by her parents to stay at Schloss Rumpenheim and at the court of Stuttgart, stopping at Munich on the way home. Her next visit to Rumpenheim, with her mother, her two elder brothers and their nurses, took place in 1871, when she was four. On this occasion they continued on to Neu Strelitz, to stay with her Aunt Augusta and her Uncle Fritz. In September 1873, when she was six and a half years old, the whole Teck family spent seven weeks at Rumpenheim, before journeying eastwards into Styria to the Duke of Teck's sister Princess Amélie, Countess von Hügel, at Reinthal, and ending with Christmas and New Year in Strelitz. In October 1876 Princess May was once more at Rumpenheim with her mother. She was there again with the Duchess in the summer of 1878, when she was eleven. During the years 1883 to 1885, when the Tecks were established in Italy, they vacated Florence in the hot weather to spend summers with the Württemberg royal family on the Bodensee, and with their Teck relations in Styria. After Princess May was grown-up she would go with her mother to St Moritz, another haunt of German royalty. In 1892, when she was in mourning for Prince Eddy, she and the Duchess of Teck spent many weeks with the Württembergs in Stuttgart and at Ludwigsburg. After her marriage Princess May went on her own, incognita and accompanied by a modest suite, to visit her Aunt Augusta Strelitz, either in Strelitz itself or at the Grand Duchess's pretty summer retreat, the Kepp Schloss, in the Saxon countryside outside Dresden.

The background of Princess May's childhood in England—the White Lodge, Kensington Palace, Marlborough House, St James's Palace—was in this way complemented by a first-hand knowledge of life in Germany. There was never any doubt in her mind that she preferred her own country. She found the old German houses uncomfortable and the etiquette at the little courts unbearably constricting. From an early age Queen Mary was passionately patriotic. Writing her first letter in French, to her grandmother, at the age of nine she ended it: '*je puis vous dire aussi le "bon jour", et beaucoup d'autres mots en français, mais je serai toujours une vraie petite Anglaise*'.3 'I certainly do *not* like Germany', she wrote in May 1892, from Schloss Ludwigsburg, to her old governess, Madame Bricka, '& alas I have forgotten all my German which makes me terribly shy— . . . I think Württemberg a primitive place, they have no idea of comfort & are so narrow minded—Thank God I belong to a great Nation!—'4

Rumpenheim and all that it signified were her mother's specific contribution to this German aspect of Princess May's background. Stuttgart and Ludwigsburg were Württemberg places, and though the Duchess of Teck had also had blood relations in the Württemberg royal family, it was primarily through the Duke of Teck that Princess May became acquainted with the formalities of the rather arid court of Stuttgart. Princess Amélie's Schloss Reinthal, and the neighbouring Schweizerhaus, or chalet, in which lived Princess Claudine of Teck, were no more than most agreeable Austrian country places in which the Duke of Teck's two sisters lived in a quiet and thoroughly morganatic way. Reinthal had no special associations. Rumpenheim was the object and the centre of a family cult. To the Cambridges, and to their royal cousins of Greece and Denmark, the Rumpenheim *mystique* was very potent. For our purposes this requires some explanation.

Before it was gutted by incendiary bombs (which also destroyed its contents) in the last war, Schloss Rumpenheim, which stands on the banks of the River Main opposite Hanau, and within driving distance of Frankfurt, was a charming and sedate eighteenth-century house, built round three sides of an inner courtyard. The Schloss was separated from the hamlet of Rumpenheim, near Offenbach, by a low wall, and access to the house was gained by an unpretentious pair of iron gates opening out of the cobbled village street. The house was white. The door and window surrounds were in pink brick. The shutters were green. The main block, overlooking the river, had two slight, square towers at either end of it; each of these contained an extra bedroom floor. From the centre of the roof of this block there rose a cupola, with a clock beneath. On summer days this white façade would be reflected in the glassy surface of the Main, so that from Hanau, or crossing over in the ferry, you saw the whole of Rumpenheim mirrored in the wide, tranquil water, upside down.

The two wings which flanked the courtyard on the landward side were lower than the main block of the Schloss. They consisted of a chain of rooms, arranged as a series of self-contained private apart-

ments. Each wing had two low archways which opened the courtyard
to the gardens. At the end of each wing there were two pavilions, with
flights of stone steps. In this courtyard, though not in the geometrical
centre of it, there grew, as there still grows, an ancient and gigantic
copper beech, luxuriant and crimson in its season. In the vista formed
by the two wings, at the open end of the courtyard, near the entrance
gates, stood a stone statue of *Diane Chasseresse*, between two horse-
chestnut trees. Behind these, lurking amid thick and melancholy
laurels, was the *Gruft*, or family mausoleum, in which, heaped with
browning wreaths, the ornate coffins of past Hesse-Cassels lay on
shelves, their dank solitude disturbed only by pious visitations of
the family on the anniversaries of various deaths. Behind this
mausoleum stood the church, a severe building with a spire. To
the left, as you looked from the courtyard towards this church,
was a woodland garden, where tall elm trees brooded over mauve lilac
bushes, and moss-grown pathways led hither and thither to miniature
temples and memorial obelisks. The river frontage of Rumpenheim
was terraced, with gravel and formal beds of flowers. Below it the
ground then shelved sharply to the river. On the garden side of the
Schloss a *Platanen-Allee* carried the terrace walk onwards to a Chinese
bath-house, which commanded a view of the water-meadows, in
which cattle drowsily grazed. From this bath-kiosk the Duchess of
Cambridge had as a girl watched, cowering, the triumphant march of
Napoleon's army into Frankfurt after the French victory at Hanau,
upon the farther shore.

There are two facts to be borne in mind about Rumpenheim.
Firstly it was a house of modest size: 'a homely whitewashed barrack
of little cells opening into one another, stiff and simple beyond words',
the late Lord Rosebery called it, when he was taken there by the Duke
of Cambridge from Homburg in 1889.5 Secondly, in its lay-out, its
appearance and its furnishings (and thus in its general tone) Rumpenheim was essentially eighteenth century: 'built quite in the style of
an old country house, with a print-room and furniture such as was
in vogue ninety years ago', wrote an Englishwoman who visited
Rumpenheim in 1824.6 Not until the eighteen-nineties, when the house
was inhabited by Prince Friedrich-Karl of Hesse and his wife Princess
Margaret, the youngest daughter of the Empress Frederick of Germany,
were alterations made at Rumpenheim. The *grüne Salon* was then
refurbished and emerged pale yellow, the old family portraits were
thinned out upon the walls, the flower-beds and the '*Bosquet*'

abolished in favour of turf and shrubs. Throughout Princess May's girlhood Schloss Rumpenheim remained untouched, and looked exactly as it had done when rebuilt by Princess Mary of Great Britain and Ireland, the daughter of George II, who had withdrawn there from Cassel with her children when her husband, Frederick, Landgrave of Hesse-Cassel, embraced the Roman Catholic faith in 1754.*

This English Landgravine's second son, the Landgrave Frederick, who had died in 1837, had left Rumpenheim in his will to all six of his children equally, on the understanding that it was to be used as a focal point for family reunions. His eldest son, the Landgrave William, had married Princess Charlotte of Denmark, and was father to Queen Louise of Denmark, the mother of our Queen Alexandra. The old Landgrave Frederick's two other sons, Prince Frederick and Prince George, had never married. They lived, two crusty bachelors, at Rumpenheim, only spending the worst months of each winter in their town house in Frankfurt. Of the old Landgrave's three daughters the eldest, Louisa, married General von Decken; the second, Marie, married the Grand Duke of Mecklenburg-Strelitz; while the third daughter, Augusta, was, as we already know, Princess May's grandmother the Duchess of Cambridge.

The married members of this family of six, together with their children, their children's wives or husbands, and, ultimately, their grandchildren and great-grandchildren, assembled every two years at Rumpenheim to spend some weeks or months together. Each family unit lived in one of the self-contained apartments of the Schloss, meeting in the main building for meals. Generation after generation played, as children, along the river bank or about the umbrageous garden, and many marriages between cousins were, as the old Landgrave had hoped when he drafted his testament, the result. The last of his six children to die was the Duchess of Cambridge who was in this way sole owner of Rumpenheim for some years. At her death it passed to the blind son of her nephew Frederick. He, having also inherited the fine Schloss at Philippsruhe, likewise on the Main, lent it to his brother Prince Friedrich-Karl, husband of Princess Margaret

* Mary, Princess of Hesse (1723–1772), born a Princess of Great Britain and Ireland, was the fourth daughter of George II by his Queen, Caroline of Anspach. Married in 1740 to the son and heir of William VIII of Hesse-Cassel, she left her husband on his conversion to Roman Catholicism in 1754 and lived at Rumpenheim in the county of Hanau. On her father-in-law's death in 1760 she administered Hanau as Regent.

of Prussia. Their son, Prince Philip, the present Landgrave of Hesse, owns the blackened, roofless shell of Rumpenheim today.

We have noticed that unexpected encounters with stray relatives while travelling formed one of the Duchess of Teck's main pleasures on the Continent. How much more rapturous, then, did she feel at Rumpenheim, where you met, as it were by appointment, a whole number of your closest cousins! Lady Geraldine Somerset* was surprised by the warmth of Rumpenheim family meetings: 'It was amusing to see [the King of Hanover's] arrival and reception,' she confided to her diary in 1863, 'the way they all kissed! I never saw people, cousins in every degree, kiss to that extent, here, there, everywhere, a dozen times over. . . .' On this occasion Lady Geraldine observed and noted for posterity 'a trait of family economy, too characteristic to be passed over: on such grand occasions as Royal and Kingly visits all the small merits of Rumpenheim are usually brought to the fore and so all the little fountains play: but this King† is blind and would not have seen them so it was an unnecessary expense—and none of the fountains played!!' During the same visit, when she was in waiting on the Duchess of Cambridge and Princess Mary Adelaide, Lady Geraldine accompanied the whole family on a rustic outing to Prince Frederick's farm at Dorfelden. '. . . We walked about there, had a very good rural luncheon after which they all got very wild, poking potatoes and squashed grapes down each others' necks and into each others' pockets, and perfectly distraught!' Lady Geraldine, who liked staying at Strelitz as much as she disliked staying at Rumpenheim, had other complaints to make against the poor old house and its inhabitants. The food was 'too infamous . . . ! *pas mangeable!*', the house was so overcrowded as to be unbearable ('letter-writing all the morning till one, and after that one never gets a moment undisturbed, they run in and out! then we dine at 5 and that *ends* the day'), the dining-room was small and stuffy, but in the

---

* Lady Geraldine Harriet Anne Somerset, b. 1832, was the daughter of the seventh Duke of Beaufort by his second wife, Emily Frances (daughter of Charles Culling-Smith). Lady Geraldine was lady-in-waiting to the Duchess of Cambridge from 1858 to 1889. After the death of the Duchess Lady Geraldine lived on in Upper Brook Street until she died in 1915. Lady Geraldine's diaries are in the Royal Archives at Windsor Castle.

† King George V of Hanover, b. 1819, d. 1878. Succeeded his father, Queen Victoria's uncle, 1851, lost his kingdom to Prussia, 1866. Blinded in boyhood by swinging a chain purse which caught him in the eye, during a walk with his tutor at Kew. Buried in the Royal Vault at Windsor by his special request.

'tropical' heat of August the 'arrangements [are] as though we were living at the North Pole in December!' She disliked being chivvied out to '*play croquet*, in this dust and nastiness, where is no turf, and *not even gravel!!*' and she equally resented the 'tremendously merry' evening games of 'mufti, slapping hands, and a kind of post'. Then there were the Tuesday receptions 'when the *whole* house stands about on hind legs all day, waiting for the going to go!'7

One of Lady Geraldine Somerset's duties was to keep the Duchess of Cambridge's diary. She omitted to mention to Her Royal Highness that she was also keeping a second diary: her own. Yet on the whole, however, there was a delicious sense of privacy about Rumpenheim gatherings. That the most unsympathetic observer could fail to enjoy summers there would not have seemed credible to the Cambridges or to their hosts. To them, Rumpenheim summers seemed perfect. Rumpenheim autumns and winters were a different matter, though; for the old Hesse brothers did not care to spend too much money on the heating, and the Cambridges and Tecks were sometimes driven to get their own firewood in from Offenbach by the cartload.

Princess May's second visit to Rumpenheim, when she was three, occurred in one such autumn. After some weeks at Rumpenheim their mother took Princess May, Prince Dolly, Prince Frank and the suite of nursery attendants on to Strelitz, which they reached on 12 October 1871. The next day the Grand Duchess of Mecklenburg-Strelitz wrote to the Duke of Cambridge an account of this arrival:

. . . Mary arrived here all safe with her delightful chicks last night, escorted by Wenchstern, who had gone to meet her at Berlin. The children are coughing, no wonder they should have caught cold from the unheated rooms at Rumpenheim; I have a cold within me ever since and now I am quite stiff with pains in my limbs. . . .8

A part of the fun of Rumpenheim lay in the fact that it overlooked the Hanau–Offenbach ferry. From the terrace or the windows, you could see who was seated in the travelling carriage or the light droshky at that moment gliding slowly into view across the water. 'On our passage over the flying ferry towed by boats, we were recognised and hailed', the Duchess of Teck wrote of her visit with her children in 1871. 'Mama, Uncles Fritz and George, Louise, Lilli, Ahlefeld, Geraldo, and Fräulein Trott received us. . . . Grand welcome and *Bewunderung*!' 'Luncheon in garden and garden-house, after which we sat quietly, for the heat was intense, till three,' she noted during the same stay at Rumpenheim; 'just as we were going in, we espied a carriage coming over the water, and in it sat Alix, Thyra, Mrs Hardinge and the General, all hiding their faces in order not to be recognised! A charming surprise for Louise.' The courtyard side of the house could also provide its own charming surprises: 'Nassau had taken leave of us, and was on the point of starting when a carriage drove up to the centre door, out of which sprang a lady who came towards us. It was dear Augusta!'9

Of her two next visits to Rumpenheim, at the ages of six and nine, Princess May retained vivid recollections. Prince Frederick, her eldest great-uncle, died some days after the second of these two visits, in the winter of 1876: 'I remember him at Rumpenheim . . . in 1873, when I was 6—he was my Grandmother Cambridge's brother', Queen Mary wrote from Badminton in 1940.10 On her way with her parents to Rumpenheim for the visit of September 1876, Princess May scribbled a pencil note to her brothers in the train: ' . . . We had a very good passage and I was not at all sick, and as Mama and Papa are now reading in the train I thought I would write a letter to you to wish you good morning pray how do you do?' This sisterly missive was completed at Rumpenheim: 'I must tell you we had such a good dinner at Cologne and Papa thought I should send you this piece of pink paper from one of our cutlets. I wrote this letter in my pocket book in the train but it was rather untidy and I could not send it to you.'11 In 1876 there were a number of children at Rumpenheim: 'so that May' [wrote her mother] 'has plenty of companions, tho' she is still too shy to care to be much with them. Poor dear May has had the tooth-ache & been rather homesick (she misses you all terribly I fear) but she is beginning to recover her spirits a little & to look less woebegone. Papa & I are in our nice old rooms up on the tip-top & May sleeps in my sitting-room, with Nannie on the sopha close to her, but she is to have her Papa's rooms, when he goes away next week.'12

The last of Princess May's childhood visits to Rumpenheim was, in its inception, more adventurous and, in its end, more tragic than any of the others. Writing from White Lodge to her elder brothers in September 1878, she told them how the journey came about. She was then eleven years old:

You will be so awfully surprised, when I tell you that yesterday Aunt Augusta surprised me very much, she asked me if I would like to go to

Rumpenheim with the Prince and Princess of Wales and cousins but I said no, as I thought I was to go alone, but when I heard Mama was there, I said yes, so Aunt Augusta said she would ask the Prince of Wales, and the Prince said yes, so I am going this evening. You can imagine in what a hurry we all are. I am very busy packing my desk and bag. Anna has gone to London to fetch some of my dresses, Baby is in despair, Mrs Ranger pretends to be crying, and Alice says the house is awfully dull.[13]

This must have been an exciting journey, for Queen Mary still recollected the details of it seventy years later. Sending a newspaper article on Queen Victoria's courier, Kanné, which had interested her, she wrote to the Librarian at Windsor Castle, in May 1948:

I am the *only* person living who knew this worthy man. . . . What a good thing it is that I retain my wonderful memory![14]

She added a characteristic note to be pinned on to the article:

1878 I went to Rumpenheim nr Frankfurt a/Main to stay with Hessian Relations—travelled with Pss of Wales & her daughters via Brussels & Cologne & Kanné was upset because Pss. of W. had not told him that another room was required for Pss. May (now Queen Mary) in the Hotel at Cologne.

This stay at Rumpenheim was rendered hideous to the Duchess of Teck by the death from typhoid fever of her beloved dresser, Brand. 'Brandie' had been with the Duchess for twenty years, and they were mutually devoted: 'Five weeks have gone by since [her death] . . .', the Duchess wrote to Queen Victoria, 'and if time has *calmed* my sorrow, it has deepened it and made the void her death has caused in my daily life, only the more apparent!—Forgive me if I have wearied you, but I know how warmly you have felt for me and how fully you can understand, how hourly and terribly I miss the faithful, loving service and devotion of Her, who for 20 years had been about me and had made all my cares and joys, her own.'[15] The Duchess of Teck was well-known to be one of those considerate and happy employers who inspire loyalty and affection in their dependants.

This death, which was long-drawn out and agonising, overshadowed happier memories of Rumpenheim. Moreover, while her maid was dying, the Duchess could not give way to her grief, since in another of the pavilions of the Schloss, Princess May herself lay ill, attacked by a violent gastric fever which seemed likely at one moment to turn into the dreaded typhoid itself. 'Cold water treatment however worked wonders, for the child,' wrote her mother,[16] 'alas! in poor Brand's case, it could not be applied, owing to all the serious complications. Since our return [to England] May has picked up most satisfactorily, tho' she still requires careful looking after and has decidedly outgrown her strength.'

Queen Victoria had never been to Rumpenheim, but she would categorically declare that she knew it was unhealthy and that the rooms were too small. This prejudice arose from a connotation of the name Rumpenheim at which we must glance before we leave the ruined old Main Schloss for ever. To the Cambridges and all their cousins the very word 'Rumpenheim' brought a nostalgic thrill. To Queen Victoria, however, it had a purely political meaning. As Hesses, Nassaus and Hanovers, the Rumpenheim families cherished an undying hatred for Prussia. They never forgave the rape of their countries in 1866, and they encouraged one of their number, Alexandra, Princess of Wales, in her fervid anti-Prussianism, an attitude which was thought, in its turn, to influence the Prince of Wales. In September 1867 the Queen of Prussia* wrote to Queen Victoria complaining that the Princess of Wales, then in Berlin, had refused to go with her husband to see the Prussian King. 'This is *too* bad & Bertie *ought* to *know* his duty better than to allow such things to *happen*', Queen Victoria wrote off at once to her daughter, the Prussian Crown Princess. 'I am *more* shocked & grieved than I can say. . . . That's all *Rumpenheim* Influence.'[17]

III

At Rumpenheim, then, Princess May and her brothers were exposed to a bitterly anti-Prussian atmosphere. The same was true of their visits to their Uncle Fritz and Aunt Augusta at Neu Strelitz. In July 1866, in flagrant contravention of the King of Prussia's personal verbal guarantee of Strelitz neutrality, Bismarck had sent the Grand Duke Frederick an ultimatum: unless he mobilised his troops im-

* Augusta (1811–1890), daughter of Charles Frederick, Grand Duke of Saxe-Weimar, had married the future King of Prussia, William I (1797–1888; German Emperor, 1871) in 1829. Reared in the liberal atmosphere of the court of Weimar, she had won Queen Victoria's friendship during a first visit to England in 1846. She maintained an intimate correspondence with Queen Victoria, which helped somewhat to alleviate the difficult position of the Queen's eldest daughter, the Princess Royal, when she became Crown Princess of Prussia by her marriage in 1853 to the future Emperor Frederick III. On the particular occasion to which the quotation above refers, the Princess of Wales was at length persuaded to perform the normal courtesy of calling on the Prussian sovereign.

mediately and handed them over to fight on the side of Prussia, his little country would be forthwith occupied and treated as enemy territory. Against his wife's wishes the humiliated Grand Duke acquiesced, saving his country from Prussian occupation. He was influenced in this capitulation by the example of his neighbour, the Grand Duke of Mecklenburg-Schwerin, who had 'behaved infamously ill . . . [and] hastily threw himself, bag and baggage, into the Enemy's camp'[18]—such was the description of their neighbour's action given by the Grand Duchess Augusta, to whom Prussia was ever 'the Enemy'.

Strelitz had thus lost its political independence, but compliance had at least saved it from the fate of Hanover, Hesse and Nassau, and it was not, like these, seized and incorporated into the Prussian State. The internal government of the Grand Duchy continued to function as before, with the Grand Duke at its head. Unlike Rumpenheim, an example of fallen royalty living as exiles on the borders of their former possessions, the Grand Ducal court at Neu Strelitz bore, after 1866, no outward appearance of change. This court had a character all its own; in a showily militaristic Germany it remained pacific. When, in 1904, her husband died, and her son Adolphus Frederick V became Grand Duke in his stead, the Grand Duchess Augusta was disgusted by the latter's '*Military* ways'. 'Strelitz that never was a Military State, suddenly is all drums and fifes,' she wrote to her niece Princess May,[19] 'such a pity, a bad imitation of Schwerin & small German Courts, whilst we *were* a Gentlemanlike *Civilian* court!' At this quiet, old-fashioned court, the advent of the Grand Duchess's mother or of her sister, with her husband and children, was a semi-state occasion.

The journey from Rumpenheim to Neu Strelitz, which lay far off in a corner of north-eastern Germany, was long and tiring. Crossing by the ferry to Hanau, the departing travellers would drive thence into Frankfurt, where they took the train for Berlin. Here, in these days before the railway had linked the Prussian capital to Strelitz, they would be met by the Grand Ducal carriage. This vehicle, drawn by post-horses, conveyed them as far as the village of Fürstenberg, on the Strelitz borders. In this village they would find the Grand Duke's own sleek horses—six of them with two postilions in black and scarlet, an outrider, a *Bereiter* and coachman and strap-hanging footmen. After a pause for food, the travellers re-entered the heavy emblazoned equipage and swung off once more through the afternoon light, at a smarter pace, towards Strelitz. To cover the distance between Berlin and Strelitz in this manner took eight hours. The horses thudded on across the level, sandy wastelands of North Germany. In summertime the workers in the fields and the villagers lined the road to wave as their Grand Duke's English relatives passed them in a cloud of dust. In winter, only some solitary peasant plodding his muffled way through the deep snow might be seen. Here and there a poplar tree broke the monotony of the featureless landscape.

Just outside the town of Neu Strelitz you came upon a belt of surprisingly splendid beech and oak woods, which had the unnatural appearance of having been deliberately planted on the dreary plain. 'All sand, flat as the hand; and the little *freundlich* town, the Schloss and charming garden and these woods, are put down upon this flat expanse of sand like an Arabian desert, as tea-cups on a tray.'[20]

Inside the Schloss at Strelitz, as the time for the guests' arrival drew near, the whole Grand Ducal court, stiff as a set of clockwork figures, would begin to take up their correct positions for the formal reception of the visitors in the great *Saal*. On such occasions the Court turned out in what the Grand Duchess Augusta, using the slang of her youth, called 'full fig': the ladies in low evening dresses with bare shoulders and jewels, the *Exzellenzen*, *Kammerherren* and other male members of the court wearing the Strelitz uniform, and their Orders, and holding their cocked hats. The centrepiece of this doll-like group was the reigning family itself: the unbending, half-blind Grand Duke Frederick, his Hessian mother the Dowager Grand Duchess, his wife, the Grand Duchess Augusta, a proud, shrewd figure with the conscious bearing of a Princess of Great Britain and Ireland, and their only child, young Adolphus, known as Doppus to his relatives. The signal which warned the expectant circle that the Duke and Duchess of Teck were approaching was the sound of the band which, stationed in the *Platz* beneath the windows of the Schloss, would clash out into a triumphal *God Save the Queen* as the Royal carriage swept clattering into the square. Amidst the cheers of the townsfolk it would dash through the Schloss gates, from its dark, silken interior a white beringed hand fluttering, inquisitive childish faces peering, blonde and blue-eyed, from its windows. In the great *Saal* the double doors would be flung open, and, while a general obsequious motion of curtsying and bowing swept through the static group of courtiers like wind through the corn, the Teck and Strelitz sisters, reunited once more, would fall emotionally into one another's arms. This scene, a pendant to those at Rumpenheim, would likewise furnish Princess May with food for thought.

Behind the Schloss at Strelitz was a lovely formal garden on a miniature scale—'*en petit-petit, très petit*, something of the old-fashioned, Versailles, style'²¹—and, farther back, a lake. The garden contained a pretty *Orangerie*, with statues round the walls, and here, in warm weather, the family dined. There were agreeable walks to be taken in such woods as the Koppel, and expeditions could easily be made to charming places outside the town. Twenty miles off, there was the small old Schloss of Hohenwieritz, for example, in which the Grand Duchess Augusta, her mother-in-law and her child, had taken refuge during the brief republican riots which the year 1848 had brought even to Neu Strelitz. Hohenwieritz was one of the rendezvous for beagling, when the huntsmen 'in greatest Melton style of red coat and top boots' would set the hounds after hare. There were also, in winter, the wild boar hunts, which, so long as he could still see, formed the Grand Duke Frederick's favourite pastime, and which he laid on when such visitors as his neighbour Mecklenburg-Schwerin, or the Duke of Nassau, came to stay. These expeditions to shoot the wild boar in the frozen wastes round Strelitz incidentally provided the Teck children at Christmas-time with a grisly annual reminder of their Strelitz uncle. Year after year he would send the Duchess of Teck a boar's head, shipped from Hamburg together with two others, one for the Duke of Cambridge at Gloucester House, the other for the Prince of Wales at Sandringham. The Grand Duke liked to write to tell his sister-in-law what kind, and quality, each head would be:

Winter has set in with great severity this year & earlier than usual [he wrote to her, for instance, in December 1875]. . . . The wild boar shooting is therefore very good this year & I hasten to send you (Posto franco) a *hure de sanglier* which I hope shall arrive in good condition, & just in time for your Christmas dinner. It is the head of a *lady* & not of a *gentleman* wild boar & perhaps less showy, but the old Master of the hunt informed me it was particularly tender, & so I send it at once & trust you will let your dear Mama partake of it. May it also be to the taste of Francis!*²²

* After her husband's death, the Dowager Grand Duchess Augusta maintained the tradition of the boar's head. 'From the Throne I sink down to the Kitchen', she wrote to her niece Queen Mary in February 1912, 'to announce to you the departure of the Wild Boars Head for George, only lately killed and prepared for sending. Will you tell him I hope he will accept it? I have addressed it to "the King" to the care of the Master of the Household, thinking this safest.'²³

Another excursion from Neu Strelitz was a drive of eight miles in the shelborne to Mirow, the birthplace of Queen Charlotte, the wife of George III, and great-grandmother of Princess May of Teck. Queen Charlotte had been born a Duchess of Mecklenburg-Strelitz. One of the nieces of the reigning Grand Duke of that day, she had left Mirow in 1760 and had married the King of England in 1761. In a wood called *der Holm*, just the other side of Mirow, the Teck children were shown 'a fine Beech tree under which Queen Charlotte had often sat & played with her *Geschwister*'. The Grand Duchess Augusta had had a branch cut from this tree, and had sent some of the leaves to Queen Victoria, who at once asked her to have the tree photographed. In January 1910, Princess May, then Princess of Wales, discovered this photograph at Windsor in a white frame with a Royal crown on it. 'I really am glad you discovered it', her old aunt wrote to her, 'as it is rather interesting (to *you* at least) that the *two* Granddaughters of the old Queen, *one* in England, the *other* again in Mecklenburgh, should have exchanged thoughts, interest and letters on this subject.'24 Her Aunt Augusta did more than anyone else to foster Princess May's chief interest—family history—and to sharpen her sense of the past. Also at Mirow was the church vault of the Mecklenburg-Strelitz family, a counterpart to the Hesses' *Gruft* amid the laurels at Rumpenheim, and to the Cambridge Mausoleum, a domed mortuary chapel, containing the coffin of Adolphus, Duke of Cambridge, at the eastern end of the parish church at Kew.

Each of Princess May's two visits to Strelitz in childhood included her participation in the festivities for Christmas and New Year. The Grand Duchess Augusta, whose spiritual home was in London, where she spent as much time as she possibly could, used to complain of the life in Neu Strelitz—'too wearying, fatiguing, oh! so tiresome! one feels so far away from life and interest and commotion of *mind*!'25 Strelitz gave the Grand Duchess no opportunity to indulge her ruling passion, the discussion of political news. She had to content herself with reading and re-reading, her lorgnette to her eye, *The Times* and other London newspapers which reached her, several days stale, via Cuxhaven. All the same, she had managed to invigorate Strelitz society by patronising the theatre and the opera (of which last she was an addict, her preference being for Donizetti and the music of her youth), and by giving dinners and balls. The Strelitz season, which her sister once tersely described as 'short but brilliant', began with the carnival in January and continued into March. The

Grand Duchess would declare that Strelitz was only tolerable in May—'*the* moment for seeing Strelitz'—when the lilacs and thorns and the pink and white chestnut trees were in rich blossom, and the 'overpowering' scent of elder and lime floated into her open window as she sat at her slanting writing-desk, penning long, lively letters to her English family. She affected to feel that a *kleinstädtlich* little court in northern Germany was no place for a Princess of Great Britain and Ireland, yet secretly she enjoyed the short but brilliant season, the entertainments of which all pivoted around herself.

By ill-luck, the two Christmases which the Teck children spent at Strelitz were overshadowed by illness—the first by anxiety for the life of the Prince of Wales, who lay for some weeks in December 1871 at death's door at Sandringham, perilously ill with typhoid fever. When better news was telegraphed from England, and all danger was past, the whole Teck family suddenly contracted scarlet fever at Strelitz in January of the new year: started by Prince Dolly, the infection spread to his brother Frank, from him to Princess May, from her to her mother, and thence to the English dressers and attendants. '[It] effectually put me *hors de writing* and all other *combat*', the Duchess of Teck wrote to her brother, in a letter in which were scattered such phrases as 'feverish tossing', 'fearful sickness and giddiness' and 'parched with thirst'. On recovery she was forced to '*vegetate* in one suite of rooms, which happily included the nurseries, the children's three rooms adjoining mine'.[26]

The next visit to Strelitz, that of 1873, was marred by the Duchess of Cambridge's stroke:

It was a *serious* Christmas this time, dearest Mamma not being able to join our Circle in the Saal [wrote the Grand Duchess] but she was able to have a Tree in her anteroom, where she gave us her presents and received ours. . . . There was again a beautiful 'Etalage' of presents and the darling chicks were delighted and brightened up the scene with their happy faces and by their childlike prattle and screams of joy.[27]

At Strelitz the Christmas Eve dinner and distribution of presents round the tall, sparkling Christmas tree was enlivened by the North German custom of *Juhl-Klaps*. These consisted of little jokes in verse, with bon-bons and chocolates or comic drawings or coloured prints attached to them, which the servants would hurl into the great *Saal* at unexpected intervals. The verses or tags would refer somewhat crudely to a peculiarity of the royal personage at whom it was flung:

a box of chocolates addressed, for example, to Princess Mary Adelaide once bore the label: 'For the private picking of Queen Gourmandiza.' Dressed up with comic noses and wigs, the children would impersonate imaginary characters. The proceedings were jolly, and became noisy. Princess May and her brothers would sleep a part of the day, so as to be able to sit up and join in the fun until ten p.m.

On 27 November 1871, at Neu Strelitz, the Duchess of Teck celebrated her thirty-eighth birthday—for though, with her warmth of heart and careless generosity, she had many of the characteristics of a Scorpio, she was in fact born under Sagittarius. She was awakened in the morning by Princess May, Prince Dolly and the baby Frank who brought her bunches of violets to her bedroom. Later, the screen concealing her presents was withdrawn and 'a charming display of most coveted gifts met my delighted gaze!' At the birthday dinner she was dressed in lilac satin, afterwards changing into 'a blue low gown' for the *soirée musicale* in her sister's apartments, where the Grand Duchess's *protégée*, a young woman named Schubert, sang solos, and the evening ended with ices and punch. A 'surprise' for this birthday was postponed because of the Prince of Wales's illness, but when more reassuring news began to come over the telegraph wires (and before the onset of the Tecks' scarlet fever) it was finally carried out. The Duchess of Teck, her mother and the Grand Duke drove out through the gates of the Schloss into Strelitz, where the townspeople were going about their business in sledges, and the frozen surface of the lake was dotted with pedestrians. Here, at the Palais Theater, she took the seat of honour and the curtain rose:

It began by four *tableaux* representing Faith (Ducke, *schön*) Hope, Charity (Gussy with the three chicks—charming!), and an allegory, my 'M' held by May as rose, Dolly as thistle, and Baby as Shamrock. Charming idea and deliciously carried out. These were followed by two very pretty pieces, the second *ein ganz deliziöses Liederspiel*, '*Ein moderner Barbar*' and '*Bleib' bei mir*' in both of which Vivi and Schubert were perfect.*28

These early experiences of Strelitz ways gave Princess May her first sight of Aunt Augusta in her own setting. She also saw her aunt frequently in London, where the Grand Duchess stayed annually in rooms of her own in the old Duchess of Cambridge's apartment at

* 'Gussy and the three chicks': the Grand Duchess Augusta and her Teck nephews and niece. 'Vivi' was one of the Grand Duchess's ladies, Vivi Molière.

St James's Palace. After the Duchess of Cambridge's death in 1889, Aunt Augusta took the long lease of a small house in Buckingham Gate, looking out upon the Wellington Barracks; she christened it 'Mecklenburg House', and here she would live when in London, surrounded by family souvenirs, sleeping in her Aunt Gloucester's former bed, and cherishing such divers possessions as a statuette of Queen Victoria at her spinning-wheel and a stuffed pheasant, which had been shot by her brother the Duke of Cambridge in Richmond Park.

These London sojourns, together with Princess May's later visits to Neu Strelitz, and the weekly correspondence kept up on both sides when the aunt was in Germany, combined to make the kindly but caustic old Grand Duchess one of the major influences in her niece's mental development and materially helped to form her view of life. On both sides it was a relationship of the strongest affection: 'it really is touching, her devotion to me and I am much more like her daughter than her niece', Princess May once wrote.[29] The Grand Duchess admired her niece as much as she loved her: 'What I love in you is the truth and straightness of your character', she told her, and she would write, too, of 'the charm of your being both serious and gay'.[30]

The large part that the Grand Duchess of Mecklenburg-Strelitz played in Queen Mary's life—and will, in consequence, re-enact in this biography—demands some consideration of her person and her character. This can be most conveniently inserted here.

IV

We have already learned a little about Princess Augusta Caroline, Grand Duchess of Mecklenburg-Strelitz—for at least some salient features of her character should have by now emerged: that she was proud of her birth, that she preferred London to Strelitz, that in her youth she had caused Queen Victoria jealousy, that she was not given to over-spending, had a kind heart but a sharp tongue, was fond of her sister Princess Mary Adelaide, although usually exasperated by her, and that, born in 1822, she lived to the impressive age of ninety-four. Yet there were other aspects of her personality and her career than these.

Princess Augusta Caroline had been born in Hanover, while her father Adolphus, Duke of Cambridge, was Viceroy. In her childhood

D

she was taken to England on visits, but her family were not re-established there until the year of Queen Victoria's accession, when Hanover became independent of the British Crown. 'Augusta Cambridge' was considered an entertaining little girl: 'I have found some old Journals amongst old Papers, written by my Swiss Governess, describing *me* as a child from 8–12 years old', she once wrote, in 1893, to her nephew, Prince Dolly of Teck:[31] ' . . . I must have been a most amusing child! certainly more so than the present generation! but not having grown up as delightful as the promise of my childhood was I think I had better end this prosy letter.' As the only grown-up English Princess of the blood royal during Queen Victoria's first years on the throne, Princess Augusta had had a very enjoyable time in London in her youth. This had terminated with her marriage, in 1843, to her cousin Frederick, the Hereditary Grand Duke—or, in simpler terms, the heir to the duchy—of Mecklenburg-Strelitz.* It had been, at any rate on his side, a love-match, but 'Fritz Strelitz' was by no means Princess Augusta's only suitor. Suggestions had emanated from the Foreign Office that she should be married to the heir of either the Greek or Belgian thrones. The Prince Consort's only brother Ernest, afterwards the ogre-like Duke of Saxe-Coburg-Gotha, had also been suspected of designs upon Princess Augusta: 'Your enjoying the Ball too so amuses me,' she wrote in old age to her niece, of a ball given at Buckingham Palace in 1911, 'in the same Gallery I danced in 71 years ago, when Ernest Coburg was expelled by force out of the Dance, because he was not to make up to me!!! what an escape I had!'[32]

Princess Augusta's married life did not prove easy. She and her husband had one surviving child only, a son Adolphus Frederick.† Within fifteen years of their wedding, the Hereditary Grand Duke began to lose his eyesight, and soon became totally blind. Moreover, he was neither an emotional nor demonstrative man: 'As to poor, dear Fritz, it is unluckily his *way* not to make any show of affection',

* Frederick William, Hereditary Grand Duke of Mecklenburg-Strelitz, b. 1819, succeeded his father the Grand Duke George, 1860, d. 1904.

† Adolphus Frederick V, b. 1848, succeeded his father as Grand Duke of Mecklenburg-Strelitz, 1904, d. 1914. He married, 1877, Elisabeth, Princess of Anhalt, daughter of Frederick I, reigning Duke of Anhalt. They had four children: Marie, Princess of Lippe, Jutta, Crown Princess of Montenegro, Adolphus Frederick VI (who succeeded his father as Grand Duke, 1914, and shot himself, 1918), and Charles Borwin, Duke of Mecklenburg-Strelitz, died of heart disease 1908, *aet.* nineteen.

the Duchess of Teck wrote in 1875, evidently in reply to a letter of complaint from her sister Augusta, 'but his *icy abord* & reserve are *more* than *trying* & must exasperate you, the more so that they contrast so painfully with (*may I say it?*) *our* warmhearted, impulsive natures.'33 Then, as we have noted, there was for Princess Augusta Caroline a sense that, by living in Strelitz, she was missing the best of life. Politics were her passion. She herself dated her interest in them from the French Revolution of 1830, which she had avidly followed in the newspapers at the age of eight.

In politics, the Grand Duchess was an extreme Tory, and an ardent foe of every kind of change. After Disraeli's death she used to keep Primrose Day piously in Strelitz, and, like the Teck family, regarded Mr Gladstone as the Devil incarnate: 'I was in the Chapel Royal today with the G O M *under* me, horrid spectacle' or 'The old *horror* is again going to stump Scotland, visiting the Aberdeens, Breadalbanes and Dalhousies! how is it possible such people can still be taken in by that wicked madman!'34 She was not in any doubt that the old order was changing for the worse: 'how people delight in a *monde renversé*', she wrote, not long before the outbreak of the Great War. She believed in the Divine Right of Kings with a religious conviction, and felt that any members of the Royal Family (herself, needless to say, included) were in this sense beings from another sphere.

In consequence of these beliefs, and of the great length of her life which spanned five reigns—from that of King George IV, whom she remembered at Windsor, to that of her niece's husband King George V—the Grand Duchess was for ever receiving a succession of mental jolts and shocks, some of a major kind—her distress at the Parliament Act of 1911, for instance—some of lesser importance. 'Did I ever tell you how shocked I was when one day I was driving up the Avenue telling the footman I wished to drive to the Statue,' [she told her niece, in reminiscence of some visit to Windsor in Queen Victoria's day] 'he asked, "Do you mean the *old Gentleman* on the copper horse?" imagine my royal and loyal feelings and horror at the modern servants calling the King and my Grandfather thus! but the Queen *roared* when I told her.'35

Next to politics, the Grand Duchess loved music, and especially the opera. She would look back on 'my happy youth, all the delight of that grand Opera-time, which I so truly enjoyed more than anything else, and I did "adore" Grisi and Mario (on the *Stage*, not otherwise)'.³⁶ She passed many happy hours at Strelitz, personally superintending the production of Italian works in the Opera House, and even appreciative of those of new composers such as Leoncavallo and Puccini. Books were likewise a source of endless pleasure to her. She especially liked reading French memoirs, but she had also a respect and affection for the poets and writers fashionable in her youth. She could, on occasion, quote—or rather misquote—Byron, as in a letter of 1884 to her niece, Princess May, then seventeen years old:

So you were at Venice! glorious old Venice! I wish I could see it once again. I remember that when I stood outside, before St Marco, I fancied myself dreaming, or having a vision, the sun shining upon the gold, mosaic front; the inside, so beautiful too—and the Doge's Palace! the Courtyard & Staircase! I had my Childe Harold in my hand

> 'I stood upon the Bridge of sighs
> A Palace & a Prison on each side.'

did you read this there? I was about your age then and oh! how I enjoyed and admired Italy's beauties and historical reminiscences; *that* was at *day* time, at *night* I was eaten up by fleas!! horrid recollection!³⁷

In person the Grand Duchess was short and, at one time, plump. In a smart bonnet, silk gown and lace *fichu* she had something of the look of a complacent partridge; she had, too, a bird-like and enquiring eye. Her neck and shoulders were much admired when she was *décolletée* of an evening and aflash with the famous Cambridge sapphires, given to her on her marriage by her mother. When she was ninety, her niece Queen Mary wrote to her: 'If you have a dinner to celebrate yr birthday you *must* wear on yr 90th birthday the pearl & diamond diadem & yr *English* orders, do please do so for my sake. Think how beautiful you will look with yr white hair and still lovely neck.'³⁸ To this the nonagenarian wistfully replied: 'Your flattering words about my "lovely neck" I can only answer, saying: *it* has departed. I have grown so thin, having to deplore the *absence* of what once was "so lovely".'³⁹ In old age the Grand Duchess would, except for state functions, dress shabbily, for she was against all forms of personal extravagance, and would not even have rubber tyres on her carriages, preferring to be shaken and rattled about as the vehicles lumbered over the cobbles of Strelitz than to indulge in an unnecessary additional expenditure. Her houses were as old-fashioned as herself, and her rooms were even more crowded with objects and photographs than those of her sister at the White Lodge. The Grand Duchess was known in London for her perfect manners, her shrewdness and her wit.

Staying at Strelitz showed Princess May a certain German way of life, but her aunt's chief contribution to her upbringing was to instil into her a pride in her English family and in her race. In 1848 Princess Augusta Caroline had declared that she would not really mind if Strelitz became a republic, as she could then withdraw to her own country and 'tumble upon Kew'. When her daughter-in-law* became in her turn Grand Duchess of Mecklenburg-Strelitz, the old Dowager derived a characteristic and not wholly benevolent amusement from watching 'Elly': 'She (Elly) however welters in happiness at her luxurious "Schloss" wearing a new Paris dress daily, Diamonds also, when we are quite *entre nous*—Yes, she does enjoy being a *Grand Duchess*! poor dear, I am glad *she* does, for I never did, I was satisfied with what I ever *was* and *am* still!'[40]

The old Grand Duchess died in Strelitz in the midst of the maelstrom of the Great War, far from the country and the family she loved. On her death-bed she sent a message to the King of England—'tell the King it is a stout old English heart that is ceasing to beat'—and the last coherent word she uttered was the single name, 'May'.

v

The Grand Duchess of Mecklenburg-Strelitz was Princess May's sole aunt upon her mother's side. On her father's side of the family she had two Teck aunts: the Princesses Claudine and Amélie. Princess Claudine had been born in 1836, her sister in 1838. Their brother, the Duke of Teck, came between them in age, having been born in 1837. They were, as we know, the children of Duke Alexander of Württemberg by his morganatic marriage with the Hungarian Countess Claudia Rhèdey, who was killed when her horse ran away with her at Vienna in 1841. It was through Duke Alexander that his son, the Duke of Teck, might—or, as Queen Victoria thought, should—have been heir-presumptive to the kingdom of Württemberg.

---

* Elisabeth, Princess of Anhalt (1857–1933), known in the family as 'Elly', married the future Grand Duke Adolphus Frederick V of Mecklenburg-Strelitz (see footnote on p. 98) in 1877.

The Württemberg succession is a complex and potentially confusing subject, which need only be glanced at here.

In the eighteenth century the ruling factor in the story of the Württemberg dukedom was the persistent absence of heirs male; since, as in Hanover, daughters could not succeed to the sovereign power and possessions. This meant that from 1737 until 1795, the dukedom had passed in succession to three brothers—Duke Charles II Eugene, Duke Ludwig Eugene and Duke Frederick II Eugene. The third of these Dukes had three sons: Duke Frederick III, who became in 1806 first King of Württemberg under the title King Frederick I, and who married as his second wife Charlotte, Princess Royal of Great Britain, the eldest daughter of George III; Duke Ludwig and Duke Alexander. Duke Frederick II Eugene had also had two daughters: Princess Dorothea Sophia, who married the Tsar Paul I of Russia, and Princess Elizabeth, who married the Emperor Francis I of Austria.

The Teck family descended from Duke Frederick II Eugene's second son, Ludwig. This Duke Ludwig married a Princess of Nassau-Weilburg, a minor royal family whose picturesque and ancient castles may still be seen at Weilburg and elsewhere along the entrancing pastoral valley of the River Lahn, a gentle tributary of the Rhine.

Duke Ludwig had a daughter, Pauline (who married her first cousin King William I of Württemberg, the son and successor of King Frederick I), and a son, Duke Alexander, who married Countess Claudia Rhèdey. King William I and his first cousin Pauline produced one son, who succeeded his father as King Charles I of Württemberg in 1864 and died in 1891, when he was succeeded by his nephew King William II. It was at this point that the Tecks should, according to their own ideas, have stepped into the picture: for King William II—'Uncle Willy' to Princess May and her brothers—although twice married, had only one surviving child, a daughter* who could not succeed him on the throne. This meant that the next King of Württemberg would be of the Austrian branch of the family, who, unlike the elder branch, were all Roman Catholics. Queen Victoria, who considered it 'in these days really ... too absurd' that the Tecks

---

* Pauline Olga, Princess of Württemberg, b. 1877, is the only surviving child of King William II (1848–1921) and his first wife Marie, Princess of Waldeck and Pyrmont (1857–1888). The King's second marriage, to Princess Charlotte of Schaumburg-Lippe (1864–1946), was childless. Princess Pauline married, 1898, Frederick, hereditary Prince of Wied.

should not have the right of succession to the Württemberg throne, also declared 'that for that reason the Württemberg Dynasty is to become Catholic is a misfortune'.[41]

Queen Victoria was, nevertheless, anxious that one of Princess May's brothers should enter the Württemberg army, a project to which their parents would never agree. 'I must honestly confess I am very much against any of our sons going into the Württemberg service until the King has assured their position in the country by giving them the *"Hoheit"* ', the Duchess of Teck wrote to the Queen in August 1892, explaining that so many of the *Standesherrn** in Württemberg were *Fürsten* (or Princes) and that this made it 'rather a difficult position for our boys and you can well understand that I do not care to expose them to what has really been the *misfortune* of their father's life!—I quite understand the reasons, that prompt you in giving the advice, contained in your most kind letter to Francis and gratefully appreciate your kindly and affectionate interest in our boys, but you must forgive me if I cannot get over this to me insurmountable obstacle, seeing that Francis *ought* to be the *heir presumptive* to the throne!'[42]

This galling position was one major source of the Duke of Teck's sense of frustration, and of his fragile nerves. Instead of living in state at Stuttgart, as the future King of Württemberg, with Prince Dolly as the future Crown Prince, he was reduced to vegetating inconspicuously in England, pruning roses at White Lodge and attending the mess of the Post Office Volunteers. The blight of morganatic blood affected his daughter also, since it would have debarred any reigning German Prince, Grand Duke or Duke from asking for her hand. As it turned out, of course, Princess May ended as Queen Consort of England, while the Württemberg throne capsized in the general shipwreck of German royalties in 1918. These facts, however, lay shrouded in the future. There could be no prevision of them to console the Duke of Teck for the fact that his father, Duke Alexander, had married for love.

No documentary evidence survives to show us what the Duke of Teck really felt about his father. Under all the circumstances his feelings for the author of his life's 'misfortune' are not likely to have been warm. The Duchess of Teck kept up amiable, daughterly relations with her father-in-law, whose 'active self-reliant nature' she appreciated, and who sent her letters illustrated with the excellent caricatures he drew. On the childish horizon of Princess May and her

* *Standesherrn* = leading court officials.

brothers, Duke Alexander did not loom very large. He was a heavy, jovial old gentleman, smelling of tobacco—'the old chap' to the Teck schoolboys, whom he would ply with black cigars they did not like, and whom he would embarrass at luncheon at the Hotel Imperial in Vienna by shouting at all the waiters to explain who his grandsons were. To Princess May he was *'Grosspapa'*, to whom she would sometimes write in her best German a dutiful letter of thanks for a brooch or a pin.

We most of us tend to deteriorate physically with age. Time had not been indulgent to old Duke Alexander of Württemberg's appearance. In his youth, when he had fallen in love with the ravishing Countess Claudia at a Court Ball in Vienna in 1835, he had been a personable young officer in the Austro-Hungarian Army, with a wasp-waist well suited to his gold-braided uniforms—Russian, Hungarian, Austrian or Württemberger—which were encrusted with his various Orders: the Andreas Order, for instance, or the Black Eagle of Prussia. At that distant moment of his brief and romantic marriage, when he was stationed with the garrison in the graceful old city of Graz upon the Mur, he had worn his hair in the modish windswept fashion of the eighteen-thirties. His face was, then, small and heart-shaped, and his moustache was trim and waxed. By the time his grandchildren first met him, all traces of these looks had gone. The heart-shaped face was embedded in rolls of fat; two double chins brimmed over the collars of the uniform he would still sometimes wear. His hair had receded, revealing a forehead that was pink and glistening. The little moustache had swollen also. Now concealing his mouth completely, it jutted out on each side of his face at a most peculiar downward angle, spreading as it went, and ending up resting upon each shoulder like a stiff grey-black fan. Gone, too, was the neat figure, which a barrel of a body had replaced. It was indeed hard to connect this bloated personage with any byegone romance.

There was one fact about Grosspapa's present position which would not have escaped a child's appraising eye: Grosspapa was quite disturbingly poor. He lived most modestly in a tiny house in Vienna. Its small rooms were thought by his grandson Frank to be 'cosy', but they contained nothing of value, the old man's best possessions being a few sabres, some Oriental weapons chased in silver, some silver bowls, some paintings of Hussars, and a handful of miniatures of himself and his wife, Claudia, during their short idyllic youth. 'He has not a single thing worth any money', wrote Prince Frank in

July 1885;[43] he had gone to Vienna with his brother Prince Dolly to represent the Teck family at Duke Alexander's funeral. Perhaps one of the nicest things the old Württemberg Duke ever did for his grandsons was to die, for it gave them the opportunity for a spree in Vienna which Prince Frank candidly described to his mother as 'heavenly'. After his death, Duke Alexander's furniture was sold to pay expenses.

Princess May only knew her grandfather for some weeks at Reinthal in 1873. He had no direct, personal effect upon her life—save by having, long ago, complicated it by giving her the heritage of morganatic blood. This was a blot which Princess May's sisters-in-law, the Wales daughters, did not forget. To the end of her life, when mildly annoyed with Queen Mary on some trifling matter, Princess Louise, Duchess of Fife, would murmur to one of her daughters: 'Poor May! poor May! with her Württemberg hands!'

Queen Mary herself always felt that she owed a debt to her Hungarian grandmother, Countess Claudia Rhèdey—for to her ancestral influence she would attribute her own sense of colour and her love for beautiful vivid things.

VI

The two Teck sisters, daughters of Duke Alexander of Württemberg and aunts to Princess May, had not inherited their Rhèdey mother's startling beauty. Their countenances were mild and pleasant. Their lives, like their interests, were provincial. They were an inseparable pair. When the younger, Princess Amélie, having married Paul, Baron, and later Count, von Hügel, moved in 1863 to Schloss Reinthal, in the Styrian hills beyond Graz, her sister Princess Claudine moved with her, and built herself a charmingly fanciful Swiss chalet, the 'Schweizerhaus', on Reinthal land less than half a mile from the big house.

Princess Claudine liked the strictly rural. She kept goats and had a row of beehives, and stored apples and honey all about her little house in any empty room. She also designed an elaborate stable in which she kept eight cows; she was happily and utterly absorbed in her miniature farm. Her sister and her sister's only child, Paul Julius Hügel, known as 'Bubi', were her passion, and when Princess Amélie died of cancer in July 1893, at the comparatively early age of fifty-five, Princess Claudine only survived her by seventeen months, dying

D*

herself, of diphtheria, in November 1894. 'Those two sisters were
wrapt up in each other! & through life never scarcely parted!' the
Duchess of Teck wrote, after Princess Amélie's death.44 Peaceable,
sensible German country ladies, these Teck aunts formed an admirable
contrast to Princess May's Aunt Augusta Strelitz, with her restless
and sophisticated mind. Nor can we imagine that they particularly
sympathised with the feverish anxieties about rank and status which
obsessed their brother Franz, first Duke of Teck.

One of the few separations these Teck Princesses were ever called
on to endure took place in the winter of 1869 to 1870 when Princess
Amélie and her husband made a journey up the Nile, and Princess
Claudine paid her only visit to England. She stayed with her brother
and sister-in-law at White Lodge and at Kensington Palace, appeared
in London Society, and was taken about to various country houses:
to Weston Park, to Grimston, to Studley Royal. She even stayed
one night at Windsor, and went out driving with the Queen in her
carriage. She was present, at Kensington Palace, at the birth, in
January 1870, of her second nephew, Prince Frank of Teck.

During this time in London Princess Claudine sat to the painter
Sidney Hodges. The result is a portrait which shows us a serene
youngish woman of thirty-three, with clear dark eyes and a soft,
demure expression, her brown hair drawn up and curled around the
top of her head, a black lace shawl over her shoulders, and about her
neck a black velvet riband, tied at the front with a bow from which
depends a jewelled locket on a golden chain. It is the very image of
the ideal spinster aunt—understanding and indulgent, if perhaps, at
times, austere. 'The Princess Claudine is so very very kind, most
anxious to do all in her power to make all comfortable,' Princess May's
nurse, Mrs Girdlestone, wrote to the Duchess of Cambridge from the
Schweizerhaus, Reinthal, in October 1873,45 'she is so nice with the
Children very kind but very *firm*.'

At five months old, Princess May had been carried off to Munich
from Stuttgart, on an icy November day of 1867, to be exhibited to
her Teck aunts. She next saw Princess Claudine in London, in 1869;
and in 1873 she and her brothers spent some weeks at the Schweizerhaus at Reinthal, between their stay at Rumpenheim and their second
Strelitz Christmas. There was then a gap of eleven years, during which
neither the Duchess of Teck nor her children saw these Princesses. In
1884 the Duke and Duchess, with Princess May and Prince Alge,
spent a fortnight at Graz, seeing the aunts daily. Finally, in 1890,

they had a two-day rendezvous with them in the medieval town of Innsbruck, at the feet of the Tyrolese Alps. Afterwards Princess May would write the aunts occasional letters, but she never saw them again.

In November 1873 the Duchess of Teck wrote an account of the family's summer and autumn movements to a friend. A part of this lengthy letter reads: 'On the 8th of October we went on via Vienna (where we only spent a few hours, and I had the melancholy pleasure of meeting the poor dear Queen of Hanover and her younger daughter Mary for the first time since 1866) to Reinthal, near Graz, the home of my two sisters-in-law. We were the guests of Princess Claudine, who has a charming villa, in the Swiss cottage style, close to her married sister's place. Here we had the pleasure of at length presenting our trio to their grandpapa.'[46] After ten days Princess Mary Adelaide and her husband returned to the seductions of Imperial Vienna, leaving the children at Reinthal 'under the charge of their kind Aunts' for another month. The children lived in the Schweizerhaus, a small, many-gabled chalet, with a gallery enclosed by glass. The gateway to the Schweizerhaus was the grandest feature of the little building; it was a fine stone arch with whorled decoration cut into it, at its summit two urns and the Teck coat of arms. The garden of the Schweizerhaus contained some statuary, and was encircled by a spiked iron paling. From the chalet it took you only fifteen minutes to walk downhill to the quiet old von Hügel Schloss.

Princess May and her brothers had the run of two gardens—those of the Schweizerhaus and of the Schloss itself. Their uncle, Paul von Hügel, a man whom neither the Duke nor the Duchess of Teck especially esteemed, would romp about with them, and he gave them the use of a donkey-carriage belonging to their cousin, Paul Julius, or 'Bubi'. This was while the fine weather lasted; when it broke, life in the Schweizerhaus had its limitations. Here we may seize the opportunity to quote at greater length from the only extant, and very graphic, letter of a person dominant in Princess May's nursery days: Mrs Girdlestone, 'dear Girdie'. We know very little about Mary Girdlestone, but this solitary letter shows her as the prototype of all English Nannies abroad. It shows, too, that she had a thorough understanding of the psychology of the children's grandmother, the Duchess of Cambridge, to whom it was addressed:

I am desired by Her Royal Highness The Princess Mary Adelaide to write an account of the dear Children to your Royal Highness. I am happy to say they are all quite well and as merry and full of spirits as ever. They so often talk of your Royal Highness and when they are to see you again once or twice in saying their little prayer God Bless dear Grandmama Prince Frank said does Grand Mama here [*sic*] us, he used to call Grandmama I want you. We have been most fortunate in fine weather since we have been here until Monday it changed not cold but rain and the roads are dreadful to day again it has poured all day and what we shall do if we stay here much longer I do not know for walking. The Princess Claudine . . . has them [the Teck children] downstairs with her after tea quite alone take [*sic*] such pains to amuse them. . . . And they are generally very good. The Princess Amélia is also very nice to play with them. . . . Their Nursery is a nice large room where I sleep with the 3 Children they have all their Meals downstairs in the pretty little dining room which is like a Nut-Shell, it is a pretty little Summer Residence and the upstairs rooms are much larger than down, but not at all the Place for Children to be shut in all day this is our first day we could not get out. My duty to Her Royal Highness the Grand Duchess and I hope she will take pity upon us, and have the dear Children soon for I shall be anxious to get home early in the year.47

The Schweizerhaus still stands behind its palings today, its delightful and bizarre appearance unaltered, although the three lanes which lead up to it are now peppered with modern villas and cottages, an overflow of the Graz suburb of Saint Peter. Schloss Reinthal, too, is still intact, hidden under the brow of the hill, and protected by thickly planted trees, predominantly fir. But while the old Schloss has been spared the fate of Rumpenheim, and was neither bombed nor burned to the ground in the last war, it suffered a long, degrading occupation by Soviet Russian troops, five hundred of whom were billeted on the present owners for several years. Soiled and surreptitiously looted, Schloss Reinthal seems today the ghost of a house, an illusion fostered by its sheltered position and unfrequented drives. Seen from across the valley at sundown on a March evening, when snow is deep and crisp upon the hills, hiding all traces of the ancient avenue which once led to the courtyard's low, wide portal, it looks a castle from a fairy-tale, the secret, turreted abode of some Styrian Bluebeard. The valley lies silent in the sunset. No puff of wind stirs the sentinel trees. Wafting slowly upwards from a hidden chimney, a curl of wood-smoke hovers above the old house's purple roofs. Somewhere in the walled garden of the Schloss, with its frozen pool and its black box hedges, a dog is baying. The sound echoes harshly on the still and biting evening air.

Schloss Reinthal is, in origin, a sixteenth-century house, constructed round the four sides of a courtyard. The old avenue which led to the front gateway of this courtyard has disappeared, and the house can now only be reached down a steep and narrow lane which brings you to a door in the garden wall. This garden wall, like the arcades that run along three sides of the interior of the courtyard, give Reinthal a secluded and protected air. The house is yellow-ochre in colour, with dark red gabled roofs; two square towers on either side of the main entrance have tall pyramidal turrets upon them, squat and strong rather than elegant. In the garden there was once an ornamental pool with a fountain playing, and elsewhere about the grounds there were twelve ponds, only one of which remains today. The garden is famous for its rhododendrons, as well as for the wide and splendid view of the valley which it commands. This view is also available from the two big drawing-rooms on the first floor, and in winter-time the snow-light is reflected through the windows and gleams on the old wood-work and on the polished floors.

It is an essentially happy and comfortable house, with an aroma of old civilised amusements and faded family attachments. You would drive in with your carriage to the farther side of the courtyard, and alight under the arcades, snug and safe from rain or snow. A shallow staircase turns upwards to the first floor, where an old glass door keeps the warmth in and the draughts out. This staircase, decorated with antlers, has an achievement of the Teck and von Hügel arms painted on its windows; together with a massive billiard-table and the old porcelain stoves in every room, these painted windows are the only relics of the von Hügel tenancy of Reinthal. The stoves are old and fine, some dark green, some white; they stand like friendly familiars, in the corner of each room, generating a pleasant heat and giving the air a tang of burning wood. The chief drawing-room has a frescoed ceiling, showing entwined wreaths and bouquets of flowers. Beyond the two large drawing-rooms is a slip-room, in which the men would smoke. 'We lunched & then walked to Reinthal [from the Schweizer-haus]', we read in Princess May's earliest and least informative Diary —that for the year 1884. 'We sat & talked in the smoking room. Papa went at 5 to Graz.'[48]

On this last visit to Reinthal, in 1884, the Duke and Duchess of Teck, Princess May and Prince Alge had travelled from Gmunden, where they had stayed at an hotel and seen 'Uncle Ernest' and 'Aunt Thyra' Cumberland* every day for almost two months. The journey

* Ernest Augustus, Duke of Cumberland and Teviotdale, KG (1845–1923), was the eldest son and heir of the last reigning King of Hanover, the blind

from Gmunden to Graz had been tedious and was vividly described by the Duchess in a letter to her eldest son in England: 'You *know how* beautiful the country is as far as Amsee & for some considerable way beyond, our route lay through equally picturesque regions, the sun lighting up the snow mountains too gloriously! Then alas! we passed through a *boggy* peat country, *au beau milieu* of which we had to wait for over an hour & ¾ at a wretched little station, at which there was absolutely nothing to be done but have some soup, or seen—Later on the landscape greatly improved again, but the day closed in too early for us to be able to see much: at Bruck, where we were joined by Papa, we had another endless wait in the dark. . . . Altho' it was 9¼ or so when we reached Graz, your dear, kind Aunts were at the station to receive us & with Paul Hügel took us to our hotel, where of course there was a breeze before we were permitted to settle ourselves in the apartment Hügel had taken for us; a very nice, convenient one.'49

What the poor Duchess gallantly termed 'a breeze' was the scene which the Duke of Teck usually made on arriving at any new hotel. These scenes were caused by the Duke's suspicion that no hotel-rooms could ever measure up to his own ideas of how a Serene Highness should live. These highfalutin notions were very unacceptable to Princess May, who was herself the soul of common sense. 'I had a letter from Papa yesterday,' she wrote to her husband in March 1898, 'very low poor thing as Hamilton has *at last* impressed him with the fact that he must economise & the idea of having *fewer* servants distresses him much—Poor man if only he was less proud & foolish about that sort of thing, what can it matter how many servants one has as long as one can live comfortably?'50 For all four of his children, but especially for his calm, reflective daughter, the Duke of Teck's theories of life formed, alas, an object lesson in how not to behave. This point needs lightly stressing, since her father's tendency to public tantrums were as embarrassing to a growing girl as her mother's volubility and anxiety to make Princess May talk.

Why the Duke of Teck should have been distressed by the rooms

George V (1819–1878). In 1878 he married Thyra, Princess of Denmark (1853–1933), a sister of Queen Alexandra, then Princess of Wales. The terms 'aunt' and 'uncle' were used by the Teck children to embrace cousins of an older generation. Ernest Augustus, Duke of Cumberland, was, in fact, the son of the Duchess of Teck's first cousin, while the Duchess of Cumberland's relationship to the Teck family through the Hesses was even more remote.

allotted to his family at the Erzherzog Johann is very hard to understand today, for these rooms are large and lofty, and arranged in a peaceful corner of this great old hotel. In 1884 the rooms could be connected with each other by flinging open the high double doors, so that it was like living in a capacious private apartment. The walls were covered in olive green silk, curtains of brocade hung stiffly from the tall windows, and behind these elaborate knotted lace curtains shut out any glimpse of the snowflakes whirling down on to the grey streets of Graz. In the bathrooms the plumbing was of the most modern and contorted variety. At the Hotel Erzherzog Johann everything, one might think, would have contributed to the Duke's comfort and to his peace of mind.

'Both Claudine & Amélie have aged a good deal in the *eleven* years that have elapsed since we met & grown very grey, but they were as affectionate and nice as ever & we *all* immensely enjoyed being together, & only regretted your & Frank's absence', the Duchess wrote to Prince Dolly of this visit. They found Schloss Reinthal 'very much improved, as regards furnishing & comfort', but the little Schweizerhaus seemed to have been neglected in favour of Princess Claudine's farm; even the garden was now full of chicken wire and scrabbling hens. 'You cannot think how devoted Aunt Claudine is to her farm, to which she devotes nearly all her time & thoughts', her sister-in-law wrote in the same letter to Prince Dolly.[51] The Tecks stayed two weeks in Graz, going each day to Reinthal, and making little expeditions to Poels, 'Baron Washington's place, whose wife is a Pss of Oldenburg', or to Countess Olga Meraviglia's 'charming villa' in Graz. Countess Meraviglia was both hospitable and gifted: 'she recites wonderfully well'.

This last journey to see the Princesses Claudine and Amélie was all too short. After two weeks the Teck family returned to Florence. Within ten years the Reinthal sisters were dead, their bodies lying in the vault beneath the black marble von Hügel monument, in the cheerless Evangelical graveyard of St Peter in Graz.

CHAPTER FIVE

EXILE TO FLORENCE

———

NEITHER IN YOUTH nor in age was Queen Mary much given to brooding over the past. Her interest was directed to what was happening all over the world at the moment, rather than to what might have happened to herself some years ago. Her children, and her brothers' children, noticed that she hardly ever discussed her own youth. As Queen Consort she was in any case far too busy to dwell much on distant years, and as Queen Dowager she maintained her vivid interest in the present, in collecting objects, and in reading historical memoirs of a much earlier epoch. Should she be asked a direct question about any part of her youth, however, she would give a characteristically plain answer. During a conversation at Sandringham in August 1951 someone asked: 'And whereabouts in Florence did Your Majesty live, and for how long?' 'Well you see,' Queen Mary replied, 'my parents were always *in short street* so they had to go abroad to economise. In September 1883 we went out to Florence and stayed in Paoli's Hotel on the Lungarno; then we stayed with cousins in Austria and so on; and then for the winter of 1884 we were lent (which suited my mother's finances) by a Miss Light, the Villa I Cedri, about two and a half miles outside the Porta San Niccolò. We came back to London in May 1885.' These few sentences precisely summarise the reasons for and the duration of the Florentine exile, which took Princess May to live out of her own country from the age of sixteen to that of eighteen years.

Both in its cause and in its effect this period was of the utmost importance to Princess May's psychological development: for the cause—the humiliatingly public financial collapse of the establishments at White Lodge and Kensington Palace—and the effect, the birth of that interest in works of art and in collecting for which Queen Mary was afterwards well known, were equally formative to character. The sad example of her parents' near-bankruptcy, the knowledge of the really considerable quantity of debt which gripped the Duchess of

Teck in its octopus tentacles—at first making it impossible to leave England at all, and then making it almost as hard to return thither— taught Princess May (and all her brothers save Prince Frank, who had unfortunately inherited Princess Mary Adelaide's happy-go-lucky attitude to money) a salutary lesson: never to live above one's income. It also taught her—far more than any number of visits to the Poor— to sympathise with people who were not well off financially. This sympathy became the source of much quiet and thoughtful generosity in later years. With these developments there went a new sense of responsibility: for it was in Florence that the Duchess of Teck first realised her daughter's innate good sense, and first began to rely on her opinion, and to ask and follow this sedate young girl's advice. Again, Princess May determined to turn this enforced exile from England to her own benefit, by studying the works of art and the literature of Tuscany.

From this moment on, Princess May never lost an opportunity for self-improvement or self-discipline. In her shy, observing way she studied people and she studied books: from this examination of the world around her there grew a private but modest conviction that she possessed certain mental capacities, which, if she were ever to be given an opportunity to focus them upon a wider screen, might prove useful in the world. In this connection two quotations from somewhat later letters of Princess May's will be relevant here. Both these letters were addressed to her French companion, Madame Hélène Bricka, one of the very few persons to whom, in her youth, Princess May ever opened her heart. In the first letter, dating from before her marriage, she wrote: '. . . I read as much as possible. But my hands are full, my father pulls me one way, my mother the other, it is good not to become selfish but sometimes I grumble at my life, at the waste of time, at the *petitesse de la vie* when one feels capable of greater things.' The second, dated some fifteen years later, runs in part: 'You write rather sadly, I wonder why? After all one tries to do one's best in the world, those who think & understand. . . . So many things appear futile, frivolous, waste of time & energy, yet they must be done as long as the world is as civilization? [*sic*] has made it, of course one often rebels *mais que faire?* I have spent all my afternoons lately going to *Museums*, how much one learns & picks up, & how much nicer than going out to tea & gossip.'[1] It was along such lines as these that Princess May's mind had already, in Florence in 1883, begun to move.

There is no need to linger over the now musty details of the Tecks' financial collapse. These are of interest to us only for their effect upon the mind and the future of Princess May. It may be recalled that already, in 1878, Princess Mary Adelaide had asked the Queen for a private loan of twelve hundred pounds and had been refused. In fact, her money troubles dated back far earlier, to the very first days of her married life in 1866. Princess Mary Adelaide practised her own daily economies such as keeping used paper from parcels, hoarding pieces of string in her bureau drawers at the White Lodge, and scrupulously snipping off any blank sheet at the end of a letter; but of the wider and more constructive forms of saving money she had no conception at all. She was one of those persons who are genuinely and temperamentally incapable of understanding the simplest finance. Such persons cannot visualise money. They have no idea whatsoever either of where it comes from nor whither it goes. Naturally a source of keen anxiety to their relations, they subconsciously and innocently rely on these for help. There comes a point in time, when their financial situation has got so notoriously out of hand, that their family feels bound to intervene. Accountants, bankers and lawyers are consulted. So soon as the total of the debts seems correctly assessed some new item turns up to increase it. The family does its best to help, raises what money it can, and places this sum in the hands of a reliable trustee. Meanwhile the erring relative is asked to go and live quietly out of England for some months or even years. This was exactly what, in 1882 and 1883, the Cambridge family, in the course of many stormy conclaves at St James's Palace, decided, with the Queen's support, to ask the Duke and Duchess of Teck to do.

A minimum of figure-reckoning will suggest the kind of situation in which poor, warm-hearted Princess Mary Adelaide had involved herself and her not very strong-minded husband. In 1865 Palmerston had persuaded Parliament to grant the Duchess of Teck £5,000 a year. To this she was able to add, with her mother's generous help, another £2,000; moreover the Duchess of Cambridge's advisers computed that in the first sixteen years of married life, her mother had given Princess Mary Adelaide in addition another £60,000. With a total income of nearly £8,000 a year, the Tecks were spending more than £15,000 a year. To set up house at Kensington Palace in 1866 they had borrowed £8,000 from Miss Coutts. By the time White Lodge was also a going concern this debt had risen to more than £50,000. They also owed £18,000 to local tradesmen, and it was these last creditors who, threatening an execution in the Tecks' houses, brought the whole matter to a head. Early in 1882 Lord Winchester was sent to Princess Mary Adelaide as an emissary from the Duchess of Cambridge to remonstrate with her and enquire into the whole position, since the Princess did not answer her mother's letters and evaded all questions about her finances. She replied to Lord Winchester that retrenchment was 'impossible' since there was 'no extravagance in her life'. Lord Winchester reported that he found her 'utterly impracticable'. The Duke of Teck, though more reasonable, seemed also quite incapable of taking the situation in hand.

All through the year 1882 and on into 1883, discussions continued at St James's Palace, between the Duchess of Cambridge, her advisers, her son the Duke of Cambridge and, while they were in London, the Grand Duke and Grand Duchess of Mecklenburg-Strelitz. These were seemingly endless discussions, 'never decided, never advancing, never becoming action'. On all sides it was urged that White Lodge must be given up, the Kensington Palace apartment shut up, and the Teck family remove themselves to live modestly on the Continent for some years. Far from giving up White Lodge the Duchess of Teck was just then having it redecorated: 'I hope you will admire our creamy walls, which are well nigh finished', she wrote happily to her boys in March 1883.[2] She complained on all sides of her family's stinginess, the particular target for her gibes being her brother, the Duke of Cambridge. Why should a wealthy brother persecute his younger sister in this manner, when he could so easily help her out of her difficulties? Such was Princess Mary Adelaide's reasoning. Failing this, the country should come to her aid and double her allowance; her popularity, she assured her exasperated relatives, was growing by the hour. The nation must learn how meanly its favourite Princess was being treated. She even persuaded Borthwick, proprietor of the *Morning Post*, to insert a leader on the subject in his newspaper. What might have been quietly hushed up and discreetly arranged, became by these wild methods a public scandal.

We have had a brief glimpse of Prince George, Duke of Cambridge, as a highly reactionary Commander-in-Chief of the British Army for close on forty years, as a man of heart who had married an actress because he loved her, and as a brother who could write a 'dear funny letter' ridiculing his love-sick sister Princess Mary Adelaide at the time of the Teck engagement. At the present point in our narrative we should look at him more closely. The Duke of Cambridge was a thick-set, barrel-chested man. He had inherited his mother's egg-like countenance, but in his case it was half-buried in a fuzzy egg-cup of yellowish-white side-whiskers and moustache. He had also inherited that 'severity of expression' which had once made the Duchess of Cambridge so daunting to her niece Queen Victoria; the Duke's variety of this expression being more masculine and more ferocious than that of his parent. He had a florid face and an angry, blood-shot eye, china-blue and very piercing. To Princess May and her brothers, 'Uncle George' was friendly, but between their parents and himself there was little love lost. No doubt this antipathy was born of many past annoyances; it is likely that Princess Mary Adelaide had been odious about her theatrical sister-in-law, Mrs Louisa FitzGeorge, while the Duke of Teck did nothing to placate 'George Cambridge', whom he regarded as a natural enemy. He would find miraculous ways of enraging the Commander-in-Chief: when, for example, the Duke of Teck's soldier servant was suspected of having stolen part of His Serene Highness's kit during the short Egyptian campaign of 1882, Teck told his brother-in-law that if he himself ever had to go on another campaign it should be with German soldiers who at least were honest. In some ways, though, the Cambridge family were not just to Teck, for having (as he thought) inveigled him into the marriage, they now turned against him in a body and accused him of being unable to control Princess Mary Adelaide—whom they well knew, from long experience, to be utterly uncontrollable. The Duke of Teck had grand ideas about his position, but he had not the reckless, inborn extravagance of his wife: 'My own liabilities are not greater than those of any other Gentleman about town, rather indolent about paying bills', he wrote to Sir Henry Ponsonby3 in May 1883. It was not to be wondered at that the Duke of Teck's nervous crises became more frequent, when he saw himself held up to the world at large, and to his own children, as a man too feeble to run his household or restrain his wife.

The Cambridge family continued to threaten and to implore: '. . . let me once again *implore* you to *give up* the White Lodge & *retain* Kensington. You & Francis cannot ever on Mays & your boys account, altogether leave London, & in a small way you can do far more in London, where you are always sure to come to, than in the country. . . . You have had a very *severe lesson*. . . . Put a good face on it, be grateful to dearest Mamma, for her generous liberality, go away for a time & return to Kensington Palace, there in a *smaller* way to live comfortably though quietly, for the future. It is the best house for *your children*, believe me, & this you should think of more than your own momentary fancies or interests.'4 These earnest but tactless words of advice are extracted from a long letter written by the Duke of Cambridge to his sister on 25 May 1883. They were not heeded. Princess Mary Adelaide continued to go about '*flott*' (as her mother called it), in London Society. She continued to redecorate White Lodge. She wrote woeful letters to her own friends, imbued with all the conscious courage of a victim: 'I am myself rather low, having very much to try me, and at present am looking for the silver lining to the dark cloud, though I keep as brave a heart as I can.'5

The Cambridge family had by now concocted a practical but not an unkind scheme, by which they agreed to unite to raise what money they could by selling some of their German securities, and to lend this sum to Princess Mary Adelaide against her expectations under her mother's will. The loan would be strictly conditional on a written promise that the money be solely administered by responsible persons nominated by the Cambridges, that White Lodge be abandoned, Kensington closed, and the Teck family withdraw to a wing of Rumpenheim, with a small apartment in Frankfurt—perhaps at the Hotel de Russie?—for each winter. Unless they should prefer living in Württemberg,* or in Graz? They could live wherever they wished, so long as it was out of England. The Tecks spurned such conditions. They said they did not really need the money. In desperation the Cambridges ended by playing their ace: a request that the Queen would summon Princess Mary Adelaide and order her to go. In this they had reckoned without the Duchess of Teck's own trump card: her ready sympathy and her winning charm.

In April 1883 Princess Mary Adelaide obediently hurried down to Osborne. Now at this precise moment Queen Victoria was in a low

* There was one moment in the spring of 1882 when that resourceful man, Sir Henry Ponsonby, Private Secretary to the Queen, entered into correspondence with Mr G. T. Gould, British Minister to the Court of Württemberg, on the possibility of the Duke of Teck being, as it were, re-inserted into the succession of the Württemberg throne. It was found that the consent of the National Legislature would be needed, and nothing more was done about it. Mr Gould declared that no member of the Royal House of Württemberg, with the exception of the King and Queen, spent more than £5,000 or £6,000 a year. He added that he was certain that the Duke of Teck would 'as well as the Duchess, be received with open arms by the whole Royal Family, with perhaps one or two solitary exceptions'.6

and very vulnerable state herself, since John Brown had died only a
few weeks before. The warm-hearted Princess Mary Adelaide was
filled with compassion for her desolate cousin. She did not like to
bother her at such a moment with her own sorrows, but if the Queen
really would be kind enough to listen for a moment she would explain
to her the predicament as she saw it. Her immensely rich brother
would not help her with a farthing, her hostile and stingy sister
Augusta Strelitz was equally unkind, they both combined to slander
her to their poor, sick mother the Duchess of Cambridge, who was
in any case putty in the hands of her 'evil genius', Lady Geraldine
Somerset. As a result of hearing this new version of the situation—
'you know it was not my fault', Princess Mary Adelaide wrote to her
on leaving Osborne7—the Queen was influenced in the Tecks'
favour; when Sir Henry Ponsonby endeavoured to put more correct
facts before her, the Queen would sharply answer: 'But I have it all
from Princess Mary.'

In the end, even Princess Mary Adelaide had to admit defeat—
although she did retain White Lodge and give Kensington back to
the Queen, after an exceedingly public auction of the latter house's
contents. On the evening of 15 September 1883, a little group of
exiles stood, surrounded by their trunks and shrouded in their travelling capes and ulsters, on the gaslit departure platform of Victoria
Station. The group consisted of the Duke of Teck, the Duchess of
Teck, Princess May, Prince Dolly, Prince Frank and Prince Alge.
They were accompanied by a German governess, two female dressers
and two menservants. The Duke of Cambridge, the Grand Duchess
of Mecklenburg-Strelitz, Lady Geraldine Somerset and several friends
and dependants were there to watch them leave at eight o'clock. 'It
all went off far better and quieter than I had feared', Lady Geraldine
noted in her journal. '*No* ovation, no scene! She [Princess Mary
Adelaide] was very composed for her, and P[rince] T[eck] and the
children were even cheerful. The person who made *most* fuss and
wept *far* most, in fact *only*, was P[rincess] A[ugusta]. . . . There were
but few people there and *no* demonstration whatever, absolutely *none*!!
no sound at all but the screeching of the engine! They steamed off
and we drove home—P[rincess] A[ugusta] *en larmes!!*'8

The Teck party travelled incognito, using the name of Counts and
Countesses of Hohenstein, the title bestowed on the Duke of Teck's
Hungarian mother when she had married Duke Alexander of Würt-
temberg in 1835. 'Even *I* used to sign myself as Victoria Mary

Hohenstein', Queen Mary said, when talking of this Florentine adventure: 'Very ridiculous we must have seemed, I must say, this utterly English family, all talking English, and maintaining the artless fiction that we were the family Hohenstein.'

The immediate destination of the family Hohenstein was Rorschach on the Bodensee, where they had been asked to stay with some of their Württemberg relations for a few weeks. After this a form of life which must have seemed to Princess May as novel as their new name was awaiting them—that of Florence in its winter season. 'It was with much regret that I heard you were gone to Florence for living in a town full of attractions & temptations to expense, made me very anxious. Some quieter & more retired spot would surely have been better.'9 These wise words were written to her cousin Princess Mary Adelaide by Queen Victoria in November 1883. By the time this prophetic letter reached Tuscany, 'Countess Hohenstein' had entered heart and soul into the cosmopolitan delights of Florentine life. Princess Mary Adelaide's hotel rooms were heavy with the scent of tuberoses and violets in December, she was hiring carriages in which to parade in the Cascine, she was giving dinner-parties, appearing in the royal box at the opera, and dancing in Cotillions arrayed in a new gown of grey satin, wearing a tiara and the splendid diamonds which, even in the worst days in London, she had absolutely refused to give in gage or sell.

II

At Rorschach, on the Swiss shore of the Lake of Constance, the whole family stayed in the fine autumn weather at the Villa Seefeld, a chalet belonging to Princess Catherine of Württemberg. The Villa Seefeld, and the bright evening lights that glanced and rippled over the placid waters of the Bodensee, formed a delicious contrast to the recent hectic summer days in London, and the real sadness of dismantling Kensington Palace, where the Duke and Duchess had lived for sixteen years, and where all their children had been born.

On 18 October Princess May, her parents and her youngest brother set off for Florence via Lucerne and Milan, the two elder boys returning to England to school. The journey to Lucerne was made 'in a very nice compartment' with an open balcony at one end. On this balcony they spent nearly all day, watching the 'grand and beautiful' Swiss scenery unfurl before their eyes. Dense smoke in the St Gotthard tunnel forced them to shut themselves into their carriage again, but once through this 'triumph of engineering art' the landscape became even more beautiful as they proceeded through the Tessin valley. It seemed a foretaste of Italy: 'Spanish chestnuts, mulberries and walnut trees, creeping vines (arbour-like) and Indian corn', the Duchess of Teck noted excitedly in her now daily journal.[10] Ever ready to be friendly, the Duchess 'fraternised' (as she called it) upon their open balcony, with the people in the next compartment—two English ladies and 'a charming, most gentlemanlike, nicelooking young Russian' whom they met again in Milan Cathedral and later saw in Florence: Prince Serge Wolkonsky from St Petersburg.* They reached Milan at eight in the evening, 'and, to our dismay, were received by an official, the Chief of Police'.

This first breach in the Hohenstein incognito was followed two days later by an invitation to the Duke and Duchess to dine at Monza with the King and Queen of Italy. The King sent his special train ('handsomely fitted-up') to bring them to Monza, where they found a warm welcome and where Princess Mary Adelaide received all the gratifying attentions due to her rank. Next day, as they travelled on towards Florence, their incognito became more fictional than ever: 'Préfets complimented us at all the principal stations. Two got into the carriage!'[11] This gay and semi-triumphal progress down northern Italy was hardly what the Cambridges had envisaged or could have approved.

At Florence railway station the English Consul, Mr Dominic Colnaghi, met them, and conducted them to Paoli's Hotel, on the Lungarno. Here the proprietor, who had been courier to Sir James Hudson, the British Ambassador in Rome, showed them over the suite reserved for them until they should have found a villa to their liking. These rooms seemed so nice that they decided to retain them for the present: for at the Private Hotel Paoli 'English comfort & tastes are considered & . . . we have plenty of sun & [are] trying to reconcile ourselves to the Florentine bad taste, displayed in *huge* patterns & *glaring* colours & *hideous* contrasts of colour, on the walls & on the ceilings', the Duchess wrote to Prince Frank, adding that they planned to make themselves 'as *snug* & *comfortable* in our really charming suite of rooms, as possible'. There was only one drawback:

* Queen Mary never lost sight of her old friends. 'I saw Prince Serge Wolkonsky, an old friend of Florence days', she recorded in her diary for 10 April 1937. 'I had not seen him for 38 years.'

there were other rooms on the same floor as theirs, though at the back. This was not to be borne: 'we had to take [them] because we could not have had a stranger lodging in the midst of us; so we shall be very *comfy*, all on one floor and close together'.[12] When Paoli rendered his first accounts to the Duke of Teck, there was some unpleasantness about these extra rooms, for which they found to their aggrieved astonishment they were expected to pay.

From the very first days of their arrival their future life in Florence began to take shape. 'The very civil Prefetto, General Corti, called', soon followed by many English acquaintances, including Mrs Purves, whose elder daughter Daisy took Princess May for walks, and taught her the intricate art of crustoleum painting in the hotel sitting-room. But the nicest surprise of all was to discover a beloved Rumpenheim cousin, 'Mimi' Princess of Anhalt, with her daughters Bathildis of Schaumburg-Lippe and the still unmarried Hilda.* 'Mimi (incog. as Countess Engern), Tilla, & Hilda! *Alle drei ganz unverändert* . . . we have just been spending a nice *gemütlichen Abend chez nous*. I hope they are going to stay on a few days', wrote the Duchess.[13] They did stay some days longer, taking their English cousins to the Piazzone where 'the band was playing, to which the small amount of *beau monde* at present in Florence were listening in their carriages . . . Tilla insisted on walking by the Arno, under a *Platanen-Allee*, because she said it reminded her of Rumpenheim! but it was so *triste* that Mimi rebelled.'[14] The Duchess of Teck herself found the part of the Lungarno beneath the Hotel Paoli windows reminiscent of Frankfurt, 'that portion of it, I mean, which lies by the Main'. But the Arno just then was 'at its worst', very dry and poor, and 'quite brown in colour' so that the outlook from the hotel was not enchanting: 'but the view from the drawing-room on the Apennines over the brown roofs is very fine'.[15]

'Just at first', the Duchess of Teck wrote to Prince Frank from the Paoli in December 1883, 'we were none of us very taken with Florence as a winter home.'[16] They disliked the 'dark, cold narrow streets, wider at the *bottom* than at the *top*'. The Florentine palazzos seemed

* Marie, Princess of Hesse (1814–1895), a Rumpenheim cousin of the Duchess of Teck, had married Prince Frederick of Anhalt-Dessau (1799–1864) in 1832. Their eldest daughter Adelheid became Duchess of Nassau by her marriage in 1851 to Adolphus, Duke of Nassau; their second daughter Princess Bathildis-Amalgonda married William, Prince of Schaumburg-Lippe, in 1862; and their third daughter Princess Hilda-Charlotte died unmarried. The Anhalts had no sons.

grim and fortress-like to their unaccustomed eyes. They noticed with annoyance that two carriages could often not pass one another in the streets. The windows of the palaces were 'barred & grated like those of a dungeon'. Princess May was frightened by the funeral processions which would wind through these gloomy streets at dusk. Their first impression of the city of Florence was that it was a severe, depressing place. Even the combined efforts of Mimi and Tilla and Hilda could not give the city more than a fleeting illusion of *Gemütlichkeit*, or of the kind of German cosiness in which the Tecks had recently been swathed at the Villa Seefeld on the Bodensee. Moreover, one and all of them felt uprooted and adrift. This was especially true of Princess May, who was considered by her father to be languishing for White Lodge.

'My daughter feels homesick for White Lodge and is often quite melancholy', the Duke of Teck wrote after Christmas to his friend Prince Edward of Saxe-Weimar who passed the letter, as was intended, to the Queen to read. 'I have no intercourse with the enemy's Camp (St James's) and the only comfort to be without a home and a wanderer in foreign lands is the satisfaction of being away from those, whose want of heart, instead of preventing a scandal only increased it by word and mouth [*sic*].' He told Prince Edward that the Society of Florence was 'very good', that they were going to many dinners and *soirées*, that the King of Italy had placed the royal boxes at all the theatres at their disposition, and had sent them wild boar and pheasants: 'But we are *not* happy. . . . Amusements, even in Italy, are expensive. Everybody is exceedingly kind to us but this does not sweeten our enforced exile.'[17] 'We think Florence rather a dull place, but of course much of our time is spent in seeing churches', Princess May wrote to Prince Dolly, in a rather unenterprising wintry mood.[18]

For an intelligent English girl of sixteen to sum up Florence as 'rather a dull place' seems unimaginative. It was, however, only a first impression, lasting some few weeks. Like her mother, Princess May soon found that Florence is 'a place that certainly grows upon one'.[19] Her earlier reaction also sheds light on her state of mind and her outlook at this moment of her life.

At White Lodge and at Kensington Palace, Princess May had led a remarkably sheltered existence. Her vision of the outside world was circumscribed: there were the houses of her royal cousins and of her mother's friends; Hopetoun House in Scotland; the *Schlösser* of various relatives in Germany and Austria. Despite her parents' debts—

or more correctly because of them since the Teck household could not possibly have lived in such state on £7,000 a year—her youth had so far been, materially, very comfortable. Both her parents' houses were well staffed by servants. Their coach-houses and stables were still at this period full of carriages and horses. Her mother was a popular Princess, the Queen's first cousin, whose doings were reported in the newspapers and whose patronage was sought by every charity. Princess May had never before lived in an hotel, nor dined at a *table d'hôte*. She was in a strange city in a strange country, the language of which she could not yet speak and where the houses seemed 'so uncomfortably arranged and so dirty, and the people always smell of garlic'.[20] Years later, when she had travelled across half the globe and fallen romantically in love with Indian and other exotic land-scapes, Queen Mary fully appreciated the thrilling charm of the un-familiar and the delicious shock of novelty. Just now this was something she had still to learn. It was in Florence that she began to learn it.

At this period, also, there was the plain fact that Princess May's education, though infinitely more solid than that of her Wales cousins Princess Louise, Princess Victoria and Princess Maud, was still narrow. This was not her fault. The education of the Teck children had long been the subject of wrangles between the Cambridge family and the Teck parents; there was once even the perilous suggestion that Aunt Augusta Strelitz should 'take charge of May' and 'form her'. In 1882 the Duchess of Cambridge undertook all financial responsibility for her four grandchildren's education, insisting that the boys must go to school, and that Princess May's rigid German governess, Fräulein Gutman, be dismissed. 'Gutman', however, travelled with the Tecks to Florence, leaving them only in the spring of 1884,* when Princess May was put into the hands of competent French and Italian teachers and began studying foreign literature.

* We do not know whether Fräulein Gutman left Florence with real regret, for on one occasion Prince Alge, who was twelve, pushed her into a fountain there. It was to Fräulein Gutman that Princess Mary Adelaide made her famous repartee about her hair-box. One evening, after seeing Salvini act, the whole family returned to the Duchess of Teck's sitting-room in the Hotel Paoli, where the Duchess began to make tea. She asked Fräulein Gutman to be so kind as to fetch the biscuits, which would be found in her hair-box in her bedroom. When Fräulein Gutman protested that she could not eat biscuits out of anyone's hair-box, Princess Mary Adelaide turned to her and said: 'If a Princess of Great Britain and Ireland can eat biscuits out of a hair-box, I presume the daughter of a Dresden dentist can?'

Now began Princess May's real education—that which, by reading, she gave to herself, and which continued for the remainder of her life. The Duchess of Teck, for her part, was not what is called 'a great reader': if she was not talking, she was trying to catch up with her correspondence, and if she was not writing letters she was indulging in one of her truest pleasures—telegraphing. 'I assisted at Alix's lunch & then telegraphed till tea-time', she wrote in a letter from Sandringham in 1880;[21] or 'I wrote innumerable telegrams'. All this frenetic activity left no leisure for reading books. 'Mama never has time [to read],' Princess May once told a girl neighbour at White Lodge, 'she pumps Dolly and she pumps me as to what we have been reading lately. Then some clever man comes to dine, and Mama talks brilliantly about the books she hasn't read and they say: "It is remarkable how Your Royal Highness can find the time to keep up with the literature of the day!" Now I *have* read the book, but I can't talk about it.' On returning a book by Carmen Sylva, which the Princess of Wales had lent the Duchess of Teck one year before, Princess May wrote to her husband, in August 1895: 'I am sending Motherdear the book, please tell her Mama has actually read it.'[22] Such remarks as these indicate how completely Princess May had to rely upon herself and upon her paid teachers when she began seriously to wish to widen her mental horizons. A very short time in Florence served to show her how much she did not know.

After the first few weeks of repining, the family began a stringent course of sightseeing, looking at churches and monasteries, driving up to Bellosguardo, to the Vincigliata, or out to the Certosa, visiting Michelangelo's house and standing in admiration before selected pictures in the Uffizi and the Pitti. Many of these expeditions were made under the sedulous guidance of Miss Susan Horner, joint authoress with her sister of 'a delightful book about Florence' which the Duchess and Princess May were reading. 'Miss Susan Horner arrived a little before two o'clock, and soon afterwards I drove with her, May, and Gutman to the Cloisters of the Recollects, or barefooted monks (now suppressed) in the Via Cavour—charming little court with beautiful frescoes in *grisaille* by Andrea del Sarto and Franciabigio',[23] runs one of many similar accounts (in the Duchess's journal) of sightseeing with Miss Horner, who later managed to interest Princess Mary Adelaide in a society she and her sister had formed with the unpromising object of promoting kindness to animals amongst the peasant children of Tuscany.

Princess May, who always loved the theatre, went frequently to see Salvini act, either with her parents or alone with Mrs Monson (one of Aunt Marie Edinburgh's ladies who had most conveniently turned up in Florence) as a chaperone. There were, too, contemporaries of Princess May's own age in Florence, to whom she would talk in her shy, quiet way: Daisy Purves and her little sister, 'the Colnaghi girls', 'the Bossi girls', 'the Home Speirs girls', Louisa Maquay, Lady Crawford's daughters, Lady Jane and Lady Mabel Lindsay. She was taken to one or two small dances at the Carnival time, and there were luncheon and tea-parties at the Villa Stibbert or the Villa Palmieri, La Colombaia or the Villa Spence.

Very far from being 'rather dull' the social life of Florence in the early eighteen-eighties was, as the Duchess of Teck quickly discovered, varied and, in patches, brilliant. The basis of it were the old Florentine families, the Corsini, the Torrigiani and others. The members of these families could be seen daily driving about the Cascine at the fashionable hour, in shining carriages, finely turned out. In their own great dim palaces they tended to entertain rarely, but when they did so they gave big dinner-parties. The English Society in Florence was the most hospitable and, many foreigners found, the most agreeable. Its recognised head was old Lady Orford who kept a weekly *salon* from ten at night till four in the morning, during which she chain-smoked black cigars.

Both in the English and the Italian Society of Florence the tone was, by London standards, unusually free. The *ménage à trois* was accepted, quite naturally, as the only civilised solution to the problems of marriage, and at Lady Orford's *salon* there was even the spectacle of a Florentine lady playing whist with her husband, her ex-husband, and her lover. Back in London, Lady Geraldine Somerset was busily at work collecting like a jackdaw every scrap of glittering Florentine gossip for the benefit of the Duchess of Cambridge. Needless to say, these scraps all went to show what a free-and-easy, indeed immoral, city Florence was, and how unsuitable for Princess May. Lady Geraldine would believe any story so long as it was against the Tecks. She heard that the Duke of Teck now insisted that the lady of every house in which they dined should personally present himself and Princess Mary Adelaide with their cups of coffee after dinner. On the 1st of January 1884 she regaled the Duke of Cambridge with a most satisfying new anecdote: 'We [the Duchess of Cambridge and Lady Geraldine] told him what we had just heard of the *grand train de vie qu'ils mènent* at Florence! of the story of the lady at whose house P[rincess] M[ary Adelaide] was at a ball and having to wait for her carriage when coming away, the poor lady waiting with her caught so severe a chill she *died* two days after!!'[24]

The richest and most brilliant Society in 1883 and 1884 in Florence was still that of the Russian nobility and aristocracy, who had for some years formed a graceful colony in the city until summoned back to Russia by a ukase of the Tsar in 1885. The withdrawal of these absentee landlords to their own estates was thought by some to have 'extinguished the social glory' of Florence; but while the Tecks were there, the Russians were still in their full glory. They were headed by Princess Woronzoff, who had a collection of jewels believed to be unique in the world, and who appeared each day wearing twelve ropes of perfectly matched pearls which reached down to her knees. Then there was the Russian-Jewish Comtesse de Talleyrand and her husband, and her husband's brother the Duc de Dino. Queen Nathalie of Servia could also be observed in the Cascine, or walking about the streets of Florence followed by an admiring crowd, for Queen Nathalie never wore a hat out of doors, and wandered from shop to shop along the Ponte Vecchio 'arrayed in a plain gown invariably of white or of black, with a single row of pearls around her neck, her abundant hair [falling] down her back in girlish fashion'.[25]

These were the personages who were now passing daily before Princess May's observant eyes. Her mother, her father and herself were often to be seen driving in the Cascine—at times in the company of some of the four daughters of the Duchess of Madrid, who had left her husband Don Carlos of Spain, at other times with Russian or with English acquaintances, or with 'lovely little Marchesa Ginori' who owned a real English barouche, a ride in which Princess Mary Adelaide particularly enjoyed: 'Mama was delighted to be in a decent carriage again', wrote Princess May.[26] 'The weather is quite spring like', she wrote on 3 March 1884 to her Aunt Augusta (for alone amongst her family Princess May kept up a regular correspondence with the Grand Duchess, who had now come to rely on her for news), 'and it is delightful to go into the country and pick wild flowers in the *poderes*. A little while ago a Russian lady gave a fancy ball, and we went to an English lady's house to see some of the people in costumes, it seems to be the fashion here for the people to show themselves first to their friends, and then go to the ball; they might just as well breakfast with their friends the following morning in costumes, as they rarely return from balls till between 7 & 8 o'clock. I don't know if it's true but I have been told so. Some of the costumes were very fine, but the ladies were over-dressed, one especially who was covered with beautiful jewels but she looked like a jeweller's shop. Last week was the end of the Carnival the last day there was a Corso in the Cascine (the sort of Hyde Park). The Italian gentlemen had 4 breaks filled with flowers which they threw to the ladies we had quantities, it was really a very pretty sight. In the evening there was a masked ball at the Pergola. We went to the king's box to see it. It was rather funny seeing the people dance, in masks and dominos.'[27]

Sometimes a glimpse could be caught of 'dreadful Ouida',[28] and the Tecks actually made friends with Ouida's rival in Florence, Mrs Janet Ross, whom the Duchess found sympathetic and 'not so loud' as she had been led to expect.[29] 'Few women possessed the charm of the Duchess of Teck,' Mrs Ross has written in her reminiscences, describing a dinner she had given for the Teck family, 'she took an interest in everybody and everything. . . . She sang some old German *Studentenlieder* with wonderful verve and looked so handsome that I could hardly take my eyes off her. . . . The young Princess was a remarkably attractive girl, rather silent, but with a look of quiet determination mixed with kindliness which augured well for the future.'[30] Another person who used the identical expression 'quiet determination' in describing Princess May in Florence was a young friend of the Duke of Teck, and a favourite of the Duchess. This was an Irish painter, trained in Paris. He was twenty-three years old, very handsome and lively, and his name was Thaddeus Jones.*

'As mother and daughter were inseparable companions', Jones wrote of the Duchess and Princess May, 'the shyness and reserve which distinguished the young Princess were, perhaps, more marked by contrast with the open genial manner of the Duchess. She possessed, however, her royal mother's sense of humour and quickness of perception. Tall, slight and graceful, her pretty features resembled those of the Duchess, although lacking in that mobility of expression which lent such a charm to HRH's face . . . it was easy to perceive that,

---

* Henry Thaddeus Jones, who was born in 1860, studied in London and at Julien's studio in Paris. Settled, 1881, in Florence. His successful career as a portrait painter was greatly due to the Tecks. In 1886 he settled in London and exhibited frequently. He moved to the United States, where he wrote his *Recollections of a Court Painter*, 1912.

underneath her maidenly reserve, there was developing the quiet determination of the *maitresse femme*.'³¹

'Mr Thaddy', as the Duchess playfully called her young *protégé*, is a most valuable eye-witness of how the Teck family seemed in Florence. Before enlisting his further aid, however, we must here record the fresh calamity which overtook Princess Mary Adelaide and her growing daughter in the early spring of 1884. On the morning of the fifth of March, at the Hotel Paoli, the Duke of Teck awoke to find that he had suffered in the night a severe paralytic stroke.

III

For reasons of her own—some memory perhaps of the Duchess of Cambridge's stroke at Strelitz in 1873 and its dire results—Princess Mary Adelaide was anxious to believe, and to persuade others, that her husband's paralytic seizure was merely a case of Florentine sun-stroke. 'I suppose you have heard by now that poor Papa has been very ill indeed. Either from sunstroke or a chill, he found on awaken-ing on the 5th of March, that his left arm was as good as paralysed; that his left leg was almost useless for walking, & that his mouth was slightly crooked', Princess May wrote to her brother Dolly several days after the event.³² 'Happily Dr Baldwin thinks that in 3 or 4 weeks he will be restored to the use of his various limbs, he can already move his arm & can walk from his room to Mama's. . . . I thought perhaps you might have heard he was ill & wondered why we had not written, but we are so much with him that I have had no time to write. . . . We have had the most lovely weather and we go on expeditions to get flowers—Jones' pictures of Mama & Papa were sent to England to go to the Academy, they were very good.' Fifteen days after the stroke, Princess Mary Adelaide wrote in her journal: 'Francis walked about the passage and into his sitting-room for the first time since his illness. Hurrah!'³³

In February 1884 the Duke of Teck had paid a very brief visit to England, to take his elder sons back to school. On his return to Florence he had seemed perfectly well, and on the fourth of March he had taken his habitual daily stroll with young Thaddeus Jones, whose company he found highly congenial. So soon as the Duke could see friends, Thaddeus Jones was asked to sit with him. The Irish youth was 'distressed beyond words at the Duke's altered appearance'.

It needs little medical or psychological knowledge to perceive that the Duke of Teck's seizure was the natural result of the traumatic year of money worries in London, and of the frequent and understandable fits of rage into which the poor man had been driven. The Cambridges affected to believe the inverse of this argument: 'I fear Franz is worse than we could take from your account of him (or rather his own dictated to you and May) what an anxiety', the Grand Duchess of Strelitz wrote to her sister from St James's Palace in April 1884.[34] 'I fancy the terribly excited state he has been in for some time, his violence, must have been caused by his approaching attack. I am truly sorry for you, poor Mary!' The dear old Duchess of Cambridge opined that the attack had been 'the result of a scene' between Princess Mary Adelaide and her husband; while Lady Geraldine Somerset spent much time interviewing every returning traveller from Florence: the British Ambassador, Sir James Hudson, who gave a *deplorable* account! . . . that he is quite altered and an old man! that the attack was a very severe one, and his memory went!'; Fräulein Gutman, who thought the Duke 'better but gives a deplorable account of him on the whole!'; Mrs Purves who told them 'his mouth and leg are now *quite* right and the hand only still weak, and when it gets tired numb'.[35] Months later, in November 1884, the Queen of Hanover added her voice to this ghoulish chorus, writing to tell Queen Victoria that she herself believed the Duke of Teck to be suffering from 'softening of the brain! and it develops itself in these frightful paroxysms of rage'.[36] This last was a complete exaggeration: but the fact remained that from March 1884 on, Princess May's father was a sick man, prematurely aged in his forties, more touchy than ever, and a perpetual source of anxiety to his children and his wife. Once again Princess May, who instinctively shrank from the sight of illness, was brought daily face to face with it in one of its most trying forms. Not only this: it was her own father who was ill. Princess May had a genuine filial affection for her father who, for all his quirks, had been always indulgent with her, was proud of her and took a connoisseur's interest in her appearance and her clothes. She and her three brothers had all inherited, in varying and modified degrees, the Duke of Teck's temper. It was now up to Princess May to impose upon herself a rigid discipline of patience, and to become neither flustered nor annoyed by the poor Duke's caprices. This she managed to do—and we must recall that she was not yet turned seventeen.

The tragedy—for such indeed it was—of the Duke of Teck's

E

seizure interfered, of course, with the family's immediate plans. They
had arranged to leave the Hotel Paoli in the month of March and to
settle in an old country house beyond the city walls. They were now
forced to postpone this move and to linger on at the Paoli. After
some weeks the Duke was well enough to be put into a carriage and
driven up to the Villa Stibbert. Here he convalesced under Mr
Stibbert's care, talking Florentine gossip with his visitors in the
great hall of the villa, which was peopled with awe-inspiring dummy
knights on dummy horses, caparisoned in full armour: 'the *tout
ensemble* resembling a remarkably well-kept museum'.

Meanwhile the Duchess began to put into operation her cherished
plan of borrowing from—or rather sharing with—its owner, a
fifteenth-century villa, I Cedri, which stands in an English garden
on the left bank of the Arno, some three or four miles from the Porta
San Niccolò, near Bagno a Ripoli. 'I went over the rooms of Miss
Light's Villa (I Cedri) with a view to our occupation', Princess Mary
Adelaide wrote in her journal. 'It promises to make a charming spring
abode for us . . . the garden is full of wild violets, and all the bushes
and flowers coming out.'37 With Princess May and Prince Alge, the
Duchess moved to the Villa I Cedri on 3 April 1884. In a few days
time the Duke joined them, and they entered upon the second, and
by far the more agreeable, phase of their Tuscan life.

Only those who have spent many months in hotels can know the
intense relief of getting out of one and back into a private house again.
The Villa I Cedri was not, of course, the Tecks' own, and they did
not pay rent for it; but the English lady to whom it then belonged,
Miss Bianca Light, had only stipulated that she should have the use
of a small apartment there when she did not wish to remain in
Florence. To all intents and purposes the Cedri was as private and
as secluded as White Lodge.

Built in the fifteenth century for the Laroni family, the Villa I Cedri
had since then had many owners. In the eighteen-forties it had been
bought by the Light family, and now belonged to Miss Bianca Light,
the sister of the President of the English Club in Florence, Major
Light, who had become a crony of the Duke of Teck and had in fact
presented Thaddeus Jones to His Serene Highness. The house is a
characteristic Tuscan villa of its period: rectangular, with a flat tiled
roof, and walls coated in yellow plaster. It stands in a garden designed
in the English fashion, but containing fine ilexes, cedar trees and
magnolias. Near the house is a very large plane tree. The country

beyond the garden wall is the olive-studded landscape of Tuscany. There are no buildings between the villa and the banks of the Arno, which here forms a wide translucent weir, its waters momentarily held in check by a low lock at Bagno a Ripoli. Throughout the villa and the garden you are conscious of the rustling sound of water slipping gently over this lock.

The Villa I Cedri was an ideal house for an invalid's convalescence and equally well suited to a shy girl of sixteen who loved to wander through the *poderi*, a pale Kate Greenaway figure in a Tuscan straw hat, picking the grey iris and the aconites: 'there are such quantities of wild flowers in the *poderes*', Princess May wrote to her Strelitz aunt,[38] 'daffodils, jonquils, anemones, narcissi & violets & hyacinths.' It was also an ideal house, as Princess Mary Adelaide soon perceived, in which to entertain friends from Florence. One of the first alterations the Tecks made at the Villa I Cedri was to have a species of 'lay-by' constructed in the narrow lane that led to the house. This lay-by permitted two carriages to pass one another. The wide bulge in the stone wall of the adjacent *podere* is still pointed out to visitors by the local peasants today, as a relic of the English Highnesses' occupation of the villa.

The main room in the house was naturally the hall, which was the height of the house and had frescoes by Fabbroni. A gallery ran part of the way round this hall, and off the gallery opened the bedrooms, the smaller dining-room and the Duchess of Teck's boudoir. The furnishings of the hall were an Italian version of Victorian or Second Empire taste. The Duke of Teck soon got to work on these furnishings, altering, as was his habit, the positions of the various circular tables, pots of fern and buttoned ottomans. They engaged a first-rate Italian cook, discovered that one could easily get 'dishes and bonbons' from Doney's (if one arranged with the British Consul to have these eatables passed through the customs barrier at the Porta San Niccolò), and that nothing was simpler in Florence than to hire a piano or buy a few mandolins. On 21 April, less than three weeks after the family had settled in I Cedri, the delicious invasion from Florence began: 'Soon after lunch Alice Shaw Stewart arrived, followed later by Alethea Lawly and Miss Carton. We went down to the hall to tea, and were joined by dear Lady Alfred and Amy Paget. It felt like *home* in dear old England', the Duchess of Teck noted on 21 April. 'When all had left Bianca took us a charming ramble down one of her *poderi* to show us the view across the Arno, to the picturesque mill, and back by a very pretty farmhouse with a wall and kind of vine-covered pergola. We hurried home to arrange the table for our little dinner-party, and gathered some heartsease and other flowers.'³⁹

The Cambridges had expressed concern that in five months at the Paoli the Teck family had successfully got rid of two thousand pounds. Princess Mary Adelaide's answer was to borrow a house, rent free. Obviously, since one had made this distinct economy, one could allow oneself to entertain a few friends. Her journal now contains familiar phrases: 'Home and dressed for dinner for eleven'—'We were a party of twenty-five in all, and sat out in front of the house'—'At half-past eight our twenty-six guests began to arrive.' There were tennis parties and mandolin parties, and big tea-parties out of doors under the cedar trees, and long spring evenings during which the Duchess of Teck would sing to her guests after dinner the songs specially composed for her by Marzials—and even, on one occasion, a Russian song written in her honour by Prince Wolkonsky, who had returned from St Petersburg. Every Saturday there was a regular dinner-party: 'Those Saturday dinner-parties', writes Thaddeus Jones, 'had already become a feature at I Cedri and were remarkable for their whole-hearted gaiety; they could not be otherwise with so genial and gracious a hostess as Princess Mary [Adelaide]. . . . After dinner the Duchess, who had a sweet sympathetic voice, invariably sang some ballads, the evenings being otherwise enlivened by charades, games and sometimes by a small dance.'⁴⁰ Very soon the White Lodge custom of having a house full of guests for the week-end was re-established in the old villa by the Arno.

Royalties, both resident in Florence or visiting the city, naturally came out to pay their respects to Princess Mary Adelaide, whose incognita was now all too literally nominal. 'The dear Grand Duke of Mecklenburg-Schwerin came alone about noon, and quite *en surprise*', we read in the Duchess's Journal for 2 May 1884; or 'After luncheon the dear Duc de Chartres was announced, and, before he left, came up to my room'. Or, again: 'The Duchess of Madrid . . . arrived just as we were starting for Florence. I sat with her in the hall for a little while, then took her in my carriage, with May, to the Palazzo Pitti.' Living so far from the city naturally obliged them to have horses and carriages of their own—how else were they to go to and fro? Moreover Princess May's art studies, the pace of which was now suddenly stepped up, required daily visits to Florence, long afternoons spent in ecstasy before the works of the Old Masters.

'Through the passage across Ponte Vecchio to the Pitti Palace', the Duchess of Teck records of one such afternoon of early summer, '... we visited *five saloons* very carefully. Titians! Raphaels! Andrea del Sartos! Van Dycks! Rubenses!—gloriously beautiful! Quite beyond everything. *Tore* myself away about seven.'[41]

So life at the Villa I Cedri near Bagno a Ripoli began to resemble life at White Lodge in Richmond Park, but with a difference. The *dolce far niente* of civilised Italian living accorded well with Princess Mary Adelaide's own easy-going temperament, lack of punctuality and love of late hours. To the day of her death she would repeat, with her delightful beaming smile of approval: 'Oh! but that is *so very Italian!*'

And what part, you may well ask, did Princess May take in all this Florentine hurly-burly, this vortex of excitements and reactions and emotions on seeing sunsets and Titians and minor royalties and vine-covered pergolas? Still in eclipse behind her mother? Still wearing a Tuscan straw hat and picking flowers in those *poderi*? The answer to such questions is: yes. Princess May did spend a good deal of her time going on quiet floral expeditions and enjoying the 'heavenly weather, just like summer; lovely blue sky, no clouds, perfectly delicious'.[42] She was also having Italian lessons and singing lessons, and she had resumed her painting. 'Directly after breakfast we went to the farmhouse in the *poderi* to watch May paint with Verwloet; Zucchelli joined us and Tommasso protected us!' wrote the Duchess. 'Devoured brown cherries brought by peasants.'[43] This was on the morning of 23 May 1884. Three days later, on the twenty-sixth, came an event of considerable personal importance to Princess May: it was her seventeenth birthday. This birthday, which rendered her for some twelve or fourteen hours the most important person in the Villa I Cedri, seems to offer a good opportunity to beg Princess May to leave her easel, her camp-stool and her paint-box, and to step forward so that we can see her more clearly in the bright, shadowless Italian sun.

It is not altogether the kindest moment to approach Princess May, since she is in the midst of drastic dental treatment. 'Much of my time is taken up with the dentist', she wrote to her brother, Prince Dolly, on 31 May. 'I have had 6 teeth stopped & 2 roots are to be taken out. Did you go to the dentist in London before you went to school?'[44] The roots were painlessly removed under laughing gas, and Princess May's birthday presents (which we will look over in a moment) compensated for that nervous anxiety inevitable upon any visit to any dentist, at any age.

Photographs taken about this time by Signor Giacomo Brogi, the photographer to the King of Italy, give us some clues to Princess May's appearance as a young lady of seventeen. Some people are naturally photogenic, some people are not, and Princess May was definitely in the second category. 'She never ought to be photographed, as they do not do her justice', said a woman who met Princess May, then Princess of Wales, at Knowsley in 1902. In photographs her hair, for example, looks dark, and in fact it was fair—not ash-blonde as Princess Mary Adelaide's had been, but of a colour that was a mixture of light brown and pale yellow, and which glinted gold in the sunlight. Already at this period she wore it dressed tightly at the temples, with a braid round the back of her head, and a bang over the forehead. This bang, or artificial fringe, had come into fashion in the middle seventies of the century, and Princess May wore it all her life. It was an elegant rather than an attractive coiffure, for it hid the forehead almost completely. Writing in 1885 to the Crown Princess Frederick to thank her for some photographs of her daughters, Queen Victoria commented: 'The dear girls are all very nice . . . [and] charmingly arranged—only I think you shld not let the girls have their hair so low—It looks like little *poodles*! The forehead, is always a pretty thing to see.' Eleven years earlier she had written, again to the Crown Princess: 'I think Alix [the Princess of Wales] does not dress her hair to advantage just now, too high & pointed & close at the sides for her small head. The present fashion with a frizzle & fringe in front is *frightful*.'45 Although she allowed her daughters the Princesses of Prussia to wear their hair in this modish manner, the Empress Frederick did not herself care for it. 'How pretty she would look', she wrote of Princess May in 1897, 'if she did not disfigure herself with her coiffure.'46

We now come to a rather crucial question: what did Princess May, at seventeen years old, look like? Is the girl in the white frilled dress who is crossing the lawn beneath the cedars (having left Verwloet standing alone in the *podere*) a pretty girl, or is she not?

Now, we can dismiss the Empress Frederick's opinion out of hand, for the Empress Frederick was by nature carping, and towards Princess May she was never quite just. There is usually a reason or a motive for almost every human being's attitude towards another human being, and in this case we need only to learn that the Empress

Frederick had secretly hoped that one of her four daughters might have married the English heir-presumptive; it somehow seemed to the Empress Frederick that a Princess of Prussia had been spurned in favour of a morganatically-born Princess of Teck. Let us listen to other, less prejudiced persons, who knew her in her youth. These speak of her beautiful 'wild-rose' complexion, of her neat figure, of her upright carriage and graceful movements. 'I suppose she really was very pretty, but one somehow never thought of her as so': this, from a friend of her youth still living today. From another we gain much the same impression: 'No, I never thought of her as pretty. She did her hair wrong, too high and tight at the sides. It was a light-brown, a yellow-brown.' Finally, since young women are ordinarily fairly well aware themselves of what they look like, a remark made by Princess May about her own appearance should carry weight: 'I am afraid', she said, 'I am too much like Queen Charlotte ever to be good-looking.'

There was indeed a close resemblance in the structure of Princess May's face—particularly about the full jaw and almost turned-up nose—and that of Queen Charlotte, the Mecklenburg Princess who had as a child played under the beech tree at Mirow and had married Princess May's great-grandfather George III. But Princess May had a facial expression all her own, a combination of charming gravity, alertness and the hope of being amused: these were the qualities which illuminated her features. Her piercing china-blue eyes missed nothing that was going on, and she had inherited from her father his sense of the ridiculous. In the depths of these blue eyes there lurked a merry twinkle. 'I can quite picture your appearance to myself', Princess May's Aunt Augusta once wrote to her: 'also can see the twinkle in your eye, or the twitching of your mouth, when any funny thing strikes you' and (Aunt Augusta again): 'I can quite see your pretty mouth smiling, your eyes glistening up at something funny you happen to see, bringing up that arch-smile of yours, so characteristic in expression.'[47] Quiet and watchful persons can often get more amusement out of life than those who talk too much and have no time to observe. Moreover, when Princess May was thoroughly amused she laughed aloud. Keir Hardie—no flatterer of royal persons— once said of her: 'When that woman laughs, she does laugh, and not make a contortion like so many royalties.' 'I always have to be so careful never to laugh', Princess May remarked on one occasion, with wistful humour, 'because you see I have such a *vulgar* laugh!'

Princess May's lifelong habit of observation was greatly aided by three assets: her piercing eyesight, her phenomenal memory for faces, and an aural clarity which enabled her to hear every word that was being said at any distance from herself down a long and cheerful dinner-table.

In these Florentine years Princess May's figure was slight, and, as the mode then was, stiffly corseted. With the example of her mother in her mind, she was determined to avoid putting on weight; in middle life she did become somewhat heavier, but then she thinned down again. In her general appearance, in fact, as in her coiffure, there was never any startling change. Here comes a curious fact about Queen Mary. She was not, as she seemed to be in public, a tall, imposing woman. All public personages tend to look larger than life; and, in later years, with her hair dressed beneath a tiara or a toque, and wearing high-heeled shoes, Queen Mary gave an illusion of height. She herself once remarked that before her hair was dressed in the morning, she was not one inch taller than her husband King George V, who was five feet six inches.

Having attempted to gain some notion of Princess May's appearance at the time of her seventeenth birthday, 26 May 1884, we may now look at her birthday presents, and at the way in which this significant anniversary was celebrated at the Villa I Cedri.

IV

Many thanks for your charming birthday letter [Princess May wrote[48] on 31 May 1884 to her eldest brother in England]. I spent a very happy birthday, but I missed you & Frank awfully. Mama gave me her carbuncle & diamond star earrings, 2 little bracelets with pearl clasps, & a plain pair of earrings, a white leather book for photos, clothes & writing paper. Papa gave a grey dust-cloak & a Japanese fan—Miss Light a brooch. Miss Alcock (a charming girl & great friend of ours) a sapphire & diamond horseshoe pin.

> Fln Gutman book of German songs.
> Anna—lovely embroidered cover for a book.
> Sir J. Hudson—bonbonnière.
> Mr ffrench—gold bangle.
> Mr Lambert—a lovely cushion.
> Mr Gaspieri—a picture in a carved frame.
> Mr Peter Wells—A lovely painted fan.
> Mr Jones—A fan painted by himself with apple blossom.
> Gdmama—£2.

This meticulous list is very characteristic of its writer: for all
through her life, both as Princess and as Queen, Princess May loved
to draw up and to check lists, to write labels and to docket objects
and pieces of furniture. It has been said of her that had she not been
Queen Consort she would have made an admirable and efficient
museum curator.

Apart from exhibiting the innate orderliness of Princess May's
mind, this list is worth a second glance. We notice in it first the
generosity so typical of the Duchess of Teck—the gift of some of
her own jewellery, of earrings, an album and clothes. Next, we
observe the equally typical parsimony of the old Duchess of Cambridge, who felt two pounds an adequate sum to give her only granddaughter on her seventeenth birthday. Indeed, Princess May was
lucky to get two pounds and not one pound ten: 'Are you sorry the
holidays are over?' she had written to Prince Dolly on 11 May of
this year, 'how you have been spoilt at St James, from Frank we hear
that Grandmama has given you £2 instead of 30/-, what a shame
that AlGe & I don't get any more.'49 A third feature of this list is
that it contains no present for her godchild from Queen Victoria,
and nothing from 'Aunt Alix' or the Wales cousins.

The Duchess of Teck had been disgruntled at having to leave
England at all. She was also a most intermittent correspondent. As a
result, she hardly ever wrote either to her mother or her brother in
England, or to her royal cousins. Even the Princess of Wales, eagerly
affectionate though she was, had become discouraged. At Christmas
1884 she sent a box of presents—diamond brooches, a photo frame,
an 'egg pencil, owl & monkey'—out to the Villa I Cedri, with a letter,
part of which reads:

My darling old Mary,
    It seems a perfect age since we parted & heard anything from each
other—& now I can stand it no longer & send you these small offerings
as a *reminder* of me—& hope they will cheer you up as little Christmas
messages from home. . . . I wonder whether you ever received my telegram
on your birthday & also my long answer to yrs on my birthday—How are
you all getting on—We all miss you terribly here & I most of all as you
know. . . . I saw dear Aunt Cambridge today—she is looking much about
the same—but complains bitterly at never hearing from you!! Goodbye for
today darling Mary fond love to dear Francis & children from us all—&
write a line to yr loving faithful old friend—& cousin—Alix.50

The Prince and Princess of Wales had thoughtfully asked the two
E*

elder Teck boys to stay at Sandringham for Easter 1884, but even this hospitable gesture elicited no thanks from I Cedri, where the delights of a new life were absorbing Princess Mary Adelaide's attention to a degree which made her neglectful of relatives and friends at home.

Princess May kept up a meagre and haphazard correspondence with the Wales Princesses: 'I had a letter from Maud this morning' or 'I heard from Toria that their ball was great fun' or again 'I had a letter from Harry [Princess Maud of Wales] to thank me for the letter & my new photos I sent her on the 26th'.[51] For the younger members of the Royal Family, Princess May's own contemporaries and former playmates, it was almost a case of out of sight out of mind. They were no longer even quite certain how long May Teck and her parents had been away. Writing, eight years later, from the Royal Yacht *Osborne*, in which he was cruising with his mother and sisters along the Italian coast, Prince George, Duke of York, wrote to tell Princess May of an incognito tour of Florence, in which they had seen as many galleries and churches as they could: 'I need not tell you anything about them . . . weren't you there for nearly two years once, I forget.'[52]

So far as Queen Victoria was concerned, she only heard from Princess Mary Adelaide from Florence upon the sudden death, at Cannes, of Prince Leopold, Duke of Albany, in April 1884. The Duke of Albany had been Princess Mary Adelaide's godson, and, in consequence, the Queen asked Princess Helena to send a detailed account of the death to Florence, together with a copy of the doctor's lengthy report from Cannes. The Queen followed this up with a grief-stricken letter—'My life seems now to be made up of grief, & loss of those who are dear & a support to me'—telling her cousin of the 'last sad ceremony' and of the plans for a marble tomb in the Memorial Chapel at Windsor, surmounted by 'a recumbent Statue of dearest Leopd.' by the Austrian sculptor Boehm.[53] Princess Mary Adelaide had found time to acknowledge all this melancholy but interesting information. She had written a deeply sympathising letter. After this major effort, however, she had become once more, epistolatorily, as silent as Prince Leopold's marble tomb. In late August another letter from the Queen arrived:

For ages I have intended writing to thank you for your last letter & by *writing*—for your pretty present.—But one event after another has crowded in upon me—that I never cld manage it, & indeed have taken a leaf out

of your book in that respect of writing. . . . Pray acknowledge this letter—
& the accompanying parcel by Telegraph—to *Balmoral*—whither we go
on the eveng. of the 1st.—I send you a recollection of your beloved God
Child & cousin—our darling Leopd & a photograph of him—& *my book*,
& Alice's. . . . Your dear Mama is I hear as well as usual!—Love to Franz
& May. Tell *her* to write to Beatrice. The Parcel cannot go with this so
please telegraph *twice*.54

There is no evidence that this letter was ever answered. By the
winter of 1884 Queen Victoria openly expressed herself as 'much
annoyed' by Princess Mary Adelaide's resolute silence. On 2 December
Queen Victoria wrote to offer to let the Tecks have back their old
apartment in Kensington, if only they would relinquish White Lodge.
To this well-meant suggestion Princess Mary Adelaide sent no reply
at all; the Queen then telegraphed to enquire brusquely why her
letter had not been answered and received in return a short telegram:
'Gracious letter received answer follows.'55

At this time, too, the Queen was getting as exasperated as were the
Duke of Cambridge and his mother over another matter involving
the Tecks. This derived directly from Princess May's seventeenth
birthday, since it now became imperative that she should be confirmed.
The religious aspect of confirmation was something about which the
Queen felt most sincerely. She was haunted by the knowledge that
Princess May remained unconfirmed, and she could not understand
the Duchess's strange evasions and delays about this matter. Confirmation also had a social significance. Until Princess May was confirmed she could not be presented at a Court, and until she was
presented at a Court she could not appear at balls or go about in
general society, either in London or even in Neu Strelitz—to which
latter, smaller capital Princess Mary Adelaide had toyed with the idea
of sending her daughter for the winter season of 1884.

The battle now joined about Princess May's confirmation became
as fierce as that over the relinquishment of White Lodge. I Cedri
was bombarded by letters from the Cambridges, and letters from
Princess Beatrice writing peremptorily in the Queen's name. In the
face of this attack, Princess Mary Adelaide deployed her customary
defensive tactics, which principally involved going quietly to ground
and pretending that there was no contest going on at all. The Queen
insisted that the confirmation take place immediately, and arranged
for the Bishop of Gibraltar to perform the ceremony. The Bishop
was prepared to meet the Tecks in Florence or at any other place

in his continental diocese which they cared to appoint. This did not suit Princess Mary Adelaide's book.

Confirmation is naturally a very serious matter. For the English Royal Family in the nineteenth century it was also an occasion for the bestowal of jewels and other presents on the young member of the family concerned. Aunts and uncles and cousins all contributed to make a Royal confirmation day an unforgettable event in a youthful life. Princess Mary Adelaide did not see why her only daughter should be confirmed in a hole-and-corner way in Florence, when it would be so easy for them all to make a trip to London, stay with the old Duchess of Cambridge at St James's Palace, and have the confirmation ceremony in the one place in which it should, in her opinion, be held—in the Chapel Royal. This proposal—which was, of course, a thinly veiled project to get back home to London so as subsequently to settle down again in comfort at White Lodge—horrified the Duchess of Cambridge, who was 'not only opposed to this plan for a score of reasons in their present position, but even quite resolved not to ask them here which she thinks would entail numberless *désagréments* both for herself and them and would be altogether a great mistake'.[56]

And so Princess May throughout her eighteenth year continued unconfirmed. By January 1885 the Duke of Cambridge had begun to change his mind on the question of letting the Tecks return to England. On one of his daily visits to his mother the Duke urged her to give her permission for this return 'on the plea that [the Duke and Duchess of Teck] are not retrenching and therefore their living abroad becomes but an additional expense'. Should they be allowed to come back to England, or should they be asked to stay where they were? Discussions at St James's Palace raged on into the spring of 1885. What Lady Geraldine called the Duchess of Cambridge's 'fruitless, bootless, always uselessly recurring "insistence" P[rincess] M[ary] "shall" give up the White Lodge' was the barrier to any agreement. During the summer and autumn of 1884 Lady Geraldine had become very bored by the topic altogether: 'the whole old story of P[rincess] M[ary] and her affairs, P[rince] T[eck] and his health, May and her confirmation, the boys and their education, Georgie [Prince Alge] and his *non*-education!!!'[57]

For us, just now, the final solution of these burning problems lies hidden in the future. All we need remember at the moment is that on her seventeenth birthday Princess May got no presents from any of her English relations (who had always showered gifts upon her in

previous years), that it became imperative that she should be confirmed, and that her mother had determined that this ceremony could
only appropriately take place in the Chapel Royal, St James's Palace,
London.

The birthday celebrations at I Cedri ended with a dinner at the
Villa La Colombaia, belonging to some English friends, the Horace
Tharps, below Fiesole. The Tharps had hung Chinese lanterns all
about their garden, and as the twilight fell fireflies came flashing to
and fro through the balmy Tuscan night. One of the guests at the
Tharps was the Baltimore girl, 'dear little Emily' Alcock, whom
Princess May had described in her list of birthday presents and their
donors as 'a charming girl & a great friend of ours'. Princess May
had grown sincerely attached to 'dearest Emily', who, like Thaddeus
Jones, had become a household pet. In 1895 Emily Alcock married
a clergyman, Mr Stone. She died in 1945. Until then Queen Mary
and she would exchange annual letters, and even occasionally meet.
'Dearest Emily—I am so grateful to you for yr kind letter & good
wishes on my *old* birthday, for I was 50 on the 26 which is really
terrible!' Queen Mary wrote to her from Buckingham Palace on 29 May
1917: 'How well I remember that birthday in Florence in 1884, one
of the few I have not spent at home—& the lovely evening in the
Tharps' garden & the fire flies—How long ago it all seems & yet
many little scenes come back vividly to one's mind; one of the saddest
parts is that except you, Alge, & myself there is scarcely anyone
living who remembers those days. Even then one had one's troubles,
one's anxieties. . . .'58

The chief of these troubles and anxieties was obviously the Duke
of Teck's health. This was much improved, but the doctors in Florence
at first urged that he should go to Bad Gastein, a precipitous cure-
station in the Tyrolese Alps. Later they changed their opinion, and
suggested Seelisberg, in Canton Uri in Switzerland. Even out at I Cedri
the heat of June proved overpowering: 'Papa . . . felt the intense heat
of those last days at Florence terribly',59 wrote Princess May to her
Aunt Augusta. On 2 July the Teck family and their attendants left
Florence at 7.40 in the morning to journey by train and lake-steamer
to Seelisberg on the Lake of Lucerne. Some forty friends gathered at
the station to see them off: 'So sorry to leave', Princess May put in
her Diary, which she was beginning to keep with regularity.

The Duke and Duchess of Teck, Princess May and Prince Alge
did not return to Florence for five months.

CHAPTER SIX

SOME SUMMER HOLIDAYS

WHEN THE DOCTORS had suggested Gastein as a suitable place for the Duke of Teck to continue his convalescence and to take the cure the perennial difficulty of finding the money to pay for a family migration of this sort cropped up. The Duchess of Cambridge was asked if she could advance two hundred pounds, since in some mystifying way Florentine living seemed to have swallowed up all the ready money available for the Tecks to draw upon. To this the old lady had agreed, on the stark principle that one invalid should help another. When the doctors subsequently pronounced against Gastein, the Duchess of Cambridge withdrew the offer of money and substituted the shop-soiled one of an apartment at Rumpenheim:

I am commissioned by dearest Mamma, now that Florence will be becoming too hot for you to remain there and you will be about making your Summer plans, to offer Rumpenheim to you as a *pied à terre* for the Summer months. You can comfortably inhabit a portion of it [wrote the Grand Duchess of Mecklenburg-Strelitz to her sister from St James's Palace on 9 May 1884]. . . . She complains dreadfully, and the older and weaker she gets, the more she will feel her pains I fear! it is a sad existence, but she is ever so good, always thinking of giving pleasure to others; this again you have an instance of, in her offering you Rph. . . . As for your never writing it really is beyond comprehension! this is my *4th* letter from here; we are so anxious about Franz and know nothing—can give no answer to all the enquiries made; what can it mean?[1]

It meant that Princess Mary Adelaide was otherwise occupied: 'Am *most busy*!' she scrawled on a scrap of paper which Princess May enclosed in her own letter to her aunt of 22 June, 'never a moment's leisure! . . . Rumpenheim much too hot for August, I fear.'[2] The Duchess of Teck had, of course, no intention whatever of going to live at Rumpenheim. So far as heat was concerned, she was perfectly right, for in high summer the plain round Frankfurt and Hanau becomes insupportably sultry, with frequent thunder-storms.

The Hotel Sonnenberg at Seelisberg on Lake Lucerne, where the family stayed for a month while the Duke of Teck took the local water-cure, was a large establishment. It consisted of three separate buildings with a 'huge table d'hôte dining room' in which two hundred people fed clatteringly at meal-times. The hotel was crammed with German tourists, some of whom were obliged to sleep on improvised beds. The corridors were uncarpeted, and the noise of stamping feet and shouting German voices echoed through them night and day, an unattractive contrast to the lulling sound of the Arno at Bagno a Ripoli. The Tecks dined at a table of their own in the bay window of the dining-room verandah, and had a pleasant, clean apartment upstairs: sufficient bedrooms and a big sitting-room with three windows looking out across the lake. At the Duchess's request, they were soon joined by their Florentine friend, old Mr Peter Wells, by young Thaddeus Jones and by Bianca Light.

At the Hotel Sonnenberg, Princess May continued her studies, getting up at seven in the morning and working until one o'clock. The afternoon was spent in the sitting-room, and at five they would walk out into the woods to pick cyclamen, or to sit and read aloud to each other under the trees. Peter Wells hired a piano for them ('The Angel!!!' Princess May exclaimed to her Diary) and they were then able to have nice little musical evenings. They also went for expeditions on the lake, and walks up mountain roads with their alpenstocks. Even an alpenstock was unable to support the full weight of Princess Mary Adelaide: 'The road was steep but with the help of our Alpen sticks we got down quite well', Princess May notes, of one such walk. 'Poor Mama's stick broke.'3

There were not many people in the Hotel Sonnenberg to whom the Tecks wanted to talk, but they made one or two pleasant acquaintances, notably the Roman landscape painter Commendatore Corrodi and his wife. Corrodi, the Duchess was delighted to discover, had actually given painting lessons to the Princess of Wales and to 'Adelheid Nassau'. He had stayed at the latter's romantic Schloss at Königstein, in the lovely Taunus hills, and in general knew 'a host' of Princess Mary Adelaide's 'belongings'. Signora Corrodi was beautiful, had a fine singing voice and was, in Mr Thaddeus Jones's slightly snobbish phrase, '*persona gratissima* with most of the royalties of Europe'. With the Corrodis, and with another family named Schwartze, the Teck party played bowls, or sat out on the terrace which was sheltered from the sun 'by a trellis of interwoven plantain trees', listening to the band. They made a disappointing overnight expedition to what the Duchess called 'the tip-top of the Rigi' to see the sun set one evening and rise the next morning, staying at a small hotel in which they had a disagreement with the waiters over opening the dining-room windows. 'It certainly is a magnificent panorama, and yet we did not feel the sight was worth all the fatigue, trouble and expense.' On the way back Princess Mary Adelaide settled 'in a seat by open side of car' as she jotted into her Journal: 'The view was beautiful; but, unluckily, I sat behind a man who smoked the whole time quite nasty cigars, so that when we reached Vitznau I felt very squeamish, and could only sit down on a bench near the landing-place and keep quiet.' She cheered up, however, on finding that even Vitznau offered pleasant opportunities for spending money: 'Feeling better, I went with the rest to look into a very pretty shop, at which we made some purchases.'[4] Princess May's Diary gives a laconic account of the expedition: 'Horrid hotel & rude people. Chilly going, at Vitznau hot. Mama felt sick. We bought some carved wooden bears. . . .'[5]

In the first week of August Prince Dolly and Prince Frank arrived at Seelisberg for their summer holidays, much to their sister's delight: 'Dolly's voice is completely changed, he speaks in a deep gruff voice. So funny!'[6] she wrote to her Aunt Augusta. To have her elder brothers with her again was a real satisfaction to Princess May for Prince Alge was still too much of a child to be a companion for her. He was a very fat little boy, and his brothers, who suspected him of being their mother's favourite, teased him mercilessly. When these summer holidays of 1884 were over, Princess Mary Adelaide took up her pen and delivered one of her rare scoldings to her elder sons:

> The one thing that distressed & worried me [she wrote, from Gmunden on 7 October] was your unkindness to poor Algy & intolerance of his, I admit trying ways, always forgetting that he is after all but a child & requires humoring a little & being treated as such, instead of only knocks & pinches & bruises & hard words—& perpetual teasing, which in itself must irritate beyond measure a nature like his—It is *unmanly* & unworthy of you & is a fault you must especially guard against.[7]

Since the Duke's water-cure seemed to have been effective the family now moved on to stay with their Württemberg cousins on the Bodensee. It was a large party that entrained in a roomy private carriage at Lucerne: the Duke and the Duchess of Teck, their children and their servants, Mr Thaddeus Jones and Mr Peter Wells with his Italian valet, Arcangelo. Mr Wells was a rich and popular old widower, who spent the winter months in Florence where his only aim was to attend as many parties each day and night as he possibly could. He had known Princess Mary Adelaide as a girl, and his wife, a Lethbridge, now long dead, had gone to her first ball at Cambridge House. He was a benevolent old egoist, with silvery hair and a 'clean-shaven contented countenance', an elderly beau whose manners bewitched every lady he met. Like young Thaddeus Jones, he had been enlisted by the Duchess to help to keep the Duke of Teck amused.

Mr Peter Wells did not smoke, and on the journey from Lucerne to Bad Horn, where the party had taken rooms in what they found to be a 'pot-house', the Hotel Horn, he sat and chatted to Princess May and her mother, whilst the Duke of Teck and Mr Jones retired to the next compartment to smoke cigars. The Duke and Thaddeus soon fell asleep, but the young painter woke suddenly to find that someone had placed a lump of strong-smelling Limburger cheese under his nose. Who had perpetrated this practical joke? He thought it must have been the elder Teck boys, since when he looked into the compartment he had earlier left he found everything as it had been before: 'Princess May and her mother talking with Peter Wells, little Algy asleep near them, a picture of peaceful innocence impossible to associate with the misdeed.' He went in to them to complain, but was met by 'general hilarity and cries of "throw the dreadful thing out of the window".'[8]

At the little lakeside station of Bad Horn, Prince William of Württemberg was waiting to receive the travellers, attended by his equerry, Hauptmann von Roeder. After greetings and presentations, Princess May and her mother drove off to the Hotel Horn, leaving the others to follow them on foot.

II

Prince William of Württemberg, the Teck children's 'Uncle Willy', was heir-presumptive to his father's cousin, King Carl I, the reigning King of Württemberg at the time of the Tecks' visit to the Bodensee. In an earlier chapter we have already had a vertiginous glimpse of the complications of the Württemberg succession in the eighteenth century. This tradition of complexity the Württemberg family managed to carry on into the nineteenth century. It is necessary to capitulate the relevant facts as painlessly as possible here.

King Carl of Württemberg was the son of King William I of Württemberg by his third wife,* Duchess Pauline of Württemberg. Duchess Pauline was her husband's first cousin, and was one of the sisters of the Duke of Teck's father, Duke Alexander—the 'Grosspapa' who gave the Teck boys black cigars when they visited him at his small house in Vienna. King Carl's wife, Queen Olga, was a Russian, a daughter of the Tsar Nicholas I. They had no progeny, so that the succession would go, on King Carl's death, to his uncle's grandson, Prince William. Prince William had married a Princess of Waldeck and Pyrmont, who had died in 1882, having borne her husband a son who died at five months old, a daughter who had died at birth, and another daughter, Princess Pauline, known in the family as 'Affie', who was automatically, as a female, ruled out of the succession to the throne. Later, in 1886, Prince William married as his second wife Princess Charlotte of Schaumburg-Lippe, a daughter of the Duchess of Teck's cousin, Princess Bathildis-Amalgonda of Anhalt. She had no children, and in consequence the Württemberg throne would pass on her husband's death to the Catholic branch of the Württemberg family—which, as we have seen, Queen Victoria regarded as a calamity and the Duke and Duchess of Teck as a gross injustice. Had it not been for that much-stressed disaster of morganatic blood, the Tecks would have had every hope of ending up in their old age as King Francis I and Queen Mary Adelaide of Württemberg; in which contingency Princess May would doubtless have married some minor German Prince.

At the moment in time—August 1884—at which the numerous Teck party poured out of the special carriage on to the wayside platform at Bad Horn, Prince William, who stood waiting for them, was not yet King of Württemberg. The cold and pompous court of Württemberg was presided over by King Carl and Queen Olga, who spent the winter months in their Schloss at Stuttgart and the spring months at Ludwigsburg, a colossal country palace near the capital.

---

* King William I had previously married (1) Princess Charlotte of Bavaria, by whom he had no issue, and (2) the Grand Duchess Katherina Paulovna, the daughter of the Tsar Paul I, whose wife had been a Princess of Württemberg, and an aunt of King William I. By this second marriage King William I had had two daughters: Marie Countess Neifferg and Sophie, the cultivated Queen of the Netherlands, who lived, estranged from her husband, at The Hague. Neither of these daughters could, of course, inherit the throne under the Württemberg law forbidding the succession of a Queen Regnant.

We shall presently have an occasion to examine both these grandiose edifices, when following Princess May on her melancholy visits to them in 1892, during one of the blackest and most unpromising periods of her young life. But now it is still August 1884: and in August King Carl I, Queen Olga, and their suite, were lingering at their summer Schloss at Friedrichshafen, on the opposite shore of the Bodensee to Bad Horn.

The Tecks had chosen Bad Horn as a temporary home because it was within walking distance of the Villa Seefeld at Rorschach, a house in which they had already stayed on their way to Florence in the autumn of the previous year, but which was not large enough to contain their present party. The Villa Seefeld was not in Württemberg but in Switzerland. It lay exactly opposite Friedrichshafen across the lake, and belonged to a portly, austere old widowed Princess, Catherine of Württemberg, who had a red, mannish face, and habitually dressed in purple and mauve. Princess Catherine was the mother of Prince William. She was also the sister of the reigning King Carl I; which meant that King Carl's heir, Prince William, was not only an uncle's grandson but an own nephew.

Besides these intricate family relationships—or more probably because of them—the Court of Württemberg was noted for another peculiarity: the intense rivalry of the various members of the royal family with one another. It was riddled with intrigue. 'I hope', wrote the wise old Grand Duchess of Mecklenburg-Strelitz to her niece, Princess May, 'you will steer clear of the family feuds at the Court of W.'9 'Of all the touchy people I have ever met in my life', Princess May wrote to her aunt of the Württemberg family, on another occasion, 'commend me to them, they would all drive me wild in a week *if I had* to live there.'10

Although the Tecks were staying at the Hotel Horn (where the food was 'indifferent') they had most of their meals, and spent a large part of every day, at the Villa Seefeld with 'dear, kind Catherine', her son Prince William and their respective 'suites'. Life at the Villa Seefeld was unexciting, but very restful: the Duchess of Teck described it as 'vegetation' and complained of the lack of variety—'as tho' life were *one unchanging round*!'11 The member of the party who probably enjoyed it most was the Duke of Teck, for the Bodensee, or Lake of Constance, is not only visually one of the finest inland seas in Europe, but was also the setting for his own carefree youth. It reminded him of an earlier, halcyon existence. In a charming letter to his four children, written during a visit to the Villa Seefeld in September 1877, the Duke had written:

> You will think me a very ungrateful Papa, for not having thanked you for your dear and kind letters and wishes for my birthday ere this, but indeed . . . we are out on Expeditions in the mountains every day and we are hardly at home except for lunch and dinner. This House is close to a beautiful and very enormous Lake, on the opposite shore of which I spent many a happy day in my earlier life and later on, and it is 25 years since I have been first. There are many relations of mine here about, first of all at Friedrichshafen, just opposite this place, over the Lake, my cousins the King & Queen. . . . There are other cousins of mine and I am very pleased to see them again and to be with them and to talk of old days, when they & myself had been children and of dear relations who had been so kind to us and are no more with us to love us and be loved by us. . . . I was out fishing on the Lake in a boat, yesterday, but tho' I was out 2 hours, I caught nothing.[12]

On the late summer visit of 1884, the Duke would take his boys out sailing on the deep lake waters. Princess May was occupied in painting, and in sitting to Thaddeus Jones, who was concocting a portrait of her in the open air with the Lake of Constance as a background 'effect'. She would also play on the beach with her cousin, Pauline Württemberg, a child of five years old, whose mother had died the year before. They would make 'a delightful seesaw with planks' for little 'Affie', while the Teck boys and their father made waterfalls in the sand. Then there were the Seegarten paths to be weeded; and farther afield, nice expeditions to shop or to look at architectural beauties in such places in the vicinity as St Gall or Ragaz. Not far from the Villa Seefeld was the lovely villa of Maria-halden, where the Duchess of Hamilton, born a Baden, was then living. The Duchess of Hamilton's daughter, Countess Festetics, was also at Mariahalden with her children, and there were frequent interchanges between the two houses, one mysterious entry in Princess May's Diary, for 23 August, reading: 'Then to Mariahalden to play lawn tennis. Alas! it had been sent to Hungary. Picked roses & then walked home & supped.'[13] Farther along the lake were the Duke of Parma, and, farther still, the Duchess of Madrid.

The interior of the Villa Seefeld also offered its own mild attractions. Chief amongst these was a large musical box, which 'Aunt Catherine' kept in her dining-room and which was played every evening. There was, too, a good deal of singing in the evenings, and a certain amount of halma; alternating at times with more strenuous diversions such as puss-in-the-corner, and a game in which 'we covered ourselves up with napkins & the people outside had to guess to whom the eyes belonged'.[14] One night the Duke of Teck improvised an exhibition of *Schattenspiele* or *Ombres Chinoises* in the coach-house, with Prince William as a chef, Thaddeus Jones as Harlequin and Hauptmann von Roeder as Columbine. The evening ended suddenly, when the Duke of Teck—who was managing the lighting arrangements behind the white sheet against which the actors performed—knocked over a lamp and set the whole coach-house on fire. Princess May noted in her Diary: 'Such fun.'

Thaddeus Jones would often perform card tricks for old Princess Catherine, whose 'august features relaxed with amused wonder' at the three-card trick: 'That three-card trick was the "Open Sesame" to the heart of Princess Catherine, in whose favour I rose high.'[15] When the youthful Thaddeus was taken away by Prince William of Württemberg to see some manœuvres in September, the Duchess of Teck wrote him a long chatty letter, ending: 'Catherine gave us an impromptu cold supper. I afterwards made myself useful sorting the cards which had all got mixed by tricks, and pressing into shape those your fingers had bent. How Catherine enjoyed those tricks! You are a great favourite with her I find.'[16]

On one evening at the Villa Seefeld, as Princess May noted in her Diary, Princess Catherine of Württemberg and her guests experimented with table-turning. They chose the massive mahogany dining-table 'which it would probably have taken half-a-dozen men to move about', and were much startled when it set off on what Thaddeus Jones describes as 'a jumping progress around the room'. The evening nearly ended in disaster. Princess Mary Adelaide who, owing to her size, tended to be accident-prone, 'got entangled in her gown, tripped and fell, with the edge of the massive table upon her'. She was not hurt, but it took the united strength of Princess Catherine, the Duke of Teck, Countess Festetics, Princess May, the Teck boys, Peter Wells, Thaddeus Jones and 'some other guests' to lever the table off Princess Mary Adelaide and into an upright position again.

One of Princess Catherine of Württemberg's greatest pleasures in life was to eat; and in this direction she was not austere. 'The food plays a very great part in this house,' the Duchess of Teck wrote on a later, similar visit to the Seefeld, 'poor dear Catherine being *almost as greedy* as her Granddaughter!—It is quite excellent, only too nourishing & there is *much too much* of it! We have *sumptuous banquets* at 1, which make me feel sleepy all the early part of the afternoon & amusing suppers at 7, with *Dicke Milch* or now & then soup to begin with! tea, wine, a hot dish & either vegetables or salad, cold meat *variés*, aspic, *compôte*, cakes & sometimes a sweet dish! The Table groaning under the weight of the several dishes!' Even the private steam-boats which ferried the members of the Württemberg family to and fro across the Bodensee were laden with foodstuffs: ' ... At 4, we re-embarked [from Villa Seefeld] in fair weather for Friedrichshafen, being regaled on board with tea, sandwiches, champagne, beer & fruit & cakes!—What a lot these worthy people do eat! A caviar toast was all I could take to myself!' wrote the Duchess of Teck, who was by no means an ascetic at the table.[17]

There was naturally a good deal of coming and going by boat from the Villa Seefeld to the Schloss at Friedrichshafen and vice versa. One day in early September the Duke and Duchess of Teck embarked at eleven-twenty-five in the morning, to present their four children to their cousins, King Carl and Queen Olga. The family party were 'all very smart', the Duchess wearing 'the brown and gold-braid toilette'. The Schloss at Friedrichshafen, a former monastery, had been bought by King Carl's grandfather as shooting quarters, and converted by the next King of Württemberg into a summer and autumn residence, about the year 1821. It is attached to the *Schlosskirche*, a baroque building with two lofty towers surmounted by onion domes, which form a landmark at this end of the Bodensee. The interior of the Schloss* contained suites of rooms with pretty stuccoed ceilings. A lofty first-floor loggia, frescoed with armorial devices, looked out over the lake. There was a charming garden, with fine chestnut trees, a pleached lime walk along the lakeside, a private harbour flanked by small pavilions, a bowling alley and a *carrousel*. 'But oh, the stiffness of the inmates!' wrote Princess Mary Adelaide. The Villa Seefeld, where the ladies had to bring gloves and fans to luncheon, was formal enough; but at the royal court on holiday at Friedrichshafen there was considerably more state.

The visitors were received by a lady-in-waiting and an equerry. Princess May and her mother were conducted to an apartment prepared for them, where they took off their cloaks. 'Here May and I

* The Schloss at Friedrichshafen, now the property of HRH Duke Philip of Württemberg, was sacked after the 1939–1945 war. The garden was also destroyed. The *Schlosskirche* alone has been, quite beautifully, restored.

sat in state, twiddling our thumbs, until at $1\frac{1}{2}$ the King . . . paid me a visit; we had arrived before 1.' King Carl of Württemberg, who was an eccentric, seemed greatly aged. He walked with a stick and dragged one leg after him, but 'evidently wished to be amiable, and was very kind in manner to the children, whom we presented to him'.[18] 'The poor King of Württemberg', wrote the Empress Frederick to her mother Queen Victoria, after his death in 1891, '. . . was very peculiar & difficult to manage & had the funniest caprices—in fact was not always "all there".'[19] The Empress said that King Carl had been managed by his wife, Queen Olga, who 'kept everything going'. Neither King Carl nor Queen Olga appealed greatly to Princess Mary Adelaide. When the Queen at length sent word that she was ready to see her relations, King Carl took them to her rooms: '*Grande embrassade et conversation forcée*', commented the Duchess of Teck, who was then taken by Queen Olga to see her collection of pictures, 'most of them gems of the modern school'. They lunched at two o'clock in the company of the suite of eighteen courtiers, and after a private talk between the Queen and Princess Mary Adelaide ('she & I have little or nothing in common') the party were taken for a drive and then delivered back to their boat: 'I breathed freely once more, the stiff formal visit being over',[20] wrote the Duchess of Teck.

Princess May's account in her Journal of this same visit to Friedrichshafen is factual and unenlightening. Already at seventeen she had initiated her system of keeping non-committal records of daily events,* seldom expressing an opinion or judgement, and making use of a vocabulary chiefly remarkable for its limitations. As usual, she had no illusions about her Diaries. 'My Diaries?' she once said years later, when Queen Consort, to a friend, 'oh *my* Diaries aren't interesting—not like the King's!'

The discretion of Princess May's Journals is, of course, all of a piece with her reserved character, but it would be true to say that even had she wished to keep another kind of Journal she would not have been capable of doing so. It is an interesting fact that the then

---

* Although Queen Mary began to keep a Diary in 1884, she let it lapse for several years, and did not take up the habit methodically again until 1891. She re-read these Diaries in her old age, as a note in the volume for 1947 reveals: 'Saturday, 26 July. Awfully hot day sat out under the trees where it was very pleasant—I am reading through all my diaries commenced in 1891—to me interesting as it reminds me of so many people and places & so forth and of our journeys.' During this process of re-reading, she would occasionally make emendations or explanatory additions on certain pages.

elder generation of the English Royal Family—in particular Queen
Victoria, Princess Mary Adelaide and the Grand Duchess Augusta—
had a genuine gift for writing which was not inherited by their
immediate descendants. Princess May forced herself to write letters,
and she wrote many throughout her life. It went against the grain,
but this was never a consideration which influenced or dictated Queen
Mary's behaviour. 'My great difficulty in writing letters is I hate it
so, it is such a waste of time', she wrote to Madame Bricka in 1892.
'Today I got up quite early and wrote letters to Papa, brothers &
Grandmama from 9.30 to ¼ to 12—Wasnt that virtuous for me who
detest writing?' she wrote again in 1898.[21] Disliking letter-writing
herself, Princess May did not especially appreciate this heaven-sent
gift in others: 'I don't want any descriptions of places, only just to
hear how you are & how you like Neuenahr & whether it is doing
you good',[22] she told her mother, in August 1893, when Princess
Mary Adelaide was taking the cure at the rural spa of Bad Neuenahr
in the tranquil Rhenish valley of the Ahr.

Incidents like the visit to the King and Queen of Württemberg at
Friedrichshafen undoubtedly increased Princess May's knowledge of,
and strong aversion for, life at the small German courts. The Tecks'
next adventures, at Gmunden, brought her back into touch with a
world she much preferred: that of the English, Danish and Greek
royal families.

III

On 10 September the Teck family party entrained once more, bound
this time for Gmunden on the Traun See in Austria. Here, beside
their third lake this summer, they settled down for two months at
the Hotel Goldenes Schiff. The Traun See is narrow and elongated,
a thin strip of green-blue water set in a cleft of the mountainous
Salzkammergut, and fed at one end by the River Traun, which tumbles
down seventeen rapids out of the lake again. The little township of
Gmunden sits at the edge of the Traun See, facing the steep mountains
of the opposite shore. It is essentially a miniature landscape—a
contrast to the gloomy grandeur of Lake Lucerne, or the wide, but
not comfortless, expanses of the Bodensee.

To the Duke and Duchess of Teck a sight of the beauties of the
Traun See was not the only objective of their visit; for at Gmunden
the Queen of Hanover, born a Princess of Saxe-Altenberg and widow

of the blind King George V,* held court, with her spinster daughter, Princess Mary of Hanover, in a large villa commanding a fine view of the lake. Also at Gmunden lived the Queen's only son, Ernest Augustus, Duke of Cumberland, his wife and their four children.† The Queen's third child, Princess Frederica (who was one year older than her sister Princess Mary), had married Baron von Pawel-Rammigen in 1880. Known to Princess May as 'Cousin Lily of Hanover', Princess Frederica lived in an apartment at Hampton Court granted her by Queen Victoria and haunted by the ubiquitous ghost of a small and active lap-dog.

The Duke of Cumberland—'Uncle Ernst' to Princess May—was a man with a very long neck and narrow shoulders. He was rather bald and wore thick spectacles. The Danish royal family thought him hideous: 'certainly one must admit poor dear Ernest is the *ugliest* man there ever was made!!!' wrote the Princess of Wales to her son Prince George, from Fredensborg Slot in 1900, 'but I like him *so* much—'²³ 'He [Uncle Ernst] looks much the same & wears awful sort of soft nightshirt collars' [Princess May told her brother Prince Alge of a meeting with the Cumberlands at Mentone in March 1898]. 'I cannot say he looks well "*en civile*".'²⁴ The plain fact was that Uncle Ernst Cumberland did not 'look well' in anything. For Princess Mary Adelaide, and more particularly for the Grand Duchess Augusta (who had never got over the rape of Hanover by the Prussians in 1866), the Duke of Cumberland was a personage of sad historic import, a dethroned King, head of the House of Guelph to which the Cambridge sisters were both so proud to belong.

In 1878 the Duke of Cumberland had married Princess Thyra of Denmark, daughter of King Christian IX and his Rumpenheim Queen, Louise, and a younger sister of Alexandra, Princess of Wales, of King George of the Hellenes and of the Empress Marie Feodorovna of Russia—Princess May's 'Aunt Alix', 'Uncle Willie' and 'Aunt Minny-Minny'. Aunt Thyra thus belonged by right of birth to that intimate group of European royalties whose knockabout humour we noticed earlier, when we were contemplating her nieces, the three Wales Princesses.

The Duchess of Cumberland's brother, the King of the Hellenes,

---

* See note on p. 86.

† In 1884 the Cumberlands' fourth child, Princess Olga, had just been born. Their two youngest children of their family of six, both sons, were born in 1885 and 1887 respectively.

with his wife, Queen Olga, who had been a Russian Grand Duchess, and their four elder children were likewise staying at Gmunden. Scattered around the shores of the Traun See there were, too, some Württemberg cousins, two or three Austrian Archdukes with their Archduchesses, the Dowager Grand Duchess of Tuscany, and, inevitably, Aunt Mimi Anhalt with her daughters Hilda and Tilla in tow. This gathering of royalties in and around Gmunden really constituted what Queen Victoria, using a phrase coined by her son-in-law Prince Louis of Hesse-Darmstadt, termed a 'Royal Mob': 'than which', she once wrote, 'I dislike *nothing more*'.25 When her eldest daughter the Empress Frederick was staying with the Danish royalties near Copenhagen in 1889, the Queen had written inquisitively: 'Do tell me when you have time a little more abt the Royal Mob at Fredensborg & I wish the dear girls wd write their impressions.' When she received the Empress's reply, she wrote again: 'That Mob of Royalty & that noise must have been dreadful & rather strange to romp & carry one another about as they do.'26 A special joke amongst these Danish and Greek cousins was to make funny noises and to yell if they saw anyone trying to write a letter: 'At this moment the whole room is full here & I can hardly write & they shout so that I must say Goodbye for today',27 the Princess of Wales wrote from Fredensborg in 1889; and it must be remembered that by this period the Princess of Wales was virtually stone deaf.

It will be grasped that Princess May had now entered an atmosphere very different from that of the staid Württemberg court. There were wild games in villa gardens, many excursions by boat, the seventeen rapids to be shot on the River Traun, pony-phaetons to be driven hither and thither. Here, too, there were accidents, although fortunately they did not this time involve Princess Mary Adelaide. 'Aunt Thyra rode' (Princess May's Journal informs us, recording an October drive, 'to a mountain' with 'Mama, Papa, Alge, Aunt Thyra, Emmy, Tuxen, & Peter [Wells]') 'but had a nasty tumble pony fell through a bridge made of planks & rolled on her. She was not hurt & sent pony home.' 'Poor little Minny [Princess Marie of Greece and Denmark] fell & nearly broke her collar bone, she suffered terribly', she wrote of an afternoon spent playing 'different games' in the garden of the Queen of Hanover's villa; and, on 15 October, 'Poor Plumpy [Prince George of Greece and Denmark] swallowed a *Kreutzer*', with an entry three days later, '*Kreutzer* came to light'. There were also serious evenings at the Queen of Hanover's villa, when Madame

Prokisch or Madame de Klenck read *Vanity Fair* aloud. 'Went', reads another Journal entry, 'to a lecture at the Queen's about catacombs.'[28]

At Gmunden, Princess May became much attached to 'all the dear Greeks' and especially to Princess Alexandra ('Alix'), who was three years her junior, and took her driving in a pony-phaeton: 'She is such a charming amusing girl, very like Louise of Wales only not at all rough.'[29] This young Greek Princess had evidently inherited the gentleness and winning charm of her mother, Queen Olga of the Hellenes.*

Queen Olga was the niece of the Tsar Alexander II of Russia. She was an affectionate, delightful woman, who was much loved by the young Waleses, and became like a 'second mother' to Prince George, Duke of York, while he was on the Mediterranean station. She preached, and practised, *'la religion de la souffrance humaine'*: 'Do you know those lovely words,' she wrote to Prince George, *'Dites que jamais vous ne marcherez sur un cœur, que vous respecterez le sentiment partout, ou vous le trouverez . . . que vous aurez la religion de la souffrance humaine. . . .* Is it not lovely?'[30] Queen Victoria wholeheartedly admired Queen Olga. 'How charming Olga of Greece is!' she wrote to the Empress Frederick, 'so handsome & so dear & charming. She has *none* of the *bourgeoiserie* of the rest of the Russian family even including our dear excellent Marie [Duchess of Edinburgh].'[†][31]

Nine years later, Queen Olga was to play a part in deciding the fate of Princess May of Teck; for, in March and April 1893, just before his engagement, Prince George was staying at the court of Athens, and had many private discussions with Queen Olga about his marriage plans. Queen Olga was very strongly in favour of the marriage with Princess May, of whom she had evidently formed a good opinion at Gmunden this autumn of 1884: 'I'm sure, tootsums, that she will make you happy, they say she has such a sweet disposition & is so *equal*, and *that* in itself is a great blessing, because nothing can be more disagreeable in everyday-life, than a person who is in high spirits today & low tomorrow.' She begged him to take an interest in all that interested his future wife: 'There are many little things

---

* When Prince William of Denmark (1845–1913) had been elected to succeed King Otho of the Hellenes in 1863, he took the style of King George I. In 1867 he had married Olga Constantinovna, Grand Duchess of Russia (1851–1926) and a niece of the Tsar Alexander II. They had, in all, seven children. King George I was assassinated in 1913.

† Daughter of Tsar Alexander II, and thus a first cousin to Queen Olga.

wch. are *dear* to a woman's heart, wch. men would think *trifles*, forgetting that our lives consist mostly of trifles, & that great events are rare.' 'I don't possess one single photo of May,' she wrote after the engagement had been made public, 'yes, one, she gave me in Gmunden years ago.'³² It would be exaggerated to say that Queen Olga's influence in the matter of Prince George's marriage was decisive, but the long quiet talks they had together that spring of 1893 in Athens unquestionably helped him to make up his mind, under circumstances which, as we shall later see, were not easy.

Even as she was romping with Alix and Minny and Plumpy in the gardens of Gmunden, or clambering with them into a rowing-boat for a turn upon the lake, the thread of Princess May's destiny was steadily, surreptitiously unwinding. Princess May had been born with a strong desire to please and to try to make herself amiable; but in that autumn of 1884 she could have no notion that the opinion her Greek Aunt Olga was forming of her would one day help to raise her up on to the English throne.

IV

After two months at Gmunden the Teck party proceeded to Graz, where, as we know, they stayed in the Hotel Erzherzog Johann, and visited the Reinthal aunts every day. From Graz they went for two nights to Venice: 'Went in gondola to hotel, Papa didnt like rooms, had a scene', Princess May records.³³ From Venice they returned to Florence to spend the winter at I Cedri. We need not spend it with them, since we now know quite enough about their Florentine exile, and—what alone matters to us—its effect upon Princess May.

In April 1885 the Duchess of Cambridge relented and told the wanderers they might come home at once. To this letter Princess Mary Adelaide replied with unexpected promptitude, explaining that it was out of the question for them to leave Florence before the end of May, as there were 'so many arrangements to make'. She added that at first they would have to stay in London because White Lodge was 'so full of things from Kensington'.³⁴ This delay affronted the Cambridges, who persisted in regarding Princess Mary Adelaide in the light of a delinquent to whom they were behaving with peerless magnanimity. It seems likely that the final reprieve came about through the intervention of the Queen, and was not unconnected with the matter of Princess May's confirmation:

I wonder how our reception at St James's will be [the Duke of Teck wrote on 30 April to Prince Dolly]. I believe that it was the Queen's doing, that our return was not delayed any longer or made dependent on such conditions, that we could not have accepted them, much as Mamas heart longed to return home.35

At last, on 22 May 1885, all was settled: the servants were paid off, the luggage was packed, the outstanding bills with Florentine shop-keepers had been considered, the necessary compartments booked in the night express. Then, on the very day they were to leave, Princess Mary Adelaide had one of her accidents.

'Our departure is postponed', wrote Princess May to her eldest brother, on 22 May, '. . . as poor Mama unfortunately had a fall last night. . . . Mama went to her bed to look for a parcel which she could not find & was so glad to find it that she said to Butty* "here it is" & in that moment caught her foot in a piece of rope of the carpet & tried to save herself but could not & fell heavily on the stone floor & bruised her left elbow & arm & strained her left side . . . tomorrow we think she will be better, she is up today & packing, but it pains her to sit down & get up.'36

Courage was one of Princess Mary Adelaide's attributes. Strapped and bandaged by Dr Baldwin, she limped into the train from Florence on the night of 24 May. At six a.m. on 26 May the Teck family debouched at Victoria Station. Princess May and her mother drove off to stay with Lady Marion Alford, while the Duke of Teck and the boys went to the Alexandra Hotel. Later that morning, washed and refreshed, they descended in a body on the Duchess of Cambridge's apartments at St. James's Palace. '[The Duke] is not altered in appearance at all, "*in seinem Wesen*" perhaps, seemingly languid and weak', Lady Geraldine Somerset wrote in her Diary, in a mood closely resembling that of disappointment.

By a coincidence, due to the Duchess of Teck's lunge for a missing parcel, the family arrived in England on the morning of Princess May's eighteenth birthday. Her life in Italy was over, and for ever. It was a time to which, in the years that followed, she would some-times look back with fond regret. It was in one such nostalgic mood that she wrote in April 1888 to little Emily Alcock, who was then in Florence, during the first spring stay of Queen Victoria at the Villa Palmieri:

* Miss Butler, Princess Mary Adelaide's dresser.

You may imagine with what interest we read of the dear Queen's magnificent reception at dear Florence, all the well known places came so vividly back to our minds & we seemed to see all the windows gaily decorated with carpets flags etc. how lovely & touching it must have been to hear 'God Save the Queen' struck up at the Piazza del Duomo & San Marco, we howled when we read the account in the Italian Papers. I can quite fancy that you missed us at the beloved I Cedri—oh! how happy those days were, I sometimes long to go back there.[37]

———————

'NOTHING could have been kinder than our reception by one and all', the Duke of Teck wrote three days after the Tecks' arrival in London, to their old friend Mr Peter Wells in Florence. '... We hope to stay a little time in town, and indeed it does one good to see every one smile their greeting from carriages and footpath, and waving their hands. It is a regular pilgrimage to Princess Mary's door, and hundreds of persons have been to write their names down here. . . .'[1] 'Here' was Alford House, in which the whole family were temporarily staying as Lady Marion Alford's guests. The Duke had already been down to White Lodge, which he found in 'such a neat and cared-for state that it is quite a delight to see it; lilacs in flower, seringas not quite out, rhododendrons just coming into bloom, in fact a second spring for us'. He had also received 'a most kind letter' from the Prince of Wales.

Absent from London for the best part of two years, Princess Mary Adelaide naturally did not want to retire to White Lodge immediately on her return. There were too many London friends to be seen—and there was Princess May's first London Season to be organised. The Duchess of Cambridge would not let her daughter and granddaughter stay at St James's Palace. The apartment at Kensington Palace was no longer at their disposal. Where could they go?

In this predicament Baroness Burdett-Coutts came once more to the rescue, arranging for them to borrow her sister's house in Chester Square. It was a small gloomy house, at the narrow end of the square near the church. They moved into it on 6 June. 'We left dear Alford House this morning and came to this tiny nutshell which can only contain Mama, Alge, myself and 7 servants Papa staying elsewhere', Princess May wrote to Mr Dominic Colnaghi, the British Consul in Florence, on 6 June 1885. 'The advantage is that it has been lent us by Baroness Coutts sister, the disadvantage is that the drawingroom contains 9 glass cases of stuffed birds, hideous prints of ancestors etc. which we can't get rid of as there's no room to store them in. This morning we went to the Guard Mounting, it poured such a bore after we have had the most lovely weather, we then breakfasted at Marlborough House and then came here. . . . I am not going out much here as the charming family don't think it good for me, I am so young you see! Only 18.'2

Princess Mary Adelaide had not been home a fortnight before she was once more at loggerheads with the Cambridge family, this time because she wished to take Princess May to a Court Concert, before she had been presented, and, of course, before she had been confirmed. In this fresh controversy the Duchess of Cambridge received unlooked-for support from her son-in-law the Duke of Teck, who likewise thought Princess May should not go about at night in London until her social position had been regularised by presentation to the Queen. The result was a lively discussion after which the Duke of Teck—whose letters alone prove that he had, by now, quite recovered from the stroke of the previous year—became unwell again for a day or two. His daughter reassured the Duchess of Cambridge in a note explaining that her father 'often has these attacks, when his brain feels as though loose and moving in his head'.3

Early in July any further argument about Princess May's *début* was precluded by the death of old Duke Alexander of Württemberg at the Styrian watering-place of Tueffer: 'Alas! our pleasant dinner on Wednesday, and the dance on Friday for poor May, are over for us!' the Duchess of Teck wrote to Lady Salisbury, 'for my Father-in-law died quite suddenly on Saturday night without illness or warning of any kind! It is a great shock to us. . . .'4 It was also a great inconvenience to them, since it flung the family—poised for metropolitan pleasures—into deep mourning. It meant that they could not even go to the theatre for six months. Mourning also prevented their attending the wedding of Princess Beatrice and Prince Henry of Battenberg* at Whippingham Church, near Osborne, on 23 July. The 'tiny nutshell' of a house in Chester Square was necessarily vacated, and by the end of the month the Tecks were back at White Lodge. 'We

* Beatrice, Princess of Great Britain and Ireland (1857–1944), youngest child of Queen Victoria and the Prince Consort, married Henry, Prince of Battenberg, KG (1858–1896), at Whippingham in the Isle of Wight in 1885. Prince Henry (called 'Liko' in the family) was the fourth child and third son of Alexander, Prince of Hesse and by the Rhine, by his marriage with Julie, Countess Hauke (created Princess of Battenberg, 1858). Like the Duke of Teck, Prince Henry of Battenberg was thus the product of a morganatic marriage.

are all so happy at being in our beloved home again', Princess Mary Adelaide wrote to a friend, 'and once more united, and I really think the Duke is better for the rest and quiet of this place. At any rate he is recovering his spirits, and finds pleasant occupation in making room for and arranging our Kensington furniture and things.'5

Before the family's return from Florence the Cambridges, in April conclave, had decided that if the Tecks returned to White Lodge they should consent to 'inhabiting the *Corps de Logis* only'. This was, of course, out of the question for Princess Mary Adelaide—whose 'favourite nook' was, in any case, an embrasure in the Green Corridor, half-way between the *corps de logis* and one of the house's convenient and essential wings. Mourning for Duke Alexander of Württemberg might restrict the Duchess of Teck's London activities, but it need in no way prevent her being visited, at White Lodge, by her numerous London friends.

Nor could her mourning for her '*Grosspapa*' any longer delay the confirmation of Princess May. The Duchess of Cambridge had wanted the ceremony performed in her own drawing-room, where she could witness it from her invalid chair. This joyless project was defeated; it was to be the Chapel Royal or nowhere. At this point Princess May unexpectedly took the matter into her own hands—one of the first occasions we can record in which she successfully pressed forward her wishes. These wishes were that she and Prince Dolly should be confirmed together. Such a spectacular switch from her usual role of quiet observer to that of an outspoken girl with a mind of her own had its effect upon her grandmother, her uncle and her Aunt Augusta. Instead of discussing Princess May's confirmation with Princess May's mother over Princess May's head, they addressed themselves to the girl herself—a scene described by Lady Geraldine's fertile pen:

The Duke, HRH [the Duchess of Cambridge] and P[rincess] A[ugusta] spoke to May about her confirmation, putting it to her plainly that she must make her choice, since Dolly's studies for his coming examination for Sandhurst cannot again be interrupted so that he can only be confirmed after the 8th July. She must choose whether she cares so much to be confirmed together with him that she will wait, in which case she must go down to the White Lodge and live quietly there till the confirmation is over,—or if she wishes and prefers to go out then she must be confirmed at once without him, for she *ought* and *must* not go out before she is confirmed and he *ought* and *must* not be interrupted in his studies. All the while

F

P[rincess] M[ary Adelaide] ostentatiously taking no part in the discussion and affecting to be in animated conversation with her dear Mrs Mitford!!⁶

During her time in Florence Princess May had not risen in Lady Geraldine's estimation, for she had answered one of that lady's acid letters by a justifiably angry protest. '. . . After Papa's illness & Uncle Leopold's death, she wrote me one of her rudest letters, you know her style, complaining in very insolent terms of Mama', Princess May had told her Aunt Augusta. '. . . I do not think she ought to be allowed to write & speak to us children about Mama & Papa in the way she does . . . for it makes it very unpleasant. I have written to her about it & given her a bit of my mind & I daresay she will be frantic & complain of me to Uncle George, but I don't care for I do not see why we should submit to her rudeness. I am sure when you were young you always stood up for Grandmama & I am sure you will approve our doing so for our Mother.'⁷ Princess May had left England in the autumn of 1883 as a shy girl; she had returned in the spring of 1885 as a determined young woman with whom the Cambridges had now to reckon, however silent she might seem. Lady Geraldine was reduced to confiding to her Journal spiteful references to Princess May's clothes: 'May (in *such* a *hideous* bonnet!!) came in while they were here.'⁸

We have sufficiently hinted at the awkward and embarrassing position in which, as a child, Princess May had often been put by one or other of her parents. These embarrassments, character-testing enough in themselves, were as nothing to the valiant part the girl now chose to play in the Teck household. This part was succinctly described by her Aunt Augusta, in a letter written to Lady Eva Dugdale shortly after the accession to the throne of King George V in 1910. 'When a child', the Grand Duchess wrote of the new Queen, 'she was shy, she had a difficult position, between her Parents so different in character, temper and tastes, yet devoted to each other; as she grew up she stood nearer to her Mother yet was ever the good Angel between them loving both. She never "came out" however being very reserved, as she had to be, until later.'⁹ The title of Serene Highness, and the right to stand with the Princesses of the Blood Royal at Queen Victoria's Drawing-Rooms, were small compensations for a youth thorny with problems and anxieties—a youth in which tact, discretion and reserve were at a premium.

With the Queen's permission, and prayer 'that every blessing may

be poured down upon the dear Children about to renew their bap-
tismal vows',[10] Princess May and her eldest brother Prince Adolphus
were confirmed in the Chapel Royal by the Bishop of St Albans on
1 August 1885 at one o'clock. The Prince of Wales and his three
daughters, the Duke of Cambridge, the Grand Duke of Mecklenburg-
Strelitz* and the whole Teck family, as well as certain ladies-in-
waiting and old servants, were present. The ceremony was followed
by a 'short address to the dear Children' in the old Duchess of
Cambridge's room, and by a luncheon party at St James's Palace.
Princess May received a good many confirmation gifts. She wrote
an account of the day to her aunt in Strelitz:

It was a very pretty service and went off very well tho' Dolly & I were
dreadfully nervous. . . . We all went over to Grandmama, the Bishop too,
& she gave me some beautiful diamond stars. Uncle Wales a beaten
gold bracelet with jewelled flowers on it. Uncle George a clasp . . . with
George III & Queen Charlotte's hair in it, which I greatly value. The
Queen diamond butterfly brooch & white ivory prayer book with words
written by herself in it. Aunt Marie Edinburgh beaten gold bracelet. Mama
small diamond necklace of her own & diamond & pearl earrings & 3 yellow
diamond wheat ears. Papa a little brooch. . . . Poor Mama was much upset
which was increased by Uncle George being angry with Mama for having
kept his carriage waiting 2 hours the day we came down here [White
Lodge], which was not her fault but stupid Butler's who as usual had not
got her things packed when the carriage came. It is too provoking.[11]

This letter to the Grand Duchess was illustrated by a little sketch
of Uncle George Cambridge's present which, as of family-historical
interest, seems to have pleased Princess May the most. The locks of
George III's and Queen Charlotte's hair were set in a circle of
diamonds on a band of dark blue enamel and diamonds, with the
monograms GR and CR in gold upon it. This clasp was intended
to be worn on velvet as a bracelet or necklet. We know that Princess
May thought that, facially, she resembled Queen Charlotte. All her
life, and especially when she became Queen Consort, she felt a strong
affinity with her long deceased great-grandmother.

Thus handsomely equipped with jewellery, Princess May appeared
at her first Drawing-Room in March 1886, standing between her own
mother and the Princess of Wales in the semicircle of Princesses and
Royal Duchesses beside the Queen's throne. At the court of Berlin
she could never have achieved this station near the throne, but Queen

* The Grand Duchess had withdrawn to Germany again.

Victoria, as we have already noticed, was open-minded and liberal about such trivia as morganatic blood. Princess May was clad in a white dress given her by her Aunt Augusta and upon this were pinned the largest of the Duchess of Cambridge's diamond stars, a 'beautiful diamond brooch' (which was also a confirmation present from her Aunt Augusta) and other diamond brooches 'put on *à la mode*', to use her proud father's phrase. She also wore the diamond necklace given her at her confirmation by her mother, Princess Mary Adelaide.

II

The period of Württemberg mourning, and her own confirmation, once over, Princess May now began to take her modest, ancillary part in public life. Always seen about with her mother, she was a silent, slim, fair girl in that epoch of the hour-glass figure, the bustle, the minute bonnet, the poodle hair-style and the muff. In January 1886 seats on the Woolsack were reserved for Princess Mary Adelaide and her daughter at the State Opening of Parliament, and a chair for the Duke of Teck.* Princess May also attended the two public state functions of that year—the laying of the foundation stone for Tower Bridge by the Prince of Wales, and the opening of the Colonial and Indian Exhibition by Queen Victoria. This last ceremony she found very moving, '. . . it was *quite beautiful* & I had a lump in my throat all the time,' she wrote to her Strelitz Aunt, 'as for Aunt Vicky [the Crown Princess of Prussia] she wept fountains over her best gown. The Queen looked very well, was most gracious & read in such a clear voice that all the people in the boxes round the Hall heard her distinctly, when she had ended the applause was deafening. . . . Albani sang "Home sweet Home" too divinely—Tennyson's ode is beautiful but we all thought Sullivan's music to it, very dull and heavy.'[12]

* Places on the Woolsack itself were traditionally reserved for Princesses of the Blood Royal at the Opening of Parliament by the Sovereign. They would sit facing the throne. The Woolsack proved, however, too high for Alexandra, Princess of Wales, a personage of diminutive stature, and in 1879 a fixed stool was placed for her, although this also was found to be of the wrong height. In February 1880 the Princesses 'seated themselves on a low bench occupying the place of the Woolsack' (*The Times*, 7 February 1880). Between the years 1881 to 1885 the seating of the Princesses on stools or ottomans below the Woolsack gradually ceased, and the custom fell into desuetude. The present system (1959) is for the Sovereign's immediate relations to occupy places reserved for them on the front benches of the House of Lords to the Queen's left.

In June 1887 Princess May played a part in the shining gaieties of the week of the Golden Jubilee, when London was looking 'bright and beautiful', and the atmosphere 'was particularly clear and there was a glow and colour about everything'.[13] 'We have all been so overworked this year that we are nearly dead', Princess May wrote in July of that year to her little Baltimore friend, Emily Alcock.[14] ' . . . I really cannot describe all the fêtes. The excitement here in London was something not to be imagined, & I believe it was this that kept us all up thro' that fatiguing time when we were on the go from morning till night—*sans relâche.*' She wrote that 'it all went off gloriously', that the weather had been superb, that 'the people . . . [were] loyal to a degree', and that the Queen's procession through the streets, the Princes riding by her carriage, was 'magnificent':

We had a little Procession to ourselves [she explained to Miss Alcock] 3 carriages. Mama, Papa, 2 Princes of Anhalt & Meiningen in one. Brothers & I in another the suite in the 3d. Mama received a wonderful ovation!!! not surprising I think considering all she has done in this Country, only a just reward I should say—

Princess Mary Adelaide was always sure of a 'wonderful ovation' in any carriage procession through London—she was enormously fat, she was greatly loved, and she had a way of tilting her plump face upwards as she waved which meant that the serried ranks of people on roof tops and balconies, who only caught sight of the headgear of the other Royalties, received the full searchlight beam of Princess Mary's smile. It was with happy tricks like these that the Queen's daughters could not and would not compete.

Now, too, began for Princess May a six years' stint of attending the Duchess of Teck on many charitable enterprises—'a function at Finsbury for Factory Girls', for example, or the opening of a new Barnardo's Home at Bethnal Green. Wherever the Duchess of Teck went in London, Princess May accompanied her. She became gradually familiar to the public as the fair-haired, grown-up daughter of their adored Princess Mary Adelaide.

Queen Victoria's attention was likewise slowly veering towards Princess May of Teck. She asked her to stay at Windsor Castle with her parents. In March 1886 she declared that she did 'not think May pretty, but a very nice girl, *distinguée*-looking with a pretty figure'.[15]

By such gentle, such imperceptible degrees did the Queen of England on the one hand, the British public on the other, become aware of the quiet charm and placid air of Princess May of Teck. Her personality dawned at first faintly on Queen and country. We might compare it to the old process of photographic development, a blurred image becoming, stage by stage, sharper: or, if we like, to the way the profile on a coin which has been placed under a thin sheet of paper will more and more clearly emerge upon the white surface when rubbed with a soft pencil lead.

III

When the Teck family had returned from Florence the Duchess of Cambridge, daily more infirm, was in her eighty-eighth year. In July 1885 she kept her eighty-eighth birthday, an event upon which the Duke and Duchess of Teck, Princess May and Prince Alge trooped to congratulate her:

Mamma was most dear [Princess Mary Adelaide wrote to her elder boys] receiving me with a charming greeting 'God bless you, my darling Child!'—& seemed charmed with my present: a huge china pot for a big plant, or small tree, & with May's water-color drawing. She had some very nice presents & the show of bouquets & baskets was wonderful & quite worthy of the flower shows at the Botanic—I am afraid to say how many, she received, so numerous were they! Poor Grandmamma felt rather faint (partly from the smell of all the exotics I think) & exhausted, so we left as soon as her dinner was brought in, Geraldine in a boiling rage because I prevented her from *forcing* poor Mamma to dictate answers to her telegrams.[16]

The old Duchess of Cambridge had begun to derive a genuine delight from her granddaughter's appearance. To Lady Geraldine's disgust she spoke of 'May' as being very beautiful, and urged that she should marry the Grand Duke Michael Michailovitch,* who was in London in the spring of 1886. This suggestion was strongly combated by the Duke of Cambridge and also by the Duke of Teck, the latter stating categorically that he would not be a party to 'sacrificing his child', that the Russian Grand Dukes made notoriously bad husbands, that Russia was a horrid country and that the Russians were

* The Grand Duke Michael Michailovitch (1861–1929), grandson of Tsar Nicholas I of All the Russias, married in 1891 Sophie Nicholaievna, Countess de Merenberg, a daughter of Prince Nicholas of Nassau and his wife, Nathalia Pushkin, daughter of the poet. Countess de Merenberg was created Countess de Torby on her marriage.

'our enemies'. Here, fleetingly, was an even more threatening prospect for poor Princess May than that which would have faced her as a Princess of Württemberg; for it would have been better, or at any rate safer, to have been bored into a stupor at the court of Stuttgart than to have been slaughtered in the Russian holocaust of 1917. Fate had neither St Petersburg nor Stuttgart in store for her. She went on dancing calmly through successive London seasons.

The ambiguity of Princess May's status as a Serene, and not a Royal Highness, now gave her father many opportunities to agitate himself about her social position. At a fête 'at the Colonies'* in July 1886 he was '*dans tous les états* because no one had been named to give his arm to May!!' The Duke of Teck had a respectful admiration for his daughter, and he was morbidly prepared to see slights where none were intended. He was even furious with a constable in Hyde Park who had 'very respectfully and civilly *according to P[rince] T[eck]'s own account*, his hat in his hand, begged May to keep her dog on a string in accordance with the rules because he had such difficulty in enforcing them upon others when they saw her dog allowed to run about loose'.[17]

The Duchess of Cambridge, who had nothing to do all day but sit brooding over her own ailments, a subject to which speculations about Princess May's future formed an attractive and roseate alternative, at one time produced the suggestion that Princess May 'ought to dance with the Ambassadors'. The Duke of Cambridge replied that it would 'only turn her head, taking her out of her position which many . . . circumstances already do far too much'. He also said that Princess May was far too young, and 'at present, at all events, has no conversation whatever'.[18] This last remark was a comment rather than a criticism.

Small talk at a dinner-party or on the dance-floor was still as agonisingly difficult to Princess May as the deportment lessons at the classes of Taglioni and Mr d'Egville had been many years ago. But if the London season was made uncomfortable for her by this conversational incapacity, there was another form of social life with which she was experimenting and which she thoroughly relished. This was country-house life and country-house parties. 'Tomorrow the people go away & others come', she wrote to Prince Dolly from Buckhurst, where she and her mother were staying with the De La Warrs in October 1885. 'I am so sorry, one gets to know people better in a country house.'[19]

* i.e., the Colonial Office in Whitehall.

The country-houses to which Princess Mary Adelaide now began to take her daughter were some of the largest in England. They could shelter and sustain a herd of guests: 'You know we went to Ashridge on the 14th for 3 days. It was quite charming there. . . . We were a large party about 40', Princess May wrote to her Aunt Augusta in December 1886; or: 'On the 20th we all went to Hatfield. What a beautiful place! It really was most delightful there. We were about 35 staying in the house.'[20] Then there was Buckhurst, Normanton, Chillingham Castle and Luton Hoo. During visits to this last house, which was rented by the Danish Minister de Falbe and his very rich wife, a series of photographs were usually taken, showing the house-party assembled in the conservatory, and grouped round the monumental central figure and chief guest, Princess Mary Adelaide herself.

As yet the name 'Luton Hoo' meant nothing particular to Princess May of Teck. It was just an agreeable luxuriously run house in Bedfordshire, where one played tennis, went on the lake in a 'tricycle boat', 'danced vigorously' till one-thirty in the morning, and chatted to Esther Gore and Sarah Churchill, little Lord Drumlanrig and Count Koziebrodzki, 'a Pole'.* So far as Princess May was concerned Luton Hoo was still biding its time. We shall later see just why and how, on a cold December evening, the two words Luton Hoo became for ever branded on her mind.

The photographs taken at Luton Hoo during that house's earlier, and harmless, intrusions into Princess May's existence show her as one of twelve or fourteen persons seated or standing amid the potted palms, climbing plants and camellias of the de Falbes' conservatory, a comfortable, elaborate place, with carpeted floor, birds in cages, an ornamental wicker wheelbarrow full of begonias and sprawling sweet geraniums everywhere. In all these photographs Princess May looks pensive. Like the other ladies round her she is rigidly corseted, and wears a high collar pinned at the throat with a jewelled brooch. Her blouse is sewn with a cataract of tiny buttons from neck to waist. In one of the photographs Princess May is playing halma, her head bent earnestly over the board as she reflects upon her next move. The

* Count Thaddeus Koziebrodzki, a young diplomat of Polish-Austrian origin, was attached to the Austrian Embassy in London at this time. He was attracted by Princess May and is said to have wished to marry her, a project which, on religious and other grounds, was not considered suitable by the Duke and Duchess of Teck.

girls with whom she is playing have raised their heads and gaze in a startled way into the camera.

In such pleasant surroundings Princess May indulged the high spirits which her native reserve, and the sense of being watched, kept in check in London ballrooms:

After lunch it cleared Mama & Sir T[homas Lauder] drove in the pony carriage, Sir H[ubert Miller] & I in the tandem Cantilupe leading the way, we drove thro' the woods, then to Hartfield to see the church, Mama didnt get out, we did. Sir T. & I locked Sir H. into the church, he rang the bell, 2 people came to see what was the matter. Oh! I nearly died of laughing— After dinner we had an exhibition of wax figures, we were the figures, I was the sleeping beauty. Sir H. the prince . . . it was too ridiculous, I laughed till I cried![21]

In common with most girls who have been brought up as only sisters in a family of boys, Princess May had by this time acquired the habit of using her brothers' slang: 'old Greville was screwed, too much wine having been unscrewed', she wrote irreverently of a Christmas Eve dinner-party with her grandmother the Duchess of Cambridge.[22] Persons still alive confirm that, when on her own with her young contemporaries in some country-house, Princess May was gay and delightful.

In the Luton Hoo photographs Princess May looks distinctly smart. Her mother, Princess Mary Adelaide, was fond of clothes, while the Duke of Teck was also interested in them; and it was their natural wish that their only daughter should look as well as possible when she went out into the world. At this time Princess May had very little pin-money to spend on clothes, and those she wore at home at White Lodge were made by the local dressmaker at Kingston-on-Thames. For London clothes she went, like her mother, to Madame Mangas, a 'first-rate' Parisian dressmaker who did not, however, charge 'tip-top prices', and who came over regularly to London, where, with a French bonnet-maker, Madame Valentine Meurice, she had 'a tiny *pied-à-terre*' in Mount Street. The Duchess of Teck considered Madame Valentine Meurice an admirable bonnet-maker—'her bonnets . . . I think remarkably pretty and am sure you will not consider *outres* or ruinous', she wrote in 1888 to her Petersham neighbour, Mrs Master. 'Her prices run from £2. 8. to £3. 3. or thereabouts, £4 representing her highest figure and are only charged for a very handsome confection with feathers and embroidery! If you want a black bonnet make Madame

F*

Meurice show you one similar to the bonnet May has just bought of her, for it is made of a particularly pretty stuff, and costs £2. 8. or should you prefer a jet bonnet, I can recommend one after the pattern of *mine* at £3. 3.'[23]

Princess Mary Adelaide's theory about her daughter's ball-gowns was that these must be of superlative quality and design. Here once more the Cambridges were shocked: '. . . the *outrageous* charge for May's ball gown, one simple *petite robe de bal de jeune fille*, white tarlatan with white beads, and the bill comes in £40 odd!!!! and what an education for a girl under their present circumstances to be taught to dress at that rate!' The Duke of Cambridge said that he would with pleasure have given his niece forty pounds to buy three dresses, 'but over £40 for *one* gown—and that a ball-gown! most probably torn to shreds the very first night she wears it!—it is monstrous', recorded Lady Geraldine.[24] The Duke of Cambridge was, of course, completely wrong; for every woman knows that it is better to have one or two really good evening dresses than any number of cheap ones. Moreover, good clothes and the sense of being thoroughly well-dressed form in themselves an antidote to shyness—or, at the least, they lend self-confidence to a girl of eighteen entering a room full of inquisitive strangers.

IV

Expeditions to London to go to a ball, or visits to country-houses formed only the brighter, frothier part of Princess May's life now that she and her parents were back in England. While hardly penurious, arrangements at White Lodge had become simpler and less lavish than they had been in days of yore. There were, for instance, fewer carriages and horses. This meant that daily excursions to London were no longer possible—a situation which at length drove the aged Duchess of Cambridge to allow Princess Mary Adelaide and her daughter to use two of her rooms in St James's Palace at the height of each London season.

The male staff at White Lodge now consisted of a Groom of the Chambers, a butler, an under-butler, two 'matched footmen', a steward and a steward's room boy. The Duchess of Teck and her daughter had two dressers each, who worked in this capacity one day on and one day off, the off-days being devoted to mending and other similar tasks. The cook, a female, was helped by a kitchen maid and a scullery maid. There was the head housemaid, old Liza, with three or four housemaids under her. Three laundry-maids worked in the laundry.

In the coach-houses the Tecks kept a barouche, a landau, a brougham, a waggonette and a dog-cart, four carriage horses, the phaeton horse, Jumbo, and one other horse. The head coachman, Kitchener, had a first and second coachman under him, with strappers and helpers. Kitchener was especially admired by his employers, for he drove their carriage to London in record time: a feat which they attributed to his having such big hands, whereas the real truth was that the police cleared all traffic points so soon as the panoplied Royal carriage hove into view. When the family went up to London for an evening, the carriage and horses put up at Collins', the jobmaster livery-stable in St James's Street opposite the Feathers public house. The footmen would then put their livery coats in the boot and go off, with the Duchess of Teck's encouragement, to a music-hall. For purely local expeditions round Richmond the carriages and horses of country neighbours were put under requisition by Princess Mary Adelaide.

For Princess May there was one major drawback to this compara-tively modest establishment: for some years her mother had no lady-in-waiting and no secretary. Making up for time lost in Florence, Princess Mary Adelaide was now embarked upon innumerable charit-able enterprises and had what she called 'many charitable irons in the fire'. Her public appearances in such connections were far more fre-quent than ever before: 'What a lot you have all been doing lately, how you survive seems extraordinary to me, who feel tired merely reading of your engagements',[25] the Grand Duchess of Mecklenburg-Strelitz wrote to her sister.

Owing to her habitual unpunctuality and procrastination the Duchess of Teck was always behind with her business correspondence, although in her disorderly way she tried hard to get through it, spending long nights sitting up writing what her daughter termed 'her everlasting & never ending mass of notes'.[26] The letters Princess Mary Adelaide received were methodically stacked in her davenport, which she kept so neatly that one of her maids afterwards remembered that she could find anything in 'Her Royal Highness's davenport in the dark'. But these trim piles of papers tended to accumulate there unanswered. Here, again, Princess May stepped into the breach, acting from that sense of daughterly duty then expected by parents of unmarried girls. It was tiring work: 'We have been fairly quiet, except

for "Charity" things which are a decided *bore*, & make poor dear
Mama both grumpy and unpunctual', she wrote to her Aunt Augusta
one December day. 'Please forgive me for not having written to you
for such an age', she wrote, again to her aunt, in February 1886, during
their first winter back at the White Lodge, 'but as I am besides Mama's
daughter, her secretary & lady-in-waiting combined, my time is very
much filled up, especially as I am also anxious to improve my mind
& read 4 mornings in the week with a very nice French lady a Mlle
Bricka, with whom I read English, french & german.'27

This letter to the Grand Duchess constitutes Princess May's first
reference to a person who, for the next six years, exercised a paramount influence upon her intellectual development: Mademoiselle
Hélène Bricka. Mademoiselle Bricka—or, as she was more usually
called, 'Madame' Bricka—was a French Alsatian lady, one of four
sisters, and a born educationalist. She was without a degree or any
specific academic qualifications, but was widely read in French,
German and English, had travelled, and had studied modern history
and social problems. It was said of her that you could never have
'dear good Hélène' in the house without learning something worth
while.

Madame Bricka now took over Princess May's education, succeeding
the Italian masters who had themselves succeeded Fräulein Gutman
in Florence. With her pupil's earnest co-operation, Madame Bricka
got Princess May's studies at last on to a wider and more modern
basis. She was soon a permanent inmate of White Lodge, where, after
Princess May's marriage, she acted as companion-secretary to the
Duchess of Teck. Madame Bricka was also liked by the Duke of Teck,
who was now indulging in the hobby of carpentry, making library
bookshelves and 'artistic arrangements in his daughter's boudoir'. 'I
never came back from a holiday', Madame Bricka once related, 'without
finding the Duke had done something to my room during my absence;
and when I used to thank him he would say "You know this is your
home, and I want you to feel at home".'28

Madame Bricka was a dominating woman, who always treated
Princess May as though she were still a child—an attitude also maintained through life by Tatry, Princess May's old French maid. In
appearance 'good old Hélène' Bricka was not prepossessing. She was
of middle height, rather stout, very near-sighted and had a mottled,
uneven complexion due, it was whispered, to burns. She wore a *toupé*
of dark brown curls, about which the Teck boys would tease her:

'New curls again, Bricka?' one of them would remark. 'What extravagance!' Bricka was warm-hearted and very excitable. Her feeling for Princess May became, over the years, devotional: 'It is so heavenly to be near my Princess,' she wrote, after Princess May's marriage, from York Cottage, Sandringham, 'always the same, if anything sweeter than she was.'[29] Madame Bricka was one of the first persons in whom Princess May had managed to inspire such deep affection: 'Dear old Hélène,' she wrote when newly married, 'I am so sorry for you, I know you will miss me more than the others, we were so much together & sympathised so much, I now requote Chapman's* words to me "You said you liked being liked, did you ever count the cost to the liker"—*que c'est vrai!*'[30]

Hélène Bricka came to occupy a place in Princess May's mental development as important as that of the Grand Duchess of Mecklenburg-Strelitz herself; but while the Grand Duchess was for ever harping on the unique position of an English Princess, and encouraging her niece's passion for the history of the English Royal Family, Bricka brought an element from the wider, outside world of freely thinking men and women into the slightly incense-laden atmosphere of White Lodge. She made her pupil read George Eliot, historical memoirs, modern history, and Blue Books on industrial and social conditions, and particularly on the 'Sweated Industries'.

It was a family joke that Bricka had first been asked to read with Princess May so that the latter should not waste her time during the endless waiting about for meals which Princess Mary Adelaide's unpunctuality inflicted upon all her family. This unpunctuality was getting not better, but worse. The Duchess of Teck would return from London or from some function two hours late for dinner, and then retire to her room to change at leisure before entering the dining-room: 'We dine—that is we ought to dine at 8 o'C. . . . it is by now 7.15 but no Mama back from Town yet', the Duke of Teck wrote to his daughter of some evening when they were dining with a Richmond neighbour, 'what a Life dear Mama leads me! . . . It is 7.30 now, no Mama yet, but I must dress and if necessary go on foot.'[31] It was said in Princess May's family that she had read all three volumes of Motley's *Dutch Republic* while waiting for her mother before meals.

Apart from widening Princess May's mental horizons, Hélène Bricka

* A clergyman of St Luke's, Camberwell, whose sermons the Duchess of Teck and her daughter greatly admired, and who would sometimes stay at White Lodge.

occupied the useful and needed role of confidante. To Bricka the girl would unburden herself of her opinions about the world at large, her parents in particular and her own character, with an unusual frankness: '*Je crois que l'atmosphère à White Lodge est très* depressing, *on y est toujours* guild *et* household worry mad!!!', wrote Princess May in her imperfect French to her old friend, '*et les choses importantes de la vie sont entièrement oubliées. Que mes sentiments sont beaux! n'est-ce-pas?*' '*Que je regrette que vous soyez si triste et que vous souffrez du Heimweh, je le comprends car souvent mon entourage m'embête, et je voudrais causer, causer avec vous pour me rafraîchir. J'aime beaucoup mes livres et ils me viennent en aide*', she wrote on a later occasion.[32]

There was, for Princess May of Teck, another advantage about Bricka. When the Frenchwoman came to White Lodge in 1886 she had had no previous experience of living with royal persons, and this gave her a salutary detachment and an independence of mind. Madame Bricka sincerely loved the Duchess of Teck as well as her daughter, but she would at times rebel at Princess Mary Adelaide's imperious and capricious ways. 'What a funny world it is!', she wrote to Prince Alge, in 1895, of an afternoon visitation by an Austrian Archduke with his Archduchess, when it had been hinted to her that she would not be 'wanted'. 'I often wonder if in heaven there will be such differences! not good enough to mix with some of them! good enough to bring up the highest in the Land! it does not make people more Loyal to be snubbed.'[33]

In later years Bricka began to undertake the education of Princess May's own children, but, becoming old and infirm, she retired to rooms in Pimlico. Here she died in the first year of the Great War. 'Poor Hélène Bricka is dead,' Queen Mary wrote to her aunt in Strelitz, 'she had been ill for months so it was a mercy, still it means another landmark gone.'[34]

v

When Madame Hélène Bricka had been finally integrated into the household at White Lodge, she began to shoulder some part of Princess May's gruelling work as secretary to the Duchess of Teck. We have so far, perhaps, mainly emphasised those aspects of Princess Mary Adelaide's personality liable to render her a problem to her daughter—taking for granted Princess May's love and admiration for her mother. Back in England in 1885, the Duchess of Teck became also an example to Princess May.

By an odd anomaly Princess Mary Adelaide, who was perfectly incapable of handling her own finances, had a marked talent for coping with those of charitable organisations: 'Her advice was sound, and her experience invaluable. Indeed, many a bazaar would have failed to pay its expenses, and probably have landed the promoters in debt, had it not been for the Princess's timely aid and practical assistance.'35 Princess May inherited her mother's wish to alleviate poverty and suffering. By acting as her mother's assistant in a thousand charitable enterprises during these years at White Lodge, Princess May served an invaluable apprenticeship in the best methods of exercising both private and institutional charity at that time.

In England, and most especially in London, in the eighteen-eighties, the field open to private charity was disgracefully large. Poverty—indeed real starvation—was widespread, and even efforts as manifold and energetic as those of Princess Mary Adelaide (who almost literally worked herself to death in good causes) could satisfy only the tiniest fraction of the pressing demands for help. The winters of 1886 and 1887, which were very harsh, caused fearful suffering among the poor and unemployed. Writing to explain to their Florentine friend Mr Colnaghi why she had not answered some letter of his, Princess Mary Adelaide told him:

The truth is all my leisure is just now taken up with humble efforts to assist in relieving the terrible distress there undoubtedly exists in many parts of London most especially of course in the East; harrowing descriptions of which have of late been given us by George Holland who works in the slums of Whitechapel.36

In the following winter, that of 1887, the Duchess of Teck wrote to her cousin the Queen (who had sent her a signed photograph for Mr Holland's Whitechapel Mission): 'You will, I know, be glad to hear that George Holland does not think the distress this winter, so great as last year, tho' alas! there is still very much want and consequent suffering owing to work still being so scarce. He left us to go back to a tea, at which several hundred *hungry* children were tasting food, many of them at all events for the first time that day! and carried off his precious picture in triumph, which he told us, he should exhibit to them.'37

The Duchess of Teck, and in this respect her daughter also, were very much of their period; that is to say that they did not wonder about or reflect upon the real social and industrial causes of the vast amount of starvation and misery current in the England of their day. Like other good and charitable persons they did their utmost to respond to any need that came to their attention, trying to stem the torrent of social injustice with little individual bricks of kindness. As she grew older and lived to see Socialist and many other basic changes in England, Queen Mary learned more and more about the causes of poverty. Her first real grounding in such matters was, however, gained from her mother, who was in this direction practical as well as limitlessly kind-hearted, and who seemed to her contemporaries the very apotheosis of the now out-moded conception of the Lady Bountiful.

  Princess Mary Adelaide gave her patronage to any charity, bazaar or organisation which seemed to her genuine and efficiently run. This patronage was never of a merely nominal character: 'When she gave her name, she gave also her time, energy, and thought.'[38] She would herself open all letters addressed to her, decide which were worthy of immediate attention, draft replies and, with her daughter's aid, classify each case in one of her charity ledgers. This was a habit which Queen Mary also adopted. Until the end of her life the Queen would open all her letters; and her assistants were often surprised at the perspicacity with which she could assess whether an application for help was genuinely worthy or bogus. The aid she gave her mother in these years at White Lodge before her marriage was never grudging; it might be tiring and at times dispiriting, but Princess May worked with a will:

May and I threw ourselves into the Guild work, which took up pretty nearly all our time through the whole of November and the early part of December [the Duchess of Teck wrote to a friend in the winter of 1887] though we had some excellent helpers. . . . May knelt so long just at first over the huge parcels and bundles, that she very nearly gave herself a *'housemaid's knee'*! Indeed she worked so energetically that she quite knocked herself up, poor dear child![39]

'Guild work' was the family term for the collection, sorting and distribution to various charities of the many thousand garments made annually by the London and Surrey branches of the Needlework Guild, a highly successful and ambitious network of charitable enterprise which had been started in a humble way in Dorset by Princess Mary Adelaide's friend, Lady Wolverton, some years before. The London and Surrey branches were under the direct inspiration and control of the Duchess of Teck. The work involved in keeping these organisations alive and in running order was very considerable. The peak months were October and November, when all the Vice-Presidents for each section sent the Presidents the bundles of new clothes made by their associate ladies during the year. In fact, the Guild work spread itself over the whole twelve months of every year. New working cells were constantly being started, pamphlets and sheets of rules sent out, new Vice-Presidents canvassed, the sudden resignations of existing Vice-Presidents countered or accepted: 'the VPs', Princess May once wrote in exasperation, 'are a decided bore'.[40]

Princess May's exertions on behalf of the London Needlework Guild continued all her life. As Queen Consort she would sally forth from Buckingham Palace each November to help the Needlework Guild ladies, who at that time sorted the clothes at the Imperial Institute. There she would sit day after day at a central table, checking lists and labels, wearing a business-like apron and with a large pair of scissors hanging from a chain round her waist. This Needlework Guild activity first began soon after the return from Florence:

Mama & I have been trying these last months to get ladies to belong to the London Needlework Guild which was founded by Lady Wolverton some years ago, & as I am, as I wrote to you before, Mama's secretary, I have to do nearly all the writing, which I have to fit in with singing lessons, reading etc. so I hope dearest Aunt you will now forgive me for not having written after the Drawing Room as I promised [she wrote to her Aunt Augusta in May 1886].[41]

The annual flood of parcels of clothing in the late autumn and early winter gave a chaotic appearance to much of White Lodge. 'I must say Francis [the Duke of Teck] behaved most angelically, and did not (at any rate, openly) resent half the house being turned into a draper's shop, or a kind of Harvey and Nicholl's storeroom', Princess Mary Adelaide wrote in 1887; or 'The billiard table in the hall was literally speaking *covered* with *over 400* Surrey Guild articles, all beautifully & most neatly tied up in bundles'.[42] Even the most stringent injunctions could not persuade some of the Guild's Presidents and Vice-Presidents to sort properly the clothes they sent, or to label them correctly. One mitten or one stocking would appear without its pair, and mysteriously lonely articles made their unaccompanied way to White Lodge, with no sender's name attached: 'The brown blanket, we found by itself in a brown paper parcel, in the toy room, was sent by Mrs Sweat of Putney.'[43]

The London and the Surrey Needlework Guilds formed but a fraction of the many charities in which the Duchess of Teck was now involved, and had, in consequence, involved her daughter. The Guilds were, in a sense, a private activity, since the canvassing for garments, their collection, checking and despatch to poor parishes were all done within the four walls of White Lodge. So as not to get a lopsided view of the charitable enterprises in which the mother, with her daughter in attendance, was so heavily engaged we must remember the numerous public appearances they were now making—'gracing' charity concerts, opening charity bazaars, new wings of hospitals, of homes for orphans or for soldiers' widows. Once again we may recall that this was, for Princess May, a two-way traffic: she was learning at first-hand about the needy and the suffering—and these, watching her visit them with her mother in their hospitals or institutions, saw this quiet, smiling girl in the reflected glory of Princess Mary Adelaide, Duchess of Teck.

VI

At that period in England the vote or nomination system for admissions into the crowded hospitals, orphanages and homes for old people or incurables still persisted. Much of Princess Mary Adelaide's time was taken up in writing letters to her friends and relations to gain their vote for some desperate case just brought to her notice. She rightly tried to interest in her charities as many of her rich acquaintances as she could. Even the collection of Guild clothes at White Lodge was made into a practical object lesson, and each year she would set one room aside for some days, in order to display the bundles to visitors, never showing 'a sign of weariness, though the daylight died, and the lamps were lit, and still the stream of visitors flowed on and the kind face of the *châtelaine* began to look very tired'. She would lead her visitors round, 'praising those who made [the garments] telling of those to whom they were to be given, and occasionally relating an amusing story of how she had coaxed a gift of clothes out of the Prince of Wales or other male relatives'.[44] The Prince of Wales was a regular contributor, either in clothes or in money, to Princess Mary Adelaide's London Needlework Guild. He gave generously, though sometimes in that 'odious chaffing mood' which his stout cousin did not relish: 'Papa says he hopes Uncle Teck won't take the best clothes for himself this time, as he sent aunt Mary some very good suits for her guild',[45] Prince George wrote in 1896.

Now that they were home again, the young Tecks had picked up the threads of their interrupted friendship with the young Waleses. A proposed visit to Sandringham in January 1886 was postponed owing to the Princess of Wales's diphtheria: 'honestly I am rather glad . . . as I should think S. would be a trifle stiff', Princess May wrote to her eldest brother.[46] In April of the same year she and her parents went to Sandringham for Princess Victoria's confirmation: 'V. was confirmed on Maundy Thursday in the little church at Sandringham', Princess May wrote to her aunt, 'it was a very pretty sight. The church was crammed. Victoria walked up the aisle with Aunt Alix & Uncle Wales—she was so nervous poor thing. . . . In the afternoon we . . . drove with 4 Hungarian horses, driven by a Hungarian coachman, we did go it fast.'[47] She also wrote a little letter to her cousin Prince George, who was then at Malta: 'Dearest Georgie, As I am staying here I think I will write to you to tell you how much I am enjoying myself. . . . Victoria received some very nice presents. Grandmama gave her 2 bangles which really is a marvellous thing as she never gives presents as a rule, & the bangles are rather pretty. . . . Yesterday we walked about, we went to the kennels, & then had tea in the dairy —Silly Harry [Princess Maud] has just made this blot I am so sorry— Louise, Toria & Maud are making such a row I cannot write any more.'[48]

As grown-up young women the three Wales sisters were at times noisy, at others melancholy and hushed, but almost invariably one or other of them was ailing. 'The health of those girls is not enough looked after', Queen Victoria declared to the Empress Frederick in 1889.[49] Of the three of them Princess Victoria was most frequently ill and for the longest stretches at a time; she had neuralgia, abscesses in the teeth, 'fever and fatigue', constant influenza, perpetual colds in the head, and at one time a bad cyst on an eyelid. Princess Louise and Princess Maud became slightly healthier after they married, but Princess 'Toria', who was not allowed to marry the man she wished since he was a commoner, settled down into an old-maidish state, ill-health her chief occupation. In the summer of 1887, however, it was Princess Louise who seemed to be, physically speaking, in the worst way. The Duchess of Teck, who was becoming restless at White Lodge, and had recently been wondering how she could best afford to go on a continental journey, snatched at this pretext to organise, and incorporate Princess Louise into, a merry family party which set off in August 1887 for St Moritz and the Italian lakes. The Duchess of Cambridge strongly resented this *giro*, and talked of 'the bosh and humbug of its being by way of being for "the sake of taking P. Louise"!! the only effect of the Prince of Wales's daughter being with them to make the whole journey more expensive!'[50]

This was the first of four visits which Princess May paid with her mother to St Moritz. It was a great success, and the short stay on the Lake of Como which followed it enchanted Princess May: 'Oh! how lovely this place is, it is perfectly heavenly', Princess May wrote from the Hotel Bellevue, Cadenabbia,[51] where she was busily reading Shorthouse's *John Inglesant*. Here they visited the Villa Carlotta and invited themselves to luncheon with the old Duchessa Melzi, at the romantically situated Villa Melzi at Bellagio, on the opposite shore of the lake. A photograph taken at St Moritz shows the Duchess of Teck and Princess Louise, standing arm-in-arm, with Princess May seated on a rock, and her brothers Dolly and Alge holding stout walking-sticks. They are ranged against a painted Alpine backcloth of mountains and forests. The three princesses wear tall flower-pot hats perched on the summit of their heads, and decorated with birds' wings and bows of ribbon.*

'I am so much looking forward to being with her as we are great friends & so fond of each other', Princess May had written of the plan of taking her cousin Louise to St Moritz;[52] but Princess Louise, who was accompanied by her physician, proved to be a disappointing travelling companion. She was ever wanting to 'see' a place to say she had been there, but once she reached it she had only one desire—to leave again. The Tecks decided that she had 'the same inert, apathetic nature' as her brother, Prince Eddy, the heir-presumptive to the English throne.[53]

Princess Louise never played a very permanent part in the life of Princess May. Her hold on reality was, like her health, imperfect, but she did not have the tricky character of her sister Victoria. In July 1889 she became engaged to Lord Fife, who was made a Duke on his marriage.

'What do you say to Louise's engagement to Lord Fife', Princess May asked her Aunt Augusta in a letter written after the announcement. 'We are very glad for her because she has liked him for some years, but for a future Princess Royal to marry a subject seems rather strange don't you think so?'[54] Queen Victoria was highly satisfied by this match: 'It is a vy brilliant Marriage in a worldly point of view as

* See plate G.

he is immensely rich', she wrote to Berlin. In a later letter the Queen described the marriage ceremony, which took place in the Chapel Royal: 'Little Louise was vy pale. . . . She was not near so pretty a Bride as my dear Children, & she was too plainly dressed—& had her veil over her face wh. *no Pcess* ever has & wh. I think unbecoming & not right. . . . The Brides-Maids . . . looked vy pretty.'55 Princess May was one of the eight bridesmaids. Her dress was of 'pink *faille & crêpe de chine* with a large watered silk sash at the back & pink rosebuds in our hair & pink rose bouquets, the presents were gold bangles with a diamond L & F with her crown & his coronet on the top, they were designed by Louise, but honestly I don't think they were very pretty'.56

After Princess Louise was married, she and her husband would spend the week-ends at their house in Richmond Park, Sheen Lodge. Miss Ella Taylor, a stout party who had sometimes acted as stop-gap lady-in-waiting to the Duchess of Cambridge in past years, and who happened to be staying at White Lodge in February 1890, wrote in a letter to her sister one Monday morning:

Princess May & I breakfasted together yesterday—Pss Mary [Adelaide] did not appear till late, so of course we were very late for church. After church we were dropped in the Park & took a walk—it was a lovely day. Pss May & I prolonged our walk after Pss Mary [Adelaide] had gone in. Coming home near the house, we saw a little pony carriage, in the shape of a low dog-cart coming along—a lady driving herself—a little Groom behind. The lady stopped it was Princess Louise Duchess of Fife—She looked so pretty—almost as pretty as her mother—with a bright colour— pretty blue eyes—lovely teeth. Looking so mischief [*sic*] & happy—She shook hands with me & then asked Pss May to take a turn with her in the Park, so the two young things drove off in great glee.—The Fifes were spending Saturday to Monday at Sheen. Pss May says Pss Louise is *so* happy.57

Like the fortuitous presence of Queen Olga of Greece at Gmunden in the autumn of 1884, the fact that the Duchess of Fife was often in residence at Sheen Lodge in Richmond Park was to have, at a given moment in time, a decisive and direct bearing upon the future of her cousin May of Teck.

VII

On 10 March 1888 the Prince and Princess of Wales celebrated their Silver Wedding. Owing to the recent death of the aged Emperor of Germany, Wilhelm I, the ball scheduled to take place at Marlborough House was cancelled, but a large family dinner-party of thirty-one was not. This last turned out to be, in Princess May's own words, 'a very grand affair'. The Queen had come up from Windsor especially for it, and on her way back to the station 'drove through the streets to see the illuminations'. 'The Princess of Wales looks younger & lovelier than ever,' Princess May wrote to Emily Alcock, describing this dinner, 'she wore white & silver at the dinner & in her hair at the back of her tiara she had a spray of orange blossom & a little orange because she said she was no longer an orange blossom but a full blown orange!!'[58] Always a ready admirer of the beautiful, Princess May had a real appreciation of her Aunt Alix's looks; even though she did not always feel she could agree with the Princess of Wales's opinions or her generally ingenuous attitude to life.

'The presents are quite magnificent', Princess May wrote to her Aunt Augusta of the Waleses' Silver Wedding. 'The ladies of society gave a lovely diamond spiked tiara. The Emperor & Empress of Russia a sapphire & diamond necklace etc. . . . Frank also dined at the dinner & looked very well in his tights.'[59] Her brother, Prince Frank, was now eighteen. He was as swarthy as Prince Dolly was fair—a tall, handsome youth with black hair and startlingly blue eyes, an irreverent sense of humour and a quick, nonchalant mind. It was, perhaps, at this dinner, or at any rate about this period, that his cousin Princess Maud of Wales began to look upon Prince Frank of Teck with a not indifferent eye.

Two months after her inspection of the Princess of Wales's presents of jewellery at the Silver Wedding dinner-party, Princess May herself acquired some further brooches and bracelets set with precious stones, for on 26 May 1888 she became twenty-one years old. The Duchess of Cambridge, the Duke of Cambridge, the Princess of Wales, the Duchess of Edinburgh and many other relations gave her jewellery. The White Lodge neighbours had arranged a surprise in the form of 'a most lovely Carriage', a phaeton complete with pony, harness, a bearskin rug for winter, a monogrammed cloth rug for summer, a foot warmer, cushions and two whips—one with an umbrella and one without. 'Saturday was such an exciting day', Princess May wrote to Prince Dolly. ' . . . In the afternoon a lot of people from Richmond came & presented me with an address & a charming pony & phaeton (a small edition of Mama's). It was such a surprise & I was so pleased & touched the money was collected all round here & a great many tradespeople subscribed.'[60] It was not Princess May but her father who made a short speech of thanks to the delegation of neighbours, headed by a former Lord Mayor of London, Sir Whittaker Ellis. At this time Princess May's self-consciousness absolutely prevented her making a speech of such a kind. All through her life, indeed, she could never bring herself to make a public address.

'At 6 we went to London Gdmama gave me a beautiful bracelet with GdPapa's cameo set in pearls & diamonds', Princess May told her brother. 'Uncle George, Aunt Augusta & Mama gave me a lovely pearl & diamond heart brooch between them. We then went to see "Bootles Baby" charmingly acted.'

The cameo set in pearls and diamonds was the last birthday present the Duchess of Cambridge gave to her granddaughter, for on 6 April 1889 the old lady died at St James's Palace at the age of ninety-one. None of her children was with her. The Duke of Cambridge was in Ireland, the Grand Duchess Augusta—who had an uncanny knack for missing her relatives' death-beds: she was out of England when her father, her mother, her sister and her brother died; and out of Germany when her husband did so—was in Strelitz, and Princess Mary Adelaide, who had not been warned of immediate danger, was having her bath at White Lodge. Twenty years later Princess May recalled 'all the misery of that dreadful day . . . when my dear Mama received the tel. telling her to come at once while she was still in her bath! & then the hurry to get ready & be off, only to arrive at St. James's too late & to find all the blinds down—Dear me, how well I remember it all.'[61]

The Duchess of Cambridge's death occurred rather suddenly, and even the Princess of Wales, who 'ran across' from Marlborough House, was too late to see her alive. Queen Victoria hastened up to London from Windsor to see Aunt Cambridge's corpse. 'I saw dear old Aunt in the same place—where we last saw her—looking so peaceful & at rest—& free fm all suffering! She looked so nice,—with a white Cap tied under her chin, her head just a little turned to one side wh gave such a look of comfort—her hands folded over her breast—& a little crucifix wh. dear Alix had brought her from Gmunden in her hands. . . .'[62] The Queen added that 'unfortunate Mary only arrived at $\frac{1}{2}$ p.2. It really was not right—not to have sent for her before. Of course she feels that. . . . Mary did not show vy much grief; she cried & later on cried again—but she will feel what she has lost. Dear Aunt said to me . . . the last time I saw her: "*Ich empfehle Dir meinen Schwiegersohn Franz*".'*

* Translation: 'I recommend my son-in-law Franz to your care.'

Although Queen Victoria was much interested in illness and almost morbidly so in death she did not usually attend funerals. For her Aunt Cambridge, however, she made an exception, and announced that she intended going to Kew Church. 'I never was at any funeral (in England) nor at any Royal one—but only my own poor darling Child's [Prince Leopold, Duke of Albany] 5 years ago & this is the *only* other one I shall! And *she* is the *last* above *me*! U. George & I are *now* the *old ones* & we must feel that!' she wrote to the Empress Frederick. 'Few Mothers live to see their Son's 70th birthday as she did! Nothing but kind & loving words have been said of her by *all*.—Full of years & honour she is borne to her grave.' The Queen was impressed by the burial service in the little church on Kew Green. She sat with Princess Mary Adelaide and the Grand Duchess Augusta— 'who looked so crushed'—close beside the coffin. 'All the others were in Pews', she wrote. 'There were quantities of beautiful Wreaths & Beatrice & I placed ours just *after* the 2d Hymn—when the coffin was carried up 3 steps (a difficult task for the 8 Guardsmen)—& placed close to the Altar at the back of wh. the Mausoleum containing the Remains of Uncle Cambridge are & something had been taken out of the Reredos so that the Coffin went a little down into it, & slid gently down. . . . I am vy thankful to have been there with my poor Cousins—the 2 eldest my contemporaries.—& it was a help to them.'[63]

At her grandmother's funeral Princess May, like all the other ladies in the nave of the church, wore a long *crêpe* veil. The Princess of Wales, who had touches of white at her neck and wrists, and her three daughters, also wore long veils, but in their case these were 'made of *crêpe lisse* so that one could recognise them'.[64]

VIII

In her last years, the Duchess of Cambridge had spent a good deal of her time, as we have seen, planning a marriage for her grand-daughter: 'H R H with her present *ideé fixe* to marry P[rincess] May!' in Lady Geraldine's words. The old lady had spoken of the Grand Duke Michael, of a Prince of Anhalt, of Lord Euston and of others; it had been explained to her that Lord Euston already had a wife having made 'a sad disastrous marriage' and being unable to get a divorce. Two years after the Duchess's death, the Prince of Naples came to London; he dined at White Lodge and Princess May sat next to him at a dinner at the Mansion House. 'He is really extremely nice, clever, agreeable to talk to, talks English very well & seems altogether a nice boy—He is terribly short & not beautiful to behold', Princess May reported to her Aunt in August 1891.[65] 'So little Naples is a nice boy?' the Grand Duchess replied, from her country retreat near Dresden, 'how all these Princes travel about! is there nothing to please you amongst them or rather some one *in* England: but, as you only *rush* about, I fancy there is no *time* for Courtship of any kind! Here in Saxony the marriage of the frightful Heir is to take place in November.'[66]

We must reluctantly conclude that in this letter the Grand Duchess of Mecklenburg-Strelitz was being disingenuous. No one realised better than herself the awkwardness of her niece's position, or how slender were Princess May's marriage prospects.

It should, at this stage, have become perfectly clear that her father's morganatic birth was likely to preclude, for Princess May, any offer of marriage from a German Princeling. She would not, in any case, have wished to go and live in Germany. According to Queen Victoria (there is no other evidence) a tentative offer had been made to Princess May by one German Prince: Ernst Gunther, Duke of Schleswig-Holstein, a nephew of Princess Helena's husband, Prince Christian, and brother to the new German Empress, Augusta Victoria, wife of Wilhelm II. In November 1891 the Empress Frederick wrote to her mother Queen Victoria:

I *cannot* help laughing to myself—when I think of this summer someone mentioning to Dona*—what a charming girl May was—& how nice it would be—if her Brother thought of her!—Dona was much offended—& said to me—that her Brother would not dream of making such a *mésalliance*!!! I laughed at her.[67]

To this the Queen promptly replied:

I am much amused that Dona turned up her nose at the *idea* of her *charming* brother thinking of May whereas I *know it* as a *fact* that he *made démarches* to obtain her hand wh. *May refused* at once![68]

* 'Dona' was the family nickname for the Empress Augusta of Germany, Queen of Prussia, b. 1858, m. 1881, d. 1921. Through her mother she was a granddaughter of Queen Victoria's half-sister Princess Feodora of Leiningen and through her father, Frederick, Duke of Schleswig-Holstein, she was a niece of Prince Christian, the husband of Queen Victoria's third daughter Princess Helena ('Lenchen').

If this offer was indeed seriously made, it was no great compliment to Princess May, since '*odious* Gunther',* as Queen Victoria called the Duke of Schleswig-Holstein, was having notorious difficulty in finding himself a bride. He ended by marrying Princess Dorothea of Saxe-Coburg-Gotha in 1898.

Her morganatic blood, and her own inclinations, prevented Princess May's being absorbed into a minor German royal family. An English marriage was, then, desirable? Certainly, but here again there was a horrid difficulty: the Duke of Teck had no fortune and his daughter would be virtually dowerless. Princess May's grandmother had left her some money in her will, but the sum was not large enough to transform her into an heiress. Only a very rich member of the peerage, like Lord Hopetoun, or the Marquess of Bath's heir, Lord Weymouth, would be in a position to marry Princess May and provide her with an appropriate social position. For we must never forget that, although on the very fringe or outskirts of the English Royal Family, Princess May was nevertheless a member of it. It was, so to speak, an honorary membership, due wholly to her mother's father's Royal blood, and, though the life-members of this exclusive club were kind and courteous to her, they were well aware of the difference in status between a Serene Highness and a Royal one. From the point of view of any marriage Princess May thus had the worst of two worlds: she was too Royal to marry an ordinary English gentleman, and not Royal enough to marry a Royalty. Or so, in the late eighteen-eighties, it seemed.

Some of these difficulties might have melted away in the rays of a real passion; but her withdrawn, reserved manner, her cool, even temperament, made it unlikely that Princess May would ever inspire a violent emotion. Nor was she herself an emotional person. It seemed most probable that any marriage she might make would be predominantly a reasonable one: not in the exact French sense of a marriage of reason, but rather a reasonable marriage to a reasonable man of reasonable rank and fortune, which would offer her remarkable character a field for reasonable activity. It was not a brilliant prospect.

* When the Duke of Schleswig-Holstein wished to marry an Orleans Princess Queen Victoria wrote to the Empress Frederick in 1894 that the idea was 'quite preposterous. . . . I feel sure she wld not take such a wretched creature as he is. . . . I wd tell the Parents what a worthless individual Gunther is if I thought they were likely to give ear to him.'[69]

IX

The Duchess of Cambridge died when Princess May was twenty-one. Three years later, at twenty-four, Princess May was still unmarried, and still leading an uneventful life at White Lodge, occupying herself with reading and study, helping her mother with charities, helping her father to remain unruffled through each day. In the letter which Miss Ella Taylor wrote to her sister Miss Alice Taylor from White Lodge in February 1890 (and from which we have already quoted the description of Princess Louise, Duchess of Fife, driving her pony phaeton through Richmond Park) she gives a charming account of a midnight conversation with Princess Mary Adelaide, who could never bear to go to bed at a sensible hour:

After dinner Pss Mary & May chatted & played Halma, & the Duke played on the pianoforte. After father & daughter had retired Pss Mary remained up talking till very late. She spoke chiefly of her children. How happy she was to have such good children—that they were so steady, contented & affectionate,—her daughter is her '*Herzblatt*'—she spoke of her with tears in her eyes—saying 'May is indeed a pearl of great price'. What I have seen of the young Princess makes me think that the mother is quite justified in saying this. She is so unaffected—sensible—with a soul above buttons—she goes on with her studies—devoting a certain number of hours every day to improving her mind—& she is always serene & contented. Many girls would chafe against what might be called the dull life here—but Pss Mary says she makes herself happy wherever she is.[70]

In fact, Princess Mary Adelaide was reaping what she had sown, for we have noticed with what care and kindly severity she and her husband had brought up their four children from childhood. We have also noticed the contrast this upbringing made with that of the little Wales cousins, who were under-educated and over-indulged by their preoccupied father and their fond and beautiful mother. These little Wales cousins were now grown up. Their parents were, just as much as the Duke and Duchess of Teck, reaping what had been sown. At Marlborough House, however, the Prince and Princess of Wales were reaping the whirlwind.

It is impossible to overstress the importance of a certain discipline, or form, in life. A formless upbringing can but produce a formless character. This axiom was currently being proved true in the Wales family, in the person of Prince Albert Victor, Duke of Clarence and Avondale, KG, the heir-presumptive to the throne of England.

Prince Albert Victor's native disposition was wayward and self-indulgent. Even Queen Victoria did not blame him for this—for, idolised by his doting mother and three adoring sisters, bolstered up in crises by the far stronger character of his brother, and demoralised by the example of his father's private life, this young Prince had had very little chance to become stable. In 1890 and 1891 the problem which Prince Albert Victor presented to his family, and particularly to the Queen-Empress, his grandmother, to whose august position he must some day succeed, had become increasingly anxious and acute.

'Prince Eddy's' mind was volatile and his emotions were variable. His life was shapeless—or what outward shape it had was given to it artificially by his equerries and his entourage. In these circumstances the Queen, herself the very essence of discipline and duty, pronounced that there was only one solution: immediate marriage with some strong-minded and sensible Princess.

We must look at and weigh the reasons which led Queen Victoria to this abrupt, irrevocable decision. To do so we must now leave White Lodge, drive up to London and enter the stone portals of Marlborough House. In this seventeenth-century palace, with a large garden shielded from the Mall by high walls, and with frescoed staircase and a frescoed hallway in which pages in royal livery sit waiting, the fate of Princess May of Teck was in the balance, in the year eighteen hundred and ninety-one.

CHAPTER EIGHT

THE DUKE OF CLARENCE
AND AVONDALE

O N 19 AUGUST 1891 the Prince of Wales's Private Secretary, Sir Francis Knollys,* wrote a letter to Sir Henry Ponsonby, Private Secretary to the Queen. This letter gave an account of 'a long conversation . . . about Prince Eddy's future' which Sir Francis had had with the Princess of Wales, in her ornate and memento-laden private sitting-room at Marlborough House. 'I told her', Sir Francis explained,

that the Prince [of Wales] would agree to

1. The Colonial expedition
2. The European *cum* Colonial plan
3. To be married to Princess May in the Spring.

From what he had told me I had expected to find her strongly in favour of the European plan, but she was not really so . . . [and she] came to the conclusion that she would prefer No. 3, and that he should marry Princess May in the Spring. . . . I think the preliminaries are now pretty well settled, but do you suppose Princess May will make any resistance? I do not antici-pate any real opposition on Prince Eddy's part if he is properly managed.1

This frank and, indeed, startling little colloquy seems suddenly disruptive of our narrative. Has it not all the brutal force of a douche of cold water received full in the face? This is as it should be: for the upshot of this conference similarly disrupted the peaceful tenor of Princess May's inconspicuous life at White Lodge. To be your mother's hard-worked secretary and lady-in-waiting one day, and to be canvassed to become a future Queen of England on the next, would give the most sedentary nature a sharp, exciting jolt.

* Sir Francis Knollys (1837–1924; created Viscount Knollys of Caversham, 1911) had been Private Secretary to the Prince of Wales since 1870 and continued in this capacity after the Prince's accession to the throne in 1901. Knollys was a strong liberal and, like Sir Henry Ponsonby, an excellent letter-writer.

For us to understand the import of the three alternatives laid before the Princess of Wales—her elegant, curled head gracefully tilted to help her deaf ears catch what Sir Francis Knollys was saying—that dusty morning of high summer in London, we must reverse our recent progress and retreat once more into the earlier past. Whatever was this 'Colonial expedition'? And what the 'European plan'? And why on earth did the Prince of Wales and Queen Victoria so much desire, in August 1891, to see Prince Eddy married to Princess May of Teck—a union which the Princess of Wales had herself urged on them, some years previously, in vain?

First, we must try to familiarise ourselves with the personality of Prince Eddy. When we have done this the talk between Sir Francis Knollys and the Princess of Wales will appear in quite another light. It will no longer seem cold-blooded, for we shall see how a conjunction of rather painful circumstances had produced, at Marlborough House, an anxious situation, to cope with which the Queen, her eldest son and her daughter-in-law turned in unison to enlist the steady-minded aid and quiet wisdom of Princess May of Teck.

In August 1891 the bachelor Prince Albert Victor was already in his twenty-eighth year. He had returned from a tour of India in May 1890, in a physical state which his grandmother, Queen Victoria, described as 'dreadfully thin . . . & pale & drawn'.[2] On his way home from India he had stopped for a few days at Athens, where he had seen much of his first cousin the Crown Princess, Sophie, Duchess of Sparta, third daughter of the Empress Frederick, and a recent, blonde, German addition to the cluster of foreign royalties who then constituted the reigning family of Greece. 'Eddy leaves tomorrow morning!' Crown Princess Sophie had written to her mother in April 1890, 'poor boy he looks still dreadfully yellow & thin! he is such a dear & so good & kind!'[3]

'Dear', 'good' and 'kind' were the adjectives most usually employed in reference to Prince Eddy by his relations. Anything superlative would have been, to say the least of it, exaggerated. Even his nearest and dearest, who were naturally bent on making the best of poor Prince Eddy, could not bring themselves to use more positive terms. Prince Eddy was certainly dear and good, kind and considerate. He was also backward and utterly listless. He was self-indulgent and not punctual. He had been given no proper education, and as a result he was interested in nothing. He was as heedless and as aimless as a gleaming gold-fish in a crystal bowl. He suffered from what Sir

Harold Nicolson in his biography of King George V has called 'a constitutional lethargy'. The Grand Duchess of Mecklenburg-Strelitz, who never minced her words and had a good command of English, was driven to use a French phrase to express her own opinion of Prince Eddy—'*qui est*', she wrote to her brother, '*si peu de chose*, though as you say, "a dear Boy"'.4

In 1891 the 'dear Boy' was a thin young man, slightly taller than his brother and his sisters, with brown wavy hair that had started to recede, an oval face, an aquiline nose, large, gentle, doe-like eyes, and a buoyant little cavalry moustache which was waxed and turned up at the ends. His neck was astonishingly long—'a neck like a swan', as one of his family termed it; when not in uniform he was thus obliged to wear an unusually high starched collar, and from this necessity there arose his nickname of 'Collars-and-Cuffs'—a nickname which his father the Prince of Wales, who dearly loved to tease Prince Eddy, would recommend to child members of the Royal Family: 'Don't call him Uncle Eddy, call him Uncle-Eddy-Collars-and-Cuffs' this chaffing parent would genially exclaim.

Prince Eddy had not inherited the temperament of either of his parents, but he had, in full measure, inherited their charm. He could, in his own languid way, be both seductive and delightful, and, as we shall see, he had already inspired one fatal passion in one foreign Princess. He was, in fact, attractive to women. He frankly preferred pleasure to any form of work.

This was not promising material from which to mould a future King of England. The House of Hanover had produced a wide variety of English monarchs, the most spectacular of whom, to date, had been King George the Fourth. If anything, George IV had suffered from an excess of vitality. There had been, so far, no Hanoverian King of England who was merely apathetic. One would have had to look back to the Plantagenets to find a parallel to the kind of English monarch Prince Albert Victor, if not 'properly managed', might turn out to be.

From his birth Prince Eddy was handicapped by feeble health. He was a puny, seven-months' child, born unexpectedly in the second week of January 1864, at Frogmore House, in Windsor Home Park: 'As this event was not expected for two months, and no preparations were made for it, the public feeling is a mixture of agreeable disappointment and ill-suppressed risibility',5 the American Minister to the Court of St James's wrote in his Journal at the time. Anxieties on the score of Prince Eddy's health were coupled, as he grew into boyhood, with anxieties about his lack of character. Sir Harold Nicolson has shown how Mr Dalton, the tutor of Prince Eddy and his brother Prince George, was determined that they should be educated together, since he judged that Prince Eddy required 'the stimulus of Prince George's company to induce him to work at all'. As a result of Mr Dalton's advice, Prince Eddy, who was not destined for a naval career, spent two years with his brother aboard the *Britannia* at Dartmouth. It was hoped that this experience would, in Mr Dalton's words, assist him to develop 'those habits of promptitude and method, of manliness and self-reliance, in which he is now somewhat deficient'. This period at Dartmouth was followed for both Princes by a world cruise in the *Bacchante*, which entirely separated them from their family for three long years. Queen Victoria had initially objected to this plan, but had been persuaded to accede to it. The two Princes returned to England in 1882. Prince George had grown into a jolly and capable youth, enthusiastic about his future naval career. Prince Eddy, now eighteen, was not noticeably improved in any way. In 1883 he was sent up to Trinity College, Cambridge, and afterwards put into the 10th Hussars, who were stationed in Dublin and had their depot in York.

Prince Eddy could not have been less interested in the Army. He did not care for barrack life, he detested field days, thought his General 'a lunatic', and hated such cavalry routine as an 'Officers' ride': 'one has to go jogging round and round the riding school in a very tight and uncomfortable garment called a stable jacket and very hot work it is I can assure you'. He liked playing polo, but did not practise enough to play it well: 'Polo', he wrote from his regimental headquarters at York one June, 'is one of the few things I really care for this time of year.'[6] Among the few other things Prince Eddy really cared for at all times of the year was every form of dissipation and amusement; these tastes might have been gay and harmless in themselves, had they been counterbalanced by any symptom of concern for graver matters.

Prince Eddy's brother officers liked him rather than otherwise, and his superiors tried their level best to place his character in the most favourable light. When there was a question of promoting Prince Albert Victor to a Lieutenant-Colonelcy, the Duke of Cambridge, as Commander-in-Chief, consulted Lord Wolseley, whose long reply includes a fairly honest opinion of the young Prince's powers. 'I think', wrote Lord Wolseley, 'H R H has far more in him than he is often given credit for, but I should describe his brain & thinking powers, as maturing slowly. . . . Some of our very best & ablest men have mentally matured with extreme slowness. . . . Personally, I think he is *very much* to be liked, has most excellent manners, thoughtful for others, & always anxious to do the right thing. He is, however, young for his age [Prince Albert Victor was then twenty-seven] & requires to be brought out. I studied him closely when staying in a country house with him, & this is the result of my study.'7 Through Sir Henry Ponsonby the Duke of Cambridge told his cousin, the Queen, that it was 'attracting remark to keep His Royal Highness so long as Major in a Cavalry Regiment and there were young men in Dublin who were rising over his head.—It was true he was not a devoted soldier but he had greatly improved in the last few months.'8

Soon after this promotion, the Prince of Wales decided that his eldest son's remaining in the Army was 'simply a waste of time—& he has not that knowledge even of Military subjects which he ought to possess. His education and future has been a matter of some considerable anxiety for us & the difficulty in rousing him is very great.'9 All this time, Prince Eddy's health was getting no stronger. At the early age of twenty-four he suffered from the onset of gout: 'I hope dear Eddy has quite recovered from his *attack of gout* (it sounds as if one was talking of an old man)', his brother Prince George wrote to their mother, the Princess of Wales.10

By August 1891 Prince Eddy's general behaviour and his emotional instability were causing his parents real anxiety. The Prince of Wales determined to pack his eldest son off on a series of extended tours of the Colonies. 'The real reason', he explained to Queen Victoria, 'why we thought visits to certain Colonies were desirable was because the voyages would be longer.'11 This exposition of a project to keep the heir-presumptive to the English throne circling the globe like a *sputnik* was set before the Queen by the Prince of Wales in his reply to a long letter in which she had expressed her own wise views on Prince Eddy's immediate future.

The Prince and Princess of Wales had for some time harboured the hope and the illusion that Queen Victoria knew nothing of their eldest son's dissipations. They were wrong. The Queen might seem to be leading a reassuringly sheltered life at Osborne or Balmoral but she had an uncanny gift for knowing what was going on in her family: 'I ask again *who* is it tells the Queen these things?' Knollys wrote to

G

Ponsonby in December 1891, when the Queen had written to her daughter-in-law one of her protests about the 'dissipated life' the Duke of Clarence was leading. These dissipations were, incidentally, sapping his already feeble physical strength.

It was in May 1890 that Queen Victoria had bestowed a dukedom on her grandson, with the double title of Duke of Clarence and Avondale. The young man had been made absurd since childhood by being forced to use two Christian names instead of one, and now he had been given a double dukedom:

'I can't make out why he should be called by *both* names, why not *Clarence*', [Prince George of Wales wrote to his mother from Bermuda in July 1890]. 'I see a lot of the stupid jokes & puns about Clarence & Avondale. I think it is a great pity, because now his names are ridiculed the same as Albert Victor was which only does harm; the poor boy seems to be doomed to have two names, why can't you darling Motherdear try & get it altered & let him only be called Duke of Clarence, which is an old English title, whereas the two together is an awful mouthful. I am sure you agree with me. In fact I think we agree on most subjects, don't we darling Motherdear? Conceited donkey!!! you will say.'[12]

The Dukedom of Avondale, a Scottish title held by George II before he became Prince of Wales, had been added on the advice of the Garter King-at-Arms because the Earldom of Clarence was already a subsidiary title of the little Duke of Albany, son and heir of the dead Prince Leopold. Queen Victoria had been reluctant to make Prince Albert Victor a Duke:

... I am very sorry Eddie shld be lowered to a Duke [she wrote to the Empress Frederick from Balmoral in June 1890] like any one of the nobility wh. a Prince never can be. Nothing is so fine & grand as a Royal Prince, —but it is very good he shld be a Peer. I dont think Georgie will ever be made a Duke in my life time. . . .[13]

The Prince of Wales's proposal to keep the Duke of Clarence afloat for long stretches at a time, and to teach him to 'take an interest & appreciate the importance which our great Colonies are in connection with the great Empire over which you rule' met with no sympathy from the Queen:

I have been thinking a great deal of what you told me of your intention of making Eddy travel, & in this I *entirely agree* [she wrote from Osborne, on 4 August 1891].

But I *cannot* do so, as regards the Colonies. Eddy's good, & above all, his aptness for his position *must* be *the one thing* to be looked at. He ought to be able to take his place amongst all the European Princes & *how can he*, if he knows nothing of European Courts & Countries? He & Georgie are charming dear good boys, but very *exclusively* English which you & your brothers are not, & this is a great misfortune in these days. . . . They have, especially Eddy, gone nowhere (excepting India) but to *English speaking* Colonies. These Colonies offer no opportunities for the cultivation of art or of any historical interest whatever. . . . This is *not* what is wanted for dear Eddy, who has been nowhere but to Denmark & once or twice, Berlin & Darmstadt. But of Italy, Spain, Austria, Hungary, Russia, Turkey & Holland (very interesting) he knows nothing. . . .

He should travel as the Prince of Naples does,—not going to Courts during their seasons, but to see things & make people's acquaintance. . . .

You know yourself, who are so fond of going abroad how it enlarges one's views & rubs off that angular insular view of things which is not good for a Prince.

I feel all this so very strongly, that I *do* hope you will listen to it & follow my advice, which is dictated by *one object only*.—Eddy's & the Country's good.[14]

To this wise letter the Prince of Wales replied from Cowes next day. The gist of his reply was that he was still in favour of the 'Colonial expedition':

. . . it is difficult to explain to you the reasons why we do not consider it desirable for him to make lengthened stays in Foreign Capitals. . . . If you think Eddy too English—it is a good fault in these days—& [will] make him much more popular at home—I admit his knowledge of French & German is not as good as it should be but it comes from his apathy & disinclination to work—or master subjects which are of such importance to him. . . . A good sensible Wife—with some considerable character is what he needs most—but where is she to be found?[15]

II

Now Prince Eddy, who was volatile, and liable to tumble in and out of love, had himself made two somewhat headlong attempts to solve his own problems by a romantic marriage with a suitable European Princess. His first passion, in 1889, had been for Princess Alix of Hesse, the sixth child of Queen Victoria's daughter Princess Alice and of her husband Louis IV, Grand Duke of Hesse and by the Rhine. Queen Victoria, who was at that moment anxious that Prince Eddy should marry a German Princess, would have greatly liked

'Alicky' as a granddaughter-in-law. But it was not to be. Princess Alix, who seems to have been not at all under the spell of her English cousin's charm, refused:

I fear all hopes of Alicky's marrying Eddy is at an end [wrote Queen Victoria in May 1890]. She has written to tell him how it pains her to pain him, but that she cannot marry him, much as she likes him as a Cousin, that she knows she wld not be happy with him & that he wld not be happy with her & that he must *not* think of her. . . . It is a real sorrow to us . . . but . . . she says—that if she is *forced* she will do it—but that she would be unhappy & he—too. This shows gt strength of character as all her family & all of us wish it, & she refuses the gtest position there is.[16]

Thus firmly did the future Empress Alexandra Feodorovna of All the Russias take the first step down the fatal path which led her to the blood-stained cellar at Ekaterinburg.

Broken-hearted in the first week of May 1890 by Princess Alix of Hesse's refusal, Prince Albert Victor was in love again by the end of that month. This time his fancy had alighted on the tall, dark-haired and distinguished-looking Princess Hélène of Orleans, a daughter of the Comte de Paris, the Pretender to the French throne. The Orleans family had come to England when banished from their own country in 1886, and had then received much kindness from Queen Victoria and from members of her family. Princess Hélène of Orleans was a Roman Catholic. By French law she was not of age, being twenty-one.

This fresh emotion had not long been fluttering in Prince Eddy's heart before the Queen, with her excellent family intelligence service, and her instinct like a Geiger-counter, got to know about it. Sending him a photograph of herself for which he had asked her, she wrote from Windsor Castle on 19 May 1890:

I wish to say a few words about the subject of your future marriage. I quite agree with you that you should not be hurried and I feel sure that you will resist all the wiles and attempts of intriguers and bad women to catch you. But I wish to say that I have heard it rumoured that *you* had been thinking and talking of Princesse Hélène d'Orleans! I cant believe this for you know that I told you (as I did your Parents who agreed with me) that such a marriage is utterly *impossible*. None of our family can marry a catholic without losing all their rights and I am sure that she would never change her religion and to change her religion merely to marry is a thing much to be deprecated and which would have the very worst effect possible and be most unpopular, besides which *you* could not marry the daughter of the Pretender to the French Throne. Politically in this way it would also be impossible.

That being the case you should avoid meeting her as much as possible as it would only lead to make you unhappy if you formed an attachment for her.

Of the few possible Princesses (for of course any Lady in Society *would never* do) I think no one more likely to suit you and the position better than your Cousin Mossy. She is not regularly pretty but she has a very pretty figure, is very amiable and half English with great love for England which you will find in very few if any others. You will be able to see her shortly.[17]

Prince Eddy's 'Cousin Mossy' was Princess Margaret of Prussia, the eighth and last child of the Emperor and Empress Frederick and afterwards Landgravine of Hesse-Cassel. A plain, nice young woman of eighteen, she visited England in the spring of 1891, and stayed with her cousins at Sandringham. Nothing came of Queen Victoria's and the Empress Frederick's hope that Prince Eddy would marry her.

What Queen Victoria did not know, and would hardly have credited had she been told, was that Prince Eddy had already begun a flirtation with the Orleans Princess, whom he was meeting at the convenient house of his sister Princess Louise, Duchess of Fife, at Sheen. Moreover the Princess of Wales and her three daughters were pressing forward the claims of Princess Hélène, for she had shown what was to these fond ladies the supreme good taste of having loved Prince Eddy passionately, and hopelessly, and in silence, for three long years. Prince Eddy was essentially impressionable. He was quickly influenced by this affectionate cabal.

In one of his infrequent letters to his brother Prince George, then as usual at sea, Prince Eddy wrote:

You probably know through the girls, who told me that dear Hélène, had been fond of me for some time. I did not realise this at first although the girls constantly told me she liked me, for she never showed it in any way. Well, soon after you left and as I knew my chances with Alicky were all over, . . . I saw Hélène several times at Sheen, and naturally thought her everything that is nice in a girl, and she had become very pretty which I saw at once and also gradually perceived that she really liked me. . . . I naturally got to like, or rather love her, by the manner she showed her affection for me.[18]

This clandestine romance was after the Princess of Wales's own heart. At her inspiration Prince Eddy persuaded Princess Hélène to promise to change her religion and to marry him. In August 1890, the helpful Duchess of Fife invited the Comte and the Comtesse de

Paris and their daughter to stay at Mar Lodge. This house, which stood upon a hillock on the north bank of the river Dee, some twelve miles from Balmoral, had been renovated for his bride by the Duke of Fife. A shapeless old hunting-lodge, with verandahs supported by rustic tree-trunks creosoted black, Mar Lodge was burned down in 1895 and replaced by the present suburban-looking mansion with scarlet roofs, black-and-white eaves and a trim Tudor garden, which stands today upon the Dee's southern bank. Here, in an atmosphere of kilts and fishing-rods, and all amidst the magenta heather and the silver birches, and at picnics beside the Devil's Cauldron on the Quoich, the romance between Prince Eddy and the French Princess burgeoned. But how was Queen Victoria to be placated, and won round?

The Princess of Wales was adroit and feminine. She well knew that Queen Victoria was a sentimentalist, and she advised the young couple to rush across country to Balmoral and to tell the Queen all. So, one August morning, Prince Eddy and Princess Hélène got into a carriage at Mar Lodge, crossed the Lynn O'Dee, and eating their luncheon on the way, reached Balmoral in the early afternoon. 'You can imagine what a thing to go through', Prince Eddy told his brother George, 'and I did not at all relish the idea. . . . I naturally expected Grandmama would be furious at the idea, and say it was quite impossible etc. But instead of that she was very nice about it and promised to help us as much as possible, which she is now doing. . . . I believe what pleased her most was my taking Hélène into her, and saying we had arranged it entirely between ourselves without consulting our parents first. This as you know was not quite true but she believed it all and was quite pleased. Hélène however had said nothing as yet to her parents which was the worst to come for her poor girl.'[19]

There now began a tortuous exchange of questionnaires and *aides-mémoires*, involving the Queen, the Prince of Wales, the Prime Minister (then Lord Salisbury), Lord Rosebery, Sir Henry Ponsonby, Sir Francis Knollys and the Lord Chancellor: the object being to establish what would be the constitutional position of the heir-presumptive should he marry either a Roman Catholic wife, or a wife who had renounced her true religion and turned Protestant. Prince Eddy at one moment declared he would willingly abdicate his rights to the succession. 'You have no idea how I love this sweet girl now, and I feel I could never be happy without her', he wrote to his brother.[20] Meanwhile the Comte de Paris was adamant and would not hear of such a marriage under any circumstances. He instructed his daughter to withdraw her impulsive offer of apostasy. In the autumn of 1890 Princess Hélène of Orleans went to Rome to plead in person with the Pope, who could only confirm the verdict of the Comte de Paris. By the spring of 1891 the whole affair was officially, though not emotionally, at an end.

Queen Victoria, who did not know her grandson very well and always saw him on his best behaviour, was persuaded that Prince Eddy would not recover from this blow for many years. Those who knew the Prince intimately thought differently. Sir Henry Ponsonby had occasion to go to Marlborough House to see the Prince of Wales one June day in 1891. He accidentally met Prince Eddy there:

> While waiting at Marlborough House before the Prince of Wales came home, The Duke of Clarence and Avondale came into the room [Ponsonby wrote to Queen Victoria]—and Sir Henry Ponsonby, though of course he did not touch on this subject, as there were others there, must say that His Royal Highness did not appear depressed but talked away in a most lively manner.

> Sir Henry Ponsonby cannot help thinking that he must have been prepared for this end for some time and that the settlement of an impossible situation must have almost been a relief to him.[21]

The legendary love of Prince Albert Victor and Princess Hélène of Orleans, afterwards Duchess of Aosta, is commemorated at Windsor Castle by a bead wreath with the single word 'HÉLÈNE' upon it, which is pointed out to tourists visiting the Duke of Clarence's elaborate tomb in the annexe to St George's Chapel. This wreath was left there on the characteristically magnanimous instructions of Queen Mary, who liked and respected Princess Hélène. There was never any doubt of the reality of Princess Hélène's love for Prince Albert Victor, who, looking to English eyes rather like a tailor's dummy, might have been considered in late nineteenth-century Paris as a trim and fetching beau. After his death Princess Hélène came to see Queen Victoria. '*Je l'aimais tant*', she told her, '*et j'ai peut-être été imprudente mais je n'ai pas pu faire autrement, je l'aimais tant;—il était si bon.*'[22] Prince Albert Victor's part in this romantic story would be more touching were it not for documentary evidence that he was, simultaneously, in love with someone else.

'I thought it was impossible a short time ago', Prince Eddy wrote, on 21 June 1891, to the beautiful Lady Sybil St Clair Erskine,* a

---

* Lady Sybil was the second daughter of the fourth Earl of Rosslyn. Born in 1871, she married the thirteenth Earl of Westmorland on 28 May 1892 and died in 1910, leaving two sons and two daughters.

debutante daughter of Lord Rosslyn, 'to —— more than one person at the same time, and I believe according to things in general it should be so, but I feel that exceptions will happen at times. I can explain it easier to you when next we meet, than by writing. I only hope and trust that this charming creature which has so fascinated me, is not merely playing with my feelings. . . . I can't believe she would after what she has already said, and asked me to say. . . . I am writing in an odd way and have no doubt you will think so but I do it for a particular reason and want you to promise me . . . to cut out the crest and signature, which would then prevent anyone understanding it, supposing someone got hold of the letter by any chance. You understand why I say this? . . . If one could only transplant oneself now and then, and then all of a sudden appear before the person one most wishes to see how delightful that would be. I am sure if it were only possible, the world would be a great deal happier than it is. Don't you think so?' There were a number of such letters, all of which Lady Sybil judiciously preserved crest and signature intact.

'I wonder if you really love me a little?' Prince Eddy wrote to Lady Sybil, one week after the letter just quoted. 'I ought not to ask such a silly question I suppose but still I should be very pleased if you did just a little bit. . . . You may trust me not to show your letters to any-one. . . . You can't be too careful what you do in these days, when hardly anybody is to be trusted. . . . It is very hot today and I feel very languid and not up to doing much. . . .'

This particular series of letters concludes with one marked by Lady Sybil: 'Prince Eddy's last letter before his death to me.' This letter, enquiring about the truth of Lady Sybil's reported engagement to Lord Burghersh, includes a sentence reading: 'Don't be surprised if you hear before long that I am engaged also, for I expect it will come off soon. But it will be a very different thing to what it might have been once, . . . but still it can't be helped.'[23]

This utterly artless set of letters from Prince Albert Victor to Lady Sybil St Clair Erskine shows more succinctly than any other written evidence the reasons which influenced his parents and his grandmother to beg him to marry suitably and soon. It also demonstrates the peculiar problems which they were ready to hand over, as though on a platter, to Princess May of Teck.

III

We must now leave Marlborough House, Mar and Balmoral and see what has been happening at White Lodge, where Princess May, entirely oblivious of these plans and projects, is still leading her useful and studious life.

On 12 June 1891, the Duke and Duchess of Teck celebrated their Silver Wedding anniversary. White Lodge had been renovated in honour of this event, and two garden parties for relations, friends and neighbours were given on successive days. The Teck family were ensconced in a tent of pale blue and cream coloured Indian silk. This tent was flanked by two 'immense baskets of flowers', a tribute from the Duke of Orleans. Amongst the presents which flowed into White Lodge was a 'loveliest of watch bracelets' sent to Princess Mary Adelaide by the Queen. Later in the summer the Emperor and Empress of Germany came over on a state visit, in the festivities for which Princess May and her parents naturally took part.

The Grand Duchess of Mecklenburg-Strelitz missed both the Silver Wedding celebrations and the Emperor's visit, for she was afraid of the influenza epidemic which had again broken out in England. '. . . this nasty Influenza . . . with daily reports, as to the number of cases and deaths; this made me nervous too, the idea of going into it, into the pested air, from here, where the air is so pure . . . I had to ask myself: is it prudent for both of us, to expose ourselves to this illness, to be laid up with it *there* for no use?'[24]

Although the Grand Duchess would not admit it, the German air was equally 'pested'. 'The Influenza is *raging*—and the Hospitals are all *crowded* with patients', wrote the Empress Frederick from Berlin in the winter of 1891.[25] The influenza pandemic of 1889 to 1890 had started in Central Asia, with a handful of cases at Bokhara in May 1889. Early in October it had reached Tomsk, and spread thence to St Petersburg. Soon it was reported that it had reached Paris and Berlin, London and New York. India, Australia, China and Central Africa were swept by it in 1890. In Europe it recurred in an epidemic form in 1891 and 1892: in January of the latter year five hundred deaths from influenza were reported in London alone. Many distinguished persons, Cardinal Manning amongst them, died from this scourge. One of Princess May's own friends, a girl of about her age, also died of the influenza. It seemed to Princess May a tiresome and potentially dangerous disease, though it was, of course, absurd of Aunt Augusta

G*

to take it so very seriously. How could Princess May suppose that this germ from Bokhara, in Central Asia, would shortly alter the course of her whole life?

The year 1891 was a busy and apparently a happy one for Princess May. Her Diary records the usual round of functions: 'In the evening Mama gave away prizes to the Young Mens Christian Association in Aldersgate Street'; 'Mama opened an industrial exhibition' at Hackney; 'Mama opened an exhibition at King Edward ragged schools, Spital-fields'; 'Went to Ly Wolverton's where Mama read & I sang to some poor men from Westminster'; 'drove to Camberwell where Mama opened the Institute & Gymnasium which Ly Wolverton gave to the Parish. The Dean & Mr Chapman made charming speeches & Mama's speech was so touching that we nearly wept. It was quite the nicest function I have ever been at.' She was also attending courses of lectures on Elizabethan literature and on social hygiene.

All of these activities were interlaced with attendance at Court Balls, frequent visits to the theatre, dinner-parties at Marlborough House and with Uncle George Cambridge. In September and October the Tecks settled, with Lady Wolverton and her niece Gian Tufnell, at the Foley Arms Hotel at Malvern; they did not go abroad this year, most likely from motives of economy. From Malvern—a place which Princess May found exceedingly pretty and rural—they made sight-seeing expeditions to cathedrals, churches, country-houses and beauty-spots in the vicinity. Princess May was much impressed with Worcester Cathedral where she was shown the tomb of Arthur, Prince of Wales, son and heir to Henry VII. We may recall that this Prince of Wales had died during his father's lifetime, leaving a young widow who had then married his only brother, King Henry VIII.

All through this year of 1891 Princess May had been seeing her cousin Louise at Sheen Lodge regularly. She had also seen a fair amount of her other Wales cousins, with the exception of Prince Eddy, who was often with his regiment at York, though he escorted Princess May round the paddocks one day of Ascot week 1891. In January 1891 Princess May had been to stay at Sandringham for six days with her parents. In late October they met the Prince of Wales for three days at Easton: 'he was perfectly charming', Princess May told her Aunt Augusta.[26] By now she was not entirely unaware of what might be pending for her in the future. Neither the Duke nor the Duchess of Teck, who were in a state of suppressed but wild excitement and high tension, said a word about the marriage possibilities to the Prince of Wales, who was thankful to them for their reticence.

In the last week of October 1891 the Tecks were given a signal as clear, as swift, as dazzling as a Bengal rocket. Princess May and her brother, Prince Adolphus, were commanded to proceed northward to Balmoral Castle without delay.

IV

When this summons to Balmoral reached them, Princess May and her parents were staying with Lady Wolverton at Coombe Wood, Kingston-on-Thames, quite close, in fact, to White Lodge. The Queen's message had taken the form of a letter to Princess Mary Adelaide who, on this occasion, replied to it with astounding promptitude. Queen Victoria had deliberately refrained from asking her cousin to accompany her children, since she wished for an opportunity to get to know Princess May on her own. Eager and indiscreet as ever, Princess Mary Adelaide hinted broadly that she herself would have liked to have been invited too:

> Only a line, [she wrote from Coombe Wood] not to keep the messenger too long waiting to thank you for your very dear letter and to say with what joy my Children will obey your gracious and more than kind summons, though I must own that I feel inclined to be rather envious! and not a little jealous at being left out in the cold and not invited to accompany them! albeit *very much gratified* at your most kind wish to have them with you for a little while.[27]

The Duchess of Teck had only been asked to Balmoral once in her life, and this had been long ago, when she and her husband had gone to stay there in October 1868. After this visit the Queen had sent her what must indeed have been a voluminous 'Hunting Stewart Velvet dress . . . as a souvenir of dear Scotland, wh.', the Queen wrote, 'I left more unwillingly than ever & wh. I hope will prove acceptable.'[28]

As the Queen aged she became more and more unwilling to leave 'dear Scotland'. Her rare guests and her Household found that the white, castellated, Germanic-looking house remained tolerable in mid-October, when the mauve Michaelmas daisies stood in stiff array in the flower-beds outside the ground-floor windows; and walks and drives were still possible on crisp golden afternoons. By the end of that month, and throughout November, however, Balmoral was cold and draughty, and sometimes snowbound as well. The Queen had a dislike of heated rooms, and would keep the windows open in the dankest or frostiest weather. The fireplaces in the main rooms at Balmoral were usually empty.

If Osborne House, in the Isle of Wight, which could only be reached by water across the Solent, was found somewhat inconvenient by the Queen's successive Prime Ministers and others whom she was obliged to see, Balmoral Castle was still more so. 'Carrying on the Government of a country six hundred miles from the Metropolis doubles the Labour', Disraeli once complained.[29] Here in her northern fastness the Queen led an even more retiring life than she did at Windsor Castle or at Osborne House. She paid a short two-week visit to Balmoral each June, travelling in a special train, with Princess Beatrice on a truckle bed in her sleeping compartment. She would go north again in August, and stay on through the late summer and the autumn into early winter. Except for Princess Beatrice and her husband Prince Henry of Battenberg, both of whom shared the Queen's daily life and moved with her when she moved, few even of Queen Victoria's own children were ever invited to stay at Balmoral. The Prince and Princess of Wales usually spent August in the old castle of Abergeldie, a grim little Scottish fortress which looks as though it had been transplanted from Touraine, and which stands a couple of miles along the Dee from Balmoral. At Mar Lodge, beyond Braemar, there lived, as we have seen, the Queen's eldest Wales granddaughter Princess Louise, Duchess of Fife.

It would be hard to exaggerate the deliberate isolation, indeed the secrecy, of the Queen's existence at Balmoral. Sometimes she was not seen by her Household or her few guests for days at a time. She would work steadily at her red despatch-boxes, at letters and at much other business, a round broken only by drives to, or picnics at, one or other of the little houses she had constructed on the Balmoral estate, her favourite retreat being the Glassalt Shiel. Even more than Osborne, Balmoral was a shrine dedicated to the memory of the Prince Consort, who had built the castle on Deeside because he thought this valley, then thickly wooded with firs and larches, closely resembled certain German landscapes which he loved. On Craig Lurigan, behind and above the castle, Queen Victoria had put up a cairn to his memory, and round this his health was sometimes drunk in whisky by his family, the Household, the ghillies and the guests. The Prince Consort's tastes and personality impregnated the house, which was filled with his portraits.

The routine of life at Balmoral was stiff and strict. Every detail of it was dictated by the Queen, who supervised the meals, the Household's curriculum, the stalking, and even the use made of the ponies in the stables. She kept in touch with her guests, Household and servants by writing notes. Cabinet Ministers loathed staying at Balmoral, which was uncomfortable, chilly and run on conventual lines. In Queen Victoria's day the house, which is naturally light and airy, was rendered gloomy by the dark marmalade-coloured paint which covered all the panelling and other woodwork. Tartan prevailed everywhere, in stair-carpets, in upholstery, in curtains. When, in 1910, Princess May, become Queen Mary, took over at Balmoral, she made radical changes in its interior, for she had inherited all her father's passion for re-hanging pictures and re-arranging rooms. One of her first steps was to have the panelling stripped and lightened, and it is now only in the back passages that one can find traces of the dark marmalade.

In the normal course of events Queen Victoria would never have dreamed of asking her Cambridge cousin's children to Balmoral—not from any prejudice against them, or dislike for their company, but simply because she would have found it embarrassing, for fundamentally the Queen was shy. In 1865 she had written to the Empress Frederick: 'I have been now *30* years in harness—& therefore *ought* to know what shd be—but I am *terribly shy* & nervous & *always was so.*'30 Her grandchildren found Queen Victoria kind and not at all formidable, but very, very shy, 'girlishly shy', in the words of Princess Beatrice's sister-in-law Princess Marie of Erbach-Schönberg. The Queen had a little diffident shrug of the shoulders, and a benevolent nervous smile which revealed her teeth, and reminded one of an amiable field-mouse. Even to people staying in the house Queen Victoria was not, of course, easy of access. She only appeared at stated hours for meals. Princess Beatrice would announce with whom or whither the Queen wished to drive of an afternoon.

This extremely small old lady of seventy-two, lame in one leg and dressed in stiff black silk, with a soft, white, lace cap upon her white hair, had an imposing dignity about her. She was surrounded by an atmosphere of genuine awe. Thickly carpeted corridors led to her private apartments, which smelled of orange-flower water. Door after door would be noiselessly opened until one reached the inner sanctum and came face to face with this diminutive figure in black.

A legend grew up in her lifetime, and has increased out of all proportion since, that Queen Victoria was an austere and alarming old lady. She was neither. She was, primarily, benevolent and anxious for others to be happy. She was liable to fits of uncontrollable laughter. She derived an innocent delight from the little old-fashioned private theatricals which her Household would organise for her amusement, and which her grandson Prince Eddy despised: 'It is extraordinary how pleased Grandmama is with such small things', he wrote to his brother Prince George in February 1891, of some 'tiresome theatricals' for which he had been summoned all the way to Osborne House, 'for she is quite childish in some ways about them. It was the same thing with the *tableaux* in Scotland this autumn. But I suppose it is because she has no other amusement, that she takes such interest and pleasure in these performances.'[31]

The Queen's favourite role, perhaps, was that of adviser to young people who were unhappy or had got into difficulties. In 1889 she had invited her Prussian granddaughter Princess Victoria to Windsor and Balmoral, wishing to help her recuperate from her disappointment at being unable to marry Prince Alexander of Battenberg with whom she was deeply in love. On another occasion the Queen helped Princess Marie Louise, one of her Schleswig-Holstein granddaughters, in an awkwardness of another kind. Her one wish was to help and to alleviate; but she liked those she advised to listen to her advice. 'Married children are very often a gt trial at 1st', she wrote in March 1880, 'but one gets accustomed to their follies as time goes on & many things right themselves; still it is very wrong of young people *not* to listen or take advice—for they have no experience. We Parents have much to go through—much to bear!'[32]

Just as in June 1889 she had invited Princess Victoria of Prussia to Balmoral with a purpose—that of trying to assuage her grief—so had the Queen a definite reason for asking Princess May of Teck in November 1891. She wanted to get to know her better, and to confirm her own opinion that the girl would make a suitable future Queen.

After arranging eighteen hundred garments for the London Needlework Guild at White Lodge on 4 November, Princess May, together with her brother Prince Dolly, caught the night train to Aberdeen at Euston Station. Her parents came to see them off. 'Reached Aberdeen at 8, red carpet & the station master to meet us, felt rather shy, he took us to the hotel close by where we washed and breakfasted. Miss Cochrane* joined us at breakfast & we left again by the 9.30 train

* A member of Queen Victoria's Household.

(we kept our saloon carriage) for Ballater', Princess May reported in a letter to her mother.[33] On their arrival at Balmoral they were met at the door by 'Aunt Beatrice' Battenberg who took them to their rooms. They lunched at two o'clock, the brother and sister sitting one on each side of their hostess, the Queen. 'Your dear Children arrived safely after 12, looking very well', the Queen telegraphed to Princess Mary Adelaide: 'Fine day. Very pleased to see them here.' 'Most dear & kind & thoughtful of her!' the Duchess of Teck wrote off to Princess May: 'I feel *sure* you are already quite *sous son charme* & becoming very devoted to "Aunt Queen"!'[34]

This important visit to Balmoral lasted for ten days. Princess May went out driving a good deal, walked alone with the Queen, attended the rehearsal and the actual performances of two theatrical pieces in the Balmoral ballroom, played with Princess Beatrice's children, and smoked cigarettes with her brother and her Aunt Beatrice in the latter's rooms. When the indifferent weather permitted, they made one or two longish expeditions, going one day as far as the Danzig and home by Mar Lodge and Braemar: 'Mar Lodge', Princess May wrote of her cousin Louise's house, 'is a funny looking place with scattered houses with verandahs which look like bungalows, I don't think it can be comfortable.'[35]

The ten days in the almost weird seclusion of Balmoral sped quickly by, and the brother and sister left for London on Saturday November 14th.

Queen Victoria was highly satisfied with Princess May's visit. She found her 'so improved in looks', and wrote of her to the Empress Frederick:

Today is again wet & cheerless. We have seen a gt deal of May & Dolly Teck during these 10 days visit here & I cannot say enough good of them. May is a particularly nice girl, so quiet & yet cheerful & so vy carefully brought up & so sensible. She is grown very pretty.[36]

To this letter the Empress Frederick sent a grudging reply: 'I am so glad to hear you are pleased with May & Dolly Teck.—I wonder whether Eddy—will ever marry May? . . . some people said there was not much in May—that she was a little "*oberflächlich*" [shallow or superficial] but you know how little worth such criticisms are in general.'[37] 'You speak of May Teck,' Queen Victoria answered. 'I think & hope that Eddy will try & marry her for I think she is a superior girl—quiet & reserved *till* you know her well,—but she is the reverse of *oberflächlich*. She has no frivolous tastes, has been very carefully brought up & is well informed & always occupied.'³⁸

The Queen had given the young Tecks a letter for their mother. In this she wrote: '. . . I never had an opportunity before of knowing May well or Dolly either, & I am so glad to find that they were soon quite at their ease with us. They are so well brought up & have such good manners wh. in the present day is not *too* frequent. May is a dear, charming girl, & so sensible & unfrivolous.—She was in great good looks.'³⁹ To this letter Princess Mary Adelaide again replied very promptly and in her most effusive vein, thanking the Queen for her praise of 'our dear Children' and for her kindness to them: 'You treated them with so much affection that they very soon lost all shyness and felt, as they tell me, quite at their ease with you, dearest Cousin. . . . When you are again at Windsor, I hope I may soon have an opportunity of kissing your dear hands and thanking you *de vive voix* for having made my May and Dolly so happy and so thoroughly at home with your dear, gracious self!'⁴⁰

Princess Mary Adelaide and her brother the Duke of Cambridge were now both of them convinced that Prince Eddy would propose to Princess May. Although his mother was now dead, the Duke of Cambridge continued to confide in Lady Geraldine Somerset, who recorded their talks in her Journal. Time had not softened Lady Geraldine. She kept her hatred of the Duchess of Teck at fever pitch, and her attitude towards Princess May can only be compared to that of Cousine Bette towards Hortense Hulot.

On 12 November the Duke of Cambridge came to see Lady Geraldine and spoke:

of May at Balmoral!! and what it means!?! he thinks just as I do, that the Queen has been told . . . 'how popular it would be'!! and has sent for the girl *pour l'approfondir* and to see what she is really like, with a view to the project!! he has not seen P[rincess] M[ary Adelaide] so knows nothing.

On 15 November the Duchess of Teck, her husband and Prince Dolly were rash enough themselves to call on Lady Geraldine to give her the latest good news. Lady Geraldine's fury became almost daemonic:

Presently the rest of the party came P[rincess] M[ary Adelaide], P[rince] T[eck] and Dolly just returned (this morning only) from Balmoral!—Evidently that is to be!!! P[rincess] M[ary Adelaide] informed me 'the Queen has fallen in love with my children! *specially May*!! she thinks her so well brought up! *so amusing*' (the very last thing in the world I should say she is!!) etc. . . . in short P[rincess] M[ary Adelaide] at all counts is satisfied it is to be! The Duke talking of May's prospects!! enchanted at them!!⁴¹

On 3 December 1891, the Prince of Wales wrote to his mother, the Queen, from Marlborough House:

. . . You may I think make your mind quite easy about Eddy—& that he has made up his mind to propose to May but we thought it best '*de ne pas brusquer les choses*' & as she is coming to us with her Parents after Xmas to Sandringham everything will I am sure be satisfactorily settled then.⁴²

The Prince of Wales was overlooking the odd streak of precipitancy in Prince Eddy's otherwise flaccid character, which had enabled him to switch his affections in one week from Princess Alix of Hesse to Princess Hélène of Orleans, and then to split these feelings equally between the latter Princess and Lady Sybil St Clair Erskine. Dear and good, Prince Albert Victor was also pliable and obedient. Once an idea had been inserted into his head, he acted on it. He was now all agog at the prospect of marrying Princess May. On the very day on which his father was writing to the Queen about the importance of a decent interval before the proposal, Prince Eddy was staying under the same roof with Princess May and her parents—that of the de Falbes' overheated house in Bedfordshire—Luton Hoo.

v

'Fine day', we read in Princess May's Diary for 2 December 1891:

. . . We left for Luton. Party Eddy, Baths & Katie Thynne, Georgie Forbes & Ida, Dudley Wards, Arthur & Clemmie Walsh, Miss Leigh, Arthur Somerset, Sir Charles Hartropp, Mrs Gregson, Mr Brownlow, Oliver Montagu etc.—

We may recall that Princess May was already familiar with Luton Hoo, where she had first met Koziebrodzki and had been photographed with Princess Mary Adelaide and the other guests in a conservatory full of camellias and scented geranium. The Tecks paid several visits to Luton Hoo, for Mr de Falbe, a quick, pleasant man with a rather bald head and an imperial, was Danish Minister at the Court of St James's, and thus *persona grata* with the Danish Princess of Wales and, through her, with other adjacent members of the Royal Family.

'We all enjoyed our visit very much', Princess May had written to her Aunt Augusta in November 1886, 'the only thing was that the heat in the house was so terrific that we nearly all died of it, it was like being shut up in a hot house.'[43]

On summer visits to Luton Hoo the young people would play at lawn tennis 'in front of the portico' while the older generation would sit out under the trees. In the evenings there was whist, and, for the young, dancing to 'a capital organ turned by one of the footmen'. In 1888 a shocking accident had occurred near Luton Hoo: 'In the after-noon', the Duchess of Teck wrote to her sister Augusta, 'Madame de Falbe and I went for a drive, and called to enquire after the poor widow of the unfortunate Colonel Sowerby, who was gored to death by a favourite Egyptian stag, which he kept in an enclosure not far from his house. . . . A servant, who looked very woe-begone, and no wonder! gave us some particulars.'[44]

In 1891 Princess May arrived at Luton Hoo on 2 December with her parents and remained there until the seventh. The day following that of their arrival was a Thursday: 'A dull day', Princess May recorded in her Diary. This entry bore reference to the weather solely, for in no other way was Thursday 3 December 1891 a dull day for Princess May. She lunched with the shooters, and walked with them afterwards. In the evening there was a County Ball at Luton Hoo. Now, in her overheated house Madame de Falbe had an overheated —and overfurnished—boudoir. Into this room, while the house guests and the country neighbours were frolicking in the ballroom, Prince Eddy led his cousin Princess May. He proposed to her, and was accepted.

'To my great surprise Eddy proposed to me during the evening in Mme de Falbe's boudoir*—Of course I said yes—We are both very happy—Kept it secret from everybody but Mama & Papa.' This extract comes likewise from Princess May's Diary.

To us, living in a completely different age to that of the eighteen-nineties, the phrase 'of course I said yes' may seem a little surprising. It is not so, in fact. At that period royal marriages were seldom made

---

* The Falbes later sent a photograph of this boudoir to Princess May, who pasted it into her photograph album. On 14 July 1918 Queen Mary, with the King and Sister Agnes, went to see Lady Wernher's convalescent home for officers at Luton Hoo. 'I had not been to Luton since I was engaged to Eddy there 27 years ago! The house is so much altered that it is difficult to make out where the former rooms were', Queen Mary noted in her Diary that day.

for love: only two of the Queen's own children, Princess Louise, Duchess of Argyll, and Princess Beatrice, known as Princess Henry of Battenberg, had married from this motive, and Princess Louise lived to regret it. Moreover, many factors would have influenced Princess May's acceptance of her cousin as a husband. She had been reared to venerate the throne, and to recognise that the first duty of any English Prince or Princess was to help support it, and add to its lustre. Character, tradition and sense of duty all combined to enforce her decision. She possessed, as we have seen, a profound conviction of her own capacities, once these were given a chance of free play: what better chance could she have for this, than to become successively Duchess of Clarence and Avondale, Princess of Wales, Queen of England? To Princess May and to all her family Royalty was a profession—the highest and the finest in the world. If we need an analogy, she was like a girl at some minor ballet-school, trained as a dancer from childhood, and now suddenly, unexpectedly, offered the prima ballerina's position at the most famous theatre in the world. Think, too, how brilliant was this sudden prospect in contrast to the obscure life she had been leading at White Lodge.

There was also one other factor involved, and this may sound paradoxical: Princess May liked her cousin Prince Eddy but she did not know him very well. As we shall observe, she began to have qualms and doubts during her short engagement, but on that evening in Madame de Falbe's boudoir not one of these had yet had any opportunity to appear.

The next day Prince Eddy went out hunting. In the evening he came to Princess May's room and showed her 'a charming telegram from Aunt Alix'. After dinner they played bezique together, the next morning ('lovely day') they were photographed, and Prince Eddy set off for London and for Windsor to announce the engagement to his parents and to seek the sanction of the Queen. Prince Dolly arrived at Luton Hoo that evening and 'was astounded to hear the news'.45 The engagement had come sooner than had been officially intended, and it was not found possible to keep it quiet. A public announcement was made. On 7 December Princess May left Luton for London. On reaching St Pancras station she was, for the first heady time in her life, lustily cheered by the crowd. It was no longer Princess Mary Adelaide who was the centre of the public's attention. The London crowd's ovation was from now on reserved for the shy but radiant figure of Princess May.

The Tecks lunched at Marlborough House where Princess May received 'a warm welcome'. In the afternoon the Queen made one of her rare sallies from Windsor to London, in order to congratulate her heir-presumptive and his affianced: Princess May.

CHAPTER NINE

THE FIRST ENGAGEMENT

———————

THERE was one individual in London, that crisp and pulsating December, who in no manner shared the Queen's pleasure, the Waleses' satisfaction, and the Teck's overt delight, at the engagement of Princess May to the Duke of Clarence and Avondale.

Was this person Princess Hélène of Orleans? No; for Princess Hélène of Orleans was not in London, but at Stowe House in Buckinghamshire; and she was on the verge of leaving England for a prolonged tour of Spain with her tactful parents the Comte and Comtesse de Paris.* Also Princess Hélène had, that autumn, sent Prince Eddy an enchanting letter releasing him from his promises, giving him her blessing and admonishing him to perform his duty as a Protestant English Prince by immediately marrying a Protestant Princess.

Who, then, if not Princess Hélène of Orleans could have failed to be gratified at Princess May's happiness? Lady Geraldine Somerset perchance? Correct! Lady Geraldine had never forgiven Princess May the letter she had written from Florence in 1884, in defence of her parents, the Duke and the Duchess of Teck. That Princess May should now become the heroine of a royal Cinderella-story annoyed Lady Geraldine Somerset beyond endurance.

On 6 December Princess May's uncle, who was also Lady Geraldine's idol, the Duke of Cambridge, had called on Lady Geraldine Somerset to tell her the news. 'Of course we discussed it all and at first had a stormy interview, alas! for I could not feign pleasure I do not feel', Lady Geraldine told her Journal. On a later visit the Duke of Cambridge further exacerbated his old friend by telling her how pleased the Prince of Wales now was with the engagement:

. . . [The Prince of Wales] says May is the most charming girl he has ever come across—(considering he has known her intimately since her birth, it has taken him some considerable time to find it out, nearly one quarter of a century!!!) [The Duke of Cambridge also spoke] of P[rincess] M[ary

* Had Prince Eddy been less previous at Luton Hoo—i.e. had he waited to propose till the Tecks' visit to Sandringham after Christmas—the poor Princess

Adelaide]'s gigantic popularity!! and more gigantic luck!! how everything has played into her hands. . . .[2]

In an entry in her Diary dated 8 December 1891, however, Lady Geraldine Somerset plays into our hands, for any evidence in Princess May's favour from so intensely prejudiced a witness carries total conviction:

I saw the Duke's carriage drive up! and out jumped May! and rushed up to my room and into my arms!! so radiantly happy one could not but be glad! P[rincess] M[ary Adelaide] had remained down in my drawing-room because of her knee, so we ran down to her and found Dolly there too, and had *grandes embrassades* and excitement and exhilaration! then they told me all the story of how it all took place at Luton, and how it has woken him up! and how bright and radiant he is and not at all shy!!

Nor does Lady Geraldine's evidence stand alone. Other witnesses confirm that Prince Eddy's feelings had once more undergone a windmill revolution, and that, having at last taken a really irrevocable decision about his future, he was blissfully contented with the result. It seems probable that Princess May had infected him with her high spirits, which were, just then, much to the fore. At Luton Hoo, on the evening of Prince Eddy's proposal, he and Princess May had, in her words, 'flitted about . . . in suppressed excitement', and, when she announced her engagement to the other girls staying in the house—who included Lord Bath's daughter Lady Catherine Thynne, Lord Alington's fiancée, Miss Leigh, and the young newly married Lady Clementine Walsh—Princess May had picked up her skirts and waltzed round and round her bedroom. It was in this euphoric mood that she had returned to London and in this mood that she now went rushing about the capital with her future bridegroom.

Princess May and Prince Eddy drove out in London incognito in the Prince of Wales's private hansom, went to hear *Cavalleria Rusticana* at the Shaftesbury Theatre, to the Court Theatre to see *The Pantomime Rehearsal*, and to 'modern Venice' at Olympia, where they floated in a gondola around a replica of part of the Grand Canal. They also

of Orleans would have been out of this country when the Clarence engagement was officially announced. This was what the Prince of Wales had kindly intended. The newspapers were (according to Lady Geraldine Somerset) 'twaddling and *asinine* over this desperate love match [Princess May's engagement] and attachment of years triumphing over all obstacles!— columns of *rot*. How Princess Hélène must laugh in her sleeve as she reads of this long devotion! and P. Alix of Hesse too.'[1]

began to choose wallpapers for the rooms at St James's Palace which had been those of the old Duchess of Cambridge and were now to be allotted to the young couple by the Queen. On 19 December Prince Eddy came to stay for two days at White Lodge, and in the week before this Princess May, Prince Eddy and the Teck parents had all been at Windsor as the guests of the Queen, who took the engaged couple into the Mausoleum to seek the posthumous blessing of the Prince Consort.

When Princess May had left Windsor after this visit, she received a letter from the Queen, part of which read:

I had no opportunity to speak to you alone, Darling Child, but I hope to do so when you come with Mama to Osborne. In the meantime let me however say *how much* I rejoice at your becoming My Grandchild & how much confidence I have in you, to fill worthily the important position to which you are called by your marriage with Eddy.

Marriage is the *most* important step which can be taken & should not be looked upon lightly or as *all roses*. The trials in life in fact *begin* with marriage, & no one should forget that it is only by mutually giving way to one another, & by mutual respect & confidence as well as love—that true happiness can be obtained.—Dear Eddy is a dear, good boy. . . .3

The Prince and Princess of Wales had both welcomed their future daughter-in-law with open arms. Each had written her a warm and charming letter to Luton Hoo, and in London she was now constantly in and out of Marlborough House. 'Lunched at Marlborough House—Then Eddy & I saw the Lord Mayor. Then I saw dear Georgie looking thin but well*—Toria & Harry were shut up in their rooms with fearful colds.'4

Apart from Lady Geraldine Somerset there was another person in London who was almost equally displeased by the Clarence engagement. This was Prince Eddy's Aunt Helena, Queen Victoria's third daughter and, since 1866, Princess Christian of Schleswig-Holstein. 'Poor dear Lenchen' had two daughters, Princess Marie Louise who had been married, in July of this very year, 1891, to Prince Aribert of Anhalt (whom she subsequently found it necessary to divorce) and Princess Helena Victoria, known to the members of her family as 'Tora'. To Princess Christian it had seemed very odd that neither of these girls should have been selected by Prince Eddy as his bride. 'Lenchen', wrote Queen Victoria on 16 December 1891:

* Prince George was convalescing from typhoid fever.

. . . is not at all pleased at May's Engagt. to Eddy, & does *not* unfortunately keep it to herself—& was (to my horror) positively rude to Mary & May at Marlborough House when we went there on Monday 7th & both Mary & Alix were distressed at it (it made me so hot) & she has been imprudent enough to speak to other people abt. it. *I cant* understand *it.* Louise [Princess Louise, Duchess of Argyll] also does not much like it, tho' she admits May is a vy nice girl & L. was quite kind & civil.—But both sisters are *jealous* of Mary's popularity. May will I am *sure* be a very nice Niece & cousin. . . . I have asked Angeli to come over to paint her, for she is a vy pretty girl,—*very* sensible & well informed, a *solid girl* wh. we want. . . .5

The Queen wrote from Osborne to Princess Mary Adelaide on 30 December:

I am glad to say H[elena] speaks most affectionately of dear May, & Eddy —& that the little cloud at M. House—was a little inexplicable *moment d'humeur* wh. I hope you will quite dismiss from your mind & forget. Do write to her in her present great trial for it soothes her to receive sympathy (& she has received a great deal).6

Princess Helena's 'great trial', just then, was a most unfortunate accident caused by the Duke of Connaught, who had inadvertently shot his brother-in-law Prince Christian of Schleswig-Holstein through one eye, which had to be removed under chloroform.

Another aunt of Prince Eddy's, the Empress Frederick, who, as we know, had also hoped to see one of her daughters transformed into Duchess of Clarence and Avondale, wrote an entirely characteristic letter to her mother the Queen:

My beloved Mama, Let me offer you most sincere & heartfelt congratulations on dear Eddy's engagement—which is, I am sure—what you, & Bertie & Alix wished! I saw lately in the newspapers how often Eddy, & May had met, so I was almost certain—the engagement was imminent! . . . Mary is indeed a lucky person,—the *one wish* of her heart has been fulfilled for her child, and I am sure she is supremely happy. May the dear young people— enjoy every blessing & happiness this Life can afford. I am indeed glad that Eddy *is* engaged & will have a home of his own, & that his future wife is not *too* young.7

So much for Prince Albert Victor's royal aunts and their reactions to his engagement. Of Princess May's three aunts, the most vocal was, as we might expect, her Aunt Augusta Strelitz.

II

The Grand Duchess of Mecklenburg-Strelitz had been taken unawares by the announcement. She was at that time heavily involved in superintending the rehearsals of Mascagni's *Cavalleria Rusticana** in the opera house at Neu Strelitz, and after the first public performance had been given that December, she wrote proudly that she had 'led the music' from her box 'as singers & musicians looked towards me'. The Duchess of Teck's triumphant telegram informing her sister of the engagement interrupted these musical preoccupations:

My heart is so full I don't know where to begin! [she wrote off to Princess Mary Adelaide] No! my astonishment! all seemed quite vague, the little I had heard about it and then arrives your telegram! I went flop down on a chair, could only tel: 'flabbergasted' and my blessing! rather a contrast, but really, I was speechless. . . . I would *telegraph* myself to the White Lodge, so as to hear it all, was it premeditated going to Luton Hoo, or came it on there by chance? and do they care for each other? It is an immense position and has ever been your hearts desire, but it is a serious, great undertaking for poor May, and to fill a Queen of England's position in present times, a serious matter; she is such a dear, sensible and well endowed creature. . . . God grant he may become worthy of her. . . . What *will* you do without May? hang yourself upon one of the fine Oak trees I suppose! . . . Oh! how dear Mama would have rejoiced . . ! to me it all is like a dream, having been out of it all! but *how* did it come on? '*je m'y perds*'. . . . What does poor Franz say? does he *cry* or *swear*?!! perhaps both! I hope it won't be too much for his head. . . . and Geraldine—*what will she say?!!!*[8]

To Queen Victoria, who had had *Cavalleria Rusticana* performed at Windsor, and who liked the music so much that she would wander about humming the 'wonderfully descriptive and plaintive' airs to herself,[9] the Grand Duchess also wrote, partly to thank for a photograph of the Windsor Castle performance of the opera which the Queen, not to be outdone by Strelitz, had sent her, partly to congratulate her on her grandson's engagement. 'I never was more astounded than when Mary's telegram arrived!' she wrote to the Queen, 'I had not been in the secret, *perhaps* because when people spoke of *it* and Mary seemed anxious for it, I always admonished her, not to think of it, thinking it never would be, therefore not wishing

* Mascagni's opera *Cavalleria Rusticana* had first been performed in Rome in May 1890; its first performance in London was at the Shaftesbury Theatre on 19 October 1891.

to encourage, even in thought, what would only raise the dear child's hopes—*if* she had any—and lead to nothing.'[10]

The Grand Duchess had just been to Remplin to attend the wedding of a Prince of Anhalt. Whilst there, she had met Kaiser Wilhelm II. On her return she wrote a long letter to her brother the Duke of Cambridge:

Just before going to Remplin I got your letter, so doubly welcome, as it gave me the first details of May's Engagement and tranquillized me, as to its being a real *'mariage d'inclination'* which till then, I had not been aware of. Well! what shall I begin by saying? that I truly rejoice at the dear child's happiness and the bright prospect of a brilliant grand future, and yet, what *may* that future be, in *our* times . . . has she the *health*, the feeling of *importance* as to her future position, as *all* will devolve upon her, will be demanded of her. . . .

Young William II said 'I am very glad, May is the wife for Eddy, I am so glad for Aunt Mary too' this was nice of him. . . . I was amused at those German *Princilians*, who had turned up their noses at the prospect of a marriage with May, now she has drawn the *first* prize, pulling sweet faces, especially when the Emp. approved so highly! Well it *is* extraordinary, according to ancient views, but it is a *blessing* the Nation wishing it, the Sovereign approving and the young people being happy! so we are so too! I hear it is to be in February already! good gracious, what a cold journey I shall have. Fritz pulls a long face, but of course, we are coming.[11]

The wedding day had been fixed for 27 February, since both the Tecks and the Waleses wished it to take place before Lent. In any case, Queen Victoria disapproved of long engagements as 'very trying & not very good': she also disliked weddings in principle—'I *hate* weddings', she wrote in 1887. 'They are melancholy things and cause the happiest beings such trials with them, bad health &c &c.'[12]

Meanwhile White Lodge had become a scene of hectic activity. 'Oh! dearest Aunt', wrote Princess May, 'how people do bother, we get trousseau things sent us on approval from all parts of England, Scotland & Ireland so that we are nearly driven mad & have not a moments peace. Then Papa gets flurried & annoyed so that I pity poor Mama with all my heart.'[13]

The Duke of Teck was, of course, enchanted at his daughter's prospects; yet even in the midst of the rejoicing he felt left out or, rather, elbowed aside. 'How well the Queen *worded* her *consent* given in Council. "Pss Victoria Mary, Daughter of H R H The Pss Mary Ad. *and* of H H Duke of Teck" quite as it is *correct*,' wrote the Grand

Duchess of Mecklenburg-Strelitz, '*thus* proving May's *descent* from a *Royal* Mother; *brave Queen!* and just what *May truly is*, according to English notions.'¹⁴ Even this moment of triumph was darkened for the Duke of Teck by the stain of morganatic blood.

The new King of Württemberg, William II (the son of Princess Catharine of the Villa Seefeld) could not come to London for the wedding, since he was still in mourning for his predecessor King Carl I, who had died in October. Princess Claudine of Teck refused to leave her Schweizerhaus at Reinthal to travel across the length of Europe in mid-winter. It rather looked as if there might be no representative of the Württemberg family at the marriage at all. Queen Victoria suggested that 'Duke William [of Württemberg] . . . who is a distinguished Officer in the Austrian Army, & generally lives at Graz' should be invited, for 'It wld *never* do to have *no one* to represent *May's father's family* & wld be *contrary to any precedent*'.¹⁵

These were only minute clouds on the White Lodge horizon. Christmas 1891 brought its own additional gaiety to the happy scene at White Lodge. At nearby Sheen, the Fifes gave a little dance on 26 December. 'We danced to a most lovely Viennese band which played several things out of the lovely "*Cavalleria Rusticana*",' Princess May wrote to Strelitz. 'It was a most charming little fête & we all thoroughly enjoyed ourselves—. . . . Our wedding is fixed for Feby 27th at Windsor & afterwards we are to drive thro' the principal streets of London on our way to St Pancras to Sandringham for the honeymoon.'¹⁶

'Goodbye to 1891, a most eventful year to me', Princess May wrote on the last page of her Diary, at White Lodge. On 4 January 1892, Princess May and her parents travelled down to Sandringham House with the Prince of Wales, the Duke of Cambridge, Prince Eddy and a numerous suite. The Prince of Wales and Prince Albert Victor had been to London to attend the funeral of Prince Victor of Hohenlohe-Langenburg, whose mother had been Queen Victoria's half-sister Princess Feodora of Leiningen. It was wintry, gusty weather, and at this funeral Prince Eddy had caught a little cold in the head. When they reached Sandringham, they found that Princess Victoria of Wales was ill. 'Poor Toria is seedy, sent to bed', her brother Prince George noted in his Diary. 'I think it is Influenza.'¹⁷

III

Sandringham House stands in the flat Norfolk countryside amidst well-kept lawns and shrubberies. It is not far from the old, grey market town of King's Lynn, and within easy distance of the sea-shore, where the waves of the German Ocean beat against the eastern coast of England. It had been bought at the Prince Consort's direction as a private property for his eldest son, after several beautiful and historic English houses had been discussed, inspected and rejected. One of its chief advantages, in the Prince Consort's eyes, was that it was very inaccessible, quite remote from any racing or gambling set, and surrounded by highly respectable country-houses like Houghton and Holkham, inhabited by highly respectable old-established aristo-cratic families; for the Prince Consort subscribed to that school of thought which believes that the pleasure-loving tendencies of such a character as Albert Edward, Prince of Wales, can be thwarted by environment. He did not live long enough to see this theory disproved.

The original house at Sandringham had belonged to Lady Harriet d'Orsay, Lord Blessington's heiress daughter whom Lady Blessington had married off to her own lover. It was a modest place, with no architectural merit. This old house had been burned almost to the ground in 1870, and the Prince of Wales had then constructed a strange long mansion of harsh orange brick and white stone, to which, as the years went by, he was always adding new rooms for guests. The grounds about the house, full of dells and pretty eminences, and the lake beneath the stone terrace, are the only fine features of Sandring-ham, for the house itself, built and designed in one of the worst periods of English taste, resembles a golf-hotel at St Andrews or a station-hotel at Strathpeffer.

In 1891 the inside of Sandringham House was dark and crowded with furniture, and with the knick-knacks which the Princess of Wales loved. The pictures consisted almost entirely of portraits of the Princess and her three daughters—by Hughes, by Luke Fildes, by Angeli—and these added to the general atmosphere of a mutual admiration society in which (as Mr John Gore has pointed out in his *Life of King George V*) the Wales family lived. In summer-time, and even in October, Sandringham was pleasant because of its garden. In the winter it was exposed, depressing and unrelievedly ugly.

The Sandringham estate was beautifully run, the farms, plantations, hedges and fences being kept in perfect condition, although the real purpose of it all was to provide sufficient quantities of game for the mammoth shooting-parties and gargantuan *battues* which the Prince of Wales liked. The tenants complained bitterly of the preservation of game for these shoots, since this ruined their crops. The nicest aspect of Sandringham in winter was the evening skating parties on the lake before the house, 'the lake and island illuminated with coloured lamps and torches, the skating chairs with glow-worm lights, and the skaters flitting past and disappearing in the darkness'.[18] Hot negus was handed out to the skaters from a tent upon the lawn. A hard winter also gave the Wales family occasions to indulge in their favourite pastime of practical jokes, when house-guests would be tripped up and rolled in the snow, or made to serve as cockshies for snowballing. Inside the house practical jokes were equally the order of the day, the Prince of Wales himself superintending the construction of 'apple-pie beds', or stuffing the pockets of some guest's evening clothes with sticky sweets—'pear-drops' and 'bull's eyes'. The Waleses would also sometimes fill their bicycle pumps with water and squirt each other and their guests with these. At dinner the Royal ladies always wore their diamonds and their tiaras, the men their Orders. In its combination of Court etiquette and conviviality the Sandringham atmosphere was, in its own way, unique.

This January of 1892 was a particularly bad one. In London a thick, yellow fog had descended at Christmas and had lasted into the New Year. The lake at Sandringham was frozen hard, and lively games of ice-hockey were in progress on it. The family party assembled to celebrate Prince Eddy's twenty-eighth birthday, which occurred on 8 January, was decimated by illness: Princess Victoria's influenza had spread to Albert Mensdorff, to the Prince of Wales's secretary, Sir Francis Knollys, to Stephenson, another member of the Household, and to Captain Holford, equerry to Prince Eddy. The Princess of Wales and Princess May were both suffering from bad colds. Prince George was still in a weak state after his recent dangerous attack of typhoid fever. What should have been a merry gathering was fast becoming sad and invalidish.

On 7 January, the day before his birthday, Prince Eddy felt unwell while out shooting. The ladies went to lunch with the shooters at Sir Dighton Probyn's house. After this meal was over Princess May persuaded Prince Eddy to walk back with her to the house, where Prince George took his brother's temperature and sent him up to bed. Princess May went and sat with Prince Eddy in his small bedroom, off a sombre corridor beyond the main staircase well. This narrow and claustrophobic little room has a bay window and a very high ceiling, and is next door to a room used by Prince Eddy and his brother as their study. So restricted is the space in this room, that Prince Eddy, lying in bed by the window, could stretch out his arm and touch the mantelpiece with his hand.

On the next day, a Friday and Prince Eddy's birthday, it was realised that he, too, had caught the influenza. 'Froze hard in the night & a little snow fell', Prince George wrote in his Diary. 'Answering telegrams for Eddy & writing letters all day.'[19] Princess May was helping, too, for she was already assuming in Prince Eddy's life the practical role she had long played in that of her mother. The Prince of Wales was always asking her to 'keep Eddy up to the mark', 'see that Eddy does this, May' or 'May, please do see that Eddy does that'. In London, in the first weeks of her engagement, Princess May's courage had begun to falter, for she was beginning dimly to realise the dimensions of her task. She had gone to her mother and said: 'Do you think I can *really* take this on, Mama?' 'Of course you can, May', Princess Mary Adelaide had sturdily replied. Had she not herself 'taken on' the Duke of Teck?

On the morning of his birthday, Prince Eddy managed to walk slowly downstairs to look at his presents. He returned to his room, unable to attend his birthday dinner, which was followed by an entertainment given by a ventriloquist and a banjo-player, and at which Uncle Teck proposed Prince Eddy's health. There was still no sense of danger, still less of impending calamity, amongst the inmates of Sandringham House. Everybody one knew had had the influenza that winter; and ill-health, in some form or other, may almost be said to have formed an integral part of the younger Waleses' design for living. Prince Eddy's family and their guests were now all taking daily doses of quinine, as a precautionary measure. 'Thanks so much for kind wishes', the Princess of Wales telegraphed to the Queen, who was at Osborne, and engaged in supervising rehearsals for a series of *tableaux vivants*: 'Poor Eddy got influenza, cannot dine, so tiresome.'[20]

On the 9th of January Prince Eddy developed inflammation of the lungs, and Dr Laking* was sent for to assist the local West Newton

* Dr Francis Laking (1847–1914), afterwards made a Baronet, was at this time Physician-in-Ordinary and Surgeon-Apothecary to the Prince of Wales. Dr W. H. Broadbent, who was subsequently knighted, had attended Prince George of Wales during his attack of typhoid fever some weeks previously.

doctor, Manby. Dr Laking diagnosed incipient pneumonia as well as influenza and telegraphed for Dr Broadbent, who reached Sandringham on the 10th. On the 11th the patient was 'going on very satisfactorily', his head was clear, his spirits good, he could speak to Princess May and Prince George, who were only allowed to peer at him over the top of the screen round his bed. On the morning of 12 January Prince Eddy was 'rather worse'. On the 13th he was delirious, shouting at 'the top of his voice' about his Regiment, his horses and his brother-officers, talking wildly of Lord Salisbury and Lord Randolph Churchill, and of how much he loved his grandmother, the Queen. His wandering mind flitted, also, around his life's various romances, and he frequently cried out 'Hélène! Hélène!' His fingernails turned blue and his lips were livid. The physicians feared the worst.

Prince Eddy's horrified parents, brother and sisters, were meanwhile congregated in the small sitting-room next to his bedroom. With them were the Duke and Duchess of Teck, and Princess May. His mother went often to sit by her son's bed, fanning him, stroking his hair and his temples, and wiping the sweat from his brow.

In the very early morning of 14 January, Prince Eddy's death-struggle commenced. It lasted six hours. Mr Hervey, the Prince of Wales's domestic chaplain, stood reading the prayers for the dying. At the head of the bed sat the Princess of Wales, holding her dying son's hand, and smiling at him bravely. Next to her was Princess Victoria, and then, sharing a chair together, were Princess Maud and Princess May. Behind these were the Duke and Duchess of Fife, the Prince of Wales and the Duchess of Teck. Dr Laking was kneeling, watching Prince Eddy's pulse. Prince George knelt at the other side of the bed, with a nurse and Dr Manby beside him. At the foot of the bed were another nurse, Sister Victoria, the Duke of Teck and Dr Broadbent. At nine-thirty-five on that morning of 14 January 1891 all was over. Prince Albert Victor, Duke of Clarence and Avondale, heir-presumptive to the throne of England, lay dead.

IV

The sudden death of the Duke of Clarence struck England like a thunderbolt. The awful speed of the tragedy, its constitutional implications, the way in which it trod upon the heels of the young Prince's engagement, created a stupendous sensation in the public mind. The Duke of Clarence had had little chance to become a popular figure, but the widespread grief was none the less genuine for that. 'It would be sycophancy to say that the hapless young Prince, who breathed his last this morning, was regarded with enthusiastic devotion or intense personal regard by the majority of those over whom he might have lived to reign if the Fates had been kinder', wrote the *St James's Gazette*. 'His unassuming, retired life had so far afforded little opportunity for such sentiments. . . . The Duke of Clarence may be said to have lived under the shadow of the shadow of the throne.'[21] All the same his illness and his death became a nine days' wonder in London, where the newsboys were screeching the tidings even as the great bell of Westminster Abbey commenced to toll solemnly out upon the frosty January air. Soon every church bell in the metropolis was tolling also. The shop-keepers put up their shutters. In the windows of private houses blinds were drawn down. The omnibuses that morning carried black flags, and on the whips of cab-drivers pieces of black riband flapped.

As in London, so it was throughout the country. Telegrams and letters of sympathy inundated Sandringham House and Osborne. In Norfolk and Suffolk this striking tragedy was felt especially deeply, for the country people of East Anglia prided themselves on having the Prince of Wales and his family upon their soil. The death of Prince Albert Victor, and the misery of Princess May of Teck, passed quickly into folk-lore, and for many years a ballad on the subject was circulated and sung, to the tune of *God Bless the Prince of Wales*, at East Anglian village gatherings and in the village pubs:

> Alas his soul it has departed,
>   How solemn came the news,
> His parents broken hearted,
>   Their darling son to lose.
> With sympathy and feeling,
>   We one and all should say,
> God rest his soul in silence,
>   And bless the Princess May!
>
> With love and true devotion,
>   They watched by his bed side,
> But all was gloom and sadness,
>   The moment that he died,

He closed his eyes for ever,
They kissed his pallid cheek,
In breathless tones his mother said,
O speak, my darling speak!

There were, in all, five verses to this ballad, and after each verse a chorus was sung:

A nation wrapped in mourning,
Shed bitter tears today,
For the noble Duke of Clarence,
And fair young Princess May.

The bereaved, desolate and romantic figure of Princess May of Teck, dressed in deepest mourning, became the symbol and the centre of a nation's grief.

v

'This is an overwhelming misfortune!' Queen Victoria minuted to her Private Secretary Sir Henry Ponsonby on 14 January, at Osborne House. 'One is too much stunned to take it in as yet! A tragedy too dreadful for words. . . . The poor Parents it is *too dreadful* for them to think of! & the poor young Bride! The Queens impulse yesterday was to go to Sandringham but Dr Reid & all—said she must not run the risk of cold & fatigue &c.'[22] The Prince of Wales also had begged his mother, by telegraph, not to journey down to Sandringham, which the Queen, with her natural spontaneous kindness, had urgently wished to do.

On the same day the Duchess of Teck, at Sandringham, wrote to her cousin the Queen:

My *aching, broken* heart's warmest deepest sympathy goes out to you. . . . The *shade* of improvement [on 11 January] was alas! too slight to build upon . . . tho' I *clung to hope even through the* terrible watch of that awful *never to be forgotten night* of agony—It wrung one's heart to *hear Him*, & to see Alix's wretched, imploring, face, Bertie's bowed head & poor May's *dazed misery*. It seemed *too much, too hard* to bear! & *for one moment* my strong faith seemed to waver, but now I am *calmer*, I am trying to say in all truth & submission: 'Thy will be done!' . . .

All today telegrams have been *pouring in* & I have been much with darling Alix & the dearest girls & *angelic* George who is a *tower* of strength to us all! and in *His* room (where he lies amid flowers, chiefly *Maiblumen*—

H

Her flower *now* being *woven* for the wedding train!—like a noble young Knight at rest, after the cruel battle with death!) ... All yesterday & till this afternoon, He looked too beautiful for words & his doating Mother & poor May could not tear themselves away—They have just 11 oclock borne him to the church. ... Bertie & Alix kindly wished to keep us on, united as we all are in a common sorrow—Our presence seems a comfort to them!—Of their kindness to our May, I cannot say enough. They have quite adopted her as their daughter & she calls Alix 'Motherdear'—& hopes you will allow her to call you 'Grandmamma'? These privileges & *two rings* are all that remain to her, poor Child! of her bright dream of happiness.[23]

Princess May also wrote to Queen Victoria:

... How too dear & touching of you in the midst of your sorrow to write to poor little me. ... Never shall I forget that dreadful night of agony and suspense as we sat round His bed watching Him getting weaker & weaker. Darling Aunt Alix never left Him a moment and when a few minutes before the end she turned to Dr Laking & said 'Can you do nothing more to save Him' & he shook his head, the despairing look on her face was the most heart-rending thing I have ever seen. ... I shall always look back with gratitude to your great kindness to darling Eddy and me at Windsor last month. It seems years ago. ... [24]

In a long letter written four weeks later to Emily Alcock, Princess May described the death-scene, adding:

How we all *lived* thro' it all I don't know, but God gave us wonderful strength to bear up for each other's sakes, & so far we are fairly well tho' the fearful heartache still remains & must do so for a long long time. For his beloved Mother it is simply too dreadful, but she is so patient so resigned, & that very 14th she said to me 'After all it makes one more link with heaven'. ... What a blessing & comfort religion is to one at such a moment of intense pain, what should we do without faith?[25]

The Duke of Clarence's body was taken from Sandringham Church to Windsor, and there, on 20 January 1892, his funeral took place. The 'most touching moment' was that in which the Duke of Teck handed the Prince of Wales Princess May's bridal wreath of orange-blossom, which was then laid upon the coffin.

Alfred Gilbert, a pupil of Boehm and a friend of Princess Louise, Duchess of Argyll, was commissioned to design and execute the funeral monument of Prince Albert Victor. This grandiose conception —which included a recumbent figure with a head of Mexican onyx* lying on a high table tomb surrounded by ivory weepers—was never,

* See plate 11.

owing to Gilbert's dilatory habits and disorderly life, completed. 'Dear Eddy's Sarcophagus is put up in the "Wolsey Chapel" and looks very fine though the figure is not yet on it!' the Empress Frederick wrote to her daughter Princess Margaret in March 1893. 'I wish Fischy could see it! Mr Gilbert—is one of the best artists living *so* full of *taste*— refined feeling & *such* a *knowledge* of art! It is *his* work.'[26]

On the day of Prince Eddy's funeral a memorial service was held in Neu Strelitz, and attended by the Grand Ducal family. All the blinds in the little North German town were drawn over the windows. 'I dare hardly think of the poor child', wrote the Grand Duchess to her brother, of Princess May, 'and yet I do nothing but think of her, feel for her, cry & sigh! And poor Mary! *after all*, to come to *this!* no! it is too distressing. My heart prompted me at once to set off and go to the sorrowing ones, but alas! my back is so bad still, I dared not go (I cannot bear the motion of a Carriage). . . . And what will happen about the Trousseau! who will pay for it and for all the expenses incurred? this is a very serious consideration . . . it is hard enough to lose poor Eddy but to be still more ruined, cannot be expected!' 'I can do nothing yet but read or write letters of condolence', the Grand Duchess wrote again a few days later, 'and read the long accounts in the Papers, that make me cry; I have hardly an eye left from this continuous weeping!'[27]

All over Europe the family tragedy at Sandringham House had made a deep impression. 'At Sousa I saw in a little weekly paper published there on Sundays, called *l'Avenir de Sousa*, the news of the Duke of Clarence's death', wrote Lord Ronald Gower in his Diary for January 1892. 'How quickly the orange blossom has been changed for the cypress spray!'[28]

In a numbed mood, and without hope, Princess May returned with her parents to White Lodge on 22 January 1892—'a sad home coming for me, such a contrast to my happy return from Luton'.[29] 'It is so difficult to begin one's old life again after such a shock,' she wrote to Miss Alcock, 'even reading, of which I am so fond, is a trouble to me & I cannot settle down to anything—As for writing I simply *cannot* write— . . . for it is so dreadful to have to open the wound afresh.'[30]

CHAPTER TEN

THE CYPRESS SPRAY

THE EVENING of the day on which Prince Eddy's funeral was solemnised was 'piercing cold'. Princess May, her parents and her brothers returned in this weather to White Lodge. It was one of a series of many dreary, melancholy evenings to come. The shocking sight of Prince Eddy's death—the first that she had ever witnessed—haunted Princess May. Everything had been given to her, only to be snatched away again. Life looked colourless and empty. Resignation to the will of God was the keynote of most of the letters she received, but this was not so easy to attain. She sent an urgent little note to 'dearest Hélène' Bricka, who was in London: 'Please come tomorrow by the usual train and bring yr things with you so that you can stay here—I saw yr lovely anchor in the chapel at Windsor, my loving thanks to you for sending it. I have so much to talk to you about, Yr loving miserable May.'[1]

In the second week of February the Duke and Duchess of Teck and Princess May were asked to come to Osborne by the Queen. They travelled down to Portsmouth by train, were met by the Duke and Duchess of Connaught—'Uncle Arthur' and 'Aunt Louisechen'*— and crossed the Solent to the Isle of Wight in the Royal Yacht *Alberta*. Princess May had only once been to Osborne, and then as a baby; she now liked the large, white airy house with its great sheet-glass windows looking out to sea, its dining-room decorated with Winter-halter portraits, its pungent and beautiful arboretum, and the newly completed Indian wing. Princess May planted a tree in the garden, was driven to Carisbrooke Castle and Norris Castle, and was shown over the little Swiss Cottage, crammed with curios. She saw much of the Queen.

'The dear girl looks like a crushed flower, but is resigned & quiet & gentle,—it *does* make one *so sad* for her', the Queen wrote. 'She is grown thinner, but otherwise is *not* looking ill. Mary has still her

* See note on p. 62.

wonderful elasticity of spirits but is much grieved & talks a gt deal about it all & has given me every possible detail. They are *most sad.*'² Princess Mary Adelaide's nature was, as we know, buoyant and optimistic. She was also a very religious woman, and she felt that nothing that happened in life could be without some Divine purpose. 'God is so loving and merciful', she wrote to the Empress Frederick about this time, 'one feels there must be a *silver lining* to the dark cloud, albeit our tear dimmed eyes cannot distinguish it.'³ This was, of course, a perfectly sincere sentiment; yet already Princess Mary Adelaide had perceived a thin silver thread of hope. Nor was Princess Mary Adelaide alone in this. The Queen, the Princess of Wales, and the whole of England had had the same idea. To understand this idea fully, we must momentarily reflect upon the constitutional effects of the Duke of Clarence's sudden death.

The death before marriage of the heir-presumptive, Prince Albert Victor, meant that the throne of England must ultimately descend to his only brother, Prince George, who was twenty-six years old and unmarried. Prince George was still recovering from a dangerous attack of typhoid fever which had laid him low in the autumn of 1891, and had brought his mother racing back across Europe from Livadia (where she had been staying in one of the Imperial Russian palaces on the Black Sea); for it had seemed at one time that Prince George might die. He was now convalescent, a thin, pale youth. His nerves were shattered by his brother's death, and he was suffering from insomnia. Should any tragedy remove Prince George from the scene—and, after Prince Albert Victor's death, who knew what fresh disaster might not bludgeon the English Royal House?—his eldest sister, Princess Louise, would become heiress-presumptive. Princess Louise was highly-strung but also apathetic. She was, moreover, married to a subject, the Duke of Fife, and she had at this time only one child, a daughter. For these reasons it was not considered that she would make a really suitable Queen Regnant. Hence it had now become vital for Prince George to marry and have a family.

'One wishes with all one's heart, that one could see Georgie & Ernie,* *suitably* & happily married, but that will be *very* difficult!

---

* 'Ernie' was the family name for Ernest Louis, Prince of Hesse and by the Rhine (1868–1937; Grand Duke 1892, abdicated 1918), eldest son of Queen Victoria's third child and second daughter Alice, Princess of Great Britain and Ireland (1843–1878), who had married Louis IV, Grand Duke of Hesse and by the Rhine (1837–1892), in 1862. The Grand Duke Ernest married firstly Victoria

So much has to be considered,—& who can guess what their tastes may be', the Empress Frederick wrote to her mother in March of this year 1892, '—& whether young Ladies will be forthcoming who return what ever feelings *they* may have! I am sure all this *preoccupies you*, & it does a great many people both in England and at Darmstadt.'⁴ All this certainly did preoccupy Queen Victoria, but she was not trying to 'guess' what young ladies might be 'forthcoming'. In her distinct opinion the young lady for Prince George was already found. Prince George must marry Princess May.

During the dreadful scenes of that January week at Sandringham the Duke of Teck, who was exceedingly distraught, had embarrassed his own family by wandering about the house of death repeating a single sentence over and over again: 'It must be a Tsarevitch, it must be a Tsarevitch.' What was the meaning of this strange and most unwelcome chant? It was this: Alexandra, Princess of Wales, had two younger sisters, Princess Dagmar and Princess Thyra. In 1865 Princess Dagmar of Denmark had been engaged to the heir to the throne of Russia, the Tsarevitch Nicholas, who had, however, died before their marriage, leaving Princess Dagmar in 1865 in exactly the same position as that of Princess May twenty-seven years later: 'instead of being Empress of Russia', wrote Lord Clarendon at the time, '[Princess Dagmar] is simply *une demoiselle à marier—such is life* as the young ladies say'⁵. In the year following the Tsarevitch Nicholas's death, 1866, Princess Dagmar of Denmark had married his brother, Alexander, who was the new Tsarevitch. The marriage had been perfectly successful; Princess Dagmar was now the Empress Marie Feodorovna, and the mother of six children. The Empress and her sister, the Princess of Wales, were bound to each other by those ties of intimate affection which distinguished the Danish royal family. The Princess of Wales had seen nothing unnatural in her sister's acceptance of the younger brother. To a German relative who had come over for the funeral of Prince Albert Victor, Queen Victoria remarked that 'the present Empress of Russia married the next brother and it is a most happy marriage'.⁶ 'From London I hear *all* from the Queen downwards, are resolved P[rince] George shall marry May!' Lady Geraldine Somerset wrote in her Diary, 'all, except P[rince] George!'⁷ Had Lady Geraldine been acquainted with the facts of the

Melita, a daughter of the Duke of Edinburgh and his Russian Duchess in 1894, and, after a divorce in 1901, he married as his second wife Eleonore, Princess of Solms-Hohensolms-Lich in 1905.

situation, instead of relying, as was usual with her, upon idle gossip, she would also have added: 'All, except Princess May.'

This highly delicate subject was, obviously, never mentioned to Princess May at this period, nor was it apparently discussed between the Wales and Teck parents. But Princess May was no fool. She was affronted and embarrassed by the idea, and her parents found that when, in March 1892, they took her abroad to recuperate from her sorrow, she refused to go back to England when they wished to do so. Princess May was, in fact, being pushed into one of the most embarrassing positions one can well imagine for a sensitive girl. Her resistance did not discourage any of her relations. They knew her to be dutiful and patriotic. They also knew that she had always liked her cousin, Prince George.

After leaving Osborne she returned briefly to the routine life of White Lodge. Late in February her father took her down to Eastbourne, and deposited her at Compton Place, a house belonging to the Duke of Devonshire, who had now lent it to the Prince and Princess of Wales. This visit to the Waleses was timed to cover the day on which Princess May should have been married to Prince Eddy, 27 February.

The family at Compton Place were very wretched. The Prince of Wales looked aged and worn. The Princess of Wales was exquisite in her mourning: a black coif edged with white on her head by day, a black veil hanging down her back in the evening, she moved about the house with a brave, melancholy smile. The Princess and all her family were enchantingly kind to Princess May: 'May has become the child of the Waleses,' the Duke of Teck wrote to his sisters at Reinthal, 'I foresee that she will be very much taken up with them.'[8] At Eastbourne, Princess May went out with her cousins in a waggonette along the downs. She went shopping with Prince George, and played bezique with him every evening, both before and after dinner. Prince George had loved his brother Eddy dearly, with the protective love of a strong character for a weak one. He liked to talk to Princess May about his 'darling boy', as he called Prince Eddy. For the rest of his life he always wrote his letters with Prince Eddy's pen. Their common desolation was beginning to draw Prince George and Princess May together.

On 27 February, Princess May wrote in her Diary:

Chilly damp day. This day is a very sad one for me for it was to have been our wedding day. '*Es wär' zu schön gewesen, es hat nicht sollen sein.*' ...

Under this entry is another one, written fifty-five years later in Queen
Mary's hand:

I read this diary again in 1947, when I was 80, and felt compelled to add
that the kind 'Uncle Wales' & 'Motherdear' gave me a beautiful *rivière*
of diamonds which they had destined for me as a wedding present, as well
as a lovely dressing bag, which darling Eddy had ordered for me as a
wedding gift. I remember I felt overcome by this kind thought.9

After nine days at Eastbourne, Princess May returned to White
Lodge. 'Mama', she wrote in her Diary, 'was delighted to see me
again.'

II

The Duke of Cambridge had offered to lend his mother's old home,
Kew Cottage, to the Tecks that February, thinking for some not very
apparent reason that this abode would provide them with a salutary
change. Princess Mary Adelaide, who was temperamentally incapable
of remaining downcast for long at a time, had quite another scheme
on foot. She had even found the person to finance it.
     Princess Mary Adelaide had never been to the South of France.
'[The countryside] you write of in such glowing terms is alas! an
unknown region to me', she had written to Mrs John Henry Master,
a Petersham neighbour who was staying in Cannes in 1888, 'tho' I
hope, some day, to feast my eyes upon it, for it must be beautiful
beyond all description.'10 This woeful spring of 1892 seemed an ideal
moment for such feasting of the eyes: 'I am very anxious that May
should have an entire change, and greatly tempted to accept Lady
Wolverton's proposal, that we should go out to the sunny South
with her, to a villa she intends taking somewhere on the Riviera', the
Duchess of Teck wrote to Queen Victoria, in February 1892.11 On
the 24th of the same month she was telling the Empress Frederick
that: 'We hope in about a fortnight to start for the Riviera, on a visit
to dear Lady Wolverton and are all looking forward to sunshine and
flowers.'12
     It seems pernickety to point out that dear Lady Wolverton's
'proposal' had as a matter of hard fact been made at Princess Mary
Adelaide's suggestion. Lady Wolverton was one of the select band of
the Duchess of Teck's wealthy friends who was always ready to help
her over silly, tiresome money matters—like Baroness Burdett-Coutts
in the early days of the Teck marriage, like Mr Peter Wells who had

paid the Tecks' debts in Florence after they had left. Lady Wolverton was perfectly ready to take a villa on the Riviera and to invite her grief-stricken royal friends to live in it with her. Princess Mary Adelaide requested that this villa should be at Mentone. Princess Mary Adelaide had learned, with interest, that the whole Wales family was proceeding to an hotel at Cap Martin, a shady, rocky promontory which juts out into the azure Mediterranean sea some two driving miles from Mentone.

We may recall, from many years earlier, that the Prince of Wales never felt very enthusiastic about his ample cousin, Princess Mary Adelaide. The tragedy at Sandringham had flung them together, but the Prince was now on the rebound and felt that he had possibly seen enough of his cousin for the time being. And was there not something vaguely indiscreet, if not indecent, in the Duchess of Teck planting her daughter thus on the Waleses' doorstep? The Prince of Wales was as determined as everyone else that Prince George must marry Princess May, and he wished them to see much of each other both in the South of France and elsewhere, but he judged it would look better if the Teck and Wolverton contingent was stationed some way off along the coast—say, at Cannes?

The Duke of Cambridge was also keen on his sister's going to Cannes, but for quite another reason: he had been begged to send her there by one of his old flames, Mrs Vyner, who owned a large villa at Cannes, and who wished to increase her local prestige amongst the English colony by being *persona grata* with the Duchess of Teck and with that figure of melancholy public interest, the mourning Princess May. The Duchess of Teck told the Duke of Cambridge that she could not go to Cannes because the Prince and Princess of Wales wanted her to be at Mentone. The Duke of Cambridge thereupon went down post-haste to stay at Eastbourne, where the Prince of Wales asked him three times in one Sunday morning whether he had yet written Princess Mary Adelaide to say that she must at all costs go to Cannes. The Duke returned to London and had 'a long interview' with Lady Wolverton, the upshot of which was that she telegraphed that evening to Mrs Vyner, and set off next day for Cannes to see 'various villas'. To make assurance doubly sure, the Duke of Cambridge himself saw Lady Wolverton into the train for the South.

The Duke of Cambridge thought that his sister 'did not quite like' his intervention; but she was powerless now that Lady Wolverton had been whirled out of reach and was house-hunting in Cannes. On

H*

the 9th of March—'horrible, cold, snowy day', Princess May noted in her Diary—the Duke and Duchess of Teck, Princess May, with Lady Katty Coke, Lady Eva Greville and four domestics, left Victoria Station for Cannes. The Duchess of Teck had a sore throat and was very hoarse. The Duke of Cambridge was at the station to see them go. Lady Wolverton had leased the Villa Clementine for her guests. Here they stayed until the beginning of May.

'Lady Wolverton's villa is charming & very *gemütlich*,' wrote the Duke of Teck, 'the terraced garden is filled with palms, and with orange, and lemon trees overloaded with fruit. All possible sorts of Southern flowering plants.' 'It is a wonderful garden,' he wrote in another letter, 'with terraces, rocks, fountains, marble statues, everything in a grand style.'[13] 'We were most fortunate in the charming Villa dear Lady Wolverton had been able to secure, much the nicest of all I have seen at Cannes for it is fitted up in English taste and with all home comforts', wrote Princess Mary Adelaide to Queen Victoria, 'and as it stands in its own delightful and very extensive garden, rather above and quite out of the town itself, we were quite *pour nous* and able to see as much or as little, as we liked of our friends, and acquaintances! no small advantage truly! . . . I never saw any place in such beauty, for the roses were out *en masse*, covering the walls, hedges and trees especially the olives, from which they *fell* in *clusters*! *une vraie pluie de roses!*'[14] '*Nous voici arrivés en Paradis, du soleil, du ciel bleu, la mer encore plus bleue, des fleurs, des orangers, enfin tout pour charmer les yeux et rendre la vie très agréable—Nous sommes enchantés*', read part of a letter to Madame Bricka from Princess May.[15]

Cannes was very full of English visitors that spring. The Tecks found a multitude of London friends and acquaintances, as well as the Grand Duke and Grand Duchess of Mecklenburg-Schwerin and other German royalties. Princess May's spirits began to revive. In her mother's words she 'lost that sad, *weary* look, her face wore, ever since her and our great sorrow and [she] is more like her old self, taking again an interest in all that goes on around her'.[16] On 24 March Princess May wrote a long and disarming letter to Madame Bricka:

Bien chère Amie [she wrote] . . . Write me one of yr *clever* letters & tell me of anything interesting *qui se passe* in the scientific, thinking world, here I hear too much gossip & one is inclined to sleep, tho' this must *not* happen to me, so I read as much as possible. . . . I moralise a good deal to myself but this doesn't help much—When I see people chaffing each other,

talking in a flighty way, I think of the tragedy of 2 months ago & wonder
'How can they go on like this when there is so much sadness in the world',
quite forgetting that they have not suffered as I have & do suffer—Curious
how thoughtful sorrow makes one—Please don't think by this that I am
always unhappy, only sometimes I feel rather miserable & it does me good
to talk out my feelings to so sympathetic a ear as your's—You know on the
whole I am in much better spirits & can laugh just as I used to do, only
when I am alone I feel the loneliness, some vague dream of something
pleasant having passed out of one's life for ever—I fear I am getting more
reserved than ever, this is a pity, what can I do to prevent it? Darling Alge
I hope will come for his holidays [from Eton], I am longing for one of the
boys, I must say I do like men & here I see nothing but women, women,
women, except Papa & he don't count to talk to—I am indeed a funny
person. Goodbye dearest Hélène Yr fondly devoted '*Chère Adorée*'.[17]

Princess Mary Adelaide's instinct had been justified, for this unexacting, easy life in a southern, flower-decked land, formed a real antidote
to Princess May's experiences that January in England. The Tecks
made many expeditions into the country behind Cannes, and went to
many quiet luncheons at neighbouring villas—the villa of Miss Alice
de Rothschild, for example, or Mrs Vyner's villa, or the Villa
Eléonore, where they found their old Florentine benefactor Peter
Wells, who was the father-in-law of Lord Brougham, to whom the
Villa Eléonore belonged. 'I have enjoyed seeing so many lovely new
places', wrote Princess May. 'Mama is quite happy here. Papa is as
usual rather trying but we are accustomed to this, wherever we are
c'est toujours la même histoire!'[18]

The Prince and Princess of Wales and their family had reached
Cap Martin on 9 March, the very day the Tecks set out from England.
For three weeks they gave their relatives no sign of life; then on
29 March Prince George sent Princess May a little note:

Papa & I are coming over to Cannes towards the end of the week for
a few days (incog.) & so I hope I shall see you then, we hope one day you
will give us a little dinner, we are going to stay at a quiet hotel, only don't
say anything about it. The others will remain here. . . . Goodbye dear 'Miss
May'. . . ever yr very loving old cousin Georgie.[19]

It was, of course, impossible for the Prince of Wales to remain
incognito at Cannes, especially with his yacht the *Nerine* moored in
the harbour, and while he and his son were visiting Princess May
and her parents daily. Their presence at Cannes caused a flurry of
excitement both amongst the English residents and the public back in

England. 'This visit of the P. of W. and Prince George is evidently
looked upon as a feeler, & Prince George seems to have spent every
possible moment at the villa that he could, & often went when his
father was not there',[20] wrote a White Lodge neighbour then staying
in Cannes with her daughter. *Galignani* already predicted an engagement, and the English newspapers meticulously recorded for their
readers every movement, at Cannes, of the Prince of Wales and his
son. 'Your account of Princess May's improved health & spirits
makes it the more probable that the engagement of the young couple
may ere this have been settled', an acquaintance of the Tecks wrote
from England to a friend. 'I am sure it would please the entire English
nation to be assured of it.'[21]

Whenever Princess May appeared in the streets of Cannes she was
mobbed by sympathisers. During the visit of the Prince of Wales and
Prince George she went with them to the flower-market, a scene well
described in a letter from the Duke of Teck to his sister Princess
Amélie:

The flower-market of this place is very pretty and is open until noon—
lilac, carnations, roses, violets and all sorts of flowers from the country.
We have already been there three times, only we can't stay too long, as
people recognise us at once and May becomes the centre of a crowd. Before
we left the market yesterday several women and elderly gentlemen offered
May bouquets of the most wonderful flowers. Most of the men asked May's
permission before offering her these flowers. It was really very touching.
The Prince and Georgy, who accompanied us, were completely enchanted
by this show of well-bred sentiment towards May on the part of perfect
strangers. In the end they had to carry all the flowers to the place where our
carriage was waiting, as I had both my hands full of purchases for the
Princess of Wales.[22]

Later in April the Teck party went to see the Waleses at Cap Martin,
and on 20 April the latter stayed three days in Cannes before moving
on to Hyères.

It had been Princess Mary Adelaide's intention to take Princess May
from Cannes to Neu Strelitz, but the Grand Duchess, who had
extended a warm invitation in February, had now changed her mind.
'Aunt Augusta arrives in London I believe on the 29th', Princess May
wrote to Madame Bricka. 'You see after all she would not arrange her
plans to suit ours so our visit to Strelitz has been given up—Funny,
isn't it? I don't mind but Mama is dreadfully hurt.'[23]

The Duke and Duchess took their daughter to the court of King

William II of Württemberg at Stuttgart instead. They only intended to pay their relations there a short visit, but Princess May did not wish to go back to England. 'The reason why we are always putting off the return to England is the rumour of a new engagement for May', the Duke of Teck explained to his sister. 'We have not spoken to her about it, but it seems she feels frightened by the prospect of an early return home.'[24]

III

Princess May and her parents travelled from Cannes to Stuttgart via Paris, where they spent the night. On this occasion they did not go to the Louvre or to see any exhibitions of paintings. They went instead to see Véry's Restaurant, 'which', Princess May noted in her Diary, 'was blown up by the Anarchists in April.' In common with every other member of a European Royal House, Princess May took a quite professional interest in anarchists. Nor was this interest an academic exercise: for she lived to know of several royal assassinations—in 1898 the Empress of Austria was stabbed to death at Geneva with a file, in 1913 'Uncle Willy of Greece'—otherwise King George of the Hellenes—was also killed. In 1900 the Prince and Princess of Wales were shot at, in Brussels, by the young anarchist Sipido, the bullet lodging in Miss Charlotte Knolly's bun. In 1906 Princess May had herself a narrow escape at the wedding of King Alfonso in Madrid.

After Sipido's attempt the Prince of Wales was always accompanied when abroad by the celebrated detective Melville, while after the Empress of Austria's death in 1898 even quite junior members of a royal family, like Princess Friedrich-Karl of Hesse, were watched by detectives and by the police. 'I *too* for the first time in my Life—have had a detective sent to look after me—here while I am travelling', the Empress wrote from London to her daughter the Princess Friedrich-Karl. 'Why Ladies of royal families should be less safe than usual I do not know—but the assassination of the poor Empress has made the authorities nervous, I suppose.' 'Albert Mensdorff . . . such a nice creature!' the Empress wrote some days later. '. . . heard at Paris— that the anarchists are supposed to have said,—they would not attempt to kill any more crowned heads—as it was too difficult & they were too well guarded but that they would turn their attention to *Princesses*, who were more easy to get at, & promised better success!!!'[25] 'They

now want to get rid of us all; even *I* have received warning letters,'
the Grand Duchess of Mecklenburg-Strelitz wrote in the same year
to her niece, Princess May, 'rather unpleasant and what can one do
against these horrible people?' The Grand Duchess had, in fact, a
definite theory of what one could and should do against anarchists.
'*My* plan', she wrote in August 1900, again to Princess May, 'would
be, to forbid and close all meetings, Associations, and to muzzle the
Press entirely, then, take up every man or woman, expressing
anarchist views, have them flogged daily, and if decided murderers,
have them tortured then blown off from a Gun! *that* is what *I* would
decree! and *you*? do you support me?'[26] Princess May, like the Princess
of Wales, was in favour of lynch-law for active anarchists. Prince
George considered 'hanging or shooting . . . much too good for . . .
an Anarchist, they all ought to be exterminated like wasps'.[27]

Having looked at the ruins of Véry's Restaurant, the Tecks and
their daughter went on to Stuttgart. Princess May had only seen King
William II of Württemberg—her other 'Uncle Willie'—once since
1884 when she had stayed at Bad Horn near Rorschach, before he had
succeeded his uncle, King Carl I, on the Württemberg throne. The
widowed Prince had meanwhile married Princess Charlotte of
Schaumburg-Lippe in 1886. At the time of this second marriage Prince
William was thirty-eight years of age and his bride was twenty-two.
They had produced no children. Prince William had brought his wife
to England in the winter of 1890 and they had, as a matter of course,
gone to White Lodge. 'We liked Charlotte very much, she is a good
honest soul tho' rather too brusque, she seems to get on well with
all the members of the Württemberg family which denotes great
tact', Princess May had written to her Aunt Augusta of this visit.[28]
Although the Empress Frederick called her 'very pleasing', Queen
Charlotte of Württemberg was not thought regal enough for her new
position. 'I heard . . . that she was too jolly & off-hand for a Queen,
and so ugly besides',[29] the Grand Duchess of Mecklenburg-Strelitz
wrote to her niece in May 1892. The Duchess of Teck liked Queen
Charlotte, but thought it sad she took no trouble about her appearance
or her clothes. The Queen's husband, the new King William II, was
a cultivated and distinguished man of aesthetic tastes. He was a great
connoisseur of horses, had one of the most famous studs in Europe,
and, in his stables, the finest milk-white Arab steeds.

The Duke and Duchess of Teck and Princess May reached Stuttgart
on the 5th of May. They drove to the Schloss, were shown their

rooms, breakfasted, and dressed to receive the Queen, with whom
and the King they afterwards lunched. Next day they called on Aunt
Vera Württemberg—the Duchess Eugene. Aunt Vera suffered from
an unusually virulent form of St Vitus's Dance. She was always
attended by a sergeant of the Olga Dragoner, whose duty it was to
pursue her down the palace corridors and catch her before she bruised
herself against the furniture.

In the evening, the Duke and Duchess of Teck and their daughter
dined, at the uncomfortable hour of six, with old Princess Catherine,
their purple-faced hostess of the Villa Seefeld in 1883 and 1884. The
Duke of Teck then went to the theatre. So did the four Teck servants.
Princess May and her mother withdrew to their own apartments,
which included a private sitting-room decorated in the style of the
First Empire. In this room they settled down to read, Princess May
beginning on the Memoirs of Baroness Oberkirch, which vividly
describe court life at Montbeliard in the late eighteenth century under
Duke Frederick-Eugen of Württemberg. Beyond the sitting-room
was a tiny writing cabinet, with a large desk set in the window-bay.
On this desk the Duchess of Teck, who travelled with a great many
personal impedimenta, had set out her photographs, her books, her
unanswered letters and a number of souvenirs.

Later that evening, Princess Mary Adelaide walked to this desk,
moved a lamp upon it, and sat down to write notes. At nine o'clock
Princess May was startled to hear her mother cry out, 'May! May!
the lamp has caught fire to the muslin curtains above my writing-table.
Call someone!!' Princess May raced to the burning curtains, hoping
at first to put out the fire with water from the bath in her mother's bedroom; but the curtain pole was high, the curtains long, and she could
not souse them easily. She then rushed out to get a footman. While he
was summoning the fire-brigade Princess May salvaged all she could
from her mother's desk—letters, pictures, a travelling watch and books.
At this point the flaming muslin curtains fell on to the desk and
Princess May fled back into the corridor and along to her own bedroom, which was adjacent to the sitting-room. Here she found
Princess Mary Adelaide saying: 'Save what you can, save what you
can, I shall lose everything in my bedroom!' The smoke was by now
very thick and the two ladies, half-suffocated, struggled to open the
windows, which jammed. Passers-by in the street outside broke the
windows open, with the immediate result that the draught fanned the
flames, and in the end it needed the fire-brigade to extinguish them.

'Happily neither May nor I lost our heads', the Duchess of Teck wrote to Queen Victoria. ' . . . But did ever anyone hear of such stupidity as to hang festooned muslin curtains *so close over a writing-table* as to be set fire to by the necessary lamp on the table?'[30]

The Duke of Teck had now hurried home from the play. The fire was over. He surveyed the charred ruins with a practised eye. 'The damage done is little', he wrote next day, 'and anyway the Schloss is insured; and the furnishings of the time of King Wilhelm I were hideous. The two damaged rooms can now at last be modernised.'[31]

Their hosts were amiable about this accident. By one o'clock in the morning Princess May and her mother were installed in the Oldenburg suite. The firemen had managed to move the pieces of furniture containing Princess Mary Adelaide's clothes out of her bedroom before they were burned. When they counted up their losses, the Duchess and her daughter found that these amounted to three Baedekers, some writing-paper, a photograph of the Duke of Teck in the uniform of the Olga Dragoner and—almost Balzacian in significance—their three signed photographs of Prince Eddy. The Empire desk beneath the muslin curtains had, in the Duke of Teck's terse phrase, 'vanished', but Princess May's imperturbability had saved her mother's most treasured belongings. 'I hear you nearly burnt the house down the other day,' Prince George wrote to Princess May, with whom he was now in regular correspondence, 'your description of it to Toria amused me immensely, I am sure you said dear! dear! dear! when you saw the curtains in flames.'[32]

Two days after the fire, the Teck family were moved to the vast old Schloss at Ludwigsburg, near Stuttgart. This move was not made because their hosts feared further pyromaniac activities, but because the King and Queen were now installed at Ludwigsburg in their spring residence—a modest, pleasant villa, named Marienwahl.

Marienwahl had been built and named by King William II for his first wife, Princess Marie of Waldeck and Pyrmont, a sister of the Duchess of Albany. It stands in its own miniature walled and wooded grounds a quarter of a mile from the vast baroque Schloss at Ludwigsburg. A stuccoed gateway leads to it. The little house itself is also stuccoed, and has the air of a Nash villa in St John's Wood. The small drawing-room has double doors opening into an even smaller inner drawing-room, which is still, as it was then, lined with dark red cashmere, the same material covering the low settees and upholstered chairs. These rooms were filled with small tables, early

nineteenth-century pictures and *bibelots*. They contained, amongst
other portraits, that of little Princess Pauline of Württemberg by our
old friend Thaddeus Jones. Through the windows of the inner
drawing-room you look out at ivy-covered tree-trunks. Before the
house is a mossy lawn, behind it lofty elm trees. It is, altogether, a
shady, mossy, charming little retreat, a contrast to its colossal neighbour, the Schloss of Ludwigsburg which, as the Duchess of Teck
wrote that May to her cousin, Queen Victoria, 'dates from the beginning of the last century . . . [and] is . . . one of the *largest in Europe*,
for it boasts several courtyards, 2 picture galleries, 2 chapels, a theatre
and 460 rooms! . . . Most of our windows', the Duchess continued,
'look out upon the *Schlossgarten*, only a small portion of which
immediately under the windows deserves however the name, for the
rest is nearly all meadow, the intersecting walks being shaded by lines
of fruit trees. The *Schlossgarten* is enclosed by an avenue of beautiful
chestnut trees, that have been in glorious blossom all this last fortnight.
The woods round here abound in lilies of the valley and we have
made several expeditions in quest of them . . . but alas! the intense
heat of the last week withered the lilies and put a stop to our afternoon
drives, for it was impossible to go out in any comfort before 7 and
that is unfortunately the *dinner-hour* here! . . . It breaks terribly into
one's day, having to go out to Marienwahl to luncheon at 1 and dinner
at 7 o'c, but I like the peace and quiet of it all, and I certainly think
May is deriving great benefit from our *séjour* here.'33

While she was at Ludwigsburg Princess May celebrated her twenty-
fifth birthday. The King and Queen of Württemberg gave a luncheon
party and a dinner party in honour of this event, and in the evening
the Olga Dragoner band played on the terrace of Marienwahl.
Princess May, whose German was more fluent than she cared to admit,
rather enjoyed talking to the young officers of the Olga Dragoner.
In another of her letters to Hélène Bricka she writes, on 21 June
1892, from Ludwigsburg:

Yes I do *not* know myself, I wish I did. Just now my character is in a
funny state of bewilderment & uncertainty, it is not pleasant. Yet I feel
that the people here have become fond of me thro' getting to know me
better. This I like for you know how I have '*le besoin de plaire*'—Yesterday
we went to a charming review here, & then there was a large lunch for the
Officers. I talked a great deal of German to those I knew & many were
presented to me so I *had* to talk. I felt I was a *succès* & was delighted—It
was amusing to see the admiring glances I received!!! You will say 'oh dear

how vain the child has become!' *Que voulez-vous?* In fact just at this moment I am very good & industrious reading *German* books, fancy me doing this and actually understanding it, wonders will never cease! I am getting A.1. in Württemberg History—Altogether quite a student.

Exactly eight days after this twenty-fifth birthday, King William of Württemberg told the Tecks that a telegram had just arrived from the Duchess of Edinburgh announcing the engagement of her sixteen-year-old daughter Princess Marie of Edinburgh—'Missy' to her family and friends—to the Crown Prince of Roumania. This piece of news was of some interest to Princess Mary Adelaide, Duchess of Teck—for Prince George, the new English heir-presumptive, had been much smitten by his cousin Princess Marie's charms in Malta in 1891. On 16 June the Tecks lunched with Aunt Vera Württemberg to meet Aunt Marie Edinburgh. 'Aunt M. was looking flourishing & seems delighted at Missy's engagement', Princess May recorded in her Diary.

IV

'Mary, & May & Francis have returned to England looking well & with recovered spirits', the Duke of Cambridge wrote to his cousin the Queen on 11 July 1892.[34]

Uncle George Cambridge had had many and frequent confabulations that spring and summer with Lady Geraldine Somerset, their constant topic Princess May's future. We may recall that as a young man the Duke of Cambridge had married an actress, for love. An elderly romantic, he could not approve of the notion that his niece should now marry her dead fiancé's brother—although, most illogically, he had been only too delighted at Princess May's engagement to Prince Eddy, a man she did not love. He regarded any suggestion of a marriage with Prince George as 'unseemly and unfeeling and horrible'. Queen Victoria had taken him into her confidence in this matter, telling him (as we know) that the Tsar Alexander III's marriage to Princess Dagmar of Denmark had proved most successful—and shrewdly adding, to the Duke of Cambridge's amazement, 'You know May never was in love with poor Eddy!'[35]

The announcement of Princess Marie of Edinburgh's engagement to the Crown Prince of Roumania—news which had stirred—had, indeed, fired—the imagination of Princess Mary Adelaide in Ludwigsburg—shocked the Duke of Cambridge and his confidante Lady

Geraldine. 'Disgusted', wrote Lady Geraldine in her Diary, 'to see the announcement of the marriage of poor pretty nice P. Marie of Edinburgh to the *P. of Roumania*!!! it does seem too cruel a shame to cart that nice pretty girl off to semi-barbaric Roumania and a man to the knowledge of all Europe desperately in love with another woman*—to clear the way for May!!! too bad.'[36] What was in fact to Lady Geraldine's eye 'too bad' was the nascent suspicion that, after all and in spite of everything, she might yet live to see Princess May upon the throne of England.

Coming back in July 1892, Princess May and her family peacefully ensconced themselves for the summer in White Lodge. This house was now run by a Comptroller, who had been installed at Queen Victoria's behest, and who handled all Princess Mary Adelaide's money affairs for her. In July 1892 this Comptroller, who was called the Honourable Alexander Nelson Hood, engaged a new steward's room boy of seventeen years of age named Hough. This youth, today an aged gentleman, can vividly recall the return of the Duke and Duchess of Teck and their daughter to England that summer. He remembers Princess May as 'a tall, slim young lady'—'very nice-looking, very polite', and dressed in half-mourning, with a ruby engagement ring upon her finger. He also remembers the general atmosphere of 'fluster', 'hullaballoo' and excitement which the Duchess of Teck generated in any household: insisting, for example, on three carriages to take the family to Richmond, when they could easily have fitted into one carriage. It was in this summer that there occurred the row with the chemist at Sheen.

Mr Alexander Nelson Hood remarked one day to the Duchess of Teck that it was extravagant to go to buy medicaments at Sheen 'when you can get it *all* at the Army and Navy Stores'. Poor Princess Mary Adelaide agreed that the Army and Navy Stores might be less expensive and more practical; whereupon the chemist at Sheen announced that if he thus lost royal patronage he would refuse to send any medicines to White Lodge in a crisis at night-time. This threat was conclusive. The Duke and Duchess of Teck continued to patronise the chemist at Sheen.

One other anecdote appertaining to this summer is characteristic and relevant. The 'tradespeople' were much given to talking about

* The Crown Prince of Roumania was in love with Hélène Vavarescu, herself the favourite of the Queen of Roumania, his aunt, and, under the name of Carmen Sylva, a not inconsiderable poetess.

Princess Mary Adelaide's debts. 'Since it seems the tradespeople are so fond of talking about me', Princess Mary Adelaide declared one day at luncheon, 'I shall stop the beer, bread and cheese!' with which the delivery-boys were regaled in the kitchen of White Lodge. 'But she was too kind a lady and nothing was stopped', adds Mr Hough.

If the tradespeople were gossiping about Princess Mary Adelaide, the White Lodge servants were gossiping about Princess May. The new steward's room boy was informed that Princess May had never, never wanted to marry the Duke of Clarence: it was 'an arranged sort of an affair'. The person she would really have liked to marry was the Duke of Clarence's brother, Prince George, now Duke of York. Such was the backstairs tattle in White Lodge.

The summer passed. The autumn passed. The winter, laden with ominous memories, was once more upon the bereaved Royal Family of England.

On 29 November Princess May and her parents went to stay at Sandringham, so as to be present at the celebration of the Princess of Wales's birthday, and to be with her on the mournful anniversary of 3 December—the day of the Luton Hoo engagement in 1891. 'Embarrassing', wrote the Duke of Teck to his sister, 'but we have to do it.'[37] The Princess of Wales's birthday proved sopping wet. 'Poured', wrote Princess May in her Diary. 'Motherdear's birthday. At 11. she was given her presents, some of them quite lovely, she was terribly upset, poor thing. We went out to lunch in a tent with the shooters, dreadful weather. . . . After tea I played bezique with George. . . . The band played during and after dinner.'[38] On 2 December 'Ella and Serge of Russia'—the Grand Duke Serge of Russia and his wife, who was born a Hesse-Darmstadt—came to Sandringham. On 3 December Princess May noted in her Diary: 'Dull wet day. This day last year was our engagement day, such a sad contrast.' On the day before the Tecks left, they were taken into Prince Eddy's bedroom, which was kept in perfect running order, just as though he were alive. A fire burned in the little grate, flowers stood about in vases, the bed was covered with a sateen Union Jack, even his soap and his hairbrushes had been religiously preserved. They then proceeded to Sandringham church, to gaze upon the memorial window given by Prince Albert Victor's brother-officers of the 10th Hussars. This stained glass window represents Prince Eddy as St George, in shining armour, with a halo.

At Christmas Prince George sent Princess May a brooch. 'Dearest

Georgie', she wrote to him on 28 December 1892. 'You cannot think what pleasure you have given me by sending me such a *lovely* little brooch—Thank you a thousand times—I am glad you like my small pin. It must be nice for you having Louise & her baby with you now, it will help to cheer you up, for I well know what a trial this Christmas has been to you all, and how much one beloved face will have been missed. The contrast between this time last year & now is indeed great! We can only trust that 1893 will be a happier year for us all than 1892. Once more I thank you for your sweet present & remain ever dearest Georgie—Your devoted cousin—May.'39

14 January, the first anniversary of Prince Eddy's death, was sadly kept at both White Lodge and Marlborough House. His mourning relatives visited his tomb at Windsor. On this day Prince George sent a note to Princess May, who replied to his letter:

It was most dear and kind of you to write to me and I am so grateful. Yes indeed the 14th was a terrible day for us all & I need hardly assure how much my thoughts and prayers were with poor dearest Motherdear & you all the whole day. . . . How we ever lived through the dreadful time is a perfect wonder to me. We spent some time in the chapel at Windsor on Saturday, how beautiful it is and how calmly & peacefully our Loved One lies there at rest from all the cares of this world. God be with us and help us bear our cross is the fervent prayer of your very loving cousin—May.40

So did a common sorrow unite in sympathy two persons ideally suited to make the long—and often lonely—journey through Life together. Fate had, like a capricious draughtsman, prepared and then torn up a first sketch for Princess May's career. The next, and final, version was in every way happier and more hopeful than the first.

It is now the moment for us to consider Prince George of Wales, Duke of York.

CHAPTER ELEVEN

THE DUKE OF YORK

———◆———

AT A DECENT INTERVAL after the death of the Duke of Clarence, Queen Victoria conferred a dukedom upon the new heir-presumptive to her throne, Prince George. At first the Queen was reluctant to revive the old York title, which had, in her opinion, many unpleasant memories attached to it. She suggested that Prince George should be made Duke of London; but she allowed herself to be persuaded that this non-Royal title would be thought too much of an innovation, and, in consequence, Prince George was gazetted Duke of York in May 1892, not long after the Wales and Teck families had met at Cannes.

The Duke of York was in every way the diametric opposite of his dead brother, the Duke of Clarence. Physically he was shorter than Prince Eddy had been. He had fair brown hair, bright blue eyes and a beard. His lips were very red: 'dear Georgie's pretty red lips & white teeth were always my delight', his cousin Princess Adolf of Schaumburg-Lippe* wrote of him in June 1892.[1] 'Georgie . . . is such a dear, & so awfully amusing', her sister Sophie, Duchess of Sparta,† wrote of Prince George on another occasion.[2] Prince George was far more spirited than Prince Eddy had been; he was neither limp nor languid, but independent-minded, candid, straightforward, and had a very high sense of duty. His special form of humour was chaff: 'Even the Captain continually says oh how I miss Pr. Georgies chaff!!!' his mother the Princess of Wales wrote to him in August 1893 from the *Osborne*, in which she was cruising in Norwegian waters, 'though you cld be very rude to him I thought!!!'[3]

---

* Victoria, Princess of Prussia (1866–1929), fifth child and second daughter of the Emperor Frederick III and his wife, the eldest child of Queen Victoria. Princess Victoria married in 1890 Adolphus, Prince of Schaumburg-Lippe (1859–1916), and secondly in 1927 Alexander Subkov (1900–1936).

† Sophie, Princess of Prussia (1870–1932), seventh child and third daughter of the Emperor and Empress Frederick, married in 1889 to Constantine, Duke of Sparta (1868–1923), who succeeded as King of the Hellenes in 1913 and abdicated in 1922.

Up to the time of his marriage, Prince George had two all-absorbing passions in his life: shooting and his beautiful deaf mother.

The predominant part played in the Duke of York's early life by his mother can hardly be exaggerated. The future Queen Alexandra inspired and exacted devotion in her children. She did not really wish any of them, sons or daughters, to marry, nor as Princess May presently found out did she make a wholly constructive mother-in-law. As a mother-in-law she was not, like the Duchess of Teck, ubiquitous and anxious to profit from the York marriage, but she was possessive, and she had no understanding of her daughter-in-law's mind nor sympathy with her ever-widening interests. Where Princess May's one object was to lead Prince George on towards new and serious ideas, the Princess of Wales's instinct was to hold him back in a mental playroom where she could reign supreme.

Prince George's naval career had naturally separated him from his family for long periods at a time. The Princess of Wales was almost as intermittent a correspondent as the Duchess of Teck, but when she did write to her distant son she did so with great charm and warmth:

I must write these few lines the last night of this dear old year just to tell you . . . *how* dreadfully I missed you for Xmas [she wrote to Prince George on the 'last day of the old year' in 1889]. There were all the tables [of Christmas presents] excepting yrs & there were all their cheery voices excepting the cheeriest of all & yr bright little face with its turned-up snout oh I did miss it & really shed a little secret tear for my Georgie dear! . . . Thank God everything went off well Xmas & I was all right this time & not knocked up—Do you remember last year & when I was ill just now with that horrid diphtheria & the night of the tree & Squirts & when we fought I with the hunting whip & you with the squirt?—It hardly seems like a year ago does it?⁴

We have observed that Prince George's three sisters lived in a state of prolonged childhood. This curious nursery atmosphere was also due to their mother who could never grasp that her children—or for that matter her grandchildren—had really become grown-up people. When Prince George was nearly twenty-five she would still write of 'his dear tear stained little face'. In May 1890 she told him in a letter:

My darling Georgie my thoughts have never left you for a moment & I miss you *intensely* there is no good denying that—which is a *'fact'* as you wld say—We have been doing a great deal since you left. . . . The Cadogans ball was a very pretty one & the girls enjoyed it—the Court ball very tiresome—Papa took in the delightful fat old Queen Isabelle of Spain & I went with the King of the Belgians a *pretty sight* indeed! we all waddled & limped together—You wld have laughed to have seen me sitting with her on the *haut pas* she looking like a fat *pâté*—but she is very amusing & good-natured. I must close now as the Post is off—Goodbye darling Georgie—God bless & keep you ever—yr loving Motherdear.5

The death of Prince Eddy had forced upon his brother a position of national and imperial importance for which he had received no training. It also caused his father and his mother to value him more dearly: 'You know my Georgie', wrote the Princess of Wales in July 1892, 'that you are everything to us now—& must give us *double* affection for the one that has gone before us!' Shortly before Prince George's engagement his mother wrote to him of the 'bond of love between us—that of Mother & child—which *nothing can* ever diminish or render less binding—& *nothing* & *nobody* can or shall ever come between me & my darling Georgie boy.'6

Hitherto, then, the Duke of York's life had suffered from a dichotomy—the cosseting he received from his mother contrasting sharply with the bluff, hard life aboard a man-o'-war. His tastes were strongly marked and simple. He had none of the problems nor the tendencies to dissipation of the Duke of Clarence. The Duke of York required neither stimulus nor dragooning. What he needed was marriage with a woman of superior intelligence and superior education, who could untether him from his excessive adulation for his mother.

II

Already before Prince Albert Victor's death the question of a bride for his brother Prince George had begun to exercise Queen Victoria's mind; for, when it seemed clear to the Queen that the Duke of Clarence was being, so to speak, side-tracked by his romance with Princess Hélène of Orleans, she had urged that Prince George at least must quickly marry to ensure the succession to the throne in the third generation. The Queen had in mind one of the two elder Edinburgh Princesses.* Prince George did, in fact, feel drawn towards the

* There were, in all, four of these Edinburgh sisters, the daughters of Queen Victoria's second son Prince Alfred, Duke of Edinburgh, and of his Russian wife, the Grand Duchess Marie, with whom (it may be recalled) Princess May used to go to tea as a child and who had the ikon-crowded bedroom at Clarence House. Princess Marie ('Missy') was the eldest, became Queen of Roumania and died in

golden-haired Princess Marie of Edinburgh, his cousin 'Missy', but in 1891 she was only sixteen. He was, however, personally timid about marriage and felt that he was too young for it: 'I quite agree with you, dearest Grandmama & understand your reasons for wishing Eddy & I to marry as soon as possible', he had written to Queen Victoria on 6 February 1891. 'But still I think marrying too young is a bad thing. . . . Then again the wife ought not to be too young; look at the poor Crown Prince Rudolph. She was certainly too young when he married her; she became very ill after her first child was born & naturally he was a very wild young man. The result was he committed suicide & killed this poor girl & brought the most terrible sorrow & shame to his poor wife & parents; that is only one instance of young marriages that I know of. . . . The one thing I never could do is to marry a person that didnt care for me. I should be miserable for the rest of my life.'

When Prince George had been stationed in Malta his ship, HMS *Alexandra*, had been under the command of his uncle Prince Alfred, Duke of Edinburgh, and so he had naturally seen much of his little Edinburgh cousins Princess Missy, Princess Ducky and Princess Sandra, who lived at San Antonio. He called them 'the dear three' and would ride beside their ponies on his own beautiful glossy horse, 'Real Jam', or drive all three of them in a high two-wheeled dog-cart with 'Cocky', a steady-going brown cob. He had also accompanied these girls and their parents to the Carnival in Valetta, where they were pelted with sugar plums by the populace: 'when we drove away the whole crowd pelted us & threw as hard as they could, & it hurt like anything especially when these things hit you in the face & on the head as we had no masks on, as it was Alfred got one in his eye which hurt him dreadfully, no, I have seen enough of that rot to last me for a life time',7 Prince George wrote to his mother.

To Princess Missy her cousin George was, in her own words, 'a beloved chum'; but he did not attract her. Had she shown signs of responding to his nascent affection, Prince George would have liked to marry her; but even in that hypothetical case he had no wish to marry in a hurry, as he told his mother. 'I quite agree with you it

1938. The second, Princess Victoria Melita ('Ducky'), married, first, the Grand Duke of Hesse, and second, the Grand Duke Cyril of Russia. The third daughter, Alexandra ('Sandra'), married the hereditary Prince of Hohenlohe-Langenberg. The fourth, Princess Beatrice ('Baby Bee'), married the Infante Alfonso of Bourbon-Orleans.

certainly wld be too soon in every way!!' the Princess of Wales wrote
to him in reply, 'particularly as the bride is not in long petticoats yet!!!
Entre nous, talking about *her!* it is a pity those children shld be entirely brought up as Germans. Last time I saw them they spoke with
a very strong foreign accent—which I think is a great pity as after all
they are English.' The Princess of Wales, in fact, was not enthusiastic
about her niece Missy.

Well & now about yr Matrimonial prospects!!! ha ha ha! [she wrote to
Prince George in April 1891]. You are *quite* right to think Grandmama has
gone mad on the subject—& it is too *ridiculous* . . . the girl being a perfect
baby yet—altho Aunt Marie begging her pardon does *all* she can to make
her *old before her time* . . . and what do you say to Aunt Marie having
hurried on the *two girls confirmation*—& in Germany too so that now they
won't *even know* that they have ever been English—particularly as they have
been confirmed in the German church. . . . Even Aunt Vicky was furious
about it—8

It was not quite just of the Princess of Wales to criticise her sister-
in-law for having the Edinburgh girls educated in Germany, for,
owing to a complex matter known as 'the Coburg Succession', this
was where they had in fact been living for some years. 'The Coburg
Succession' concerned the dukedom of Saxe-Coburg-Gotha, which
was then held by the Prince Consort's brother Ernest. 'Terrible old
Uncle Ernest', as Princess Missy called him, had a faded old wife, the
Duchess Alexandrina, who worshipped him; but they had no children.
It thus became necessary to find an heir for Coburg, where Uncle
Ernest held court in a highly raffish and even disreputable manner,
surrounded by a horde of *Jäger* and proletarian flatterers, and almost
wholly absorbed in the pursuit of young women. Prince Alfred, Duke
of Edinburgh, had been selected, and he and the Duchess with their
children were installed in the charming pink-stuccoed Gothic Revival
castle of the Rosenau, on a hilltop outside the city of Coburg, waiting
for ogreish Uncle Ernest to die—which in 1893 he did.

The Duchess of Edinburgh had never liked England. Reared at the
Imperial Court of St Petersburg in the singular state and glory that
surrounded an only daughter of the Tsar, she did not much care for
the low rank she found to be hers in England, where she came behind
all Queen Victoria's daughters as well as behind the Danish Princess
of Wales. She thought English an ugly language, and, as her children
refused to speak her favourite language, French, with her, she had

them educated in German, choosing for this purpose an anglophobe German governess. The Duke of Edinburgh might wish his daughter to marry the heir-presumptive to the English throne: the Duchess of Edinburgh did not.

In 1892 a tentative proposal of marriage on Prince George's behalf was made to the Edinburgh parents, who submitted it to their daughter Princess Marie. Influenced by her governess, as well as by the fact that she was not anxious to marry her cousin, she turned it down. It was very shortly after this that the Duchess of Edinburgh contrived the engagement of her daughter with Prince Ferdinand of Hohenzollern-Sigmaringen, the adopted heir-apparent to the rickety Roumanian Throne. The affair had been so hastily concluded that the Duke of Edinburgh's permission was not asked until it was too late. It was over this stroke that Aunt Marie Edinburgh had been so jubilant when Princess May had seen her at Ludwigsburg in the summer of 1892.

Everyone in the Royal Family was very much startled by the speed of this Roumanian engagement. 'I have bn expecting to get a telegram fm you abt Missy's Engagement, which has us all by surprise', Queen Victoria wrote to the Empress Frederick. ' . . . it seems to have come very rapidly to a climax. The Country is vy insecure & the Society—dreadful—& she is a mere Child, & quite inexperienced! —Of course the marriage cannot take place till next year; Missy herself wld *not* have Georgie. . . . It was the dream of Affie's* life. I believe Ferd. [the Crown Prince of Roumania] is *vy* nice.' The Prince of Wales was very angry at this snub to his son. He was cold to his brother and sister-in-law the Duke and Duchess of Edinburgh, who now declared that they had really wanted Princess Marie to marry Prince George. 'I fear Bertie is very angry—' wrote Queen Victoria, 'but he is unjust & wrong. Affie & Marie wished for Georgie & fm a worldly point of view it was so much better & gter a match than this one! There was no *running* after this as Bertie says—& Marie did *not* go to Potsdam for *that*, but because *Dona*† had pressed her so much & *wished* Missy for *odious Gunther*!' Prince George's feelings had not been heavily engaged. 'Poor Georgie', wrote Queen Victoria, '. . . is not bitter.' The Queen was developing a great admiration for her grandson. 'I think dear George so nice, sensible, & truly right-

* 'Affie' was the family nickname for Prince Alfred, Duke of Edinburgh.

† The Empress Augusta of Germany, Queen of Prussia, consort of the Emperor William II.

minded, & so anxious to improve himself', she wrote from Balmoral in June 1892.9

In the autumn of 1892 the Princess of Wales wrote to her son, now Duke of York. 'So the *Xtians* have been following you about with their lovely Snipe! well it *will* be a pleasure to welcome that beauty as yr bride—when may we expect the news? You see she is quite prepared to take you by storm by already offering you her contrafeit in a frame!!'10 This forlorn hope on the part of 'poor Lenchen' (that Princess Christian of Schleswig-Holstein who had made herself so unpleasant about Princess May's engagement to the Duke of Clarence one day at Marlborough House, in the Queen's presence) found no reinforcement in the English Royal Family. Princess Helena Victoria of Schleswig-Holstein, known in the family as 'the Snipe' on account of her very long nose, might indeed have made an admirable wife for Prince George, since she was kind-hearted and highly intelligent. But, save by her parents, the idea of such a marriage was never seriously entertained.

The tale of Prince George and Princess Marie of Edinburgh may incidentally serve to show us that Lady Geraldine Somerset's interpretation of motive was not invariably exact. A vivid reporter of the spoken word, she usually attributed the lowest motives to others, and thought life blacker than it was: 'what a rotten false world it is from end to end' was one of her most characteristic comments. We have seen that she interpreted the swift Roumanian engagement of Princess Marie as a family plot 'to clear the way for May!!!' This was, of course, a complete misconception, for while the Duchess of Edinburgh apparently preferred to find a German husband for her daughter Missy, she was not in the least interested in 'clearing the way' for Princess May.

The Edinburgh engagement was announced at the beginning of June 1892. The Grand Duchess of Mecklenburg-Strelitz was now in London, and she had set to work to influence her brother the Duke of Cambridge in favour of a marriage between Prince George and Princess May. 'How she has thoroughly be-Mayed him!!' wrote Lady Geraldine crossly, 'all the bosh about how clever her letters are, how well she writes etc. . . . He told me of P[rincess] M[ary Adelaide's] room at Stuttgart being on fire . . . they saved all the things in it, except three photos of P[rince] Eddy.' The Grand Duchess also told her brother the Duke of Cambridge that she was 'quite satisfied May has never been in love and is *most* unlikely ever to be so'.11

The Duke of York was, in fact, fortunate in the matter of Princess

Marie of Edinburgh. In Roumania his cousin Missy developed into a very theatrical personage, authoress of an extremely clever book of Memoirs, but as neurotic and self-satisfied as her cousin Kaiser Wilhelm II, whose character hers, indeed, slightly resembled. She would not have proved a satisfactory help-mate for Prince George.

III

After the refusal of 'Missy of Edinburgh' to marry Prince George, the Queen fell back upon her original plan that he should marry Princess May. The Queen had set her heart on it. The country expected it. The newspapers were full of rumours and reports: 'all the *beastly* newspaper bosh' as the Princess of Wales called it: 'Did you among other announcements see yrself *arm in arm*!! (walking in Richmond Park) with poor May!!'[12] In February 1893 the *Observer* telegraphed to Sir Henry Ponsonby to ask if it were true that the engagement was to be announced on the night of 11 February. 'Thanks for the information I had not heard it before and cannot find out any one in this house who has', he telegraphed back from Osborne. 'Excellent answer', minuted the Queen. 'Pray show it the P. of Wales & let the Queen have copies.'[13] By February 1893, in fact, Princess May had been forced into an acutely embarrassing position, which was not made easier by the Duchess of Teck and Princess May's brothers, who at this time talked openly of a probable engagement. The Queen, the country, and, of course, the Teck parents were determined on the marriage. The Prince and Princess of Wales were, at this moment, less enthusiastic. 'The Prince of Wales must not prevent the marriage. Something dreadful will happen if he does not marry',[14] Queen Victoria wrote superstitiously to Ponsonby at this time.

The attitude of the Prince of Wales and his wife is easily explicable, for the proposed switch of a bride from a dead Prince to his living brother seemed to carry with it the implication that Princess May had not really cared for Prince Eddy at all. Princess May was somewhat in the position of Emily Tennyson, when her fiancé Arthur Hallam, the hero of *In Memoriam*, had died in 1833; the Hallam family expected her to live on in lonely desolation, cherishing his memory, 'leading' as they put it 'the life of a nun'.

Prince George, on his side, was nervous and bewildered. He was still in despair over his brother's death, and anxious about the new position into which this had thrust him. His health was not robust, and his lack of self-confidence had not been helped by Princess Marie of Edinburgh's refusal to consider him as a husband. Moreover, he had no means of knowing what Princess May's attitude to himself might be, nor whether or no she fitted into the category of 'a person' who cared for him enough to marry him. He had several long talks with Queen Victoria, with his father, and with Sir Henry Ponsonby. Essentially an honest and humble-minded young man, he was at this moment also a puzzled and dispirited one.

It was pointed out to the Duke of York that he must now virtually abandon his career in the Navy. On the 1st of September 1892 he had paid off the *Melampus*, spent the day at White Lodge and set out for Heidelberg, where he worked hard at German for two months. The Prince of Wales declared that no one could learn a new language in only two months. 'Do you think he will learn very much German by going to Heidelberg?' the Duchess of Sparta wrote to her mother the Empress Frederick, 'poor boy it will bore him dreadfully staying there all alone.'[15] Prince George did not like sight-seeing or travelling. In this respect he was unlike his future wife.

In the spring of 1893 the Princess of Wales had the sensible idea of taking Prince George with her to Greece for a respite from his anxieties:

You will be glad to hear my letter has been written & sent off to Grand Mama—& I told her—that I thought you required a complete change and rest before settling down in life—& that I intended & proposed to take you. with me on the Yacht for a short time . . . and I also mentioned that a long engagement was a great mistake under the circumstances & the marriage I thought cld not be till June. . . . So you see my Georgie boy I hope that things will be made a little easier for you now . . . & that in the end it all will be crowned with happiness for you both—I too am worried to death about it.[16]

On 4 March 1893 the Princess of Wales, with the Duke of York, Princess Victoria, Princess Maud and a suite left London for Genoa, where they joined the Royal Yacht *Osborne* and cruised down the coast of Italy, reaching Athens via Sicily, Corfu and Corinth. They were back in London again by the end of April. During this stay at Athens, Prince George and Princess May exchanged a number of affectionate letters. Princess May wrote of water-colour exhibitions and theatres, and also of her visits to Princess Louise, Duchess of Fife, at Sheen:

I think it particularly nice of you answering my letter so quickly & I am very much touched by it [Prince George wrote to Princess May on 31 March]. You & Aunt Mary have often been in my thoughts lately, because I noticed so many little things which were 'truly Italian' & not to be found in any other country, perhaps a good thing too, dear! dear! I am glad that you often go & see Louise at Sheen, she has written to me how pleased she is when you come & see her. . . . You say that I will think your letter dull, on the contrary, as you told me all you had seen & what you had been doing & it interested me very much, if half the people who write letters, wrote as well as you it would be a blessing. . . . I hope [this letter] won't bore you too much, when you are stop & throw it away.[17]

Such diffidence was very characteristic of the Duke of York.

It was a cold and windy spring in Athens. 'The weather has been something too vile for words—all these days . . . which is such a pitty [sic], because we wanted Athens to look its best just when Aunt & cousins are here!' Crown Princess Sophie wrote to her mother, 'the first two days it poured & yesterday blew a hurricane which has knocked down many of the best trees in the garden, which looks quite sad to see them lying over the road, all smashed!!' In spite of these gales, the visitors managed to enjoy themselves, driving up to Tatoi or walking to Phaleron with the Duchess of Sparta, who was pregnant, following them in her carriage. They also entertained their cousins on board the *Osborne*. 'Our lunch on board was such fun yesterday, we stuffed ourselves full like pigs, at lunch & tea!'[18] The Spartas' children, with their English Nannies, Mrs Lorne and Mrs Thorpe, would also rush screaming about the royal yacht. These English Nannies were the only non-Germanic and non-Greek element about the court of Athens. Just before the Wales party's arrival, a very unwelcome incident had occurred in the Duchess of Sparta's household, when a German nursery-maid, named Marie Weber, sent to Athens by the Empress Frederick, committed suicide:

You can imagine my *horror* and distress on getting the following telegrams yesterday before Luncheon from Sophie [wrote the Empress Frederick from Buckingham Palace in March 1893]:
'Marie Weber tried to commit suicide this morning—fell off Parthenon, state very serious. Will you let Parents know.'
Then a second:
'Poor Marie just dead. Will you break awful news to Parents—will write to him later.'
Is this not too dreadful! Poor unfortunate—miserable girl! How *could*

she commit such a piece of sin & folly! She must have been mad. . . . You can imagine my anxiety—for such a shock & such scenes—should harm my Sophie. . . . Poor darling such impressions are very bad for her![19]

As a result of this episode, the Greek royal nursery relied in future upon phlegmatic English girls for assistance.

Other things besides the weather, and the shock to the Sparta household of Marie Weber's suicide, were just then starting to cause grave difficulties in the Greek royal family. All was not well at the court of Athens, and this greatly distressed the Princess of Wales, whose brother, formerly Prince William of Denmark, was now, as we may remember from Gmunden, King George the First of the Hellenes: Princess May's 'Uncle Willie' (pronounced 'Veelee').

The Greek children whom we briefly met scrambling about the gardens of the Queen of Hanover's villa at Gmunden were now grown up. In 1889 the eldest son, the Crown Prince Constantine—'Tino' to his family—had married Princess Sophie of Prussia: the two children with the English Nannies (whom it had been hoped Marie Weber would aid) were those of this Crown Prince and his Crown Princess. King George of the Hellenes had as we know a Russian Queen, Olga. She had married him when she was only seventeen, and her youth, combined with the King's fear that he would be accused of submitting to Russian influence, had prevented him from ever discussing Greek politics with his wife. The habit of reticence had grown upon him with the years; forgetting that his sons were now of age—the identical mistake made by his sister the Princess of Wales about her own children—he told them nothing of what was happening in the country. Some extracts from a very long letter from the Empress Frederick to her youngest daughter 'Mossy' (the Princess Friedrich-Karl of Hesse who now lived at Rumpenheim) sum up this awkward situation. The Empress is relating a conversation with the Princess of Wales at Windsor:

I had a long talk with dear Aunt Alix—who I found *so—sensible—*& *'feinfühlend'*—She says at present the state of things in the family—at Athens are very sad,—it worries her—& makes her very unhappy! she says poor Aunt Olga is miserable about it, and cried bitterly at Copenhagen!— . . . Aunt Alix . . . deeply regrets that uncle Willy does not & cannot remember that his sons are grown up now! He does not take them into his confidence . . . the consequence is that they are *very* bitter, and have become very antagonistic to him. . . . Aunt thinks that *Tino* has been *most* unjustly used. . . . Aunt says the King has often *very good reasons* for what he thinks & does but never explains them to Tino!!—Aunt thinks it *very* hard for the sons that they are treated as children. . . . Aunt admits that Uncle Willy *is* rather tyrannical in the family—although he is such a good Father. . . . Aunt says the King complains that when the sons are altogether—or with their Mama,—& talking in an animated way—the moment he comes in the conversation ceases & every one is silent, or that they get up & go away, & he feels that very much indeed. . . . Aunt says—her Brother is devoted to Sophie. . . . Aunt also thinks that wicked people abuse Tino's friends to the King. . . . Aunt is so afraid that if things go on like this there will be 2 parties in the Kingdom—one for the King & the other for his sons! . . . One must *hope* things will go better! Please tell Fischy all this.[20]

Perhaps the Prince of Wales learned a lesson from this example of family disunion at the court of Athens; for when he himself came to the throne he took an infinity of trouble to instruct Prince George in the intricacies of constitutional Monarchy.

It was during this spring of 1893 in Athens that Prince George had a series of quiet and intimate and self-analytical talks with his beloved Aunt Olga, the Queen of Greece. The Queen, who had taken a fancy to Princess May as long ago as 1884 in Gmunden, urged him to propose to her on his return to England.

IV

In February the Dowager Empress Frederick of Germany, who was also Princess Royal of Great Britain, was paying one of her annual visits to her mother in England—where indeed she was when she received the telegram about the nursery-maid's suicide in Athens. On 22 February, when she was at Windsor Castle, Princess May and her mother also arrived there to stay. 'May is a smart *Erscheinung*,' the Empress wrote to her youngest daughter, 'still all in black of course, but she seemed to me a little stiff & cold! I hear her praised on all sides and by those who know her well. . . . She is certainly very nice in manner—&c but I do not think she has much charm or is very fascinating! She may have been shy with me seeing me again after all this sorrow! and it is a shy and difficult position for her—as the newspapers are perpetually talking of her Betrothal to Georgie.— Aunt Mary [Princess Mary Adelaide] I find grown a good deal older. —& all traces of her beauty gone.'[21]

Like Lady Geraldine Somerset, the Empress Frederick tended to

I

look upon the gloomier sides of life. Her experiences in Germany had indeed been melancholy and frustrating, and the death from throat cancer of the husband she adored and admired, just after his accession to the German throne, had been a bitter blow, followed up as it was by the persecution of the Empress by her eldest son, Wilhelm II. She was a highly educated woman, and owed this fact, together with her love for works of art, to her father the Prince Consort. In manner she was lugubrious and tended to cry woe. Her constant smile was over-sweet and struck some people as an affectation or an insincerity. She was almost as small as her mother Queen Victoria, she was tearful, she dressed in deep mourning and she wrote long letters to her three younger daughters every day. Her cult for her infant grandchildren, and for any babies anywhere, amounted to a mania:

As regards the *Baby* [of the Empress's eldest daughter, the Princess of Saxe-Meiningen]—I think you are hardly a fair judge [Queen Victoria wrote to the Empress Frederick in July 1880]. Hardly anyone I know has such a *culte* for little Babies as you have, & young people are generally not so wrapped up in them.—I know dear gd. mama went into such extasies over them, so that *I* felt the *reverse*. I think there is so much contradiction in young people that they often *show* just the contrary.[22]

This maternal cult, which was not shared by Queen Victoria, was not shared by Princess May either. Here again the Empress Frederick found fault: 'May . . . does not seem to have the passionate tenderness for her little ones wh. seems so natural to me', she was to write from Osborne four years later. 'She has something very cold & stiff—& distant in her manner—each time one sees her again one has to break the ice afresh;—but I like her very much & she & Georgie seem so happy & contented together;—she is liked by the whole family,—I do *not* think her clever—& she is a little heavy & silent—*alle ihre Gedanken, Ansichten und Auffassungen erscheinen mir ziemlich banal, alltäglich und conventionell,**—conversationally—but I should say she . . . would certainly never do—or say a foolish thing.'[23]

It is probable that the Empress's eager sympathy and anxiety to discuss Prince Eddy's death made Princess May, at Windsor Castle that February of 1893, more withdrawn and reserved than ever. 'I was glad to see more of May yesterday before she left,—& she made a very nice impression upon me! I fancy that there is hardly a doubt

---

* Translation: 'All her thoughts, views and ideas appear to me to be rather banal, commonplace and conventional.'

—that she will one day be Georgie's Bride—and—have the first position in Europe, one may say in the world! She is a good steady girl I am sure and will always do her duty', the Empress wrote; only to change her mind a few days later, after a dinner-party at which she had again met Princess May at Marlborough House: 'Georgie was such a Duck too. I suppose May is the right wife for him—many think her rather dull—& superficial!—I feel there is not much "*Geistiges Leben*" or many "*Geistige Interessen*" . . . May has many excellent qualities and advantages.' Later in March the Empress went to luncheon at the White Lodge: 'the House is such a nice old thing with a charming garden—looking into the splendid Park. Then I had tea at Louise Fife's and—looked at her charming House—Sheen Lodge—, & walked about her garden! drove home with Uncle Bertie! Her event may come *any* moment!—Her little girl is a sweet little thing.—What a comfort she has so nice a place near London—to be laid up in.'[24]

The Fifes' 'place near London' was not only valuable to be laid up in. It had already served as a rendezvous for Prince Eddy and Princess Hélène of Orleans, and it now chose to play in Princess May's life the part earlier adopted by the de Falbes' house at Luton Hoo. After leaving Athens in early April, Prince George had gone on an official visit to Rome. He returned to London on 29 April, and went down to Sheen to stay with his sister. On the second of May he dined at White Lodge. This meal, which followed both on his recent correspondence with Princess May, and on the newspaper publicity about their probable engagement, may well have been nervous and embarrassing. It seems likely that Princess May dissuaded her mother from leaving Prince George and herself alone together. Next afternoon the Duke and Duchess of Teck discreetly set off, in two separate carriages and at separate hours, for London, vacating the house for a possible visit from Prince George. Princess May had arranged to go to tea that day with her cousin Princess Louise, Duchess of Fife, at Sheen. Here she found Prince George, in the company of his sister Princess Louise, his brother-in-law the Duke of Fife, and the newly born Fife baby, Princess Maud. It was a strained moment, but the problem was solved by Princess Louise's skilful and spirited resort to the tone of Wales family chaff. 'Now, Georgie,' she said, 'don't you think you ought to take May into the garden to look at the frogs in the pond?' Beside the pond Prince George proposed to his cousin May of Teck. He was accepted. 'We walked together afterwards [after tea] in the garden and he proposed to me, & I accepted him', Princess May told her Diary. 'Louise & Macduff were delighted. I drove home to announce the news to Mama & Papa & Georgie followed. He went back to Sheen after dinner. We telegraphed to all the relations.'[25]

Telegraphing was, as we know, an irresistible sport to Princess Mary Adelaide. At ten-thirty p.m. that May evening she was still telegraphing, and not to all the relations only but to most of her personal friends. A Richmond neighbour was aroused at dawn the next morning by two telegrams—both, of course, sent through the Richmond public post office. These read: 'May engaged to Duke of York' and 'Unless announced in papers keep engagement secret'. The engagement was in fact, with the Queen's permission, announced that day.

'One can only think of the engagement with very mixed feelings', was the Empress Frederick's comment in a letter to the Crown Princess of Greece, 'but with many prayers for their future, so important for their dear parents, the whole family, and the country. I am sure the very fact that Georgie is to marry May will give great pleasure in England. Aunt Mary Teck is overjoyed, as well she may be and Grandmama [Queen Victoria] thankful that something is settled for Georgie. Still, over all, there is a mist of sadness and melancholy.'[26]

The principal parties to this engagement—that is to say the Duke of York and Princess May of Teck—were not aware of this mist of sadness. They agreed together that poor Prince Eddy would have been delighted at their engagement, and that he was indeed undoubtedly rejoicing over it in another, better world. The final verdict on Princess May's second engagement comes best from her husband. On 22 December 1911, King George V wrote:

We suit each other admirably & I thank God every day that he should have brought us together, especially under the tragic circumstances of dear Eddy's death, & people only said I married you out of pity & sympathy.

That shows how little the world really knows what it is talking about.[27]

———————

'THE WEDDING OF GEORGIE is to be in the first week of July, & alas! in the Chapel Royal', wrote Queen Victoria on 13 May 1893. 'Windsor is lovely for a marriage in the summer—but I quite feel it cld not be *after* the sad funeral in St George's. . . . The Chapel Royal is . . . small & *very* ugly. Alix has reached Venice. She ought to have come over for the Imperial Institute.'[1] The Princess of Wales had lingered in Athens, still wearing deep mourning for Prince Eddy. She had thus purposely avoided being in England at the moment of the York engagement. She had also missed the opening of the Imperial Institute by Queen Victoria on 10 May, an occasion on which Princess May and Prince George were 'very much cheered' by the crowd. From Venice the Princess of Wales sent a letter to Princess May:

God bless you *both* and let me welcome you back once more as my dear daughter and grant you all the happiness here on Earth—which *you* so fully deserve—with my Georgie—which was alas denied you with my darling Eddy . . . you know *how* much I have always loved you—& how glad I am that you will still belong to us . . . and I hope that my sweet May will always come straight to me for everything. . . . Ever yr most loving & devoted old Motherdear.[2]

The summer of 1893 was one of great, indeed almost tropical heat. 'The heat is awful today, over 80° in my room & I am nearly dead, but still I must write you two lines to tell how much you are in my thoughts', wrote Prince George on 24 May in one of his now daily notes to Princess May.[3] 'On Monday we went to see Louise Fife at Sheen,' Queen Victoria had written a few days before this, 'a nice little place but it was vy dark tho' vy hot & has been vy thick & muggy all these days & so oppressive.—The Baby is a pretty little thing but very small. The Rhododendrons are in the most splendid bloom really quite a marvellous sight, quite dazzling & most beautiful

... everywhere in the Park, but more near Virginia Water & the Rhododendron Drive.'4

This sultry, oppressive weather lasted all through the eight weeks' engagement which ended with the wedding day, 6 July. As this climax drew nearer and nearer, the nerves of the young couple became more and more strung up. To begin with, the Duchess of Teck would never leave them alone together. Prince George complained of this to his fiancée, who replied that Princess Mary Adelaide was 'so obstinate ... I felt like a little devil & I have not forgiven her yet'.

The fact is [this sagacious letter continues] that we are all in a worried bustled state of mind & things irritate & annoy us which otherwise we should not bother about, I know I am always losing my temper with somebody or something & I assure you this is not generally the case, as I know only too well how much bad tempered people make one suffer. This is a simply *horrid* time we are going through & I am only looking forward to the time when you & I shall be alone at Sandringham. . . . I am very sorry that I am still so shy with you, I tried not to be so the other day, but alas failed, I was angry with myself! It is so stupid to be so stiff together & really there is nothing I would not tell you, except that I *love* you more than anybody in the world, & this I cannot tell you myself so I write it to relieve my feelings.5

To this letter Prince George replied the same day with a long, affectionate note, a part of which reads:

... Thank God we both understand each other, & I think it really unnecessary for me to tell you how deep my love for you my darling is & I feel it growing stronger & stronger every time I see you; although I may appear shy & cold. But this worry & busy time is most annoying & when we do meet it is only [to] talk business. . . .6

Engagements are well known to have nerve-racking moments; and we may think that this particular engagement, with all its antecedent sorrows and rumours, generated a pitch of nervous tension all its own. Also Princess Mary Adelaide drove her daughter hard during these weeks: 'Simply tell Aunt Mary that you won't do any more and that I don't wish it',7 Prince George wrote on 12 June. 'I hope you are quite well again, I am nearly *dead*',8 wrote Princess May some days later.

Wedding presents rained down upon the pair, and so, towards the end of June, did foreign royal wedding guests, headed by Prince George's grandparents, King Christian IX of Denmark and Droning

Louise, known in the family as Apapa and Amama, who arrived with Uncle Valdemar of Denmark on the 30th June and were met by the Tecks and the Waleses at the railway station. Then there were deputations to be received, fourteen hundred presents to be looked at and sorted, gala performances at the Opera and at various theatres, and all this in torrid heat and in naked conditions of publicity. They were cheered in the Park, they were cheered in the streets, they were cheered at the Children's Parade at the Botanic Gardens.

Princess May was also sitting to von Angeli and to Luke Fildes for her portraits: 'I must say that it is a great shame making you sit to all these artists just at this time', wrote Prince George.9 Yet despite nervous exhaustion, Princess May was fundamentally happy: 'I don't think you have any idea of how happy I am and how much I appreciate your kindness to me for as I said the other day—the more I feel the less I say, I am so sorry but I can't help it. . . .', she wrote.10 There was also, as well as everything else, the important matter of Princess May's trousseau to be dealt with.

As we may well imagine, Lady Geraldine Somerset's reactions to the accomplished fact of the York engagement were vitriolic. It had been bad enough to see Princess May become a national heroine at the time of the engagement to the Duke of Clarence, so swiftly followed by his death. But that Princess May should reappear upon the national stage in, so to speak, the Second Act, Lady Geraldine found too much to bear. 'It is clear there is not even any pretence at love-making. May is radiant at her position and abundantly satisfied, but placid and cold as always, the Duke of York apparently nonchalant and indifferent',11 she jotted down in her kindly way, after a conversation with the Duke of Cambridge and the Grand Duchess Augusta. None of these three critical persons took into account the natural reserve of Princess May, the nervousness of Prince George. Nor had they seen the letters from which we have just quoted extracts, nor a sentence in another letter from Prince George dated 3 July, only three days before the wedding: 'It is just two months today that we were engaged, how quick the time goes, I loved you then very much, now I adore you, I feel so happy that I don't know how to thank you enough for having made me so.'12

Lady Geraldine Somerset took a morbid interest in the question of who could have paid for Princess May's first trousseau, that bought at the time of the Clarence engagement. 'The question of payment for the trousseau does not seem to worry her at all', she had written of a talk with Princess Mary Adelaide in the spring of 1892, 'in view I suppose of utilizing it for this coming occasion!'[13] In fact, rather naturally, a new trousseau had been constructed, for clothes that were the height of fashion in December 1891 would no longer have looked so in May 1893.

Instead of a train embroidered with *Maiblumen*, with their sad memories of the death-chamber at Sandringham, Princess May's wedding dress now had a more conventional train of silver and white brocade, woven on the looms of Spitalfields (for one of the Duchess of Teck's manifold activities was the patronage of the domestic silk industry of England) and embroidered with a design of rose, shamrock and thistle in silver on a white ground. The bridal veil was the same as that worn by Princess Mary Adelaide at her wedding at Kew in June 1866. This was a small veil. It hung down from the back of the head and seemed to Lady Geraldine Somerset to be 'only an elongated lappet!'

It may be recalled that Princess May's Aunt Augusta Strelitz had also speculated, soon after Prince Albert Victor's death, as to who would pay up for her niece's now useless trousseau. This time, on the new engagement, she and her husband the Grand Duke contributed the handsome sum of one thousand pounds for this purpose. 'I for my part [wrote the Grand Duchess] alone will further contribute some beautiful flounces of black lace, I bought, some time ago, on your Mamma's recommendation. I never have made use of them. If you tell her, she need get no black lace for you.—I wish that it was in my power to contribute to your *future* happiness as I am doing now to your trousseau for you know, dear May, how deeply and truly I love you!'[14]

Aunt Augusta's unaccustomed generosity was of the greatest value to the Teck family, for Princess May's second trousseau was on a truly princely scale. The 'Royal Wedding Number' of the *Lady's Pictorial* described forty outdoor suits, fifteen ball-dresses, five tea-gowns, a vast number of bonnets, shoes and gloves: and this was but 'a portion of the trousseau'. 'Princess May', they wrote, 'cannot be called a dressy woman and has no extravagant taste in dress, preferring always to look neat, lady-like and elegant, to keeping in the forefront of fashion.' She was, they added, 'no mere fine lady'. Even so, this was an elaborate period in women's clothes: the bustle had gone out to be replaced by the long, rather narrow, bell-like skirt, made top-heavy by great billowing leg-of-mutton sleeves, and tight bodices. Tea-gowns and matinée-gowns played a large part in the trousseau, as well as travelling capes, travelling wraps and driving capes. The phrases used for the materials, as well as for the way they were made up, bespeak a considerable sartorial complication: bodices 'arranged in *bebé*-pleats', *berthes*, 'straw-colour wrought with crystal beads', much ruching, 'graduated tucks', '*rouleaux* of blue velvet', 'Russian braid', '*vieux-rose miroir* velvet', a 'Sir Joshua Reynolds toned white satin', many dyed ostrich feathers, 'reseda velvet', an embroidered black silk 'shot with myrtle-green', walking-costumes 'built of Harris tweed, which is very business-like'. Each of the out-door dresses and costumes had its own small bonnet, replete with feathers, velvet strings, bead embroidery or clusters of artificial flowers. 'The hem is finished with a zigzag folded band of brocade, each upward point tipped with a satin rosette' is one of many sentences which give a good visual idea of the whole. It was a wardrobe to make any woman happy. The clothes were all made by exclusively English dressmakers: Linton and Curtis, Scott Adie and Redfern.

Equally lavish were the presents, in which jewellery and plate predominated, and which were valued at £300,000. Prince George's wedding presents were kept at Marlborough House until King Christian and Droning Louise could see them; they were then removed to join Princess May's immense display at the Imperial Institute, where they were shown to the public at so much a head for the benefit of the Victoria Fund. Everything went to emphasise the fact that, in the words of one of the newspapers: 'already our sweet Princess May has assumed an absolutely different position in our eyes. She is no longer our pretty favourite girl-Princess, associated for the most part with the quiet home-life of White Lodge. She is the third greatest Royal Lady of Great Britain.'[15]

Elaborate in clothes, the age was also fulsome in its attitude towards Royal persons. Readers of national dailies and weeklies were assured that 'no young lady of the present day—Princess or otherwise—is more thoroughly grounded in the English classics, or more happily at home in modern literature than is our future Queen'. She was described as a brilliant linguist, a lover of Goethe and Schiller, an admirer of Longfellow. Her white-painted boudoir at White Lodge was represented as a temple of the Arts; even the tiny shelf beside her armchair received its measure of praise: 'a little shelf to hold conveniently one's cup of tea, or a vase of flowers, or a tiny volume taken up for the moment and as unexpectedly laid down'.

I*

This perfervid tone would have turned the head of Princess Marie of Edinburgh; it had no effect whatever on modest Princess May. One newspaper even went so far as to say that should she ever wish to do so, Princess May could pick up her pen and with ease write an excellent book.

Meanwhile the wedding day approached. Ten bridesmaids had been chosen: Princesses Victoria Melita and Alexandra of Edinburgh, Princesses Maud and Victoria of Wales, two little Battenberg children, two little Connaughts, Baby Bee of Edinburgh (also a juvenile) and —to Princess Christian's mortification—Princess Helena Victoria of Schleswig-Holstein: 'the Snipe'. At least three of these bridesmaids would have liked 'to be in Princess May's shoes' themselves. This colloquialism seems to render apposite one last detail about Princess May's trousseau: 'Princess May' (we resort once more to the lady reporter of the *Lady's Pictorial*) 'wears her boots and shoes with quite low heels and with pointed toes and has a very difficult taste in such matters.' Was this not, indeed, an archaic world when to have 'a very difficult taste' was a compliment?

On the morning of the wedding day, 6 July 1893, Princess May sent Prince George a pencilled note from Buckingham Palace, where she and her mother were staying:

> I should much like to give you a wedding ring if you will wear it for my sake—I therefore send you herewith one or two to try on for size—Let me have the one you choose at once & I will give it to you in the chapel. What . a memorable day in our lives this will be. God grant it may bring us much happiness. I love you with all my heart. Yrs for ever & ever—May.[16]

On that morning, before starting for the Chapel Royal, Prince George accidentally caught sight of his bride down the long, long vista of one of the red-carpeted corridors of Buckingham Palace. He swept her a low and courtly bow. This gesture she never forgot.

II

Princess May's wedding day dawned bright and fair. All London was astir early. Great crowds assembled along the route, the stands were thronged, there was a general clattering of soldiers and officers, the triumphal crash of military music rent the summer air. Splendid equipages ferrying the guests to the Chapel Royal passed spanking to and fro. The streets were decorated with tall Venetian masts and flowery garlands. The crowds were bigger than for the Golden Jubilee.

At eleven-thirty the first of the carriage processions, gleaming with scarlet and gold, left Buckingham Palace, taking a route up Constitution Hill and round through Piccadilly to St James's Street and so to the Chapel Royal. This procession consisted of twelve open state landaus, each drawn by four cream-coloured horses. Seated two by two in these landaus were almost all the royal persons we have yet encountered, and several, like the Tsarevitch Nicholas, whom we have not. Special cheers greeted the Duke of Cambridge, who with his sister, the Grand Duchess of Mecklenburg-Strelitz, and his brother-in-law, the Grand Duke, occupied the fourth carriage. The twelfth and last landau was greeted with deafening applause—for in this landau the sad Princess of Wales, ethereal in white satin and shimmering with diamonds in the sunlight, was wafted by like some spirit from another world. The Princess of Wales looked wan and mournful, but every now and then a charming smile flitted over her pale features, when she realised the warmth of the reception awarded her by the serried ranks of people marshalled beneath the full-blown plane-trees and upon the dry brown grass of the Green Park.

The second procession, that of the bridegroom with his father and their suite left the Palace at eleven-forty-five. Next followed the Queen's procession. The Queen drove in the 'Glass Coach' attended by the Great Officers of State and by a Sovereign's Escort of the Household Cavalry. 'I drove in a sort of state coach with many windows', the Queen wrote afterwards to the Empress Frederick, '& 4 of the Creams, but the heat was perfectly awful.'17 Also in the Queen's coach there drove—ecstatic, beaming, triumphant—Princess Mary Adelaide. The Duchess of Teck was now sixty, and this was her finest hour. The secret hopes, the anxious cares, the disappointments of a quarter of a century were that summer's day being crowned by total success. This was, in fact, the apotheosis of Princess Mary Adelaide. Her passage, beside the Queen, to the Chapel Royal was greeted by roar upon roar from the Londoners she loved.

The final procession was that of the bride. Supported by her father, the Duke of Teck, and her eldest brother, Prince Adolphus, Her Serene Highness Princess May of Teck was seated in the last carriage of this procession. In her simple dress of white and silver, and her small lace veil fastened with a diamond Rose of York, she greeted the crowd's applause with her 'sideways smile', and with a little nervous gesture of her white-gloved right hand.

At the doors of the Chapel Royal a hitch occurred. It had been overlooked by those preparing this complex cavalcade of royalties that the Queen, taking the short route down the Mall to St James's Palace, would be liable to arrive before anyone else. This is exactly what happened. Instead of arriving last (the Sovereign's correct position on all such occasions) the Queen reached the Chapel first, and there was only one gentleman usher to receive her. Princess Mary Adelaide stepped into the breach. Indicating to her Queen and cousin a room to the left of the Chapel, in which she suggested Her Majesty should wait, the Duchess of Teck, with Miss Thesiger in attendance, swept rapidly and imperiously up the aisle to assume her station by the altar. Miss Thesiger was following her when she felt a little tug at her skirt. She heard a voice saying firmly 'I am going first', and the Queen advanced alone, passing Princess Mary Adelaide—a little old lady leaning heavily on a stick, her inscrutable light-blue eyes glancing to right and left, a white lace bonnet nodding on her head. 'H M was not at all perturbed by the incident, only saying that she was glad it had happened so, for it was very amusing to see everyone come in.'[18]

The Queen of Denmark—Droning Louise of Rumpenheim associations—was the next to arrive, with her grandson the Tsarevitch and the Princess of Wales. They were speedily followed by the bridegroom and his father. Last came the bride with her attendant bridesmaids. Leaning stiffly on her father's arm, Princess May gave little twitching smiles to those she recognised amongst the guests in the Chapel as she advanced towards the altar. 'Dear May looked so pretty & quiet & dignified', wrote Queen Victoria. 'She was vy. simply & prettily dressed—& wore her Mother's Veil lace.—The Bridesmaids looked vy. sweet in white satin, with a little pink & red rose on the shoulder & some small bows of the same on the shoes.'[19] Prince George gave his answers distinctly, 'while May, though quite self-possessed, spoke very low'.[20]

At the end of the short wedding service, the royalties returned in state to Buckingham Palace. Princess Mary Adelaide drove once more alone with the Queen in her carriage. Her excitement was now running away with her, and her jovial, frantically waving figure wholly eclipsed that of the tiny widowed Queen, whose vague, tremulous efforts to acknowledge the thunder of the crowd were totally obscured by the robust and unbridled enthusiasm of her cousin, Princess Mary Adelaide.

Here we may with the greatest confidence hand ourselves over to another eye-witness, who has a good deal to say. Lady Geraldine Somerset has at times played for us the obliging part of a Greek chorus: she will now act in the capacity of one of those radio reporters, to whom listeners are switched in the middle of a news programme. Only, unlike the radio reporter of some scene in a distant part of the globe, Lady Geraldine speaks to us (and with the greatest clarity) not from far away but from long ago:

'May's Wedding Day!' Lady Geraldine wrote in her Journal on the night of 6 July 1893, 'the greatest success ever seen or heard of! not a hitch from first to last, not an if or a but!! everything went *absolutely à souhait!* first of all it was the *most heavenly* day ever *could* be—such a summer's day as you get solely and only in England—not the heavy oppressive atmosphere of yesterday, but the *most brilliant* glorious *really* tropical sunshine with tropical heat,—yet with it mercifully air from time to time refreshed one and recovered one! quite perfection. I was up at 6 and breakfasted at 8 . . . arrayed in the beautiful grey satin . . . the town was alive!! swarms everywhere! but the police arrangements so good, the moment I showed my pass card I had not the least difficulty in getting through! Piccadilly was beautifully decorated; but anything to equal the loveliness of St James's Street I never saw—it was like a bower from end to end . . . garlands of green across and across between the Venetian masts with bracelets of flowers suspended from them, *too* pretty.

'I went to the Household pew in the Chapel Royal . . . it was all so admirably arranged I think everybody in the Chapel could see well! The first to enter the Chapel was the Queen followed by P[rincess] M[ary Adelaide] who drove *in* the Queen's carriage from Buckingham Palace!! will her head be still on her shoulders tomorrow! I believe it will have expanded and blown to the moon!!—The Princess of Wales looked *more lovely*—than ever!—none can approach her! but I was sorry for her today. May with the Duke of York standing at the Altar!! and for the Princess *what pain.*

'What was *extremely* pretty to see was, the very profound bow or curtsey each one of the Royalties made to the Queen as they came to the *haut pas* and the Prince [of Wales] having first made her his bow then kissed her hand and kissed her. Two things displeased me about May's *entrée*, first that she was not veiled *at all*!! her veil hung in a little tiny narrow strip but a couple of inches wide *quite* at the *back* of her head only like an elongated lappet! secondly that instead of coming in the *exquisite, ideal* way the Pss. of Wales did at her wedding with her eyes *cast down*—too prettily—May looked right and left and slightly bowed to her acquaintance! a great mistake. The children bridesmaids were too delicious.

'When the ceremony was over and all the Royalties had departed we had a tremendous block getting away—got to Buckingham Palace where ensued a very long wait. At length there was a movement which became a crush! to the end—we all by this time famished, after our 8 o'clock breakfasts, saw a room most temptingly spread with round tables covered with food, at the open door of which we were stopped in the most tantalus fashion! Eventually we saw all the Royalties, from the next room, defiling in two and two into the tempting room and settling themselves at the tables—whereupon the doors were shut. And then at last we all went on to the Ball Room, where were some five or six standing buffets—at which we found much needed refreshment.

'At length getting hold of Lord Carrington we asked whether the Queen was not going to make a *tournée?* and found NO! that "all was at an end and over! and we could go home when we liked!" The Duke had just moved off when in came Dolly, we consulted him as to our seeing her go and he advised us to come to the balcony of P[rincess] M[ary Adelaide's] sitting-room and led us through 2 miles of corridors! till we got to her room which was the very central balcony of the whole façade of the Palace. We were in clover,—till one of the pages came to say the Queen was coming to this balcony to see them go!! out we rushed not knowing whither to go!!—found ourselves in the corridor amid a mass of Princesses—further we spied Mlle Bricka—so we rushed to join them,—and found it was just opposite the door of May's room where she was changing her dress. After a longish delay she came out in a cream coloured gown trimmed with gold—with her father, mother, brothers and P[rincess] A[ugusta] with whom I had a little talk. May kissed us all and went off—we saw her and the Duke of York get into the carriage receive the shower of slippers and drive *au pas* round the Quadrangle amid cheers and as they passed under the portico we rushed into the bedroom and from the balcony saw the Prince [of Wales], the Duke of Edinbro: the Duke [of Cambridge]! and all the Princes standing round the *grandes grilles* of the outer railing and as the Duke and Duchess of York drove into the Mall shower them with rice! Then they drove along the Mall with the magnificent Blues amid ringing cheers.'[21]

Also standing with Queen Victoria on the central balcony of the Palace were the Duke and Duchess of Teck. 'Poor Franz sobbed bitterly when Auld Lang Syne was played as they drove away. It is a horrid moment', the Queen wrote.[22] Princess Mary Adelaide likewise broke down. 'The dear Queen was perfectly angelic', she wrote to her daughter next day, '& held Papa's hand all the time, while on the balcony; on which I remained seated long after the escort had passed out of sight & the *hum* of the cheers had died away, & most of the family had departed, watching with Arthur & Papa the troops go by & the crowds disperse—Then slowly and sadly I undressed; had tea *sola* in the large centre room & finally went for a drive with Papa in our barouche.'[23]

Princess Mary Adelaide's life's dream was fulfilled. Her only daughter would one day be Queen of England. Like some great artist who has accomplished his last and finest work of art, there was little more for Princess Mary Adelaide to do on earth. From this moment of complete achievement her health began to decline. Life without her 'May'—but alone with the ailing and irritable Duke of Teck—held few charms for her. 'What Mary will do without May, I cannot think', wrote Queen Victoria, 'for she is her right hand.'[24] The fair, the sage, the hopeful young Duchess of York now stands full in the limelight, which glistens on the gold braid of her white dress and on her golden hair. Around her mother, the lovable and valiant Princess Mary Adelaide, the shades of night are slowly gathering. She has only four more years to live.

III

Their Royal Highnesses the Duke of York, who had exchanged his naval uniform for a frock coat and top hat, and the Duchess of York in a dress of cream-white Irish poplin braided with gold, a little shoulder cape of the same white poplin and over this a similar cape in lace, on her head a small golden bonnet trimmed with white ostrich plumes and white rosebuds, and tied under the chin with white velvet strings, drove through the densely-thronged City to Liverpool Street. Here they got into the train for Sandringham. At Wolferton station an open carriage, with an escort of the Royal Suffolk Volunteers, awaited them. They drove from Wolferton to York Cottage on the Sandringham estate, which was to be their country home for the next thirty-three years. The road from Wolferton was grey with dust, which the horses' hooves disturbed. When they reached the front door of their cottage Prince George's frock coat was white with dust, while Princess May's Irish poplin and lace cape had turned a blackish-grey. They were both in the last stages of exhaustion.

Sandringham was, under all the circumstances, an odd choice for the Yorks' honeymoon. 'The young people go to Sandringham to the Cottage after the Wedding wh. I regret & think rather *unlucky* & sad', wrote Queen Victoria to her eldest daughter.[25]

BOOK TWO

DUCHESS OF YORK

1893–1901

CHAPTER ONE

LOVE IN A COTTAGE

———

IT WAS NINE O'CLOCK of that July night, 1893, when the Duke of York and his bride, in the tired and dusty state we have just witnessed, reached York Cottage, Sandringham. When the front door closed behind her, Princess May found herself standing in a minute, low-ceilinged hallway, with a door on her right and a door on her left. A short dim passage stretched before her. Beyond the left-hand doorway a small staircase wound up to the first and second floors.

Her Royal Highness wearily mounted this unpretentious flight of stairs, turned to the right on the first floor and immediately found herself in her bedroom, which overlooked a pond upon which the wild duck were quacking in the dusk. Next to this bedroom was Her Royal Highness's little dressing-room, fitted up with white-painted shelves and cupboards, and containing a capacious safe for jewellery. Here, that first evening, Her Royal Highness found Tatry, her dresser from White Lodge days, a temperamental elderly Frenchwoman with a dark yellow face, a cottage-loaf coiffure, and screwed-up, sharp-seeing eyes behind wire-framed spectacles. Also on the first floor was the Duchess of York's boudoir—or as Princess Mary Adelaide called it, 'May's sanctum *orné*'.

York Cottage stands upon the brink of a reed-choked pond in one corner of the Sandringham deer park, some five minutes walk from Sandringham House. This pond, which the inmates of York Cottage dignified by the name of 'The Lake', teems with roach, and has an island in it, where rhododendrons glowed magenta that July. A hooped bridge connects the strip of lawn before the cottage with the island, from which a leaden pelican stares down into the water in a melancholy way. Beyond the pond and island stretches the park of Sandringham, in which Japanese deer then roamed. Such was the outlook from the Duchess of York's bedroom window. It was hardly an improvement on her charming airy apartments at White Lodge. Her Royal Highness felt both tired and strange.

The Prince of Wales had given York Cottage to his son as a wedding-present; the little house, and the ground on which it stood, now belonged to Prince George. Formerly known as 'The Bachelors' Cottage', the queer little building had been designed to house the overflow of male guests from the 'Big House' at Sandringham. The plans had been drawn up by a Colonel Edis, a retired officer who was the Prince of Wales's favoured architect, and boasted of this Royal connection in his London club. Doubtless, Colonel Edis had much to recommend him, but there was one drawback about employing him in the capacity in which the Prince of Wales had done: Colonel Edis was not really an architect at all.

The Bachelors' Cottage had been odd enough before it was altered to house the Duke and Duchess of York; by the time Colonel Edis had done his best upon it, it was odder still. As the years went by, and the York family increased in size, haphazard additions, dictated by necessity, were made to York Cottage. It became a rabbit-warren of tiny rooms connected by narrow passages, in which Royal pages and tall footmen would sit or stand, blocking the way.

Colonel Edis had conceived this bijou residence in several styles— Tudor black-and-white, Victorian Gothic, 'the attractive local stone-layering', and a certain element of pebble-dash and rough-cast. Outside, York Cottage was all gables and hexagonal turrets and beams and tiny balconies. It resembled those improbable houses which children can concoct with a box of Swiss or German toy bricks. Inside, at the date of the Yorks' marriage, the space at York Cottage was noticeably restricted: on the ground-floor was a drawing-room, which could be so to speak extended outwards on to the lawn on sunny days by affixing a big awning over the French windows; a dining-room with a bay for the breakfast table; and Prince George's study, which lay to the left of the front door, was pitch dark from the laurels which pressed against its little windows, and had stretched upon the walls the scarlet cloth then used for French uniforms. Opposite this room was another small one used as a reception room for visitors. The kitchens were in the basement. The whole house reeked, before each meal, of food. There was an insufficient number of baths.

It was in this cottage that Prince George and Princess May— become successively Duke and Duchess of York, Prince and Princess of Wales and King and Queen of England—lived for thirty-three years. Prince George adored York Cottage. Despite the sturdy protests of his devoted secretary Sir Arthur Bigge* who considered the place unsuitably small for its purpose, the Duke clung to it. He very much disliked entertaining, and the restricted space at York Cottage provided an excellent excuse for his not doing so. Also, like his cousin the ill-fated Tsar Nicholas II, who preferred the tiniest rooms at Tsarskoe Selo to any other apartments in his numerous palaces, the Duke of York genuinely liked small rooms, for they reminded him of the cabins of ships in which his early youth had been so cheerily passed. 'The King who loves small rooms in a cottage is miserable in a huge room here—Gobelins tapestry, huge panelling, Grinling Gibbons carving', Sir Frederick Ponsonby wrote to his wife from Chatsworth, in December 1913. 'It is not unlike a room at Hampton Court. . . . The Queen however likes the *cadre* and is quite happy.'[1]

II

Princess Mary Adelaide had told Miss Ella Taylor, if we remember, that Princess May 'makes herself happy wherever she is'.[2] Princess May was now determined to think York Cottage 'charming', and this in spite of her justifiable irritation at finding that the whole house had already been done up and furnished by Prince George without any reference to her taste. She had looked forward to choosing, to buying, to arranging: everything had been done for her by the Duke of York, who considered that he had thus saved Princess May trouble. He could not comprehend why she did not seem grateful to him for his forethought.

In December 1892, Prince George had been over York Cottage several times with 'Maple's man', and, assisted by his father the Prince of Wales, and by his eldest sister Princess Louise, Duchess of Fife, he had chosen patterns for all carpets and wallpapers. The furniture was also bought from Maple's, and was very modern. Maple, who had supplied pieces of furniture for some of the main rooms at White Lodge, was a London emporium much patronised by English and European royalties: 'We spent I don't know how many hours at Maple & Liberty!' the Crown Princess of Greece wrote to her mother

* Arthur Bigge (1849–1931), who had been introduced to Queen Victoria by the Empress Eugénie in 1880, was assistant to Sir Henry Ponsonby from that year until 1895, when he succeeded Ponsonby as Principal Private Secretary to the Queen. From 1901 until his death in 1931 he was Private Secretary to the Duke of York, serving him both when he became Prince of Wales and King. He was created Lord Stamfordham in 1911.

from London in July 1896. 'I screamed at the things to Tino's horror, but they were too lovely! *No* those shops I go mad in them! I would be ruined if I lived here longer! — Divine shops!'3 The Crown Princess of Greece was buying furniture for an English cottage she was building in the woods of Tatoi, above Athens. In 1895 she had written to ask her mother to obtain for her the plans of the 'adorable' cottage at Osborne: 'Georgie sent us kindly the plans of his little house at Sandringham', she explained. Crown Princess Sophie wished to 'compare which is best!'4

Princess May, then, found to her real chagrin and disappointment that York Cottage was already fully furnished and that the furniture was there to stay. With the exception of some pieces still being made in Edinburgh for the drawing-room, the first home of her own she had ever had was thrust on her complete. This would have annoyed any bride; but to Princess May, who had inherited all her father's love for arranging rooms, it was indeed frustrating. There was a further, much more serious, disadvantage to York Cottage. Living in it meant that Princess May was cheek by jowl with her parents-in-law.

'I am sorry their Country Quarters are so near Sandringham, it mixes them up so entirely with the present Wales surroundings,' the perspicacious old Grand Duchess Augusta wrote to her brother the Duke of Cambridge, 'they had far better have their own Entourage & friends.'5 York Cottage might have been specifically sited and planned to facilitate unannounced calls from the members of the Wales family at any moment of the day or night. There was no sense of privacy, inside or out, about York Cottage.

The honeymoon of Prince George and Princess May in these cramped surroundings was interrupted after thirteen days by the arrival at Sandringham House of the Prince and Princess of Wales with their two younger daughters Princesses Maud and Victoria, the King and Queen of Denmark and Prince Valdemar of Denmark. For the next eight days York Cottage was subject to perpetual jolly invasions by members of this party. The Princess of Wales would drop in at tea-time, her many dogs cavorting at her heels, or send a note asking the young couple up to the 'Big House' for dinner, followed by a game of *Kegelspiel*—for a bowling alley on the pattern of that at Rumpen-heim had early been installed in Sandringham House. On one occasion the Princess and her two daughters even came and sat with the Duke and Duchess of York while they were having their breakfast in the turret-alcove of their dining-room.

It must have been during this week at Sandringham that a suspicion, soon a certainty, first crossed the Princess of Wales's mind: it seemed as though she were no more the object of her son's undivided affection. Not long after this discovery a change was evident in the adjectives which the Princess of Wales applied to her daughter-in-law: 'sweet May' was now 'poor May'. This new attitude proved infectious. It was adopted by Princess May's unmarried sisters-in-law, Princess Victoria and Princess Maud. They, who had rated Princess May perfect before her marriage, now began to criticise her behind her back. 'Now do try to talk to May at dinner, though one knows she is deadly dull', Princess Victoria once said to a guest at Windsor; and there was much more in the same vein. The very fact that Prince George's wife was a young woman of superior intelligence, of thoughtful mind and wide intellectual interests formed a silent reproach to the Princess of Wales and her daughters. When Queen Victoria had written to Princess May: 'the trials of life *begin* with marriage'[6] she had, as the young Duchess of York was now learning, written nothing but the truth.

'I sometimes think that just after we were married we were not left alone enough & had not the opportunity of learning to understand each other as quickly as we might otherwise have done', Princess May wrote to her husband, with her customary good sense, in August 1894, '& this led to so many little rubs which might have been avoided. You see we are both terribly sensitive & the slightest sharp word said by one to the other immediately gave offence & I fear that neither you nor I forget those things in a hurry.'[7]

III

If engagements are notoriously trying to the nerves, honeymoons can often prove even more so. The circumstances of Princess May's honeymoon were almost the reverse of ideal. The day after their arrival at York Cottage there was a very bad thunderstorm. Princess May had always been allergic to thunder, which frightened her and made her feel ill. The succeeding days were at once warm and rainy. Often they could not go outside the cottage, but remained cooped up in the tiny rooms. Neither of them was much given to self-expression. Long though they had known each other, it took some time for their mutual shyness to evaporate.

Prince George was accustomed either to the manners of the quarter-deck, or else to the uncritical praise and chaffing endearments which his mother and his sisters showered upon him. He now found himself, alone in a small cottage in the rain, with a highly sensitive and cultivated girl who did not care for naval manners, and was far too intelligent and honest to indulge in flattery or pretend that she agreed with him when she, quite frequently, did not. Prince George felt at a loss, and sometimes he reacted like a spoiled child. It is to Princess May's singular credit that, under these conditions, and in the first weeks of their marriage, her husband fell deeply in love with her. By nature direct and monogamous, he never wavered from this devotion for the rest of his life.

'I know I am, at least I am vain enough to think that I am capable of loving anybody (who returns my love) with all my heart and soul, & I am sure I have found that person in my sweet little May', Prince George wrote to his wife some months after the honeymoon. 'You know by this time that I never do anything by halves, when I asked you to marry me, I was very fond of you, but not very much in love with you, but I saw in *you* the person I was capable of loving most deeply, if you only returned that love. . . . I have tried to understand you & to know you, & with the happy result that I know now that I do *love* you darling girl with all my *heart*, & am simply *devoted* to you. . . . I *adore you sweet May*, I can't say more than that.'[8] Is it not a most remarkable tribute to Princess May's qualities of mind and soul that she had been able not only to cope with the difficulties offered by her own and her husband's shyness and differing tastes but to inspire such a true and lasting devotion in Prince George? But Princess May had had to contend with difficulties all her young life. Her experiences now stood her in admirable stead.

The first week of the honeymoon passed quickly. In between showers they went out driving in a new carriage given them by the people on the Sandringham estate; when it poured they re-hung pictures, moved furniture, played cards, or read. Princess May discovered that her husband liked reading aloud; this was a habit he had acquired at Marlborough House, when he would read aloud to his mother the Princess of Wales while her hair was being done at eleven o'clock in the morning.

Georgie is a dear . . . he adores me which is touching [Princess May wrote to Mme Bricka in the first week of the honeymoon]. He likes reading to people so I jumped at this & he is going to read me some of his favourite books—Yesterday he read part of Greville's memoirs to me, most amusing —It makes life *very* pleasant doing things together in this way & I am very glad I am married & don't feel at all strange, in fact I feel as if I had been married for years & quite settled down—This cottage is very nice but very small, however I think we can make it charming.9

Princess May also wrote to the Duchess of Teck about how much they were enjoying Greville's 'amusing tho' spiteful' memoirs. Princess Mary Adelaide told her sister the Grand Duchess, who despatched a warning note to York Cottage: 'I hear you are reading Greville's *Mémoires*, they are entertaining but full of lies, which I can certify having lived through a great part of the time he so falsely relates.'10 'Your Parents', wrote Aunt Augusta in the same letter, 'still in the whirlpool of London life have borne up well after parting from their dear child; I dread what the return to White Lodge will be! yet the happy letters from both of you give them so much pleasure, that your happiness will prove their best support!'

The Duke and Duchess of Teck did not visit York Cottage until November of the year in which their daughter became Duchess of York. They then went and stayed at the Cottage for some days, which included Princess Mary Adelaide's birthday. The Yorks' stables, designed to hold sixteen horses, were just being completed; Princess Mary Adelaide thought these stables too large for the Cottage, just as she thought the Cottage too small for the Yorks. 'This is the *perfection* of an *ideal* Cottage! but far too small for their establishment & requirements', she wrote to Prince Alge. '*Each room* is *charming* in its way & everything is in perfect taste & most cosy & comfortable —I delight in my bedroom, but I doubt if it be as large as our pink violet room!'11

To Princess Mary Adelaide it was perfectly clear what York Cottage needed: it needed enlarging. If her daughter was condemned to live in this ornate hutch on the Sandringham estate, the least the Prince and Princess of Wales could do would be to add some rooms to it. 'We had a *comfortable*, tho' blowy journey, through a great part of which, we all 3 *dozed*!' Princess Mary Adelaide wrote to her daughter in February 1894, after another visit to York Cottage, '& on reaching London, I drove off to Marlb. H. with Falbe. . . . "Motherdear" was expecting me & I was shown into the pretty tapestry room downstairs, where she very soon joined me—She was *most sensible* about the adding on to York Cottage . . . so I hope I have put all satisfactorily *en train*!'12 The result of these negotiations was that the Prince of Wales readily agreed to the first of a series of enlargements of York

Cottage, and himself suggested the addition of a spacious billiard-room—'which', Prince George wrote to his wife, 'would of course be a charming idea & so useful as a smoking room, but it all depends on the money'.[13]

Princess May had succeeded in imposing a semblance of her own taste upon certain of the rooms at York Cottage, but she sometimes found that her arrangements were liable to alteration by her mother-in-law the Princess of Wales:

Motherdear, sisters & Charlotte* lunched with me today, for a change as we lunched with them yesterday [the Duke of York wrote to his wife, then in London, in October 1894]. Mama afterwards moved the furniture in the drawing room, which certainly gives ever so much more room, & I think looks much prettier, of course if you don't like it . . . we can move it all back again in a minute, we took nothing out of the room nor put nothing new in.[14]

To this piece of news Princess May sent a tactful but not unadroit reply:

I am so glad 'Motherdear' tried to arrange our drawing room she has so much taste, & it certainly looked much too stiff, only I thought that as the Scotch furniture had not come, it was scarcely worth while to waste a lot of time arranging it when [it will] have to be changed.[15]

That 'quiet determination' which Princess May had first displayed as a girl of sixteen in Florence had now matured. It came in very useful to her in the domestic politics of her relations with her husband's family, although it did not necessarily increase her popularity with them.

When all the Waleses were at the 'Big House' surrounded by their smart London friends, the Duchess of York's position was a solitary one. Quiet and serious, anxious to be allowed to read in peace and to go on improving her mind, she had to compete single-handed with all the rattle and fun up at the Big House. Nevertheless she and her husband were building up between them a solid and secure relationship which no amount of chaff or criticism from any direction whatsoever could affect.

* Miss Charlotte Knollys (1835–1930) was the sister of Sir Francis Knollys, later Lord Knollys (1837–1924), Private Secretary to King Edward VII. Miss Knollys was lady-in-waiting to Queen Alexandra from 1870 until the Queen's death, and was her inseparable friend. Miss Knollys was also concerned with the education of the three Wales Princesses.

IV

There was a new annoyance in store for Princess May on her honeymoon. She had to go into full mourning. On 18 July she received a letter from her mother telling her that the younger of the Teck aunts, Princess Amélie, Countess von Hügel, was dangerously ill. '*Amélie schwer erkrankt*', Princess Claudine had telegraphed from Reinthal. Countess von Hügel died on the 20th, after a new operation for malignant tumour. 'I imagine', wrote the Duchess of Teck in a long letter to Queen Victoria, who always relished clinical detail, 'mortification must have set in before the end.'[16]

Princess May was sorry to hear of her Aunt Amélie's death, but she was most concerned over its effect upon her father. 'I am so grieved for dear Papa to whom it will be such a sorrow. . . . Fancy poor me having to go into mourning, with all my new coloured gowns, such an expense too as I have so few black clothes', she wrote to her mother. 'I have sent home for the things I left there, the very things you scolded me for *not* giving to Tatry.'[17] Although black suited Princess May, she hated to wear it. It was galling to have to go about again in the mourning dresses dating from Prince Eddy's death, just when she wanted to look her best in her lovely new clothes. Her full mourning for Princess Amélie of Teck was, however, temporarily lightened during the first two weeks in August. Regardless of the honeymoon, Queen Victoria told the Duke and Duchess of York that she expected them at Osborne, to help to entertain their cousin, Wilhelm II, the German Emperor.

On her honeymoon at York Cottage Princess May had become aware of the web of personal problems which was waiting for her in her married life. At Osborne she experienced for the first time the full and public splendours of her new position.

CHAPTER TWO

THE POWER
AND THE GLORY

———————

'THIS HAS BEEN a vy gay week—Cowes crowded with people', Queen Victoria wrote on 5 August 1893. 'Dear Georgie & May had a vy pretty & hearty reception on Monday Evg.—Sailors, flags—900 School Children—Soldiers fm Trinity Pier almost—up the Hills to the Lodge & our Tenants inside the grounds. The Evg. was bright & fine.'¹

This reception at Cowes was Princess May's first taste of the kind of public life she would now constantly be leading as Duchess of York. All the ships in Cowes roads were jaunty with flags in honour of the newly-wedded pair. Travelling down from London with an equerry and a lady-in-waiting the Yorks had been met at Portsmouth station by the Duke of Connaught and by Lord Clanwilliam. They crossed to the Isle of Wight in the *Alberta*, and were ceremonially welcomed ashore at Trinity Pier by the Prince of Wales, his nephew the Emperor of Germany and other royalties. A carriage with four horses took them swiftly up the decorated road to Osborne House, where they were received at the entrance by the Queen herself, attended by Princess Louise, Duchess of Argyll, the Duchess of Connaught, Princess Victoria of Schleswig-Holstein and 'the little Connaughts & Bats'.* 'After a short talk', Princess May wrote to her mother, 'we were shown our rooms downstairs, under those we had last year, & opening on to the pretty terrace. We each have a sitting & dressing room—After tea I drove with Grandmama in the grounds, this place is looking quite lovely, so fresh & green, & I am quite in love with it. It was a perfect evening. . . .'²

From the windows of these ground-floor rooms, Princess May could gaze out across the terrace, the lawns and the scented shrubs to the gap of bright blue sea. The soft splash of the fountain was the

* i.e. the children of the Duke and Duchess of Connaught and of Prince and Princess Henry of Battenberg.

only sound upon the evening air. Osborne was at its best in summer-time, when the great magnolias, which smelt of lemons, were withering upon the Italianate terrace, and the red rambler roses, then a novelty, were in flower. 'There was also jasmine on those terraces', writes one of the Queen's granddaughters, 'and jasmine has always filled me with a sort of ecstasy.'3 'I wish you could look out at the sea with me today out of my window', wrote the Empress Frederick, from Osborne, earlier in that same year, 1893. 'It is like a turquoise—and the long soft shadows under the evergreens and the velvety turf—and the delicate tracing of the branches of the oaks—chestnuts &c . . . look lovely!—All the little white sails of the fishing boats on the Solent! —How I love this view—.'4 The Empress Frederick, a large part of whose childhood had been spent at Osborne, liked to walk along the private beach there, collecting shells. 'I took a long walk— . . . Through the woods & down by the sea! The water was gently rippling —with a little lazy splash on the beach—and the birds were singing.' 'Oh I did wish Fischy could have seen all the lovely green fields & turf and the *quantities* of evergreens!' the Empress wrote to her daughter the Princess Friedrich-Karl of Hesse. 'I am never tired of going down to the beach—and wandering in the wood—& listening to the Birds!'5

Queen Victoria's routine at Osborne was as stringent as that at Balmoral, but she was, inevitably, less secluded. She might be seen each morning breakfasting out in the garden, under a green-fringed parasol tent, surrounded by her Indian servants, her highlanders, and her dogs, with perhaps one or two of her daughters 'in nervous attendance' and a lady-in-waiting clad in black. Every object on the Queen's breakfast table, except her cup and saucer but including her egg-cup, was made of solid gold. Princess May shared these open-air breakfasts: 'Every morning at breakfast Grandmama asks me "Have you heard from Mama yet?"'—to which I am obliged to say no which is rather sad for I am simply longing to get *one* line from you',6 she wrote that August to her mother, then taking the cure at Bad Neuenahr.

'I cannot say how much pleased I am & we all are with dear May', wrote Queen Victoria during this visit. 'She is so unaffected & sensible, & so very distinguished & dignified in her manner—& vy civil to every one.—She is vy pretty & the more you see her, the more I like & admire her. . . . I really feel *quite happy* abt this dear young *ménage*—whom may God bless & protect.'7 Queen Victoria was now even more lame than she had been when Princess May and Prince

Dolly had stayed with her at Balmoral in 1891: 'Beloved Grandmama', wrote the Empress Frederick in the spring of 1893, 'is looking *very* well—in the face—her smile & voice & complexion as young as 20 years ago,—but she has great difficulty in moving and getting about —in getting up from her chair.'[8] At Osborne the Queen would drive at a foot's pace about the grounds in her chair-carriage, drawn by a pony which was the exact replica in miniature of the four cream-coloured horses which drew her carriages in London. After dinner, she would remain seated at a round table near the door of the drawing-room, any guests with whom she wished to speak being ushered up to her and subsequently ushered away again.

During these two weeks at Osborne in August 1893, Queen Victoria deliberately made a great fuss of the young Duchess of York, thrusting her to the fore, and implicitly indicating to her what her position now meant. The Queen's daughetrs were instructed to follow the same course: '*All* the Aunts push me on & make such a fuss about me while I laugh in my sleeve & say to myself "Dear me how times have changed, 'tis a funny world"—Well one lives & learns!'[9] Princess May confided to her mother. Queen Victoria had sent the Duchess of Teck a 'nice telegram' about Princess May. 'I feel much flattered at the nice tel. she sent you about me', wrote Princess May. 'She goes on telling "Motherdear" that I look so distinguished & am so nice, to which she (Motherdear) replies "I found that out years ago & told you so". Rather amusing. Not?'[10]

On the evening of their arrival at Osborne House, 31 July, there was a great dinner-party in the Indian Room there. This Indian Room had only been completed the year before. It had been thoughtfully planned, and was much admired. The room was large, and vaguely Oriental; it was hung with Indian stuffs and lighted with electric bulbs concealed in some large blue vases given to the Queen by a body of Parsee merchants for her Golden Jubilee. The long table shone with silver, and was decorated with flowers in fine silver bowls. 'We were 55', wrote Princess May. 'The Indian Room is magnificent & it was such a pretty sight. I sat next to William who made himself most agreeable, Uncle Arthur sat on my other side. Fancy me, little me, sitting next to William, the place of honour!!! It seemed so strange. . . . After dinner great presentation of German suite & others, military, naval, etc. I talked my *best* German. We got away at 11.30.'[11]

It was a very gay fortnight. Princess May was always on show: 'I drove with her [the Queen] to West Cowes where the people wished to see me. The people were most civil', for example.[12] 'So you are pleased . . . with your reception at Osborne. . . ?' Aunt Augusta enquired from Neu Strelitz, 'which I have been following daily in the Court Circular, as from the flaming descriptions in Cowes Articles. Poor Dear, to have married a Sailor! but he too is not quite firm on Sea; oh! it is always a nasty Element, though so grand to look upon from a distance!'[13] These last remarks bore reference to the fact that Princess May was always very sea-sick; when she was on board a ship she had a constant feeling of constriction at the back of her neck and a pain behind her eyes. This affliction made her later ocean voyages with her husband a great trial to her.

Princess May enjoyed these weeks on the Isle of Wight, for everyone laid themselves out to please her, and she was able for the moment to forget the more complex aspects of her marriage. She wrote her mother long accounts of all her doings, including descriptions of her own clothes:

You may like to know that the 1st evening at dinner I wore my white *broché* satin low with the Iveagh's tiara, Gdmama's necklace, the Kensington bow in front of the bodice, & the Warwicks' sun on the side. I wish you had seen me, I think you wld have thought I looked tidy. The 2d evening I wore Mrs Mason's black square gown, which is lovely & last night a lovely little grey gown from Mangas, with the combined counties pearls, & Richmond's pearl & diamond brooch in my hair.[14]

I I

At Cowes, most of the Royal Family lived aboard their yachts. The Prince and Princess of Wales, with Princess Victoria and Princess Maud, were on the *Osborne*. Princess May would visit her mother-in-law and her sisters-in-law, who at Cowes were always dressed in white and wore yachting caps, and whose cabins were strewn with trinkets, and, of course, filled with photographs. Also at Cowes was the Imperial German yacht, *Hohenzollern*. This housed the Kaiser and his suite and had its own band.

At this period Kaiser Wilhelm II was still liked by most of his English royal relations, from his grandmother Queen Victoria downwards. The Prince and Princess of Wales were in a minority in distrusting and disliking him. Princess May herself always liked 'William', and was pleased by the attentions he paid her, for he was a distinct admirer of his cousin George's bride. 'I think him looking well & less stout', Queen Victoria wrote of her German grandson to his mother, the Empress Frederick, this August of 1893.[15] In spite of his ferocious moustachios, and his uniforms, Kaiser Wilhelm II was not, visually, an imposing figure: 'ungraceful, nervous and plain' and lacking in 'atmosphere'.[16] But when he wished to charm, the Kaiser could be very winning. In February of that year he had been on a state visit to Neu Strelitz where, despite her Hanoverian and Guelphic loyalties, the old Grand Duchess had fallen under his spell. He always talked English with her and with the Grand Duke: 'quite like an *English* Nephew having but eyes and attention for *me* and Fritz',[17] the Grand Duchess wrote of a visit she and the Grand Duke had paid to the Emperor at Potsdam. On his arrival at Strelitz that February day in 1893 the Kaiser had embraced the Grand Duchess warmly:

At 12.30 the Train ran in, he jumped out of the Carriage *direct* into my arms!—he always has his fun with me—she coming next to be embraced. William II drove with Fritz & Dolphus—all three in Lancer Uniform— in an open Barouche with 4 horses 2 Outriders, then came a Chariot with the Empss & myself, Elly following with her Chicks and 9 Carriages with Suites besides, following ours, all in Red Liveries of course. Thank goodness the sun was shining brightly upon the snow. . . . Orders were showered about, '*de part et d'autre*' Dolphus getting the Hohenzollern Chain.[18]

Despite the antipathy between the Prince of Wales and the Emperor William—in itself one of the minor causes of the First World War— the Duke and Duchess of York kept up a friendly if intermittent relationship with the Kaiser, whom in 1900 they asked to be godfather to their third son Prince Henry, now Duke of Gloucester. In March 1908 they both went to Cologne, so that Prince George could inspect a German regiment, the 8th Cuirassiers, of which he had since 1902 been Colonel-in-Chief:

W. has made me Col. of the 8th Cuirassier Regt which is quartered at Deutz near Cologne the late Gd Duke of Weimar was their last Chief. You would be surprised to see yr spouse walking about with a helmet on which looks somewhat like an extinguisher on a candle, I feel like that too [Prince George wrote to Princess May from Berlin in January 1902]. Of course the uniform didn't fit & I have spent hours with different tailors trying on . . . & I have absolutely walked miles in the Schloss as W's rooms are at the other end of the Castle & every minute I have to come back & put on another uniform.[19]

'W. wishes at this moment to be extra civil, but without offence I fear it is only to . . . throw dust in our eyes—*his country* cannot disguise its *true* feelings against us—and all *his future* will show it with a vengeance',[20] wrote the Princess of Wales, in a letter very characteristic of the violent anti-Prussian sentiments which she wished to instil into her son.

To Princess May, with her youthful experiences of German courts, there was a certain glamour about the Kaiser. Sometimes she thought he made 'royalty ridiculous'[21] but on the whole, until the Great War, she had a respect and liking for him. The last time that she saw the Kaiser was in 1913, when, as King and Queen of England, she and her husband proceeded to Berlin to be present at the wedding of the Duke of Cumberland's son Ernest Augustus to the Kaiser's only daughter, the pretty and popular Princess Victoria Louise.

It was noticeable that after the Armistice of 1918, neither King George V nor Queen Mary was ever heard to say a harsh word about the ex-Kaiser. They felt sorry for him, and considered that in his Dutch retirement he behaved with dignity and restraint. In October 1938, the ex-Kaiser sent Queen Mary the first letter he had written to her since the war—a note of congratulation from 'Yours affte cousin —William' upon the Munich agreement, which both he and Queen Mary, in common with many other people, supposed would avert a Second World War. Queen Mary sent this note on to King George VI, asking him to have it placed amongst the Royal Archives:

Enclosed [she wrote] will touch and interest you as it did me, . . . Poor William he must have been horrified at the thought of another war between our 2 countries—I have written to him & told him I was sending on the letter to you.[22]

That summer of 1893 the possibility of a war between Germany and England did not cross the minds of those assembled so gaily, so happily, for Cowes Week. Only the news that Uncle Ernest Coburg was, at last, dying came to mar the pleasures and the animation of these August days; and, save for Queen Victoria whose brother-in-law he was, no one really cared much about 'terrible Uncle Ernest' Coburg. It was a week of flags, of bedecked yachts, bouquets and triumphal arches, of cheering and staring and clapping: and the heroine of it all was the graceful Duchess of York.

K

III

During their fortnight at Osborne, Princess May and her husband had both found time to give sittings to the Danish painter Tuxen, who had been commissioned to execute the official picture of their wedding in the Chapel Royal.* The Duchess of Teck looms large in Tuxen's picture, for she is seated on a chair almost in the centre of the canvas, and the spectator looks, as it were, over her shoulder towards the bride and her bevy of bridesmaids at the altar. Princess Mary Adelaide sat to Tuxen in the Armoury at St James's Palace, wearing her tiara and a 'low body': 'I like the arrangement of the picture very much & think it on the whole, very promising!' she wrote to her daughter. ' . . . by the time I had sat for an hour, or so, I was quite recognisable altho' not flattered!—What a pity, as I am to be such a prominent figure in the picture there can only be a *back*, or *side* view of my lovely person!'[23] The Tecks had first met Tuxen at Gmunden in 1884, when he had gone with them on that rather eventful expedition during which Princess Thyra, Duchess of Cumberland, and her pony had fallen through a plank bridge.

In 1893 Princess May was painted three times—by Heinrich von Angeli, who painted an oval head and shoulders portrait which the Queen had given to the Duchess of Teck; by Tuxen for the state wedding group; and by Luke Fildes. In 1895 Edward Hughes produced a large portrait in the grand manner, showing Princess May, dressed in yellow satin and muslin, and wearing many jewels, sitting rather daintily on a carved stone garden seat in the shade of a tree. Her right hand holds a bouquet of tea-roses in her lap, she leans her head pensively upon her left hand.

All this outburst of portraiture was one more symptom of the dignity of Princess May's new position. In earlier years she had merely sat to Thaddeus Jones for fun; now, as Duchess of York, she was being solemnly recorded for Posterity.

The Hughes portrait, which is not an attractive work of art—or which, to be strictly correct, is not a work of art at all—was suspended over the mantelpiece in Prince George's study in York House. It was so big that the cornice had to be cut away to fit the picture in. Prince George's desk was in the middle of his study facing the mantelpiece, and so he gazed up at the Hughes portrait every day. Access to this study, which was on the ground floor, could only be gained through

* See plate 13.

the room in which the Duchess of York dealt with her own correspondence at her own desk; when both sets of doors stood open, the Hughes picture appeared at the end of the vista. It was framed and glazed and from some angles its vast surface reflected the many little photographs and pictures of ships with which the Duke of York had covered the other walls of his room.

York Cottage, Sandringham, represented the private life of Princess May and her husband; the stage for their public life was York House, St James's Palace. At Sandringham they had an admirable chef, and their standard of living was very high; at York House it was sumptuous but economical. King George V is too often referred to by historians as 'a man of simple tastes'; it was but a comparative simplicity. King George was just as much a perfectionist in living as his father. He expected, and obtained, the ultimate degree of civilised English comfort and style in all the outward details of his life. Foreign royalties were amazed at the atmosphere of peace combined with ease and wealth which reigned in the various households of important members of the English Royal Family. There were none of the abrupt movements, the strident ejaculations, the spur-clicking, the general clatter, the exaggerated, noisy deference which surrounded the princes of Germany. Quiet but luxurious, a household such as that at York House outwardly resembled the household of a British nobleman. Its equivalent could be encountered nowhere in royal circles on the Continent.

In *A King's Story* the Duke of Windsor has admirably described the complex organism which in his youth formed a Royal Household —the Comptroller, the equerries, the ladies-in-waiting, the Private Secretaries, the legion of servants both indoors and in the stables. The object of all this retinue was to protect the Royalty in the centre of the hive from any form of avoidable anxiety and from crude contact with the outside world, so as to preserve Him or Her healthy, serene, and intact for the performance of Royal duties with the maximum of efficiency and the minimum of worry. Augustus Hare, who met the Duke of York staying at Elvedon in November 1895, wrote in a letter to Lord Halifax, afterwards published:

Anything more odious or annoying than being a prince certainly cannot be imagined. Such a wearisome round of dullest duties and painful 'pleasures' as it is their life's work to live in like a treadmill. Then, every fault of manner, far more of conduct and character is commented, dwelt on and exaggerated. I should be sorry for any Prince but am really dreadfully sorry for this one, as he would have been charming, and might have been extremely happy if the misfortune of his birth had not condemned him to the severe and miserable existence of princedom, in which all minor faults are uncorrected.[24]

Hare also remarked that 'princes have no chance—no chance at all—conversationally, as no one ever contradicts them; no subjects are aired but those which they choose for themselves, and the merest commonplaces from royal lips are listened to as if they were oracles'. It was to this ingrowing and unnatural form of living that Princess May now had to accustom herself. Her family and friends noticed a change in her manner: she rigidly suppressed her high spirits and became, if anything, even more reserved than before. The sense of being constantly watched haunted her, and she felt as self-conscious and as shy in public as she had in childhood in Taglioni's dancing room. One by one the barriers were going up between Princess May and the real world. It was not until the last decade of her life, during the 1939–1945 war, that Queen Mary managed happily to resume the sort of contact with ordinary men and women which she had experienced at White Lodge as a girl, and from which her marriage to the Duke of York had severed her.

What we might term the inner defence lines at York House consisted of a Private Secretary and equerries for the Duke of York, and ladies-in-waiting for the Duchess of York. At the time of her marriage it had become imperative for Princess May to select and appoint ladies-in-waiting. When she had almost become Duchess of Clarence and Avondale in 1891, Princess May had, with her mother's assistance, chosen two ladies, both of whom Queen Victoria thought far too young. 'I am in hopes', she had written to Princess Mary Adelaide in December 1891, 'that the Ladies for May have *not both* been *definitively* settled for they are really too young particularly Ldy Clementina Walsh, who is *not* 21—& the other is only 23!! *None* of the Pcesses who married ever had a Lady younger than themselves & *one* at least shld have been older. It is so necessary to have some one to be a help.'[25] This time, Princess May began modestly with only one lady-in-waiting, Lady Eva Greville. When in 1895 Lady Eva married a Warwickshire gentleman, Mr Frank Dugdale, she was from then on assisted at York House by Lady Mary Lygon, one of Lord Beauchamp's daughters with whom Princess May had made friends during her time at Malvern in 1891. In 1897 Princess Mary Adelaide's old friend and lady-in-waiting, Lady Katty Coke, was also gazetted to the Duchess of York's household, as an extra lady-in-waiting. When late in 1901 the Duke of York became Prince of Wales, and he and Princess May moved across the road to Marlborough House, the number of her ladies was again increased; and on King George's accession in 1910, she naturally appointed a full Queen Consort's Household, which included both ladies-in-waiting, who had in this case an ornamental or ceremonial function, and Women-of-the-Bedchamber, who did the work of answering those letters not dealt with by the Queen's Private Secretary. The Queen's ladies-in-waiting travelled to and from the Palace in two-horse broughams from the Royal stables, Women-of-the-Bedchamber in one-horse broughams. Queen Mary instituted a system of rosters for the Women-of-the-Bedchamber, since she had observed that her mother-in-law, Queen Alexandra, with only Miss Charlotte Knollys as her constant companion and amanuensis, had fallen completely under this lady's influence. At present, however, in York House in 1893, the Duchess of York was assisted by Lady Eva Greville alone.

'Little Bird Eva', as Princess May and her mother called Lady Eva Greville, was the only daughter of the fourth Earl of Warwick and was seven years older than her mistress, the Duchess of York. She was diminutive and somewhat plain, though very animated and amusing. She very soon became first-rate at her job. When Lady Eva became engaged to Mr Dugdale (who was subsequently incorporated into the York household) the Duchess of Teck was worried that 'the necessarily altered relations will not make every day life henceforth so easy to May, whom Eva *relieved* of so much—having so thoroughly worked herself into her position, as to be quite May's *right-hand*—May will now have to have 2 ladies! I wonder if her choice will fall on Clemmie Walsh, or if she will look out for an *unmarried* lady?'[26]

'Little Bird' was a great favourite with Princess Mary Adelaide, who rushed up to London one evening after dinner in May 1896 to be present at the birth of Lady Eva's first child, an event of which the Princess wrote her daughter a long and vivid account, characteristically ending this report on a sleepless night spent partly in Lady Eva's bedroom and partly nursing the new-born baby in the nursery: 'It was 6 before I got away . . . & I had a delightful drive home, in the early morning lovely, clear sunshine!'[27] After the First World War Lady Eva Dugdale had a stroke and had to retire from her position with the Queen. To Queen Mary's great sorrow she died in July 1940: 'Poor Eva Dugdale died yesterday, I had known her for 55 years! Luckily I went to see her in May when I went to Salisbury, she was very ill then, so it is a happy release.'[28]

A part of the functions of Lady Eva and of the Duke of York's equerry, Colonel Derek Keppel, was to be present with the Duke and Duchess at meals, a tradition which, as the Duke of Windsor has pointed out, meant in years to come that the York children were hardly ever alone with their parents. At the beginning of the marriage however, before any of their children had yet appeared, the custom of having an equerry and a lady at meal-times meant that Prince George and Princess May were themselves seldom alone together, either at York Cottage, Sandringham, or at York House, St. James's.

IV

'So now you are installed at St James's dear old St James's!' Princess May's Aunt Augusta wrote to her from Strelitz in July 1893. 'I always now have it before my mind's eye, since I know you housed there! *ohiemé!* shall I ever be able to go there again? if so, *you* must take me there, all by ourselves, for I know I shall break down, and yet—I am sure dearest Mama would be glad to know *you* in her old Rooms. I shall not like to see *mine* inhabited by *"Dieu sait qui"*.'[29] The Grand Duchess harboured a real nostalgia for her mother's rooms at St James's Palace, now York House: 'what dear and often sad recollections are there for me and my very old fashioned heart, that clings to all that is *past*, this modern people will not understand', she wrote to Prince Dolly in 1895.[30] Other members of Princess May's family were not so enthusiastic: 'alas! St James' does not boast a *Sunny* room', Princess Mary Adelaide had written in 1875, after the Duchess of Cambridge's stroke.[31] 'This is a beastly house & I think very unhealthy', the Duke of York wrote to his wife in August 1895;[32] and, again, this time in 1899, 'I hate this house more than ever when you are away.'[33]

The fact is that York House was then, as it is now, an awkward house to live in. To begin with, it is not, like Marlborough House, a separate entity, standing in its own garden. York House forms but one part of the large, rambling, red-brick Tudor Palace of St James's, which, assembled round a series of courtyards, lies at the bottom of sloping St James's Street and has its garden frontage on the Mall. St James's Palace also contains the Throne Room and other state rooms, in which Levées used to be held; the Lord Chamberlain's

Office, and a good number of apartments traditionally assigned by the Sovereign to members of the Royal Family, or of the Household.

York House has seventy-five rooms, and of these the few really good ones all face due north. It is a thin, potentially gloomy house, with a small entrance hall: 'The staircase and *entrée* are very small but very pretty', wrote the Empress Frederick of the Yorks' 'gorgeous new abode' in 1894. 'They have fine large lofty rooms, a very fine large Bed room in wh. poor Aunt [Cambridge] died & where I saw her last—3 Salons—a dressing-room & bath room for each! I did not see the dining room or the other rooms!'34 The main rooms into which the Empress Frederick failed to penetrate were three. There was first the dining-room. This had painted panelling, with niches holding oriental vases, a portrait of the Prince of Wales built into the over-mantel, which was modern and elaborate, and bronze lamps in the form of female figures supporting frosted white globes. A glass firescreen, an expandable circular mahogany dining-room table, abetted by a set of heavy mahogany chairs with padded leather seats, and a high Coro-mandel screen completed the equipment of this room, which looked out into the street and, on dull days, seemed rather like a tank. Next, across the hall from the dining-room was Princess May's sitting-room, in which she would conduct business—a room given a slightly mascu-line air by leather sofas and leather armchairs. A glass screen contained photographs of most of her relations; above her desk stood a naked figure of Hermes. The lamps in this room were porcelain, and the shades were made of soft material and were flounced. Beyond this room there lay, as we have seen, the Duke of York's study dominated by Edward Hughes' portrait of Princess May over the fireplace.

Upstairs were the three 'Salons' which the Empress Frederick admired. These are large, fine rooms with very high ceilings, and they open one into the other with double doors. In the Yorks' day they were lit by heavy crystal chandeliers and by wall-sconces, and were filled with tall feathery palms in pots as well as with a profusion of lilies, roses, lilac and other flowers in vases which stood about on various small tables. There were screens with glass tops and gilded frames, ottomans and sofas covered in striped silk, vitrine-tables filled with snuff-boxes, *étuis* and miniatures: the whole gave an impression of comfort, taste and wealth. On this same floor, and opening out of one of the drawing-rooms, was Princess May's bedroom, which con-tained a polished brass bedstead surmounted by a richly draped canopy screwed to the ceiling, white-painted furniture, a crucifix and some religious pictures, as well as a quantity of family photographs, including a large photograph of Prince Eddy which hung high up beside the bed. It was a simple, comfortable bedroom; and although, as at York Cottage, Princess May found that much of the furniture for York House was already in place when she arrived there, the bedroom bore the mark of her own distinctively personal touch.

The remainder of York House was taken up by 'passages interrupted by unexpected flights of steps leading to unsymmetrical rooms' crammed with furniture. These passages, with their sudden flights of steps, made the upper regions perilous in the dark: 'I know how distressed you will be when you learn that I fell down that horridly dangerous step from the night nursery into the passage, *tout de mon long*,' wrote the Duchess of Teck to her daughter in 1894, 'arriving on my hands & knees! (I fear *mon écriture s'en ressent!*)'35 'She might have been killed, & Peters who heard the fall, nearly died of fright as when she ran up to Mama she found her lying quite still & thought she was dead',36 Princess May wrote of this accident to her husband. 'There is a very good electric light at the top of the stairs & it ought [to] have been turned on', replied the Duke of York,37 who had been having rather a trying time lately with his mother-in-law, for in 1894 Princess Mary Adelaide was seldom out of York House. She could not, as in old days when it was her mother's house, actually stay there, but she visited it frequently to see her daughter, and she also used the house for purposes of her own: 'Mangas & Maurice will be in London all *this* week & as I want to see them both, may I do so *chez toi* some morning or afternoon?'38 she asked Princess May in a letter of February 1894. Lady Geraldine Somerset had derived a certain *Schadenfreude* from what she had learned about the internal arrangements at York House: 'Meanwhile also there seems many a *désillusion* preparing for P[rincess] M[ary Adelaide]!!' she had written in her Journal at the time of the York engagement, 'the Duke of York having it seems a pretty just appreciation of his future mother-in-law, has taken pains to arrange his house that it shall be impossible for her to sleep at St James's!! and announced he will not have her to dine with him "as he likes to dine punctually".'39

The Duke of York—inevitably aided by 'Maple's man'—had prepared York House in much the same thorough way that he had got ready York Cottage. Once again Princess May found herself faced with the accomplished fact of an already decorated house. But York House was larger and needed much more furniture; and there was also far more scope for weeding out and re-arranging existing pieces than at York Cottage. Both Princess May's parents helped her with their advice:

Sid [Sidney Greville] . . . met us, Papa & me, at St James's, the frame-maker's where, as I have already told, we found a charming screen for Louise & accompanied us to the 2 shops in North Audley Street, of which Emily had told us & which have often attracted our attention, (*your's* & *mine*) when driving past [Princess Mary Adelaide wrote to her daughter soon after the marriage]—Biddie, who is a working upholsterer, has been commissioned by Papa to make a sketch for the corner of the boudoir & is abroad just now picking up ideas; he has some lovely things & 2 sofas, I much admire, & want you to see—Conrahd's is a much larger shop, with a *splendid* show & 2 corner arrangements, we are both in love with! tho' possibly they may not quite suit your boudoir; he has however a sofa, which Papa reflects upon for you. Leaving the other two to go to Sinclairs furniture depot in Shaftesbury Avenue, I did some commissions at shop doors *en route* for Warwick House.[40]

As the years went by, York House looked, to its inmates' eyes, better and better: '*York House devient tout à fait jolie avec toutes nos belles choses*', Princess May wrote to Bricka in March 1897, '*mais comme maison elle n'est pas très confortable. Nous avons donnés 2 grand diners, un grand succès et il parait qu'on était enchanté.*'[41] 'Some Audiences in the evening completed my day's work', wrote the Empress Frederick during a busy spree in London in that same March, 'and dined (5 covers)—with Georgie—May—Aunt Alix & Toria at York House! It was so cosy & nice—& they have such pretty things—good servants & an excellent cook!—We talked almost only of Greece!!'[42]

York house naturally benefited at birthdays and Christmases: 'Yr Parents ask what I wish for, well I told Toria I want a pretty screen for the Green Drawing Room, if Motherdear asks her, Toria knows all about size & the sort of color I should like',[43] wrote Princess May to her husband one spring. 'Mama gave me your beautiful red & gold *portière* which I think very handsome,' she wrote in 1895 to her brother, Prince Alge, who was in Mhow, 'I shall use it as a piano cover in our red drawing room as the color just matches, many loving thanks for sending it me.'[44]

A White Lodge neighbour, who went to tea with Princess May in the spring of 1894, found her 'resting on a satin sofa' in the Red Drawing-Room. 'A coverlet of white satin, embroidered with May

K*

blossoms was over her feet; the room was panelled in crimson brocade. She shewed us her bedroom after tea. I thought the outlook from all the windows very depressing, one saw nothing but grimy London walls.'

Princess May was reposing on her satin sofa because this tea-party took place only a few weeks before the birth of her first child, whom Queen and country confidently expected would be an heir male to the heir-presumptive to the British Empire.

v

At Cowes in August 1893, Princess May had perceived the more radiant and delightful aspects of her new and important position as Duchess of York. At York House, that following winter, she had been gratified by the luxurious setting in which she now lived. With the approaching birth of her first child in the early summer of 1894 she discovered the reverse of the medal, for she became the object of an amount of attention on the part of the country and of the Royal Family which she did not relish. The birth of the child was expected in mid-June and it had been intended that it should take place at Buckingham Palace. It was, once more, a hot summer, and, at Princess May's own instigation, the doctors urged that she should go instead to her parents' house, White Lodge in Richmond Park, to await the birth in peace and quiet. The Duke and Duchess of York accordingly moved to White Lodge on 4 June. Even here the peace and quiet were only relative. White Lodge was now connected by telephone with East Sheen. 'The movements of the Royal couple have been watched with keen interest, and day after day large numbers of people have assembled in the vicinity of the Lodge in the hope of catching a glimpse of Princess May and her husband', wrote the Richmond correspondent of *The Times*.[45]

The Royal Family were as eagerly expectant, indeed as impatient, as the English public. 'Dear May keeps us waiting a little, but it must be very soon',[46] Queen Victoria wrote that June. 'No Telegram about dear May! *we* had so reckoned upon it so each time the door went open we jumped up, hoping!'[47] wrote the Grand Duchess Augusta from Neu Strelitz. 'I hope we shall soon hear good news of May', echoed the Empress Frederick[48] from her new country house near Kronberg, Friedrichshof. The Yorks went over several times to see Queen Victoria at Windsor: 'Dear May . . . is looking wonderfully

well, only a little pale & is vy active & *s'arrange si bien*, with blue
lace & other very becoming arrangements that one sees very little.'49

Princess May found the onset of maternity, with, in her case, its
attendant publicity, disconcerting. She heartily agreed with the views
on the subject of Queen Victoria, who wrote in April 1893 to her
eldest daughter:

> It is really *too dreadful* to have the first year of one's married life &
> happiness spoilt by *discomfort & misery*; I have a most lively recollection
> of what it was before you were born—All sort of fuss & precautions of all
> kinds & sorts—displaying every thing & being talked abt & worried to
> death of wh. I think *with* perfect horror—in addition to wh. *I* was furious
> at being in that position.50

Female members of the Royal Family found that Princess May never
wished to discuss the matter: 'She . . . does not wish it remarked or
mentioned', wrote the Empress Frederick ruefully, after seeing
Princess May at Osborne before the birth of the Yorks' third child.51
To the Empress Frederick any and every detail connected with the
birth of so celestial a being as a human baby was of paramount interest.
Her letters to her married daughters were always full of advice, and
she was for ever despatching English midwives to Athens to look
after Princess Sophie, Duchess of Sparta. The Empress once again
concluded that Princess May was 'very cold and stiff' and very
unmaternal.

At last, at ten o'clock in the evening of the 23rd of June,
1894, Princess May's first son was born. Telegrams as numerous as
flights of swallows in a summer sky were released from White Lodge,
while a myriad more telegrams of congratulation flew thither and to
Windsor Castle. Every royalty in Europe, every public body in Great
Britain and the Empire, sent their congratulations. In Neu Strelitz
the Grand Duchess was beside herself with excitement:

> I still am in a *twitter* can hardly take in the immense happiness of the
> moment! of this great Historical Event! are *you* not beside yourself? [the
> Grand Duchess wrote to her sister Princess Mary Adelaide]. I am! and long
> to *squeeze* everybody who comes in my way. Bruère* was the first, who got
> a *hug*, such as she never had before, then followed old Hueber, *howling*,
> Willichen and of course Elly with her girls. . . . Before and after—(and *in*
> Church people *winked* at me) and loudly congratulated me; on Parade I

* The Grand Duchess's German dresser.

was received with 'God save the Queen' when, of course, I *howled*. Oh it is so delightful! ... I came to my room yesterday morning, saw a Telegram laying, but thinking it came from Fritz first read my Prayers quietly, then opened it, read 'George' good Heavens! I could hardly read on and there it was 'a son, both doing well!' down I went—mentally—on my knees, tears of gratitude and happiness flowing, streaming, and the hugging *followed*. I tel. to Georgie, you, the Queen, Wales's, George, and here to Aldefeldt, Mathilde of Saxony, Dss Anhalt, Hélène, oh! I longed to telegraph all over the world! ... 52

On the White Lodge lawn a marquee was quickly set up and in this a book was installed in which callers could inscribe their names; in the first day over fifteen hundred persons came to do so. 'Additional accommodation has been temporarily erected for carriages, and to prevent people from getting too near the house a temporary hurdle fence has been erected at some distance from the railings. Several constables are on duty to preserve order', reported *The Times'* correspondent.53 Such was the generous welcome given by the world to a Prince who, after a brief reign as King Edward VIII, is today the Duke of Windsor.

On 27 June Queen Victoria, accompanied by various members of her family and by a suite, travelled from Windsor to Richmond by special train, and visited White Lodge. Writing to point out to the Empress Frederick that 'it seems that it has never happened in this Country that there shd. be 3 direct Heirs as well as the Sovereign alive!' the Queen described this visit:

I went over yesterday with Beatrice, Nicky, Alicky, &c to see May & the Baby who is a vy fine strong Boy, a pretty Child. May I did not see, as it was rather too soon & the Doctor specially wished she shld be kept vy quiet, but she is perfectly well & Dr Williams said one could not be a stronger & healthier parent than she is—wh. is a gt. thing for the future.—
The Newspapers have charmingly written Articles.—But oh! what a frightful contrast is this horrible assassination of poor M. Carnot! The 2 Events were almost paralel [*sic*] & the contrast too awful. It is like the murder of Henri Quatre! They ought not to have allowed the people to crowd round the Carriage. It is vy unsafe. It is too shocking. He was a good Man, & one feels so much for her.54

A month after this visit, the Queen and her family again descended on White Lodge, this time for the christening of the infant Prince. Queen Victoria and her grandson the Duke of York had had several exchanges of letters about the child's prospective names, since the Queen wished, as usual, that he should be called Albert, explaining that 'This will be the *Coburg* line, like formerly the Plantagenet, the Tudor, . . . the Stewart, & the Brunswicks',55 while Prince George and Princess May had determined to 'call him *Edward* after *darling Eddy*'.56 ' . . . You write as if *Edward* was the *real* name of dear Eddy was called by [*sic*], while it was *Victor Albert* which Papa again & again said was his *real* official appellation—& all his monograms were *VA*.'57 The upshot of all this was that the York baby, wearing a Honiton lace robe, and blessed with twelve godparents, was christened Edward Albert Christian George Andrew Patrick David. To his parents and his family he was soon known as 'David'.

Princess May's punctiliousness was legendary. She had now, as always, performed the duty that was expected of her. Having ensured the succession to the throne of England in the fourth generation she might now have hoped to rest peacefully on her laurels; but there was little domestic peace, that June and July, at White Lodge in Richmond Park.

VI

After six somewhat trying weeks at White Lodge, Princess May left England with her parents and her brother, Prince Alge, on 4 August 1894. She and her mother established themselves at St Moritz for a month. The baby, Prince Edward, was left under the care of his nurses and of Bricka at White Lodge. The Duke of York went to Cowes. 'I was sure you wld miss yr sweet *May* & tutsoms baby very much & it was a pity she had to leave you for St Moritz, but never mind once in a way does not matter so much', wrote the Princess of Wales, a large part of whose own life was now spent away from her husband, and who was just then in Russia. ' . . . Give darling May my very best love & kiss sweet baby from Granny whenever you see them!!'58

The Princess of Wales was, as we have noticed, a difficult mother-in-law; equally so, but in another way, was Princess Mary Adelaide. During those June and July weeks at White Lodge she had exasperated the poor Duke of York. While separated from his wife that August he took the opportunity to unburden himself in a long and sensible letter, complaining of the way in which Princess Mary Adelaide—'Maria', as he liked to call her—seemed to have been overshadowing their lives throughout the year. 'I am very fond of dear Maria', he wrote rather desperately, 'but I assure you I wouldn't go through the six weeks I spent at White Lodge again for anything she used to come in & disturb us & then her unpunctuality used to annoy me too dreadfully. She was always most kind to me & therefore it made it impossible for me to say anything. . . . And in London too it was very bad in May & beginning June, she was always running in & out of St James's so that I saw you very little & it used to make me angry. . . .'[59] 'I well know how true it is', Princess May replied, from St Moritz, '& it used to fidget me dreadfully when I was laid up to feel that we could hardly ever be alone without being interrupted.'[60] 'It is one of the small things in life which can just prevent one being absolutely happy & if it could be altered my happiness would be perfect; you know what I mean',[61] Prince George wrote in answer to this frank admission.

Princess May's Diary for 1894 shows that her mother was, indeed, 'always running in & out of St James's'. 'Mama came at 4.00 p.m. and stayed till 8.00 p.m.', we read, or 'Mama lunched and stayed till after 8.00 p.m.' The Duchess of Teck and her husband would frequently lunch or dine at York House and, apart from these meals, hardly a single day there passed without a call from Princess May's mother. Princess Mary Adelaide had become so accustomed to leaning on her daughter for advice and help that without her she felt lost. 'She forgets', wrote Prince George, 'that you are married & only remembers that you are her *only* daughter (which perhaps is unfortunate for me) as she has been used to ask your advice on everything, & naturally wants to do so still, I wish she would use a little more tact.'[62] 'You might try and mention it to her in a casual sort of way', he wrote in another letter at this time.[63]

The fact was that both the Duke and the Duchess of Teck missed Princess May horribly. They could not adjust themselves to life without her. The Duke of Teck was becoming weekly more cantankerous and difficult to cope with; while the reaction from the emotional strain of the years 1892 to 1893—the Duke of Clarence's death, the triumph of the York wedding—had left Princess Mary Adelaide in a low, weak, dispirited state. In the summer of 1894 the birth of her grandson at White Lodge rallied her, though, as we have seen, she continued to try to lead a vicarious existence based on Princess May's marriage.

Some weeks after the birth of Prince Edward of York, however, another event in the Teck family provided Princess Mary Adelaide with an exciting new interest, which diverted some of her attention and her energies away from the York household. This event was the engagement of her eldest son to Lady Margaret Grosvenor, the third daughter of the first Duke of Westminster, who was then one of the richest men in the whole of England. 'It is a vy *good* connection— ... & she will doubtless be well off',[64] wrote Queen Victoria when announcing to the Empress Frederick this 'piece of news ... wh. has come as a surprise to every one'. 'Dolly in love is indeed a changed being, they are so happy, Margaret is a charming girl, we like her so much',[65] Princess May wrote to her Aunt Augusta.

Prince Adolphus of Teck, who was now twenty-six, was an officer in the 17th Lancers; he had been out to India in 1888–1890, and on his return he had startled his sister and his parents by his blond good looks. By 1894 he was beginning to go bald. Prince Dolly was generally popular. He was adored by his sister, and greatly liked by his brother-in-law the Duke of York, who wrote: 'I never met a nicer fellow, I think him quite charming . . . he has got such excellent manners & is so quiet & nice, he really shoots very well.'[66] Earlier that year, 1894, in one of her weekly letters to her eldest daughter, Queen Victoria had mentioned her anxiety that the two unmarried Wales sisters should marry, and had told her that the Prince of Wales had suggested 'Dolly Teck'. The Queen did not think this would be a good match. The Empress Frederick agreed with her:

> With regard to darling Bertie's sweet girls I can only say—that I do *not* think—Dolly Teck—or Ernie [Hohenlohe] *charming* as both young men are would—do—for British Princesses—his daughters & yr Grand daughters—*as no other* Pcess (of Wales) has married a foreign Prince;—it *would* be desirable that they should marry some one of a reigning family— Max of Baden—wd perhaps be Grand Duke some day—and young Lippe is at any rate not a *mediatised* Prince. Ernie is far more suited in Rank and position to Tora [of Schleswig-Holstein]—than to Maude or Victoria. . . . Of course I would write to Bertie with pleasure,—I am only so afraid of displeasing dearest Alix— . . . or—of appearing to meddle in her family affairs,—but it really is *not* wise—to leave the fate of these dear girls— '*dans le vague*'.[67]

As it happened, Princess Maud of Wales was not interested in Prince Adolphus of Teck, but in his brother, Prince Frank; while Prince Adolphus was interested in neither of his Wales cousins, but in Lady Margaret Grosvenor.

The only person who was not particularly pleased over the Westminster engagement was, typically enough, the Duke of Teck. He had cherished a hope that Prince Adolphus might marry Princess Pauline, the daughter of King William II of Württemberg; and in any case he set, as we know, inordinate store by royal blood: '*Votre père est toujours impossible, vous savez ce que je veux dire*', Madame Bricka wrote to Prince Alge in July 1895 about Princess Adolphus of Teck who was then staying at White Lodge; '*si la petite était une lourde Princesse allemande, comme votre père la trouverait charmante. Et quand on pense que les rois autrefois épousaient des* Ladies.—*Son humeur est plus terrible qu'autrefois, tout le monde en souffre.*'[68] Whatever her father may have thought, Princess May was enchanted at the thought of seeing her favourite brother happily married: 'I assure you I am so excited about it I hardly know what to do',[69] she wrote to Lady Meg on 28 July 1894. Princess Mary Adelaide was also pleased. She began to initiate Lady Meg Grosvenor into the mysteries of Guild and other charity work, and to help with her trousseau and the plans for the wedding, which was to be at the Duke of Westminster's palatial house in Cheshire, Eaton Hall. The Westminsters also had a fine town house in London. This Princess Mary Adelaide found most convenient. There was to her a certain quiet appeal about the solid wealth of the millionaire Duke of Westminster, who later proved to be an open-handed friend.

Prince Dolly, with Lady Meg and the Duke of Westminster, were among the many persons who came to 'take leave' of Princess May and her parents at Victoria Station on 4 August 1894. Princess May was travelling incognita as 'Lady Killarney', but she was, of course, attended by a lady-in-waiting, an equerry and the requisite dressers and footmen. Her mother had a similar retinue. The Duke of Teck and Prince Alge were heading for the Bodensee, to stay with Uncle Willie Württemberg; while Princess May, her mother and their suites proceeded to the Hotel Victoria, St Moritz Bad. 'Poor Mama is so delighted to have me with her again alone, that it makes up for a good deal & touches me deeply', Princess May wrote to Queen Victoria from this hotel. 'Mama is flourishing and walks very well.'[70]

In those days the fashionable season at St Moritz was not the winter for ski-ing, but the height of the summer, for walking and inhaling the mountain air. This was Princess Mary Adelaide's fourth visit to St Moritz, and Princess May's third: 'The drive from Chur we thought lovelier than ever & we are having heavenly weather', Princess May wrote to Prince Dolly. 'There are not many English this year. . . . The Duchess of Aosta is here . . . also Vera & Elsa & Olga. Hélène Mecklenburg-Altenburg, & Asy Mecklenburg are here, besides Elizabeth Anhalt & poor blind Alick. Quite a cousinly gathering! Vivi Molière we found here & only fancy I recognised her tho' I had not seen her for 18 years.'[71] To recognise her Aunt Augusta Strelitz's lady-in-waiting, Mademoiselle Molière, whom she had last seen during the Tecks' visit to Neu Strelitz in 1876 was indeed a feat of memory, for in 1876 Princess May had been only nine years old; yet, as we have already remarked, her memory can only be described as phenomenal. Vivi Molière had recently been on the Lake of Como, in waiting on the Grand Duchess Augusta, who was staying incognita as Countess Nemerow, at the Villa d'Este, where she made the acquaintance of the composer Leoncavallo: 'Vivi, "*qui ne veut que s'amuser*" does not amuse me, runs about all day long, and she is my only resource', the Grand Duchess had written to her sister. ' . . . Vivi *smokes* with Leoncavallo!!! plays at Billiards etc. . . . all our hawthorn Trees are out and in blossom, a Chesnut next a Magnolia and so on; then the Nightin*girls* scream, too enchanting.'[72]

This month at St Moritz was distinctly gay, and revived Princess May, who had been exhausted, and Princess Mary Adelaide, who had been depressed. The day after their arrival their sitting-room at the Hotel Victoria was rearranged, under the direction of Princess May who was lying on the sofa. The Duchess of Teck had been to see the Duchess of Aosta. When she got back at five o'clock she 'found our little salon transmogrified into a *most cosy snuggery*! by means of our stuffs, cushions, photos &c. . . . Huge lovely baskets of carnations & other flowers, the gift of Madame & Miss de Planta were brought in. Dressed after 8 & supped *à 6* at 8½.—Then played patience during a most disturbing & very heavy thunder & hailstorm—To bed in good time. . . .'[73]

Although Princess May could not, of course, foresee it, this was in fact her penultimate time abroad with her mother. It was also, for her, one of the last periods of real freedom. 'This place is doing both Mama & me a world of good, the air is so refreshing', she wrote to her husband. ' . . . I hope I shall return quite strong again, but up till now my nerves are still somewhat shaky which is a bore. We have made our rooms so pretty & comfortable & mine is full of your & darling baby's photos.'[74]

The little English party were happy and carefree: they made many

expeditions in the carriages called *Einspanner* to find wild pinks, or
to join the Leo Rothschilds on a picnic, or to admire the view down
into Italy, or to watch the eagles soaring in the clear blue sky around
the mountain peaks. They had coffee in various inns and chalets,
made purchases at familiar shops, and on one day helped the owners
of five shops which were on fire to salvage what they could of their
goods: 'We were out shopping about 12.30 today & as we were
passing a shop a gentleman came out & told us the shop was on fire',
Princess May wrote to Prince George. 'We immediately tried to get
hold of some people to fetch the fire-engines but they were so slow
that 5 small wooden chalets & contents were burnt to the ground.
It was horrid to see it all, we helped as much as we cld packing up
things etc. . . . Nobody was hurt—But as you can imagine it was a
great shock to us all & our nerves feel rather shaky in consequence.'75

   In the evenings there were concerts in the *Kursaal*, or private entertainments in their own 'cosy snuggery' or in that of the Duchess
Eugene of Württemberg. 'Supped 8¼ & hurried down with May to
Vera's sitting-room, to hear Hélène [of Mecklenburg-Altenburg]
sing—', Prince Mary Adelaide wrote in her Diary. 'Rather disappointing, as she had to accompany herself & to bend forward all
the time on account of her shortsightedness.'76 On one Sunday
morning they went to service at the French Huguenot Church:
'Pasteur Ruffet preached a gloriously beautiful sermon on the conversion of St Paul, one which went to one's heart & *thrilled* one
through & through!' [Princess Mary Adelaide notes]. 'I think I never
heard him more eloquent, or more impressive! When he drew a
picture *de la mère convertie*, we felt he was addressing himself to us
two *à propos* of the bringing up of our precious baby—I came out
quite *emotionnée* & went for an hour's walk up a delightful path
behind the French church, towards the Johannesberg & Hahnensee.'77

   On the last day of August 1894 Princess May arrived home at
York House. Her mother had gone on to join the Duke of Teck in
Württemberg. Early in September the Duke and Duchess of York
attended functions in Birmingham and in Liverpool, after which they
went to stay at Balmoral and at Mar Lodge. They had already stayed
in Scotland in August and September of the previous year, 1893.
They were to go to stay there for many, many autumns to come.
Already, in the first full year of marriage, the pattern and rhythm of
Princess May's new life was being established. This rhythm, these
regular migrations from London to Sandringham, from Sandringham

back to London, from London to Cowes, from Cowes to Scotland, were only interrupted by exceptional events—such as, in 1914, the outbreak of the First World War, or, now, in October 1894, the death at St Petersburg of Tsar Alexander III of Russia.

VII

The death of the Tsar Alexander III came as a severe shock to the Wales family. 'Uncle Sacha', the husband of the Princess of Wales's sister Dagmar, had been ill for some time, but he was only forty-nine when he died. He had reigned thirteen years, having succeeded his father, Tsar Alexander II, who had been assassinated in 1881.

'This news is too awful', Princess May wrote to her husband on 1 November, from White Lodge, '& I feel for you all with all my heart. . . . I only hope precious Toria won't be ill. . . . My head gets quite bewildered in thinking of all our dear ones in their sorrow & misery.'[78] The Tsar's death was all the more disturbing and dramatic, because it came only a few weeks before the projected marriage of the Tsarevitch Nicholas and Princess Alix of Hesse Darmstadt and by the Rhine, that granddaughter of Queen Victoria who had refused to marry Prince Eddy in 1889. The Tsarevitch's engagement had been long delayed by Princess Alix's hesitation over changing her religion to that of the Orthodox Church, a step to which she had ultimately agreed. It was a love-match: 'I never saw two people more in love with each other', wrote Prince George to Princess May. 'I told them both that I could not wish them more than that they should be as happy as you & I were together. Was that right?'[79]

The day after they heard of Uncle Sacha's death, Princess May and Prince George gave the Duchess of Teck and Prince Alge dinner at York house. They dined without the lady-in-waiting or the equerry so as to be, in Princess May's words, ' "en famille" & sympathise in this tragedy'.[80] Princess Mary Adelaide was not emotionally affected by the Tsar Alexander's demise, since she had scarcely known him. She may have been a shade too buoyant at this meal, for she wrote of it to her new confidante, Lady Meg Grosvenor: 'We found Georgie terribly low & had in consequence a very silent & depressing dinner à 4—I had a glimpse of Louise, Victoria & Maud, all of course much cut up & am thankful for them, that they are off to York Cottage today. . . . Baby was angelic & actually smiled &

laughed at his *"Grannie"* out of his bassinette, when he ought to have been going off to sleep!'[81]

The Prince and Princess of Wales had at once set off for St Petersburg to attend the late Tsar's obsequies, which were to be shortly followed by the new Tsar's wedding. To Princess May's distress, a message soon came through from St Petersburg to say that the Prince of Wales wished the Duke of York to join them there immediately. 'We are in despair', wrote Princess May. By this time Prince George and Princess May very much disliked being separated. Also Russia was a notoriously dangerous country for royalties, who had to be closely guarded day and night. 'I think it quite enough', wrote Aunt Augusta from Strelitz, 'to have *one* Heir apparent in Russia and that *Two* are too much! How sad though all one reads from there and what a moral as well as bodily fatigue those everlasting *Orthodox* Ceremonies must be! they are made to drive *all* feeling out of them.'[82]

Princess May bade her husband farewell at Wolferton Station, Sandringham: 'That saying "good-bye" this morning was awful, & I did it so badly too, for I felt so miserable', she wrote to him. ' . . . Anyhow I know that you understood what I felt & what agony it was having to take leave. It poured so heavily that we had to return in the closed carriage, & then Toria & I looked at the portfolios & chose some pretty little paintings for my room which Rainbow will have framed—I also looked at the pieces of silk I thought would do for the chairs, but fear they are not quite suitable & must try something else. After lunch it still rained so . . . that we gave up going out, & sat all together in the little sitting room & Victoria stuck in photos in yr book & mine, while Harry read & I wrote & read etc. We *all* felt very chippy & wretched.'[83]

With her usual prescience, the Grand Duchess of Mecklenburg-Strelitz had foreseen how wearying and interminable the Tsar Alexander's funeral ceremonies would seem to the European mourners. Sixty-one royalties and their suites had foregathered in the marble and malachite apartments of the great palaces of St Petersburg. For seventeen days the body of the late Tsar lay in an open coffin in the fortress church of St Peter and St Paul; thousands of his subjects passed through the church day and night, while hidden choirs chanted, and a priest stood by the coffin intoning the Scriptures. The church was lit by a myriad lamps, and the atmosphere was hot and almost foetid. Each day, directly after lunch, the Prince of Wales and all the other relatives of the late Tsar processed to the church in full uniform for the second of the two daily services. 'After the service was over', Prince George wrote of the first of seven he attended, 'we all went up to [the] coffin which was open & kissed the Holy picture which he holds in his hand, it gave me a shock when I saw his dear face so close to mine when I stooped down, he looks so beautiful & peaceful, but of course the face has changed very much, it is a fortnight today.'[84] In between these services, they walked about the streets of St Petersburg, which were damp and foggy and hung with black; they went to Fabergé's shop, to the Hermitage, to the Artillery Museum, and to see one or two famous churches. The rest of the time was spent with the Russian, Greek and Danish cousins. Prince George was staying at the Anitchkoff Palace.

At length, on 19 November, the late Tsar's body was put away, after a service lasting two and a half hours. The Duke of York was one of the pall-bearers: 'we carried him & lowered him down into the vault where all the members of the family are buried, it was most impressive & sad, & I shall never forget it. Darling Aunt Minny was so brave & stood the whole time & never broke down once.'[85] On 26 November the new Tsar and Princess Alix of Hesse were married in the chapel of the Winter Palace.

Prince George arrived back in London in the first week of December, and went down to meet his wife at Windsor Castle, whither the Queen had somewhat capriciously summoned her. 'I received a telegram from Grandmama saying she hoped I would join sisters at Windsor on 29th & that we would *all* stay there till Uncle & you returned. Oh! what a shock!' Princess May wrote to Prince George.[86]

During the Duke of York's absence in Russia he had written long letters to his wife every day, and so had she to him. This separation, coming so soon after the St Moritz one, served to prove to both of them that they had become essential to one another. 'I really believe I should get ill if I had to be away from you for a long time', Prince George wrote from St Petersburg to Princess May.[87]

VIII

One of the subjects about which Princess May and her husband corresponded during Prince George's stay in Russia had been the most convenient date for Prince Dolly's wedding that November. Just when this had been satisfactorily arranged so as to suit the Westminsters, the Tecks and the Yorks, a telegram from Graz reached

White Lodge. This told the Duke of Teck that his remaining sister, Princess Claudine, had suddenly died of diphtheria at her Schweizerhaus at Reinthal.

Princess Claudine had in her later years become increasingly eccentric; she would rise at four-thirty in the morning to ride about the countryside on a white horse, followed by her dogs but unattended by a groom. She wore her white hair cut short like a man, and was entirely absorbed in her little farm. When she went down to church on Sundays at St Peter in Graz her coachman would remain at the church door holding her dogs on a leash. The death a year earlier of her sister Amélie had affected her profoundly, and she had lost the wish to live. She died, however, at an inconvenient moment for her relatives, since all the wedding plans of her nephew, Prince Dolly, were set awry by mourning.

The Duke of Teck, with Prince Alge to look after him, set out for Graz to attend the funeral. 'On account of infection', Princess Mary Adelaide told Queen Victoria, 'the body was not allowed to pass through the town, but had to be taken straight to the cemetery, where poor Francis & Alge met it. No one is allowed to go into the house, which is now being disinfected . . . I have . . . been obliged to ask the Westminsters to put off the wedding until the 12th of Decr., for which date it is now fixed.'[88]

This postponement of Prince Dolly's wedding was awkward for everyone, but particularly so for Princess May, for her husband now asked her whether it would matter his not attending the ceremony at Eaton Hall, since this would interfere with his shooting at Sandringham. In her sensible, obliging way, Princess May agreed that Prince George must not interrupt his shooting; but when she reached Eaton Hall—a house of gigantic size, in which three hundred and forty people were sleeping during the wedding festivities—she found that the Westminster family were hurt that the Duke of York had not come too: 'From little things I heard last night I gathered that your not coming was a disappointment to all, & I must *honestly* confess that now that I am actually here I do see that your coming to the wedding would be a *great* civility & personal kindness . . . so that I do *press* you to come', Princess May wrote to Prince George. 'Remember no one has influenced me about it. I only act on my own judgement & think it is right you should come . . . yr telegraphing to *me* to propose yrself just for the wedding wld be the proper thing to do.'[89] Prince George, who admitted that he had felt 'uncomfortable'

about not going to Eaton, and had even feared that he would receive
a telegraphic command from Queen Victoria to do so, complied
immediately with his wife's request. 'You are a dear angel to have
done as I asked and I am most grateful to you',[90] she replied. Princess
May concealed this kindly manœuvre even from her mother, who
attributed Prince George's arrival to the Prince of Wales's persuasion.
This tiny incident over Prince Dolly's wedding shows once more the
complete confidence of Princess May's relationship with her husband
in the first year and a half of their marriage.

The Eaton Hall wedding was on a scale of grandeur which the
Duchess of Teck found most gratifying. On the evening that the
bridegroom, his parents and his sister the Duchess of York arrived
the town of Chester was illuminated by electric light and by soldiers
holding torches. The presents were numerous and valuable: 'Happily
the taste of the period is good, so that there is nothing very objection-
able among the number and wonderful to relate not many dupli-
cates',[91] Princess Mary Adelaide wrote in her account of the proceedings
to Queen Victoria. On the wedding morning Princess May and her
mother assisted at the bride's toilette, and after the ceremony and the
luncheon were over they 'ran out' to watch Prince and Princess
Adolphus of Teck drive off in a high phaeton drawn by two greys
with a postilion, preceded by two outriders, and escorted by the
Cheshire Yeomanry. Princess Adolphus 'looked *quite charming* in her
go-away gown of sapphire blue velvet, trimmed with sable, and cape
and toque to match; a kind of victorine of glorious sable, given her
by the dear old Baroness Burdett Coutts completed the costume'.[92]

From Cheshire, the Duke and Duchess of York returned to London.
A week later, after visiting Windsor for the annual service in the
Mausoleum on 14 December (the day of the Prince Consort's death)
they went down to Sandringham for Christmas, which was always
celebrated at the Big House in a lavish manner which their eldest son
has described in his memoirs as: 'Dickens in a Cartier setting.'[93]

'Dined at home the last evening of the Old Year', Princess May
wrote in her Diary on 31 December 1894, '& so goes another year!'

CHAPTER THREE

IN THE SHADOW

FOR the Duke of York, and even more for the Duchess, the
last six years of Queen Victoria's reign—from January 1895
until her death in January 1901—were years of inanition. It is
a matter of history that up till the very last, infirm and almost blind,
Queen Victoria guarded her prerogatives jealously, and did not allow
the Prince of Wales to share any part of her work. The result, as is
well known, was that when he did finally ascend the throne as King
Edward VII, he knew next to nothing of the business side of a constitutional monarchy. The Prince of Wales had sought refuge from
this enforced idleness in a purely social life, for which the Queen
criticised him, without however offering him any interesting or constructive alternative. If the Prince of Wales was thus kept far away
from the hub of government, we may fancy how much more remote
from it was his son and heir, the Duke of York. Prince George and
Princess May were living all too literally 'in the shadow of the shadow
of the Throne'.[1]

Until the outbreak of the Boer War in 1899, the Duke and Duchess
of York had a minimum of official engagements each year: 'a function'
every few weeks at Lancaster or at Liverpool or at Halifax or at
Brighton, perhaps; a visit to Coburg or to Copenhagen for a royal
wedding; two state visits to Ireland in 1897 and in 1899; their part to
play in the festivities of the Diamond Jubilee year. The Duke of York
minded this inactivity less than his wife did, for to him life was, in
Mr John Gore's words, 'an idyll in the 'nineties'. Prince George had
never expected to be heir-presumptive, nor did he particularly enjoy
the position. He was perfectly contented to lead the quiet life of a
country gentleman at Sandringham. As Mr John Gore has pointed
out this Sandringham life gave Princess May's talents no scope whatever: she was not even permitted to help or to influence local institutions in the neighbourhood, since these her mother-in-law regarded
as her own private sphere.[2] Princess May's up-to-date ideas on the
role of women in modern life found no understanding or encourage-

ment from the Princess of Wales, whose charities were manifold but haphazard. In the first years of her marriage Princess May thus had more leisure time on her hands than she had ever had at White Lodge. Her intellectual interests, as we have noticed, isolated her from the Wales family. Except for the births of her three eldest children, this was a period of frustration for the Duchess of York.

In these latest years of her reign, the Queen emerged more and more frequently from her retirement. She now once more held her Drawing-Rooms in person, instead of getting her eldest son and daughter-in-law to deputise for her. 'We saw dear Gangan ready for the drawing-room!' the Empress Frederick wrote to her youngest married daughter in 1894. 'You cannot think how nice she looked!'3 The London public saw more of the Queen, too, driving out from Buckingham Palace with a Sovereign's Escort of the Household Cavalry:

When we drove to the Railway station there were crowds of people out as it was bright and fine, and many carriages in Hyde Park! [wrote the Empress Frederick, of a journey with her mother the Queen to Windsor in February 1894] If only Fischy could see the Life Guards, those beautiful men! with figures like statues and *so* well dressed—& those *lovely* Horses, —the men all ride & sit like gentlemen with such *light* hands! The Horses all playing with the bits—& their black coats shining like satin! Papa always said—he never saw any thing more perfect, than their '*Erscheinung*' and their riding!4

The sunset of the Victorian Age was indeed singularly lustrous. The London Season of 1895, a year which had begun with a great frost which killed many thousand birds, and caused very great suffering and unemployment in London, was socially brilliant. 'There have been a good many foreign royalties over in England this summer which has given *éclat* to the season',5 Princess May wrote to her brother Alge, who was in India. Ascot week 1895 was marked by the Prince of Wales's victory with Persimmon:

Tuesday we had a delightful day at the races! [the Duchess of Teck wrote, also to Prince Alge] glorious weather! a very fine procession up the course! *12* Psses & in all *20 royalties* filling *5* carriages, for Marie Edin. Coburg, with 3 daughters & her Roumanian son-in-law are at Bagshot; & great fun for Uncle Wales won *2* races & we all *won* our *money*! I cried with excitement at his first victory with *Persimmon*, & cheered when *Florizel* 2 won him Her My's *Gold Vase*.6

Princess May enjoyed the Ascot gaieties as much as did the other members of the Royal Family, but she was not interested in racing as such, nor did she feel in the least attuned to the racing and gambling circle of which her father-in-law was the centre; neither did she care for the segment of London Society then already being called 'the smart set'. These persons were quite aware of the Duchess of York's attitude towards them. They retaliated by accusing her of intolerance. *'Il n'y a pas de doute que je ne suis pas populaire parmi de certains gens'*, Princess May wrote to Madame Bricka, in reply to a letter about this 'smart set', *'pourquoi je ne sais pas, puisque je me donne un mal infini pour plaire, on me trouve trop* "good", *trop* "particular"—*Certes je n'aime pas leurs* "goings on". . . . *C'est égal j'irai mon chemin, et j'ai plus de diablerie en moi, qu'on ne crois! N'est ce pas, ma chère?'*[7]

The smart set might resent the Duchess of York's lack of frivolity, but she was, during these years, acquiring the esteem of more interesting and more fastidious persons. 'I had never before had the opportunity of making any real acquaintance with the Duchess of York', Lord Rosebery wrote to Queen Victoria at this time, 'and I hope I may be allowed to say that I was greatly struck with her excellent sense and her unaffected directness of judgement, which seem to me to promise a career of the greatest usefulness to her country.'[8] We have already quoted Augustus Hare's opinion of the Duke of York; in another volume of *The Story of My Life* we find an intelligent account of his acquaintanceship with the Duchess of York. Hare first met Princess May staying at Swaylands, one autumn in the eighteen-nineties:

I have been a week staying at Swaylands to meet the Duchess of York, and as there were scarcely any other guests, saw a great deal of her, and was increasingly filled with admiration for the dignified simplicity and single-mindedness, and the high sense of duty by which her naturally merry, genial nature is pervaded, and which will be the very salvation of England some day. Before her scandal sits dumb: she has a quiet but inflexible power of silencing everything which seems likely to approach ill-natured gossip, yet immediately after gives such a genial kindly look and word to the silenced one as prevents any feeling of mortification. All morning the Duchess was occupied with her lady in real hard work, chiefly letters, I believe; in the afternoon we went for long drives and sight-seeings—of Penshurst, Knole, Groombridge, Hever, Ightham, and she was full of interest in the history and associations of these old-world places. . . .[9]

These were the impressions which a sensitive and cosmopolitan man, who was in no way a royal snob, gained of Princess May in the early years of her married life.

II

'Great & Greater Britain is *ringing* with & *re-echoing the cry* "*A Boy!!!* What *Joy!!!*" & I think I cannot begin this letter with any more appropriate phrase!'[10] the Duchess of Teck wrote to Prince Alge in India on 20 December 1895. Her reference was to the birth, six days earlier, of Princess May's second son, Prince Albert, afterwards King George VI.*

Prince George and Princess May had learnt their lesson from their trying experiences at White Lodge before and after Prince Edward's birth the previous year. This time they arranged that the birth should take place at York Cottage, and without the co-operation of Princess Mary Adelaide, who was not invited to see her new grandson until the first week of January 1896: '*Je vais très bien et suis si contente d'avoir Mama içi maintenant*', Princess May wrote to Bricka on 9 January 1896.[11] With her customary tact, Princess May had succeeded in conveying to her mother that Prince George liked to see his wife alone. 'In the afternoon I walked or wrote till tea-time, which I took with May in the boudoir, remaining with her until George came up from his tea, when I *discreetly retired* & wrote in the sitting room downstairs, till dressing time',[12] the Duchess of Teck informed Prince Alge in one of her long 'journal-letters' from York Cottage after the birth of Prince Albert.

Princess May had arranged for her parents to be kept fully informed of the events at York Cottage. Letters from the midwife 'dear Green' and from Lady Eva Dugdale provided Princess Mary Adelaide with bulletins on her daughter's health: 'I can't help thinking your dear R H may care to have a line from the "Little Bird",' Lady Eva wrote from York Cottage on 17 December, 'especially as it has just come from the presence of the beloved little Princess. It is such a happiness to

---

* Prince Albert Frederick Arthur George, known in the Family as 'Bertie', created Duke of York 5 June 1920, succeeded to the Throne as King George VI after the Abdication of his brother King Edward VIII on 10 December 1936. On 26 April 1923 the Duke of York married Lady Elizabeth Bowes-Lyon, ninth child of the 14th Earl of Strathmore. On his death on 6 February 1952, at the age of fifty-six, King George VI was succeeded by the elder of his two daughters, who now reigns as Queen Elizabeth II.

see her so well . . . she is so bright, her voice so strong, quite able to hear her letters read & laughs & takes an interest in everything.'[13] This letter—one of several from the Cottage signed 'I am, with all respect, Your Royal Highness's Little Bird'—was copied out by Bricka for despatch to Prince Alge in India. 'Dear May . . .', wrote Queen Victoria, 'is *unberufen* very strong. She gets through these affairs like nothing.'[14]

The Yorks' second son had unluckily been born on 14 December, the anniversary of the Prince Consort's death. 'I am afraid dear Grandmama you were rather distressed that he was born on the 14th that doubly sad day to you & all our family', wrote the Duke of York to Queen Victoria, 'but we hope that his having been born on that day may be the means of making it a little less sad to you.'[15] The direct result of the child's birth on what the Queen's immediate family amongst themselves called 'Mausoleum Day' (from the annual service in the Mausoleum at Frogmore which they were all expected to attend) was that he was christened Albert: 'Dear Grandmama we propose with your permission to call him *Albert* after dear Grand-papa',[16] the baby's father wrote. 'It is a great pleasure to me that he is to be called *Albert*,' the Queen told the Empress Frederick, 'but in fact, he cld hardly have been called by any other name.'[17] Princess Mary Adelaide, who did not care for the name 'Albert', wrote to Prince Alge that the Queen had insisted on this name: 'but *George* will be his *last* name & we hope some day may *supplant* the *less favoured* one!'[18]

Prince Albert of York's christening, fixed to take place on 3 February 1896, was postponed owing to the unexpected death of Prince Henry of Battenberg, the husband of the Queen's youngest daughter Princess Beatrice. At the age of thirty-eight, Prince Henry had volunteered for service with the Ashanti Expeditionary Force and succumbed to fever on his arrival at Sierra Leone. 'So I see the Christening has been put off!' the Grand Duchess Augusta wrote to Prince Dolly from Strelitz, 'rather odd, that a Babe can't be made a *Christian* of, because poor Henry is dead!'[19]

Known as 'Liko' to his relatives, Prince Henry of Battenberg was the third son of Prince Alexander of Hesse by his morganatic marriage with the Polish Countess Hauke. To Queen Victoria's surprise and annoyance, he and Princess Beatrice had fallen in love with one another when they had met at Darmstadt in 1884. They had married in the following year. Soon 'Liko' Battenberg became indispensable to the Queen, rousing her from the morbid condition into which John Brown's death in 1883 had plunged her. Prince Henry of Battenberg's death in 1896 was thus not only a great personal sorrow to Princess Beatrice, but an almost mortal blow to the aged Queen. 'Isnt it too sad about poor Liko?' wrote Princess May to Prince Dolly. 'Poor At Beatrice it is awful for her, her whole life ruined, one's heart bleeds for her in her fearful sorrow—What will the Queen & she do now, those 2 women quite alone, it is too sad & depressing to think of.'[20] 'Poor poor Beatrice!' the Duchess of Teck wrote from Eaton Hall to Princess May. ' . . . She is never out of my thoughts & for the poor dear Queen too I deeply grieve, for poor, dear Liko was the one being, who brought a little of the outward world & of life & animation into her otherwise so monotonous, deadly dreary existence! her daily round of duty!'[21] Early in February the Duchess of Teck was asked down to Osborne by the Queen. Here she found both Queen Victoria and Princess Beatrice in tears; moreover, the atmosphere at Osborne was not improved by the behaviour of Princess Louise, Marchioness of Lorne, who had gone out of her way to be disagreeable to her sister Princess Beatrice: 'Louise has alas! froisséd her terribly', wrote the Duchess of Teck, 'by calmly announcing, that she (Louise) was Liko's confidant & Beatrice, nothing to him, indicated by a shrug of the shoulders!— This Beatrice told me herself— . . . To Helen she was equally unkind & after doing her utmost to set Uncle Wales against Helena, she—on going away—ignored her—Charming behaviour truly—The whole place is ringing with it.'[22]

Prince Albert of York's postponed christening took place at Sandringham, when the funeral of Prince Henry of Battenberg in the Isle of Wight was over.

The Duchess of York had now given birth to two sons in the first two years of her marriage. Her family, and the British public, considered this an eminently satisfactory achievement. The Duke of Clarence's death had left a legacy of anxiety behind it; and there was general rejoicing at the fact that the heir to the heir-presumptive to the throne now had a brother who could, if necessary, inherit his rights to the succession. 'I am delighted', wrote Prince Frank of Teck to his mother, in December 1895, 'that they have got their king guarded.'[23]

Prince Frank of Teck was then on his way to India. He was, as usual, in disgrace.

Princess Mary Adelaide and her husband had taken great pains to
bring up their children carefully, wisely and well. In the cases of
Princess May, of Prince Dolly and of their youngest boy Prince Alge
they had every reason, that December of 1895, to congratulate themselves. Princess May was Duchess of York. She was now the mother
of two sons and she would in all probability one day be Queen of
England. Prince Dolly had made a rich and very happy marriage and
was enjoying his army life. Prince Alge, who was only twenty-one,
was likewise proving a good soldier and seemed set for a distinguished
career. For these three of their four children all augured well. There
remained their second son, Prince Francis or 'Frank'.

From his boyhood, when he had been expelled from Wellington
College for tossing the headmaster over a hedge, Prince Frank had
never fitted into the sober pattern of semi-royal life. He was the
cleverest and the most amusing of the three Teck Princes. 'He was
such fun, very like his mother', one of his relations says of him.
Prince Frank had certainly inherited Princess Mary Adelaide's vitality
and zest for life, as well as her gift for descriptive writing. He had also
inherited her hopelessness about money. Prince Frank lived in a
permanent state of debt, was elegantly dressed on credit, and made
rash and heavy racing bets which he could not win but which he
equally could not afford to lose. By 1895, the year of his second
nephew's birth, Prince Frank, like his parents before him, was urged
by his family to leave England. He was not, however, given a choice
of places of exile. India, he was told, was his destination. Before leaving
the country Prince Frank went down to lunch with the Queen at
Windsor Castle: 'I gave him my Photograph as you wished', Queen
Victoria wrote to Princess Mary Adelaide, '& also told him I hoped
I shld hear good accounts of him & *that he wld be vy steady in every
way*—& he said he "wld try". I hope he will be able to resist
temptation.'[24]

Soon poor Prince Frank was writing long letters to his family from
Ganeshkind, Mahableshwar, Poona and Quetta: 'This sarcophagus of
a place', he wrote of Mahableshwar; and, of British India generally,
'I can only surmise that this land was meant as an example of what to
expect in the world below'.[25] These letters were in parts bitter, but
in the main gay. They suggested to his relatives that Prince Frank
was irritatingly unrepentant. Princess May had no comprehension of

the flippant. She was puzzled and annoyed by the tone of her brother Frank's missives: 'Today I heard from Frank, a long letter from Mahableshwar, written in his very flippant style which honestly I cannot understand.'[26] Prince Frank refused to be impressed by his sister's illustrious position. 'Tonight is a big ball—so little Franky must rest *à la* May', he wrote to the Duchess of Teck from Ganeshkind in September 1896, 'and so dear Mama your little boy will finish his letter shortly.' 'I . . . was much amused at Master & Mistress York going to Newmarket. I think I must write and warn her simple soul against the evils of the race—I shall send her a betting book as X-mas pres.',[27] he wrote, again to his mother, a few weeks later.

Disquieting to his more serious-minded sister, Prince Frank was, needless to say, the favourite son of Princess Mary Adelaide, for he had those salient faults which, in a son, are dear to a mother's heart. She loved, too, his sense of humour, and his buoyancy of spirit, which resembled her own. Prince Frank was an affectionate son. In his letters from India he would chide his mother for not taking more care of her health: 'Now I am credibly informed that you have been more than naughty and that the doctors are distressed about you . . . all your friends tell me you don't look well—so you must take care of yourself and submit to injunctions and . . . tell your charitable friends to "go to hell" say this once in a loud voice and the only bother you'll have is to hear from them no more.'[28] In August 1896 he wrote describing what he conjectured to be the current state of Princess Mary Adelaide, of the White Lodge coachman, Kitchener, and of the White Lodge steward, Adams:

So now the year is on the wane and all the trying time of the season once more over—in which time not only have you done too much, but worn—in all probability the very tissues of your body to bursting point—I can picture to myself Kitchener's feelings, now trying to restore his horses to animal life again*—and Adams' feelings on reckoning the cost of the midnight or rather morning oil—fact is you've been horrid naughty—and May—in the role of head nurse and '*chargé d'affaires des choses internelles de votre Altesse*'—is now posted over you to see to the *régime* being carried out.[29]

* The late Lord Cambridge, formerly Prince Adolphus of Teck, would describe to his children how their grandmother the Duchess of Teck, leaving White Lodge very late for some function in London, would lean from the window of her brougham and cry to the coachman: 'Fly! Kitchener! Fly!'

In some ways Prince Frank of Teck's character was as weak as that of his dead cousin the Duke of Clarence, but he did not, like Prince Albert Victor, suffer from languor or from lethargy. Stationed in Dublin with his regiment he had been 'surrounded' in his mother's words by 'a dangerous set, who flatter him & turn his weak head'.³⁰ Although he made fun of his own family, Prince Frank was not above fussing about his precedence at a dinner-party, in a way all too reminiscent of his father, the Duke of Teck. When he was sent out to India in 1895 his wise old aunt, the Grand Duchess of Mecklenburg-Strelitz, urged that his commanding officer there should be 'told *why* he is sent out, and what his racing, betting and horse propensities are, so that he may keep an eye upon him, or else [he] will play the Prince and the dashing Dragoon and make them do as he pleases, won't he?' she wrote to Prince Dolly in August that year.³¹

The immediate cause of Prince Frank's Indian exile was a once famous bet at Punchestown, by which he lost, at one fell swoop, ten thousand pounds. Prince Frank had neither ten thousand pounds, nor even one thousand pounds with which to gamble. Like his mother before him, he relied upon his family to extricate him from his commitment. Headed by Princess May, who could always be relied on to help any of her brothers with any money she could spare, they rallied round him. So soon as a satisfactory arrangement had been made, Prince Frank's spirits began to rise again:

Thank God poor foolish Frank's wretched bet has been settled & he writes from Dublin in a cheerier tone than one could have expected after so *awful* a *shock* & *terrible* a crisis! of which I am feeling the effects now both *morally* & *physically!* [Princess Mary Adelaide wrote to Prince Alge in July 1895] but it is all important he should leave Ireland with as little delay as possible & we are looking out for a staff appointment in India, or the Colonies, for him, so as to get him away from his undesirable acquaintances. . . . People seem very kind about it, they pity him for having been *entrapped* & express themselves *sincerely sorry* for me. . . . I cannot say enough in praise of darling May, who at once came to the rescue, & dear Georgie! & Dolly, who insists on paying ½ the yearly interest on the money raised—The other ½ Papa & I have undertaken.³²

There was a strong streak of outrageousness in Prince Frank's character which his sister the Duchess of York could not appreciate. Even the annual memorial service for the old Duchess of Cambridge at Kew church, a mournful family occasion always followed by a luncheon at the Duke of Cambridge's house on Kew Green, seemed comic to Prince Frank: 'Alix . . . sent me a splendid epistle & full of news', he wrote to his mother from Ganeshkind, '—whilst you were apparently praying at Kew—with the rest of the family—or perhaps quarrelling at the Luncheon—.' When, by the united efforts of his relatives, the Dublin bet had been settled, he at once suggested to Princess Mary Adelaide that he should resign from the army and go to try to make money in South Africa. 'I feel confident I should get on capitally with Cecil Rhodes', he wrote, '. . . no doubt one would come across a curious crew—those who have fled the country others who have been broke racing gambling etc.—in fact much like little self.'33 His family were, however, determined he should go to India, for apart from his 'betting and horse propensities' Prince Frank was causing them concern by his prolonged attachment to a much older married woman, who exercised a total control over his plans and wishes. It was this liaison which had precluded Prince Frank's fulfilling his mother's heart's desire by marrying his cousin 'Harry'—Princess Maud of Wales.

IV

Princess Maud of Wales was Princess May's favourite sister-in-law. She was gentle and she was pretty. 'I paid May & Georgie a visit too, & Maudie dear', the Empress Frederick wrote to her youngest daughter from Windsor in February 1895, 'whose foot and leg are much better!—She did look so pretty—& fresh—like a little rose— with her bright eyes,—and dear intelligent expression, she and Victoria are two such Ducks! I cannot understand their not being married they would be such charming wives.'34 One of the chief reasons why, in 1895, Princess Maud and Princess Victoria were still not married was that their mother the Princess of Wales was loth to lose them. In June 1894 the Queen had written to the Empress Frederick an account of a conversation she had held with the Prince of Wales about his unmarried daughters: 'I told Bertie what you wrote to me a little time ago abt. them & he answered me he knew your kind wishes for the future wh. he quite shared but that Alix found them such companions that she wld not encourage their marrying & that they themselves had no inclination for it, (in wh. I think that he is mistaken, as regards Maud). He said he was "powerless" wh. I cannot understand.'35 Queen Victoria knew, of course, that Princess Maud cherished an unreciprocated love for Prince Frank of Teck, who liked his

L

cousin but, owing to his own emotional entanglement, did not even trouble to answer her letters. In June 1894 the Princess of Wales's nephew, Christian, later Crown Prince, and finally King, of Denmark —'a giant & vy. like his Mother', according to Queen Victoria—was in London. It was hoped that he might marry one of the Wales Princesses: 'Alix', wrote Queen Victoria, 'to whom I said I had hoped something for the girls said—she wld. be vy. glad & wld. like it, but she feared the girls thought him too young for them.'³⁶ In the following year, 1895, Princess Maud became engaged to Prince Christian of Denmark's younger brother, Prince Charles, who was elected ten years later to the Norwegian throne when he took the style and title of King Haakon VII.

'*Et que pensez-vous du mariage de la Princesse Maud avec son cousin?*' wrote Madame Bricka to Prince Alge in November 1895. ' . . . *Que j'en suis triste. Si le Prince F[rank] avait voulu? . . . Sa conduite envers cette petite était cruelle; il ne répondait à ses lettres, et vous savez qu'on ne peut toujours jouer avec le cœur d'une femme. Pauvre petite elle l'a bien aimé.*'³⁷ Princess Maud and her family were rather worried lest Prince Frank's parents the Duke and Duchess of Teck should feel hurt at the engagement. Princess May, with her customary tact, ascertained that this was not the case: 'please do not for a moment think that they are angry about it, for after F's foolish behaviour in the summer they had given up all hope of the other', she wrote to Prince George.³⁸ The Duchess of Teck found 'Karl of Denmark' 'a very goodlooking boy'. '[He] seems *charming*!' she wrote, 'but looks *fully 3 years* younger than Maud, has *no money*, they are not going either to give him a *house*, . . . there is *no sort* of *time* fixed for the wedding, Aunt Alix saying "they must wait!" her usual form of proceeding!— I say, as Maud is the *parti*, let Karl enter the *British* Navy, but to this I hear the Queen of Denmark is strongly opposed . . . so, as usual, *procrastination*!—My feeling is, Maud does not care for him enough to leave England for his sake & live in Denmark & I dread her finding this out when too late.'³⁹

Princess Maud was married in July 1896, while Prince Frank of Teck was still fretting in India. 'When is Harry to be married—', he had written to his mother from Mahableshwar in April, 'do please dont forget & get her a present from me.'⁴⁰ Princess Maud, or 'Harry' as she was called in the family, was one of the easier members of the Royal Family to please when it came to what her mother the Princess of Wales once called 'that gruesome present choosing',⁴¹ for Princess

Maud had definite tastes: 'At Hayward', wrote Princess May to her husband before Christmas 1896, 'I saw several nice things, I ordered the cigarette holder & think I have found a tiny thing for you to give Harry to hang on one of her long chains.'[42]

After her marriage Princess Maud went to live with her husband in Copenhagen, where for the first few months she was happy. 'Maud & Charles dined, both in very good spirits, Maud looked lovely in a pink chiffon teagown, much pleased with herself & with her house & full of talk',[43] Princess May wrote to her mother from York House in September 1896. This Danish marriage left Princess May with only one unmarried sister-in-law; but that sister-in-law was Princess Victoria.

Prince Frank of Teck never married. As the years went by he became alienated from his sister Princess May for a variety of reasons, one of them being that after their mother's death he gave the famous Cambridge emeralds to his elderly lady-love, and another that Princess May tried to help him with money and good advice. The Duke of York also helped him financially, but Prince Frank was one of those who find the burden of gratitude too heavy to bear.

At the beginning of the new reign in 1901 Prince Frank fancied himself much in favour at Court. Having left the army he was still without a proper income and without an occupation. 'I saw Frank several times in London, he is still busily occupied in doing nothing', Prince George wrote to Prince Dolly in December 1906.[44] Prince Frank was losing his looks and becoming fatter, but he was as carefree and debonair as ever, driving about London in a smart electric brougham and ingratiating himself with his little nephews and nieces by buying them lavish presents at shops at which he knew that their parents had accounts.

Prince Frank died suddenly in 1910, as the result of a small, mismanaged nasal operation. During his illness he had become reconciled to his sister, by that time Queen Mary. For some years before his death he had at last found a vocation in working hard to raise funds for the Middlesex Hospital. In these earnest labours he had proved himself a worthy son of his mother Princess Mary Adelaide.

v

Three months before Princess Maud's marriage to Prince Charles of Denmark, the Duke and Duchess of York had represented Queen

Victoria at two other family weddings: that of Princess Alexandra (the third daughter of the Duke of Edinburgh—now Duke of Saxe-Coburg-Gotha)—to Prince Ernest of Hohenlohe-Langenburg* at Coburg, and that of Princess Louise of Denmark (the eldest daughter of the Princess of Wales's brother the Crown Prince of Denmark) to Prince Frederick of Schaumburg-Lippe†, at Copenhagen. Leaving England on 14 April 1896, they did not return home until 14 May.

These official visits to Coburg and to Copenhagen were the first which Princess May had made abroad in her capacity as Duchess of York. They were very different in tone from her previous experiences of continental royalties. She was no longer a low-ranking Serene Highness to whom flirtatious young officers might pay compliments, but the wife of the heir-presumptive to the English throne. 'A great many people came up to be presented to Her Royal Highness, and both Mr Monson and Mr Bambridge have told me since, how much interested people were in seeing Her Royal Highness: and what a great and charming impression she made on all', Princess May's new lady-in-waiting, Lady Mary Lygon, wrote to the Duchess of Teck from Coburg. ' . . . The [German] Empress wore a flame coloured velvet dress, embroidered in gold. Her Royal Highness wore a pink dress embroidered in silver: and her diamonds looked magnificent.'[45]

The Yorks travelled to Coburg by way of Darmstadt, where they spent one night at the Neues Palais as guests of their cousins the Grand Duke and Grand Duchess of Hesse Darmstadt and by the Rhine. Although the Grand Duke and Grand Duchess had been dancing until four o'clock in the morning, they went punctiliously to the railway station three hours later to receive the Duke and Duchess of York: 'We got here after 7 this morning. Ernie & Ducky met us at the station, so kind of them, & we drove with them here', Princess May told her mother. 'It is very comfortable & nice & so pleasant to be surrounded by photos & pictures of Grandmama, the Aunts, Uncles etc., in fact all the relations at home so that one feels quite at home & *gemütlich*.'[46] 'Ducky', the Grand Duchess of Hesse

* Prince Ernest of Hohenlohe-Langenburg ('Ernie') was a grandson of Queen Victoria's half-sister Princess Feodora of Leiningen (1807–1872) who had married the 4th Fürst of Hohenlohe-Langenburg, whose name was also Ernest, b. 1794, d. 1860.

† Prince Frederick of Schaumburg-Lippe (1868–1945), first married Princess Louise of Denmark (1875–1906) and, after her death, married as his second wife Princess Antoinette of Anhalt (b. 1885) in 1909.

Darmstadt and by the Rhine, was an elder sister of the Coburg bride, Princess Alexandra of Edinburgh. She and her husband the Grand Duke accompanied the Duke and Duchess of York on the long onward journey by train to Coburg the next day. This journey took seven hours. At Coburg there was, again, an official reception at the station, by a family group headed by Uncle Alfred Edinburgh, now Duke of Saxe-Coburg-Gotha: 'We arrived here at 2.30 on Thursday,' Princess May wrote from Schloss Ehrenburg, Coburg, 'Ernie & Ducky came with us in our carriage, & we were met at the station by U. Alfred, Missy & Ferdinand, Sandra, Baby, etc.—General embracing & presentations of suites—Drove to Palais Edinburgh, comfortable nice house, where At. Marie received us. Lunched & then we came over to this nice large Schloss where we are installed in the rooms Grandmama had 2 years ago—They are furnished in a terribly old fashioned style but we are quite comfortable & have lots of room .... Sandra is delighted with your & Papa's present which is very pretty & will be most useful to them, they have *very* few presents, such a contrast to our mass.'47 The 'nice large Schloss' of Ehrenburg, built in 1543 and containing a Gobelin room, much Empire furniture, some good pictures and a well-stocked library, had been re-faced in the neo-Gothic style by the Prince Consort's brother, 'terrible old Uncle Ernest', the late Duke of Saxe-Coburg-Gotha. With a spacious public garden before it, the Schloss stands in the centre of the old town of Coburg, which lies picturesquely among the foothills of the Thuringian Forest. The exterior of the Schloss resembles the work of the English architect Barry, and seems out of place in the town, with its many medieval and Renaissance buildings and its historical connections with Martin Luther and the German Reformation.

The civil and religious ceremonies of the Coburg wedding passed off pleasantly, the second becoming somewhat emotional, since both the bride and her youngest sister burst into tears during the sermon: 'Poor Baby seemed much upset during the service—The sermon was rather long', wrote Princess May.48 From Coburg the English party set off northward through Hanover and Hamburg for Copenhagen, which they reached ten days before the date set for the Danish wedding. This respite was spent by Princess May in sightseeing: 'I had no idea that this town contained so many interesting things,' she wrote to her mother, 'how you would enjoy seeing them, I really think you & Papa ought to come here once, I am sure Amama & Apapa would like it—They are kindness itself to us, most charming to live with, so amiable & doing all they can to make us happy & feel at home.'⁴⁹ Princess May was much appreciated by the King and Queen of Denmark and their court: 'Her Royal Highness has created quite a sensation here,' wrote Lady Mary Lygon, 'I was told that both the King and Queen had quite lost their hearts to her: and everybody I meet talks to me of her beauty and charming gracious-ness. Her Royal Highness is very well, excepting for a sore throat, which is the result of talking very loud to the Queen.'⁵⁰

On the Sunday before the day fixed for the Copenhagen wedding, the Danish family and their guests were filled with awful consternation by the receipt of a telegram from Gmunden. This informed them that the eldest son of the Duke and Duchess of Cumberland, Prince George William, or 'Plumpy', was apparently dying of 'Gelenktyphus'. It may be remembered from Princess May's visit with her parents to Gmunden in 1884 that Princess Thyra, Duchess of Cumberland, was a sister to the Princess of Wales and a daughter of the King and Queen of Denmark: she was thus aunt to Princess Louise of Denmark, the bride of this particular wedding. The state ball and other festivities were cancelled. Telegrams from Gmunden arrived frequently by day and by night. In fact Prince George William recovered from this dangerous illness, preserved by Providence to be killed when driving his motor-car too fast at the age of thirty-two in 1912.

Just after this bad news had reached the court of Denmark the family of the bridegroom, Prince Frederick of Schaumburg-Lippe reached Copenhagen in force. These comprised the bridegroom's father, who was stone deaf and wore an ear-trumpet slung round his neck—'everyone in consequence tries to avoid him';⁵¹ the bridegroom's mother, his two brothers and his two sisters; the reigning Prince of Schaumburg-Lippe, a tall man chiefly remarkable for having a bad squint in both eyes; his wife, Princess Bathildis, who was born an Anhalt; the Grand Duke and Grand Duchess of Luxembourg, Prince Julius of Glucksburg, Prince Carl of Sweden and last but certainly not least Princess May's Aunt Hilda Anhalt—who, as we may recall from Florentine and other meetings was the sister of Princess Bathildis ('Tilla') of Schaumburg-Lippe. Princess Hilda of Anhalt was, in Princess May's opinion, very much aged. She contributed an authentic note of doom to the nuptial scene by repeating, 'Ach! wie furchtbar!'* over and over again as each telegram arrived from Gmunden. 'It really irritated us all particularly Amama', wrote

* 'Oh how terrible!'

Princess May, '& now Amama dreads Aunts Adelheid & Bathildis singing the same song!'[52] The marriage took place on 5 May at eight o'clock in the evening, in one of the saloons of the Crown Prince's palace: 'As we all sat in armchairs round the drawing room, it was a little difficult to realize that we were taking part in a religious ceremony!'[53] wrote Lady Mary Lygon. Four days later the Duke and Duchess of York set off via Cologne for Paris, where they lingered for the inside of a week before returning to London.

This was Princess May's first visit to the 'Danish Family'. She was interested by Copenhagen, grateful for the affectionate kindness of the old King and Queen and thoroughly bored by what Prince George called the 'dawdle & waste of time'[54] that was the rule at the court of Denmark. 'The life here is very tiring as one is all day waiting about, & one has no time to oneself',[55] she wrote on a subsequent visit to Copenhagen; and 'the 6.30 dinner is our despair & the endless evening afterwards with cercle is a bore.'[56] These early dinners were followed by 'much extra eating' as the long evening wore on; the food was bad and elaborate—'very rich jammy sauces and nothing plain or eatable', according to Sir Frederick Ponsonby.[57] The court stood about till almost midnight, or, as an alternative, played Loo and Patchesi for hour after hour.

On such exceptional occasions as the 1896 wedding, the old King and Queen of Denmark gave grand dinner-parties and other formal entertainments; but they and their six children were really happiest leading a very simple life, which did not, however, include any intellectual exertion. The Princess of Wales cared for her Danish home 'much more than for anything else'.[58] She knew—and resented it—that Prince George, Princess May and Princess Victoria found the court of Denmark excessively dull. She attributed this to their being 'so spoilt': 'Greville was delighted here & not at all dull as you imagine it is alas', she wrote to Prince George from Fredensborg Slot in August 1900, 'only my dear children who are so spoilt that they think everything dull where there is no shooting!! or where they can't exactly do as they can at home voilà tout!!!—and it distresses me sometimes, as it is apt to make one become selfish at last! when one never goes out of the way to do what others like & only what suits one self best— Naturally it wld have pleased poor Apapa just to have seen you & dear May whom he likes so much for a little here! & I as well—the whole family flattered themselves that it wld also have pleased you to have seen them once again. . . .'[59] 'Yes, alas poor Toria has of course to go to D. with Mama, it will certainly do her no good I fear & she hates it so',[60] Prince George wrote to Princess May before another of the Princess of Wales's frequent excursions to her native land.

In 1896, the year of Princess May's first visit to their court, the King of Denmark, Christian IX, was seventy-eight years old, and his wife Droning Louise, who was tiny and elegant, with sparkling eyes of periwinkle blue, was seventy-nine. Their eldest son, the Crown Prince Frederick, had married Princess Louise of Sweden and Norway in 1869. They had eight children. The Crown Princess was known in the family as 'The Swan', and to her younger relatives as 'Aunt Swan'. Aunt Swan was 'so religious' that she never went out into Copenhagen Society: 'she is a good soul but a little queer in the head & very difficult to get on with as she is so stiff',[61] wrote Princess May that April 1896. The King and Queen of Denmark's other children were, as we know, the Princess of Wales, King George I of the Hellenes, the Dowager Empress of All the Russias, and the Duchess of Cumberland. There was also Prince Valdemar of Denmark, who was the youngest of the family and had married a Princess of Bourbon-Orleans, a Roman Catholic and a daughter of the Tecks' old friend the Duc de Chartres. Through their mother Droning Louise, born a Princess of Hesse, these six children of the House of Denmark were all devoutly anti-Prussian—a fact which we have seen that Queen Victoria deplored as '*Rumpenheim* influence'.

Queen Victoria had little use for the Queen of Denmark, whom she judged 'false, intriguing & not wise'.[62] The Queen was also irritated by Droning Louise's deafness, for it was through her that this hereditary defect had entered the Danish Royal family, and might, via the Princess of Wales, have passed into that of England. The Princess of Wales suffered fearfully from being so deaf, and in her case deafness was intermittently accompanied by noises in her ears which she described as being 'like a railway train'. 'Poor dear she is *so* deaf that it makes me quite sad & she looks so pathetic sometimes, trying to hear what we are saying and laughing about',[63] Princess May once wrote to her Aunt Augusta. The Princess of Wales would never speak about her deafness to her own children, but on one occasion she wrote to Princess May: 'You my sweet May are always so dear & nice to me—& whenever I am not quite "*au fait*" on account of my *beastly ears* you always by a *word* or even by a turn towards me make me understand—for which I am *most grateful* as nobody can know what I often have to go through—.'[64] When, in 1908, there was a scare that Prince Edward of Wales might become deaf, his father wrote, 'Glad Laking & Tod have both seen David & that they hope with proper treatment that his deafness will go . . . in my family one can't be too careful about ears.'[65]

In 1898, two years after the wedding of Princess Louise of Denmark, the Princess of Wales implored Prince George and Princess May to go again to Denmark, bringing with them Prince Edward, then four years old. The reason for this urgent request was that Queen Louise of Denmark was dying, and wished her great-grandson, the little Prince Edward, to see her before she died. 'In some ways it is rather tiresome that we have to go for so short a time', Princess May wrote to her Aunt Augusta, 'but as poor Amama is so very ill we cannot do otherwise. I will try & write from there if I have a moment which I think seems doubtful.'[66]

The Queen of Denmark died a few weeks after this visit. 'So our dear Louise's sufferings have ended!' the Grand Duchess of Mecklenburg-Strelitz wrote to her brother the Duke of Cambridge on 29 September 1898. 'I hear it this instant and that she expired at 6 o'clock this morning! how all *old* memories spring up, *your* old affection for each other, *our* long sisterly friendship of nearly 70 years! she clung to and cherished the memory of old Hanover days and Rumpenheim!' 'Her feeling for family and old associations', the Grand Duchess wrote of Droning Louise, 'was very great and true.'[67]

VI

In the August following the weddings at Coburg and Copenhagen, and that, in London, of Princess Maud of Wales, the Duchess of York took her mother to the Engadine, on what proved to be the last of Princess Mary Adelaide's many, many journeys abroad. Princess Mary Adelaide had, as usual, been doing too much, and she was worn out. The doctor at St Moritz declared that she must diet, rest and go to bed early. 'In fact I must lead the life of an invalid, how tiresome for you', she said to her daughter on hearing this verdict.[68] Princess May replied that she had come with her mother on purpose to look after her. It was during this stay at St Moritz that Prince Frank wrote the letter already quoted in which he referred to Princess May as 'head nurse'.

The weather in the Engadine that summer was remarkably bad, and the English party found they could do few of their favourite

L*

expeditions. It rained day after day. Princess May was always much affected by the weather, of which she kept a conscientious record in her Diary. A clever little French girl was staying with her parents in the same hotel as the English Royalties. She used to watch them at meals at the small wooden tables in the restaurant. Today an old lady, she clearly remembers the Duchess of York being 'very very cross' about the rain at St Moritz: 'Hang the weather!' she would impatiently exclaim. The child also thought, or was told by her elders, that Princess May 'looked German—she was of the heavy German type'. Despite the weather, Princess May was in good spirits: 'Last night Countess Larisch . . . gave a small dance on purpose for me which was really great fun & I thoroughly enjoyed it. . . . We had a *cotillon* which was charmingly arranged by Ct Larisch (son) and I danced a great deal, so you see I am quite frisky & anxious to enjoy myself', she wrote to Prince George.[69]

Leaving St Moritz at the end of the month, Princess May and her mother travelled via Zürich to Frankfurt, where they stayed a couple of days before going to visit the Empress Frederick in her new country-house at Kronberg. From Frankfurt they went one afternoon to Rumpenheim. 'Home to lunch', Princess May records on 3 September, '& then we drove to dear old Rumpenheim. Mossy & Fischy were not there but we went all over the house & garden, the church & vault, in fact saw everything, it was interesting seeing all the things I had not seen for 18 years—We spent nearly three hours there & got home at 6.40. We drove to Rumpenheim thro' Offenbach & returned over the ferry.'[70] This farewell visit to the scenes of her youth affected Princess Mary Adelaide deeply: 'Mama found all the pictures & things she knew so well in old days.'[71] 'Your visit to Rumpenheim with May', wrote Prince Frank from Ganeshkind, 'must have conjured up a varied assortment of recollections and, as Emily writes, you visited every room—I feel sure, that that one in which poor Nanny* lived, was not missed—one might almost say a death or a birth in every bedroom.'[72]

On the day after the Rumpenheim tour, the Duchess of York and her mother, with their attendants, took an evening train at Frankfurt for the half-hour's journey to Kronberg. Here they were met at the station by the Empress Frederick: 'A. Vicky met us at the station & we drove with her here where we had tea in the garden & grounds which are so pretty & we came in in time to dress for dinner.'[73] In

* See pages 89–90 for the death at Rumpenheim, in 1878, of the Duchess of Teck's beloved dresser, Brand.

1889 the Empress Frederick had bought a fine site at the foot of the beautiful Taunus hills near Kronberg, and here she had constructed a long imposing house. Its architecture was inspired by that of the Elizabethan manor-house of Flete in Devonshire, but with Italianate details, medieval German turrets, a wide terrace and a tower. It was called Friedrichshof in memory of the Empress's husband the Emperor Frederick III. 'Friedrichshof is a Country House & not a "Schloss" according to german ideas', the Empress wrote to Queen Victoria, 'though it has a *bit of a* tower & a terrace. It is more comfortable & compact than Babelsburg or Reinhardsheim but about that size, & with that amount of accommodation. As many rooms as Bagshot, I should think.'74 She put the Queen on her mettle by adding that she did not think her mother would care for Friedrichshof: 'You say you are afraid I shall [not] like your new Home, as I dont like what is *old* & dark as dear Papa disliked all the English Country seats & said they were all made so dark and with our vy dark & dull climate every thing shld be light & bright as here & at Osborne. But I like mediaeval things',75 the Queen replied from Balmoral.

The Empress Frederick was above all else a woman of great taste, with a profound knowledge of works of art. She filled Friedrichshof with fine pictures and tapestries, bronzes and French furniture. It was, as it remains today, a very comfortable house indeed. The Fried-richshof collections stirred Princess May's nascent interest in works of art: 'We spent two charming days with Aunt Vicky at Friedrichshof, it is such a beautiful place with such lovely things in it all collected by her—She was so dear & nice to us',76 she wrote to Aunt Augusta. Princess May was installed in the 'Greek Suite' on the first floor of Friedrichshof, to the right from the main staircase. 'May has your rooms,' the Empress wrote to her daughter Crown Princess Sophie, 'it is always a pang for me to see anyone else in them, but you will not mind May using them, I know how much you like her. It is indeed pleasant to have them, especially as everyone here says May is your image. She is so sweet and charming and sensible, and her being like my Sophie drew me towards her. She is in great good looks, and of an evening wears a pink satin gown, which suited her so well. I think people admire her much here.'77 'I am flattered you find me like May', the Crown Princess answered, 'but fear I never had her nose mouth or complexion or lovely coloured hair!'78

At this period of the nineties, Princess May's looks were at their apogee. 'Pss May is looking remarkably well & in such good spirits',

a member of her suite had written to the Duchess of Teck from Balmoral the previous autumn. 'She was quite superb in white & many
diamonds on Monday night & made quite a little sensation coming
down into the dimly lighted Concert room by the staircase at the side
of the stage, with the footlights shining upon her brightly as she
followed the Queen into the room.'[79] The Empress Frederick's new
admiration for Princess May's appearance did not prevent her establishing the fact that her nephew's wife wore a false front of hair over
her forehead: 'The towsel and fringe like a thick sponge over the
forehead suits Aunt Alix but no one else', she wrote to her daughter
Sophie at this time. 'It spoils Maudie's pretty face, and May wears
a wig front, and Charlotte is quite disfigured by it.'[80] The Empress
held strong views on how young women should dress. In 1898 the
Crown Princess wrote to her mother to enquire about a most exciting
rumour that had just percolated through to the distant court of
Athens. This was that ladies in London Society were using make-up
on their faces. 'To my satisfaction', the Empress replied, from Drumlanrig Castle, 'I can tell you that not *one* of all the young ladies I saw
at Dalmeny, Gosford, Hopetoun or here were painted, powdered or
laced or got up or wearing fringes, but fresh and lovely as English
and Scottish maidens should be in the bloom of health and youth.'[81]

From Frankfurt the Duchess of Teck went on to Bad Nauheim
and Princess May set off homewards. On the channel boat, she met
Princess Hélène of Orleans, who was now Duchess of Aosta. 'She
looks so well', Princess May reported, 'but I think he has a disagreeable expression & I am glad I am not his wife!'[82] Passing through
London Princess May went to join Prince George in Scotland, where
later in the month they helped to entertain the Russian Tsar and
Tsarina, who had come over to visit Queen Victoria. Owing to the
fear of anarchists, the Tsar was not permitted by the Russian security
men to set foot in London or any other large city, and he had thus
been invited to Balmoral.

Princess May had loved this time abroad with her mother. 'I felt
so low when we parted at Frankfurt that I nearly cried so I had to
walk away quickly to gulp down my tears, what a pleasant time we
had together, it really was delightful, particularly the last part with
all the interests of seeing Rumpenheim, Frankfort & Friedrichshof
with you, we really must take another journey together for we suit
so well & like the same things & you are so delightfully keen about
everything',[83] she wrote to Princess Mary Adelaide.

Alas! for Princess Mary Adelaide, Duchess of Teck, there were to be no more journeys, either with or without her daughter: no more alpine panoramas, no more walks by mountain torrents or past vine-covered pergolas, no more unexpected encounters with foreign cousins in *Platanen Alleen* or in the *Fürstlichen Zimmer* of some German railway station. Never again would she see the friendly façade of Rumpenheim mirrored in the Main waters, never again watch the sun setting across the Bodensee. The only journey that awaited her in the coming year 1897 was the last, long journey through the unknown landscapes and mysterious regions of the dead.

VII

In 1897, the glorious year of the Diamond Jubilee, Princess May celebrated her thirtieth birthday. A month before this, on 25 April, her third child and only daughter, Princess Mary of York,* was born. So soon as Princess May had recovered, she was told that her mother had just undergone a serious emergency operation at White Lodge, but was making good progress towards convalescence. In this same week occurred, too, the terrible charity bazaar fire in Paris, in which many eminent persons, including the Wittelsbach Princess, the Duchesse d'Alençon, perished. One of Princess Mary Adelaide's first actions on regaining consciousness from the chloroform was to order wreaths to be sent in her name to the Paris funerals of the victims. 'This fire at Paris is the most awful Catastrophe almost ever known,' wrote Queen Victoria on 5 May, 'to think of poor Sophie Alençon being one of the victims is *too*, *too* dreadful! It makes one *shudder*. Mary† is going on quite well & recovering slowly.'[84] In another letter the Queen added the latest grisly detail from Paris, which was that all that had been found of the Duchesse d'Alençon was 'the head'.

On getting back home from abroad in the autumn of 1896 Princess Mary Adelaide had resumed her gruelling round of social and charit-able activities. She was visibly overtired and ill, but she never relaxed. 'I fear we can never alter H R H, she has never yet taken care of

---

* Princess Victoria Alexandra Alice Mary, b. 25 April 1897, m. 28 February 1922 Viscount Lascelles (succeeded as 6th Earl of Harewood, 1929, and d. 1947) and has two sons the 7th Earl of Harewood and Hon. Gerald Lascelles. After the death of her father's eldest sister in 1931 Princess Mary was, in 1932 declared Princess Royal, the title held by her aunt since 1905.

† i.e. Princess Mary Adelaide, Duchess of Teck.

herself. What will England be without her? I feel too sad for words',[85] wrote Hélène Bricka, who foresaw the worst.

Princess Mary Adelaide was also enduring with stoicism the now rapid mental and nervous deterioration of her husband the Duke of Teck: 'he, poor dear man, seems really to have softening of the brain', the Empress Frederick wrote from Windsor in March 1897, 'and one does not quite understand what he means,—he laughs about nothing & cannot find his words.'[86] 'I was indeed sorry to hear your account of papa, tho' I gathered that he had gone down hill from the *Geschwistern* letters',[87] wrote Prince Frank to his mother from India. '. . . Papa looked in about 3.30,' Princess May wrote to her husband from York House, 'he is looking well, but I thought him terribly confused about things in general & he jumps so from one subject to another.'[88] All this naturally preyed upon Princess Mary Adelaide's mind and affected her already poor state of health. She now became subject to prolonged fainting fits. After one of these, while staying with her friends the Walshes at Warfield in October 1896, she broke down in tears, murmuring: 'I don't want to die yet. I cannot leave my children—my sons want me still.'[89]

Princess Mary Adelaide's convalescence after her operation was surprisingly swift. This was primarily due to her will-power: 'We all laughed at the message you sent Motherdear, "that there is some life left in the old dog yet",' wrote Prince George, 'it was so like you.'[90] There was a good deal of life left in Princess Mary Adelaide, as her letters to her daughter from her sick-bed go to show:

I am making *wonderful progress*, say *nurses* & *Drs!* taking roast lamb & mint sauce, boiled mutton, roast chicken, asparagus, spinach &c—besides *invalid turtle soup* brought by *kind Ly Mayoress* & every kind of jelly! . . . My bed is placed in front of window overlooking beech tree, still pink leaved! & I can watch the bicycles fly past.

'Mary Lygon', she wrote in another letter, '. . . brought me a *huge* bunch of *heavenly* dark red roses from Beauchamp—So kind! People *spoil* me with attentions & my room is a *perfect bower* of flowers! . . . Tatry will amuse you with the account of my *return* to *frivolity* yesterday & displaying to an admiring circle the spring gowns & evening toilette, ordered of Madame Moreau but never yet tried on. . . . I have desired Moreau to show you some patterns suitable for *me*, for *you* to *choose* from for Jubilee *day* & Buck. P. Garden party &c.'[91] Princess Mary Adelaide was determined not to miss the Diamond Jubilee festivities. She attended the Palace garden party in a wheel-chair, and figured in the carriage procession to and from St Paul's on the Jubilee Day itself.

Princess Mary Adelaide's appearance in the Jubilee procession, her first in public since her illness, was greeted with applause: 'Never before had a Princess of Great Britain and Ireland received such an ovation', writes her biographer. '. . . Men women and children cheered her to the echo, and handkerchiefs and banners were waved as a token of joy and thankfulness for the preservation of a life so dear to the working men and women of this country.'[92] Owing to the Queen's great lameness, the Diamond Jubilee Thanksgiving Service on 22 June 1897 was held on the steps of St Paul's Cathedral. This was an innovation of which, needless to say, the Grand Duchess of Mecklen-burg-Strelitz disapproved: 'No! that out of door Service before St Pauls!' she wrote when she first heard of the plan, in April, 'has one ever heard of such a thing! after 60 years Reign, to thank God in the Street!!! who *can* have started such an idea, and how could the Queen adopt it?—'[93] Nevertheless the Grand Duchess came over to take part in the service and in the family entertainments at Buckingham Palace and Marlborough House. 'Buckingham Palace', wrote the Empress Frederick at this time, 'is like a beehive, & the place is so crammed we do not see so very much of one another.'[94] 'Here all are more or less off their heads', the Grand Duchess wrote to her nephew Prince Dolly from London that June, 'only May keeps her head on her shoulders alright.'[95]

In August the Duke and Duchess of York left London for an official three weeks' visit to Ireland. They were the first members of the Royal Family for several decades to visit Ireland in this way. Their reception by the amiable Irish crowds was deceptively loyal:

. . . What a grand success! & glorious triumph far beyond the *most sanguine expectations*, I might even say hopes! your visit to Ireland has been [wrote Princess May's proud mother] to quote the words of the Parnellite correspondent of the Daily Graphic: '*a triumphal procession!*' . . . How admirably you & Georgie both bore your part through it all! how well, charmingly, he spoke! how you won *all hearts!* . . . I am . . . proud of *you*, my own darling child for having made so delightful an impression on every one, high & low! & everywhere & having so *materially helped* to win over Ireland to *loyalty* & an altered view of things as regards the Throne & royal family! for this is what I really believe the effect of your visit will result in!—But now *we must* agitate for the *hire*, or *purchase* by the *nation* of a royal residence in Ireland. . . . Possibly it might be a wise move to get some patriotic nobleman, or landowner, to *lend* you a place as an *experiment* before you are committed to anything. . . . I enclose . . . a most kind gift from our dear Baroness B. Coutts, confided to my charge, to replenish your *empty purse, vidée par* your Irish expenses.[96]

The project for an Irish residence for the Duke and Duchess of York did not find favour with Queen Victoria. Lord Salisbury's Cabinet discussed it in November 1897. They agreed that it would be 'a salutary measure', and stated that they were ready to provide the money for it. No further steps were taken, however, when it was ascertained that the plan was not acceptable to the Queen. 'What a pity the Queen does not approve of an Irish Home for the Yorks', wrote the Grand Duchess of Mecklenburg-Strelitz to Prince Alge; 'it is a great mistake, they did their *work* so well, now she ought to carry on the good that has begun.'[97] 'Papers still full of Irish Triumphal progress and May's dresses', Prince Frank, who was now in Egypt, wrote to his mother on 9 October, 'tho' I see she is criticised for not smiling when she bows.'[98]

VIII

On their return from Ireland, the Duke and Duchess of York stayed with the Queen at Balmoral, after which they came south to London and thence to York Cottage, Sandringham. Towards the end of October, Princess May left Sandringham to spend a few days at White Lodge. It was Guild time, and she found the house full of the familiar piles of clothing, of packages and sacks, with her mother supervising the lady helpers from the neighbourhood. Princess May, too, set to work. 'We unpacked Guild things all day long', she noted in her Diary for 25 October 1897. 'Mama & I dined at home while Papa & the others went to the play—& we had a nice long talk afterwards. Mama was not feeling quite well.'

The next day, a Tuesday, Princess Mary Adelaide stayed in bed: 'I sat with her', wrote Princess May, 'in the morning & afternoon.'[99] In the evening the Duchess of Teck was markedly worse. The doctor decided on a second emergency operation and sent for Mr Allingham, the surgeon, who operated at twelve-thirty at night, while Princess May, Prince Alge and the Duke of Teck waited downstairs. 'I feel so awfully miserable as you can imagine & I pray God that all may yet be well but I feel so frightened', Princess May wrote to her husband that evening. '. . . I feel in an agony of fright but I am thankful I am in the house so that I know what is going on—instead of having to be sent for.'[100] Two hours after the completion of the operation, Princess Mary Adelaide's heart failed. She died at 3 a.m.

All that day, which was one of thick fog, members of the Royal Family converged on White Lodge. The Duke of York drove down from London: 'All the relations came down in the course of the day', Prince George wrote in his Diary, 'including Motherdear who returned later to Sandringham. Very busy answering & opening telegrams. Uncle Teck is quite brokenhearted but calm. . . . My Darling May is wonderful, so brave & calm, but very tired.'[101] During Princess Mary Adelaide's last hours the Duke of Teck had sent the Princess of Wales an urgent telegram asking her to come down to White Lodge:

. . . so of course I got ready at once [the Princess of Wales wrote to the Grand Duchess of Mecklenburg-Strelitz] & before I left the house I heard from poor May saying *all was over!* . . . On arriving at White Lodge I found everyone plunged in the most terrible grief—he poor Man heartbroken utterly crushed—poor darling May & her two brothers calm but in perfect despair—Uncle George very much upset—Bertie was also there having come up from Newmarket with the former—Sister Louise also there . . . and poor dear Geraldine was there—& so nice & feeling—We had a long talk together. Darling May who so far bears up wonderfully well took me upstairs at once into dear Mary's room! where she was lying in her *last* long sleep—She looked *so* beautiful calm and peaceful with such a happy expression on her dear face. . . . She reminded me so of dear beloved Aunt Cambridge too when I saw her dying.[102]

Letters and telegrams poured into White Lodge: 'never, never in this world can there have been anyone so full of love & sympathy & thought for everyone—& no one so universally beloved', wrote Lady Eva Dugdale to Princess May, '& her memory & all the good she has done must live for ever. . . . I am sending a little cross of violets to Windsor & I am trying to get some edelweiss to put with it, for dear Princess Mary is so associated with some of the happiest days of my life spent at St Moritz with her & you—that I should like a little remembrance of those times to go with her.'[103]

From what we have seen of Princess Mary Adelaide it will come as no surprise to learn that she had never made a will. She had, however, left verbal instructions with the Duke of Teck to ask if she could be buried in the Royal vault at Windsor: 'Mama told Papa on more than one occasion that she had a great wish to have her last resting place at Windsor . . . as she particularly disliked the idea of being buried in the damp vault at Kew in spite of her Parents being buried there', Princess May wrote to the Queen. 'If you approve of this I know you will be doing an enormous kindness to poor dear Papa.'[104] The funeral took place on 3 November: 'It was dreadful having to leave her there & to return home without her who was *the* centre of all to us as you know', Princess May wrote to her Aunt Augusta. 'It seems impossible to realise that darling Mama, of all people in the world, so full of life & happiness, should have left us, it is awful awful, & I dread to think of how we can live without her— For Papa it is cruel & his sad state makes it so much worse, he was so dependent on Mama for everything, & now God knows what he will do.'[105] 'That you should have been there to see her those last days, will ever be a sad comfort to you', the Grand Duchess had written to her niece, 'but now *all* will rest upon you, poor child, and you will have to do and think for them all.'[106]

As so often before, the Grand Duchess Augusta was perfectly right: everything connected with the Teck family now devolved on Princess May, who had to take decisions, sort papers and try to help her father divide jewellery and other possessions. The worst problem of all was the Duke of Teck, who was now mentally in a very bad way indeed. 'Dear Mama has left us at a very trying time', Prince Alge wrote about his father, 'and just now her advice and kindness would indeed have been a boon.'[107] Having bidden farewell to Princess Mary Adelaide, we may now do so equally to the Duke of Teck; for, after an unsuccessful visit to the Court of Württemberg, where his cousins found him too much of a responsibility, he lived on in seclusion at White Lodge, looked after by a doctor and male nurses. Even the sight of his own children unbalanced him, and when he died in January 1900 Princess May, whose three brothers were by then on active service in South Africa, had not been permitted to see him for many months. 'Poor Franz Teck's death is a happy release for him—', the Prince of Wales wrote that January, '& he has virtually been dead to us for nearly two years!'[108] The Duke's body was laid beside that of Princess Mary Adelaide in the Royal vault: 'It was sad to see U. George [Cambridge]—nearly 81—leaning on his stick & watching the coffin of his Brother in law so much his junior in years descend [into] the vault—', wrote the Prince of Wales to his sister the Empress Frederick.[109]

Fate had thus deprived Princess May of both her parents. In her

1. Portraits of HRH Princess Mary Adelaide, Duchess of Teck and of HSH Francis, Duke of Teck, circa 1866

(*From the paintings by Henry Weigall Jr. in the possession of the 2nd Marquess of Cambridge*)

2. HRH the Duchess of Teck with her daughter Princess May and two elder sons, 1873; two photographs of Princess May of Teck in 1874
(From photographs by W. & D. Downey by permission of The Radio Times Hulton Picture Library)

Princess Catherine of Württemberg
(*From a photograph in the possession of H R H the Princess of Wied, Princess of Württemberg*)

3. Duke Alexander of Württemberg, father of the Duke of Teck
(*From the painting in the possession of the 2nd Marquess of Cambridge*)

4. Schloss Rumpenheim, near Offenbach
(From a gouache drawing in the Royal Library at Windsor Castle)

5. HRH Princess Augusta, Duchess of Cambridge
(From the portrait painted by Heinrich von Angeli in 1877
and now at Windsor Castle. Reproduced by gracious
permission of Her Majesty the Queen)

6. Princess May of Teck with her three brothers, circa 1886
(From a photograph in the possession of Mr. T. Baylis)

7. HRH the Duchess of Teck with Princess May in the garden
at White Lodge, circa 1888
(From a photograph by R. Craigie)

8. Princess May of Teck in 1890
(From a photograph by Russell & Sons)

9. HRH the Duchess of Teck with Princess May, Prince Adolphus and Prince Alexander of Teck. The fifth member of the group is Princess Louise of Wales
(From a photograph in Queen Mary's album taken at St. Moritz 1887)

Princess Mary with her elder brothers Prince Adolphus and Prince Francis of Teck in the garden at White Lodge. June 1891
(From a photograph in Queen Mary's album)

10. Prince Albert Victor, Duke of Clarence, with members of his staff, outside Marlborough House in June 1890

(From a photograph; by permission of the Radio Times Hulton Picture Library)

11. Monumental effigy of the Duke of Clarence from his tomb, designed by Sir Alfred Gilbert, in the Memorial Chapel, Windsor Castle (*By gracious permission of Her Majesty the Queen*)

12. Princess May (on extreme right) and her mother, in mourning for the Duke of Clarence, Cannes 1892

(From a photograph in Queen Mary's album, annotated: 'Mama, Mr. Aubrey Fitzclarence, Lady K. Coke, Self, Count Vay, Miss Tufnell, Lady Arran')

13. The marriage ceremony of Princess May of Teck and the Duke of York, 6 July 1893
(From the picture by Tuxen at Buckingham Palace. Reproduced by gracious permission of Her Majesty the Queen)

14. York Cottage, Sandringham, at the time of the honeymoon
of the Duke and Duchess of York, July 1893
The drawing-room at York Cottage
(From photographs in Queen Mary's albums)

15. TRH the Duke and Duchess of York, Christmas 1893
(From a photograph in the possession of H R H Princess Alice,
Countess of Athlone)

16. HRH the Princess of Wales, afterwards Queen Alexandra

(From a photograph; by permission of Radio Times Hulton Picture Library)

17. TRH the Duke and Duchess of York, with the Emperor and Empress of Germany, the Duke and Duchess of Saxe-Coburg-Gotha and other relations at the Coburg Wedding, April 1896
(From a photograph in Queen Mary's album)

18. HRH the Duchess of York, with her brother Prince Alexander of Teck (afterwards Earl of Athlone), at Langford, Derby, in August 1899
(From a photograph in Queen Mary's album)

19. TRH the Duke and Duchess of York, with Queen Victoria and
other Members of the Royal Family, in the garden at Osborne
House, August 1898
(From a photograph in Queen Mary's album)

Queen Victoria at work, circa 1898
*(From a photograph in the possession of
Bridget, Lady Victor Paget)*

20. HRH Princess Augusta Caroline, Grand Duchess of
Mecklenburg-Strelitz
*(From a photograph in the possession of H R H Princess Alice,
Countess of Athlone)*

Victoria Mary
1900

21. HRH the Duchess of York, 1900
(From a photograph in the possession
of Lady Cecilie Goff)

22. HRH Victoria Mary, Princess of Wales, in her sitting-room at
Malabar Point, Bombay, during the visit of TRH to India in 1905
(*From a photograph in Queen Mary's album*)

23. Two photographs of Her Majesty Queen Mary on board the
Medina, on the way to India for the Delhi Durbar, November 1911
(From Queen Mary's albums)

24. Two photographs of King George V and Queen Mary in
India, 1911–12
(From Queen Mary's albums)

25. Queen Mary being greeted at the railway station of Neu Strelitz
by her Aunt, the Dowager Grand Duchess of Mecklenburg-Strelitz,
then ninety years of age, and by her cousins the Grand Duke and
Grand Duchess of Mecklenburg-Strelitz; August 1912

(From a photograph in Queen Mary's album)

26. Queen Mary in the First World War: with King George V and Sir William Robertson at Aldershot, and the Queen making a private visit to a street shrine in Hackney. Both in 1916 (*From photographs in Queen Mary's albums*)

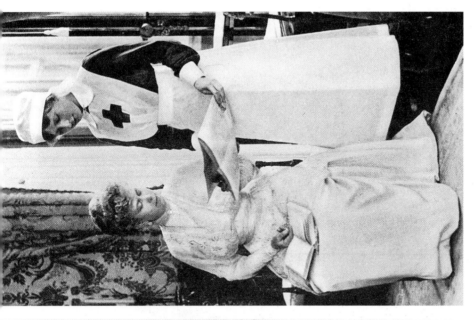

27. Queen Mary and Queen Alexandra, November 1916; Queen Mary, at the time of her Silver Wedding celebrations in July 1918, with her daughter, now HRH Princess Royal
(From Queen Mary's albums)

Opening of Parliament
Dec: 9th 1924

28. King George V and Queen Mary on their way to the
Opening of Parliament, 9 December 1924
(From a photograph in Queen Mary's album)

29. King George V and Queen Mary in the garden of Adelaide
Cottage, Windsor Home Park, in the autumn of 1935
*(From a photograph in the possession of Princess Alice, Countess of
Athlone)*

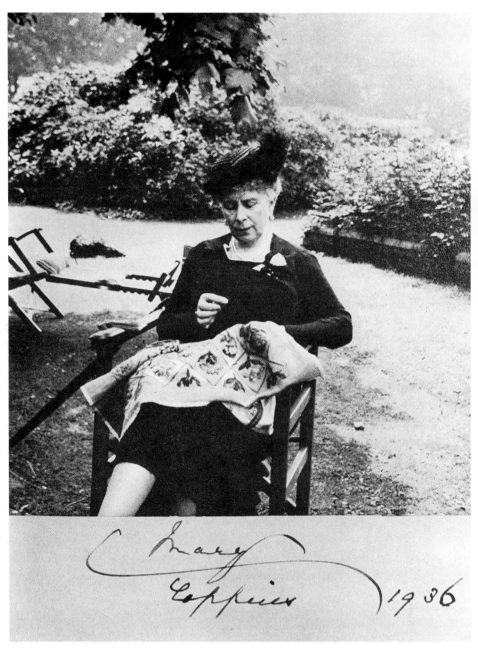

30. Queen Mary in the early days of her widowhood
(Photograph taken at Coppins, Iver, in June 1936; from Queen Mary's album)

Leaving Westminster Abbey

31. Queen Mary leaving Westminster Abbey after the Coronation of King George VI and Queen Elizabeth, 12 May 1937

(From a photograph in Queen Mary's album)

32. Queen Mary, aided by her Despatch Riders, cutting down a tree
at Badminton, autumn 1942
(From a photograph in the possession of Sir John Weir)

Queen Mary, accompanied by her brother and her sister-in-law,
Lord Athlone and Princess Alice, on her way to inspect the crater of
a bomb just detonated in St. James's Park, 26 April 1946
(From a photograph in Queen Mary's album)

desolation she turned to her Aunt Augusta, with whom she now became more and more confidential and intimate. After her mother's death she passed a wretched winter in England and then, in the spring of 1898, arranged to join the Grand Duchess of Mecklenburg-Strelitz in the South of France.

Princess May found her aunt in dire need of comfort and support, for just then Berlin itself and every little court of Germany was ringing with a scandal which concerned the Grand Ducal family at Neu Strelitz.

In the weeks immediately preceding the Duchess of Teck's death, the Empress Frederick had been hinting at this scandal in her letters to Queen Victoria. 'But you have left us all in great & painful suspense by your allusion to some dreadful report abt the M.S.s & I have cyphered to beg you to say what it means', Queen Victoria wrote impatiently to her eldest daughter on 9 October 1897. 'The other day when May was here, she said that the eldest girl of Adolphus was vy unwell w. *enemia* to such an extent as to necessitate her being sent away at once to a warmer climate as she was in a state of *Melancolia*. This must be in connection with what you just have heard.' The Empress remained inexplicit: '. . . I really must scold that you continue to speak of something *dreadful* wh. if true wld make the whole Strelitz & Anhalt family wretched for ever & then refuse to say anything but go on in the same strain in every letter!' wrote Queen Victoria. 'You shld never have said anything if you wld not say *what* is supposed . . . it is too unpleasant to have such hysterical hints thrown out—without saying what it is!'[110]

The scandal at Strelitz, which made radical newspaper headlines in its day, is only of interest to us since it shows us Princess May's wisdom and open-mindedness, as well as her loyalty and affection, at their best. Pale, sad and tired, the Duchess of York set off to join her Strelitz aunt at Mentone on 1 March 1898.

CHAPTER FOUR

'GOOD BYE TO
THE OLD CENTURY'

———

TRAVELLING AS LADY KILLARNEY, and accompanied by the Dugdales, her dresser and two other servants, the Duchess of York arrived at Mentone to find her aunt installed in the annexe of the Hôtel du Louvre. The Grand Duchess's rooms were on the first floor with balconies, and Princess May took over the ground floor, which had a large terrace. 'One feels like in a private house, not like in an Hotel', her aunt had written to her beforehand.[1] The Grand Duchess's suite consisted of her gentleman, Herr von Lucke, and her lady-in-waiting, Frau von Heyden, known as 'Oh! Matilda!' Also with the Grand Duchess—and indeed the actual reason for the old lady's presence at Mentone at all—was her eldest grandchild, Marie, Duchess of Mecklenburg-Strelitz, who was then a girl of nineteen. 'Marie', wrote Princess May, 'is a nice girl but oh! so badly dressed, so very German which is scarcely a pretty fashion.'[2] On the way to the Coburg wedding in April 1896 Princess May had had a rendezvous on the station at Brussels with Aunt Augusta, who was bound for England with her two granddaughters: 'They looked so nice I thought', Princess May wrote of her young cousins, '*mais les toilettes!!!* Oh!'[3]

The sad little story of young Duchess Marie of Mecklenburg-Strelitz need not in itself detain us long, for its sole interest today is in the light it throws upon Princess May's moral courage and true nobility of character.

Marie Strelitz had a younger sister Jutta and two brothers, Adolphus Frederick and Charles Borwin. They were the four children of the only son of the reigning Grand Duke and of the Grand Duchess Augusta—the Erbgrossherzog Adolphus Frederick, who had married Elisabeth, a daughter of the reigning Duke of Anhalt. We can recall from Princess May's childhood visits to Strelitz the extreme formality, indeed the rigour, which prevailed in the etiquette of the Grand Ducal court at Neu Strelitz. The same atmosphere was to be found in the Erbgrossherzog's Palais, which was situated at the end of the Schloss-strasse, opposite that Alte Palais in which Princess Mary Adelaide's birthday entertainment had taken place in 1873. The Erbgrossherzog's Palais was inhabited by the Hereditary Grand Duke, his wife and his four children. His two daughters were in the hands of governesses, who formed a screen between them and their parents, so that these latter had no real contact with their children. The two girls were reared in a total ignorance of life: when their grandmother announced to them the birth of Prince Edward of York, the eldest Strelitz girl thought it ' "very odd" that May should have a Baby!' 'Why?' the Grand Duchess wrote to her niece, 'I don't know, unless she thinks of her as one near her own age.'4

Inflexibility of mind and habits has dangers all its own. Rigidity of manners is analogous to the rigidity of a carcase, for like a carcase it can breed corruption. The result of so much stiffness in their sur-roundings was that the two daughters of the Erbgrossherzog Adolphus were supervised but not looked after. In 1897 it was suddenly brought to the incredulous Erbgrossherzogin Elizabeth's attention—very late in the day—that her eldest daughter seemed to be about to have a child.

In the tempest of recriminations which followed this discovery it was established that the real cause of the misfortune was one of the many inflexible rules of the Grand Ducal court: that all the lamps in all the rooms, including those of the young Duchesses' bedrooms, were carried in by the footmen and never by the maids. The responsi-bility for the crime was quickly traced to one Hecht, a young married footman who was immediately dismissed without a character. When he applied for another position in the neighbourhood, his prospective employers wrote to the Hofmarschallernt of the court of Strelitz to ask why he had left. They were told that Hecht had been dismissed for stealing. Hecht thereupon took the train to Berlin, and consulted a lawyer. This lawyer happened to be a Social-Democrat. He released the story to the eager anti-monarchical press of the capital. The Strelitz family thereupon pensioned off Hecht, but omitted to stipulate that he must first leave Strelitz. He stayed on in the town, hoping to extract more money by his presence.

Meanwhile the story had spread from court to court across Europe. Queen Victoria told the Grand Duchess Augusta that she had heard it from the Empress Frederick, adding: 'I believe she has done much harm in writing to all the Courts!'5 At Strelitz the wretched Duchess

Marie's parents would have nothing more to do with her. They insisted on the child being sent away at once. 'It is too awful & shameful & almost sinful to send the poor Baby away', wrote Queen Victoria. 'I hear fm a reliable source that the *family* have forbidden that poor unhappy girl's name ever being mentioned *in* the family. . . . I think it too wicked', the Queen wrote in a later letter on the same subject.[6] The Grand Duchess Augusta alone of her German family championed her granddaughter, in whose fundamental innocence she believed: for it was clear that the girl had been either terrorised by Hecht—as the Grand Duchess thought—or 'drugged', which was Queen Victoria's theory. The German Emperor fancied she had been hypnotised, a possibility also entertained by the Duke of York.

It will be seen that under these curious circumstances the fact that the Duchess of York went publicly to stay with her young cousin, and was to be seen driving with her daily, was indeed a noble and protective gesture. On Princess May's advice her Aunt Augusta went with her to see Queen Victoria, then at Cimiez, and told her the whole story. The Prince of Wales was also talked round by Princess May. 'He has been so kind about it', Princess May wrote to her husband, '& At A. is so grateful to her *English* family for behaving so well & upholding her views—At. looks much better & happier since I came.'[7] 'I certainly think the English relations have behaved better & are more sensible about it all', Prince George replied. 'The parents are the worst & ought to be ashamed of themselves.'[8] The old Grand Duchess never forgot that the attitude of the 'English family' was almost solely due to the energy and sense of justice of Princess May.

It was not the sort of situation with which Princess May had ever been faced before. But her quiet gift for coping with the difficulties of life now amounted to a kind of genius. Her only regret was that she had not been consulted earlier on: 'The more she [Aunt Augusta] tells me about it the more I feel how utterly the whole thing was mismanaged—What a pity when it could easily have been arranged to send the girl away on the plea of ill-health',[9] she wrote from Mentone to Prince George.

The poor young Duchess Marie was fated to have an unhappy life for many years to come. Her parents refused to see her, and they would not even attend her wedding to a Frenchman, Comte Jametel, nearly twenty years her senior, in 1899. This marriage proved a failure, since Comte Jametel was found to have married Duchess Marie for her money, and continued his very public liaison with a Spanish

Infanta. After many legal difficulties and with the loss of her fortune she divorced him in 1908, and later made a second, happier marriage. Throughout all these troubles, her 'Aunt May' continued to give her moral support; for once the Duchess of York had taken up a cause she invariably saw it through.

II

Princess May's day with her Aunt Augusta at Cimiez was but one of many occasions on which she saw and talked with the Queen in the year of the Diamond Jubilee. Queen Victoria, whose attitude towards several of her own children was detached, was now very fond of Princess May: 'Each time I see you I love & respect you more & am so truly thankful that Georgie has such a partner—to help & encourage him in his difficult position',[10] she wrote in October 1897 from Balmoral. In these last years Princess May was seeing much of the Queen: if we take 1898 as typical, we find that she spent twenty-nine days with the Queen at Osborne, eight days at Windsor Castle, one day at Cimiez, visited her four times in London, stayed for six days at Balmoral and went there four times again from Mar Lodge. When the Queen died in January 1901, Princess May wrote: 'I cannot tell you how miserable I am at the dear Queen's death as she was always so kind to me & ever a good friend & counsellor—The last few years we have been so much with her & our chicks too that we shall miss our visits sadly.'[11]

Nevertheless even Princess May found the Queen's system of cross-examination (which the Princess of Wales frankly dreaded) rather exhausting: 'I like Balmoral for about a fortnight', she wrote to her husband in 1895, 'but I honestly think that longer than that is rather an ordeal as the everlasting questions & the carefulness of one's replies is extremely fatiguing in the long run, however as she kindly asks us to stay I suppose we had better do so.'[12] 'I quite believe you were much cross-questioned about here & everybody', the Princess of Wales had once written to Prince George from the court of Denmark, '—but I hope you were careful in what you said.'[13] The Queen's probing questions alternated with excellent advice. 'I hope that you will brush up & practise Georgie's French & German also', she had written not long after the Yorks' marriage, '—for you *must both* be *able* to speak it with foreigners—& with so many relatives. Uncle Bertie speaks both languages so well that it is very essential you shd do so. You shd *not* speak English to them when they come here as I observe you do.'[14] In March 1899, the year of her own eightieth birthday, Queen Victoria showed the Duchess of York another mark of favour: she asked her to accompany her on her southward migration to the Hotel Regina at Cimiez near Nice.

The Queen, with Princess Henry of Battenberg, her ten-year-old son Prince Leopold of Battenberg, Princess Victoria of Schleswig-Holstein, Princess May and a large suite travelled from Boulogne by special train. It was a moment at which English people were not much liked by the French: 'There were quantities of people lining the route & everybody was *most* civil & the reception was a *very* good one to the gentlemen's great joy, not a hiss or a boo—', wrote Princess May to Prince George. 'Gdmama had an escort & I assure you it made me feel quite lumpy to see how pleased all the people looked & what a reception she had—All the arrangements were perfect—At Boulogne there were quantities of people. . . . We breakfasted at Tarascon at 9 —with Gdmama where we stopped an hour.'[15] 'I am delighted with my comfortable rooms in this nice hotel, a most charming bedroom & sitting room adjoining which Mr Waring has done up specially for me!' she wrote in the same letter. 'The view from my windows is splendid—'

Queen Victoria much enjoyed her sojourns in the South—whether in the Hotel Regina at Cimiez or the Villa Palmieri in Florence—for to her these seemed more of a change than they did to her Court. In reality the change was one of locale only, the routine of the Household remaining unaltered by such journeys. 'I suppose you keep exactly the same hours as at Windsor', Prince George wrote to Princess May at Cimiez, '& dine at 9.15. I think that is a mistake in the South of France.'[16] Every detail of the installation of the Court was carefully supervised, and even the writing-paper was identical in form, quality and printing with that of Windsor Castle or Balmoral, the only difference being the words 'Hotel Regina, Cimiez' beneath the embossed crown. The Queen's drawing-room at the Hotel Regina had red wall-paper, and contained some indifferent pictures lent by an old picture-dealer in Nice. The dining-room next door had 'a vulgar, glaring paper' on which hung copies of the full-length Allan Ramsay coronation portraits of George III and Queen Charlotte. Guests invited to dine with the Queen were assembled in a brightly lit ante-room. At half-past eight they were shepherded into the drawing-room, lined up, and uneasily awaited the entry of the Queen, who would come into the room leaning on the arm of one of her Indian servants, who wore a gold-striped turban. After dinner, the Queen would sit in the centre of the drawing-room, receiving her guests each in turn for a short talk. At eleven o'clock precisely the Queen retired. The evening was at an end.

At eighty, Queen Victoria was now, so far as reading and writing went, almost hopelessly blind. The constitutional implications of her failing eyesight were potentially grave, since she could no longer keep a grip on affairs which were the Sovereign's prerogative, and might thus leave her successor with diminished constitutional powers. Her Private Secretary and his assistants were made exceedingly anxious by this situation, since the Queen still refused to take them into her confidence, and relied entirely upon Princess Henry of Battenberg (Princess Beatrice), whose duty it became to read her mother the telegrams, memoranda and despatches which the Queen could no longer read for herself. 'The result', wrote Frederick Ponsonby, one of the Queen's assistant Private Secretaries, to his mother in August 1898, '. . . is that the most absurd mistakes occur & the Queen is not even *au courant* with the ordinary topics of the present day. Imagine [Princess] B[eatrice] trying to explain the vaccination question or our policy in the east. Bigge or I may write out long *précis* of these things but they are often not read to H M as [Princess] B[eatrice] is in a hurry to develop a photograph or wants to paint a flower for a Bazaar. . . . Apart from the most hideous mistakes that occur . . . there is the danger of the Q's letting go almost entirely the control of things which should be kept under the immediate supervision of the Sovereign.' 'The sad thing is', young Ponsonby wrote in another letter, 'that it is only her eyes nothing else. Her memory is still wonderful, her shrewdness her power of discrimination as strong as ever her long experience of European politics alone makes her opinion valuable but when her sole means of reading despatches, *précis*, debates etc. lie in [Princess] B[eatrice], it is simply hopeless.'[17]

The situation was further complicated by the immense confidence which the Queen insisted on placing in the famous Munshi, a low-caste and mischief-making Hindu who had taken the privileged place of John Brown in the Queen's daily life. The Queen's Household loathed the Munshi: 'The Indian servants behind her chair looked rather splendid,' a surviving member of Queen Victoria's Household recently remarked, 'we could take that, but the Munshi was so personally repulsive and disagreeable that he was impossible. He made endless

trouble, too.' On this last visit to France the Queen had been determined to take the Munshi with her. This would have involved his
eating with the ladies and gentlemen of the Household, who 'put their
feet down at this and refused'. The Queen's personal secretary, Miss
Harriet Phipps, remonstrated with the Queen, who became so incensed
that she swept all the objects off her writing-table on to the floor. The
Household then prepared to go on strike or to resign in a body. The
Prime Minister, Lord Salisbury, who was coming down to Windsor,
was appealed to by the Household. He told the Queen that the French
were 'such odd people' they might laugh at Her Majesty about the
Munshi. This had momentarily the desired effect. The Munshi was
left behind, but not for long. 'Gdmama again spoke about the $M----i$
who to the despair of the poor gentlemen arrived today', Princess
May wrote to her husband from Cimiez on 1 April. 'I was most
guarded in my replies.'[18]

During these weeks at Cimiez Princess May was constantly with
Queen Victoria. 'I drove with Gdmama to Villefranche while the others
paid visits. You would have laughed at me sitting with Gdmama's
purse in my hand giving her one franc pieces to throw to the beggars,
some such awful frights too, with horrible disfigurements! Most of
the people we passed on the way bowed most politely.' 'At 4 I drove
with Gdmama and she talked about all sorts of things all the time &
was most cheerful,' Princess May wrote, again to her husband, 'she
talked very kindly of you & said she was so glad we got on so well
together as in these days it was such an example to others! She really
was most dear & kind & I was very glad to have this opportunity of
being alone with her.'[19]

This stay at the Hotel Regina at Cimiez was Queen Victoria's last
time on the Continent, for on 11 October of that same year, 1899, the
Boer War broke out. The European public regarded the Boers as
heroes, and England was vilified to such a degree that it was deemed
unsafe for English Royalties to expose themselves to probable insults
by travelling in either France or Germany. 'It is, if a justifiable and
even a necessary war, a deplorable affair', wrote a diarist of the time,[20]
'and one feels regret at the nineteenth century closing with England
placing all her strength in destroying a small Dutch Republic.'

III

It will be remembered that the Boer War opened that autumn and
winter of 1899 with a series of fearful disasters for the small force of

fifty thousand men which had been hastily despatched to the veldt. Names such as Magersfontein, Spion Kop and Nicholson's Nek now filled the newspapers, and after the 'black week of Colenso' in December newsboys were forbidden to shout out the latest bad news from the South African cablegrams. Society women from London flocked to Cape Town to do amateur nursing. The roll of dead and wounded mounted steadily. Then in the spring of 1900 there came the relief of Bloemfontein, of Kimberley, of Ladysmith and finally of Mafeking, this last modest victory being greeted in London with delirium by the crowds who 'mafficked' in the streets all night long. After the relief of Ladysmith Queen Victoria came up to London:

Cold day [Princess May's Diary for 8 March 1900 records]. At 12 At Alix fetched us in her carriage & we drove to Buck. Palace to see the Queen arrive from Windsor—It was a most thrilling sight & the place was packed with people. The members of the Houses of Lords & Commons met the Queen in the Quadrangle & sang 'God save the Queen'—We then went to see Gdmama for a minute. . . . We dined with the Queen. Family party of 12. The large crowd outside cheered & sang 'God Save the Queen' all the time & Gdmama went to the window after dinner much to their delight. Tosti & his wife sang & played. Very pleasant evening—'

At the taking of Mafeking Prince Alge of Teck was mentioned in despatches as 'a very promising Cavalry Officer, quick and always cool and collected'. 'I am so glad Alge is named so nicely', wrote Princess May to her husband. '—How pleased poor Mama & Papa wld have been—'[21]

The outbreak of the Boer War affected Princess May's life in two ways. Her brothers Prince Dolly, Prince Frank and Prince Alge all set out to fight in South Africa in the winter of 1899. She felt their absence very much, particularly that of Prince Dolly who was, as we have seen, her favourite brother. She was also naturally much concerned about their safety at a period when so many of the families of her friends and acquaintances were thrown into mourning by a shot on the veldt. The war also increased the public activities of the Duke and Duchess of York considerably. The Prince of Wales 'had become busily involved in co-ordinating and centralising the numerous independent volunteer agencies which came into being in various parts of the country to collect funds for the relief of soldiers and sailors on active service, their wives and families'[22]—for the soldiers, who had suddenly become as popular as they had been in England during the

Crimean War, were woefully underpaid. It was at this time that Kipling was commissioned to write *The Absent-minded Beggar*, which was sung in every music-hall throughout the country:

> When you've shouted 'Rule Britannia', when you've sung
>   'God Save the Queen',
> When you've finished killing Kruger with your mouth,
> Will you kindly drop a shilling in my little tambourine
> For a gentleman in khaki ordered South?

While the Prince of Wales was thus occupied, and the Princess of Wales was busying herself in her kind haphazard way about nurses and hospital ships, the Duke and Duchess of York took over many of the Waleses' duties. They likewise concerned themselves with the welfare of the troops. Princess May diverted much of the produce of the Needlework Guild (which was still a flourishing concern) to provide comforts for the men in hospitals in South Africa.

On 31 March 1900, in the very midst of the Boer War, Princess May's fourth child, Prince Henry of York* was born. Lord Roberts, the hero of the hour, was asked to stand as one of the baby's god-parents, and telegraphed his acceptance from Bloemfontein. Four days later came the attempt of the youth, Sipido, to assassinate the Prince and Princess of Wales in Brussels. They were seated in their railway carriage at the Gare du Nord: 'The ball was found in the carriage to-day, having passed between our two heads', the Princess of Wales telegraphed. 'I felt it whizzing across my eyes.'[23] 'The attempt at Brussels was too horrible; no wonder poor Alix had not recovered on arriving at Copenhagen', wrote the Grand Duchess of Mecklenburg-Strelitz. 'What an escape they both had!' she wrote in another letter, 'as Alix was sitting near Wales! how awful it must have been!'[24] 'Well thank God beloved Papa & I escaped from the wld be assassin on our way here!!!' the Princess of Wales wrote from the Amalienborg Palace to Prince George. '. . . it *was* a narrow shave indeed which God alone mercifully averted—Thank God I was with Papa & shared the danger in full. It wld have been much worse hearing of it afterwards.'[25] 'Good sometimes comes out of evil', Prince George reminded

---

* Prince Henry William Frederick Albert, b. 31 March 1900, was created Duke of Gloucester at the time of his marriage in November 1935 to Lady Alice Montagu-Douglas-Scott, third daughter of the seventh Duke of Buccleuch by whom he has two sons, Prince William and Prince Richard of Gloucester.

his mother, '& I am certain the affair at Brussels, will if possible, make you two more popular than ever.'[26]

One direct effect of Sipido's attempt was that, after it, the Prince of Wales and other members of the English Royal Family abroad were even more strictly guarded. 'I must tell you that Melville the celebrated detective also came with us, he will always go abroad with Papa now, the result of Sipido's attempt', Prince George wrote from Coburg to Princess May in August 1900, '& I must say I think it is quite right in these days, when there are so many anarchists about.'[27] In July of that year King Umberto of Italy had been assassinated. The fear of anarchists was growing. When Princess May was staying in the Engadine in 1903, she was asked by the Swiss authorities to avoid Geneva: 'So Sir C. Green told you that the Swiss authorities would prefer yr not going to Geneva, I think they are quite right,' wrote Prince George, 'the place is always full of Anarchists & brutes, remember the poor Empress of Austria.'[28]

After the victories of 1900, the Boer War seemed to the British public to be virtually ended, although the Boers, with peculiar resilience, continued to fight on. All three Teck Princes had come home by December 1900, 'Thank God my three dear brothers are back again & well', Princess May wrote to little Emily Alcock. ' . . . They have all become much more serious since the terrible war experiences they have gone through & no wonder for they must have seen dreadful sights.'[29]

The Boer War was almost over. The nineteenth century was drawing to its close, and so was the life of Queen Victoria. In the winter of 1900 the Queen was frequently drowsy and began to suffer from aphasia. She did not recognise Lord Roberts when he came to see her on his return from South Africa. Her family felt that her anxiety over the course of the Boer War was killing her, for in an odd way they could not admit that, like other mortals, the Queen was dying of old age.

'Good bye to the Old Century', Princess May wrote in her Diary for 31 December 1900. 'My old loving heart will be with you in the ensuing Century as it is and has ever been in this!' wrote Princess May's Aunt Augusta to her niece from Strelitz.[30]

BOOK THREE

VICTORIA MARY,
PRINCESS OF WALES

1901–1910

CHAPTER ONE

THE NEW CENTURY

AS THE NEW CENTURY dawned, Queen Victoria lay dying at Osborne House, a tiny wasted figure in white on the great canopied bed from which she could in old days gaze (through wide high windows which the Prince Consort had designed) out at the arboretum and the sea. On the evening of Tuesday 22nd January 1901, she died there peacefully, in the presence of almost every one of her immediate descendants, and in the Kaiser's arms. Prince George had been summoned to Osborne on the previous day and Princess May, with the Duke of Connaught and his daughters, arrived just before the end:

We got there at 5.30 only just in time to see beloved Grandmama alive for she passed away at 6.30 p.m. surrounded by us all [Princess May recorded in her Diary]. It was too sad for words. At about 10 we had a short service in her bedroom, darling Grandmama looked so lovely & peaceful dressed all in white with lace, & the bed covered with flowers. The thought of England without the Queen is dreadful even to think of. God help us all.[1]

This quiet fading out of life made an impression on Princess May, whose previous experiences of death had been the noisy and frightful delirium of Prince Eddy at Sandringham in 1892, and her own mother's sudden collapse after an emergency operation in 1897. 'The Queen looked so beautiful after death, like a marble statue, & much younger', she wrote from Osborne on 27 January to her Aunt Augusta. 'Now she lies in her coffin in the dining room which is beautifully arranged as a chapel, the coffin is covered with the coronation robes & her little diamond crown & the garter lie on a cushion above her head—4 huge Grenadiers watch there day & night, it is so impressive & fine, yet so simple. You would howl if you could see it all—We go from time to time & the feeling of peace in that room is most soothing to one's feelings.'[2]

The death of Queen Victoria has been often described in print— imaginatively by Lytton Strachey, and in its constitutional and historical implications by other biographers. Its coincidence with the birth

M

of the new century seemed to everyone symbolic. Throughout Great Britain and the Empire the Queen's demise created consternation, and in every court and chancellery of Europe it aroused interest, speculation and concern. In our case we may limit ourselves to the smaller canvas of how this death affected Princess May.

First there was the change of status. No longer the wife of the heir-presumptive to the heir-apparent, she was now the wife of the direct and actual heir to the British throne. Next there came the change of name. The Duke of York now automatically inherited the dukedom of Cornwall, which was traditionally held by the heir to the throne and which, with its vast estates and properties of every kind in the West of England, provided a sufficient income with which to keep up the pomp and fulfil the duties of Prince George's new role in life.

Known throughout the greater part of 1901 as Duke and Duchess of Cornwall and York, Prince George and Princess May did not become Prince and Princess of Wales until 9 November of that year, the new King's birthday, and after they had returned, as we shall see, from an extensive tour across the globe. 'We are to be called D. & Dss of Cornwall & York and I don't think the King intends to create G. Pce of Wales. . . .', Princess May wrote to Bricka from Osborne in January 1901.3 Prince George's new private secretary, Sir Arthur Bigge, 'strongly dissented at the very start from King Edward's decision' against immediately creating the Duke of York Prince of Wales.4

Princess May, who was above everything else a traditionalist, disapproved of this delay quite as much as Bigge. 'I believe this is the first time that the Heir Apparent has not been created Prince of Wales!' she wrote to her Aunt Augusta on 3 February 1901. 'I dislike departing from traditions.'5 With this letter she sent her aunt some pressed flowers from the late Queen's bedroom at Osborne. The old Grand Duchess replied:

Need I say, I wept over those flowers that had layed by Her side? But, when my tears were dried my *ire* was up & hot that the legitimate historical Title is not to be continued nor borne by you & George! Oh! what a terrible mistake so to upset old traditions! and *why?* because *he* will not be superseded? what can it be else? . . . The 'Dauphin' can't be suppressed nor the Pce des Assturias [*sic*] in France & Spain. What reason can the King give?6

The reason for the delay would seem to have been that the new

King felt that the titles of Prince and Princess of Wales were so connected in the public mind with his consort and himself that confusion might arise if Prince George and Princess May assumed these names too abruptly. Queen Alexandra, also, was personally much attached to a title which for nearly forty years she had adorned by her elegance and beauty; later she would always address an envelope to Princess May as 'Her Royal Highness Victoria Mary, Princess of Wales' and never to 'Her Royal Highness, the Princess of Wales'. In fact when the Wales title was finally conferred on Prince George a good many muddles about letters addressed to Princess May and to her mother-in-law by members of the public did, as Queen Alexandra may have foreseen, occur.

There was a third major change in Princess May's life in 1901. This was a change of residence. York House would have to be abandoned in favour of Marlborough House, and a larger establishment kept up there. Already, during the old Queen's lifetime, there had been a plan for the Yorks to move from York House to Clarence House, which 'Aunt Marie Edinburgh-Coburg' had relinquished after her husband's death. 'We must talk over St James's,' the Grand Duchess had written to her niece from Strelitz about the Clarence House plan, 'a move of *yours* from *there*, is a death blow to *me*, but then, perhaps I shall no longer be there to see it; it also appears to me considering the Queen's age, that a move, *before* the *next*-coming one, is only a double trouble!'[7] Being of the Queen's own generation, the Grand Duchess Augusta did not share the general family conviction that her cousin and Sovereign was immortal.

The move to Marlborough House—which Princess May was able to arrange and decorate as she pleased—did not take place until April 1903, for the new King and Queen had first to modernise Buckingham Palace, which had not been touched for fifty or sixty years, before they vacated Marlborough House. Queen Alexandra, moreover, at first refused to leave Marlborough House. The new King came one day in February 1901 to see the Grand Duchess of Mecklenburg-Strelitz (who was then in London) at Mecklenburg House: 'I met him on the Staircase', the old lady reported to her brother the Duke of Cambridge, 'where he kissed my hand and later embraced me most warmly. He sat with me for an hour and a half, talking on all subjects, telling me all about the dear Queen and family matters, begging me as an *English* Pss to tell Alix that it is a duty & necessity to live at the Palace, this he said twice over.'[8] A month later the Grand Duchess went on a tour of inspection of Buckingham Palace with the new Queen: 'I tried to encourage her, assuring her, her pretty things would make it all look very nice. Her chief object was to get "Charlotte well lodged"!'9 This was Miss Charlotte Knollys, on whom Queen Alexandra relied profoundly in the course of her not always happy married life.

King Edward was surprised and annoyed to find that his daughter-in-law intended redecorating Marlborough House; he felt that what had been good enough for him should be good enough for the new Prince and Princess of Wales. 'I hope . . . yr father . . . was not very angry with you about M.House,' Princess May wrote to Prince George, 'that question quite weighs on my mind as surely he must know we really cannot go into a filthy dirty house—*not* even to oblige him.'10 It was only in the metropolis that Prince George and Princess May moved house. In December 1901 King Edward distressed his son and daughter-in-law by offering them Osborne, which they did not want, would hardly ever have used, and in any case could not have afforded to maintain. The King was very insistent about this offer, and in this he was seconded by Queen Alexandra. 'Just returned from tea with "Motherdear",' Princess May wrote to her husband from York Cottage on 12 December 1901, 'she spoke to me about Osborne . . . she says that of course if we cannot take it the old place will have to go to rack & ruin. I told her we were going to talk it over & see what could be done.'11 In the end Osborne House became a convalescent home for officers. The old Queen's apartments, left exactly as at the time of her death, were locked up. They were only opened to the public in 1956. When Princess May and her husband happened to be in the Isle of Wight they used a small house on the Osborne estate named Barton Manor.

In 1901, also, there was a rather vague project, probably initiated by Princess May, to get away from York Cottage by leasing the splendid old Norfolk house built for Sir Robert Walpole, Houghton Hall. 'I went all over Houghton one day', wrote Queen Alexandra to her son, '—it is certainly a very fine old place which might be made beautiful—but take *my good advice* and *do not* be *in a hurry* to bind yrself in any way this first year at any rate—Wait quietly & see how things will turn out—& you will find plenty to do with yr money by & by & *this next* year of all with so much moving about & additions in every way! & also let us be *near each other* this winter at least.'12 Nothing came of the Houghton project. Princess May, her husband, their growing children, their Household and their servants remained cooped up in York Cottage for another twenty-four years.

While Buckingham Palace and Marlborough House were being renovated, a great deal of swift clearing up was going on at Windsor, where the King would stump through the rooms and corridors of the Castle wearing a pot-hat and using a walking-stick as though he were out-of-doors, accompanied by his dogs and by Lord Esher. They would turn out cupboards and empty drawers, and rearrange pictures and furniture. Princess May thought all these changes too precipitate: 'it is always best to do such things very *piano* & with much reflection', she wrote from Buckingham Palace to her Aunt Augusta in 1915. 'Many things were changed here & at Windsor much too quickly by our predecessors as you well remember.'[13] Many innovations in the sphere of Court appointments were also being made with what seemed to Princess May and to her aunt an unwise speed: 'Altogether as you say the changes seem to be rather rapid, the reason probably being that they want to get everything properly started & in working order before the Coronation, for we all know how many things had gone to sleep in dear Grandmama's time from want of being used oftener',[14] she wrote to the Grand Duchess in May of 1901.

In Queen Victoria's day members of the Royal Family were not allowed to roam at will about the Castle, and it was almost with a sense of pioneering that Prince George went down there to stay with his father in November 1901:

This, I must say, is a most comfortable house, the furniture is not beautiful but quite nice & there is more room than I thought there was. My room opens out of Papa's & is on the ground floor; then I have got a writing table next to his in his sitting room, he wished it so. Sidney is now doing boxes with him while I am writing this. Fancy that being possible in dear Grandmama's time; anyhow it shows that Papa & I are on good terms with each other [he wrote to Princess May].[15]

The proximity of these desks seems to offer us an occasion to re-examine the personality of King Edward VII, whom we have seen on many occasions as 'Uncle Wales'. 'Uncle Wales' was now King of Great Britain and Ireland, and of the British Dominions Beyond the Seas, Emperor of India. 'Motherdear' was Queen Consort and Empress. What was the effect upon their personalities, and their relationship to their son and daughter-in-law, of this new, august position?

11

When he ascended the throne in January 1901, King Edward VII was fifty-nine years and six months old. He was not young for his age. In 1898 he had fallen down a spiral staircase at Baron Ferdinand de Rothschild's gigantic house in Buckinghamshire, Waddesdon Manor, and broken his knee-cap; his convalescence from this painful accident had been complicated by pleurisy, and in the last years of the old century his attacks of breathlessness, attributed to bronchitis but also caused by excessive smoking, had been frequent and bad. He began his reign feeling ill, exhausted and depressed.

The new King's favourite brother Alfred, Duke of Edinburgh and Saxe-Coburg, had died five months before their mother Queen Victoria. His favourite sister the Empress Frederick was dying of a particularly agonising form of spinal cancer in her castle at Kronberg. The King had, too, waited so long to succeed to the throne, and had been kept so constantly at bay by Queen Victoria where anything political or constitutional was concerned, that he had become disillusioned. It almost seemed as though he had reached the throne too late. At certain moments of his reign he even toyed with the idea of abdication in favour of his son; but these were only moments of grave depression, for he soon found that he enjoyed being King.

Unlike Queen Victoria, Edward VII tended almost invariably to take the advice of his Ministers. At first he concentrated to what was thought an excessive degree upon the minutiae of precedence, Court etiquette and dress. He was deeply wounded at the opening of his reign to find that even a sober, loyal newspaper like *The Times* gave vent to the general doubts about whether a man with his particular interests and taste for gaiety would be likely to make a good Sovereign. So shielded had he been by his friends and his entourage, that it had scarcely been brought home to him that he had for many decades been the subject of public criticism. People expressed themselves as delighted but also astounded, that the new King looked 'so regal' in the funeral procession of Queen Victoria, that he was capable of making a very moving Declaration before the Privy Council at his accession, and that he had definite, conciliatory, intelligent and original ideas about foreign affairs. The delight was gratifying, but the astonishment was less so. The new King felt not only ill and tired, but aggrieved and misjudged.

Owing to Queen Victoria's jealous grip on her prerogatives, King Edward VII had much to learn about the business of Kingship. He began by making two or three blunders in his relations with his Ministers, but with his usual charm he apologised for these and attributed them to his own inexperience. His charm and genuine kindliness were very helpful to him at the beginning of his reign. When he lost his temper he was always quick to apologise, with his guttural geniality and his laugh which was like the sound of tearing linen.

King Edward was determined to restore to the English Court the glamour which Queen Victoria's long widowhood and quiet ways had diminished. His short reign of nine years did indeed demarcate what is now known as the Edwardian Era, a period in which wealth rather than intellect or noble birth was valued at the Court. This was not an atmosphere in which Princess May moved with marked enjoyment. Her decorous domesticity and serious manner were more than ever the target for the gibes of the 'smart set', to whom they seemed to constitute an unspoken rebuke. Here was one of the reasons which made the Australian voyage of 1901, during which the Duke of Cornwall and York opened the first Federal Parliament of the Commonwealth of Australia, so helpful to Princess May, for, to her surprise, she found herself immensely popular in Australia. 'You will see that your humble servant has found great favour with the Australians,' she wrote to Hélène Bricka from Melbourne, 'rather different to at home where they always find fault with what I do or do not do.' In another letter, also to Bricka, of November 1906, Princess May referred to 'old me who am always criticised & generally condemned, at least by some people'. She naturally resented such criticism, which she knew to be fundamentally unfair. '*Il parait qu'on s'étonne* "that *I* did it all so well",' she had written during the state visit to Ireland in 1897, 'but only give me the chance & I will do the things as well as anybody, after all why shouldn't I?'[16]

King Edward invariably treated his daughter-in-law with great kindness, but she never felt wholly at her ease with him. Now that he was not only her father-in-law but her King, her attitude towards him was even more formal than before. Her reverence for the Monarchy as an institution, and thus for the person of the Monarch himself, invested her father-in-law in her eyes with an aura so bright that it almost made her blink, although her innate prudence taught her to distrust the revolutionary changes in social and Court life which King Edward introduced. She also distrusted the complete absence of forethought which seemed to characterise the daily life of the new King and Queen. 'I wish we could have saved Cambridge Cottage when dear U. George died', she wrote to the Grand Duchess in June 1910, after King George V's accession, 'but then you see George & I were never asked or consulted about such things which was a pity considering this concerned our sons, but then alas there *never never* was *ever* any thought of what might occur in the future, & this I have always deplored.'[17] The existence of Queen Alexandra was notably planless, and such plans as were made were always frustrated in their execution by her eternal unpunctuality—which is said to have once dislocated the whole system of express-trains in north-western Europe, since the Queen had kept her special waiting for some hours. The Princess of Wales's inability to be on time had always worried Queen Victoria, and it greatly annoyed King Edward, who was the soul of exactitude. 'The King', wrote Princess May from Windsor Castle one January, 'is so easy to live with, very punctual & one knows exactly what one is to do which is agreeable & not waiting about. We still hope "Motherdear" may join us but she still suffers much from neuralgia & depression & feels up to nothing.'[18]

III

The new Queen's relationship with her daughter-in-law Princess May was, as always, outwardly friendly. They wrote each other affectionate notes; but, as we have already seen, they had few sympathies in common. 'It interests me to hear that she (May) is rather shy of Q. Alix,' wrote the Grand Duchess of Mecklenburg-Strelitz to Prince Dolly (now, since his father's death, Duke of Teck), 'they never were on a very intimate footing, both cling to their *own* family not making friends with others—at least this is my impression.'[19] Queen Alexandra and her daughter Princess Victoria never forgot that Princess May was, in their eyes, imperfectly Royal; oddly enough, Queen Victoria had thought precisely the same thing about Queen Alexandra herself. Long, long ago, in December 1865, Prince and Princess Leopold of Hohenzollern-Sigmaringen had paid Queen Victoria a visit at Osborne. Princess Leopold's Christian name was Antoinette. 'Oh! if Antoinette were in Al:'s place!' Queen Victoria had written. 'She is *so* much more *sympathique & grande dame.* Our good Al: is like a distinguished lady of Society but nothing more!' 'What you say about dear Antoinette is I think quite just,' she wrote a week later, again to her eldest daughter in Berlin, 'I did not mean that she was cleverer than Alix—but she is softer, more affte, & a *real Prss*—wh. the other is *not.* But poor Alix

has had and has no chance in the *milieu* she is in, who can't educate
or develop her.' All the same Queen Victoria was very susceptible to
the Princess of Wales's charm and to her child-like innocence of
character. 'Nothing cld be dearer & nicer than she is,' she wrote, in
November 1866, 'I never saw a *purer* mind—it is *quite charming* to
see her & hear her.—She looks delicate. I do love her dearly.'[20]

By a strange anomaly, King Edward when he came to the throne
was almost as exclusively jealous about his prerogatives as his mother
Queen Victoria had been. Queen Alexandra found that she was rele-
gated to a rather powerless and almost obscure position. She confided
in the Grand Duchess of Mecklenburg-Strelitz—who had indeed
helped to make the Wales marriage in 1863:

I had a long talk to Alix about her position as Queen [the Grand Duchess
wrote to Princess May in June 1901] she says, *he* does not permit her taking
it, as he takes everything to himself lets her do nothing in the way of
carrying out her duties; for instance, he did not even let her give the Prizes
for the Red Cross which she has done hitherto; he says he is in an exceptional
position and must take all the honours to himself![21]

Princess May thought, on the other hand, that the new Queen did not
work hard enough or take her position with sufficient earnestness:

Your account of yr visit to the Royal Academy interested me, yes it was
a pity At Alix did not go, but alas when she once gets *stuck* at Sandringham,
it is difficult to move her, I had so hoped that in her new position as Queen
all this would have improved, & I do feel that it is very important that one
should take a lively interest in Art or in anything connected with the good
of one's Country. . . . It does not look well either for her so constantly to
leave *him* alone as she does.[22]

When her husband became King, Alexandra, Princess of Wales, was
fifty-six. Her appearance was the wonder of her family and of the
public too. 'Really to look at her one cannot imagine her age, for she
looks too marvellously young', wrote Princess May four years later,[23]
on her mother-in-law's sixtieth birthday. Those who preserve a look
of youth into late middle-age are usually persons whose characters
retain strata of immaturity; the child-like innocence and manner of
the new Queen were in this sense the corollary of her prolonged
beauty. As often happens with those who look too young for too
long, there was now a certain rigidity about Queen Alexandra's
expression and her gestures.

M*

Queen Alexandra had retained all the winning impulsiveness and spontaneity that had endeared her to the English when she had first appeared in their country in 1863 as 'the Sea-King's daughter from over the sea'. These she kept to the end of her life. Visiting a hospital during the First World War, she noticed that one patient looked very downcast and on enquiring why she was informed that one of the man's legs would be stiff for the rest of his life. She immediately went over to him and told him not to worry, as her own leg had been stiff for years. 'But look what I can do with it', she exclaimed, and with a gymnastic movement she swept her leg over the seat of a chair by the soldier's bed. On another occasion a young footman from Mar Lodge, who had accompanied Princess Louise to Sandringham for Christmas, was found by Queen Alexandra gazing dreamily out over the snow-covered garden. 'You look lonely', she said, 'and I cannot bear anyone to be lonely in my house at Christmas time.' She asked him his name, and after a long talk with him she disappeared, enjoining him to remain where he was. A few minutes later the Queen returned, holding in her hand a little leather case containing some gold links. 'Now these are my personal present to you,' she said, 'you will get your ordinary presents at the Tree tonight.'

It happened that this particular young Scotsman from Mar Lodge had had the special pitch of voice which Queen Alexandra could hear, for her deafness usually padlocked her into a lonely world in which she could not follow the general conversation of her family and friends. From this she suffered with intensity. This deafness, combined with her husband's infidelities, often made the new Queen's life a rather miserable one. She sought refuge from her sorrows in her devotion to her son and to her grandchildren, as well as in her frequent visits to her beloved home in Denmark.

It will thus be seen that, for its two chief characters, the new reign and the new century in England opened wearily. A further sadness had now to be faced by the King and the Queen, for the long-planned voyage to Australia and Canada of their son and daughter-in-law, which would involve a separation of seven and a half months, could brook no more delay. King Edward was loth to lose his son, at just this moment, for such a length of time; but the Secretary of State for the Colonies, Mr Joseph Chamberlain, declared that the Duke of Cornwall and York must fulfil the obligation he had undertaken to open, in the King's name, the first Australian Federal Parliament. He and the Duchess were due to sail, with a large suite and an escort of

cruisers, on 16 March 1901. They were due back in England on
1 November.

An ancillary reason which made the King and Queen unwilling to
see their only son embark just then was that he was once again not
very well. A severe attack of German measles at Osborne had prevented him, and consequently Princess May, from attending Queen
Victoria's funeral in January, and just before the opening of Parliament
in the following month he collapsed again and had to stay in bed.
Princess May went to see the King open Parliament on her own. She
found it 'a very fine sight & . . . very well done. All the ladies in
black against the peers red robes looked particularly well, we all wore
high gowns trimmed with crape, & points & crape veils, with diamonds on them, & lots of jewels on our gowns & our orders—Aunt
Alix looked beautiful in the robes & the Crown Jewels & Grandmama's dear little diamond crown on her head with the crape veil
flowing from it—Uncles Wales read the speech well in a good clear
voice—All together it was very fine & one felt very *emotionée*. I have
had a fearfully busy week in London choosing black clothes for our
visit [to Australia] & every sort of thing besides, extremely bewildering
and leaves one rather with a permanent headache',[24] she wrote on 16
February to her Aunt Augusta, who was at that moment setting off,
unannounced, for London, to see what was afoot at the new Court.

As the only living Princess of Great Britain and Ireland who could
clearly remember the Coronation and the court of King William IV
and Queen Adelaide, the Grand Duchess of Mecklenburg-Strelitz now
came into her own as an authority on royal precedents—for Queen
Victoria had been so long on the throne that at her death no one had
any clear conception of the etiquette of a Court presided over by a
King and a Queen Consort.

I send you one little line to tell you from At. Alix that she has been told
that on the demise of a reigning sovereign Queen the Mistress of the Robes
exists no more [Princess May had written to her Aunt Augusta the previous
month]—Now At. Alix can hardly believe that this is so, so she begs you
will let me know what happened when William IV came to the throne &
who Queen Adelaide had? Not a soul seems able to give any information
on so many subjects which will have to be settled so do pray come over
to England & lend your valuable aid.

'Aunt Alix', wrote Princess May in the same letter, 'is quite ready to
do what is right if only she is told, but just at present everyone is
quite at sea—& there is no-one but you who could help her—'.[25]

This role of an historical authority appealed strongly to the old Grand Duchess. She ordered her mourning clothes to be packed (together with grey dresses 'in case of a birthday') and set off for London accompanied by her granddaughter Marie (now Comtesse Jametel and still unhappy), and her Strelitz lady-in-waiting 'Oh! Matilda' Heyden. Aunt Augusta was burning with curiosity about the new Court. She also saw in the change of Sovereign an opportunity for socially re-instating her granddaughter Marie—to whom the King, the Queen and all the Royal Family were indeed very kind. She wished, too, to say good-bye to her niece May before the Cornwall-and-Yorks' departure for the Antipodes.

IV

An invitation for the Duke and Duchess of York to visit Australia and New Zealand had first been sent by the Governments of those countries in January 1898. It had been refused by Queen Victoria, on the grounds that, in her seventy-ninth year, she could not possibly do without her grandson, and that his absence from England for a long period would throw too much public work upon the shoulders of the Prince of Wales and the Duke of Connaught. The Prince of Wales himself was in favour of the projected tour; in 1868 he had been much impressed by the publication of Dilke's *Greater Britain*, the first book to reveal to the British public that they had an Empire at all. Ever since reading this book, the Prince had felt that first-hand knowledge of the Empire was, for an heir-presumptive to the British throne, of far greater importance than any amount of visits to European courts. It was this conviction which had led him to persuade the Queen in 1879 to permit Prince Eddy and Prince George to set off on the three-year cruise of the *Bacchante*, and it was a subsidiary motive (though not, we may recall, the main one) for the 'Colonial plan' to send Prince Eddy spinning off round the world in 1891.

During the Boer War when the Empire troops fought so valiantly in South Africa, the Queen at last agreed that it was only right that the Duke and Duchess of York should proceed to the Antipodes as a gesture of gratitude from herself and from the Mother Country. Her death in January 1901 was not allowed to interfere with plans for the voyage, by then in an advanced state of preparedness. The only change it made was that there were to be no state dinners or state balls, which in fact relieved the Duke and the Duchess of a certain amount of additional strain. It also meant that the Duchess and all her ladies would have to wear black, save on board ship and in the tropics, when white or grey were permissible. 'Toques', wrote Lady Mary Lygon, who with old Lady Katty Coke and Mrs Derek Keppel, was one of the Duchess of Cornwall and York's three ladies on the tour, 'are a great difficulty—as there is so little variety in *all* black ones.'[26]

The itinerary of the tour was now also more ambitious. The Royal party were to proceed first to Melbourne, by way of Gibraltar, Malta, Port Said, Colombo and Singapore, visiting Brisbane and Sydney, then on to New Zealand and Mauritius, and home by South Africa (where the war was still dragging on) and Canada. It was a novel and almost daunting prospect, in a day when such an extended tour of the Empire had never yet been undertaken by a member of the Royal Family. 'Of course it is a long way to go & I suppose we should be away about 5 months, but it will be very interesting & I think it is right! we should go,' Princess May wrote to her Aunt in Strelitz in September 1900, 'especially after the fine way in which Australia has come forward during the war. . . . We should leave the children in charge of my Parents in law—I can quite see yr surprise on this announcement, particularly as you know what a bad sailor I am, but it shows how keen I am to go, that I consider this quite a minor consideration.'[27] The girl of sixteen who had been homesick in Florence in 1883 was now a woman of thirty-three with an unquenchable curiosity about new places and strange scenery. 'How plucky you are, dear Love, I admire you!' the old Grand Duchess replied, 'even feeling keen about going out there! I am sure there will be much to interest you but oh! *the voyage!* the distance, the leaving the darling Chicks behind! well! I will say no more. . . . I can only admire your courage, and love you the more!'[28] 'She is a chip of the old block!' the Grand Duchess wrote of their niece to her aged brother the Duke of Cambridge.[29]

The ship selected for the voyage was the P. & O. liner *Ophir*, of only seven thousand tons and ten thousand horse-power. She was temporarily commissioned in the Royal Navy and, of course, entirely refurnished. Prince George had warned Princess May in November 1900 that decisions about the decoration and furnishings of their cabins must be taken swiftly. She thereupon, to Prince George's delight, settled all these matters in the short space of one morning. Accustomed to his mother's procrastination, he complimented his wife on her efficiency. 'You certainly are a good woman of business, but that I always knew you were, to have settled everything so quickly.'³⁰ The fabrics used in the *Ophir* made the ubiquitous rose-bud chintz of the old Royal Yacht *Victoria and Albert* look painfully out-of-date. On the *Ophir*, the 'drawing-room' was upholstered in pale blue brocade, with many easy chairs and sofas and a deep pile carpet. The dining-room—'rather gaudy'—had red morocco-covered chairs and a small music gallery for the band. The Duke and Duchess had each a bedroom and a sitting-room, crowded with photographs and panelled in white. Their wash-stands were of alabaster and onyx; one, worth two hundred pounds, was cracked during installation. Privileged friends of the Royal Family were given passes to go down and inspect the luxuries of the *Ophir* before she sailed. These were generally admired, though not by the old Grand Duchess of Mecklenburg-Strelitz who was, of course, unable to resist a 'rather fatiguing day' looking over the ship at Portsmouth. 'I went down to Portsmouth', she wrote to her brother in March 1901, 'to see the *Ophir* an enormous Vessel, with, what they call "every comfort"! these appear to me very small, with sea-sickness at the bottom of it all!'³¹

The Grand Duchess did not go down to Portsmouth for the last leave-taking on 16 March 1901, but said good-bye to the travellers at Waterloo. The leave-taking had been preceded by a family dinner-party at Marlborough House, at which the King nearly broke down and cried. At the final farewell on board the *Ophir* itself, King Edward choked back his sobs when giving the toast of his son and daughter-in-law at the end of luncheon, and the Duke of Cornwall and York was so moved that he could scarcely reply. Queen Alexandra and Princess Victoria wept freely during this meal, and several of the attendant ladies were also 'moved to tears'. At the end of this emotional repast the King and Queen boarded the yacht *Alberta* and for two miles led the way. 'It was horrible when you passed in the "Alberta" on your way to Portsmouth, May & I came down to our cabins & had a good cry & tried to comfort each other', Prince George wrote to his mother from Gibraltar. 'I must say this is a beautiful ship & she has easy motion, better than any one I have been in before.'³² 'I paid poor Alix a long visit yesterday', the Grand Duchess Augusta wrote of the Queen on 18 March, 'when she told me all about it, crying all the time.'³³

The cruise of the *Ophir* was like all cruises. When it was rough those who were bad sailors disappeared to their cabins, when the weather was good they played deck-games, did gymnastics, and read

and wrote on deck. There were sailors' sing-songs, there was Crossing
the Line, there was steam heat in the Indian Ocean.

The Duke and Duchess of Cornwall and York were received with
full honours at Gibraltar, Malta, Port Said, Colombo and Singapore.
Princess May hated the sea. 'I *detest* the sea,' she wrote to Hélène Bricka
from the middle of the Indian Ocean, 'I like seeing the places & being on
land, the rest of it is purgatory to me & makes me miserable & depressed,
so please don't envy me.'34 She had a swing-cot installed by bluejackets in her cabin, a place in which Prince Alge of Teck, who was
also on board, considered that his sister May spent altogether too much
time. He thought she would have felt less ill if she had looked at the
waves and come more often into the open air. On 30 March the
Duchess of Cornwall and York had her first sight of the East. 'Very
curious seeing all the Arabs in the town & the curious buildings my
first glimpse of the East', she wrote in her Diary at Port Said. 'It
rained rather hard all the time.'35

So far as the politics of Empire went the effect of the *Ophir* cruise
was all that had been hoped, and more. The Duke and Duchess
were welcomed everywhere with immense and loyal enthusiasm. As
Mr John Gore has pointed out, the tour also widened Prince George's
view of the world and gave him much-needed self-confidence. For
Princess May it was her first real chance to show what she had always
been convinced she could do if but given her chance. 'Her Royal
Highness has quite got over all her shyness abroad, and almost enjoys
a procession', wrote Lady Mary Lygon. 'Her smile is commented on
in every paper and her charm of manner; in fact, she is having a
"*succès fou*" especially as no one was prepared for her good looks all
photographs being caricatures.' 'Her Royal Highness as usual is
winning golden opinions', Lady Mary wrote again, from Sydney, 'and
the Duke is now supposed to be the shy one!'

'The Duke has of course been splendid too—but she took the
whole of Australia and New Zealand by storm', Lady Mary further
wrote, this time from Albany in Western Australia, 'and every state
has successively fallen in love with her looks, her smile, and her great
charm of manner. She is at last coming out of her shell and will electrify
them at home as she has everyone here.'36 At the Opening of the
Federal Parliament in Melbourne, Princess May won particularly high
praise: 'G. & M. bowed right round, & very well they did it, M.
reminding me of Mamma & I felt quite proud of her',37 wrote Prince
Alge to his eldest brother on 17 May.

The prototype of all subsequent Commonwealth tours by members of the British Royal Family, the cruise of the *Ophir* was very exhausting. From England the Queen, and sometimes the King also, would write to the Duke and Duchess of Cornwall and York urging them 'to rest more'. 'It is all very well for you & Papa to say we mustn't do so much but it is impossible to help it', Prince George wrote to his mother. 'Our stay in each place is so short, that everything has to be crammed into it.' 'Darling May is of the greatest possible help to me & works very hard, I don't think I could have done all this without her', he wrote to Queen Alexandra on another occasion, from Sydney. 'Everybody admires her very much which is very pleasing to me. I hope you are as proud of your daughter in law as I am of my wife.'[38]

Her first sight of the East, her first experience of the civilisations of Australia, New Zealand, Canada and the Cape, gave Princess May much food for thought and strengthened her inherent patriotism, and her belief in her country's Imperial mission. Lady Mary Lygon was, however, wrong in thinking that the *Ophir* cruise had permanently cured Princess May's shyness; being, so to speak, on her own helped to alleviate it, for in these distant portions of the globe there was no one to accuse her of dullness behind her back, and no one to remember her morganatic blood or to deem her insufficiently Royal. When she came back to England, her natural reserve reasserted itself in the more familiar surroundings: 'I wish I were not such a snail in its shell', she wrote to Bricka in November 1906, during a large house-party given by Lord Derby at Knowsley, 'but at nearly 40—it's difficult to alter the habit of a lifetime—I know this rather spoils life but *que faire?*[39]

One direct result of the long voyage in the *Ophir* was to increase, if that were possible, Prince George's admiration for his wife. 'Somehow I can't tell you, so I take the first opportunity of writing to say how deeply I am indebted to you darling for the splendid way in which you supported & helped me during our long Tour,' he told her in a letter from Windsor after their return home, 'it was you who made it a success. . . . If you had not come with me, it would not have been at all a success. . . . Although I have often told it you before, I repeat it once more, that I love you darling child, with my whole heart & soul & thank God every day that I have such a wife as you, who is such a great help & support to me & I believe loves me too.'[40] Letters such as this, containing sentiments which Prince George was never able to express by word of mouth, gave Princess May a profound pleasure and satisfaction. Together with her mother's stamina, she had inherited Princess Mary Adelaide's devout wish to be of use in the world. 'You know what a pleasure it is to me to do everything in my power to help you in any way I can & I am so very grateful to you for all the dear kind things you say in your letter', she replied. ' . . . I hope my darling that as long as you & I live you will ever rely on me to do what I can to help you, now more than ever in yr new & very responsible position. . . . Thank God I think we get on very well together, & after what you told me the other day of the sad lives of poor Missy & Ducky, we should be even more grateful to feel that so much sympathy exists between us 2. in our married life & that we should be so wonderfully well suited to each other in every way.'41

We may here conveniently remark that, during this world tour, Princess May consistently exercised that uncanny power of self-absorption in a specific object which, granted only to men of genius, is at the disposal of every woman. Thus, she could surmount the horrors of sea-sickness, the exhaustion of shaking hands with three thousand strangers in one afternoon, the intense contrasts of climate (which she hated), because she was helping to weld her husband's future reputation, and because she was fulfilling a purpose in which she believed with all her mind and soul. She could, for these same reasons, burst the bonds of her own shyness and self-consciousness. Back in London, where the tempo was less intense and where so unique an effort was not yet required of her, she quietly withdrew once more into her 'shell'. It was not until her husband himself ascended the throne that a sustained and almost superhuman concentration of the will was demanded of Princess May.

v

On their return home on 1 November 1901, the Duke and Duchess of Cornwall and York were met at Portsmouth by the King and Queen. Back in London they drove in procession from Waterloo Station to Marlborough House, in which King Edward and Queen Alexandra were still living. While stopping at Mauritius on their way to the Cape they had heard of the death of the Empress Frederick at Kronberg, an event which had caused her brother the King much unhappiness.

On 9 November 1901, the King's sixtieth birthday, Prince George was at length proclaimed Prince of Wales; in January of the New Year, 1902, the new Prince and Princess of Wales ceremoniously took their places at the Opening of Parliament on chairs of state placed for them below the dais of the throne, and facing the House. On this occasion the King wore the uniform of a Field-Marshal, while the Queen had a long crimson ermine-lined train held up behind her by pages. Round her waist was a girdle of diamonds that reached to her knees.

For Princess May the spring of 1902 was uneventful: there were some 'functions', some visits to East End clubs, to the British Museum, to shops and to the theatres when she was in London, combined with short periods at York Cottage and week-ends at Midland and West Country houses. In April she and Prince George went to Denmark for a stiffish fortnight for the celebration of the old King's eighty-fourth birthday.

The great event to which everyone in London was now looking forward was the Coronation of the King and Queen, fixed for 26 June. The preparations went on apace, and soon the main streets through which the procession would pass took on that back-stage air insepar-able in London from the erection of wooden stands, barricades, flag-poles and Venetian masts. Already in January 1902, the route for the Coronation procession next June was published, together with plans for a subsequent drive through London. 'Do tell me, when you have time, what the route of the Procession means,' wrote the Grand Duchess of Mecklenburg-Strelitz to Princess May, 'are these 14 miles to be passed with the *Crown on the head* . . . or is it to take place next day? it is impossible to understand what is meant.'42 'You ask about the Coronation route,' her niece replied, 'well as far as I can make out we only drive to the Abbey & back that day, the following day we drive round the town in open carriages & bonnets . . . no question of robes & coronets which is an invention of the fertile press . . . there are limits to one's endurance.'43

Princess May's Aunt Augusta was much perturbed by all the inno-vations instigated by the new King. Was it true that peeresses were no longer to wear diadems in the Abbey? Why had the colour of the Princesses' robes been changed? She had written down her memories of William IV's coronation for Queen Alexandra's benefit: 'I put down in writing for her, of what I recollect of the old Court; this she is glad to have, as it shows what The Queen Consort had to do and where she stood and walked. Now it appears, this is to be altered, yet

she hopes to put it right for you, some day, when you take her place',
she wrote to Princess May. 'Imagine,' she wrote again, of Queen
Alexandra, 'she was told, she was to stand bye, mute & still, no
presentations at the Drawingroom but to *him*; I told her Queen
Adelaide had them presented all, she having to kiss Duchesses, March-
ionesses (Count^{ss} I dont know) with two kisses, then one kiss down
to Earls daughters, after which giving her hand to be kissed, and the
men kneeling on one knee. I recollect washing Q. Adelaide's hand
afterwards fetching water from the King's Closet. It is extraordinary
that nobody knows anything more about the last Reign but one! Do
remember what I have been writing for personal use some day.'[44]

June approached. London was bedecked, and the foreign royalties
and deputations from the Empire had begun to arrive in the capital.
Twelve days before the date for the coronation the King and
Queen, accompanied by the Prince and Princess of Wales, Princess Victoria of Schleswig-Holstein and the King's surviving
brother the Duke of Connaught with his wife, left London for a
ceremonial review at Aldershot. 'The King had a bad attack of lumbago
& could not get up', Princess May noted in her Diary for 15 June.
Next day Queen Alexandra reviewed thirty-one thousand troops in
his stead. On the 17th the King was not well enough to drive in semi-
state from Windsor to Ascot. On the 23rd it was announced that he
was suffering from acute appendicitis and was to be operated on next
day. The Coronation was indefinitely postponed. 'The consternation',
wrote Princess May, 'which the postponement of the Coronation
festivities caused was sad to witness.'[45]

Sad indeed it was, and also very alarming. The operation for appendicitis was then quite novel, and was regarded with distrust; in Princess
Mary Adelaide's day a German cousin of hers who had suffered from
her *Blinddarmentzündung* had been regarded as doomed to one of the
more painful of the numerous varieties of death. Rumours flew about
London that the King was 'sinking fast'. 'I have never felt anything
like the physical and mental oppression of the day in London', wrote
an eye-witness on 27 June. 'It was hot and airless and muggy—the
decorations flapped about in an ominous manner—and gloom and
consternation were in every face. The King's age etc. is much against
him—but he has a wonderful constitution which may carry him
through. . . . I was very sorry for the Prince of Wales, for everything
had to be decided by him; and besides his *great* devotion to his father
—the feeling that at any moment he might find himself King of

England must have hung like a horrible nightmare on him. He does not like responsibility and though he has aged much in the last eighteen months—one could wish for him another two or three years of respite and preparation.'[46] 'Oh, do *pray* that Uncle Wales may get well,' Princess May said through her sobs to Hélène Bricka, 'George says he isn't ready yet to reign.'[47]

The King's illness, which was followed by a successful and comparatively brief convalescence aboard his yacht at Cowes, threw a heavy burden of responsibility upon Prince George and Princess May. As Prince and Princess of Wales they were obliged to entertain the European royalties now gathered so fruitlessly in London, and to take leave of them with becoming grace. When a new date for the Coronation was fixed there remained of all the foreign representatives and their suites, only the Special Mission from Abyssinia. The Coronation procession of 9 August 1902 consisted almost entirely of Imperial and Colonial deputations and thus took on, in Lord Rosebery's tactful phrase, 'something of the character of a family festival'.[48] 'Fine but dull and cloudy', Princess May wrote of the Coronation Day. 'At 10.45 we started in state for Westminster Abbey. Got there at 11. . . . Beautiful impressive service. . . . Very fine sight. . . . Very good reception from the large crowds in the streets. . . . Dined at home.'[49] 'My Princess', wrote Lady Mary Lygon of Princess May, 'attracted a great deal of admiration, as she walked down the Abbey, with Eva [Dugdale] and I staggering under her heavy purple velvet and ermine train.' The Princess of Wales's ladies wore dresses of white satin with a design of feathers in *diamanté* 'all up the front and round the skirt'; 'which *I* think', Lady Mary had written earlier, 'will be prettier than the gold and silver of the Queen's ladies.'[50]

After the Coronation, the new Princess of Wales repaired to Scotland with her children. They installed themselves in the little Dee-side castle of Abergeldie, near Balmoral. This was to be their Scottish home for the next eight years. Princess May was feeling tired and despondent that summer. She was also expecting her fifth child. 'I shall soon have a regiment, not a family', Mr John Gore tells us that Prince George remarked about this time.

VI

'The Dee-side is not attractive in August', the first Lord Esher once wrote firmly. 'Cold, grey and unwinning.'[51] That August of 1902

Dee-side was at its least seductive. Princess May and her children arrived at Abergeldie in pelting rain, which continued for several days on end. 'I trust you will ... be pleased with Abergeldie', Prince George, who felt dubious about this, wrote from Cowes. 'The garden anyhow is charming and you can pick flowers & eat fruit.'[52] In fact none of the flowers was out at Abergeldie, and the fruit on the old, rain-drenched garden walls was rotten before it was ripe. There were some strawberries, but that was all: 'The garden here too is not bright & pretty yet, the strawberries however are ripe', wrote Princess May in reply. 'Really this weather is too depressing & I feel quite in the blues & wretched.'[53] She had, anyway, not looked forward to her stay at Abergeldie: '*je n'aime pas ce château-là*', she had written before leaving London to Bricka, '*tandis que Balmoral je l'adore.*'[54]

The small fortress of Abergeldie, which has a medieval tower and a walled garden, stands within easy distance of Balmoral. It is not, however, on the Balmoral estate but on the Gordon estate, and the Royal Family, who regarded it as 'making a hole' in their property, were never able to persuade its owner to sell it, but could only take Abergeldie on lease. In Queen Victoria's time it was inhabited by her eldest son and daughter-in-law, and now that King Edward and Queen Alexandra were naturally going to reside at Balmoral, Abergeldie Castle was handed on to the new Prince and Princess of Wales. For Queen Alexandra, and in consequence for Prince George as well, 'dear old Abergeldie' was another of those places invested with a family mystique by the fact that she and her children had lived there. 'Ah that dear old place how I used to love being there in old times & when you were young & tiny & we all so happy together', she wrote to her son in September of 1902. '—It seems a long *long* time since then—& all is so changed now! Last time *we* were there was with darling Eddy—& since then I cld not bear to stay there again! How comfortable it was then & the drawing room I had succeeded in making quite pretty—I daresay May & you have also made it nice.'[55]

During the weeks she was at Abergeldie alone with the children, while her husband was at Cowes and later in the month at shooting parties, Princess May gave way to unusual bouts of despondency. 'I really regret not having gone to Frogmore instead of coming here this year, for I cannot get out & it is so gloomy & depressing for me I am in despair. If this weather goes on like this I shall return to England by myself for I cannot stand the gloom & cold.'[56] Prince George at once offered to give up his shooting at Studley Royal and come north to comfort Princess May. 'Pray do not think of giving up your visit to Studley for me', she replied. 'I am much touched at your kind offer but I fear that nothing & nobody will dispel this awful depression, the only thing I long for is sun & to be able to sit out all day but this is a hopeless dream.'57 Abergeldie contained only one sitting-room, and this was not large. Princess May's bedroom, which had a coved ceiling and was set in the thickness of the tower, overlooked the garden. 'This is a small house but quite comfortable', Lady Mary Lygon, who was in waiting, wrote to her sister Lady Ampthill, 'and the garden would be charming *if* any of its flowers were out.'58

While the rain continued, Princess May set to work to reorganise such sparse comforts as the interior of the dour little castle could offer. When the weather improved slightly she went round the garden with the gardener, 'suggesting various things for him to plant another year',59 and urging that the three fine old cherry trees should have creepers planted at their roots. By 1905 the Abergeldie garden was well in hand. 'The garden here is looking very pretty', she wrote in August of that year, 'but owing to the want of rain the sweet pea hedge is not as pretty as last year.'61

Princess May had not inherited her father's truly German passion for growing flowers and for gardening. She liked the results, in the form of cut lilac or roses or lilies of the valley to put about her rooms. She also loved pictures of flowers. But, to her, flowers were not of interest in themselves—they were auxiliaries to living, and served to give pleasure to oneself or, equally important in her eyes, to others. 'I am indeed glad to know . . . that you were able to give pleasure with the flowers from here', she wrote from Sandringham to Hélène Bricka in July 1905. 'Oh! were it but mine own & then what a lot of joy one could give to so many people, I wish the dear Queen wld realise this for she likes doing kind actions & here is a way at her elbow, & only to give the orders—but there is no one to remind.'61

As August succeeded August, year by year, Princess May began to get accustomed to Abergeldie. She even succeeded in making the house comfortable with new carpets, papers and heating. On rare, fine summer days she arranged picnics and expeditions which took the little family party outside the grim walls of Abergeldie. 'We had a picnic lunch at the end of the lake', she wrote to Prince George of a day spent at the Glassalt Shiel, with her children, her mother-in-law and Princess Victoria, '& they drew the lake with nets for fish which

we had for lunch & tea. . . . Tea we had at Alt-na-gui-thi-sach—
Mama was in tearing spirits, amusing herself like a child—Toria is
only pretty well.'[62] 'It really is not so bad here when the weather is
fine', Princess May wrote to her Aunt Augusta from Abergeldie in
1909, 'but in bad weather oh!!!!'[63]

VII

The breathless nostalgia which enveloped Queen Alexandra whenever
she thought of dear old Abergeldie was as nothing to that in which
she indulged before leaving Marlborough House for Buckingham
Palace. For some months she clung to this house like a limpet to its
native rock, writing to her son, in August 1901 of 'tearing oneself
away from the *old Home* here Marlborough House! that I *feel* will
finish me! All my happiness & sorrows were here very nearly all you
children born here all my reminiscences of my whole life are here—
& I feel as if by taking me away from it a chord will be torn in my
heart which *can* never never be mended again!! but I dare not think
of it even—'[64] Prince George was, as always, charmingly sympathetic
to his mother: 'Of course the idea of leaving yr old home is terrible
to you now' [he replied] 'but I feel sure that after you get comfortably
settled in the new house, & I know your rooms will be lovely with
everything that modern art & science can produce, the pang of parting
with the old, will in some degree be lessened.'[65] At length, on 27 March
1902, the King and Queen left Marlborough House for good, and
established themselves in Buckingham Palace. A month later the Prince
and Princess of Wales inspected the house from top to bottom: 'It is
an enormous house & I think will do up well', Princess May noted
in her Diary.[66] 'We have not yet got into Marlborough House as
it will take at least 6 months to clean, do up & arrange', she wrote to
little Emily Alcock during that wet August of 1902 at Abergeldie.
'We shall have a busy time doing it all & finding places for the
numberless things we possess—In some ways this will rather amuse
me as I think I have inherited Papa's love of arranging rooms, but
Marl. House is very large & it will be alarming to tackle at first I
fear—'[67]

We have so far only peeped into Marlborough House, on that hot
summer's morning of 1891, when Sir Francis Knollys was discussing
Prince Eddy's marriage project with Prince Eddy's mother in her
small, much-furnished boudoir. 'I thought Alix's [rooms] always too

small and so full besides', the Grand Duchess of Mecklenburg-Strelitz
wrote of Queen Alexandra's apartments at Marlborough House.[68]
Since this house was to be Princess May's home from 1903 till 1910,
and, again, when she was Queen Dowager after 1936, we should now
examine it a little less cursorily.

Marlborough House had been hastily erected by Sir Christopher
Wren between the years 1709 and 1710 for the first Duke of Marlborough and his Duchess. The two main staircases and the great
saloon were frescoed by the painter Laguerre with gory battle-scenes
from the Duke of Marlborough's victorious campaigns. It is built of
red brick with stone coping, and, in Sir George Arthur's words, is
not 'one of Christopher Wren's happiest architectural efforts, but its
rooms are "handsome".'[69] It stands within its own green garden,
behind high walls, on the Mall, to the East of St James's Palace. To
Princess May and Prince George one of its greatest merits was its
seclusion, for since it had its own courtyard, and a portico under which
carriages could drive to the front door, Marlborough House offered
what York House could not provide: privacy when its inhabitants
alighted from or stepped up into, their carriages. At York House
there were always little knots of sightseers waiting near the front door
to watch the royalties come and go. Royal personages make a sufficient
number of professionally public appearances to be justified in expecting
a certain measure of privacy in leaving or returning to their own
thresholds. This welcome privacy the new Prince and Princess of
Wales found at Marlborough House.

In the nineteenth century Marlborough House had first been lived
in by William IV's widow, the Dowager Queen Adelaide, and later,
as we know, by Albert Edward and Alexandra, Prince and Princess
of Wales. During both these tenancies the house, which is indeed
naturally dark, had seemed sombre: 'I am quite delighted you both
like your rooms and am sure you have made them lovely, less full or
gloomy than they were before in Alix's and the Dowager's time',
wrote Aunt Augusta to her niece. 'I got so many *snarling* scoldings
from the latter in my very young days *there*, that I think the remembrance makes me dislike that house, but now, when I some day, shall
see it with *you* in it, I am sure it will look like sunshine upon me!
Oh! when shall I be there?'[70]

At Buckingham Palace and Windsor Castle, King Edward directed
every part of the re-decoration, for, except for the arrangement of her
own and of Miss Charlotte Knolly's rooms, such matters did not

interest Queen Alexandra. At Marlborough House this situation was reversed, for recognising Princess May's superior taste and gifts, Prince George let her have her own way, protesting only occasionally about tiny details: 'there seems to me to be too much money to be spent on gilding, I hate gilding',[71] for example. In the days of the previous occupants, the ceilings and elaborate cornices at Marlborough House, as well as much of the panelling had been painted what Princess May called 'the ugly pink and green'.[72] These were now painted white, with a modicum of good water-gilding to relieve the plainness: 'the plainer ceilings are a great improvement', wrote Princess May in October 1902.[73] The ground floor of Marlborough House was taken up by a suite of lofty reception-rooms, while on the first floor were the private sitting-rooms and bedrooms of Prince George and Princess May.

Work on Marlborough House continued through the summer, autumn and winter of 1902. In March 1903 Princess May and her husband left York House—which had by now become 'our dear old Home'—for Buckingham Palace where they stayed for a few weeks until Marlborough House should be quite ready. During this period Princess May and her Ladies performed 'Herculean labours' in arranging furniture and hanging pictures, working eight hours a day. On 4 April she and her husband took up residence, driving in two shut carriages to Marlborough House, where they were received by the housekeeper. Princess May's first letter from her new abode was written to her Aunt Augusta, who was greatly touched by this civility: 'We are fairly comfortably installed already & are quite delighted with our own rooms which I really flatter myself are pretty & most comfortable', she wrote. ' . . . This certainly is a beautiful house & the garden is the great attraction.'[74] The garden was a great attraction for the children in particular, and the new baby, Prince George,* born on 20 December 1902, could lie out there in his perambulator in the shade, just as his mother Princess May had lain in her canopied cot in the garden of Kensington Palace, near the effluvial pond, some thirty-five years previously. Prince George and Princess May now had a family of five children, four sons and one daughter.

Once the interior of Marlborough House was completed, a ticklish

* Born at York Cottage, Sandringham, on 20 December 1902, Prince George Edward Alexander Edmund was created Duke of Kent at the time of his marriage (29 November 1934) to Princess Marina, daughter of Prince Nicholas of Greece by whom he had three children, the present Duke of Kent, Princess Alexandra and Prince Michael of Kent. He was killed on active service 25 August 1942.

question arose: what would Queen Alexandra think of it? The re-decoration of any house by a successor seems in itself a silent criticism of the previous occupant's taste, and Princess May feared 'semi-sarcastical words' as her Aunt Augusta called them. However, she and Prince George took the plunge. On 10 May 1903 they gave their first family dinner-party, to the accompaniment of Gottlieb's Vienna Orchestra, which played light music—the sort of airs which a new maid at Marlborough House was astonished to hear Princess May whistling to herself as she walked briskly along an upper corridor. 'The house looked lovely & the dinner went off well', Princess May noted in her Diary. Besides the King and Queen, she had invited Prince Karl of Denmark, Princess Louise Duchess of Fife with her husband, the three Teck brothers with Princess Dolly, now Duchess of Teck, her old uncle the Duke of Cambridge (who was eighty-four, and was in the last year of his life), the Duchess of Albany and her daughter Princess Alice (soon to be Prince Alge's wife),* and six other relations and friends. All the guests signed their names on the back of the gold-rimmed menu card, which Princess May kept with other such mementoes, loose in her practical scarlet and green Letts quarto Diary. 'Motherdear, Alix—the first dinner in our beloved old home', scribbled Queen Alexandra.[76]

In July, the new Prince and Princess of Wales became more adventurous. They gave a great ball for eleven hundred and fifty guests, building a temporary ballroom for this over the garden. This artificial ballroom had white plaster pillars: 'it reminded me somewhat', wrote Lady Mary Lygon, 'of the banqueting hall at Madras.'[77] The host and hostess went to bed at four in the morning and left three hours later for Plymouth and Truro, where they had 'functions' to perform. Entertainments on this scale were of course the exception, not the rule. Life at Marlborough House was as peaceful as life at York

---

* On 10 February 1904, the twenty-nine-year-old Prince Alexander of Teck (Earl of Athlone, 1917) was married, at St George's Chapel, Windsor, to Princess Alice, eldest child and only daughter of Queen Victoria's fourth son, Prince Leopold, Duke of Albany (1853–1884) and his wife Helen, Princess of Waldeck and Pyrmont (1861–1922). This marriage gave particular pleasure to Princess May: 'I am in a great state of excitement over it', she wrote to her Aunt Augusta, ' . . . for I seem always to have "bemothered" Alge all my life, he being 7 years younger than me—The two ought to suit very well, as she has been well & sensibly brought up & I have always been fond of her.' 'It was a most cheerful wedding,' Princess May wrote in another letter, 'no crying & At. Helen behaved like a brick—.'[75]

House had been. 'We have had 3 delicious summer days, such a joy after all the gloom', Princess May wrote during one typical English summer. 'I am writing in the garden, George sits near reading, & the children play cricket, a truly domestic scene!!!'[78] 'Here I am back in London once more', Prince George wrote to his wife one August, '& am now sitting in the garden in our usual place under the trees writing this letter, it is very sad to see yr chair empty & I can't say how dreadfully I miss you darling, I expect every minute to see you coming out of the house.'[79]

It was in this manner, then, that Princess May faced the new reign and the new century. She was Princess of Wales, she was now the mother of four little Princes and one little Princess, she lived in increased splendour, and at Marlborough House. These were the outward changes in her circumstances. Inwardly she remained as reasonable, as studious and as anxious to be constructive in life as ever. The domestic simplicity which was to stamp the reign of King George V already marked the diligent and honourable daily lives at Marlborough House of the new Prince and the new Princess of Wales.

TRAVEL AND TRANSITION

HE London Season of 1903 was the first really brilliant one
of the Edwardian Court. That of 1901 had been eclipsed by
the mourning for Queen Victoria, that of 1902 by the King's
critical illness. May, June and July 1903 set the tone which the English
Court was to keep up until the death of King Edward in 1910. The
dull afternoon Drawing-Rooms of the old Queen were now replaced
by sparkling evening receptions at Buckingham Palace. The rich but
rather various Society which King Edward VII and Queen Alexandra
had collected around them when they were Prince and Princess of
Wales was now to be found thronging their entertainments at
Buckingham Palace and Windsor Castle.

During Ascot week, 1903, there was a great ball in the Waterloo
Chamber at Windsor Castle; it was the first ball to be given at Windsor
for sixty-three years. 'The ball on Friday was a great success & a
lovely sight, we danced in the Waterloo Gallery & supped in St
George's Hall', Princess May wrote to her Aunt Augusta. 'About
900 people were present. Unfortunately at the beginning of the ball
while Dolly was dancing with Victoria, his spurs caught in Mrs *George*
Keppels awfully long gown, & he & Victoria fell heavily on their
backs. Poor Victoria hurt her head & back very much & felt so faint
& giddy she was unable to dance any more, & Dolly was also shaken,
not being a light weight to fall—It is such a pity that ladies will wear
long flowing garments made of chiffon at balls for of course, they
catch round the men's legs.'[1] 'But oh! poor Dolly's and Victoria's fall,
truly grievous,' Aunt Augusta replied, 'she who is already so delicate.'[2]

In April 1902 King Edward had placed Frogmore House in Windsor
Home Park at the disposal of Prince George and Princess May. It was
there that they now always stayed and entertained during Ascot week.
Frogmore House, which had been built in the reign of William and
Mary, became Royal property when purchased by Queen Charlotte
in 1792. A pretty old cream-coloured building, with a long colonnade,
rooms of convenient size and a large ballroom, Frogmore House still

looks as it did after it had been altered for Queen Charlotte by the architect Wyatt. It was at Frogmore that Prince Eddy had been born in 1864. Queen Victoria liked to use the secluded Frogmore garden for writing letters and working at her despatch-boxes. 'I am sitting in this dear lovely garden', she had, for instance, written in 1867, 'where *all* is Peace & quiet & you only hear the hum of the bees the singing of the birds & the occasional crowing & cackling from the Poultry Yard! It does my poor excited, worried nerves— good!—'[3]

Princess May now used Frogmore for much the same purposes. Whenever she could get away from London for a few days she would bring her children down to Frogmore, where they would play beside the lake whilst she sat and read or wrote letters beneath a big lime-tree. 'It is too divine here & everything is looking lovely, the house charming & fresh & the garden & grounds a dream',[4] she wrote to Prince George from Frogmore one July. Later on Princess May replanted in the Frogmore garden a lilac-tree from Rumpenheim, which her grandmother the old Duchess of Cambridge had brought over many years before and put in the Cambridge Cottage garden at Kew. Even after her husband became King and they lived at Windsor Castle, Queen Mary would come and spend long summer afternoons at Frogmore, and towards the end of her life she arranged the interior of the house as a kind of family museum. But, as Princess of Wales, she regarded Frogmore primarily as a place of refuge in which to recuperate from the fatigues of London life. 'I am altogether rather limp & not up to much which is a bore', she wrote from Frogmore to her Aunt Augusta in May 1903, after describing the almost incredible series of London activities in which she had latterly become involved. 'In fact I am too energetic & try to do more than I am up to but you know how difficult it is to pull up—No doubt a week's rest here will do me worlds of good.'[5]

The end of that summer, 1903, found Princess May still 'rather limp', and so in August she set off attended by Lady Eva Dugdale and her husband for a short Swiss holiday at Beatenberg above Inter- laken. Even Princess May's incognito journeys were now more pompous than of yore. 'We had a most comfortable journey & we found the no. 3 saloon very nice & it runs well', she wrote to Prince George of the Royal railway carriage in which she had travelled, 'but think of me wishing to travel incog in that huge carriage with E R VII painted in large letters on it!!!'[6]

The hotel at Beatenberg proved a disappointment, since the rooms were too small and there were no walks in the vicinity. It had been recommended to Princess May by Fehr, the King's courier, who had travelled out with her: 'I cannot understand how Fehr cld have recommended this place', she wrote to her husband, 'but if you see him pray don't pitch into him as he is rather upset & distressed that I don't like it.'7 Princess May and her party only remained at Beatenberg two nights, going down subsequently to Interlaken to stay at the Hotel Jungfraublick, which was built beside a pretty wood and had large airy rooms. It was, by a coincidence, the very hotel in which Princess Mary Adelaide had stayed with her sister the Grand Duchess of Mecklenburg-Strelitz in 1864. Ruined for Lady Eva Dugdale by the news that her mother, Lady Warwick, had suddenly died, the weeks at Interlaken were otherwise happy and calm. 'Do you know', wrote Princess May to Prince George, 'the roads are so good here that it wld have been rather fun to have a motor car to go about, 2 people in the hotel have their own.'8

II

The advent of the motor-car, so soon to revolutionise the tempo of life all over Europe, had coincided with the very last years of Queen Victoria's reign. 'Our drive', Princess May had written from Mentone, when she was staying there with her Aunt Augusta in 1898, 'was somewhat disturbed by an odious motor car which kept on passing us & then slowing down, it smelt so nasty & made such a noise.'9 By 1901 motor-cars had even entered the precincts of Hyde Park: 'the Motors spoil & frighten ones drives,' wrote Aunt Augusta from Mecklenburg House in June 1901, 'going *within* the "file" even, noisy and stinking besides.'10

All her life long Princess May was interested in modern developments; from being 'odious' motor-cars quickly became in her eyes convenient and enviable possessions:

Only think what George & I did this afternoon, we went in Ld Shrewsbury's *motor car* (driven by him) down to Hampton Court which George had never seen [Princess May wrote to her aunt in April 1903]. I really enjoyed the drive very much & we flew . . . [we] have just returned at *7.15*, it took us *38* minutes to get back—I feel you will nearly have a fit at me going in a motor.11

The Grand Duchess replied with alacrity:

And now to your drive in a Motor-Car! yes, I very nearly had a fit and quite screamed out to myself . . . oh! dearest child, how could you? *38m.* too, about 20 miles, I believe. It really actually took my breath away. George never to have seen Hampton Court also all but took my breath away!— how was this possible?[12]

With Princess May to decide was to act. In July 1903 only three months after this expedition she was writing of drives in 'our motor-car' in Cornwall, where she and Prince George were staying with the Mount Edgcumbes.

In the acquisition of this motor Prince George and Princess May were at least two years behind the King and Queen. 'We had a splendid motor down there', Queen Alexandra had written to her son in June 1901, of a sojourn at Sandringham, '& I did enjoy being driven about in the cool of the evening at *50 miles*!! an hour!—when nothing in the way of course only!—& I must say I have the greatest confidence in our driver—I poke him violently in the back at every *corner* to go gently & when ever a *dog, child* or anything comes in our way!'[13] Princess May distrusted her mother-in-law's love of speed. She had never got over her fright at being driven by Queen Alexandra in her pony-trap along the winding Princess's Walk at Sandringham, for the Queen, who had exceptionally fast ponies, would drive round the bends like the wind. The Grand Duchess of Mecklenburg-Strelitz persisted in thinking motor-cars 'horrible', 'dangerous' and 'so un-Royal', but they were soon part of the everyday equipment of those who could afford them, and for members of the Royal Family, with their life of constant movement, they were, of course, invaluable.

Bicycling, which had come into vogue for women as well as for men in the last decade of Queen Victoria's reign, did not appeal to Princess May, although her husband and his sisters were all bicycling enthusiasts. On wet afternoons when these latter would bicycle round and round the ballroom at Sandringham House, Princess May confined herself to pedalling a large tricycle.

Other novel amenities were also coming into everyday use. York Cottage and Frogmore House, as well, of course, as Marlborough House, were on the telephone by 1902: 'I talked to G. on the telephone in the evening & he told me the Procession in London had gone off very well & that the King had had a wonderful reception', Princess May noted, for example, in her Diary for 25 October 1902. All their houses were now lit by electric light, and Princess May often spent an evening listening in to an opera or a play on the Electrophone, an excellent Post Office service now long discontinued which enabled one to be connected, through head-phones, with any major London theatre or music-hall one wished. Already in 1896 and 1897 Princess May and Prince George had been 'to see the Cinematograph',[14] both at the Alhambra Theatre and at Marlborough House, where private cinematograph exhibitions were occasionally given. The Coronation procession of King Edward VII was filmed; soon news-films became fairly common. Even Aunt Augusta, who loathed all modern inventions, was mollified and indeed seduced to see a film of herself receiving Princess May at Neu Strelitz. 'We went to see you and us Kinephotographed, so amusing and so like us all, truly diverting', she wrote to her niece, and, in another letter: 'The film-picture was a real success ... we spent near 2 hours there, really amused in a clean new Hall, no smoking allowed. As everything now is international, perhaps *our* Film may come to England some day!'[15]

Meanwhile, at Friedrichshafen, and indeed very near the old Württemberg Schloss which Princess May knew so well, Count Zeppelin was at work on his airship. 'Newspapers also take up much of my time,' the Grand Duchess of Mecklenburg-Strelitz wrote to her niece one September, 'first Zeppelin who bores me terribly, as they are mad about his invention, make me sick of it.' 'Really, the Papers are so full of horrors', she wrote again, 'then of all people, even Sovereigns now flying up into the air.'[16] It was to be expected that a personage as implacably old-fashioned as Aunt Augusta should dislike motorcars and even more so airships. Princess May, on the other hand, was intensely curious about the astonishingly fast strides being made in such directions during King Edward VII's reign. 'How quickly the two Centuries have grown almost into opposition to each other and so quickly too!'[17] the Grand Duchess astutely remarked in a letter of 1911. 'I so agree with what you say about the ideas of the two centuries being so totally different & it has come so rapidly too', was Princess May's mild reply;[18] for one of Princess May's cardinal maxims was that 'one must move with the times'.

III

In 1904, Princess May had a glimpse of a European court which, beside her father-in-law's renovated and modernised establishment, seemed, as indeed it was, almost archaic; for on 18 April of that year she and her husband paid, as Prince and Princess of Wales, a state visit to the old Emperor Franz Josef at Vienna. This glimpse of an almost legendary figure, and of a court at which the etiquette had not been changed for several centuries, appealed to Princess May's historical sense: 'You can imagine what it was to *me* to find myself there, knowing the feelings Mama, you, Gdmama & Papa had for him & Austria', she wrote to her Aunt Augusta. 'It thrilled me & we must talk it all over.'[19]

The reception at the railway station at Vienna Princess May found 'most alarming'!—for there, waiting for the English Royalties, were the Emperor himself, several Archdukes, the members of the British Embassy (who included Prince and Princess Dolly, now Duke and Duchess of Teck, Prince Dolly being the British Military Attaché to the Imperial Court), as well as a Guard of Honour. Princess May who 'looked very charming in heliotrope', was handed a bouquet of orchids, put into a carriage with her own lady-in-waiting, and taken in procession to the Hofburg, Prince George driving with the Emperor, who was now seventy-three years old. Prince George was wearing the uniform of his Hungarian Regiment, the 72nd Pressburg, from which the Guard of Honour was drawn. At the Hofburg, all the Austrian Archdukes were ranged at the head of the staircase—'another ordeal'; and in the adjoining room were all the suites. 'It will be rather alarming, having all those strange people presented,' Aunt Augusta had correctly predicted, 'seeing the long line before one, having to say a word to each, but I am sure you will pass this ordeal well and where a word may fail you, a sweet smile will take its place!'[20]

Princess May found it 'all delightful tho' tiring, everyone so kind & *the* Emperor charming'.[21] The Prince and Princess of Wales were allotted twelve apartments. They dined with the Austrian suite attached to them and their own Household; for the Emperor dined at five, went to bed at eight, and rose at four a.m. daily. There were a series of balls, supper-parties and visits to the Opera House during the four-day visit, and once again Princess May scored a personal success. 'She is much better looking than any of the Archduchesses', wrote the loyal and patriotic Lady Mary Lygon to her sister, '—also they are very stiff—so everyone raved over the ease and charm of the Princess's manners.'[22] Princess May danced till four in the morning, being partnered in the *Cotillon* by the Archduke Leopold Salvator on one night, by Prince Elias of Parma on the next. There was a large

N

luncheon party at Schönbrunn, where Princess May examined every room of that extensive and elaborate palace, and also drove round the grounds with the Emperor in a carriage called a '*Pirutchade*', which 'dates from about 200 years', and which formed a distinct contrast to King Edward VII's electric broughams.

Prince George left Vienna for one night to shoot capercailzie, whilst Princess May concentrated on seeing as many of the wonders and beauties of the spacious old Imperial city as she could crowd into four days and a tight social schedule. Try as she would, Princess May could never repair the grave faults in her husband's youthful education. He had never been taught to be interested in works of art or in objects and places of historical interest, for which Princess May herself had developed an undying passion. 'With all my love of history you can imagine what a pleasure all this has been to me,' Princess May wrote on a subsequent visit to Paris, where she had been shown Versailles, Chantilly and Fontainebleau, 'alas for my poor George all these things are a sealed book, such a pity & so deplorable in his position! & he misses so much that is interesting in one's life.'[23]

From Vienna, the Prince and Princess of Wales proceeded to pay a State Visit to Stuttgart, where Prince George invested Princess May's cousin, King William II of Württemberg, with the Order of the Garter. Since the court of Württemberg was in mourning for Queen Charlotte's brother, who had just died, there were no formal festivities for the English visitors. 'Here it is "*gemütlich*", Willy & Charlotte so kind, & the former old friends glad & pleased to see me again. My German is almost fluent & they are surprised I can talk it so well, which is flattering! I got on capitally last night after the investiture, at the *cercle*, talking to the Ministers, & George struggled manfully with German too. We drive during the day to pretty spots in the neighbourhood, the country looks lovely with the fruit trees out.'[24] The last occasion on which Princess May had been at the court at Stuttgart was that sad sojourn there with her parents after the death of Prince Eddy in 1892, when Princess Mary Adelaide's sitting-room caught fire.

Fascinated though she naturally was to see the court of the Emperor Franz Josef in action, and flattered though she felt by her reception and her personal success there, Princess May retained her critical sense. Forty years later she remarked in conversation to a friend that the collapse of the Imperial systems in Austria and in Russia had come as no surprise to her, since she had never conceived how an order so stiff and hierarchical, and so totally detached from the people of those countries, could possibly survive in a free and modern world.

IV

In the March which preceded this April visit to Vienna, Princess May's uncle, the Duke of Cambridge, had died at the age of eighty-five. 'We received the sad news at Portsmouth', wrote Princess May to her Aunt Augusta, '& returned at once to London—We went to Gl[oucester] House where we saw him looking so peaceful in his bed, *very* very pale but the features handsome & very like Mama I thought. . . . It upset me very much as you can imagine for dear Uncle had always been so dear & nice to me ever since I was quite a tiny mite, that I shall miss him dreadfully, of late years, especially since my marriage, we had become fast friends, holding the same views on many subjects, as with you, dear Aunt, & I greatly enjoyed my talks with him, when we were allowed to be alone.'[25] This last phrase bore reference to the old Duke's sons, the FitzGeorges, who were constantly in attendance on him and did not much like the rest of his family seeing him alone; for the Duke of Cambridge was exceedingly rich, and possessed much splendid plate, many family pictures and jewelled snuff-boxes. He had once made Queen Victoria a written promise to leave these back to the Royal Family in his will. This he did not, however, do, and the FitzGeorges reaped all. Most of the best objects were sold by auction, after Princess May and other members of the old Duke's family had been given the chance to buy in what they liked at valuation.

Unlike his sister Princess Mary Adelaide, the Duke of Cambridge had made a will, but he had never had a catalogue made of his numerous family possessions. This Princess May regretted: 'Alas there is no real catalogue of where the things came from, which rather takes away from the interest of some of the smaller *bibelots*', she wrote to her Aunt Augusta. '—The sons do not even know by whom some of the pictures are—Of course in time this may be ascertained. The plate is so fine, both gold and silver, & such a quantity of it. The sons say there is so much to be looked thro', so many things that have not been touched for years, that they scarcely know where & how to begin.'[26] The comparative chaos of the Duke of Cambridge's possessions impressed once more on his niece Princess May the essential importance of making catalogues and notes about her own growing collection. This was a work after her own heart. In the same way, towards the end of her life, she docketed and arranged her papers for a future biographer, sometimes writing on an envelope containing, say, a German letter to Queen Victoria from some relation, the disarming superscription: 'Nice letter about *me*.'

The Duke of Cambridge was accorded a military funeral. The service was in the Abbey, and the Duke's body was then borne in solemn procession to Kensal Green cemetery, where he had wished to be buried in the same vault as his dead wife Mrs FitzGeorge, the former Miss Louisa Fairbrother. 'I only deeply regret that he will not be laid to rest in the Family Vault at Windsor, and is to be taken to a strange resting place, so far away from us all!' wrote his sister the Grand Duchess of Mecklenburg-Strelitz.[27] 'As for the funeral', wrote Princess May to her aunt, 'to my mind it was the most impressive & beautiful sight . . . I have ever seen, too upsetting for words, & I cried floods all the time. . . . The sight of the funeral *cortège* passing Buck. Palace was magnificent in the brilliant sunshine & the absolute silence of the crowds had a wonderful effect. At. Alix was so feeling & dear to me, we stood together, she feels Uncle's death very much indeed.'[28]

As we have noticed earlier, the Grand Duchess Augusta had an uncanny gift for missing the death-beds of her nearest relations. She had not been present in England when her mother the old Duchess of Cambridge had died in 1889, nor in 1897 when her sister Princess Mary Adelaide did so. Similarly she was still in Strelitz, trying to make up her mind to come to England, when her brother George Cambridge expired that March of 1904. Lady Geraldine Somerset, who scarcely ever missed an opportunity to make herself felt, scolded the old Grand Duchess for not coming over to see her brother before he died: 'I had a *vile* letter from Geraldine, really a nasty one, upbraiding me for not being there', she wrote to Princess May from Strelitz, 'saying that *I* had put off my journey *then* when dear Mamma died, as *now* I was doing, etc. . . . really too bad of her, when it was *her*, who never wrote how much weaker poor Mamma had become. Meanwhile I could not travel now, having a nasty cough and feeling very unwell, besides weather atrocious, so that I dare not venture out even!'[29]

Cambridge Cottage, the late Duke of Cambridge's house at Kew, was, however, filled with furniture and pictures, a part of which belonged to the Grand Duchess; so that in the April of the year her brother had died, the old lady crossed the Channel and, establishing herself as usual at Mecklenburg House, set to work to sort out her own possessions at Kew for transfer back to Strelitz. Her husband, the Grand Duke of Mecklenburg-Strelitz (Princess May's 'Uncle Fritz') had been very unwell for some months. 'Poor Uncle', his wife had written to Princess May in 1903, 'is not an easy patient to manage, patience being required, and this, I know, I am not famous for! he has such odd fancies, he makes poor me answerable for impossible things and if ever I give in for a day, to rest, he is angry and *will* not understand, that his state of health makes me anxious, or depresses me; poor man, he *never* understood me and *so* it will go on to the end; this has ever been one of my hardest trials during my long married life, together with many others!'[30] The Grand Duchess's long married life of sixty-one years came to an abrupt close that spring; for, on 29 May 1904, whilst of course she was in England, the old blind Grand Duke died at Neu Strelitz. 'At 12', wrote Princess May in her Diary for 30 May 1904, 'I heard the news of poor Uncle Fritz Mecklenburg's death the night before—I went at once to poor Aunt Augusta who was very much upset at the news.' 'Very wet day', she recorded on 31 May. 'We saw poor Aunt Augusta off from Victoria Station at 11.' In accordance with the custom of describing corpses initiated by Queen Victoria, Aunt Augusta sent Princess May a detailed account of how 'dearest Frederick' looked in death:

His features are quite beautiful in death [she wrote] so finely marbled, and as he lays there, one can see what a real Gentleman he was and what blood he had in his veins, his colour has darkened a little, otherwise he is unchanged. I am glad I can see his dear face still! but it is all so dreadfully sad, and seems so strange to me to see Dolphus running about, giving orders, doing all himself (like others do) he had a Special to meet me half way to Berlin; tried to keep up and praised me for showing the brave old Guelph![31]

'I do feel so much for you in your loneliness, it must be a great trial, & before everything used to centre round you & Uncle', wrote Princess May imaginatively to her widowed aunt, '& now the blank void the emptiness must be hard to bear—The silence too in the large Schloss where so much went on before—I picture it all to myself—'[32] 'My life here is so quiet, so deadly still, that it is quite appalling,' the Grand Duchess wrote to her niece from Strelitz, 'it is so odd not to be asked for orders or in fact for anything; I feel so useless, and still cannot quite take in, that dearest Uncle is gone and I am never to see [him] or hear his dear sonorous voice again; I even sometimes get up in a hurry to ask him something, some good advice, he was ever so ready to give me!'33 This was a sensation which Princess May understood only too well: 'I know that feeling so well', she answered, 'of thinking "Oh I will ask - - - that". I had it so strongly after dear Mama's death—& it is such a shock to feel they are gone & cannot reply, yet sometimes when ones feelings & ideas are fixed on a subject, one feels that they wish one to do it, almost as if one were pushed, is not this strange?'34

In late July Princess May herself set off for Strelitz, to try to bring her aunt some comfort. With her usual astuteness she immediately sized up the situation at Neu Strelitz, where the old Grand Duchess did not at all enjoy her new position as Dowager, nor the fact that her son 'Dolphus' and her daughter-in-law 'Elly' were now in charge. 'We see a certain amount of Dolphus & Elly & they are so nice with At A.', Princess May wrote to her husband. 'It isn't always easy for them & when one lives here, one reads between the lines! Dear Aunt, is so agreeable so amusing, but not easy in every day life for them. Particularly now in the altered position. . . . What a lot of nice family things At Augusta has, I am going to help her to make a catalogue while I am here, because of course, as usual, no record of anything has been kept.'35

v

'The pleasure I always have in receiving your dear letters', wrote Aunt Augusta to her niece in January 1905, 'was rather marred by the secret imparted to me! such a surprise, so unexpected! I will write what my Hessian Gdmother said to her Daughters on such occasions *"Vous aurez un cœur de plus à vous aimer"!'*36 Princess May, already the mother of five children, was expecting another baby. Prince John* was born on 12 July 1905.

We have already noticed, at the time of the birth of her first son Prince Edward, that Princess May shared Queen Victoria's views on pregnancy. She was delighted with each baby once it was born, but

---

* Prince John, who died suddenly at the age of thirteen on 18 January 1919, early developed epilepsy and was segregated from his brothers and sister. He lived happily, with his own Household, at Wood Farm, Wolferton, on the Sandringham estate.

the long preliminary period of feeling ill and of forced inactivity distressed her. She felt both depressed and conspicuous. 'Of course it is a great bore for me & requires a great deal of patience to bear it', she had once written to her husband on this subject, 'but this is alas the penalty of being a woman!'37

It is possible that Princess May's innate distaste for all the processes of childbirth may have tinted her rather detached attitude to her children. She was not, as the Empress Frederick had averred, an unmaternal woman, but, like her husband Prince George, she had no automatic or spontaneous understanding of a child's mind or ways. Her children were a source of pride to her, but they were also a source of wonder. Mr John Gore, in his *Personal Memoir of King George V* —a book to the writing of which Queen Mary contributed much wise advice—has shown that the King's relationship with his sons was not, to say the least of it, ideal. With the best possible intentions, King George V frightened and subdued his children. When they were very young he embarrassed them by chaffing questions, and as they grew up he alienated them by continual criticisms, interspersed with fits of impatient anger. Their happiest childhood memories were of the rare periods when they were alone at Frogmore or at Abergeldie with their mother, whilst their father was shooting in the Midlands or yachting at Cowes. Princess May would then deploy for their benefit all her gaiety and charm, all the pent-up high spirits of her youthful days at White Lodge. Her husband was to some extent a repressive influence upon her, and after he became King she saw him as invested with the mystique of the Monarchy. 'I have always to remember', she once remarked to a friend when discussing her sons, 'that their Father is also their King.'

The Duke of Windsor has lucidly explained in his memoirs how much the strictness of King George V as a parent impeded the Duke's own development and that of his brothers. 'The laws of behaviour', he writes, 'as revealed to a small boy tended to be ruled by a vast preponderance of "dont's". But with Mama life was less severe. Although she backed up my father in all matters of discipline, she never failed to take our side whenever in her judgement he was being too harsh with us.'38 The later correspondence of Queen Mary and King George reveals many instances in which she would defend or shield the conduct of whichever of her sons was currently in most disfavour with their father. One further passage from the memoirs of the Duke of Windsor, who has evidently inherited the literary flair of his grandmother, Princess Mary Adelaide, Duchess of Teck, is relevant here. Writing of his early schoolroom years and of the strange educational régime instituted by that muscular Christian, Mr Henry Hansell, he gives this touching vignette of Princess May at York Cottage:

It was my mother's habit to rest in her boudoir before dinner, and this hour she saved for us. At 6.30 we were called in from the schoolroom. She would be in *negligée* resting on the sofa; and, when we were gathered around her on little chairs, she would read and talk to us. Looking back upon this scene, I am sure that my cultural interests began at my mother's knee. The years that she had lived abroad as a young girl had mellowed her outlook; and reading and observation had equipped her with a prodigious knowledge of Royal history. Her soft voice, her cultivated mind, the cosy room overflowing with personal treasures were all inseparable ingredients of the happiness associated with this last hour of a child's day.

Being also practical by nature, my mother utilised the time to teach us how to make woollen comforters for one of her many charities. She supplied each of us with a wooden ring into which were fitted upright brass pegs. While she read, we busily looped the wool yarn around each peg, thus forming, by means of a succession of crochet stitches, a comforter five feet in length.[39]

Several of the Household of those days who are still living emphasise how immensely 'cosy' was the atmosphere at York Cottage of an evening, the children gathered with their mother round a lamp-lit table playing some educational card-game—cards with the counties of England on them for example—while their father was shut into his library alone, working at his stamp collection, or reading *The Times* newspaper. Yet it cannot be denied that, between them, King George and Queen Mary managed to be rather unsuccessful and somewhat unsympathetic parents. They were too often surprised by the simplest manifestations of childishness in children. Why was their eldest son so 'fidgetty', so 'jumpy' as a tiny boy? 'David was "jumpy" yesterday morning, however he got quieter after being out, what a curious child he is', Princess May wrote when Prince Edward of York was scarcely two years old;[40] or 'Baby was delicious at tea this evening, he is in a charming frame of mind & I hope he will be nice when you return darling tomorrow. He often calls for "Papa" & seems to miss you very much—I really believe he begins to like me at last, he is most civil to me.'[41]

Always busy, and always protected from the harsher sides of life by Private Secretaries, equerries and ladies-in-waiting, Princess May and her husband sometimes overlooked the simplest of nursery facts. It took them three years, for instance, to discover that Prince Edward's first nurse was trying to turn her charge against his parents, and that she always pinched him before bringing him into the drawing-room, so that he would cry and be sent upstairs again in disgrace. Equally, they were astonished when this unusual nurse had a nervous break-down and when they thereupon learned that she had not had one single day's holiday for three years. The régime at Marlborough House and at York Cottage, at Frogmore and at Abergeldie was not of course in any way analogous to the stiff procedures of the court at Strelitz, through which the young Duchess Marie had come to grief; but it remains true that quite often Prince George and Princess May did not know precisely what was afoot in nursery or schoolroom. Princess May was, too, a little overwhelmed by the responsibility of rearing a future King of England, and was so anxious that her eldest son should grow up a paragon and an example that he was at one moment in danger of becoming precocious. Her ideas of suitable entertainments for children were at times a shade austere: 'David arrived from Sandringham', she wrote in her Diary in February 1907, when her eldest son was twelve years old. 'I took him to see some water colours of gardens by Mrs Crofton in Bond Street & also to Graves' Gallery where we saw pictures by Sir Richard Sankey.'[42]

Just as Princess May was unaware of the behaviour of Prince Edward's first nurse, so she remained entirely contented with the dull and disastrous educational system of the Princes' tutor, Mr Hansell. 'I have taken lately to be present at the boys history lessons', she wrote in 1905 to her Aunt Augusta. 'I must say Hansell teaches it well & they really answer the questions very nicely—taking a real interest in what he tells them. This pleases me immensely as you know how devoted I am to history.'[43] Princess May also regarded her children with the family-historical eye. Was her daughter not a little like Queen Charlotte? How nice it was that her eldest son seemed to resemble Prince Eddy! She preferred to see them separately, one at a time. 'I can so well understand your preferring to enjoy them *singly*!' wrote Aunt Augusta one day in 1907, '6 all of a heap is rather much! though a blessing that they are *there*! talking to him [Prince Edward] alone & hearing him express his opinions makes it possible for you to instil your views into his, so necessary in modern times. I do the same with my Gdsons who, Heaven be praised, *listen* to me!'[44] 'Yes,' replied

N*

Princess May, 'I always feel that they pick up so much from one when they are young, I know I did from my Parents in so many ways, things one never afterwards forgets & which are so valuable—I do so hope our children will turn out common-sense people which is so important in this world—We have taken no end of trouble with their education & they have very nice people round them so one feels all is being done to help them.'45 It would be quite erroneous to suggest that Princess May was not devoted to her children. What she had minded most about leaving England for the Australian and Canadian tour of 1901 had been the long months without seeing them. 'When I went', she remarked to a friend in 1901, 'the older children were big enough to miss me, and the younger ones had grown and altered so much that when I got back, they seemed like little strangers round the table.'

During the *Ophir* cruise of 1901, Princess May was constantly worried by letters from her old governess Madame Bricka, who was then in charge of the children's education, telling her how much King Edward and Queen Alexandra were spoiling their grandsons. Lessons would be interrupted, deferred or cancelled. Queen Alexandra would descend on York Cottage and insist on bathing the baby, whether it was his bath-time or not. She would let her grandsons pour salt and pepper into her glass, and would roguishly quaff this mixture to their great delight. She also thought she understood children better than her daughter-in-law did:

You say that David asks so many questions which are sometimes awkward & difficult to answer [she wrote to Princess May in 1901]—& therefore he ought not to be left with nurses only—I quite agree to the *latter* . . . I assure you David does not ask anything more wonderful than *most children* of his age & certainly little Bertie & baby Mary—ask just as many funny things as he did before you left.

Another extract from this long letter will go to show how much basis there was for Princess May's anxiety during the *Ophir* cruise; for self-justification is almost invariably revealing:

You ask me [Queen Alexandra wrote about Prince Edward] about Bricka & his french—well all I can say is that she has been giving him lessons & had *him to herself all the time here* & at *Windsor*—since you left excepting our two visits to Sandringham—The reason we did not take her there was that [Doctor] Laking particularly asked that he might be left more with his brothers & sister—for a *little while*—as *we all* noticed *how* precautious [*sic*]

& *old-fashioned* he was getting—& quite the *ways* of *'a single child'*! which wld make him ultimately a 'tiresome child'—laying down the law & thinking himself far superior to the younger ones—It did him a great deal *of good*— to be treated the *same* as Bertie—who is after all very little younger than he—the same difference as there was between Eddy & Georgie—In *that short* time his Education was *not* neglected—you may be sure—About his *French* I confess I know very little as *I never interfere* in his lessons with Bricka & she told me she did *most* in *English* with him & David himself declares that he cannot speak french yet, though I think she *always* speaks french to *him during their dinner.*[46]

Nineteen hundred and five, the year of the birth of Princess May's sixth and last child Prince John, brought with it another long period of separation from her children, for on 19 October 1905, Princess May and her husband set out for Genoa, where they boarded the battleship *Renown* and set sail for Bombay. They did not return from this State Visit to India until the middle of April 1906.

VI

Princess May set to work to prepare for this Indian expedition with her usual quiet competence. 'We . . . are having a nice restful time, I am reading books on India which are most interesting, I read nearly all the morning when I have not letters to write', she wrote to Bricka from Abergeldie[47] one day in early autumn. Princess May's system of reading up—or as her children called it 'Mama's swatting up'— information about a new country before she went there was now a regular part of her routine. Sir Walter Lawrence, a man of wide Indian experience and a former private secretary to Lord Curzon during his Viceroyalty, had been chosen as Chief of Staff for the tour. He went several times to Marlborough House to discuss details with Princess May and her husband, and he reminded Princess May that it would be the first time a Princess of Wales had set foot in India. Sir Walter was much impressed by Princess May's knowledge: 'Thanks to the amount of Indian reading which I have done I really am not so ignorant about India as most of the English women here are', wrote Princess May from Agra in December 1905, again to Bricka. 'In fact Sir W. Lawrence told me one day "I consider you have a very good grasp on Indian affairs, quite remarkable in a woman". I felt much flattered & repeat this for yr ears only as you know what trouble I took to get the right books. The religions too

I know something of, Hindu, Mohammedan, & Buddhism. All this knowledge, however small, helps one to take a keen interest in all one sees & I therefore enjoy to the utmost every detail of the wonderful sights.'[48]

Back in London from Abergeldie at the end of September 1905, Princess May also set to work getting clothes for her long and sultry sojourn in the East. 'I am delighted to hear that you have now finished trying on all yr dresses & I hope they fit well', wrote Prince George, in his masculine way. 'In all the papers I see long accounts of them.'[49] Away in Strelitz, Aunt Augusta had also seen, and studied, these long newspaper accounts: 'Your Dresses amuse me to read about; so many too! and *who* is to *pay*? the one for the Tiger hunt gave me the shivers!'[50] On this Indian trip Princess May was once again dogged by royal mourning. This time it was 'beloved Apapa's death' (the demise of the aged King of Denmark) news of which reached them at Mysore in January 1906: 'This event has cast a gloom over our visit here', she wrote to Aunt Augusta, '& we feel so sorry that this should have happened now. . . . It is tiresome too on account of my clothes as I can only wear white now, & all the coloured clothes upon which I had to pay hundreds have had to be put away! Such a waste!'[51]

The battleship HMS *Renown* was in every way an improvement on the *Ophir*, and the journey out was unexpectedly enjoyable to Princess May. From Genoa they went down the Italian coast to the Bay of Naples, and then through the straits of Messina. 'Yesterday morning we steamed thro' the Straits of Messina, & at 10 the Mediterranean Fleet came out to meet us & performed some very pretty manœuvres for our benefit.'[52] This comment indicates the gradual change in Princess May's point of view: the prim, timid girl from White Lodge was now thoroughly accustomed to life on the larger scale. Stranger sights than fleet manœuvres, stranger experiences than any of the *Ophir* tour awaited Princess May in India. 'Fancy you "Miss May" on an Elephant', Queen Alexandra wrote to her daughter-in-law from Sandringham that December of 1905. 'I can hardly [see] you perched up there.'[53]

In the tale of Princess May's development this Indian journey of 1905–1906 is of cardinal importance. Her Household noticed that she was 'quite different in India', and indeed that marvellous sub-continent, with its manifold varieties of scenery, cultures and religions, was to her an astounding revelation. It stirred her emotionally, and it would be no exaggeration to say that Princess May fell in love with India. Ever afterwards a certain dreamy note would enter her voice when she spoke of India: 'lovely India, *beautiful* India', she used to murmur like some incantation. She was never able to adapt her mind to the idea of the constitutional independence granted India in 1947. 'When I die', she remarked at that time, in whimsical reminiscence of Queen Mary Tudor, '*INDIA* will be found written on my heart.'

Princess May had set off for India in a mood which could almost be described as one of gusto. On the last day of September she had made a descent on Portsmouth to look over the *Renown*: 'I am delighted with the "*Renown*" & so will you be,' she wrote to Prince George (who was still at Abergeldie with the children), 'she looks lovely painted white & her boats so smart, white & green. All the cabins are charming & comfortable & are such a success. I am sure you will be pleased—It was lucky I went down as there were several little faults, & things had been forgotten, which make all the difference to one's comfort—When I had finished looking at everything we had tea on deck as it was a nice afternoon & the band played. . . . Altogether I enjoyed my day amongst the *dear* Navy!'[54]

Both during the voyage and in India itself Princess May wrote regularly to her Aunt Augusta, describing how they dined on deck ('which is pleasant') or how in the Suez Canal she watched 'many caravans coming from the East to Cairo, the camels laden with bales & goods, & the hot dusty Beduins walking alongside'.[55] One interesting effect of her unbridled enthusiasm for India and the Indians was that her letters suddenly became far more vivid, and bore much more resemblance to those of her mother Princess Mary Adelaide. The old Grand Duchess noticed this at once, and congratulated her niece, who replied:

I am so glad to know that you like my letters & descriptions from India, for personally I was rather disgusted with my style of letter-writing here. I do not seem to be able to concentrate my thoughts whilst writing, & thus I fancied my letters would seem somewhat disjointed. We travel so fast & see so many beautiful places & scenes, that many things escape my memory whilst writing but as long as you are satisfied all is well.[56]

It is just this absence of concentration, and this disjointedness, that give Princess May's letters from India their life and charm. But she remained unaware of the basic fact that, in letter-writing, spontaneity is all.

During their four months in India, Princess May and Prince George travelled far and wide. Often they slept in their special train, but on numerous other exciting occasions they would be the guests of some Indian prince or English Governor. 'The Maharana with native chiefs met us at the station on Saty & we drove here thro' rows of fine looking retainers, some in old armour, a wonderful scene', Princess May wrote from Udaipur. 'The lovely white Palace stands very well, high up, overlooking 3 lovely lakes with pretty islands dotted about.' 'We are now staying with the nice Maharajah of Bikanir', she wrote again, this time from Gujner. ' . . . we especially admired his fine camel corps. . . . We drove to a charming red sandstone Palace he has built. . . .' 'Here I am in Ld Kitchener's splendid camp for the Manœuvres, the tents are like rooms & even have fireplaces in them & electric light! . . . I saw something of the manœuvres today from an elephant, not a comfortable mode of riding, tho' one sees capitally.' . . . 'Yesterday we had our interesting drive through the Khyber Pass & lunched at the fort at Lundi Kotal'; '48 massed bands played'; 'The Palace at Gwalior is a fine building. . . . The Maharajah showed us his jewels which are really magnificent.'[57] Princess May moved through India as though in a dream; but, enraptured though she might be by the spectacular and luminous beauties of princely life in India, she also insisted on walking *incognita* about the side streets of some big city, looking at the mud dwellings of the poor and making purchases in the shops. 'In this way one sees various phases of the life in this country, thus adding to one's store of knowledge which is always pleasant', she wrote to her Aunt Augusta from Dehra Dun in March 1906. 'It is sad to think that we shall soon be leaving India to which I have become deeply attached.'[58]

Characteristically enough, Princess May also kept herself abreast of English and European news whilst on this Indian tour. 'Just heard that Balfour has resigned', she wrote from Peshawar on 2 December 1905; or 'What a pity Dolphus got into such a mess over Ratzeburg'; or 'Yes I had heard about Cecile's hopes & I believe Charlie's wife is the same. What a pity Alix Schwerin is not. Her sister Marie Louise Baden is, could it only be a son this time & break the Baden curse'; or 'Fancy Dss W. of Mecklenburg dying of over smoking—such a pity people can't do things in moderation'.[59]

After a short visit to Burma, the royal party returned to India, and embarked at Karachi: 'Left our dear train with real regret', Princess May confided to her Letts Diary.[60] 'It all seems like a beautiful dream

& one forgets the small discomforts & the fatigue of it all in the joy of having been able to make that wonderful journey', she wrote to her aunt from Karachi.[61] 'We steamed away about 6 our band playing "for auld lang syne" which was most upsetting. We went on the bridge & watched dear beautiful India vanish from our sight.'[62]

In India Princess May's love of the picturesque and also of the beautiful had been amply satisfied. Her passion for acquiring information was, too, assuaged in India. When she and her husband, in Prince George's words, 'set their heads towards home' they both felt enriched by all that India had shown them. 'Really we left with sincere regret that wonderful country where we have received nothing but kindness & sympathy', wrote Princess May.[63]

CHAPTER THREE

THE LARGER SCALE

———

ON THEIR WAY HOME to England Prince George and Princess May stopped in Cairo for a week: 'I did not ascend the Pyramid, it was too much of a climb', Princess May told her Aunt, 'but I did ride a camel and really rather liked it —The Sphinx I thought most disappointing.'[1] From Cairo they proceeded to Corfu, where they found the King of the Hellenes and were soon joined by King Edward VII, Queen Alexandra and Princess Victoria who were aboard the yacht *Victoria and Albert*. 'You may imagine how pleased we were to see each other again—The King looks well but Motherdear looks very sad & tired after her great sorrow,* however we hope that the air and sunshine out here may do her good. . . . This is a lovely place & when we arrived here we found Uncle Willy here on bd his yacht the "*Amphitrite*" & he has been most kind in arranging expeditions & drives for us in the pretty country which is looking too deliciously green & pretty.'[2]

'Uncle Willy', Queen Alexandra's brother the King of the Hellenes, had withdrawn to his villa on Corfu to avoid the rigours of Passion Week in Athens. So soon as these taxing seven days were over, the King of the Hellenes returned to Athens, his yacht being followed into the Piraeus by HMS *Renown* carrying the Royal party from India. Athens provided what (as we know) Queen Victoria used to call 'a royal mob' of relations. 'Went on bd the Yacht & met all the Greek relations there', Princess May wrote in her Diary. 'U. Willy, At. Olga, Tino & Sophie, George, Nicky & Ellen, Andrea & Alice, Christo, Tino's boy, Louis & Drino Battenberg. Landed with them all & went by train to Athens. Drove to the Palace. Gaily decorated streets, crowds etc. . . . Dined *en famille* at 8.30, 18 of us.'[3]

The day after that of this family gathering, Princess May set about serious sight-seeing in Athens. 'I went with the Tinos & Toria to the beautiful Acropolis & we saw the Parthenon, the Nike Temple, the Propylaea, the Museum etc. Beautiful view from the top', she

---

* i.e. the recent death, in January 1906, of Queen Alexandra's father, King Christian IX of Denmark.

recorded.4 After tea with the Duke and Duchess of Sparta Princess May went to investigate the British School of Archaeology, and to arrange for its director to take her over the Museum the next morning. 'I specially admired a bronze figure of Paris', she noted, '& the small Tanagra figures. There is also a small marble statue of Minerva which is like the colossal statue of Minerva which stood in the Parthenon made of gold & ivory.'5 This morning at the Museum was followed by a visit to the Stadium where the Olympic Games were to be held, a drive to Phaleron Bay and a dinner-party for one hundred and eighty guests in the Palace. The court of Athens was still in mourning for the King of Denmark, father to Queen Alexandra and King George of the Hellenes: 'We ladies all wore high black gowns & long crape veils & looked very lugubrious!' Princess May wrote in her Diary of this slightly massive entertainment. The rest of this short visit to Athens Princess May spent in motoring to Marathon, watching the Olympic Games, looking at Byzantine churches, the theatre of Dionysus and the Theseus Temple. On 24 April they took leave of their relatives at Athens and set out in *Renown*, homeward bound.

II

During the absence in India of Princess May and Prince George their young cousin Ena,* the only daughter of Princess Beatrice, had become engaged to the King of Spain, Alfonso XIII. This marriage, which obliged the bride to change her religion and become a Roman Catholic, aroused all the latent anti-Catholic feeling of a large portion of the English public. 'Beatrice', wrote Prince George in March from Gwalior, where he was on a shooting expedition while Princess May was sight-seeing at Lucknow, 'is advised on her return to England to keep Ena quiet somewhere, at Osborne, & not to bring her to London as the feeling is so strong.'6

'So Ena is to become Spanish Queen! a Battenberg, good gracious!' Princess May's Aunt Augusta had written to her from Strelitz; for Aunt Augusta, we may recall, did not share Queen Victoria's sane views on the subject of morganatic blood. The Spanish courtship had taken place in 'Cousin Lily'—Princess Frederica of Hanover's—villa

---

* The second of the four children of Queen Victoria's youngest daughter and Prince Henry of Battenberg, Princess Victoria-Eugénie, known as 'Ena' in the Royal Family, was born in 1887 and married in 1906, King Alfonso XIII of Spain (1886–1941).

at Biarritz: 'Lily has all the grand affair on hand & it will be a nice expense to her', the old Grand Duchess had added.7 'Did you see that ridiculous Photo of them all, *laughing*, Beatrice leaning down over the young Lovers spreading her arms out like an Eagle, Lily grinning, no, too funny & not Royal!'8 Aunt Augusta asked in another letter. In the old Grand Duchess's eyes the Spanish engagement of 1906 had almost every disadvantage: the Battenberg connection, the change of religion, and the fact that the King of Spain's motor-car had played a much-publicised part in the proceedings at Biarritz. 'Love-making in the Motor-Car, Miss Cochrane as *Elephant* next the Chauffeur, certainly *new* for stiff Spanish Etiquette!'9

Whilst at Gwalior, Prince George had received a letter from his father King Edward, informing him that he might send him as his personal representative to the Madrid wedding at the end of May. Prince George despatched this piece of news to Princess May at Lucknow. 'I do hope that if Papa really sends you to Madrid that I may be allowed to accompany you, it wld be so interesting to see a Spanish King married & then I have known Ena since she was a baby,' she replied, 'you might try & arrange this for me, for I believe I was a help to you at Vienna, wasn't I, & my goodness that was stiff.'10 'Of course darling I would like you to come with me to Madrid,' Prince George answered, 'you are always a help to me anywhere, that you must know.'11 As it turned out the Queen-Mother of Spain, Queen Christina—whom Princess May found 'charming, so nice & dear & Austrian'12—asked King Edward to send Princess May to Madrid with her husband. 'Queen Christina specially asked the King whether I could not go with G—so I feel quite flattered.'13

With a refurbished wardrobe and a bundle of notes on Madrid and on Spanish history provided by Bricka, Princess May set off with her husband and a large suite for Madrid in the last week of May 1906. She had already been to see the future Queen of Spain depart from London: 'This morning', she had written on 24 May to her aunt, 'we all went to see her off, a trying moment for the poor child & I felt so sorry for Aunt Beatrice—I do hope Ena will get on well in Spain, I think she is a sensible girl & may do good there, anyhow she is full of good intentions—but I don't know whether she realises what a difficult future lies before her.'14 'Yes,' replied the old Grand Duchess, 'I am sure Ena has no idea of her *real* future, now all is flowers and cheers! how long will this last in such a Country as Spain?'15 The doubts expressed by both Princess May and her wise old aunt were in fact justified: for the Spanish life of Queen Ena began with an assassination attempt on her wedding-day, and has ended in exile beside the Lake of Geneva.

Princess Marie of Erbach-Schönberg, a Battenberg aunt of Queen Ena, has left, in her excellent book of *Reminiscences*, a long and vivid account of how the Spanish wedding of May 1906 seemed to the foreign royal guests.[16] She has recorded the pageantry and the pomp, the heat and the dust of these days in Madrid; and, of course, the incident of the anarchist's bomb thrown at the royal nuptial coach— which killed many onlookers in the street and on the balconies, smashed the chain of the King's Order on his breast, spattered the bride's wedding dress with blood, and swept all the assembled royalties with panic; all the assembled royalties save Princess May: '[Frederica of Hanover] told me . . . how you were *the* one who had shown proper feeling, in your deportment, when that horrible Bomb was thrown', wrote Aunt Augusta proudly to her niece.[17] 'The wedding atmosphere was, of course, dissipated', writes Princess Marie of Erbach-Schönberg in a somewhat understated passage of her memoirs.

The transport of so many European royalties to Madrid in the dead heat of late May was a problem in itself. Princess Marie of Erbach-Schönberg left Paris with her husband in a *train de luxe*, which also contained the Grand Duke Vladimir of Russia and his suite, and the Prussian, Austrian, French, Swedish and Siamese envoys. At Biarritz the Archduke Franz Ferdinand of Austria was added to the company. 'Everybody was complaining of the *train de luxe*', writes Princess Marie. 'The dirt was indescribable. At eleven o'clock we reached the Spanish frontier, Irun, where we all had to get out to change trains. A lighted waiting-room with sentries before it was prepared presumably for the princely guests, but there was no one there to conduct us to it. We stood about a long while, and gradually other royal personages appeared—Andrew of Greece, Prince Ludwig Ferdinand and Prince Alfons of Bavaria, the Hereditary Prince of Monaco, Prince Friedrich-Heinrich of Prussia, and many suites.' The platform was so badly lit that the royalties found difficulty in recognising one another, and the confusion became 'perfectly indescribable' when another trainload of princely personages came hissing into the wayside station of Irun. Aboard this second *train de luxe* were the Prince and Princess of Wales (Prince George and Princess May), together with Prince Dolly of Teck and his wife, and all their chamberlains, equerries, ladies-in-waiting, dressers and footmen. This arrival was watched by Princess

Marie of Erbach-Schönberg and the Grand Duke Vladimir 'from
amidst the crowd'. After an hour's wait, the combined contents of
these two trains were packed into a new, Spanish, *train de luxe*, and
whirled off through the hot night towards Madrid. 'At midnight,'
records Princess Marie of Erbach-Schönberg, 'we all met in the dining-
car and tried to refresh ourselves with cooling drinks.' They reached
Madrid at three p.m. of the next day: 'Red carpets, guards of honour,
anthems, uniforms of every description, attachés with gold-embroi-
dered coats. The Infanta Maria Thérèse, sister of the King, with her
husband, greeted us, also Don Carlos of Bourbon, the widower of the
Princess of Asturias. The departure of the guards of honour followed
a long wait in the *salon*, until by degrees all the royal personages with
their escorts had driven away.'

Next came the drive 'through a not very pretty part of the town' to
the Palacio Real—a' brightly illuminated palace, which dominates the
town like a colossus'. The long procession of carriages wound its way
uphill through ornamental gardens and, by way of 'splendid wrought-
iron gates' into the great courtyard in which, amidst the deafening
sound of braying trumpets and beating drums, troops of soldiers
were drawn up. Each carriage-load of arrivals was greeted by lords-
in-waiting and halberdiers, to the strains of the appropriate national
anthem, and then conducted to the peristyle of the staircase, where
they found the young King, his mother, the rest of the Spanish royal
family and those guests who had already arrived. They were then
marshalled in procession and taken through rows of ladies-in-waiting
in full evening dress, into the great reception rooms. 'The heat was
indescribable and Prince Albrecht of Prussia . . . fainted.'

Prince George and Princess May were, of course, amongst the few
privileged personages who were actually lodged in the Palacio Real
—envoys of lesser status being boarded out in the other palaces and the
Grandees' houses of the city. Princess May was fascinated by the
Spanish court, beside which the Imperial Court of Vienna seemed
positively modern—for, in the Palacio Real in Madrid, there reigned
an etiquette which had not been altered since the reign of Philip II.
She and Prince George were lodged in 'cathedral-high' apartments,
to and from which they were solemnly conducted by a Spanish Duke
before and after every meal and every ceremony or entertainment.
Vast marble colonnades stretched before them in every direction. The
doors of each room were guarded by halberdiers with pikes. As the
Prince and Princess of Wales left their apartments an official would

clap his hands, and every halberdier would present arms, passing from one to another the cry: '*Arriba Princesa! Arriba Principe!!*' This sixteenth-century routine appealed strongly to Princess May's vivid historical imagination.

The morning of the wedding-day, 31 May 1906, dawned warm and golden. In the great courtyard of the Palacio Real, beneath a cerulean sky, the forty state coaches waiting for the guests lumbered round and round, each drawn by six white or six black horses carrying nodding crests of pink or orange ostrich plumes upon their heads. The procession went at a foot's pace to the small old Gothic church of St Hieronimo, which has a long flight of steps (on this occasion covered with scarlet carpets and with flowers) leading up to it. The Prince and Princess of Wales were in the front row of pews, the King of Spain sitting awaiting his bride upon a royal throne set at right-angles to the altar.

It was on the way back from the ceremony that Morales tossed his bomb—a small, black, smoking, insignificant-looking object, which was seen dropping from a window in the Calle Mayor, just as the coach containing the King and his bride was passing the Italian Embassy. Aimed at the roof of the royal coach, the bomb fell ahead of this, and landed amongst the six sleek and caparisoned horses which were slowly drawing the vehicle through the dense, vociferous crowds. The Marchesa di Tolosa and her child, who were watching from a balcony, were killed outright; so were many people in the crowd and several soldiers; all that was found of one of the footmen on the royal carriage was his boots. Amidst scenes of uproar the King and Queen, pallid, shaken and covered with blood and bomb-splinters, scrambled down from their carriage and mounted into the *coche de respetto*, an empty coach which (by tradition) followed immediately behind theirs. In this they proceeded to the Palacio Real. When she got back to the Palace, to be received by her horrified mother and the great number of royalties there assembled, Queen Ena could only repeat again and again: 'I saw a man without any legs! I saw a man without any legs!'

The family luncheon which followed the wedding ceremony was feverish and gloomy. No one could eat anything and, in Princess Marie of Erbach-Schönberg's words, 'every attempt at cheerfulness failed miserably'. Aunt Marie Edinburgh-Coburg who was in Madrid with her youngest daughter Baby Bee, did not enliven the proceedings by 'heavily repeating' in French: '*Moi, je suis tellement accoutumée à ces sortes de choses*'—for Aunt Marie was, as we may remember, a Russian, and had lost both her father and her brother by anarchists' bombs. It was not just the shock of the attempt on the life of the young King and Queen; the rumour was buzzing around the luncheon table that the assassin had tried to get into the church with his bomb concealed in a bouquet of flowers. The church of St Hieronimo is small, and it is unlikely that, had Morales succeeded, any of the more distinguished guests would have escaped alive. Luncheon over, the royalties retired to their rooms to telegraph news of their own safety to their nearest and dearest. Princess May telegraphed to her Aunt Augusta.

Dearly loved May! [wrote the Grand Duchess] I am so horror stricken that I really don't know what to write; it is all too terrible, too awful, to think what *has* happened & what *might* have befallen *you!* poor Ena too! the *most* endangered! . . . I am feeling so anxious all along! I am sure your stay at Madrid has been interesting but in what terrible danger you ever were floating![18]

Princess May, who earned the admiration of her suite and of the other royalties by her calm demeanour at this dreadful time, replied to her aunt:

. . . well we have been thro' a most unpleasant experience & we can only thank God that the anarchist did not get into the church in which case we must all have been blown up! Nothing could have been braver than the young couple were, but what a beginning for her. . . . I saw the coach one day, still with blood on the wheels & behind where the footmen were standing—apart from the horror of this awful attempt the visit to Madrid was most interesting but oh! the heat was nearly as bad as India & made one feel quite exhausted. . . . I liked seeing the fine pictures, palace, Escurial, Armoury etc.[19]

None of the royal guests much enjoyed the next days in Madrid. The would-be assassin was not found for seventy-two hours, the police precautions were woefully inadequate—'*damn* these Police!' the Prince of Wales was heard to exclaim—and the public seemed permitted to roam at will about the colonnades of the Palacio Real, and almost into the very apartments of the apprehensive foreign guests.

The visit to Madrid had been interesting, but it had also proved what Princess May called 'unpleasant'. Everyone was rather glad to leave. 'This fortnight', the Archduke Franz Ferdinand remarked to

Princess Marie of Erbach-Schönberg, on leaving Madrid, 'has been equivalent to a campaign.'

III

One week after their safe return from the Madrid wedding, Prince George and Princess May set off once again on their travels, this time aboard the Royal Yacht *Victoria and Albert*, and headed for the fjords of Norway, to attend the coronation at Trondheim of the Norwegian King and Queen. 'A letter this time from the far North!' wrote Princess May to her Aunt Augusta, 'how we do travel about to be sure. . . . We had lovely weather at first but then it turned cold & we had much wind & rain which was unpleasant for landing from the yacht in evening dress when the boat jumps up & down!'[20]

The King and Queen of Norway were new, and so was their kingdom. United to Sweden for ninety-one years, the Norwegians had won their independence in 1905, when the Union was dissolved. There was then the question: should Norway become a kingdom or a republic? After some hesitation, and under the influence of Kaiser Wilhelm II, a royal but democratic constitution was agreed upon, and Prince Charles of Denmark, the second son of the King of Denmark, was elected to the throne under the title of King Haakon VII—or, as Aunt Augusta preferred to call it, 'Hakoon VII'. Prince Charles, as we know, had married Princess Maud of Wales, the favourite sister-in-law of Princess May. It was to see this couple crowned in the old Gothic cathedral of the little northern town of Trondheim that Prince George and Princess May had now come north. As there were no hotels in Trondheim, they lived aboard their yacht. The only other royal representatives at this homely coronation were the Grand Duke Michael of Russia, Prince Friedrich-Heinrich of Prussia and the Crown Prince and Crown Princess of Denmark— 'being', as Princess May explained to her aunt, 'the only people who have yachts.'[21]

To the old Grand Duchess of Mecklenburg-Strelitz, and indeed to Princess May herself, the idea of an elected Monarch seemed a contradiction in terms: 'too horrible', wrote Aunt Augusta, 'for an English Princess to sit upon a Revolutionary Throne!' 'So Maud is sitting on her very unsafe throne—to say the least of it', she wrote in another letter, 'he making speeches, poor fellow, thanking the revolutionary Norwegians for having *elected* him! no really, it is all too odd!'

' "Motherdear" will not like it either', she added, 'besides they have but that one *peaky* Boy.'[22] Aunt Augusta did not at all approve of Prince George and Princess May attending the Trondheim coronation: 'A *revolutionary* Coronation! such a *farce*, *I* don't like your being there for it, it looks like *sanctioning* all that nasty Revolution. . . . What a whirl of things of all kinds, you will have in your brains! people, Countries, climates etc., and how will you ever find your way through them all? only, that you have an extraordinarily well-shaped mind, so can weather all these various impressions.' 'How', Aunt Augusta again enquired, 'can a future *K*. & *Q*. of *E*. go to witness a Coronation *"par la grace du Peuple et de la Révolution"*!!! makes me sick and I should say, *you too*.'[23] 'The whole thing', Princess May replied, 'seems curious, but we live in *very* modern days.'[24]

Like her sisters, Princess Louise, Duchess of Fife (whom her father King Edward VII had now created Princess Royal) and Princess Victoria, Queen Maud of Norway suffered from congenitally delicate health. In her case this took the form of nagging neuralgia, together with a weakness in the legs which rendered her incapable of walking in solemn procession to the cathedral at Trondheim to be crowned. None the less, she played her part in the ceremony well. 'The Coronation ceremony', wrote her sister-in-law, Princess May, 'was fine & impressive—Very well done & both Charles & Maud did it all in a dignified manner & both looked very well with the Crowns on their heads. The Norwegians seem to be nice friendly people & are very enthusiastic and Charles & Maud appear to get on very well with them all. They have such a nice entourage. . . .'[25]

Princess May liked Norway. 'Norway is certainly a grand country & the scenery is so beautiful, a mixture of Scotland & Switzerland', she wrote. The innocent and placid little town of Trondheim, straggling along its fjord, and with the spire of the only Gothic cathedral in the far north of Europe soaring above the flowering cherry-trees, also pleased her: 'The shops here are charming & I have bought some very nice furs, enamelled things & china.'[26] On their arrival at Trondheim in the *Victoria and Albert* they had anchored off the island of Ravnkloa in the Trondheim Fjord. The King and Queen of Norway, with their little son Prince Olaf, came aboard the *Victoria and Albert* off a royal launch, the King wearing the uniform of a British admiral and the Order of the Bath. As King Haakon stepped aboard, the British yacht hoisted the Norwegian flag to the sound of martial music and the hoarse murmur of the cheering crowds of Trondheim citizens lining the distant shore. Princess May had had the sensible idea of bringing her young daughter Princess Mary with her to Trondheim. Princess Mary was nine years old and this was her first trip abroad. 'Little Olav is a dear,' wrote Princess May, 'he has fallen in love with my Mary who is rather shy & blushes at his advances, she is happy as the day is long at being with us here & we actually took her to the Coronation & she behaved quite beautifully thro' the long service.'[27]

In Kristiania (now Oslo), their capital, the new King and Queen of Norway had the immense pilastered Kongens Slot (or Royal Palace) at their disposal, but in Trondheim there had been no royal residence, and a charming, roomy frame-building, the Stiftsgaarden, had been quickly renovated for them before the Coronation. '[Charles and Maud] have quite a nice house in the town but it is too small to put anyone up, it has been charmingly furnished & done up for them as a present from the people here',[28] wrote Princess May. After a fortnight of festivities in Trondheim, including displays of *Heil-Gymnastik*, a choir of school-children, and a '*defilir cour*' at which six hundred persons passed before the King and Queen of Norway, the English Royal party steamed off through the fjords, where Prince George went fishing, whilst Princess May admired the dramatic scenery of this part of Norway.

On the free and easy ladies of the Norwegian court Princess May created a 'rather stiff' impression. They were surprised to find she was unable to converse with them in Swedish or Norwegian, but judged her to be impressive, elegant and '*imposant*'—a Norwegian adjective implying natural dignity. They particularly admired her pale embroidered gowns and fine jewels.

IV

Back home from the Norwegian coronation, Princess May retired to Frogmore House, while Prince George went racing at Newmarket and Goodwood, and, subsequently, yachting at Cowes. The remainder of the year was occupied by the customary routine migrations: from Frogmore to London, from London to Scotland, from Scotland to London again, from London to Sandringham for the family festivities at Christmas. Before proceeding to Sandringham, Princess May went to pay a visit to her friends Lord and Lady Mount Stephen, at their beautiful Jacobean house, Brocket Hall in Hertfordshire. This couple played an important role in a side of Princess May's life which was now becoming increasingly important to her: her passion for collecting objects, and, specifically, objects connected with the history of the Guelph family—a passion which she once described as 'my one great hobby'.[29]

This love of collecting, which Princess May had inherited from her father and in which she was warmly encouraged both by her brother Prince Dolly and by her old Aunt Augusta, was now developing into a guiding interest. It appealed to her historical sense, to her liking for order and for cataloguing; it also formed an antidote to, and an outlet from, more wearying sides of Princess May's daily round. For the years 1906 to 1910 were not exciting years for the Prince and Princess of Wales. As we have learned, they felt no special sympathy for the social side of the Edwardian epoch; nor did King Edward VII, kindly and affable though he invariably was towards his son and his daughter-in-law, allow them any very tempting share in public life during his reign.

On 26 May 1907 Princess May celebrated her fortieth birthday. Her character was by now set in its final mould, but she continued to extend the frontiers of her knowledge of intellectual and artistic things, and she now diligently began to build up those collections for which she was afterwards famous. In this work two of her strongest supporters, and also benefactors, were Lord and Lady Mount Stephen.

Princess May's long friendship with Lady Mount Stephen dated from the days of her earliest youth. Born Gian Tufnell, Lady Mount Stephen was the niece of that same Giana, Lady Wolverton, who had been the Tecks' neighbour at Coombe, had founded the Needlework Guild, had taken the villa at Cannes to which the Duchess of Teck and her daughter had retreated after Prince Eddy's death in 1892, and had in many other ways aided the Duchess of Teck both with her numerous charities and in her periodic financial landslides. Gian Tufnell had become the Duchess of Teck's second lady-in-waiting in 1895, and had in 1897, suddenly and very much to everyone's surprise, married the Canadian railway millionaire Lord Mount Stephen, a man many years her senior. She was one of Princess May's few really intimate friends, for they were bound to one another by the strongest of all ties in friendship—a common memory of much past happiness amongst those now dead. With Lady Mount Stephen, Princess May could recall the life at White Lodge, with all its ups and downs; the wit, vitality and benevolence of the Duchess of Teck; the gay sojourns and the laughter at St Moritz; the whole fabric, in fact, of her own lost youth. Blessed with wealth as great as her knowledge of works of art,

Lady Mount Stephen helped Princess May in her collecting in much the same way that her aunt Lady Wolverton had helped the Duchess of Teck in other directions.

With a heart full of gratitude I gaze upon that splendid & interesting collection of silver which belonged to my Great Aunt [wrote Princess May in a letter typical in its tone of her extensive correspondence with Lady Mount Stephen]. Many many affect. thanks for this beautiful gift which is so much appreciated by me—Then the little Wedgwood scent bottle is so pretty, I have never seen one like it, a delightful addition to my room at Windsor—no one will notice the crack![30]

'I am delighted', she wrote in another letter, 'with the beautiful Enamel of George IV and thank you most gratefully for it, a charming addition to what I consider is your & "dear George's" collection'; or 'The Battersea tea caddy is too lovely and will go so well with my pale blue collection.' Sometimes Lady Mount Stephen was not so successful:

It was too dear of you trying to get it for me [Princess May, by then Queen Mary, wrote of a portrait of Charles II which came up at Sotheby's auction rooms in September 1920] but one really cannot give these ridiculous prices for the sake of sentiment for it was not a beautiful picture, merely interesting, however my gratitude is none the less warm—I too find it difficult to pick up anything of historical interest except by paying huge sums & then the things are not worth it which is annoying to my business like mind, a sentiment which 'dear George' will highly approve of!!![31]

Lady Mount Stephen's role in the life of her Royal friend was not merely the easy one of a benefactor; they would discuss sale-rooms and galleries, exchange marked sale catalogues, and pore over each other's newest acquisitions with the zeal of true collectors. 'It was such a pleasure showing you my rooms on Sunday as you are so very appreciative of detail & worthy of all the beautiful objects which are ever a constant joy to me', Queen Mary wrote in 1914. 'It always seems strange to me that there can be people to whom these things mean & say nothing to them, I confess I pity them as they miss much in life.'[32]

A pioneer amongst the modern Royal Family in this field—she herself felt that one would have to look back to Queen Caroline, wife of George II, to find a Royalty in England who would have fully approved her taste—Princess May was also imbued with a missionary spirit. 'The charming little George IV pocket book & the frame with the commemoration of the Pce & Pss of Wales' marriage I shall give to my eldest son as I am doing all I can to encourage his collecting family things', she wrote, again to Gian Mount Stephen.33 'Happily I have induced George to get almost as keen as I am about family things which I know you will be glad to hear of',34 she wrote about her husband to Aunt Augusta.

The commencement of this large collection of objects and pictures of Royal historical interest may be said to date from the gradual dispersal of the old Duke of Cambridge's effects by his sons the FitzGeorges in the years immediately following his death in 1904. As we have seen, the Duke of Cambridge had made no catalogue; and as the fine family plate, the miniatures, the jewelled snuff-boxes turned up piecemeal in the sale-rooms, Princess May was often bewildered. 'Oh! dear, oh! dear if only I could find the history of all these things, how interesting it wld be, but alas there is no inventory, nothing', Princess May wrote to her Aunt Augusta in 1909. 'I am very busy now seeing that our various inventories are correct & that everything is entered as far as possible with its history. It is really rather wonderful what we have managed to collect & get together since we married, quite a creditable collection of family things and of others, without spending much money over it. I confess I feel rather proud of our endeavours I hope you won't laugh at me.'35 'You really are doing a good work in trying to *save* as many historical as family relics, as other objects relating to our Family or History',36 Aunt Augusta replied.

Both as Princess of Wales and as Queen Consort, Princess May's instincts were in essence conservative; she would never, for instance, have dreamed of initiating a collection of contemporary pictures (most of which she indeed abhorred). Her aim was to preserve as much of the old world of manners and traditions as was possible, before all was engulfed in oblivion by the swift developments of modern times. This passion for conservation and for order was manifest in all her activities—she would pull ivy off a wall to preserve its seventeenth-century brickwork, and in the Second World War she set to work with a will at Badminton (where she was then living as the guest of her niece's husband the Duke of Beaufort) to promote locally every form of government salvage campaign. To collect, to preserve, to docket, to tidy and to put in order were primary objectives all through her life.

In this great task of the visual documentation of the history of the English Royal Family, Princess May was initially handicapped by two factors—the lack of interest of the other members of the family then living, and her own patchy knowledge. The first handicap she ignored, and, as we have just seen, she even managed to fire her husband with an intermittent interest in family things. The second handicap she surmounted by studious reading, by making full use of her prodigious memory, and by taking every opportunity to look at the collections of continental royal relations:

I quite forgot to tell you [she wrote to her Aunt Augusta in April 1908, recounting a visit to the Grand Duke of Hesse-Darmstadt-and-by-the-Rhine] that when Ernie showed me the old Schloss at Darmstadt which he has arranged very well in suites of rooms of different periods of German style, furniture, pictures etc. (family things of course) all to correspond, I was thrilled at finding a picture of Gdmama's grandparents of Nassau Usingen, as also a picture of Landgravine Mary's husband with the Garter, also with his Darmstadt wife & of her Mother, these I recognised from yr Strelitz pictures, Ernie was delighted at my keenness & interest & told Mossy I was 'splendid' in my knowledge of history!!! You will laugh at me & think my head is being turned in my old age of nearly 41—but as I feel about 25 I don't mind.37

This predominant interest in family relics, or in pictures depicting earlier English and German royalties, undoubtedly impeded Princess May's appreciation of the greatest works of art. It has been said that art to her meant iconography—and royal iconography at that. On a tour of the magnificent collection of pictures at Petworth House, for example, the picture which interested her most was one by an indifferent artist depicting the Apotheosis of Princess Charlotte. Moreover, since her stay as a young girl in Florence from 1883 to 1885, Princess May had had limited opportunities to develop a connoisseur's eye. Apart from Madame Bricka, who was not interested in works of art at all, there had been no strong instructive influence to mould Princess May's mind. All she knew she had herself acquired by painstaking reading and careful observation, by cross-examining museum curators, art-dealers and collectors whenever these crossed her path. To take an analogy from another art, that of literature, it is relevant to note that she first saw *Hamlet* given on the stage when she was seventy-seven, and that she was first enthralled by the novels of Tolstoy and of Dostoievsky when she was over eighty years of age.

In the public mind the interests and predilections of royal persons become automatically magnified. Thus the legend of Queen Mary's infallible knowledge of works of art and objects of virtu is a trifle exaggerated—as she, in her sincerely unpretentious way, would have been the first to acknowledge. She gained a thorough acquaintanceship with English Royal iconography of the eighteenth and nineteenth centuries; she could usually identify the better-known marks on English china, and could recognise, in furniture, the works of Hepplewhite or Chippendale; but she never bought a good painting in her life.

To maintain a just and balanced vision of the life of Princess May in early middle age, it is however essential to bear in mind this crescent passion for family history and for discovering and retrieving objects dispersed from the Royal collections in the past. This passion provided her with an absorbing hobby, a ceaseless and zestful amusement, and incidentally enriched the Royal collections with many first-rate pieces of furniture or plate which had been lost to them through historical upheavals, or by mere negligence in years gone by. Concurrently with this main interest Princess May indulged in the subsidiary one of accumulating articles of lesser value which appealed to her personal taste: Battersea enamels, late jades, miniature elephants of agate with jewelled howdahs, small tea-sets in gold or silver, *papier-mâché* workboxes, tiny water-colours of flower-gardens, glass paintings and so on. By these more heterogeneous collections she expressed her innate love of detail. They provided her with many happy hours.

v

The visit to Darmstadt during which Princess May had surprised her cousin the Grand Duke by her knowledge of family history occurred in March 1908. It immediately followed on a two-day visit to Cologne, where Prince George inspected his Cuirassier Regiment while his wife examined the Cathedral Treasury and the other sights of the old Rhenish city. From Cologne they proceeded to Paris, where they stayed a fortnight. This Parisian interlude was not an occasion of State —but all the same it was a symptom of the anxious political situation in Europe; England and France, for their own safety, were now drawing closer together. Another outward manifestation of this fact soon appeared in London in the shape of the Franco-British Exhibition at Shepherd's Bush, which Prince George opened in May 1908 in pouring rain.

In Paris Princess May indulged her love of sight-seeing to her heart's content. She visited the Louvre, the Panthéon, the Musée des Arts Decoratifs, St Etienne du Mont and many other places of note, sometimes with her husband but more often alone. She even drove as far afield as Chartres Cathedral to see 'its very fine windows'. With her innate impatience over 'trying-on' at dressmakers, she refused all the tempting offers of the greatest Parisian *couturières*, and concentrated on doing as much sight-seeing as she could. This holiday in Paris was, in fact, one of Princess May's very last journeys abroad; for her husband's accession to the throne in 1910, combined with his genuine hatred of continental travel, kept her in England. Moreover, the outbreak of the First World War in 1914 precluded her for four long years from visiting the Continent, save to make a tour of British war hospitals. The continental phase of her life which had begun with her first visit to Rumpenheim as a child of five months, was closing.

Although from now on circumstances thus prevented Princess May from indulging in continental sight-seeing, she continued to widen her knowledge of the houses, cathedrals, abbeys and churches of her own country. Each year she would go to stay with friends in the country for a few days—with the Shaftesburys at St Giles in Dorset, for example, or with the Mount Stephens at Brocket Hall. Her intense interest in the past made her an easy guest to entertain: in five days at the Shaftesburys' house in October 1908 she thoroughly examined Romsey Abbey, Winchester Cathedral and College, Castle Hall, Kingston Lacey, Sherborne Castle and Sherborne Abbey, Cranborne Manor, Christchurch, Somerley and St Cross. Equally, she began about this time a diligent study of places of interest in London itself—partly for her own amusement, partly to show her children such sights as the Tower, Westminster Abbey, St Paul's, the Soane Museum and the many churches built by Sir Christopher Wren within the City precincts. During this same period she would also go to the theatre and to the Opera some thirty-five or forty times a year, for she had inherited her mother's passion for the stage. Some of these theatre visits were to charity matinées, but on the whole they were made for pleasure, and they were thoughtfully chosen so that Prince George, who did not care for the serious drama, should not be bored:

I have been doing some rather nice things this week [she wrote about this time to her Aunt Augusta]. I visited the old Charterhouse buildings in the City dating from the 18th century, quite an interesting old place. Then we went to the Record Office where we saw some wonderful old archives, papers, books & so forth, & the Domesday book. . . . The King has nearly got rid of the cold he could not shake off in London & seemed much better. Friday we had a Matinée in aid of a children's home I am interested in, a great success & we got £870—Yesterday I visited the Incurable Hospital at Putney, so you see I am fairly busy & in an energetic mood!³⁸

In the last three years of King Edward VII's reign, his bronchial colds, sometimes accompanied by sudden fainting fits, became more frequent and recalcitrant. The political situation, both at home and abroad, also worried him to a degree that undoubtedly affected his health. To some of his family, who witnessed the terrible fits of breathlessness which seized him, it appeared that the end of his reign could not be far distant—yet when this came, it seemed as abrupt and shocking as death always does. For Prince George and Princess May the King's death was particularly to be dreaded, for it would thrust them from a peaceful and semi-private existence into one of shadow-less limelight and awe-inspiring responsibility. When King Edward VII did in fact die, on 6 May 1910, Prince George's sense of loss and sorrow was made still harder to bear by his own fears of his inadequacy for the position he had now to fill. In this crisis of his life he had two supports—his secretary Sir Arthur Bigge; and his calm devoted wife, Princess May.

To Princess May the opening of the year 1910 seemed little different from the opening of the year 1909. At Marlborough House, that February, she was busy reading books about Africa, for a journey to that continent was planned for her husband and herself in August. Princess May wrote to Bricka that she found it difficult to become really interested in Africa: '*Franchement cela m'ennuit, il n'y a pas de traditions, rien qui vous attire—Mais il faut bien en savoir quelque-chose, je ne veux pas paraître comme une ignorante! Oh, celà par exemple non!!!*'³⁹ In March she visited the Aeroplane Exhibition and saw an aeroplane in flight; in April she went to the Private View of the Royal Academy. The King was also at this Private View; he had returned from Biarritz the day before, after yet another alarming bronchial attack, of which, however, he had made light. On 1 May he took his son and daughter-in-law—Queen Alexandra being at Corfu—to the Opera to see an indifferent performance of *Rigoletto*. The next day Princess May went with her sons to Westminster Abbey, where Archdeacon Wilberforce showed them the remains of the Saxon pillars of Edward the Confessor's church by the light of a lantern. The day after this was the anniversary of the engagement of Prince George and Princess May seventeen years before; she took her sons to tea at Kew, and then to the Palace Theatre to see the Russian dancers. On 4 May there is the first mention in Princess May's Diary of any real anxiety about the King: 'We felt very much worried about Papa.' On 5 May the whole Wales family went to Victoria Station to welcome Queen Alexandra and Princess Victoria, who had posted back on receipt of the bad news about King Edward. At ten o'clock in the morning of 6 May Prince George went to the Palace and stayed there all day, sending for his wife at seven o'clock that evening. At a quarter before midnight King Edward VII died quietly while oxygen was being administered. 'What a loss to the Nation & to us all. God help us—We left the Palace soon after 12', Princess May records. 'Mama bore up wonderfully & never left Papa's side.'⁴⁰ 'I have lost my best friend & the best of fathers', Prince George wrote in his Diary. 'I never had a word with him in my life. I am heart-broken and overwhelmed with grief but God will help me in my great responsibilities & darling May will be my comfort as she has always been.'⁴¹

Thus, in the short space of two days, was the whole structure of Princess May's life irrevocably changed. That for which her mother Princess Mary Adelaide had hoped and prayed, that for which Queen Victoria had shrewdly planned, that which the old Grand Duchess of Mecklenburg-Strelitz had often pictured to herself in happy day-dreams in her boudoir in the Schloss at Strelitz, was now suddenly an accomplished fact. Princess May was Queen Consort of Great Britain and Ireland and of the British Dominions beyond the Seas, Empress of India.

From Strelitz the Grand Duchess sent a letter post-haste to the new Queen's brother Dolly: 'She will', wrote Aunt Augusta, 'indeed be a Queen!'⁴²

BOOK FOUR

QUEEN MARY

1910–1953

CHAPTER ONE

'NO BED OF ROSES'

T HE NEW KING, who was proclaimed under the style of King George V at St James's Palace at nine o'clock on the morning of 9 May 1910—a ceremony which he and his family watched 'from the boys' window' at Marlborough House across the way—was a man of firm principle and also of fixed prejudices. One of these prejudices was a hatred of everything complex, including double names: he had always pitied his brother Prince Eddy for having been publicly known as Prince Albert Victor and subsequently created Duke of Clarence and Avondale. In the same way he had never liked the fact that his wife 'May' signed letters and official papers with her first two names: Victoria Mary. He now told her that as Queen she must drop one or other of these names. They both of them agreed that she could not very well be called Queen Victoria and so she was styled Queen Mary. 'I hope you approve of my new name Mary', she wrote to her Aunt Augusta on 15 May 1910. 'George dislikes double names & I could not be Victoria, but it strikes me as curious to be rechristened at the age of 43.' The name of Princess May must, therefore, now disappear from our text, to be replaced by that of Queen Mary. But we must not forget that this change of name implies no change of character: the regal figure known to posterity as Queen Mary remained Princess May at heart: the girl from White Lodge, the Duchess of York, the Princess of Wales and Queen Mary are the same individual whose life we have been slowly tracing. They are all one and all of a piece.

'Yes,' Queen Mary continued in the same letter from Marlborough House to her old aunt, 'I regret the quieter, easier time we had, everything will be more difficult now & more ceremonious & I dread leaving this *beautiful* old house which I love. I do truly regret your not being able to come to England now, there is so much we could talk over together. I am sorry you have a gumboil.'

Both King George and Queen Mary found the opening weeks of the new reign nerve-racking. There was in the first place the late

King's funeral to be organised and attended; the many foreign royalties who came over for this function had to be suitably received, and entertained. The widowed Queen Alexandra made things no easier by insisting at this funeral upon a precedence which was not hers by right; in this she was supported by her sister the Dowager Empress of All the Russias, who had come to London for three months and was insisting that at the court of St Petersburg the Dowager Tsarina held precedence over the wife of the reigning Tsar. On this point of precedence at the funeral, Queen Mary naturally and typically gave way to her mother-in-law; but it proved to be only the first of a multitude of small difficulties which Queen Alexandra kept raising at her sister's instigation. Until the arrival in London of the Dowager Empress—'Aunt Minny'—everything had gone smoothly. Queen Mary wrote discreetly to her Aunt Augusta, explaining how Aunt Minny's presence impeded plans and arrangements, since the Dowager Empress took her widowed sister down to Sandringham, where they stayed virtually *incommunicada*. 'I understand every word, expressed & *not*, & have *feared*, what you so gently allude to!' the old Grand Duchess answered. 'May that pernicious influence soon depart!'[1]

'I confess', Queen Mary wrote in another letter to Strelitz just three weeks after King Edward's death, 'I am now very tired after the strain of the past weeks & now as you know come all the disagreeables, so much to arrange, so much that must be changed, most awkward & unpleasant for both sides, if only things can be managed without having rows, but it is difficult to get a certain person to see things in their right light. Everything at this moment appears to me to be chaos & with my methodical mind I suffer in proportion, no doubt some day all will be right again but for the time being everything seems unsettled & upset. You will as usual enter into my feelings & know what I am going through. It is a pity in some ways being so sensitive because one suffers so much more, still I suppose it makes one better able to understand other people & to enter into their feelings.'[2] Once again, her youthful training in tact at White Lodge was proving invaluable.

In his will King Edward VII had left Sandringham House to his widow for her lifetime. In London the Queen Dowager agreed to retire from the Palace to live once more at Marlborough House, but she would not say when this move was liable to take place; for difficult as it had been to persuade Queen Alexandra to move into Buckingham Palace in 1902, it was now just as difficult to persuade her to move out of it again in 1910. The jewels of the Queen Consort provided another vexation: 'Alix retaining *the* lovely little Crown I do not approve of', wrote the Grand Duchess. 'Oh! were *I* there instead of Minny!! more I dare not say.'³ Queen Alexandra was not acting from any motive of small-minded jealousy, indeed she seemed not to be acting from any positive or identifiable motive at all: 'the odd part', wrote Queen Mary, 'is that the person causing the delay & trouble remains supremely unconscious as to the inconvenience it is causing, such a funny state of things & everyone seems afraid to speak.'⁴

Apart from these tiresome family difficulties, Queen Mary found herself faced by a cohort of questions—some important, some trifling —demanding an answer. Complaining once more to her aunt, of the 'hourly interruptions' to which both she and King George were now being subjected she wrote: 'There is nothing more fatiguing & quite wears one out. It is far less tiring to work at one thing for 3 hours than to have to turn one's thoughts to different subjects every few minutes, jumping from an important subject, to some minor one, & vice versa, oh! I know it well. . . . Here we continue to have cold weather, we are very busy with dull things of all kinds, getting on *very* slowly with business, *not* very lively & I wish the old life were coming back, I don't like this, anyhow as it is at present, perhaps some day it may be better, at least I hope so.'⁵ 'The position', she wrote a few weeks later to her aunt, 'is no bed of roses.'⁶

The position of Queen Consort was not only no bed of roses, its scope had never been officially defined. It was, so to speak, whatever you felt inclined, or had the ability, to make it. Queen Charlotte had concentrated on domesticity and the upbringing of her very large family. The Queen of George IV, who had never, in any case, sat beside him on the throne, had been noticeably undomesticated. Queen Adelaide, another German, had not made much impression upon her husband's subjects' consciousness. Queen Alexandra had been decorative and generous and gay. What would Queen Mary do? How would she interpret her role as Queen Consort? To those who knew her at all this was not an open question.

We noticed, many chapters back, at the time of Princess May's engagement to Prince Eddy, that she was not of a passionate nature. Yet she was, in fact, consumed by one single abstract passion, which ruled her life, and dictated her whole conduct in her new position. This was her passion for the British Monarchy. The fact that the new King-Emperor was her husband and her cousin—the 'Georgie' she had known since childhood—in no way diminished in her eyes the lofty, solitary splendour that invested the person of the Monarch. From now on she sacrificed everything to his needs and to the preservation of his peace of mind, thinking of him before she thought of anyone else, her children and, of course, herself, included. Queen Mary was not in the least afraid of her husband, but she would no longer contradict him even in the family circle; she would no longer protest save in private or by letter when he was unfair to one or other of his sons, or lost his temper with any of them. That power of absolute concentration upon a single objective which she had first displayed during the Australian tour of 1901 she now brought permanently to bear upon the King's daily life. The tact which she had acquired as a youthful intermediary between her mother and her father during their wrangles at White Lodge was now devoted to smoothing the King's path. She believed that all should defer to the King's slightest wish, and she made herself into a living example of her creed. Outwardly this was not a spectacular part to play. Inwardly it required a constant and dramatic exercise of imagination, foresight and self-control.

This sublimation of herself to her ideal of the British Crown meant that Queen Mary would often be misjudged and rated 'dull' and 'cold' —for her reserve of manner was now as great as ever, indeed it became greater than before. In a letter to Lady Eva Dugdale, written a few days after Princess May had become Queen Mary, the old Dowager of Mecklenburg-Strelitz recalled for how many years her niece had remained shy and reserved:

She never 'came out' however being very reserved, as she had to be, until later, nor did I realise or get to know her real character, until she came to me in 1898, a real Angel of mercy at that terribly sad and trying time for me;* then only did I find in her, all that is wonderfully combined in her whole being! the warm heart, the clear, good and quiet judgement in all things, her gentle reserve and yet coming forward when it was right, I not only loved, I respected and admired in her all the great qualities she possesses, then by degrees felt more & more, that she would some day fill her place and be a real Queen as she must be! I have not mentioned how greatly her intellect, her knowledge of History etc. enhances all the rest for this you know, as you do what I have written above, yet to write or really describe or judge such a character in full, is more than I am able to do. In all my grief it is to me an immense relief to read and hear her named and praised.7

* The Grand Duchess was, of course, referring to Princess May's visit to Mentone at the time of the Neu Strelitz scandal over the Duchess Marie.

We may note here that Queen Mary herself considered that her new position of Queen Consort had upon her the effect of diminishing her shyness. 'Untrue', she minuted beside a passage in the proofs of Mr John Gore's *Personal Memoir* of King George V.* 'I used to be rather shy but after the King succeeded & when one shared the central figure with the King this feeling vanished.'

For Queen Mary her husband's accession to the throne incidentally brought with it a new source of personal disquiet, and one which took her wholly by surprise: she found she saw him much less than in the old comparatively care-free days when he had been Duke of York and later Prince of Wales. The reasons for this, obvious enough to any man, were not ones which readily appeal to women: the new King had, for the first time in his life, an immense amount of work to get through each day. He would work at his 'boxes'—the red leather official despatch-boxes in which all Cabinet and other papers came to him—far into the night; and especially in the first year of his reign he had a multitude of decisions to take over Household, Coronation and other non-political matters. Looming high above these were the great political issues of the day—notably the House of Lords Reform Bill, which had puzzled and distressed King Edward VII in the last year of his life.

Neither in youth nor in middle-age was King George V verbally demonstrative, and, since he and Queen Mary were together without a break from the death of King Edward in May until a short visit King George paid to Sandringham at the end of October 1910, Queen Mary had no yardstick by which to judge whether her husband thought she was being a helpful Queen Consort or the reverse. Downcast by this lack of an overt approval, she began to fear that they were as she termed it 'drifting'. Her delight was therefore all the more intense when, on 31 October 1910, she received a long letter of gratitude from her husband from Sandringham, of which the following extracts contain the pith:

* Queen Mary read and annotated the proofs of Mr John Gore's admirable book on her late husband's life (published 1941) during the early part of the Second World War, when she was living at Badminton. In discussing this passage with Mr Gore (who had gone down to Badminton to see her), the Queen told him that she had often observed that someone who did not care for gossip and preferred to talk about serious topics, was condemned by others as 'shy' and 'dull'. 'You all go on as if I had been *stutteringly shy*!' Queen Mary remarked with vehemence, 'but I can assure you I wasn't as bad as that!'

o*

As the Messenger is going directly I must write you a few lines for him to take. Fancy this is the first letter I have written to you since . . . our lives have been entirely changed by darling Papa having been taken away from us. You have never left me for a single day since that sad event. I fear darling my nature is not demonstrative, but I want you to understand, that I am indeed grateful to you, for all you have done all these busy months for me & to thank you from the bottom of my heart for all your love & for the enormous help & comfort which you have been to me in my new position. I can't imagine how I could have got on at all without you, I shall never forget it. . . . My love grows stronger for you every day mixed with admiration & I thank God every day that he has given me such a darling devoted wife as you are. . . . God bless you my sweet Angel May, who I know will always stick to me as I need your love & help more than ever now.[8]

Queen Mary replied that this letter had given her 'such untold pleasure'.[9] 'What a pity it is you cannot *tell* me what you write for I should appreciate it so enormously—It is such a blessing to know that I am a help to you.' 'I am glad my letter pleased', King George answered from York Cottage on the next day. 'I really am full of feeling & sentiment & am very sympathetic but somehow I always find it difficult to express what I feel except in a letter, especially to the person I love & am always with like you darling. . . . I feel lost when you are not there & everything seems out of gear.'[10]

All the same, during his first years on the throne, the King found that he had, from time to time, to deliver little written reassurances to his wife; and she found that she must be satisfied with these rare but heartfelt tributes. 'I could not possibly get on without you, & you are the greatest comfort to me', he wrote to her, for instance, in the summer of 1911. 'Of course I always wish to tell you everything but sometimes I am so tired after having talked to people all day that I have no time or forget to tell you things, but it is not because I don't want to.'[11] In her replies Queen Mary displays a disarmingly feminine streak: 'It seems so quiet here without you & I miss you very much, in spite of seeing you so little when you are here, this still rankles & annoys me.' Or: 'I miss you very much as I always do when you are away, tho' I can't say I ever see much of you *now*.'[12] This was, in fact, a matter which later proved easy to adjust, once King George V had settled more smoothly into the alarming and absorbing routine of Monarchy; but in their first years upon the throne they both suffered from a sense of strain: 'I am glad to know by letter', wrote Queen

Mary in July 1913, 'that I really am of use to you in the tiring & strenuous life we have to lead. Thank God I am (*unberufen*) fairly strong and can get through the work pretty well tho' I must confess I am often dreadfully tired.'[13]

The possession of power brings troubles and anxieties all its own —and Queen Mary was swiftly finding that even the limited power of a British Queen Consort, which might best be defined as the power of doing good, is no sinecure. Her central aim was to protect her husband as much as possible and to encourage his first hesitant steps along the weary uphill path of kingship. This, as we have seen, she had to do while herself receiving merely intermittent reassurance that she was doing it well. She had also to exercise her tact in her relations with her predecessor as Queen Consort, her mother-in-law Queen Alexandra. Then, in these first months, there were an enormous number of problems connected with the Royal palaces, the Household, hospital and other charitable patronage, and the preparations for the Coronation, fixed for 22 June 1911. 'Life is *too* fatiguing for me, I have *too* much to do, to think of, I am getting worn out & people bother one so, I am sick of the everlasting begging for favours of all kinds!' she wrote to old Hélène Bricka[14] some months after King George's accession. While Queen Mary was in this state of overwork and anxiety her second brother, Prince Frank, died suddenly at the age of thirty-nine.

In the summer of 1910 Prince Frank had had a minor nasal operation. Prematurely released from hospital he had gone northward to join his sister the Queen at Balmoral. There they had spent a happy week together, resuming the old affectionate relationship which Prince Frank's follies had suspended for so many years. He was still not quite well, however, and when the King and Queen returned to London Prince Frank was left in Scotland in the care of Queen Victoria's old doctor, Sir James Reid. Pleurisy developed, he was hurried to London, operated upon, and then died. Queen Mary was overwhelmed by grief:

Indeed [she wrote to her husband] you were more than feeling & kind to me about dear Frank, whose death is a great sorrow & blow to me, for we were so very intimate in the old days until alas the 'rift' came. I am so thankful I still had that nice week with him at Balmoral when he was quite like his old self & seemed to be so happy with us & our children.[15]

At Prince Frank's funeral in St George's Chapel, Windsor, Queen Mary, who scarcely ever showed emotion in public, broke down and wept freely. 'Dear Frank's coffin lies with that of dear Mama', she told her Aunt Augusta in a letter describing the current arrangement inside the Royal Vault. 'I think she would have wished this as she was especially devoted to him. The Vault looks very nice now, & is well lighted & arranged. The King lies on the stone in the centre for the present. Ultimately he is to be moved to the Memorial Chapel where Eddy & Uncle Leopold are.'[16]

II

'People are of course speculating even now what the new Court will be like and they anticipate a good deal of change', wrote Mr Cornwallis-West to his daughter, Princess Daisy of Pless, just after the funeral of King Edward VII. 'I know the new Queen better than I do the King —and have a high opinion of her good sense and courtesy. It is said the King is a bad linguist which, if true, is unfortunate.'[17] By 'people' Mr Cornwallis-West meant, of course, 'people in Society'; these foresaw, and feared, a reversion to the more staid and domesticated Court life of Queen Victoria's time. They spoke sarcastically of the opening of 'a sweeter, simpler reign'. What did the real 'people', the people in the streets, think?

In his life of King George V, Mr John Gore has put on record the two main rumours about the new King current in London at the beginning of his reign. One was that the new King drank, the other was that he had no interest in the national sport of horse-racing. The alcoholic rumour arose from the fact that King George had a loud voice and a bluff manner. It was also due to the fact that chronic indigestion had given him a patchy complexion. One of the most abstemious of men, the King was partly amused, partly annoyed by this rumour. As to his being uninterested in racing, he soon proved this to be baseless.

Apart from these two rumours about the new King, there was the equally absurd but slanderous piece of gossip that he had married the daughter of an English Admiral at Malta in 1890, and that this mythical union invalidated his marriage to Queen Mary and made their children illegitimate. This ridiculous story had been brought to Sir Henry Ponsonby's attention as early as 1893,* when it had been published in

---

* The Duke of York, who at first treated the story as a joke, announced to Princess May one morning during their engagement: 'I say, May, we can't get married after all! I hear I have got a wife and three children!'

the *Star* newspaper. No action to deny it publicly was taken, however, until in 1910 a journalist named Edward Mylius resurrected the legend in a seditious Parisian publication, *The Liberator*. King George V determined to put an end once and for all to what he termed 'a damnable lie'. Mylius was at once prosecuted for criminal libel and condemned to twelve months' imprisonment. During the trial it was proved that the King had not even been in Malta at the time of the alleged marriage, and that of the Admiral's two daughters one was totally unknown to him, while the other had been presented to him twice in her life—once at the age of eight, and a second time after both she and the King were, respectively, happily married. Naturally enough the Mylius case caused a stir: 'What did you say to that law suit about George's being married before?' Queen Mary wrote to her Aunt Augusta on 4 February 1911. 'So many people believed it that when this scoundrel Mylius was found with the incriminating papers it was thought better to prosecute, & the result has been quite admirable & I hope the story is now doomed. The papers have been so nice & the people quite charming over this somewhat unpleasant occurrence.'

About Queen Mary herself there were two conflicting rumours, both of them also untrue. Members of the Court decided, because she invariably deferred to her husband's wishes, that the Queen was afraid of the King; members of the public, observing that the Queen looked taller than the King did, and—at first—failed to smile at him in public, concluded that the King was afraid of the Queen. By contrast with Queen Alexandra's winning ways and lissome figure, the new Queen may have appeared rather intimidating and stiff; we may also recall that Princess May's appearance had always been more admired at the courts of Berlin and Vienna than in English Society. 'Stately' and 'imposing' were the adjectives now most often used about this appearance:

I now come to Queen Mary . . . [wrote a contemporary in 1936]. For the past twenty-five years she has been one of the handsomest women in Europe. Her quarter of a century on the throne has given her whole personality poise and her manner assurance. . . . Scores and scores of times I have heard Americans and foreigners rave about the stately and imposing grace of Her Majesty's appearance and bearing at a Court, a Court Ball or other important function. I have never known any Empress or Queen who could wear a quantity of superb jewels with such ease and simplicity and without appearing in the least over-laden. Queen Alexandra could successively wear a great many jewels, but I have sometimes thought her slight figure a little overborne by them; it is never so with Queen Mary.[18]

It was indeed true that Queen Mary could display a quantity of jewels upon her person as amply as her mother Princess Mary Adelaide had done. She now, moreover, had serious jewels to display. Two random extracts from her dress-books for the Coronation Year Courts of 1911 are suggestive of the panoply with which she was now, on state occasions, arrayed. For the Second Court, 10 May 1911, the entry reads as follows: 'White & gold *broché* silk gown. Train of white satin embroidered silver & gold. Jewels: diamond crown, rows of diamonds forming collar, with large necklace under, lesser South African Stars, the Koh-i-noor, Star of Africa. Orders: the Garter, two family orders, & the Crown of India.' For the fourth and last Court of that season, Queen Mary wore a 'gown of cloth of silver with rich embroidered overdress of trellis design, wrought in pearls and floss silk. Train of silver tissue & lace. Pearl and diamond tiara, City collar between rows of diamonds, four rows of Crown pearls, diamond stomacher and brooches. Orders: the Garter, two family and Crown of India.'[19]

In her customarily methodical way—a relic of her days at White Lodge as well as of her German ancestry—Queen Mary kept in her own handwriting a list of all the clothes she ordered for the Coronation Year, together with the names of the makers and the prices of each item. The aggregate amounted to more than £2,000. The colours and the materials are indicative of her personal tastes—'gold and white', 'grey and silver', 'white *broché* with roses', 'mauve cut velvet', 'yellow satin', 'muslin with large roses', 'muslin with convolvulus', 'pinky mauve muslin', 'muslin with hollyhocks'. She was never fond of wearing strong colours, although occasionally a 'periwinkle blue' occurs in her dress-books; it was not until 1930 that she ventured to wear red. 'The Queen', wrote Lady Bertha Dawkins from Windsor in 1930, 'wore a red soft velvet dress with fur, which looked magnificent; she has never worn red before.'[20]

Queen Mary thought that she liked clothes as much as any other woman, but she found the hours spent with the dressmakers 'a bore'. 'We are getting on well with all the Coronation arrangements, & I with my tiresome *trousseau* of clothes which has meant endless trying on', she wrote to her Aunt Augusta in May 1911 from Buckingham Palace. 'The fashions are so hideous that it has been a great trouble to evolve pretty *toilettes* out of them, however I hope some of the gowns will be a success.'[21] We may here note a fact often overlooked by those who always commented on Queen Mary's 'stylisation', and praised her for never having altered her appearance—the toque, the coiffure, the parasol—for twenty-five years. This fact concerns the influence of her husband King George upon his wife's way of dressing.

Already in 1905 the King, then Prince of Wales, had replied to a letter in which Princess May complained of the tiring business of choosing dresses: 'I am sure you have chosen some pretty ones & I generally approve of them, I mean the stuff, but not always the fashions which these stupid dress makers always will make even when you tell them not to.'[22] Left to herself, Queen Mary would certainly have followed the current fashions, in a modified and dignified form, far more freely; but King George's conservatism forbade this. Once or twice, after the First World War, the Queen attempted to wear wide-brimmed hats in the summer; this found no favour with the King.

King George's conservatism which, as Mr Gore has explained, made it very hard for him to understand or sympathise with the younger generation, contemporaries of his own children, was due to a strong wish for everything to remain as it had been when he was a boy. This wish was in itself a corollary of his sisters' somewhat immature outlook, and of his mother's appearance of eternal youth. He had not wished to become heir to the throne in 1892; his happiest hours were always spent with the friends of his early years in the Navy; he retained until his dying day the handwriting of a schoolboy; and he wished his wife to grow old looking exactly as she had looked when they had first become engaged. Queen Mary's stylisation, which endeared her to the British public and indeed to the whole world, making her uniquely recognisable everywhere, was not, therefore, due to a deliberate decision of her own. It was a manifestation of her husband King George's deep-seated loathing for change. The 'May' to whom he had proposed at Sheen in 1893 must be for ever 'May'; and by the time he died in 1936 it was too late for Queen Mary to alter an appearance—even had she by then wished to do so—which had become at once famous and beloved. This instinct, whatever its origin, was in its effects a brilliant one. The reign of King George V witnessed violent social and other upheavals. Throughout all these, the Monarchy remained stable, safe and an example of old-fashioned rectitude and simplicity. King George subconsciously realised that to be stable in so public a position is not enough; one must look stable as well.

III

'I so understand your disliking the change of abode,' the old Grand Duchess of Mecklenburg-Strelitz wrote to her niece Queen Mary in December 1910, 'your saying "here one can never find anyone" so well describes the discomfort of the bigger Palace.'[23]

By 'the bigger Palace' Aunt Augusta meant of course Buckingham Palace, in which the new King and Queen took up residence in temporary quarters in December 1910. 'It is rather strange & lonely here without you & the children & I feel rather lost', Queen Mary wrote to her husband from the Palace, into which she had moved four days before he did. 'Oh! how I regret our dear beloved Marl: Hse, the most perfect of all houses & so compact. Here everything is so straggly, such distances to go & so fatiguing. But I ought not to grumble for they have been very anxious to make me as comfortable as possible & these rooms are very nice & I have a good many of my own things round me.'[24] 'I am sure the rooms are very comfortable, the distances are great but it is good exercise for you as you never walk a yard in London',[25] the King replied.

It would be incorrect to use the word 'rambling' to describe a large building symmetrically constructed round four sides of an inner court-yard; yet this is indeed the effect made by the interior of Buckingham Palace, with its apparently innumerable narrow passage-ways, its vast sombre throne room, its ballroom, its various dining-rooms, its great picture galleries alternating with nests of small sitting-rooms and bed-rooms, its landings and staircases, and its acres of red carpeting. There is certainly nothing 'compact' about Buckingham Palace. Bought by George III in 1762 as a dower-house, and reconstructed by Nash for George IV, it was never occupied by any Sovereign until Queen Victoria. After the Prince Consort's death, Queen Victoria came to London seldom; Buckingham Palace, only used for Courts or on such an occasion as Princess May's wedding in 1893, was left untouched for forty years. During this stagnant period the Prince of Wales, after-wards King Edward VII, would refer to his mother's London Palace as 'the Mausoleum'. So soon as he himself succeeded to the throne in 1901, King Edward gave orders for the renovation of Buckingham Palace, and also sanctioned plans to widen the Mall and make it into what his daughter-in-law termed 'a fine wide carriage road going straight to the entry gate of the Palace'.[26] The throne room and the ballroom were redecorated, and so was the private suite of the then

King and Queen: 'We then went to Buck. Palace & saw the alterations in Their Majesties suite of rooms.' Princess May had noted in her Diary in April 1902: 'Some are very nice, others less so.'[27]

Settled in temporary rooms in Buckingham Palace in December 1910, King George and Queen Mary were not able to move into their permanent suite until the following February. During her first few weeks at the Palace, Queen Mary was still regretting the loss of 'our beloved Home' as she now called Marlborough House: 'Buckingham Palace', she wrote to her eldest son on 10 December 1910, 'is not so "*gemütlich*" as Marlborough House.' The King and Queen moved into their permanent suites in February 1911: 'Well at last *me voilà* writing to you from my *new* rooms which we took possession of last Wedy', Queen Mary wrote on 26 February. ' . . . I feel more at home now, glad that this *great eruption* is at an end & that one can begin to turn one's thoughts to other things, tho' I confess much is left still to do in the Palace as so much has been removed & must be replaced—I am trying to rehang the pictures in the various rooms according to family, date, etc., not an easy task when one has miles of corridors to cover to find anything—however I hope to do it in time if my legs hold out.'[28] 'I really am beginning to like our new rooms', she wrote again that March, '& to feel more at home in them, they certainly have turned out pretty and are not as full of things as Motherdear had them.'[29] 'I expect you will think May's rooms rather empty, but then you have so many more things than she has', King George wrote tactfully to his mother.[30] Down at Sandringham, Queen Alexandra had got wind of the radical alterations which Queen Mary had made in the private suite at Buckingham Palace: '*Our* dear old rooms', she wrote to her daughter-in-law. ' . . . I shall indeed be very curious & anxious to see them & how you have arranged it all. Yes the sitting room with its nice & pretty bow window is certainly very cold & draughty in the winter—particularly where my writing table stood —I wonder where you have put yours—and the lovely bedroom with its pretty arches—which I hear you have *removed* how is that arranged—'[31]

A large part of each day of the last three weeks of February 1911 —Sundays, of course, excepted—was spent by Queen Mary in the private apartments at Buckingham Palace hanging pictures, placing furniture and arranging miniatures, snuff-boxes and valuable china in vitrines: 'I began to arrange my sitting room & place the furniture', she noted in her Diary for 7 February. 'A most tedious job and nothing fits in.' Aided by the Dugdales she slaved away hour after hour; and, as a result, on 24 February she could triumphantly record 'Eva dined with me in my green room which looks charming'. Soon the system Queen Mary had herself devised of devoting a single room to some particular date and style of furniture received the accolade of official approval from the Director of the Victoria and Albert Museum himself: 'I then saw Sir Cecil Smith who was delighted with my Chinese Chippendale room, he wanted to see it because he is busy arranging little rooms of various styles at the V. and A. & he said seeing my rooms wld help him very much indeed—he is such a nice man & full of knowledge.'³²

While this reorganisation of the rooms in Buckingham Palace was hard work, it incidentally provided Queen Mary with an agreeable diversion from the myriad problems now facing her daily in her new position as Queen Consort—for, as the late Lord Crewe once remarked, 'the best form of relaxation is to do some other kind of work'. We may here remark that Queen Mary was never able to relax in the modern sense of the term, nor had she the remotest wish to do so; to her 'resting' meant lying down for an hour before dinner and reading or being read to by one of her ladies—in either case it meant using and improving her mind. This habit originated in an older generation; she had perhaps learned it from her Aunt Augusta, who, writing to her in April 1910, told her: 'I am reading the Duc de Morny's Life, rather too much in detail yet entertaining in many ways, as I know most people named in it. I read 60 pages last night, by way of *resting!* You & I *rest* in the same old fashioned way, don't we?'³³ One of Queen Mary's strongest aversions in life was to wasting time, and to those who succumbed to that gentle temptation. 'I like energy & doing & seeing things, but the way people fritter away their time & their vitality doing *absolutely* useless things makes me furious',³⁴ she once wrote, in 1909. If she had to sit for her portrait, someone would be detailed to read aloud to her while she was sitting; she would even on occasions write letters while her hair was being dressed for the day.

The work in Buckingham Palace that February of 1911 also prevented Queen Mary from dwelling too nervously upon something which, for her and for King George V, was fast assuming the shape of an imminent threat: their Coronation. 'It will be a great ordeal', she wrote to her eldest brother, '& we are dreading it as you can imagine.'³⁵

IV

Queen Mary entered upon the Coronation Year of 1911 in a mood flickering with anxiety, humility and awe. She shared her husband's profound sense of responsibility and dedication; but in her case this was enhanced by her historical instinct, her consciousness that both she and the King were direct descendants of Alfred the Great, and that they were soon to be crowned and anointed at Westminster Abbey with a religious ceremonial which in its essentials dated back to the dawn of the British Monarchy. In Strelitz the old Grand Duchess was brooding over letters written to her at the time of King Edward VII's crowning, in 1902: 'There is one of "Motherdear",' she wrote to Queen Mary, 'so alarmed at her coming Coronation, and now it is you, who have to face it, and yet, you will dread it less as you will be filled with the spirit of Historical interest and of the grandeur of the Ceremony, which she cannot have felt as you will.'[36] Queen Alexandra had been more affected by the visual and aesthetic aspects of the Coronation ceremony: 'nothing in this world comes up to it', she wrote to Queen Mary, '—having felt & gone through it all myself only 9 short years ago—*how* beautiful & solemn it was & quite ineffaceable from ones mind for ever—& the heavenly music—adding to it all.'[37]

In the months leading up to the day in late June selected for the actual Coronation ceremony, Queen Mary had little time in which to indulge her feelings, for she was, in her own way, kept as busy as the King. In a letter written on New Year's day 1911, she described her life at that time: 'We have just returned from church', she wrote from York Cottage, Sandringham, 'where our Rector preached a most touching sermon which of course reduced me to tears. One enters on this New Year with very mixed feelings as you can imagine, the whole task seems so stupendous, so difficult, one can only pray for guidance & courage to be given us—The work too is very fatiguing for George, who being extremely conscientious & anxious to be *au fait* of everything, reads all that is sent him & their name is legion. I, in my way, also seem to have much to do, to decide, things I must do myself in which no one can help me however willing.'[38]

The programme mapped out for the new King and Queen for the year 1911 was indeed enough to make anyone apprehensive. 'My only fright is you do *too* much at first—', Queen Alexandra wrote to her daughter-in-law, '—& this year so *full* of functions that you might both collapse—Do *please both* of you not *pledge* yr *selves* at first to undertake more than any *human people* can stand. . . . I speak like an old woman from sad experience—so please both of you remember my words & act accordingly.'³⁹

It was, of course, the novelty of the 'functions' to be performed which was particularly unnerving. We might think that by now both King George and Queen Mary would have been inured to public appearances. To a limited extent this was so: but never before, save on their Empire tours, had they occupied the high and lonely centre of the stage. There was their first Opening of Parliament to be faced, their first Courts, the Coronation ceremony itself, the first big review of the Fleet by the new King, their first official visits as King and Queen to Scotland, Ireland and Wales. Of all these various functions, the King and Queen found the Opening of Parliament most trying to their nerves. This ancient and beautiful ceremony, in which the King and Queen, crowned and robed, slowly advance into the House of Lords amidst a deadly silence, hand in hand, to take their places upon the thrones beneath the canopy, is carried out before an audience—the assembled Lords and, later, Commons—which is one of the most critical and also quizzical in the world. The Monarch then reads the Speech prepared by the Prime Minister and his Cabinet, outlining the legislation proposed for the coming Session of Parliament. Many years later King George told Lady Cromer that he had always insisted on this Speech being printed in very large type, because he had never been able to overcome the nervous trembling of his hand while he was reading it.

The first Opening of Parliament by King George V took place on 6 February 1911. 'I must say', the new King wrote to his mother after it was over, 'that I think opening Parliament the most terrible ordeal I have ever gone through. . . . The House of Lords was crammed with people & so many I knew which made it worse. We were afterwards photographed by Downey in the robing room. . . . I got your dear telegram just as we were getting into the coach which is not uncomfortable but very high. The cream coloured horses were rather unruly & the leaders shied right across the street every time they came to a band.'⁴⁰ 'The opening of parliament', Queen Mary told her Aunt Augusta, 'went off well. . . . It was a great ordeal for us & rather nervous work but we got thro' it all right & G's speech was not so bad I think. . . . What I liked best was wearing Grandmama's crown & the ribbon star & badge of the Garter! I know *you* will understand what *I* felt.'⁴¹ Shut away down at Sandringham, Queen Alexandra had spent that morning thinking about the Opening of Parliament. 'My darling May', she wrote. ' . . . My thoughts have never left you today & have followed you step by step to Westminster & in the House of Lords & on yr way back from yr first Opening of Parliament—Were you both very alarmed & shy & *emotionné* as we were the *first time* particularly! I wished all the same I cld have had a peep at you! What did you wear? & did the cloak of Gd Mama's do? Did you wear the big or small crown please tell me it interests me to hear also what Jewels you wore etc.—I always *heard* & felt my heart beating loud all the time we were seated on that very conspicuous place.'⁴²

Besides this round of daunting new official duties to perform, the King and Queen were invited to attend a number of great dinner-parties given in their honour by members of the nobility. Once again, Court mourning restricted these latter activities, for early in May Queen Alexandra's 'Uncle Hans'* had died. 'I dined with the Dss. of Devonshire but did not stay for her ball owing to Uncle Hans of Glucksburg's death', Queen Mary noted in her Diary; or, again, a few days later: 'We dined at Derby House. . . . We left before the Ball owing to our mourning.'⁴³ To King George, who disliked such grandiose entertainments as much as he disliked foreign travel, this curtailment of a potentially long evening devoted to pleasure was thoroughly welcome; Queen Mary, for all her shyness, enjoyed a ball —and in any case, as we know, she hated wearing mourning.

As Coronation Day drew irrevocably nearer, the tempo of life inside Buckingham Palace mounted. Almost from the day of his father's funeral a year before, King George had become involved in conferences and committees over plans for his Coronation. One of the major problems concerned the housing and entertainment of those foreign royalties who had declared their wish to attend the ceremony. 'The amount of Guests of all kinds who have announced themselves is quite overwhelming, *all* George's first cousins of all nationalities have asked to come, it will be a motley gathering',⁴⁴ Queen Mary wrote to her Aunt Augusta, with whom she was now maintaining an even more frequent correspondence; for it will be recalled that the old Grand Duchess's memory went back to the Coronation of King William IV and Queen Adelaide in 1831, and she was ever ready with advice. The Grand Duchess was annoyed that the Mecklenburg-Schwerins

* Prince Johann, a younger brother of Queen Alexandra's father, King Christian IX of Denmark.

were going to London for the Coronation, for she had hoped that her own son 'Dolphus', now Grand Duke of Mecklenburg-Strelitz, would be the only Mecklenburger present. 'It is not true', Queen Mary reassured her aunt, 'that Alex Schwerin was invited as an English Pss for George invited no one, people proposed themselves & the Gd Duke asked whether they might come. Even U. Alfred's daughters are not coming except Missy—U. Ernest wishes his 2 sons who are coming, to be styled Duke of Brunswick-Lüneburg *not* Cumberland which I think is such a pity—'45

As a tribute to his wife, King George had given the Order of the Bath to her two surviving brothers, and had wished to create Prince Dolly a Royal Highness. This style, for which his father the first Duke of Teck had pined all his life long, Prince Dolly prudently refused, since he did not wish to seem to benefit by his sister's new status. The King had also given the Garter to his wife's first cousin, Adolphus, Grand Duke of Mecklenburg-Strelitz. This rare honour, which delighted his mother the Dowager Grand Duchess Augusta, gave its recipient immense pleasure. From being vaguely anti-British he switched overnight to become an ardent Anglophile: 'he now *signs himself*, Adolphus *KG!* so this proves a great change in him or rather in his very foolish over-German views', Aunt Augusta wrote to her niece the Queen. 'This K G so startled me I quite hopped on my chair.'46

To Queen Mary's intense regret, one beloved relation was missing from the reunion in London that June: her Aunt Augusta. 'Do you know I think you simply *must* come for our Coronation, do think of it anyhow as a possibility, fancy how nice it wld be for *me* to have my Mother-Aunt!'47 she had written to the Grand Duchess in June 1910. The Grand Duchess, now in her eighty-ninth year, felt unable to face the journey: 'Oh! that would have been *my fourth* [Coronation], but this I dare not think of, unless some Aerobike takes me to fly across! shall I venture?!!'48 Instead of appearing in person, she wrote her niece letter after letter of enquiries, to all of which Queen Mary somehow found time to send kindly, diligent replies. Why were the Princesses' mantles to be violet instead of the traditional blue? Because Aunt Alix had selected violet for them at her Coronation, and as this was only nine years back the Princesses wished to economise by using their mantles again. Why was Queen Mary's train to be borne by six Earls' daughters? Because Queen Mary had checked up on precedents: 'You ask about Earl's daughters instead of pages to hold my train.

On looking thro' the old records they found that hitherto all *Queen-Consorts* had 6 Earl's daughters to carry their trains & no one seems to know why Motherdear had pages. . . . As you know I am a great advocate of Precedent so I said I wld choose Ladies & I have found 6 very pretty girls who will match.'⁴⁹ Why was *Rosenkavalier* to be given at the Gala Opera?—'I hope', the Grand Duchess added, 'this novelty will not be selected for the Gala Performance, for it is the most improper Opera, in existence, even the *male* singers declared their horror at having to sing such words, and the females were more than scandalised!'⁵⁰ The answer to this question was simply that 'it is not true that "Rosen Cavalier" has been chosen for the Gala Opera'.⁵¹ Nor was it true, as Aunt Augusta had been told, that the Archduke Franz Ferdinand, heir to the Austrian throne, was coming to London with his morganatic wife the Duchess of Hohenberg and was insisting on her being treated with archducal honours.

During these weeks the King and Queen were exposed to a hailstorm of queries needing immediate decisions. Even the nearest members of their own family did not spare them. 'Mama came here to tea', Queen Mary wrote to King George of a visit from his mother to Buckingham Palace in June 1911, '& says Louise is so hurt her girls* cannot wear Princesses robes, Mama quite sees the difficulty but thinks they ought to wear trains & each have a young lady to *carry* them. What do you think?'⁵² 'With regard to Louise's two girls', the King replied, 'I can't help it if she is hurt at their not wearing robes, but it would not be right. Certainly they can have trains, which can be carried by young Ladies, if the Schleswig Holstein girls did last time & are going to again now. . . . What a lot of trouble everyone seems to give. Why doesn't she come & ask me herself if she wants all these things.'⁵³ Throughout these trying weeks, Queen Mary retained her cool judgement, although by 18 June, four days before the Coronation ceremony, even she admitted to her aunt that her head was 'rather in a whirl'. 'How you get through all your work is a marvel to me, *my* head whirls only reading of your doings', the old lady answered, 'and what must be the stress on your mind having to think of and to arrange and settle all these things. With all the serious thoughts in my head yet could I not help smiling at your having a "rehearsal" with the Archbishop, as to placing the Crown on your head; too amusing to think of this *scene*, so like you to have it all *right*!'⁵⁴

* i.e. Princess Alexandra and Princess Maud, who had been born in 1891 and 1893 respectively.

Up until the very eve of Coronation Day, the King and Queen were receiving deputations, meeting foreign royalties, giving 'family luncheons' and huge banquets. On 21 June, the day before Coronation Day itself, they went to the International Horse Show at Olympia: 'Received a wonderful ovation from crowds of People', Queen Mary records in her Diary. 'Home by 5.30. Mossy & Fischy, George & Marie of Greece, & Jutta & Danilo of Montenegro came to tea.'

That night the King and Queen dined alone with their two eldest sons and went early to bed.

V

Although it improved later in the summer, the weather of June 1911 was windy and cool. Frequent rainstorms had been causing the London public, and the vendors of seats on the stands set up along the coronation processional route, some disquiet. In the whole month of June there were only five good days. Coronation Day, the twenty-second, was not amongst them.

'Dull but fine—Our Coronation day', Queen Mary recorded in her Diary. King George's comment in his Diary was longer, but it was equally characteristic: 'It was overcast and cloudy with slight showers, & a strongish cool breeze, but better for the people than great heat.' The weather of Coronation Day, 1911, thus formed a sharp, symbolic contrast to that of the July morning, eighteen years before, when Princess May had, for the first time in her life, driven in state from Buckingham Palace as the central figure of a carriage procession. She was then driving to be married at the Chapel Royal; we may recall the sparkling sunshine of that July morning, and the cheers of the surging crowds. Her prospects then had seemed gay and exciting; her prospects now were a lifetime of dedication and responsibility. The overcast sky suited her serious mood.

There were other and obvious differences between the Coronation procession of 1911 and the wedding procession of 1893: the cumbrous golden Coronation coach, the cream-coloured horses with their trappings of scarlet leather and 'a touch of lavender blue decorating their manes'; the troops from all over the Empire; the foreign royalties in their strange uniforms. Then, too, the cavalcade of 1893 had issued straight from the gates of Buckingham Palace and on down the Mall; in 1911 the procession was forced to wind its way round an island at the Palace end of that newly widened avenue. Upon this island now stood the gigantic Victoria Memorial, unveiled by King George in the presence of the German Emperor and Empress the previous May. This colossal monument, planned by King Edward VII as a tribute to the greatness of England during his mother's reign, shows Queen Victoria, regally robed, gazing stonily down the Mall. The giant Imperial effigy bore small relation to the tiny, shy, kind old Grandmama King George and Queen Mary had loved; but it formed, under their very windows, an ever-present reminder of their new responsibilities and obligations. Perhaps also on that morning of June 1911 the statue of the dead Queen may have recalled to Queen Mary's mind how many other beloved figures of her youth were no longer living to rejoice at her Coronation and to sustain her with their sympathy. Princess Mary Adelaide, Duchess of Teck, who had found herself the most loudly cheered of all those taking part in the procession of 1893, was dead. The Duke of Teck, at whose side the timid Princess May had driven to her wedding, was dead. Prince Frank was dead. King Edward VII was dead. Uncle Fritz Strelitz was dead. Of the main personages of the older generation who had taken prominent parts in the 1893 procession only Aunt Augusta Strelitz and Motherdear were still alive: but the old Grand Duchess was far away in Strelitz, praying and weeping all morning as the loyal Strelitzers flocked with bouquets to congratulate her on her niece's Coronation Day, while Queen Alexandra had retired with her unmarried daughter to Sandringham. The absence of the Queen Dowager from Westminster Abbey was in accordance with tradition, for Queen Adelaide had not attended her niece Queen Victoria's Coronation; but this time it was also due to an obsession which was temporarily haunting Queen Alexandra—that the 1911 Coronation should by rights have been the Coronation of her dead son, Prince Eddy, and not of her second son, Prince George. '*Eddy* should be King, not *Georgie*', she kept saying, to the embarrassment of her entourage.

In this sense Queen Mary, alone inside the Coronation coach with her husband who was now also her King, went to her crowning unsupported by the affections of those who had loved her most. Her elder brother Prince Dolly had sent her flowers on the day before the Coronation; her younger brother Prince Alge managed to break through the crowds outside the Palace late on Coronation Day to congratulate his sister personally. But already the new Queen was finding encouragement and warmth in that quarter on which most English monarchs have ever been able to rely for affection: the London crowd. 'Sometimes I drive with the children in the park & I am really quite touched at the nice reception we get from all classes, they all look so pleased to see one & crowd round the carriage', she had written three weeks earlier. 'It is a great encouragement when I think of all that lies before us.'[55] 'Magnificent reception both going & coming back', she wrote in her Diary of Coronation Day. 'There were hundreds of thousands of people who gave us a magnificent reception', King George recorded. 'The Service in the Abbey was most beautiful & impressive but it was a terrible ordeal. . . . Darling May looked so lovely & it was indeed a comfort to me to have her by my side as she has been ever to me during these last 18 years.'[56]

Some days after the Coronation ceremony, Queen Mary wrote a long letter about it to her Aunt Augusta:

You may imagine what an intense relief it is to us that the great and solemn Ceremony of Thursday is well over [a part of this letter reads] for it was an awful ordeal for us both especially as we felt it all so deeply and taking so great a responsibility on our shoulders—To me who love tradition & the past, & who am English from top to toe, the service was a very real solemn thing & appealed to my feelings more than I can express—Everything was most perfectly & reverently done—The foreigners seemed much impressed & were most nice & feeling. . . . Everyone regretted yr enforced absence & no one more than I did but you wld have found it most agitating —I never ceased thinking of you the whole time—[57]

The widely televised Coronation of Queen Mary's granddaughter, Queen Elizabeth II, in 1953, has made the meaning as well as the formulae and ritual of the Coronation ceremony familiar and it would be superfluous to recapitulate these in detail here. It is, however, necessary to emphasise the effect upon Queen Mary of the religious content of the ceremony of dedication through which she passed on 22 June 1911; and it will be convenient at this point to consider very briefly a subject which we have not yet examined, but which was a guiding factor in Queen Mary's life—her religion.

Like her mother, Princess Mary Adelaide, Queen Mary was by nature a deeply religious woman. Also like her mother—and indeed all her Hanoverian forebears—she preferred simplicity in religious expression. She disliked ritual and was not at all interested in doctrinal matters. As a girl in Florence she had sometimes gone to mass at one or other of the Roman Catholic churches of that city, but this was primarily to hear the singing, and, at that time, she would probably have agreed with her mother in regarding Roman Catholic ceremonies as 'mummery'. As she aged, she became more and more tolerant, not only of Roman Catholicism, but also of the religions of the East. She had read a good deal about these latter beliefs, partly to prepare herself for the Indian tour of 1905, partly because she was genuinely interested. 'We went to church this morning', she wrote to her husband from Dresden, where she was staying with her Aunt Augusta in August 1904, 'nice church, but the sermon was "rot", it lasted 27 minutes & consisted of abusing motors, sport, killing animals for eating purposes, I don't know what the man was driving at—He also impressed on us that Buddhism and the Brahmin religions were better than ours in many ways—I have long thought so, but it is scarcely for a Ch. of England clergyman to tell one so! I cannot say I felt edified.'[58] Naturally punctilious in attending church services, Queen Mary none the less found the truest expression of her religious convictions in private prayer; her Diaries contain several simple, pious and humble prayers which she evidently used daily. 'I think it was very dear of you to pray for what we want,' she once wrote to her husband, 'I did too, I always pray for everything I want to happen whether it comes or no.'[59]

For Queen Mary, then, the ceremony of the Coronation was not only of consequence for its historical implications, but for the way in which she felt it to sanctify her new position, and to invoke God's aid in shouldering her new responsibilities. It was to her, as to her husband the King, a source of hope and strength.

HER IMPERIAL MAJESTY

K ING GEORGE V had not forgotten the irritation he had felt in 1901 at his father's delay in creating him Prince of Wales, the traditional title borne by the heir-apparent to the British throne. The new King was therefore determined that his own eldest son Prince Edward—known to his family as 'David'— should not be kept long waiting for this honour. Very soon after his own accession, the King decided to create his son Prince of Wales on 23 June 1910, the young Prince's sixteenth birthday and the day selected for his confirmation. 'I cannot help feeling sorry', wrote Queen Mary, 'that my poor child of 16 should already be in the position he occupies, without being older & having more preparation, still as you know we have done our best for him & we can only hope & pray we may have succeeded & that he will ever uphold the honour & traditions of our house.'[1]

In the following year, 1911, the Prince of Wales was invested with the Order of the Garter, and it was in Garter Robes that he did homage to his father at the Coronation. In July of Coronation Year, the King and Queen, returning from a state visit to Ireland, went to Caernarvon Castle. Here, within the ruined battlements, King George V presented his eldest son to the people of the Principality of Wales, in a ceremony which 'had been allowed to lapse for centuries'[2] and which was now revived at the instigation of Mr Lloyd George. 'It was a most pictur-esque & beautiful ceremony', Queen Mary recorded in her Diary, '& very well arranged. David looked charming in his purple and miniver cloak & gold circlet & did his part very well. The heat was awful.'[3]

In his memoirs the Duke of Windsor has described this Welsh occasion. He has recalled how deeply he resented the 'fantastic costume' designed for it, which consisted of white satin breeches and a mantle and surcoat of purple velvet edged with ermine. He was afraid of what his naval friends at Dartmouth—where he had been training as a naval cadet since 1907—would think of him. 'There was a family blow-up that night', he writes, 'but in the end my mother, as always, smoothed things over.' 'You mustn't take a mere ceremony so seriously', Queen Mary told her son. 'Your friends will understand that as a Prince you are obliged to do certain things that may seem a little silly. It will be only for this once.'4

King George, in consultation with Queen Mary, had decided that a complete change must now be made in the education of his eldest son. For four years Prince Edward had led a happy and comparatively carefree life at Dartmouth, receiving the same specialised training which his father had received before him. This training was designed to equip a youth as a first-rate British naval officer, but it was not especially relevant to the duties of a Prince destined one day to become King of England. The Prince of Wales's tutor, Mr Hansell, persuaded the King that the Prince should go up to Magdalen College, Oxford. This was Mr Hansell's own old college, and he was himself to accompany the Prince to Oxford and to supervise his studies there. 'Why is he to be an undergraduate?' enquired Aunt Augusta in a letter to Queen Mary from Strelitz, 'surely this cannot be true! it is too democratic and why? and why does his Tutor *again* accompany him? Pardon me for making these remarks, only I feel so strongly in feelings and notions of *old* that I can't help expressing my fears, thinking of the future.'5 In between the various Oxford terms, it was arranged that the Prince of Wales should spend some weeks in France to improve his French, and a longer period in Germany, to improve his German. In Germany it was suggested that he should stay with his mother's relations at Stuttgart and at Neu Strelitz.

This continental project was seemingly Queen Mary's own idea; she herself wrote to ask her Aunt Augusta whether 'David' could come to stay at Strelitz for most of the three months he was to spend in Germany. The old Grand Duchess, at eighty-nine, understood young people better than did her niece: 'Will he not be awfully bored in this small place, his Gentlemen the same, there being no sports, nor Games of any kind, such as they are all accustomed to', she wisely enquired in reply to Queen Mary's letter; 'to be bored for 3 months is trying!'6 'There wld be no question as to his being bored (or the gentlemen either)', Queen Mary promptly answered, 'he is quite a contented person & never rushes about after amusement.'7 Queen Mary, in fact, was still labouring under that not infrequent parental delusion which leads mothers and fathers to fancy that their children share their own tastes. Since she hated 'rushing about' she assumed that her eldest son felt the same; and when, in after years, this energetic and inquisitive young Prince began that life of constant movement for which he soon became famous, she was as bewildered as King George, who characterised his son as 'terribly restless'.[8] As it turned out, the Prince of Wales did of course find the atmosphere of the court at Neu Strelitz dull and constricting: 'I began', he tells us in his memoirs, 'to invent plausible excuses for going to Berlin, a gay city in those pre-war days. There I had my first taste of night life.'[9]

Queen Mary watched the course of her eldest son's Oxford studies with a grave attention: 'The various tutors give good reports as to his work,' she wrote, 'but he must read more & think more for himself which is most necessary in his position.'[10] 'I think he has come on,' she wrote of 'David' in 1912, 'we have good reports from his tutors but they want him to read more, as so far his knowledge is too superficial.'[11] The difficulties, and indeed the potential dangers of her son's position caused Queen Mary a good deal of anxiety. One of the few persons in whom she confided on this subject was her old friend Lord Esher. 'The Queen walked me up and down the river for nearly two hours', he wrote in his Journal, of a visit to Balmoral in September 1912, 'talking over every conceivable detail of the Prince of Wales's character, education, temptations, etc. etc. I have promised to write her some notes on *l'Education d'un Prince*.'[12] As we have earlier observed, Queen Mary's affection for her children was always mingled with apprehension and surprise.

Two years at Oxford, several months in France and Germany, were thus expected to fill the gaps left by his Dartmouth training in the Prince of Wales's general education. So determined were his parents and Mr Hansell that no time must be lost, that they inflicted upon the young Prince of Wales one of the first great disappointments of his life: they decided that he should not accompany them to India for the spectacular Coronation Durbar at Delhi in the winter of 1911 to 1912.

II

Derived from the Persian noun *darbar*, the Indian word *durbar* has always had a double meaning. It most usually signifies a consultative meeting of chieftains for the purpose of taking administrative decisions; its secondary signification is a ceremonial gathering to pay homage. It was in this latter sense that the word was used to designate the three Imperial Durbars held at the ancient city of Delhi during the brief period of history in which Great Britain possessed and ruled her Indian Empire.

At the first of these Durbars, held in 1877 by Lord Lytton, then Viceroy, Queen Victoria had been proclaimed Empress of India, a title assumed at Disraeli's urging in 1876. The second Delhi Durbar, that of 1903, was presided over by Lord Curzon when he in his turn was Viceroy. It celebrated the accession to the Imperial throne of the King-Emperor Edward VII. Eight years later, on 12 December 1911, came the third Imperial Durbar. This, the most splendid, the most solemn and the most expensive of the three, was also the last. Accompanied by his Queen-Empress, the King-Emperor came in person to hold the Durbar, at which he announced the Government's dramatic decision to transfer the seat of Imperial Government to the ancient capital of Delhi. Strongly criticised at home by the Conservative Opposition, who declared that the blunt proclamation of such a radical change was unconstitutional since it should first have been debated in both Houses of Parliament, the announcement also perplexed the swarming crowds in the great amphitheatre at Delhi: for Indian superstition, based on India's past history, told them that the move of the Government of a ruling power to Delhi had always been followed by its downfall. Thirty-six years after the Coronation Durbar of 1911, the peoples of the Indian peninsula achieved their constitutional liberty. It is therefore no exaggeration to say that the glories and pageantry of December 1911, which seemed to most of those who witnessed them to be the apogee of British power in India, were in fact its swan-song.

For the purposes of our study of Queen Mary's life the Delhi Durbar of 1911 is of great psychological importance, less for the effect which it had upon Queen Mary herself, than for its effect upon the King. King George V returned from India in 1912 with a new self-confidence, and a new conception of his position as King-Emperor. 'Those who best knew him', writes Mr John Gore, 'are generally agreed that the Indian Durbar visit greatly influenced the King's character. They consider that that tremendous experience, the magnificent ceremonial among those millions of his subjects many of whom felt for him and hailed him almost as a god, convinced him finally and for his life of the majesty of his office and of the magnitude of his responsibilities . . . the dizzy and lonely heights of his position as King-Emperor were brought home to him.'[13] On Queen Mary's mind, the Durbar ceremonial also made an indelible impression. 'Yesterday's Durbar', she wrote after the great day of homage was over, 'was simply magnificent & too beautifully arranged, I am still quite under the influence of Imperialism it inspired.'¹⁴ Her feelings were, indeed, shared by the Englishmen and women who were present at Delhi that sunny December morning almost fifty years ago. Great Britain's Imperial power in India seemed to them magnificent, benevolent and permanent. Only a handful of the actual participants in the Durbar ceremonies felt any doubts upon the effect of the Durbar and the durability of British rule in India. One of these few was Lord Crewe, then Secretary of State for India, and considered by many of his colleagues to be the wisest man in Asquith's Cabinet. In later years, when plans for the building of New Delhi were under way, the King came to believe that he would be held personally responsible for the merits or defects of the new city. 'He considers', wrote Crewe, 'the work will be connected with his name in India. . . . This seems an exaggerated view, though no doubt the Royal visit will be remembered when, in Sheridan's words, "all of us are dead and most of us are forgotten".'¹⁵

It was King George himself who had suggested that he should go out to India to hold his Coronation Durbar in person. When he had first broached the subject to the Prime Minister in September 1910 it aroused no enthusiasm in the Cabinet. 'It was entirely my own idea to hold the Coronation Durbar at Delhi in person', the King wrote in his Diary, 'and at first I met with much opposition.'¹⁶ This opposition took several forms: objections on the ground of expense, for was it not both unwise and prodigal to hold so pompous a public ceremony at a moment when large parts of India were, as usual, in the grip of famine? There were also grave objections on the ground of security risks, for in the six years which separated King George's accession from his visit to India as Prince of Wales in 1905, anti-British revolutionary movements had made great headway there. Then there was the question of how this country would get along without its King for a period of three whole months. But the King would not be deflected: his experiences in India in 1905 had convinced him that bureaucratic government was unsuited to India, and he hoped by his personal appearance at Delhi to strengthen and re-emphasise the powers of the hereditary princes and ruling chiefs, whom he persisted in regarding as beneficent and paternal influences. In the end the Cabinet gave way, and active preparations for the Durbar commenced in London and in India. King George V thus became the first English Monarch to visit the East since Richard Cœur de Lion, and the only

British King-Emperor to visit his Indian dominions in imperial state.

Once the decision for the King-Emperor, accompanied by the Queen-Empress—for Queen Mary had soon scotched a plan to leave her behind in England as Queen-Regent—to go to India had been taken, a litter of fresh problems raised their heads. First of all, what was the King-Emperor to do at Delhi once he got there? Was he to be crowned at a second Coronation ceremony? Was he to crown himself? The King personally favoured what Lord Crewe called 'a Napoleonic auto-Coronation', but to this there were two insuperable objections: on the one hand the Archbishop of Canterbury pronounced that even an auto-Coronation required a Christian religious ceremony, and that it would be absurd to hold a Christian religious ceremony before an audience almost wholly composed of Mohammedans and Hindus; on the other hand Lord Crewe, supported by the Cabinet, explained that it would be a dangerous precedent to have a separate Indian Coronation, since it might lead, in after years, to the assumption that a King of England was not Emperor of India until he had been crowned at Delhi. Yet some ceremony there must be: 'One's instinct', wrote Lord Crewe to the Viceroy, Lord Hardinge, 'is to avoid the theatrical, but it does not follow that the instinct is sound, as we have got to impress the people of India, not some more or less cultivated persons over here.' Crewe suggested that the King should at a given moment advance to the front of the arena, receive the crown from the Viceroy who would be holding it up on a velvet cushion, and place it on his own head to the sound of massed bands followed by a general salute. 'The Crown would be brought from here,' Crewe added, 'what Crown it would be is a matter for future decision.'[17]

It was finally decided that the King-Emperor would enter the arena already crowned, with the Queen-Empress, wearing her 'best diadem' on top of a crimson velvet cap of maintenance, at his side. So far so good; until it was discovered that it was illegal to take any part of the Regalia, let alone the crown itself, out of the realm. Sir Walter Lawrence then suggested that a special Indian crown should be made in London, taken out to India and left there. The Indian princes, Sir Walter pointed out, would be only too glad to give individual jewels, thus reducing *pro rata* the estimated cost of a new crown, which worked out at some £60,000. Crewe and the Cabinet, foreseeing and dreading this as a precedent for a multiplicity of local crowns all over the Empire, vetoed the plan. The crown must be made in London,

P

taken to India, brought back again and broken up. To this the King sensibly replied that such a course would offend Indian visitors to London, who would be looking forward to seeing the Indian crown sparkling amidst the rest of the Regalia in the Tower. The result of all these discussions was a compromise: a new Indian crown was constructed by Garrard's, taken out to India on the *Medina* in a special safe, placed on the King's head in private in his tent and publicly worn by him throughout the Durbar ceremonies. It was a noble, but not a light, crown. 'Rather tired after wearing the Crown for $3\frac{1}{2}$ hours,' the King wrote in his Diary for 12 December 1911, 'it hurt my head, as it is pretty heavy.' The Crown of India was then brought back to London and placed in the Jewel-house of the Tower where it may be seen today.

The King-Emperor's part in the Durbar ceremonial was no sooner settled than a new point was raised: what was the Queen-Empress to do in India, and, further, was Queen Mary Empress of India at all? 'The humble origin of the enquiry', wrote Crewe to Hardinge, 'was a query from Lever Brothers, of Sunlight Soap fame, as to whether the Queen is Empress of India or not. I suppose the information is needed for purposes of advertisement.' The King immediately proposed to issue a proclamation defining Queen Mary's Indian status, but Crewe opposed this, since he felt 'that nothing ought to be done to throw doubt on the fact that the Queen derives the title from her marriage, as the Consort of the Emperor'.[18] He added that in his own view Queen Alexandra was now the Dowager Empress of India.

Next came the problem of the entry into Delhi, which was to take place in solemn procession through the gate used in olden days by the Mogul Emperors. This was not to be an elephant procession; but would not the Indian crowds expect that at least the King-Emperor and the Queen-Empress should pass through their midst aloft upon bejewelled elephants? Would it not be suitable, for instance, for the Imperial couple to enter Delhi together upon a single giant elephant? Lord Curzon had ridden an elephant at the Durbar of 1903; but the present King was determined that the Durbar of 1911 should be more popular in character than that of Lord Curzon, and declared that he would enter Delhi on horseback. In the event he was so obscured by the cluster of equerries and of high officials also riding horses, that, clad in the uniform of a Field-Marshal and wearing a topee, the King-Emperor passed unnoticed through the crowds. Queen Mary followed behind him, in the first carriage of the procession. This was drawn by six horses and had a couple of *chuprassi* in scarlet and gold perched upon the dickey. One of these *chuprassi* held the Golden Fan, the other the Empress's Golden State Umbrella—both symbols of royalty to Indian eyes. Opposite the Queen-Empress in her carriage sat the Duchess of Devonshire and Lord Durham. Finding that the *chuprassi's* heavy state umbrella tended to tilt backwards and to give no shade, Queen Mary unfurled her own white parasol as an auxiliary and held this above her head.

Many other details of the 1911 visit to India proved teasing to those trying to organise it. The King was determined on getting in as much tiger-shooting as he could, for, as we know, the sport of shooting held him with what Crewe once called 'an unholy fascination'. 'The fact is', wrote Crewe to Hardinge, 'that it is a misfortune for a public personage to have any taste so strongly developed as the craze for shooting is in our beloved Ruler. One may be grateful that the taste itself is not pernicious, but in such a case as this, his perspective of what is proper is almost destroyed.' The trouble here was that the King, having refused to visit the Madras Presidency on the score of lack of time, wished instead to set off six hundred miles from Delhi for a week's shooting. Crewe and Bigge felt that this would 'give an air of flippancy to the tour' and ill accord with the King-Emperor's role in India as 'a semi-divine figure'.[19] Also, if the King-Emperor went shooting, what was to happen to the Queen-Empress? 'It would hardly do, would it, for her to begin in Calcutta without him?' Crewe asked Hardinge.[20] This last conundrum was quickly solved, for Queen Mary was never at a loss as to how to dispose of her time; she announced that she would very much like to go to Agra to have another quiet look at the Taj Mahal and at Itmadaddaulah's tomb, and that she proposed to spend Christmas week investigating the remote and pristine native states of Bundi and Kotah. 'Today', she wrote from Buckingham Palace on 12 October 1911, 'I did shopping with Mary & Eva as I had to get presents for a Xmas Tree I am to give the native children at Kotah, knives, mechanical toys & dolls are what I have chosen.'[21] There proved to be twenty-eight of these native children, offspring of the Maharao Rajah of Kotah's Thakurs.

'This visit', wrote Queen Mary to her Aunt Augusta a few weeks before setting sail for Bombay, 'will be far less tiring than that of 5 years ago.'[22] The preparations were, in fact, the most fatiguing part of the project, for once again Queen Mary had to provide herself with a new wardrobe. 'There is no truth in the cutting you sent me about my intention to wear the Irish lace train at the Durbar,' she wrote to her husband, 'it is the usual invention of the papers—You know I am wearing a purple velvet train like your's only much shorter, it will be trimmed with gold braid & bordered with ermine.'[23] In 1911 women's fashions no longer permitted of full skirts; Queen Mary, like her ladies, found the new narrower skirts difficult to manage in Delhi, where the streets had been thoughtfully oiled to keep down the dust. After noticing that her Mistress of the Robes, the Duchess of Devonshire, looked askance at her efforts to gather up her narrow skirts out of the oil, Queen Mary arranged to be attended by two small Indian boys whose sole duty it was to help her at such moments, and who followed closely behind her.

At ten o'clock on the morning of 11 November 1911 the King and Queen left Buckingham Palace in a carriage procession to Victoria Station, where a great gathering of relations, government officials and foreign diplomats was assembled to take leave. Their train left for Portsmouth, where they boarded the *Medina* under a black, forbidding sky. After a family luncheon party their guests left them at half-past two, 'Queen Mary supporting Queen Alexandra to the gangway'.[24] As the three tugs began to ease the *Medina* from the quay the threatened storm broke; the passenger liner and her four attendant cruisers put to sea in a tempest. The bunting which decorated every ship of the Home Fleet was torn and lashed by the gale, and the receding Portsmouth shore showed to the departing travellers as a mushroom bank of shining wet umbrellas. King George stood upon the bridge. 'I shall never forget that moment', he wrote to his mother Queen Alexandra, 'when I saw you moving from the window of the railway carriage as we slowly steamed away from you into the wind & rain.'[25]

III

The *Medina*, which had been temporarily commissioned in the Royal Navy for the special purpose of conveying the King and Queen and their suite to Bombay and back again, was a brand-new ship of the Peninsular and Oriental Company. She was built of steel with reciprocating engines and twin screws. Her burden was thirteen thousand tons. The ship was designed to accommodate six hundred and fifty passengers; the royal party, including the King and Queen, numbered twenty-four in all. Space, therefore, was no problem, although the luxurious cabins prepared for the royal party had been placed so far forward 'as to be very trying in a seaway', and the King and Queen soon exchanged their quarters for storm cabins further aft.

In the Bay of Biscay the ship, with her attendant cruisers, ploughed through a heavy storm; almost all the passengers and many of the sailors as well were taken ill. In those days of peace the men of the Royal Navy had little opportunity to experience long heavy seas, and the sailors of the *Medina* were now to be seen stumbling about their duties as the ship rolled and lurched. Apples were issued to them which they munched as they worked in the hope of alleviating seasickness. Queen Mary, who was, as we know, a notably bad seawoman, did not leave her cabin for some days. Even King George was seasick: 'I had not been ill for years', he wrote to his mother on 14 November. 'May remained in bed till this morning, the Ladies & all the maids & servants disappeared for two days. The poor cruisers had a very bad time of it & took the seas right over them. . . . I have just sent a message to Alfonso & Ena on passing Spain.'[26] One of the only exceptions to the general sea-sickness on the *Medina* was a Windsor cowman who was in charge of the three cows on board; he had never seen the sea before in his life, but he survived the storm unperturbed.

After Gibraltar the *Medina* entered calm warm waters. The King and Queen sat on deck reading, with one or two ladies and gentlemen in attendance, while the band played. 'Our band is quite excellent & plays morning & afternoon & we spend our time on deck reading which is very pleasant & is a nice rest,' wrote King George, 'the first real rest I have had for $1\frac{1}{2}$ years.'[27] Queen Mary also loved the band. 'We have a beautiful band on bd, the Marine Artillery', she wrote to her Aunt Augusta, '& it plays 3 times a day, morning, afternoon & evening which is really delightful.'[28] This royal enthusiasm for the Marine Band was not shared by all the members of Their Majesties' suite. The band's repertory was limited, and they constantly succumbed to the temptation of playing the King's favourite piece, *In the Shadows*, over and over again. 'The band played at eleven o'clock in the morning', writes the official artist to the expedition, the painter Percy Jacomb-Hood. ' . . . The band played again in the afternoon, and again at dinner in the evening, and afterwards in the after-saloon on deck. There are certain tunes which they played frequently which, hearing now, bring back to me hot and sleepy afternoons, with the wash of the sea outside my cabin window, as I tried to work, and the conductor's foot stamping time on the deck just over my head, while John Fortescue in the cabin next to me was trying to write, and intermittently (nay, *without* intermission) calling down curses on that - - - - band.'29

Besides being the official artist accredited to the royal party, Mr Jacomb-Hood was commissioned by *The Graphic* to supply sketches of the journey out and of the events at the Durbar. His editor was particularly anxious to receive pictures 'of what he called *vie intime* on board'. Accordingly one morning Sir Derek Keppel knocked at the artist's cabin door with a message from the King. 'If you want a *vie intime* sketch, the King says "now is the time"—the Queen is on the promenade deck signing a lot of her photographs.' Jacomb-Hood hurried on deck, to find 'a pretty scene': 'The Queen hard at work signing photographs, which Sir Charles Cust who stood by her side, handed to her, Miss Baring, seated at her feet on the deck, and assisted by one of the Queen's sailor-boy attendants, sorting them out (there were four different photographs) and laying them on deck to dry. The King was reading in a chair close by, while two ladies sat not far off. I worked at this till lunch time, when the King invited me to lunch at their table, and I sat next to the Queen. . . . The King was very jolly and talkative. . . . The Queen, speaking of the number of godchildren she had, said that they were so numerous that she had to have an inventory of them made.'30 Jacomb-Hood was later allowed to do sketches of the King and Queen: 'Their Majesties', he writes, 'were both "bricks" about sitting, and I am their devoted subject; they are both so pleasant and thoughtful.' He also sketched members of the suite, and did drawings of 'the four sailor-boys who acted as messengers for the Queen, two being always within hail of her. She thought', he adds, 'they had such nice faces, and so they had, having been specially picked for her by Sir Charles Cust.'31

Despite the band and the 'very pleasant' party accompanying them, Queen Mary found life on board ship as uneventful as ever. 'We had sports for the men yesterday', she wrote as they neared Bombay, '& we gave prizes afterwards, they seemed to enjoy it all very much— But it is monotonous to a degree on bd, luckily I can read a great deal.'32 The books which Queen Mary read on the voyage out were mainly books on India and Indian problems or Indian life and religions: interspersed with these were some current novels—books by A. E. W. Mason, for example, or by Marjorie Bowen. We may remember how much old Sir Walter Lawrence had been struck in 1905 by her knowledge of India—'quite remarkable in a woman' he had told her. This knowledge had been gained by serious and systematic study. During the year 1905 she had read no less than thirty-six books on Indian subjects, and none of these could be called 'light reading', for they included Lyall's *British Dominion in India*, Noble's *Web of Indian Life*, *India, its Administration and Progress* by Sir John Strachey, *Indian Polity* by Sir G. Chesney, as well as biographies of such men as Warren Hastings and Lord Dalhousie, viceregal memoirs by Lord Dufferin and many other historical works. On the *Medina* in 1911 she renewed her acquaintanceship with some of these books, and also read a good deal of Kipling. The European life in Indian stations interested Queen Mary less than that of the native states; the only Indian Kipling she had hitherto known had been *Wee Willie Winkie*, which she had read in 1891, and read again now aboard the *Medina*. On the *Medina*, too, she read *Plain Tales from the Hills*, *From Sea to Sea*, *The Naulakha* and the *Barrack Room Ballads*.

It is unlikely that the mordant sarcasm of *Under the Deodars* or *The Story of the Gadsbys* would have appealed to Queen Mary, for she did not like fun being made of institutions which she regarded seriously. She had once, for instance, warmly congratulated Madame Bricka upon burning a copy of Balzac's *Petites Misères de la Vie Conjugale*—the only volume of Balzac, incidentally, which Queen Mary ever read. But if the greatest masterpieces of English as well as European literature were, in the most literal sense, closed books to her, Queen Mary did not waste her time. She had by now made herself exceedingly well informed, and she was as ready to impart information as to garner it. 'Shy she was, at first, but not in the least dull', wrote A. C. Benson of a meeting with the Queen at Cambridge some years later, '—very well informed about current topics and people and historical people, easily amused, and the somewhat severe lines of her face melting into great geniality. . . . I liked her voice and her quick direct replies.'[33]

As the *Medina* steams steadily eastward to the persistent strains of the Marine Artillery band it is easy to picture Queen Mary sitting in her chair on the deck, a lady-in-waiting not far off, and two of the sailor-boys within hail; on her lap a book of Indian history, an expression of careful concentration in her bright blue eyes.

IV

The *Medina*, with its attendant cruisers, reached the shores of India on the 2nd of December, a Saturday. Anchor was dropped two miles off the flat coastline of the Bombay Presidency just as the sun was rising above the palm-trees on Malabar Point. Soon the Viceroy, the Governor of Bombay and other high officials came aboard the ship to welcome the King-Emperor to his Indian Empire. They returned to the shore, there to await the landing of King George and Queen Mary upon the Apollo Bundar, where a pavilion in the Saracenic style had been erected over a dais on which stood two imperial chairs of state. Behind this pavilion was a great archway copied from the best known of the Assyrian palaces, the Palace of Khorsade; farther back was a second archway designed in the Mohammedan style; and behind this again rose an archway made of giant cotton-bales. These features, symbolising the mixed origins of the merchant community of Bombay as well as the chief source of the city's wealth, were on a more grandiose scale than anything that had greeted the King and Queen when, as Prince and Princess of Wales, they had visited Bombay in 1905. On that occasion the streets had twinkled with little oil-lamps at night, and the festooned greetings hung across the house-fronts had been of a more personal nature: 'Sir Jamset-jee-Jee-Jee-Bhoy and family wish long life and happiness to George and Mary', for example. The preparations for the reception of the Imperial couple in 1911 were far more solemn, and in keeping with the sacred character of the King-Emperor's role.

In dead calm and suffocating heat the King-Emperor and his Consort crossed the water, which shone like burnished brass. They set foot on Indian soil to the sound of a salute of one hundred and one guns. King George was wearing the white uniform of an Admiral of the Fleet, with the ribbon and star of the Star of India; Queen Mary was dressed in a gown of yellow flowered chiffon, slashed by the brilliant blue of the Garter ribbon. She also wore the King's Order and the Star of India; on her head was a plate-like hat of straw, heaped high with artificial roses to match her dress. 'We had a splendid reception at Bombay on Saturday', she wrote. 'Crowds of people in the gaily decorated streets & all beaming. Heat intense & we were glad to stay on bd instead of at Govt. House. . . . It is marvellous to me being in India again, I who never thought I should ever see it again. I am *so* glad I came.'34

Through streets gay with flags and bunting, every pavement and window in which was crammed with sightseers who also stood upon the roofs and clung upon the balconies, they drove to Government House. As she gazed about her with her quick, all-seeing eyes, Queen

Mary felt once more that sense of elation which her first sight of India had brought her six years before. Once again she revelled in this world of strident colours, where snow-white turbans jerked and nodded in the sharp sunlight, where Indian women stood swathed in stuffs of crude vivid pink or turquoise blue or acid green.

After four days in Bombay the King and Queen set off in the Imperial train for Delhi, past bedecked wayside stations smothered in brilliant bougainvillea and crowded with spectators, past neem-trees about which the green parrakeets darted and flashed. The official entry into Delhi through the Gate of the Elephants was equally exciting: 'Splendid picturesque reception', Queen Mary wrote to Strelitz. ' . . . It was a wonderful sight this morning, George rode and I followed in a carriage with the Mistress of the Robes & Lord Durham—Very grand & I felt proud to take part in so interesting & historical an event, just the kind of thing which appeals to my feelings of tradition —*You* will understand.'35

The preparations at Delhi were on a scale without precedent in the history of British India. On the wide, marshy plains beside the Jumna River a vast canvas city had been reared. It covered forty-five square miles and housed a quarter of a million persons. Each camp vied in luxury with the next, but the most lavish of all were, of course, the six great tents furnished and arranged for the King-Emperor and his Consort: there was a drawing-room, an ante-room, an office, a boudoir, bedrooms, and a dining-room that connected with the state reception tents. The Queen-Empress's apartments were lined with *vieux-rose* silk, hung with embroideries and carpeted with the most valuable Oriental rugs. Queen Mary thought this camp 'beautifully arranged': 'we have', she wrote, 'real rooms & are most comfortable.'36

The five days immediately preceding the actual Durbar ceremonies were spent by the King-Emperor in granting private audiences to the native Princes of India. 'George is really splendid', wrote his wife, 'entering into the spirit of it all & the Indian chiefs are simply enchanted with the reception he has given them, receiving them all singly.'37 There were also many ceremonies, processions and tournaments. Although her part in all these was naturally secondary to that of the King-Emperor, Queen Mary was kept busy during these days with some activities of her own. These included her reception of a deputation of Indian ladies, headed by the Maharani of Patiala, who presented her with 'a large square of emeralds of historic interest, engraved and set in diamonds, and a necklace and pendant of emeralds,

P*

set in rosettes of diamonds.' In the message of homage read out to the Queen-Empress by the Maharani there was a passage explaining that it was mistaken to suppose that simply because the ladies of India lived in *purdah*, they were 'strangers to that mighty process of evolution which manifests itself beyond the limits of its four walls'. The message also referred to the long reign of peace which British rule had brought to India. In her reply, Queen Mary assured the ladies of her own 'increasing solicitude for those who live "within the walls",' and said that she had learned 'with deep satisfaction' of the evolution taking place within the limits of *purdah*. 'The jewel you have given me will ever be very precious in my eyes', she added, 'and whenever I wear it, though thousands of miles of land and sea separate us, my thoughts will fly to the homes of India, and create again and again this happy meeting and recall the tender love your hearts have yielded me. Your jewel shall pass to future generations as an imperial heirloom, and always stand as a token of the first meeting of an English Queen with the ladies of India.'38 As we have noticed earlier, Queen Mary seldom made a public speech or read an address; on the rare occasions when she did so her words were apposite, and were largely written by herself.

The Durbar of 12 December took place upon the plains by the Jumna, inside two concentric amphitheatres—the larger one constructed to hold a hundred thousand spectators, the smaller one to accommodate the princes, rulers and notables of the Indian Empire. In the very centre of all was a dais two hundred feet across, surmounted by a series of smaller marble platforms, on the topmost of which two thrones of solid silver encased with gold stood waiting upon a cloth-of-gold carpet and beneath a golden cupola sixty-eight feet from the ground. A crimson-carpeted causeway led from this pavilion to a smaller one, used in the Homage ceremony. Fifty thousand troops paraded in the arena on the Durbar morning. The massed bands numbered more than one thousand six hundred instrumentalists, but, since amplifiers had not then been invented, the watching crowds heard little and for them the Durbar ceremony 'had to be one of sight rather than of coherent sound'.39

The organisation of the Durbar, was, in fact, the last word in perfection; but on the very morning of the great day, a fault was discovered which might have jeopardised the solemnity of the whole ceremony. The King-Emperor and his Consort, wearing Imperial robes, the King his crown, the Queen her diadem, were to enter the arena seated side by side in one of the great state barouches, equipped with C springs, from Government House. At the back of this barouche were perched the two inevitable *chuprassi* in scarlet and gold uniforms, the Imperial Crown embroidered in gold upon their breasts. These two *chuprassi* had been carefully chosen for this honour; they were very old veterans, and they found the cumbrous Imperial state umbrellas which they were to hold over the heads of the King and Queen too heavy to keep upright. Without these umbrellas the Imperial couple, in their weighty velvet robes, would have been exposed to the relentless, beating rays of the midday sun. In consequence, the officer in charge of the Royal stables had that morning hastily concocted 'a very rickety awning' over the carriage; it was supported by flexible bamboo canes wound round with cheap gold and silver tissue bought in Delhi bazaar. 'The whole thing wobbled horribly directly the carriage moved', wrote an eye-witness who was summoned at the last moment to help to cope with this hideous problem. 'All that I could suggest', he wrote, 'was the strengthening of the uprights by arched brackets supporting the roof, and also by, as nearly as possible, invisible "stays" of wire or string. As the carriage drove into the arena with Their Majesties, later on, I was dreadfully conscious of our flimsy *shamiana* set up on it. If it had collapsed, what an awful anti-climax that would have been to the Durbar of the King-Emperor and his proclamation.'[40] The *shamiana* held; the proclamations were read; the homage of the Princes of India was received; and the Delhi Durbar of December 1911 passed into Imperial history as an unqualified success.

The strange beauty of the amphitheatre, the superbly timed ceremonial, the symbols of Empire held behind the throne—these last including maces five feet high with ornamented motifs of the lotus-flower, the king-cobra and the Tudor crown—impressed the two central figures on the golden dais beneath the golden dome fully as much as they did the spectators. 'The Durbar yesterday was the most wonderful & beautiful sight I have ever seen & one I shall remember all my life', King George V wrote to his mother. 'We wore our robes & I the new crown made for the occasion. May had her best tiara on. ... I can only say it was most magnificent, the clothes & colours were marvellous. .... I had six pages & May had four to carry our robes, they were either young Maharajahs or sons of Maharajahs & all wore beautiful clothes of white & gold with gold turbans & they did look nice.'[41] At the Durbar Queen Mary had worn the fine jewels given her by the ladies of India, but her chief adornment had been the famous emeralds which had belonged to her grandmother the Duchess of Cambridge. 'Mama's Emeralds appearing *there* amused and pleases me', wrote the Duchess of Cambridge's surviving daughter, the old Augusta Strelitz. 'What would she have said to her Grandchild's Imperial glory? in which I so rejoice!'[42]

v

'I parted from George on Sat. 16th after our wonderful 10 days at Delhi,' Queen Mary wrote to her Aunt Augusta from Jaipur on 20 December 1911, 'he went to Nepaul to shoot while I left for Agra which I wanted to see again & for a tour in Rajputana. I had a delightful 2 days at Agra seeing the beautiful Taj again & the fine old Fort built in the Moghul Emperors' time as well as various other smaller places I wished to revisit—Then I came on here where I had a kind welcome from the Maharajah who is a charming old gentleman but who does not speak English. I have just returned from a wonderful old Palace & town built in 1188 which is now deserted & I am going this afternoon to see another place. I leave tomorrow for Ajmere & then to Bundi & Kotah. You will forgive only a line, it is so difficult to find time to write.'

Queen Mary enjoyed this fortnight on her own in the states of Rajputana. She spent Christmas Day at Kotah, where she first distributed 'small presents' to her suite, then visited the tombs of the Maharao Rajah's ancestors and afterwards spent some time afloat upon the River Chumbal in a launch: 'There were high rocks with jungle on each side', she noted in her Diary of this river expedition, '& we saw monkeys, a panther & 4 bears which was most exciting but none of the gentlemen got a shot.' Later in the day she gave her Christmas-tree entertainment to the Maharao Rajah's Thakurs' children, followed by a Christmas dinner-party for her suite. The next day she 'motored out to a little summer palace where a quantity of crocodiles live in a tank. A man fed them with pieces of meat. We had tea & returned home.' There was also a mild tiger-shooting expedition arranged for Queen Mary's benefit: 'We motored to a little building close to the jungle & went in *Tam-jams* or *palkis* to the *machans* into one of which I climbed by a ladder with Ld Shaftesbury, Evie & Venetia. We saw a bear, a nilghai, & some wild boars the first beat & heard a tiger behind us. The 2nd beat I saw the tiger beautifully 40 yards away coming towards us but Lord S. had his back to him & could not get a shot as he bounded away.'43 Lord Shaftesbury has described how, on this occasion, it was Queen Mary who saw the tiger before anyone else did so. She was sitting in the tree-hut, knitting, and suddenly remarked, pointing to the jungle with one of her knitting-needles: 'Look, Lord Shaftesbury, a tiger.' For some seconds, on the principle perhaps that a cat may look at a King, the animal stood transfixed, glaring with its green eyes at Queen Mary, who returned the steady gaze. The animal then disappeared into the undergrowth before Lord Shaftesbury had time to take aim.

We may here notice that Queen Mary, while she always sublimated her personality in public to that of King George, was not at all averse to doing 'functions', expeditions and sight-seeing on her own. She was happy visiting the old Palace of Amber on an elephant, she was happy going for 'a short drive in a bullock-cart'. 'All the people turned out & salaamed & were most civil', she recorded of another occasion in Rajputana; or 'Reached Guna at 5. where I inspected the 38th Central India Horse & had tea with the officers & their wives'.44 In this sense she was more self-sufficient than her husband, who confessed to a sense of incompleteness in the absence of his wife. 'Each year', he wrote to her from his shooting camp in Nepal on 22 December, 'I feel we become more & more necessary to one another & our lives become more & more wrapt up in each others. And I am sure that I love you more each year & am simply devoted to you & loathe being separated from you even for a day. Especially now in my present position with the enormous amount I have to do & with all my many responsibilities I feel that I want your kind help & support more than ever. And I must say you invariably give it me, I greatly appreciate it & thank you from the bottom of my heart for all the love & devotion you always give me.' 'You say', he wrote in another passage of this same letter, 'you were proud of being my wife, I repeat that I was very proud of being your husband & I feel that our coming here to India as the first Emperor & Empress has certainly proved itself to be what I always predicted, a great success & one which will have far reaching effects & I trust lasting effects throughout this great Empire.'45

King George and Queen Mary met again at Bankipore on 29 December: 'My train was shunted to join G's', the Queen recorded in her Diary. 'Crowds of people at the station.' From there they proceeded to Calcutta which Queen Mary called 'too European for my taste & not really Indian as the other places I have visited are'.46 A week later they returned to Bombay, and on 10 January they set sail again in the *Medina* for the homeward journey. On that last day the King-Emperor and the Queen-Empress sat once more enthroned in the Saracenic pavilion on the Apollo Bundar; King George read his speech of farewell and, as he told Queen Alexandra, 'actually broke down; I simply couldn't help it'.47 To Lord Crewe he said that he had been so much moved at the last sentences 'that he could hardly finish'. 'As he told me', wrote Crewe, 'it flashed across his mind that he would never see India again, and the thought was too much for him.'48 'Very sorry to leave dear India', Queen Mary wrote in her Diary, 'where we have had such a wonderful time.'49

VI

The day after the great Durbar ceremony of 12 December, King George and Queen Mary had been informed by wireless telegram of the wreck off the Moroccan coast of the P. & O. liner *Delhi*. Amongst the passengers on board this ship were King George's eldest sister, Princess Louise, by then Princess Royal, her husband the Duke of Fife and their two daughters Princess Alix, aged twenty, and Princess Maud, aged eighteen. They were on their way to Egypt and the Sudan, where they were to winter in that warm climate for the fourth consecutive year, since the Princess Royal, like her sisters, suffered from weak health, and spent a good part of her life taking measures to combat this.

The *Delhi* had gone aground off the coast of Morocco in heavy seas; several passengers and sailors were drowned, and many lifeboats were pulverised upon the rocks. HMS *Edinburgh*, under the command of Admiral Cradock, had sent out a boat into which the Fife family, some of the last passengers still aboard the *Delhi*, had jumped; for the Princess Royal and her husband had firmly refused to leave the ship before the other passengers had done so. 'We descended the long steep ladder, & jumped in as the boat rose', the Princess Royal wrote to her brother the King in a long, graphic letter, which he received at Aden: 'We got on alright but waves were huge, they swept down on us & filled the boat, we bailed, but not any good, water came up to our knees & she sank! flinging us all out! We floated in our belts—waves like iron walls tore over us, knocked us under, Admiral Cradock gripped my shoulder & *saved* me!—Thank God my Macduff & children both on beach but had been *under* too, it was an awful *moment*, our clothes so heavy, & we were breathless & shivery, we ran to get warm as best we could—I lost my poor bag. . . . It is an extraordinary nightmare, & we are indeed grateful to be *all* here & alive still—but I am *very* achy! I hope you can understand, what I have written.'⁵⁰ 'I have received two letters from dear Louise', King George wrote to his mother, 'giving me a description of all the terrible experiences they went through on bd the "*Delhi*", she certainly seems to have behaved most bravely & I am proud that she is my sister.'⁵¹ Recovered from their alarming experience, the Fifes went on to Khartoum and Cairo. In January they set off for Khartoum for the second time, to attend the consecration of the Cathedral there. 'We were so peaceful and contented steaming up the Nile', writes the Princess Royal's elder daughter, in her privately printed account of this winter in Egypt, 'reading, writing and sketching, which gave one the opportunity to collect one's thoughts and replenish one's mind. This was all cut short by a great tragedy suddenly cast upon us. My father caught a chill, which developed rapidly, and in ten days he died of pneumonia. . . . It seems to be generally thought that my father died as the result of the shipwreck, but this was not so.'⁵²

News of his brother-in-law's death was received by King George just as the *Medina* was steaming towards Gibraltar. Both the King and Queen Mary had liked the Duke of Fife, known in the family as 'Macduff'. 'I am so terribly upset at poor dear Macduff's sad death from pleurisy in Egypt that I can think of nothing else, but of poor Louise's grief and despair', wrote Queen Mary from Gibraltar. 'It is too sad to think that only 6 weeks ago they were saved from shipwreck & that now he is no more. . . . One longs to help but what can one do when one is miles away? . . . Of course *all* festivities here have been given up which is a great disappointment to the poor people on shore, & we have only done strict *duty* functions today, a vile day & raining heavily, too disagreeable but suitable to my feelings—Poor George feels dear Macduff's death very much, as I do too, for I was very fond of him. This will be a fresh trial to "Motherdear" who was just beginning to have a few people to stay with her at Sandringham & to be a little more cheerful.'⁵³

On 4 February 1912 the *Medina* entered the English Channel in a snowstorm, to be greeted by the Home Fleet. Met at Portsmouth on the 5th February by the Prince of Wales, as well as by Queen Alexandra and Princess Victoria clad in deepest mourning, the King and Queen entrained for London, where, despite a lowering sky and a bitter north-east wind, cheering crowds lined the pavements of their route to Buckingham Palace by Whitehall and the Mall. Next day there was a great service of Thanksgiving at St Paul's Cathedral. 'Of course', wrote Queen Mary, 'poor dear Macduff's death has considerably spoilt our homecoming, it is dreadful to be again in mourning & really at St Paul's with everyone in black, it seemed more like a funeral service than one of rejoicing. However such is life & one must make the best of it.'[54]

CHAPTER THREE

A LINE OF THEIR OWN

ONE BY-PRODUCT of the success of the Delhi Durbar and of the wide publicity given to it in the British press, was to increase the personal popularity of the new King and Queen at home. 'I went out driving in an open carriage with the Queen in the Park yesterday afternoon, & everybody crowded to see Her Majesty', wrote Lady Bertha Dawkins to her daughter in April 1912. 'There was hardly anybody there when we first went through on our way to visit the Queen's old maid in her lovely rooms at Kensington Palace, & on our way back, there were excited crowds.'[1] 'Whit Monday', Queen Mary wrote to her Aunt Augusta in that same year, 'we drove in Hyde Pk & Battersea Pk where there were large crowds who gave us a nice friendly welcome.'[2] The public were quick to recognise and to encourage the new tone of the new reign; King George was, as always, touched and surprised by any evidence of public affection and approval. 'I really do think people do appreciate all the hard work we have had', he wrote to Queen Mary in the summer of 1913 after he had been three years on the throne.[3] 'Yes', she replied, 'I quite agree with you that people are appreciative of the work *we* are trying to do for the Country in general.'[4]

Yet despite this growing popularity, the months that followed the King and Queen's return from India were sombre. Less than three weeks after they had landed at Portsmouth, they returned thither for the purpose of receiving the widowed Princess Royal and her two daughters, who had brought home the Duke of Fife's coffin aboard HMS *Powerful*. 'Awfully sad meeting with Louise', Queen Mary recorded, 'tho' she & the girls were wonderfully composed.'[5] Queen Alexandra wrote to Queen Mary that it had seemed to her 'as if *we two* felt poor dear Macduffs being *brought home* like that!! in his coffin more acutely than any one present. . . . It was all *so simple so natural* & so infinitely sad—And what a saintly heroine our poor darling Louise has become! . . . a *changed being* who can bear every cross now!'[6] Mourning for the Duke of Fife curtailed the King and Queen's social activities; and just as they were emerging from this comparative seclusion that spring, Queen Alexandra's eldest brother, King Frederick VIII of Denmark, died suddenly after a short reign of six years. 'The sad news of poor U. Freddy's death . . . came as a great shock to us all as we had heard he was better', wrote Queen Mary in May 1912 from Aldershot. ' . . . It is all very sad and his dying in the street quite alone makes it worse. . . . We return to London on Monday & have of course cancelled all Social Functions for the present, only doing *duty* ones—It is rather hard on us, having been shut up on account of poor Macduff all the late winter, now to have another mourning & to be unable to carry out our engagements.'7 'I am following your movements from daily papers and read of your leaving Devonshire H. before the Ball,' her aunt wrote to her that June, 'it is so annoying these Mournings falling in the Season, so can well understand how they are inconvenient in many ways.'8

There were far more serious causes for Queen Mary's depression that spring of 1912 than the gloomy inconvenience of royal mourning. During Mr Asquith's Government the sullen revolt of factory workers and miners against disgraceful living conditions, long working hours and low wages had gathered momentum; from 1907 on the country had been swept by a gale of industrial strikes. Coronation Year, 1911, had been marred by a brief but costly railway strike, while on their return from India the King and Queen were greeted by the great coal strike of the spring of 1912 'which lasted five weeks and cost the country the loss of thirty million working days'.9

Her humanity and her patriotism combined to make Queen Mary take these strikes very much to heart. In her thoughtful, well-informed way she pondered over them, though it was their effects rather than their causes which, at that moment, she chiefly understood. 'I am so horrified and distressed at these awful strikes which mean so much unnecessary misery & suffering', she had written in a letter of August 1911.10 She, like the King, contributed generously to funds to help the unemployed, but the strikes, as against the unemployment, bewildered her. 'If only one could act', she wrote with her usual energy during the coal strike of 1912, 'but like this one feels so impotent, & all this time our blessed & beloved country is in a state of stagnation & misery—Most people seem to go on as if everything were in a normal state, but we feel the whole thing too much to take it lightly.'11 Almost as soon as the coal strike was over a transport strike was declared, forcing Mr Asquith's Government to use dictatorial powers to suppress it. 'Now', wrote Queen Mary as this new strike broke out, 'we have a transport strike which may become very serious—really we have no luck, one tiresome thing after the other.'[12] She and the King had hoped to be able to pay certain state visits on the Continent during the months following the Delhi Durbar, but it soon became clear that this was out of the question. 'We have been obliged to give up the idea of our foreign visits which we had hoped to accomplish this Spring', the Queen wrote in a private letter, 'but really with our Country in the state she is in we feel we cannot make any plans & must remain here in London for the present.'[13]

Today, viewed across the chasm of two World Wars, the problems which beset King George V and Mr Asquith's Cabinet in the first three years of the new reign may seem of minor import: yet in their day the Parliament Bill, the Home Rule agitation with its attendant threat of Irish Civil War, the industrial unrest, the mushroom growth of Keir Hardie's Labour Party provided grave preoccupations. There were in addition the activities of Mrs Pankhurst and her followers, which, from seeming silly escapades, had, by the spring of 1912, become a serious nuisance to people in public life and above all to the King and Queen. It was in that year that London Suffragist women and girls of every class began a campaign of smashing plate-glass and other windows with hammers which they carried hidden in their muffs. 'We were very much upset because of the Suffragette Movements', Queen Mary noted, for example, in her Diary for 4 March 1912, 'smashing windows & behaving in an extraordinary way. George was kept informed by Sir Edward Henry.' It was not to be expected that the Queen, with her love of the orderly, could sympathise with the obstreperous Suffragettes. She would laconically record 'many Suffragette *contretemps*' in her Diaries. When, in what she described as 'a most sensational' Derby, Queen Mary witnessed the suicidal gesture of Miss Emily Wilding Davidson, who threw herself under the hooves of the King's horse as it was rounding Tattenham Corner, her first thought was for 'poor Jones' the jockey 'who was much knocked about'. The death of Miss Davidson was at first concealed from the Queen, who merely recorded that 'the horrid woman was injured but not seriously'.[14] 'Those horrid suffragettes burnt down the little tea house (modern) close to the Pagoda in Kew Gardens yesterday morning at 3 a.m.,' Queen Mary wrote on another occasion in 1913 to her Aunt Augusta, 'There seems no end to their iniquities'; and, again, in March 1913: 'When George opened parliament on Monday some

tiresome suffragettes rushed out in the Mall & tried to present peti-
tions, of course the police caught them, but it caused a scene &
looked undignified.'[15] Queen Mary found a ready sympathiser in
the old Grand Duchess, who compared the English Suffragettes un-
favourably with the 'more rational' *Frauenbewegung* of Germany.
'Can these females not be shut up on some Island?' she asked.[16]

By 1914 even Buckingham Palace itself was not safe from the Suffragettes. Although Mrs Pankhurst, newly released from prison, was
re-arrested when she headed a procession of women who attempted to
storm the Palace in the summer of 1914, in early June Their Majesties'
third Court was interrupted by Miss Mary Blomfield, a daughter of
the distinguished architect, who fell on both knees 'when passing the
Royal presence and cried in a loud shrill voice, which could be heard
throughout the Throne Room, "Your Majesty, won't you stop tor-
turing women?" ' Miss Blomfield was removed by Sir Douglas Dawson
and the Court went on. 'The King and Queen', ran a newspaper report
of the incident, 'showed no sign, and the proceedings were not interrupted for an instant. Eye-witnesses describe the bearing of Their
Majesties, and the continuance of the ceremony, as a masterpiece of
dignity and composure.'[17] In fact Miss Blomfield had been taken out
before she had completed her protest against the forcible feeding of
Suffragettes in HM prisons, as Queen Mary's Diary entry for 4 June
1914 makes clear:

Fine day, rather cooler. George & I received three Maori chiefs at 11—
Sat out in the garden most of the day. We held our 3rd Court in the
evening and a tiresome suffragette came & fell on her knees before G. &
held out her arms in a supplicating way, saying 'Oh! Your Majesty stop'
when she was gently escorted out by Douglas Dawson & John Hamilton.
Very unpleasant.

Although in the 1914–1918 war Queen Mary developed a great
admiration for the courage and self-sacrifice of Englishwomen in a
national crisis, she had been born with the intelligent woman's critical
attitude towards others of her sex. 'If only the worst passions were
not aroused,' she wrote during the 1911 wave of strikes, 'Liverpool is
really terrible & as usual it is the idiotic short-sighted women are the
worst offenders & egg the men on.'[18] This comment she made in a
letter to King George, for to no one else did she commit her own
political views to paper. Because, fully aware of the discretion essential
in the Consort of a Constitutional Sovereign, she never expressed her

political feelings, this did not mean that Queen Mary did not have any. She was earnestly interested in the subject, and could not dismiss it as Queen Alexandra was wont to do. 'Really', Queen Alexandra had written to her in August 1911, at the time of the Parliament Bill, 'to *ruin* the Country in this way seems *madness*—How I hate politics & all what follows worries & mostly miseries.'[19]

As we know, Queen Mary's political views in her youth had been formed in the ultra-Tory atmosphere of White Lodge, where the name of Gladstone was anathema. By the time she became Queen Consort the policies of Gladstone had begun to seem almost Conservative by comparison with the measures initiated by Mr Asquith's Cabinet, and with the positively nightmarish plans of Keir Hardie and his followers. At first Queen Mary tended to blame the Government for the strikes, but here she was sharply corrected by King George. 'I think you are a little hard on the Govt.', he wrote to her. 'They have really been doing all they can to find a solution to this most serious state of affairs.'[20] He added that he had that morning sent off telegrams to the Prime Minister, as well as to Churchill, Lloyd George and Buxton (all members of the Cabinet) to congratulate them on the handling of the strikes. 'You scold me for blaming the Govt.', replied Queen Mary, 'well, I do think the unrest is due to their extraordinary tactics in encouraging Socialism all these years & in pandering to the labour party; but I quite agree the Govt has behaved splendidly the past week in averting what might have become a national disaster. . . . I have felt the long strain very much, after all there is a limit to one's endurance.'[21] This sentiment satisfied King George: 'I quite understand what you mean when you say you blame the Govt about the strikes, yes no doubt through their very stupid & unwise speeches last year they have done much to put class against class, but now that the strikes [have] begun you admit they have behaved well, that is what I meant to say.'[22] One of Queen Mary's closest friends, now dead, once said that if asked to sum up Queen Mary's character, she would have done so in these words: '*Magnanimity and breadth of mind*.'

Socialism was a subject about which, at that time, Queen Mary knew little. She was no more interested in the theoretical than the majority of women, and she judged political creeds by their results. During the war her friendship with such an outstanding Radical as Mary Macarthur led her to modify her views about Socialists, and it was in great part due to her quiet and intelligent influence that King George's relations with his first Labour Ministers were so notably harmonious.

But even before the outbreak of war her first impulse to blame the strikes upon the Socialists waned in the face of her natural curiosity and her sense of justice. We have seen that initially she was more concerned with the strikes' effects at home and abroad than with the causes of the industrial unrest themselves; but very soon both she and the King began to feel that it was a part of their duties to examine living conditions in the industrial regions for themselves. Inspired by this conviction, King George and Queen Mary undertook a series of tours of the mining and industrial areas in 1912 and 1913. These royal tours were then an entirely novel idea. By contrast with the post-war activities of the Prince of Wales and his brother the Duke of York they were limited in scope and in duration. They were, however, a pioneering venture and for the first time in history they brought the British Monarchy into direct touch with the great industrial population of Wales, the Midlands and the North. 'About this time', wrote Mr D. C. Somervell, 'people began to realise that the King and Queen were striking out on a line of their own.'[23]

II

The King and the Queen made their first quiet and tentative experiment along this 'line of their own' during a three-day visit to South Wales in June 1912. The official purpose of this visit was the declaring open by the King of the Welsh National Museum and of a new Research Laboratory in Cardiff College. For two generations functions such as these had been the normal or traditional part of British Royalty; but on this occasion one-third of the Welsh visit was allotted to a tour of the colliery areas of Glamorgan and the black, overcrowded Merthyr Valley. As usual, Queen Mary reported these Welsh experiences to her aunt in Strelitz. 'A very weary tho' gratified niece takes up her pen to write', she began:

. . . Our visit to the mining districts on Thursday was a great success & we had a marvellous reception right in the heart of Keir Hardie's constituency who will not have liked it! It was a long hard day by motor & train lasting from 10 a.m. to 7.30 p.m.! & the constant bowing & noise of the cheering made the visit very fatiguing, however we are assured on all sides that our visit wld do more to bring peace and goodwill into the district than anything else & that we had done the best days work in all our lives! so with that we must rest on our laurels.[24]

The chief pleasure of the Grand Duchess's old age was reading the accounts of her niece's doings in the English newspapers. 'I followed you all along even into the Coal Mine, for I have been in one, in Wales, in 1849,' she wrote, 'wearing a *hood* over my head, not a hat with *white* feathers! that will have suffered!'25 Queen Mary replied that she had not actually gone underground in her hat with white feathers but had merely seen 'the surface working of a mine'.26

Although the original suggestion for this tour of a mining district in which notoriously bad conditions had led to much recent unrest may have come from the Cabinet, it was King George, and still more Queen Mary, who gave the little expedition a new twist. After watching the King receive an address from the mine-owners, Queen Mary went with him to the pit-heads of the various collieries, riding in the colliery trams and chatting with the men and boys as they emerged grimy from beneath ground. They also examined the stables of the pit-ponies. In the midst of it all Queen Mary flustered the officials by demanding to see the interior of a typical Welsh miner's cottage. When, after some hesitation, her request was granted she refused to confine herself to Mrs Thomas Jones's best parlour in the tiny house in Bude Street, but penetrated into the kitchen where she perched herself upon a kitchen chair. After drinking a cup of tea, and accepting the gift of an old mug, the Queen proceeded to examine the rest of the cottage, which she pronounced airy and clean. The news of this perfectly natural behaviour spread like wildfire through the valley. Later in the day, the King and Queen, who were touring the area by train and motor-car, were startled when a bouquet of pink carnations with two postcards attached was tossed into their compartment. Upon the postcards were the words: 'With love from Mabel' and 'With love from Annie'.

This first experiment in June 1912 was followed up in July by a short tour of some of the industries and minefields of Yorkshire. For this visit the King and Queen stayed at Wentworth Woodhouse, a vast but not especially attractive eighteenth-century building, set among pleasure-gardens blackened by coal-dust. It was while they were here that there occurred, one evening, the Cadeby Colliery disaster, in which several miners lost their lives. Although they had only just returned to Wentworth after a heavy day the King and Queen immediately got back into their motor-cars and drove by night to the colliery: 'Too tragic', wrote Queen Mary. 'We motored over late in the evening to express our sympathy personally, which was much appreciated, it was awfully upsetting seeing the poor people who had lost relatives.'27 As she talked to the bereaved families at the pit-head, it was observed that the Queen, whose control over her emotions was usually adamantine, had tears pouring down her cheeks. It was after this incident that the King and Queen were welcomed by the glass-blowers of Stairport singing the refrain:

> Kind kind and gentle is she
> Kind is my Mary.

In 1913 they continued their exploration of industrial England while staying at Crewe Hall, whence they visited the Potteries. This visit, like the others, demanded considerable organisation on the part of their hosts: 'Though it only lasts three days', Lord Crewe wrote before the visit, 'it seems to take almost as much arranging as the Durbar.'28

Today these tours of 1912 and 1913 do not seem startling, but to a public accustomed to the more formal appearances of King Edward VII and Queen Alexandra in open landaus, these examples of the human touch came as a revelation. Queen Mary's conception of the role of Queen Consort was becoming clearer; her simple and straightforward approach, her very lack of glamour, appealed strongly to the working-men's wives with whom she talked upon practical housekeeping subjects which interested her as much as they did them. 'A foolish woman said to me, "How gracious she is—every inch a queen",' a contemporary diarist has noted of an afternoon's meeting with Queen Mary. 'Now that was *exactly* what she was not. She had no majesty of mien, or ease or stateliness. She looked a hard-worked and rather tired woman, plainly dressed, doing her best to be civil to nervous people. It made me feel a sort of affectionate admiration. . . . I should like to meet her again, and I feel a curious kind of personal regard for her, and a warmth about the heart.'29

We may here see how Princess May's early training in philanthropy and social work by her mother at White Lodge, as well as her reading of reports on industrial conditions under the guidance of Madame Bricka, was turning to account. The Labour politician, Miss Margaret Bondfield, once remarked that Queen Mary would have made an excellent factory inspector. The Queen had indeed a certain grasp of essentials; she would not for instance be dazzled by the bright scheme of decoration of a new ward in a maternity hospital, but would quickly perceive, and point out, that unshaded lights were bad for the babies' eyes. It was soon noticed that her questions were intelligent, and that her interest was never simulated. She garnered information wherever she went, and, as we know, her memory was good.

The new King and Queen felt more at their ease with British working people than they ever did with members of London Society or with foreign royalties. Lord Esher has recorded a meeting with King George and Queen Mary at the London Polytechnic in the summer of 1912: 'They are really at home among that class of person', he wrote. 'So like Queen Victoria.'30 Whatever fashionable persons in the metropolis might say about the 'dull tone' of the new Court, the country at large was slowly becoming aware of the new Queen Consort's particular qualities and aims. 'Only give me a chance & I will do the things as well as anybody, after all why shouldn't I?' she had written to Bricka fifteen years earlier.31 That chance had now come.

III

In these early years during which she was investigating and expanding the sphere of a Queen Consort's useful activities Queen Mary was much aided by King George's confidence in her, even though this confidence went often unexpressed. In several senses her life upon the throne was easier than that of her mother-in-law Queen Alexandra had ever been, for Queen Alexandra had found herself as much frustrated by King Edward's jealousy for his royal prerogatives as by his open admiration for other, younger women. Moreover, as Queen Dowager, 'Motherdear' had become increasingly retiring; her widowhood increased her natural distaste for public functions and much of her time was spent in her beloved Copenhagen, or visiting her daughter Queen Maud of Norway in the Kongenslot at Kristiania, as Oslo was then still called. Queen Alexandra had never been an adept at planning her life, and once King Edward was dead she felt lost and lonely: 'It is very sad seeing her like this so "hopeless & helpless" & one feels so sorry for her', Queen Mary had written sympathetically of her mother-in-law in the spring of 1911, when King Edward VII had already been one year dead.32

The year 1912 brought Queen Alexandra two sharp fresh sorrows in the deaths of her eldest daughter's husband the Duke of Fife and that of her brother King Frederick VIII of Denmark; while in 1913 occurred the assassination of her favourite brother King George of Greece. It was only at Sandringham, where she caused inconvenience by continuing to live in the 'Big House' while King George V and Queen Mary were cramped into York Cottage with their children, their Court, their retainers and such guests as Ministers 'in attendance', that Queen Alexandra noticeably affected Queen Mary's life. In London her influence upon Buckingham Palace was no more than mildly disruptive: 'having made my arrangements for the day', Queen Mary wrote about this time, 'dear Mama suddenly announces herself to lunch or tea & everything has to be altered.'³³ Cabined by her sorrows and by her deafness, the old Queen Dowager was now a figure of romantic pathos, to whom her daughter-in-law was imaginatively kind.

In June 1912 there fell the fiftieth anniversary of Queen Alexandra's first arrival in England, as the ravishing 'Sea-king's daughter from over the sea' about to be engaged to the young Prince of Wales. This Jubilee was celebrated by the inauguration of Alexandra Day, when ten million artificial wild roses, made of linen or, more expensively, of silk, were sold in the streets of London in aid of the hospitals. The roses had been made by cripples and by the blind, and they were dispensed to the public by a horde of girls clad in white dresses caught in at the waist by sashes of scarlet—the Danish national colours. They wore straw hats heavily trimmed with artificial roses. The climax of the day was a drive by Queen Alexandra, wearing mourning and her peaked widow's bonnet, in an open landau filled with roses, and with Princess Victoria by her side. Queen Alexandra had never cared for such public appearances, and now in her sorrowing state she very naturally shrank from the cheerful enthusiasm of the crowds on what she modestly termed 'that tiresome Alexandra day'. 'I tried hard to get out of it this time', she wrote to Queen Mary when the second Alexandra Day loomed up in June of 1913, 'but . . . am told it wld be the greatest *snub* to all the poor people who put in their penny—so go *I* must—!' As year followed year Queen Alexandra's dislike of the publicity of 'Rose Day' grew: 'that horrible *Rose day* drive! which I dread more & more every year,' she wrote in 1918, 'I think you will soon have to take my place driving round London on that occasion! as I feel I am getting too old & stupid for those pleasures!! particularly now when ones mind is so sad & dreary.'³⁴ It is indeed easy to understand Queen Alexandra's genuine distaste for this ordeal: a distaste which, with characteristically generous courtesy, she took care to conceal.

IV

The summer of 1912 witnessed another anniversary which closely concerned Queen Mary. This was the ninetieth birthday of her Aunt Augusta Strelitz, and it fell in mid-July. The Queen's two surviving brothers, Prince Dolly and Prince Alge, proceeded to Neu Strelitz to attend the festivities.

The mind of the old Grand Duchess was as alert as ever, and she still spent many hours reading the newspapers and volumes of political memoirs; but her deafness was now much increased, and she was obliged to use an ear-trumpet. She also suffered periodically from sciatica and from sleeplessness. She found the ninetieth birthday celebrations gratifying but exhausting. 'I got over the terrible fatigue, by Gods mercy,' she wrote to Queen Mary,

had Speeches to make, even one from the Balcony! to Schools, Torchlight Processions one day, seven on 20th, to thank the Minister and Burgomaster for a very fine Address, (painted) with 15,582 signatures from high and low of the whole Inhabitants of this Country! . . . all were immensely pleased, also the old Farmers, who came with a *heart* of flowers, with a big 90 in the centre. As for the baskets of flowers, and flowers in all shapes, they cannot be described, only the heat made them fade so quickly. The Court gave me a fine gold vase, the States a magnificent Silver Table for flowers. . . . Children & Gdchildren, three very handsome English gold Stands. . . . I felt rather nervous and shaky, tho' otherwise I hope not the worse but how I am to get over reading, partly answering 4–5 *Sacks* full of *letters*, I don't know! it is hard labour![35]

Queen Mary had not seen her aunt since King George's accession. Her last visit to Strelitz had been in April 1910, shortly before King Edward's death. For her niece's birthday present in Coronation Year the old aunt had had her own portrait painted. With this Queen Mary was delighted. She hung it in her sitting-room opposite the oval Winterhalter portrait of her mother the Duchess of Teck, which had been brought up from Cambridge Cottage, Kew. 'All the family here admire it enormously', she wrote from Buckingham Palace, '& it was *the* centre of attraction among all my presents. The likeness is really good & the painting "well finished" which I like not like the modern school.'[36]

The Coronation of her niece had reminded the British public of the existence of the old Grand Duchess of Mecklenburg-Strelitz, who was pleased to find herself the subject of newspaper articles. 'Home Papers occupy themselves much with old me!' she wrote. 'Scraps being sent me about you and me! it is kind, I am not all forgotten, but why I have suddenly become so extraordinary a personage I can't imagine!'[37] Some of these newspaper articles had confidently predicted that Queen Mary would go to see her aunt in Strelitz before leaving for the Delhi Durbar in November 1911, but this had been baseless. 'When shall we two have a really proper talk, we have so much to say to each other',[38] Queen Mary had written from Balmoral in October 1911.

Her wish to see her aunt again was so strong that in the summer of 1912 Queen Mary actually asked her husband if she might go to Strelitz that August, taking her daughter, Princess Mary, now fifteen, and the Dugdales with her. King George, who knew that she seldom asked anything for herself, readily gave his assent, and Queen Mary wrote off to suggest a date in August to her aunt, stressing that the visit would be *quite informal*—'I should come quite *incognita* & want no fuss whatever,' she wrote, 'let it be a visit from a very devoted niece to her very dear Aunt. I feel quite excited at the prospect of our meeting again and only hope your answer in your next letter will be "yes".'[39] Aunt Augusta replied with a triple affirmative:

Yes! Yes! Yes!
My most dearly beloved May! I am so agitated at the delightful thought of seeing you again and *soon*, that I can hardly write to express my joy! my heart quite leapt whilst reading your letter, so full of dear kind affectionate words, I never dreamt of the possibility of your coming in this way, only hoped it would be possible for you, during a *State* visit next door,* to run over here for a day! now I am, oh! so happy and thankful! . . . *Most* delightful is your proposal to bring Mary. . . . All your letter is a delight to me. . . . There will be no need for a low dress, and as you always are very smart any high gown is sufficient; in Summer too these are always worn on the Continent. How I shall enjoy my talks with you. I am sure they will revive me!—[40]

On the platform at Neu Strelitz railway station Queen Mary found Aunt Augusta waiting to receive her on a strip of red carpet. The diminutive old lady was dressed in black, with a little black bonnet ornamented with a tuft of white feathers and tied with velvet strings under her chin.† Behind her stood her son Adolphus and his wife— the reigning Grand Duke and Grand Duchess—together with their

* i.e. to the Emperor and Empress of Germany at Berlin.
† For a photograph of this meeting, see plate 25.

elder daughter Duchess Marie. The Grand Duke, a burly, bearded figure was strapped into Prussian uniform with the spiked helmet or *Pickelhaube* on his head. This scene of welcome was recorded by cinematograph: 'The film-picture was a real success!' wrote the old Grand Duchess to her niece in the autumn of that year, 'representing the moment of our meeting, you bending down to embrace me, Elly & Marie next, Dolphus only from the back, then the second film shows Mary stepping forward, Fred behind her, you walking in front, all so speakingly like.'[41] 'Aunt is wonderful, looks rather thinner & is rather deaf but otherwise unaltered', Queen Mary reported to King George. 'I have rooms near her, Mary below, Mary delighted at coming here & seeing something new, awfully interested in looking out of the window in the train & very observant. I had a little talk with Aunt just before lunch with the Dolphus's at 1 & later I shall drive with Elly just to get some air.' 'We have all our meals with Dolphus & Aunt comes if she likes & feels up to it', she wrote two days later. 'Last night 2 or 3 extra people came & At looked so well in an evening gown with fine jewels—Later I sat with Dolphus & Elly & we smoked a little.'[42]

This August week at Strelitz was, on the whole, dull and rainy but, spent in talking over the past and the present, looking at the Grand Duchess's miniatures, family mementoes and photograph albums and making little motor expeditions to Hohenwieritz and the family vault at Mirow, the days glided happily by. To the amazement of her family, the old Grand Duchess suddenly announced her decision to take her first motor-car ride: 'I have done a thing I never thought could happen namely driven with Aunt in a motor!!!' wrote Queen Mary to the King. 'Only think of our surprise when she announced to us Sunday afternoon her wish to accompany us in the motor to Mirow, 20 miles from here where there is a pretty old Schloss & where there is the family vault. Of course we did not go fast but she was not nervous & only complained of slight back ache on our return. It was a delicious warm day at last & we had a charming afternoon & tea in the garden.'[43] These were the last days which Queen Mary ever spent with her beloved Aunt Augusta, for although she and King George managed to go to Strelitz during their Berlin visit in the following year, it was only for a few hours.

'How quickly the time flew at Strelitz', Queen Mary wrote to her Aunt from London. 'I never knew a week pass more quickly—Both Dolphus & Elly's kindness touched me much, they treated me as a

real cousin and I felt quite at home, in fact it was all *"sehr gemütlich
und verwandtschaftlich"*.'44 'How still it feels now you are gone, the
doors again closed!' her aunt wrote to her sorrowfully, 'but there is
so much of pleasure and hearts satisfaction for us to remember that I
am living by that.'45 'She was too dear so perfect in everything, Queen
and yet May, only she overworks herself; her visit has been a real
delight to all', the Grand Duchess told her eldest nephew, Prince
Dolly.46

v

Queen Mary's last words to the old Grand Duchess as the train for
Calais pulled out of Neu Strelitz station had been: 'Next year!' 'God
grant this hope may come true', was Aunt Augusta's comment.

The King and Queen had hoped that in the new year, 1913, they
would at last be able to pay an official visit to the German Emperor and
Empress at Berlin; but the threatening state of European politics led
the Foreign Secretary, Sir Edward Grey, to urge that this was no time
to alarm France and Russia by such a formal affirmation of friendship
with Germany. The First Balkan War, which had broken out in
October 1912, was still in progress, and though a peace was patched
up in May 1913 by the Treaty of London, the Second Balkan War
followed in June and lasted until August. On 18 March, while at
Windsor Castle, the King and Queen heard the news of the assassination of their uncle the King of Greece: 'In the evening', Queen Mary
recorded in her Diary, 'we received the shocking news that poor dear
Uncle Willy of Greece had been assassinated at Salonica—G. was
terribly upset—We heard by telephone from Marl: House that poor
Mama was in a great state of mind at the death of her favorite brother.
It is a great tragedy.'47 'Here we are all in pitchy black again!' wrote
one of the Queen's ladies from Windsor next day.48 In May an attempt
was made to assassinate the Grand Duke of Baden. The Emperor
William of Germany escaped a similar attempt at Karlsruhe.

Queen Mary was following world developments with her usual
studious but now also apprehensive zeal. In September 1912, at
Balmoral, she had helped the King to entertain the Russian Foreign
Minister, M. Sazonoff, who was making a tour of foreign capitals, and
had come to this country for talks with Sir Edward Grey. 'We found
Monsieur Sazonoff the Russian Foreign Minister very pleasant & easy
to get on with and I believe his conversations with Sir Edward Grey
here were fairly satisfactory', she wrote. 'I drove him about in motor

or carriage to see the beauties of this place & he seemed to enjoy himself, he talks perfect English.'[49] 'I think he enjoyed his stay here', King George wrote to Queen Alexandra of Sazonoff's visit, '& he made himself most agreeable, May took him for long motor drives every afternoon.'[50] In November 1912 the new German Ambassador, Prince Lichnowsky, who had been appointed on the death of Marschall von Bieberstein, arrived in London with his wife and 'made a good impression' on the King and Queen: 'both talk English well & she is nice looking, pleasing & bright, loving music & art & I don't think she cares about sport so why they said so I don't know', Queen Mary reported.[51] 'They are delighted at being here so I hope it will be an influence for good.'

The King and Queen had always liked the Emperor William, and, though they distrusted German intentions in Europe, they were pleased to be invited to the wedding, in May 1913, of the Emperor's only daughter Princess Victoria Louise to their cousin Ernest Augustus, Duke of Brunswick-Lüneburg. As a grandson of the last King of Hanover and a son of Princess Thyra of Denmark, sister to Queen Alexandra, Prince Ernest Augustus was doubly allied to the English Royal Family. To Queen Mary this marriage with the Prussian Princess was of historical interest, since it put a term to the feud between the Houses of Hohenzollern and of Brunswick which had lasted since the Emperor William I's seizure of Hanover in the war of 1866. The engagement gave particular pleasure to the old Grand Duchess of Mecklenburg-Strelitz, to whom the young Duke of Brunswick's father sent a special messenger to tell her '*all*—of course in strictest confidence, due to me, he said, as "*Doyenne*" of the Guelphic House, having a *right* to know; this was really most kind of him. All I heard is very reassuring as to *my* views', she wrote to Queen Mary when thanking her for a 'dear letter beginning with thoughts of *me* when receiving the announcement, then so perfectly approving of Ernest's dignified words to his old Hanoverians. I only hope they too will be quiet in their speeches and for the present feel thankful both Houses are no longer at enmity.'[52]

Sir Edward Grey persuaded the King that any Royal visit to Berlin for the Brunswick wedding, which took place in circumstances of imperial pomp on 24 May 1913, must be regarded as a private family affair. 'Owing to the unsettled state of Europe', Queen Mary explained, 'we have decided not to pay any *official* visits this year but as William very kindly asked us to go to Berlin for his daughter's wedding we have accepted this invitation as a purely family gathering.'53 All the same the King and Queen of England were, of course, received at the Berlin station with appropriate state. 'Arrived Berlin 11.30', Queen Mary recorded. 'Met by William & Victoria & all the Princes and Princesses—Drove to the Schloss. Very pretty sight. Excellent reception. We went to our rooms which are charming. Family luncheon at 1. We saw William & Victoria's rooms. Paid visits to Auwi & Alix* & to Fritz & Lotte† & drove in the *Thiergarten*. Large dinner in the evening of 80 people. Talked to a good many people.'54

Although Queen Mary could not know it, this 'purely family gathering' at Berlin, with its colossal banquets and *Defilir Cour*, its gala operas and military parade at Potsdam, its friendly calls of one group of cousins upon another—was the last of those assemblies of European royal relations which Queen Victoria used to dread and which the Duchess of Teck adored. It was the final appearance of the 'royal mob', the last time that King George and Queen Mary would see the German Emperor and Empress, the Tsar Nicholas and the Tsarina. However uncertain the state of Europe might seem, there was a deceptive air of stability about this ceremonial life in the great palaces of Berlin: no one, least of all Queen Mary, could suppose that within five years William and Dona, Nicky and Alicky, Mossy and Fischy, Auwi and Alix, Fritz and Lotte and almost all the other royal cousins whom they met in those May days in Berlin would be deposed, or exiled or assassinated or living in impoverished retirement. 'We left Berlin at 5.35 for London,' Queen Mary noted with her customary precision, 'William & Victoria accompanied us to the station—Took leave of them all with regret after charming visit.'55 'I cannot tell you how very much we enjoyed our visit to Berlin or how touched we were at the kindness shown us by William & Victoria & indeed by everybody. It was a most interesting time & so beautifully arranged in every way, nothing could have gone off better.'56

In the middle of the Berlin festivities, on 26 May 1913, Queen Mary had celebrated her forty-sixth birthday by paying a few hours' visit to her Aunt Augusta at Neu Strelitz, with King George and their suite. This, too, proved in fact to be a farewell. She never saw her Aunt

---

* Prince Augustus William of Prussia (1887–1949) and his wife Princess Alexandra Victoria of Schleswig-Holstein-Sonderburg-Glucksburg (b. 1887, div. 1920).

† Prince Eitel-Friedrich of Prussia (1883–1942) and his wife Sophie Charlotte, Duchess of Oldenburg (1879–1942).

Augusta, who died in 1916, again. This was a more formal visit than that Queen Mary had made on her own in 1912. Once again it was recorded on a film: 'Fancy, our going *kissing* all over the world', wrote Aunt Augusta, 'but it is impossible to stop those horrid Kino-men.'[57] 'Too amusing George & you appearing in a photo embracing! I believe it already appeared in a London paper', her niece replied. '. . . We are glad you liked our Household who were thrilled at making the acquaintance of George III Granddaughter and of so charming a personality. . . . I am so thankful you are none the worse for our visit, not too tired or over agitated, for even I felt quite agitated at being received at Strelitz by you all in state, with George, my mind going back to our Mecklenburg descent & our being the first English King & Queen to visit the home of our mutual Gt Grandmother & Gt Gt Gdmother as well as of our very dearly loved Aunt. I thought too of dear U. Fritz.'[58]

As at Vienna in 1904, Queen Mary in 1913 scored a personal success at the court of Berlin. 'All I have heard and read about your Berlin visit, is full of praise and admiration!' her Aunt wrote from Strelitz, 'a Lady (in Attendance there) told me, she never saw anything like your magnificent Dresses and Diamonds, and your regal appearance, the Wedding Toilette surpassing all!'[59] Queen Mary had indeed succeeded in dazzling the court of Berlin by her appearance at the wedding service of Princess Victoria Louise; her gown was of Indian cloth of gold with a woven design of flowers and a corsage embroidered in gold. Her train was of fine Irish lace lined with gold tissue and having a deep gold border embroidered in gold. Upon her head she wore a crown of pearls and diamonds, around her neck a diamond collar, with the large crown diamond necklace beneath this and the lesser Stars of Africa as a pendant. Her corsage was ornamented with diamond bows, pearl drops and the 'smaller South African pendant' and as Orders she simply wore the Garter and the Prussian Order. While she was not, as we have seen, innately majestic in everyday life, Queen Mary could, when she wished, adorn herself with a regal splendour. On such occasions as the Berlin wedding she regarded these trappings of Majesty as a patriotic duty to her country and to the throne.

The British Ambassador in Berlin, Sir Edward Goschen, confirmed the old Grand Duchess's view of the impression Queen Mary had made in Berlin: 'He believes your and George's visit will prove of *lasting* good',[60] the Grand Duchess reported to her niece of a letter 'all about your Berlin visit', written to her by Sir Edward Goschen.

Q

This was probably no more than an expression of loyal sentiment on Goschen's part, for he cannot have believed, as the old Grand Duchess naturally did, that the future of European politics was any longer in the hands of Kings and Emperors. In this last year of peace before the holocaust of the 1914 war, the Emperor William seems to have lost control of the foreign policy of his militaristic country and, as King George came to realise in 1918, the Kaiser was probably personally less to blame for the final outbreak of hostilities than he was thought to be in 1914. To some extent the Emperor William was swept forward, powerless, by the torrent of events.

VI

Only thirteen months lay between the wedding ceremonies at Berlin and the outbreak of the First World War. Last months of peace, they were not peaceful, for this period was no lull before the storm. We might, rather, find an analogy in a long oppressive August day upon some Swiss or German lake, when distant thunder crackles and lurches round the mountain peaks of the horizon, now reassuringly remote, now ominously near. The experienced fear it is a storm approaching, the optimists fancy it is a storm going away. But when we think of 1913 and of the spring of the following year we make an error if we picture a whole European generation gazing for portents at the sky. In England attention was specifically directed to the storm hanging over Ireland, and only a few thoughtful persons of those in authority glanced fearfully southwards to Europe, south-eastwards to the Balkans.

At Sandringham the New Year opened almost gaily. Queen Mary herself tried to strike an optimistic note. 'Last night', she wrote on 2 January 1914, 'we all dined with Mama & even danced afterwards much to the enjoyment of the young people. God grant that this year may be a peaceful one & that the clouds over these dear Islands may disperse!!!'[61] It had for some years been the Queen's habit to paste into the front cover of her Diary one of the New Year cards she had received which had especially appealed to her. For 1914 she selected a card with the quatrain:

> May every hour of every day
> And every day the whole year through
> And every step along Life's way
> A *Benediction* be to you.

The new year of 1914 proved, alas, one of the least blessed of the twentieth century.

The state of the world in these pre-war months was rendering King George V desperately anxious and unhappy. Queen Mary reflected his mood. Apart from the natural anxiety she felt, international politics now impinged upon Queen Mary's actual life more positively than before. At Sir Edward Grey's instigation, the French President Monsieur Poincaré had been invited to pay an official three-day visit to London in the month after the return of King George and Queen Mary from Berlin. Since the President's wife did not accompany him, Queen Mary's part in these formalities was confined to presiding with the King over a large banquet—'G. made a nice speech in French', she recorded, '& the President made a charming reply'[62]—and at a State Ball, at which Monsieur Poincaré confessed that he felt embarrassed at not knowing how to partner the Queen in a quadrille. In April 1914 the King and Queen repaid this visit by a state journey to Paris. 'Of course I wanted to go to Vienna first but Sir Edward Grey will not hear of it!' Queen Mary wrote to her Aunt Augusta.[63]

Queen Mary looked forward to this Paris visit with considerable apprehension. 'How I hate having to go there when matters are so unsettled here; especially as one feels so acutely how England has fallen in prestige abroad,' she wrote in April, 'I really feel so ashamed I shld prefer to hide—certainly not to have to smile & make oneself agreeable when one's heart is not in it, but then nobody gives one the credit for having a heart or feeling things in these days—It seems to me that "*finesse*" has gone out of the world, that indescribable something which was *born* in one & which was inherited thro' generations.' 'I rather dread the next days as you can imagine,' she wrote to her aunt just before starting for France, 'it will all be rather difficult and unusual.'[64] Although she did not, of course, share her Aunt Augusta's persistent view of France as a regicide nation, Queen Mary was very much aware that this would be her first state visit as Queen of England to a foreign republic. Some of her mother's greatest friends had been the Princes and Princesses of the exiled House of Orleans, and Queen Mary herself had always known and liked the Empress Eugénie. France was at that time the only great European country without a court, and thus had no royal cousins amongst whom visiting royalties could relax. The Paris visit would in this sense prove the very opposite of that to Berlin, where King George and Queen Mary had found themselves in the midst of a large family party of related, hereditary royalties.

Unlike her husband, Queen Mary spoke good French, was well acquainted with French literature and admired French furniture and *objets d'art*. But as a country France had never bulked large in her experience. She had first been to Paris with her mother in 1883, to consult the American dentist Evans who had rescued the Empress Eugénie in 1871. She had, as we know, been in Cannes after Prince Eddy's death in 1892, she had stayed at Mentone with her Aunt Augusta in 1898, and for a few weeks with Queen Victoria at Cimiez in 1899. During the 1898 sojourn in Mentone she had formed a tentative project to meet her husband in Paris for Easter, but this he had turned down. 'I don't dislike Paris, but I don't particularly care for it', he had written, pointing out that it would be cheaper and quieter to spend Easter at York Cottage, Sandringham.[65] 'I quite understand your not wishing to come to Paris & am not angry, I only thought it wld be nice for a change as I find life in general very dull—unless one has a change sometimes',[66] she had replied. Ten years later, in 1908, on their way back from Cologne and Darmstadt when Prince and Princess of Wales, they had spent a fortnight incognito in Paris, staying at the Hotel Bristol and seeing the sights; but although this visit included a large dinner-party with the President and Madame Fallières at the Elysée Palace, it had been essentially of a private nature and without overt political implications. There was thus something a trifle intimidating in the prospect of the 1914 state visit to a capital Queen Mary did not know well, and where there was no court, and no royal protocol. It was to some degree a venture into the unknown, or at any rate into the unfamiliar.

Queen Mary need not have worried. From the moment she and the King landed at Calais it was clear that they were in for a success. The arrival of the English King and Queen in Paris was to the French nation a reassuring symbol of the Entente Cordaile; the state drives and the Gala Opera were welcomed by Parisians who had been starved of official spectacles since the subsidence of the Second Empire. Queen Mary's manner, clothes and jewellery were greatly admired: '*C'est le Printemps même*' the crowd were reported to have murmured as, with Madame Poincaré beside her in the carriage, she passed along the sunlit streets lined with chestnut trees in flower, wearing a gown of pale blue *crêpe de soie* with a hat piled up with bluish white ostrich plumes, round her throat ropes of magnificent pearls. '*Elle a beaucoup de dignité*', was another popular comment, '*elle a son chic à elle*'. 'To know *you* at Paris, in this wonderful way, I hardly can take in!' her aunt wrote from Strelitz. 'Your Entry has been most successful, only the idea of *you* and Mme P. together in the State Carriage of nice Imp. Eugénie was not genial to me. . . . Your appearance, looks, Toilettes, gracious smile, bearing are nicely commented upon in German papers; this is a pleasing surprise to me, coming from that quarter.'67

The enthusiasm of the Parisians, the crowds milling round the carriages as they made their way to the Opera, enchanted Queen Mary, whose Diary of the three days takes on—for it—a positively euphoric note: 'Wonderful reception & crowds of people'. . . . 'Crowds in the streets in spite of late hour'. . . . 'Wonderful reception during the 9 miles drive [to Vincennes for a Military Review]'. . . . 'We had a charming welcome & were given presents . . . beautifully decorated streets'. . . . 'Crowds of people in the streets both going & coming back & lovely illuminations'. . . . 'to Autueil to the Races. Crowds of people, very kind receptions.'68 'The weather was glorious (summer weather),' she wrote in a letter, 'the Bois looking too lovely, chestnuts out & flowers, also the *bois* at Vincennes. . . . It has been a curious & interesting experience & shows anyhow that the French people wish to be on good terms with us.'69

For one of the very few times in her life Queen Mary found coming back to her native land an anti-climax. 'The weather in London', she recorded of the day of their return home, 'was dull & cold.'

VII

Late in the afternoon of 28 June 1914 King George V received the news of the murder by a Servian student at Sarajevo of the Archduke Franz Ferdinand and his morganatic wife, the Duchess of Hohenberg. 'The significance of the crime', Mr John Gore has pointed out, 'did not instantly strike him or the Government and the nation, though it was otherwise with many of the European Embassies in London. Of the British press only two dailies recognised the assassination as the match of Fate which would set Europe ablaze.'70 It was the personal and dynastic aspect of the murders which at first affected King George. 'Terrible shock', he noted in his Diary, 'for the dear old Emperor.'71 Queen Mary, who had much liked both the Archduke and his wife when they had stayed as guests at Windsor Castle the previous year, also tended to look at this fresh assassination as just one more crime committed by the anarchists:

The horrible tragedy to the poor Archduke & his wife came as a great shock to us [she wrote], particularly as they had been our guests so very recently, and we were really quite attached to them both. Poor Emperor, nothing is he spared, he also sent us such a nice telegram. I think it is a great blessing that husband & wife died together, making the future less complicated with regard to the position of their children—[72]

'Dreadful for the poor old Emperor', she recorded in her Diary for 28 June.

Four weeks later the real implications of the Sarajevo murders had become more sinisterly clear. 'The news from Austria & Servia sounds very serious', Queen Mary noted in her Diary on 26 July, and 'Austria has declared war against Servia!' two days later. 'God grant we may not have a European War thrust upon us', she wrote to her aunt, '& for such a stupid reason too, no I don't mean stupid, but to have to go to war on account of tiresome Servia beggars belief!'[73]— and this sentiment of incredulity was indeed that of most Englishmen and Englishwomen in those midsummer weeks of 1914. The throb of events quickened: 'War news still very serious', Queen Mary's Diary records for 29 July—'War news very grave' two days later—'G. received any number of telegrams with War news which were not satisfactory' on 1 August; and, on 2 August:

War news very bad. Germany has declared war on Russia—and will probably attack France—Louise & Maudie, Dolly & Alge came to see us. Walked with G. in the garden—After dinner a large crowd assembled in front of the Palace & sang 'God Save the King' and we went on the balcony & had a very good reception—The Govt has not yet decided what our action is to be.

The next evening the King and Queen were again called out on to the balcony. They responded three times. By the evening of the following day England was already at war:

Fine. Awful day of suspense [Queen Mary recorded on 4 August]. Several of the family came to see us—At 12. we sent an ultimatum to Germany & at 7 p.m. she declared war on us. It is too dreadful but we could not act otherwise. We went on to the balcony at 8 p.m. & again at 11.15. after the news of war having been declared was out.

Standing by the King's side that night upon the central balcony of the bright new façade of Buckingham Palace, Queen Mary gazed down upon the surging patriotic crowd below, who were cheering the beginning of an adventure destined to end in the deaths of millions, the ruin of much of Europe, and the dissolution of the old and seemingly stable political and social order of the world in which she had been brought up. Neither the two figures upon the balcony, nor the thousands who milled round the Victoria Memorial below, could know how cruelly long the war would last, nor what would be its devastating effects.

For the moment it was the evidence of unity between Throne and Country in a national crisis which most impressed Queen Mary. 'One thing I can say & this is that both of us are heart & soul trying to do our level best for our beloved Country at this supreme moment of trial', the Queen wrote next day to her friend Lady Mount Stephen, who had offered her services for war-work, and had sent Queen Mary a gift: 'We have the feeling of being supported by the people which is the great & glorious thing—I am so pleased with the charming frame, another kind thought of yours—'[74]

CHAPTER FOUR

A WAR-TIME QUEEN

ON THE DAY preceding the declaration of war, Queen Mary had telegraphed to Lady Bertha Dawkins:* 'Come at once. You may not be able to travel tomorrow.' On arriving at Buckingham Palace, Lady Bertha was summoned to Queen Mary's sitting-room. Here, all amongst the Chippendale and the satin-wood furniture, the air scented by great Canton vases of summer garden flowers, the Queen told Lady Bertha that war seemed inevitable. 'One or two things remain clearly in my mind about that day,' Lady Bertha afterwards related, 'the horror of Her Majesty at the prospect of war and the resolution of her voice.' The Queen explained that 'we must have everything ready' and that she did not 'want to have that state of things which prevailed during the Boer War'—for as Duchess of York she had been shocked by the amateurish and unco-ordinated efforts of the volunteer ladies' organisations which had haphazardly despatched to the Cape 'comforts' which the soldiers did not want, while failing to provide the necessities which they did.

This horror at the prospect of European war, and this anxiety to organise volunteer workers were not, of course, exclusive to the Queen, but they were at that moment rare enough in Great Britain, for here the war opened in conditions of chaos and enthusiasm. In a published extract from his Diary for the day war was declared the Duke of Windsor (then, of course, Prince of Wales) has described 'the unparalleled demonstration of enthusiasm' which greeted the

* Whose turn of waiting it was in August 1914. Lady Bertha Dawkins [1866–1943] was the fourth daughter of the first Earl of Lathom. Lady Bertha, who married Major Arthur Dawkins in 1903, was left a widow with one daughter in 1905, and entered the Household of Queen Mary (then Princess of Wales) as Woman of the Bedchamber in 1908. Queen Mary was much attached to Lady Bertha, on whom she largely relied for aid in her Guild and other charity work: 'I am much pleased with my choice as she is well informed & agreeable & our tastes suit, such a blessing', she had written of Lady Bertha Dawkins in March 1908.[1]

appearance of his parents the King and Queen upon the centre balcony of Buckingham Palace that night of 4 August. 'The people', he recorded, 'remained singing, cheering and whistling for another 3 hrs & I was lulled to sleep by their fearful shindy at 1.30.'[2]

Nowadays it is hard to recapture the mood in which the British public embarked upon the 1914–1918 war. Once war was declared bewilderment and incredulity gave way to determination and, on the part of those who set off for France, to crusading zeal. But the mood of many people was, in these first weeks, dominated by what Miss Violet Markham has termed 'the mentality of the South African War. None of us', she writes, 'realised that we were to be stripped of all our toys and all our comforts. Some deluded souls talked of the war being over by Christmas.'[3] At first, as was to be expected, the outbreak of the war and its immediate tragic consequencies were seen in personal rather than in national terms. As another observer noted in those early days of war, 'Society people' tended to look upon it 'as a sort of picnic, chequered by untoward incident', and that this section of the community 'fuss more about casualty lists than the fate of our army. There will be a rude awakening if as Lord K[itchener] thinks, this war goes on for years.'[4] The general view was that the war would be short and that it would be exciting. In any case it disrupted the dull routine of most daily living. It might prove gruesome, but it was a novelty.

Although the Navy took up its war-stations with a smooth speed, and although an Expeditionary Force of modest size and with no reserves of heavy artillery was safely ferried over to the French coast, the outbreak of war found the country at large totally unprepared. The first tangible effect of the war was the immediate announcement of a moratorium followed by a rush of unemployment which, in the first weeks, spread across the country like a plague. Men and women were thrown out of work, while the wives and dependants of the fighting men suddenly transported abroad were left without proper provision. A National Relief Fund was opened for voluntary contributions, but since there were no precedents for the scale and scope of problems brought into being by a World War, it was not at first realised how much more than private charity was needed. Within one month of the opening of hostilities, nearly two hundred thousand women were already out of work; and we should remember that in 1914 the number of employed women was infinitely lower than it was in, say, 1939. Here was a problem with which the Queen, by a capable

Q*

and intelligent personal use of Royal patronage, was ideally placed to deal.

We should by now have gathered that four of Queen Mary's dominant characteristics were patriotism, a love of order, an earnest desire to relieve distress and a concern about social conditions. It would not be historically true to attribute to the Queen the ultimate solution of the problems of war relief or of the employment of women in Great Britain during the First World War, for this was the achievement of hard-worked members of committees as well as of officials of government departments. Yet it is just to re-emphasise that she, who was never content to act merely as a focal point, gave the lead. Sir Harold Nicolson has described King George V's 'tasks and duties as the leader of an Empire at war' as 'manifold and incessant'. In a different way, the Queen, too, now had an opportunity to play her part upon a national scale—a part for which her whole life's training had equipped her, and one which many earlier Queens Consort would have been neither competent nor prepared to take on.

The Queen seized the initiative with energy. Already on the 5th of August, before the war was twenty-four hours old, she was laying her plans: 'Very wet day', she noted in her Diary for 5 August. 'Set to work to make plans to help the existing Organisations with offers of clothing & money etc.' 'Poured all day', we read in an even briefer entry for 6 August. 'Very busy seeing people about the various Relief schemes.'

II

In the first bewildering week of the war there seemed to be two ways, and two ways only, by which female volunteers could aid the war effort. One was by knitting socks and stomach belts and by making shirts for the soldiers, the other was by collecting money and clothing to relieve the new unemployed and the destitute. Ready to hand the Queen had her own well-tried organisation—the Needlework Guild of old White Lodge days which, now re-christened Queen Mary's Needlework Guild, had grown considerably, and could be quickly expanded to meet immediate needs. Her other asset was the King's permission to use the vast state apartments at St James's Palace, looking out over Friary Court, 'where', as she wrote in her Diary for 8 August, 'I am to arrange my Relief Clothing Guild.' On that same day, 8 August, she also went to inspect the offices of the National

Relief Fund which had been given quarters in York House and for which the Prince of Wales, supported by his mother, issued an appeal which netted a quarter of a million pounds in the first twenty-four hours. She likewise looked in that afternoon on the Red Cross organisation which was beginning to function at Devonshire House.

Wherever Queen Mary went that day she found ladies feverishly busy—knitting, sewing, sorting, packing, making lists. But were these hives of industry enough? Not only was the answer to this question in the negative; it very soon transpired that most of this hectic and well-intentioned activity was defeating its own ends. The more fiercely the voluntary ladies worked, the more women were dismissed from clothing and other factories, and the more piece-workers found themselves waiting in their homes for orders which no longer came. 'Do everything in your power', Mary Macarthur* begged an influential friend, 'to stop these women knitting!'

This unforeseen effect of the patriotic fervour of the Needlework Guild ladies, as well as that of those of other voluntary organisations, was laid before Queen Mary. Grasping the essential point, she at once applied herself to examining alternative, and more ambitious, schemes put up to her. By 15 August Lady Bertha Dawkins was writing to her daughter: 'The Queen & I are frightfully busy trying to get through a scheme for helping poor women who have no work owing to the war.' 'This morning', wrote Lady Bertha two days later, 'the Queen went over to Friary Court with me, & she was deluged with questions.' Of a subsequent visit a few days later Lady Bertha wrote: 'This morning I spent with the Queen at Friary Court, settling all the vexed questions, & my goodness! it was hot in those rooms, I felt quite faint standing a long time, & had to go & sit down by an open window.'[6] These three random extracts from Lady Bertha's letters reveal three facts about Queen Mary's attitude at the beginning of this great national crisis: the speed with which she assimilated the idea that work, not charity, must be provided for unemployed women; the practical way in which she reversed the conventional role then still

* Mary Macarthur (1880–1921) made herself, in her short life, the champion of the working women of Great Britain in her capacity as Secretary to the Women's Trade Union League and became an outstanding figure in the progressive movements of the country. 'She improved the conditions of hundreds of thousands of the most helpless and pitiable women in the country, and that not in a material sense only', writes her biographer, Mrs Mary Agnes Hamilton. ' . . . Her action, her example, her achievement, won for all women a new status. The world looked at them differently and they looked differently at themselves.'

ascribed to Royalty—that they should ask, not answer, questions; and the further fact that, with Lady Bertha's aid, she was able to 'settle all vexed questions'. The Queen had long had a private rule that her patronage of any organisation or institution was never to be merely nominal, and she now tackled the problems of war-time with all the firm efficiency she had displayed in days gone by, when helping her mother Princess Mary Adelaide at White Lodge.

On 17 August it was announced from Buckingham Palace that the Queen was in consultation with 'industrial experts and representatives of working class women', on a plan she had under contemplation 'to collect money for schemes of work for women unemployed on account of the war'. It was added that voluntary aid was intended 'to supplement and not supplant paid labour'. Three days later the Queen's Work for Women Fund was triumphantly launched, as a subsidiary of the National Relief Fund. The money collected was to be used to initiate, and at first to subsidise, sensible, business-like projects for employing women now out of work. The administration of the whole scheme was vested in a new Committee, the Central Committee for Women's Training and Employment, to which the Queen promptly offered her patronage, and on which it was privately believed she would have liked herself to serve. The composition of the Committee,* like its aims, was so original as to be a complete innovation; and, since it comprised a variety of potentially conflicting political elements, it was clearly impossible for the Queen to sit upon it. She therefore confined herself to scrutinising the progress of the Committee's work, hearing verbatim reports from the Chairman or the Honorary Secretary, and to supporting, and when necessary helping to implement, its decisions. The Central Committee began at once to sit at Wimborne House, under the adroit chairmanship of Lord Crewe's young wife. The creation of this Committee was due to the vision of one of the most remarkable women Scotland has ever produced—Mary Macarthur, who also became its Honorary Secretary.

In 1914, at the early age of thirty-four, Mary Macarthur, who came from a well-to-do middle-class family in Ayrshire, was already the recognised champion, indeed the saviour, of the exploited working women of Great Britain. The Florence Nightingale of women and children in the Sweated Industries, she had organised the Sweated

* The committee of thirteen women, later expanded to a committee of fifteen, was designed to give a proportional representation to all three political parties, Liberal, Labour and Conservative.

Industries Exhibition of 1906, held in London on the model of a similar exhibition arranged by German philanthropists at Berlin in 1905. As Princess of Wales, Queen Mary had, upon her return from India, insisted on touring this exhibition, and she had astonished those in charge of it by her pertinent questions and her considerable knowledge of the atrocious situation which it revealed. By her dedication, her common sense and her radiant personality, Mary Macarthur had changed the conditions of women who, in Edwardian days, were still being paid three-farthings an hour for intricate sewing work, and who made such articles as fine blouses for sixpence a piece, these garments being afterwards sold in Bond Street for twenty-five shillings. She had led the fight of the chain-makers of Cradley Heath, women who worked a fifty-hour week at their own backyard forges for a total weekly pay of seven or eight shillings, whilst their children of four or five years of age squatted on the ground at their feet manufacturing 'presentable chains'. She had headed strikes like that of the jam-makers of Bermondsey, had forced a Select Committee enquiry upon a reluctant Government, and had successfully fought the established men's trade unions on behalf of her own Women's Trades Union League. In 1911 she had married the radical Will Anderson, who in 1914 was elected Chairman of the Labour Party. With colleagues such as Miss Margaret Bondfield and Miss Gertrude Tuckwell, she had, in fact, liberated hundreds of thousands of her countrywomen from a life of slavery.

This brilliant firebrand was not the kind of woman with whom the Queen had ever come into direct personal touch. The Queen's position, combined with her inherited distrust of anything too radical, had hitherto shielded her from such contacts. But, just as it had needed the Crimean War to make Queen Victoria and her advisers turn to Florence Nightingale, so it was now seen that Mary Macarthur's gifts, vision and powerful influence were necessary to organise the women's war effort in 1914. Ignoring any advice to the contrary, the Queen requested Lady Crewe to bring Mary Macarthur to see her at Buckingham Palace. The result of this meeting startled the most sanguine. Queen Mary and Miss Macarthur recognised each other's qualities instinctively, and on her side the Queen further realised not only how much she and Mary Macarthur could help the cause they had at heart, but how much she, personally, could learn from her. 'Here is someone who *can* help and who *means* to help!' Mary Macarthur excitedly shouted at Gertrude Tuckwell, on her return from Buckingham

Palace to the offices of the Women's Trades Union League in the Gray's Inn Road. Soon jocular members of the Labour Movement were referring to 'the strange case of Mary M. and Mary R.'

Mary Macarthur was not in that category of persons who can be vanquished by a royal smile or who tend to modify their point of view at some mild sign of Palace favour. She had, indeed, no automatic reverence for the Monarchy as such, for, had she ever had the leisure to think about that institution, she would probably have accepted the now outmoded Labour Movement viewpoint which saw the throne as the apex of a social system which permitted the existence of such horror as the working conditions of the women at Cradley Heath, in Birmingham, in the East End of London, in Dundee, in Nottingham, in Kidderminster or in Kilbirnie. It was thus in a somewhat sceptical frame of mind that she set out for Buckingham Palace that day with Lady Crewe. She did not have to wonder long, for the Queen was as deeply impressed by her sincerity as she was by that of the Queen. 'The Queen does understand and grasp the whole situation from a Trade Union point of view', she told a colleague after one of her many subsequent audiences at Buckingham Palace. 'I positively lectured the Queen on the inequality of the classes, the injustice of it. I fear I talked too much again', she related of another audience. The Queen listened carefully to all Mary Macarthur had to tell, and she asked her for lists of books on the serious social topics they discussed.

The Queen not only took an intense interest in the decisions of her Central Committee, but frequently went to look at the practical results achieved. 'I had a most *interesting* afternoon today seeing various training centres in connection with my fund', she wrote in February 1915. 'I was quite delighted & elated. Miss Macarthur simply beamed & the visits were a great success.'7

At the end of the war, the Queen would have liked Mary Macarthur to have been rewarded in the Honours List, but she and the King were advised* that since Miss Macarthur had naturally not dissociated herself publicly from the very radical speeches her husband had been making during the Coupon Election campaign, this would not be suitable. She did, however, show her concern during Mary Macarthur's fatal illness, which ended in her death in 1921, by sending her messages and flowers. Queen Mary subsequently became patroness of the Mary

---

* Presumably by Lloyd George, who loathed Mary Macarthur and her work.

Macarthur Holiday Homes for Working Women,* the first of which was opened at Ongar in 1924, and she always maintained a characteristically kindly interest in the career of Mary Macarthur's only daughter.

III

For the first ten weeks of the war the King, and consequently the Queen also, did not leave London. These were ominous weeks of uncertainty, as the Germans advanced towards Paris and the Channel ports. The summer harvest fields of Flanders and north-eastern France were rotten with the corpses of the slain. Late in the autumn when the first Battle of the Marne had stabilised the Western Front, and the opposing armies had settled down into the unforeseen state of siege warfare in the field that was to last for the next four years, the King and Queen snatched a brief respite at York Cottage, Sandringham. 'We went to our Cottage last week for 5 days just to get a little change, & hope to go again soon for a little', the Queen wrote to her Aunt Augusta, 'but we must be here a good deal as we have much to do & I confess I almost felt restless in the country.'[8] It was York Cottage that provided the King and Queen with their short periods of real relaxation in the years of war. Balmoral was naturally closed for the duration and Windsor, virtually dismantled, was within such easy reach of London hospitals and of the convalescent homes in the country near the capital, that it provided the King and Queen with no real respite from their war-time round.

Buckingham Palace was soon put upon an austerity footing. Members of the Household—three of whom were killed in the very first weeks of the war—had volunteered, as had, too, many of the domestic staff. Carriage horses were sent from the Royal stables to do ambulance work, and Royal carriages employed to convey wounded men from the railway stations. A plan to turn the Palace itself into a hospital was rejected when it was found that the building was too old-fashioned and too inconvenient for such a purpose. As winter

---

* Queen Mary opened the home at Ongar in July 1924: 'I was so glad to be able, in this way, to show my deep appreciation of poor Mary Macarthur's untiring work on behalf of my "Work for Women" fund during the war', she wrote to Lady Crewe from Goodwood on 29 July 1924. 'The visit to the home gave me the opportunity of meeting those workers with whom I do not often come in contact & I was glad that this was so. Mats for the bedrooms have already been chosen & I am also sending a few pictures to adorn the walls.'

drew in, more and more women in deep mourning were to be seen hurrying about the London streets. One bereaved mother asked the Queen, through Mr A. J. Balfour, if she would not take the lead in discouraging the wearing of full mourning in favour of a simple purple arm-band. Although she disliked mourning intensely, the Queen replied that this was a personal matter which each lady must decide for herself, and that for her to make a public statement about it might constitute 'interference with the liberty of the subject'.

At the end of November 1914 the King paid the first of his visits to the front. Queen Mary would have liked to go too:

> My own darling Georgie dear [she wrote on 29 November], I felt very sad at seeing you go today on your important mission, without me, for all these years I have thank God been able to accompany you on all important journeys during our married life, so I feel it rather having to stay at home. I think you were quite right to go and it will be such a help & encourage-ment to officers & men in their arduous work. I am afraid you will find it very tiring, having so much motoring to do but I hope you will have good weather & that it will not be very cold. . . . God bless & protect you my own darling Georgie dear ever your very loving wife—
>
> May.9

As always whenever they were separated from one another, King George and Queen Mary exchanged letters daily. He wrote to tell her of his tours of hospitals at Boulogne, of clearing stations and hospital ships, and of his inspections of new-arrived contingents of Empire troops.

> What a very interesting letter I have to thank you for [the Queen wrote on 2 December]. . . . I was so pleased to hear as my thoughts are always with you, wondering what you are doing—It must have been splendid seeing the Indians; the clearing hospital a sad sight I fear, the aeroplane being *un*successfully shelled (thank God), & your being so near the fighting, all this has interested me beyond words. How splendid your driving with Mr Poincaré thro' *our* troops in France, you must have been thrilled, & have felt awfully proud of being their King! I know I should be. . . . So glad Poincaré & all seem so optimistic.10

There was in fact very little for Monsieur Poincaré or any other Allied leader to be optimistic about at the close of 1914, while the following year, 1915, proved, in the words of Sir Winston Churchill, 'disastrous to the cause of the Allies and the whole world'.11

Although no longer recent history, the course and the main features of the First World War are still sufficiently well remembered to make any recapitulation in this book as needless as it would surely be irrelevant. In retrospect these four years of war seem, as it were, a climatic unit—a single long dark winter over Europe, made lurid by the bursting of shells and the roar of gun-fire, and drenched in a warm, steady downpour of young human blood. It was the fate of King George, one of the kindliest and most pacific men who ever lived, and of Queen Mary, with her hatred of suffering and her inherent dread at the sight of illness or of the maimed, to shepherd their subjects through this apparently unending season when Death was stalking the continent of Europe in forms more horrible than any conceived of by Holbein or by Dürer, producing dispassionately the holocausts of the Somme or the *Kindermord von Ypern*.

Save for the bombs 'thrown' (as it was still termed) from Zeppelins, and which caused more anger than actual casualties, the war of 1914–1918 was fought on the other side of the Channel and it might have been possible for a proportion of the British public to ignore the battles that were being waged for them abroad. For the King and Queen this was never possible, for they knew and they saw too much. Even the hours of repose which Queen Mary sometimes snatched in the garden of Buckingham Palace, where a tent had been erected for fine weather, were haunted: 'Since several days the weather has become warm & delicious, the flowers & lilacs are coming out & the freshness of everything is really beautiful,' she wrote in May 1915, 'one could be happy *if* only this terrible load of anxiety did not exist —I am writing to you in the garden once more, so the time passes after all these long months.'[12] Even in the comparative peace of Buckingham Palace garden the King and the Queen did not wish to forget the war, for they had placed the garden at the disposal of wounded officers, after whom they were always enquiring, and one or two of whom they would constantly summon for a chat.

Severally or together, day after day, week after week, month after month, year after year, the King and Queen continued to perform their duties—inspecting the men of the New Armies who were going out to be killed or blinded or crippled or gassed in the trenches, encouraging those who had returned wounded or with missing limbs, trying to comfort some of the families of the tens of thousands who would never return, touring munitions plants, calling at food centres, for ever smiling and bowing and waving, never showing the exhaustion or the dull despair which filled their souls. Of all these war-time activities, it was the hospital visiting which they felt most deeply: 'You can't conceive what I suffered going round those hospitals in the war', King George afterwards confessed to a lady of the Court; and Queen Mary suffered with him. It was soon noticed, however, that if the Queen suspected that hospital officials were trying to show her the less bad or more presentable cases amongst the convalescent or the 'disabled' she would at once seek out for herself men who were in a worse way. 'We have rebegun visiting hospitals!!!' she wrote to one of her sons in November 1916. 'Oh! dear, oh! dear.'[13]

The photographic histories of the First World War contain page upon page of press photographs of the King and Queen at this work. There are also many hundred photographs of the Queen alone, or with her daughter beside her, arriving, inspecting, bending over a hospital bed, tasting or serving at soup-kitchens—always smiling the compassionate smile which became increasingly an effort of self-discipline as month followed month. Like these photographs, her Diary entries for these years record innumerable similar episodes and events:

Showery with fine intervals [we read for Thursday 18 February 1915]. At 2.20 we went to Milbanke Hospital to see 214 of our badly wounded soldiers who were prisoners in Germany & have been exchanged. It was very pathetic seeing so many men without arms, legs, eyes, etc. They were all wonderfully brave & patient & so thankful to be home again.

Or, in the same year:

Lovely day. Sat out. At 2.30 we motored to Gifford House Roehampton to see about 120 wounded soldiers—we then went to Dover House just opposite which is a convalescent home for officers who have lost arms & legs. We saw Capt: Brough (an exchanged prisoner) who had lost both arms—but he seemed wonderfully cheery.[14]

Sometimes the Queen would seek a few hours' peace at Frogmore or at Adelaide Cottage, Windsor. 'I went one day to Windsor, just to see the roses at Adelaide Cottage & the gardens which are really so lovely & peaceful, & little Frogmore too was looking so nice— Such a pity we cannot be there more', she wrote in a letter to her Aunt Augusta, in which she had described her hospital visiting ('the pluck shown fills one with admiration').[15]

Even York Cottage took on a different aspect: 'Owing to the Zeppelin visit last week', she recorded of their arrival at Sandringham in January 1915, 'we had a guard of 120 Grenadiers (3rd Batt:) under the command of Major Hamilton as well as 2 naval guns with Mr Holden RA in charge. A curious experience in this ordinarily quiet & peaceful spot!'[16] 'We had quite exciting times here!' wrote one of the Queen's Women-of-the-Bedchamber from York Cottage, Sandringham, some months later. 'We were all, maids included, after tea sitting listening to the Gramophone, when Sir Charles Cust put his head in & said "Come, a Zepp. can be heard", so out of the front door we went into the dark, wrapped up in rugs & coats, the Queen in the King's fur coat, & we did hear a distant dull thudding, but it must have been a long way off, so we came back into the house. Sir Charles had heard 3 Bombs fall before he called us, & the detective, Spencer, heard 6. When we got in, all the lights went out, & the King was frantic & somebody caught it!'[17]

Infrequent on the east coast, Zeppelin raids soon became an intermittent feature of London life; a wire-mesh net was stretched across the top of Buckingham Palace, and some elementary air-raid precaution rules for the Palace inmates drawn up. These rules the King and Queen tended to ignore, as a typical entry in the Queen's Diary for October 1915 shows:

At 8 we heard that 3 Zeppelins were coming!—At 9.30 we were sitting in G's room when we heard a distant report (presumably a bomb) so we went on to the balcony when the gun in the Green Park began firing & searchlights were turned on. This went on for 10 minutes or so. We did not see the Zeppelin but Derek saw it quite plainly from his house in Buck: Gate. We then heard some bombs being dropped & were told later that some had fallen in the Strand & elsewhere, killing 8 people & injuring 34. All was quiet by 10.15.[18]

Air-raid victims were now added to the list of the war casualties whom the King and Queen hastened to visit. 'Fine', Queen Mary recorded in her Diary three days after this Zeppelin raid. 'George & I went to the Charing X Hospital to see the victims (men and women) of the Zeppelin raid, many very sad cases & one boy of 17 dying having had his lung pierced by a bit of a bomb. Most sad.'[19]

The Queen also took the initiative in arranging for the despatch to the various Fronts of presents and tokens designed to alleviate for the fighting men the irony of successive Christmases on the battlefield. 'I have ordered for Sir Courtauld Thomson to take to the Dardanelles some wallets or packets & also some small writing blocks for the wounded which he told me wld be greatly valued as a *personal* gift from me', she wrote, for instance, to King George, when he was touring munitions centres in the North in September 1915.[20] It was shortly after this tour that the King set off for his second visit to the Western Front from which, in the words of Mr Gore, 'he returned a permanent war casualty'. On 28 October 1915, his horse took fright during an inspection of the 1st Wing, Royal Flying Corps, at Hesdigneul, reared up and fell back on top of the King, who was brought back to England in agony.

IV

King George V had sailed for France on 21 October, a month of bitter cold, with occasional sunny interludes. In her letters to him, Queen Mary described her day to day life: 'I motored with Mabell Airlie to Richmond Park where we had an hour's delightful walk, the lights & shades were so beautiful on the turning leaves' or 'Today I visited some workrooms in Chelsea where a quantity of ladies are making hospital requisites for my Guild', or she would write of the success of a charity matinée at the Empire Theatre, or of the condition of Uncle Christian Holstein who was ill,* or of how Queen Alexandra— 'in very good spirits and very talkative'—had just been to lunch with her. In the King's absence Lord Stamfordham was keeping the Queen informed of the war news: 'How tiresome the French are', she wrote, 'forcing our hand to send troops to Salonica, such a wild goose chase and most unfair on our poor men.'[21]

Once again, she minded the separation from the King at this moment: 'I was very sorry', she wrote to him, 'for my own sake that you had to go for I flatter myself that in these anxious times I am of some help to you & that you like having me near you, for tho' there is not much one can say or do, the mere fact of having sympathy near one is surely a help. Of course I know what your going to France means to our brave troops & you are so right to go, I only hope the weather will be fine and that your days will not be too tiring.'[22] 'So you talked to a wounded German, and another was dying from our gas, how horrible! but it was their own fault as they started using the gas', she wrote two days later, after receiving one of her daily missives from the King.[23]

It was on returning from tea with Queen Alexandra and Princess

* Prince Christian of Schleswig-Holstein, husband of Queen Victoria's fifth child and third daughter Princess Helena, survived until 1917.

Victoria at Marlborough House on 28 October that the Queen got the first news of King George's fall. The gravity of the accident—which was, for obvious reasons, much minimised in the public bulletins—was at first concealed from Queen Mary to allay her fears. 'Bigge met me with the news that George had had a fall from his horse in France & tho' luckily not badly hurt he was much shaken & the Drs Sir Anthony Bowlby & Bertrand Dawson advised quiet & rest for a week. Too unlucky', she noted in her Diary for 28 October. On the next day the Prince of Wales came over from France to tell his mother details of the King's condition. On 30 October the King was X-rayed, and it was found that no bones were actually broken: 'It is a great mercy nothing is broken or injured', the Queen wrote to her Aunt Augusta, 'for it was a severe fall, the horse rolling on him twice.'[24] 'It was a great relief and comfort to hear that the X-rays showed that no bones had been broken, and that all being well you will soon be able to return home', Queen Mary wrote to the King on 30 October. ' . . . Altogether you are having a really beastly time, my only comfort is that all might have been so much worse, broken bones & what not? Everybody here so kind, sympathetic & nice about you. Harry arrived today looking well, much distressed about you. . . . I have had telegrams from Alfonso, Ena, Queen M. Christine, Christian, Gustaf Sweden, etc. & have answered them all.'[25] On the day following the despatch of this letter, King George was conveyed back to England by hospital ship and on a stretcher: ' . . . you can't think how thankful we shall all be to get you back and every preparation is being made to make all as comfortable as is possible under the circumstances', wrote Queen Mary. 'Nobody to meet you *anywhere* and I will wait in my room until *you* send for me, for I presume you would rather be settled in your bed before you see me.'[26]

The King's convalescence proved lengthy and extremely painful, for further examination on his return to England revealed that he had in fact sustained a fracture of the pelvis. For Queen Mary the King's illness meant not merely anxiety, but also additional work, since she deputised for the King on such occasions as the inspection of the 33rd Division on Salisbury Plain on 8 November, or the decoration of Indian Native Officers later in that month. 'George sat in the Audience Room, fully dressed for the first time', Queen Mary's Diary records for 20 November; and, on the twenty-second of the same month: 'Dull and cold. G. went out on his terrace for a walk for ten minutes.' On 8 December the King dined with his family for the first time. Two days before Christmas the Royal Family went down to York Cottage for Christmas and New Year. This was the usual family party, enlivened this time by the singing of songs and the playing of a newly-acquired gramophone. 'In the evening after dinner, I had to play accompaniment for comic songs sung by the Queen, Princess Mary & 3 Princes till we went to bed', wrote Lady Bertha Dawkins who was in waiting. 'They did make a noise! the Queen was surprised to find that I could play & read.'[27] The King's health seemed to the optimistic Lady Bertha to be improving: 'He is ever so much better & looks very well indeed, but his leg still bothers him, as he gets neuralgia in it, & that makes him walk lame at times.'[28]

In fact, after the accident at Hesdigneul, King George V, who had never been a robust man, was often in actual pain. This pain, bravely concealed, told upon his nerves and thus upon his temper, which as we know had always been irascible. Although he lived another nineteen years, King George's family and household, to some extent also his advisers, 'realised', in the words of Sir Harold Nicolson, 'that he was never quite the same man again.'

So, in 1915, there was added to Queen Mary's many other sorrows and responsibilities a new, nagging cause for apprehension: her husband's health.

v

As well as visiting wounded and disabled soldiers, sailors and airmen in hospitals and convalescent centres, the King and Queen took a lead in entertaining at Buckingham Palace those who had been discharged. In March 1916 Queen Mary wrote to her Aunt Augusta an account of a typical series of these parties:

For three days this week we have given entertainments to wounded soldiers & sailors in our Riding School, over 2000 have been able to come & enjoyed it I am glad to say—Everything was very well organised & arranged for their comfort. They had tea first in the Coach Houses, members of our family presiding at each table, & being helped by the ladies & gentlemen of our household, & various friends of ours—The entertainments consisted of various artistes, acrobats, conjurors etc., an excellent choir singing songs of which the men knew the choruses, & sang them most lustily. How you would have liked being present, it was all so informal friendly and nice—We are much pleased at the success of our entertainments.[29]

To Aunt Augusta, too, she wrote of the sinking of the *Hampshire* in June of the same year, when Lord Kitchener and all his staff were drowned. In the war years, the King and Queen had become personally attached to Lord Kitchener: 'I feel quite stunned by the news & so sorry for G. who will feel his death terribly', Queen Mary wrote in her Diary for 6 June. To her aunt she described Lord Kitchener's loss as 'a great blow & personal grief to us which you will understand —You will I know remember standing in the Corridor here just outside my father in law's rooms, to make *his* acquaintance after his return from SA in 1902. But we all here are determined to carry on the work which he started, tho' with aching hearts for his loss— We had seen much of him during the last 22 months, he was a real friend, like a rock & always straight & full of confidence.'[30]

We may recall that Queen Mary's aunt, Princess Augusta Caroline, the Dowager Grand Duchess of Mecklenburg-Strelitz, had been born early in the reign of her paternal uncle George IV. Her survival so far beyond her own era, and right on into the midst of the First World War, seems in one sense miraculous; yet for the old English Princess, shut away in the Schloss at Neu Strelitz, amidst the sand-dunes and pine-trees of the north, it was infinitely sad. Her only son, the Grand Duke Adolphus, had died two months before the outbreak of the war, and it was now her beloved grandson 'Fred', a bachelor and an anglophile, who was reigning in Mecklenburg-Strelitz under the style of the Grand Duke Adolphus Frederick VI.*

The new Grand Duke was devoted to his grandmother, shared many of her views, and listened hungrily to her reminiscences; but even his love could not nullify the despair she felt at seeing her 'two countries', that of her birth and that of her adoption, fighting a European war, and with weapons and methods of a brutality of which her own contemporaries had never dreamed. As the war raged on, the old Grand Duchess felt ever more isolated, ringed round by the flames of anti-British propaganda, and dependent wholly for her happiness on her correspondence with her niece Queen Mary—which was maintained through the good offices of the Crown Princess of Sweden, a daughter of the Duke of Connaught. Aunt Augusta wrote, uncomplainingly, of the personal discomforts the war had brought her —the lack of staff in her Schloss, for example, which even meant that she had no one to push her wheel-chair about the pretty eighteenth-century garden paths or in amongst the pots and statues of the

* Adolphus Frederick VI, who never married, committed suicide in 1918.

Orangery. She could occasionally seek comfort in a brief visit from some equally isolated Englishwoman—Daisy, Princess of Pless, for instance, for whom the young Grand Duke Frederick cherished a passion which was thought to have prevented his marrying. But, indomitable as ever, the old Grand Duchess set to work, at the age of ninety-two, to make herself into an unofficial, small-scale, prisoners-of-war bureau, trying to gain information on the fate or whereabouts of the sons or grandsons of her English friends—requests sent on to her by Queen Mary—or writing to her niece in England for news of those of her German ones. In the winter of 1916, when the Grand Duchess was well advanced into her ninety-fifth year, her powers began to fail. She took to her bed, where she lay for a month, sleeping much of the time, but for the rest of it perfectly lucid and listening to letters or English newspapers being read aloud to her. Early in December she died quietly, sending from her death-bed a message of loyalty to King George V, and uttering, as her last word, the single name: 'May.'

Queen Mary received the news on 6 December, in the midst of the Cabinet crisis which was harassing the King and which resulted in the succession to the Premiership of Lloyd George:

Fine [we read in her Diary for Wednesday 6 December 1916]. I heard that my most beloved Aunt Augusta died yesterday morning after a month's illness which I had known of. She suffered little pain, only great weakness and slept much. A great grief to me, having been devoted to each other. Received many kind letters & telegrams. I went to Marshall & Snelgrove's to see the beautiful flowers made by the 'Flower girls Guild'. Mama & Toria came to tea. G. spent a busy day interviewing Ministers & so on. Mr Bonar Law informed G. that he was unable to form a Government & G. sent for Mr Lloyd George & asked him to do so.

'I wrote', she recorded next day, with her natural restraint and simplicity, 'many letters in connection with dear Aunt's death.'[31]

The death of those we love loses none of its shocking finality by having been expected. In the midst of one of the worst moments of the war, Queen Mary felt her Aunt Augusta's death with a grief all the more intense because the number of those to whom the Queen had been able to give her heart had always been restricted by the limitations of an unemotional nature. Ever since the death of Princess Mary Adelaide, back in 1897, the Grand Duchess of Mecklenburg-Strelitz had assumed in her niece's life, as we have seen, a truly maternal role. Of late years, by force of circumstance, Queen Mary had seen her aunt less; but she had been regaled with the old Grand Duchess's weekly letters—gay, trenchant, original in expression, downright in their views. Whenever she had felt misunderstood, or was suffering more than usually from her inherent difficulty in what would now be called 'putting her personality across', Queen Mary had had the secure, comforting knowledge that away across the cold North Sea, in the flat wastelands of northern Germany, was one heart on which she could ever rely, one mind attuned to her own, one affectionate old admirer who followed her every movement with eager enthusiasm, one judge who understood and applauded the task she had set out to do, and who felt that she was doing it well. She could write to her Aunt Augusta as she had written to few people in her life.* This outlet, so essential to someone at once sensitive, discreet and not over-endowed with the divine gift of self-expression, was now blocked by death.

VI

For Queen Mary, as for everyone else, the last two years of the war were more anxious and more wearying than ever: 'The length of this horrible war is most depressing', she wrote to Lady Mount Stephen in 1916. 'I really think it gets worse the longer it lasts.'[32] Growing unrest amongst munitions and engineering workers caused the Cabinet to ask the King and Queen to undertake even longer and more extensive goodwill tours of industrial and shipbuilding areas. Writing after a particularly taxing week which they had spent seeing smelting furnaces or shipyards in Newcastle, Liverpool, Barrow and elsewhere in the North, King George, who went on to Scapa Flow, wrote to Queen Mary to thank her and to say how 'tired, worried & depressed' he felt:

I can't ever sufficiently express my deep gratitude to you darling May for the splendid way in which you are helping me during these terrible, strenuous & anxious times. Very often I feel in despair & if it wasn't for you I should break down. Everybody seems to give one extra worries in these days. It was dear of you coming with me last week, it helps enormously if you come, I only hope you were not too tired, the great heat of course made it worse, but I know the visit did good. I miss you now abominably. . . .[33]

* Mlle Bricka, to whom she would in old days unburden herself, had died in July 1914.

'I am glad to feel I am a help to you in these dreadfully anxious &
strenuous times when everything is so difficult in every way', Queen
Mary replied, admitting that she had 'felt very tired', and adding,
'what a pulp one's brain becomes when one is over-worked as we
often are'.34 The Queen's hair was now turning grey, and she had
begun to suffer from neuritis in one arm. In the summer of 1917 the
doctors urged her to rest: 'as usual there is plenty to do', she wrote
to her son Prince Henry from Aldershot that July, 'so that the "rest"
idea has not been carried out, tho' I confess once or twice I have not
accompanied Papa on his inspections'.35

Even in this unwonted state of exhaustion, the Queen was alert to
discover new ways in which she might be of use. In 1917 and 1918
she became deeply interested in the problem of the permanently
disabled, and began to study such solutions to it as 'Dr Putti's method
of using the muscles for artificial arms'.36 She paid frequent visits to
the hospital to which she had lent her name at Roehampton: 'Very
warm fine day', she wrote of such a typical visit in July 1918. 'At
2.40 we motored to Roehampton to see the hospital for limbless
soldiers. Received by Col: McLeod, Miss Munn, Sir Ch: Kincardine,
Miss D. Myers etc. We saw the newest arms & legs & the men showed
us what they were able to do. We visited the workshops, & talked
to the officers from Dover House. A nice afternoon.'37 She would also
go to Brighton to see 'my workshops for limbless soldiers the same
as at Roehampton',38 and on 25 July 1918—the day on which she also
attended the memorial service for the Russian Imperial Family at the
Russian Chapel in Welbeck Street—she went to a house in Belgravia
to examine 'a new artificial leg which has just been invented'. These
constructive and therapeutic aspects of war hospital work appealed
to Queen Mary, for here were thoroughly practical schemes which
she could aid.

The news of the fate of the King's cousin the Tsar Nicholas II and
of his family trickled through to England slowly. On 15 March 1917,
the day after the death at Clarence House of the Duchess of Connaught, Queen Mary added a note to her Diary: 'We heard that a
revolution had broken out in Russia, that Nicky had abdicated for
himself and his son & that Misha* had been named by Nicky as
Emperor but Misha had only accepted the throne on condition he was

* The Grand Duke Michael Alexandrovitch, b. 1878, was then the only
surviving brother of the Tsar Nicholas II. He married Nathalia Sheremetvsky
in 1911 and was assassinated in 1918.

chosen by the Russian people.' Two days afterwards she recorded that 'Minny'*—the Grand Duchess George Michailovitch—'came to tea with us & we discussed the surprising events in Russia'. The Queen's next Diary reference to the Russian Revolution comes over a year later, on 24 July 1918: 'The news were confirmed of poor Nicky of Russia having been shot by those brutes of Bolsheviks last week, on July 16th. It is too horrible & heartless—Mama & Toria came to tea, terribly upset at the news.'

The real meaning of the first Russian Revolution of March 1917 escaped not only the British public, but the British Government as well. It was regarded as the satisfying replacement of a corrupt, inefficient, autocracy by a more responsible form of Government, and it was not foreseen how soon Russia would be out of the war. The effects of this were somewhat counterbalanced by the entry into the war of a new ally, the United States of America, in the same year, but none the less the total collapse of the Russian armies, followed by the signature of the Treaty of Brest-Litovsk, greatly increased the danger of an Allied defeat.

In 1917, the year in which she reached her fiftieth birthday—'I am 50!—dreadful!' she noted in her Diary for 26 May—Queen Mary paid her first war-time visit to France, from the 3rd until the 14th of July. Based on the Château de Beaurepaire, near Montreuil in Normandy, she spent a busy and, to her, interesting fortnight motoring about the country, visiting hospitals, aerodromes, nurses' hostels and casualty clearing stations. The King, who had crossed the Channel with her, was engaged on a separate tour of duty. The Queen also found time to indulge her passion for historical sight-seeing, looking over the cathedral at Amiens, and the cathedral and other churches of Rouen, and, with the Prince of Wales as companion, the battlefield of Crécy. 'It was probably', she wrote, 'the first time that a Prince of Wales had visited the scene since Edward the Black Prince was there at the time of the battle.'[39] Wherever she went, she was welcomed by the French people, and received bouquets and addresses from the local Mayors. 'Motored to Hesdin at 11.15', reads a typical Diary extract for this visit. 'Received at *hôtel de ville* by Mayor who read me a speech & gave me flowers. Saw fine tapestries. Walked on to balcony & bowed to populace below. Visited casualty clearing station

* Queen Alexandra's niece, Marie, Princess of Greece and Denmark (1876–1940), had married the Grand Duke George Michailovitch (1863–1919), who was assassinated at Petrograd. Known in the family as 'Greek Minny'.

& saw motor ambulance convoy. Lunched at Sir Arthur Sloggett's *château* & met several people. Visited Headquarters of "Tanks"— Genl Ellis—very interesting.'[40]

By 1917 the German submarine campaign had succeeded in creating a very serious food shortage in Great Britain. Once more the King and Queen took the lead, still further reducing the already austere war-time standard of the Royal table by adopting rationing. Days when the Court was in residence at Windsor were now partially spent in planting potatoes at Frogmore: 'We again went to Frogmore to finish planting our potato plot & worked from 3 to 5. Got very hot & tired', Queen Mary's Diary for April 1917 records.[41] At Sandringham long wet afternoons were spent by the Queen and the Household picking up horse-chestnuts, which were needed for munitions factories, while schoolchildren on the Sandringham estate and in the neighbouring Norfolk villages were set to work collecting scrap iron, jam jars and old glass bottles, the Queen afterwards inspecting the results. Early in the war the King had been persuaded to set an example to the nation by renouncing all alcoholic drinks in the Royal residences for the duration of the war. It was an example which was not followed by the country at large, but it added to the general fatigue of life in the Royal establishments.

Unbearable though the first three and a half years of the war had been, the worst crisis was still to come. On 21 March 1918 the Germans opened their final all-out offensive on the Western Front: 'Not very good news from France', Queen Mary recorded in her Diary. 'We all feel very anxious.' For several days it seemed as though the offensive might be successful, and that the war might after all end in a sudden German victory. The King hurried over to France, leaving Queen Mary in a state of anguish and suspense:

I fear there is heavy fighting near Arras [she wrote to the King on 28 March] but Ld Cromer seemed to think the War Office people were fairly satisfied on the whole—As for myself I have never in my life suffered so much *mentally* as I am suffering *now* & I know you are feeling the *same*. One must just have faith & believe that God cannot allow those huns to win & that our brave & gallant troops will be able to withstand the onslaughts, in spite of the overwhelming numbers of the enemy—God bless and keep you my own beloved husband.[42]

But Queen Mary was never content merely to wait. She now made a point of going to see the wounded from the new battlefields, so soon as they arrived in London. At times these men were difficult to locate:

'This afternoon we went to St Dunstan's', she wrote in the same letter to the King, 'because I found out that the *big* London hospitals of 700 beds or more only had about 25 patients from the last fighting which meant going thro' endless wards to find a couple of patients just come in, so I felt this was really useless & visited St Dunstan's instead.'

The German offensive was broken. As mid-summer 1918 approached hopes of victory for the Allies were running high. On 6 July the King and Queen celebrated their Silver Wedding, amid public festivities in London which included a semi-state drive to a Thanksgiving Service at St Paul's Cathedral and a presentation at the Guildhall. At length, in November, the war came to an end. 'Heard that William had abdicated & his son renounced his right to the Throne', Queen Mary noted in her Diary for 9 November 1918. 'What a downfall, what retribution to the man who started this awful war.' Two days later she was able to record the Armistice: 'Dull first, rain in the afternoon. The greatest day in the world's history. The armistice was signed at 5 a.m. & fighting ceased at 11. U. Arthur came to breakfast & at 11 we went on to the balcony to greet the large crowd which had formed outside. At 12.30 we went out again & the massed bands of the Guards played the National Anthem & patriotic songs & the anthems of the Allies. Huge crowds and much enthusiasm. The Army Council, the Lords of the Admiralty & members of the air board came to offer congratulations. At 3.15 we drove to the city in pouring rain & had a marvellous reception. . . . The Prime Minister came to see us at 7. U. Arthur & Patsy came to dinner, afterwards we went on to the balcony, the band played popular songs, & we had another wonderful scene. A day full of emotion & thankfulness— tinged with regret at the many lives who have fallen in this ghastly war.'43

And so for the King and the Queen, as for thousands upon thousands of Londoners, the war ended as it had begun—with an excited, shouting crowd asurge beneath the gas lamps in front of Buckingham Palace, cheering the two well-known figures who, aloft upon the brightly-lit central balcony, seemed at that moment to symbolise the nation's joy. They were the same King and Queen whom Londoners had congregated to cheer in that same place upon the evening of the 1911 Coronation and upon the evening of the outbreak of the War in 1914; but now a sense of true gratitude strengthened the more conventionally loyal enthusiasm of the past. The demonstration was, in fact, a personal tribute to this King and to this Queen.

Seen from the central balcony itself the crowd below looked much the same as on previous occasions—only larger, only wilder, only more vociferous. Nothing could indicate to King George V and Queen Mary, as they smiled and gestured to the throng below, that they were in fact saluting a new world. Insulated as they largely were by tradition and by their entourage the King and Queen would have to learn slowly for themselves just how disillusioned and how impatient that new, post-war world might prove. It was not merely a quarter of a century, it was a whole epoch that lay between this damp, fog-laden evening of November 1918 and that halcyon sunlit morning of July 1893, when Queen Victoria, the Duke and Duchess of Teck in tears at her side, had stood upon this very balcony to watch Princess May drive off with her husband down the Mall towards her honeymoon at Sandringham.

Hitherto, as we have witnessed, Queen Mary's life had demanded from her a series of sharp psychological readjustments, efforts of which her stoic work in war-time England had so far been the most triumphant. To what degree, and in what way, would she prove capable of adapting herself to the years immediately ahead—the 'Gay Twenties', a period, for the great majority of British people, of near-starvation and of sullen despair?

CHAPTER FIVE

THE NINETEEN-TWENTIES

THE FIRST MONTH of the first full year of peace, 1919, was scarred for Queen Mary by the sudden death of her sixth and youngest child, Prince John. A large, handsome boy of thirteen, Prince John had long been subject to epileptic attacks. For this and other reasons it had been judged best by his doctors that he should be segregated from his family and from his contemporaries; since 1917 he had been living, with his own establishment and in the care of his devoted nurse, Mrs Bill, at Wood Farm, Wolferton, on the Sandringham estate. On 18 January 1919 he died there in his sleep. 'At 5.30', noted his mother in her Sandringham Diary for that Saturday, 'Lalla Bill telephoned to me from Wood Farm, Wolferton, that our poor darling little Johnnie had passed away suddenly after one of his attacks.* The news gave me a great shock, tho' for the poor little boy's restless soul, death came as a great release. I broke the news to George & we motored down to Wood Farm. Found poor Lalla [Bill] very resigned but heartbroken. Little Johnnie looked very peaceful lying there.' 'For him it is a great release', she wrote to her old friend of Florence days, Emily Alcock, 'as his malady was becoming worse as he grew older, & he has thus been spared much suffering. I cannot say how grateful we feel to God for having taken him in such a peaceful way, he just slept quietly into his heavenly home, no pain, no struggle, just peace for the poor little troubled spirit which had been a great anxiety to us for many years, ever since he was four years old—The first break in the family circle is hard to bear but people have been so kind & sympathetic & this has helped us much.'¹ On 21 January Prince John was quietly buried in the little graveyard of Sandringham church.

* In after years Queen Mary used to remark upon the 'curious' fact that she had lived to see three of her five sons die sudden deaths, and that in each case—that of Prince John in 1919, that of the Duke of Kent in 1942, and that of King George VI in 1952—she had been apprised of the event by telephone.

While, conscientiously, she could not let herself repine over Prince John's death and although he had not been able for many years to play his part in family life, his loss saddened Queen Mary. During the war she had had moments of anxiety for her two elder sons, each of whom was at times in danger on the battle-fronts; now that that anxiety was over, and just as death had ceased to be the ubiquitous spectral companion of the last four years, her youngest son had died. Reticent by nature and by taste, Queen Mary spoke and wrote little of this personal sorrow, but it lowered her resistance to the gloom of the post-war months during which, despite the public celebrations of victory, it had become evident to her and to the King that peace was not shaping out as one had hoped that it would. 'Alas', she wrote in the same letter to her American friend, 'the end of the war seems to have brought great unrest behind it, it seems such a pity that as all classes had worked so well during the war, it is not possible now to work for the reconstruction of the world—it would have been a splendid opportunity to have come together.'

Peace was signed on 28 June 1919. Queen Mary, who had spent that morning inspecting her old home, York House, now being made 'nice & comfortable' for the Prince of Wales, and had then been conducted round the United Medical Mission's Exhibition at St Martin-in-the-Fields by the Bishop of Stepney, heard the news at tea-time. 'At 4.45 we heard that Peace had at last been signed with Germany. Thank God', she recorded. 'At 6 firing of salutes & we went on to the balcony & bowed to the enormous crowd in front of the Palace. The band played. Very fine moving sight. Stayed till 6.45. We went out again at 9.15 & stayed till nearly 11. More cheering etc. The searchlights over London & the rockets were very pretty.'² In London, in the following weeks, the signature of the Treaty of Versailles was celebrated by an Allied Victory Parade, a royal River Procession in barges, presentations of congratulatory addresses in the City, many fireworks, and mass dancing by children in the parks. The King and Queen also gave a garden-party at Buckingham Palace for ten thousand war-workers and another, for debutantes, which was designed to replace the pre-war Courts. In June the King's Birthday Parade was revived and in the same month Royal Ascot was resumed with a reassuringly pre-war elegance: 'Our carriage', noted Queen Mary, 'had 4 greys while the other 7 carriages had bays. A good turn out after 5 years of war. We had a good reception. Saw & talked to lots of friends. ... Lovely drive across the park.'³ 'Ascot', the Duke of Windsor has written of this occasion, 'was brilliant, with everybody out in grey toppers as before the war.'[4]

The Prince of Wales, who, at twenty-five, was busily setting up on his own at York House, and Princess Mary, now twenty-two years old, were the only two of Queen Mary's five children to be in London in the early days of 1919. Prince Albert had been transferred from the Navy to the Air Force after the Battle of Jutland. Prince Henry was a cadet at Sandhurst. Prince George was in his first year at Dartmouth.

Now that their four surviving sons were either quite grown up or very nearly so, they were a source of pride but also of concern to their parents. The peculiar charm and popularity of the Prince of Wales were a great satisfaction to Queen Mary, who appreciated his looks quite as much as she had in her youth appreciated those of her blond eldest brother, Prince Dolly: 'quite a pleasure to look at him', she would write to the King about the Prince of Wales.[5] Her one regret during the 'very wonderful day' of her Silver Wedding Anniversary in 1918 had been that 'our darling David was unable to be with us'.[6]

Not only did his mother think the Prince of Wales winning, intelligent and handsome, he had in her eyes the further and supreme merit of looking like 'the old Royal Family'. He was her eldest son and he was heir to the British throne. Yet with him as with all her children, the Queen often found communication inhibited and difficult. She would approach a delicate subject she wished to discuss with one or other of them in an oblique manner, and frequently she seemed at a loss how to approach such a subject at all. 'David dined with me in the evening, we talked a lot but of nothing very intimate',[7] is typical of the sort of comment which she would send to King George on the now rare occasions when she and her husband were separated.

This habit of reserve might be thought to have nicely counterbalanced the outspoken and indeed intemperate criticism which King George would without warning launch, like some ballistic missile, at now one, now another, of his sons. In fact it did not have this effect, nor did it make it easy for Queen Mary's children to confide in her, to tell her what they were really thinking, nor to fathom what she really thought. Her children, moreover, could not know how often, whether by a word in private or by a letter, Queen Mary would explain to their father some piece of conduct on their part which he had misjudged or misunderstood. Since their mother never discussed her own childhood with them, they remained unaware of the origins of Queen Mary's silence and discretion, which dated back to the old hectic White

R

Lodge days when she had been nicknamed 'the Peacemaker' by her brothers and when she had, in the words of Aunt Augusta which have already been quoted, 'a difficult position, between her Parents so different in character, temper and tastes, yet devoted to each other . . . ever the good angel between them, loving both'.[8] In moments of crisis, Queen Mary's reserve was a strength, but it could also be, to her family, a barrier. 'Through all this anxiety she has never once revealed her feelings to any of us', the Duke of York told his eldest brother when the latter returned from Africa at the time of the King's grave illness in December 1928. 'She is really far too reserved; she keeps too much locked up inside herself.'[9]

Meanwhile, the young Prince of Wales was swiftly coming to personify for millions the longings and the aims of the new post-war generation, with its driving wish for freedom from tradition and convention, whatever the cost. This was, to say the least of it, an unusual role for any member of the British Royal Family, and it was one which, naturally enough, Queen Mary could not altogether understand.

II

'I had two hours with the Queen', Lord Esher had written in his Journal in October 1915. ' . . . She is proud of the Prince of Wales. I tried to make her see that after the war thrones might be at a discount, and that the Prince of Wales's popularity might be a great asset.'[10] Three years later, in 1918, Lord Esher was proved right. At the end of the war the three great Imperial thrones of continental Europe—those of Austria, Germany and Russia—had fallen, the throne of Greece seemed liable to subside at any moment, and even in placid Holland there was strong republican feeling which made the fate of the House of Orange-Nassau appear uncertain. All the royal relations of King George and Queen Mary in Germany had lost their rights and positions: 'Uncle Willie' Württemberg had abdicated, the young Grand Duke of Mecklenburg-Strelitz had done likewise and also shot himself, the Duke of Saxe-Coburg-Gotha ruled in Coburg no longer, and both branches of the Hesse family were deprived of even nominal power. Only the Kings of Italy and of Belgium, of the three Scandinavian countries and of the more ambiguous kingdoms of Central Europe survived. The Spaniards, who had taken no part in the war, retained the monarchical system for another twelve years only.

Reflecting on what she rightly called 'the turmoil' in which her German relatives were struggling in 1918, Queen Mary thought with satisfaction of the apparent popularity and stability of the British throne. 'It has all been very wonderful and gratifying that after all these 4 years of ghastly warfare the people did crowd here to *us* the moment they knew the war was practically over', she had written to her third son, Prince Henry, from Buckingham Palace in November 1918.[11] 'This has repaid us for much hard work and many moments of keen and bitter anxiety.' All the same the words written by Lord Cromer in 1918 and quoted by King George VI's biographer, Sir John Wheeler-Bennett, were true enough: 'In spite', wrote Lord Cromer, 'of the unceasing labours and devotion to public duty of the King and Queen during the last three years the fact remains that the position of the Monarchy is not so stable now, in 1918, as it was at the beginning of the War. It seems therefore imperative that in the critical times with which the Country is now faced no stone should be left unturned in the endeavour to consolidate the position of the Crown. The Crown is the link of Empire', continued Lord Cromer, 'and its fate is inseparable from that of all British Possessions.'[12]

The hero of that brief hour, the American President Woodrow Wilson, was then making republicanism seem visionary and romantic. Many thoughtful people in this country wondered openly whether even so liberal and constitutional a Monarchy as that which nominally ruled Great Britain and the Empire might not be, somehow, out of date. That the Monarchy emerged intact from this difficult time was due partly to the solid British sense of tradition, and partly to the quiet and upright personalities of King George V and Queen Mary; but, as the politicians were swift to recognise, the vigour and the modernity of outlook of the heir to the throne were a national and Imperial asset which must not be wasted. In her perceptive way Queen Mary realised this also: 'I think David ought to return home before *very* long', she wrote to King George three weeks after the Armistice,[13] 'as he must help us in these difficult days, he is quite ready to do anything we want, for I had some capital talks with him while he was here and he was most sensible.' This was the background of the four tours across the world which the Prince of Wales undertook between 1919 and 1925. These tours meant that he was away from home for many, many months at a time. During them he found himself the centre of unparalleled orgies of popular enthusiasm which proved as exhilarating as they were exhausting.

Queen Mary was enchanted by her son's success abroad. 'We are much looking forward to the return of our dear son after his triumphal (I think I may say this without being vain) tour for such it has been', she wrote to an old friend, '& the touching letters I have received about him are a great pleasure to the King and me—He must have a good rest now which he badly wants, free from functions & photographers & being able to lead a healthy life in the country with ordinary country pursuits.'[14] 'What a splendid reception David got in New York,' she wrote to the King on the occasion of the Prince's first visit to the United States, during his tour of Canada in 1919, 'he really is a marvel in spite of his "fads" & I confess I feel very proud of him, don't you?'[15] The chief 'fad' which distressed the Prince of Wales's parents was what they both termed his 'restlessness'; for, filled with happy memories of their own more staid journeys to Australia and India in days gone by, they did not fully realise the exacting demands being made on their son in these vast tours of Empire nor that these demands were hardly calculated to instil a love of calm into an already enquiring and dissatisfied nature. 'David came to tea in the tent, he certainly looks better & seems quieter', Queen Mary wrote to King George in July 1921. ' . . .—He admits he is quite "played out".'[16] Her love of sightseeing made her envy the Prince of Wales his visits to such countries as Japan which she had never seen, and she enjoyed unpacking the 'delightful little Japanese things' in lacquer which he would bring back for her. 'I fear I do not share yr wish to have lived in a Japanese house with Jap: food & to have had to sit on the floor,' she wrote to him from Aldershot Pavilion in May 1922,[17] 'I much prefer European ways but I quite agree with you that Orientals do not make European houses appear really comfortable. They trust too much to Maple & Co & then add finishing touches of their own which make the whole seem incongruous. What you write about the Imp: Jap: family is most curious I did not know they were run in such an odd way by their Govt.'

Neither the King nor the Queen felt attuned to the desire for pleasure which, a most natural reaction amongst a whole young generation that had managed to survive four years of world war, seemed symbolised by the Prince's activities when off duty. 'I see David continues to dance every night & most of the night too', King George wrote to the Queen in August 1925. 'What a pity they should telegraph it every day, people who don't know, will begin to think that he is either mad or the biggest rake in Europe, such a pity!'[18]

Queen Mary was, as a matter of fact, far more equipped to sympathise with the 'fads' and the general behaviour of the youth of the nineteen-twenties than was King George, whose conservatism on such matters was now like granite. Her curiosity about life was undimmed; she even once asked Sir Frederick Ponsonby to teach her some of the new dance-steps of the period, a lesson interrupted by the entry of the King who expressed himself so violently that she never ventured to repeat this timid experiment.

Queen Mary's own dislike of 'rushing about' was, we may recall, but one more effect of her mother Princess Mary Adelaide's passion for it: 'At last the season is over,' she had written to her Aunt Augusta from White Lodge in August 1891, 'rushing about does not suit me, tho' Mama & Papa *thrive* on it.' 'How I do dislike all the flying about all over the place', she had written about the same time.[19] The phrase 'flying about' was in this context metaphorical; but now that she had lived to see her eldest son literally flying about in his own aeroplane she was interested rather than disapproving. Her only anxiety was that this life of constant movement was over-taxing his nerves and his strength, and that these long journeys abroad might unfit him for settling down into married life. For in the early twenties, the question of their elder children's marriages had, of course, begun to occupy the minds of Queen Mary and King George. From an historical and constitutional point of view they wished to see the direct succession to the throne secured in the second generation; from the parental point of view they both believed the state of marriage to offer certainly the safest and possibly the happiest solution to the problems of human life.

But who was there, in the topsy-turvy post-war world, that the Prince of Wales, the Duke of York and their sister could appropriately marry?

III

Ever since the days of George the Third—three of whose sons had, in open contravention of the Royal Marriages Act of 1772, contracted marriages with commoners—the problem of finding husbands or wives for the children of successive British Sovereigns had proved an anxious one. The marriages of two of George III's daughters to German Princes had not been popular, since it was felt that English dowries were being squandered to support small German principalities.

Although Queen Victoria had herself married a German Prince, and had welcomed her eldest daughter's marriage to the Crown Prince of Prussia, and her eldest son's marriage to a Princess of Denmark, she had suspected, as early as 1869, that such foreign alliances were unnecessary and were becoming out of date. 'Times have changed,' she wrote in that year to her eldest son, who had objected to his sister Louise's betrothal to the Marquess of Lorne, 'great foreign alliances are looked on as causes of trouble and anxiety, and are of no good. What could be more painful than the position in which our family were placed during the wars with Denmark, and between Prussia and Austria? Every family feeling was rent asunder, and we were powerless. . . . You may not be aware, as I am, with what *dislike* the marriages of Princesses of the Royal family with small German Princes . . . were looked on, and how in former days many of our Statesmen like Mr Fox, Lord Melbourne and Lord Holland abused these marriages, and said how wrong it was that alliances with noblemen of high rank and fortune, which had always existed formerly and which are perfectly legal, were no longer allowed by the Sovereign.'[20] 'I feel sure', she added, 'that *new* blood will strengthen the Throne *morally* as well as physically.'

What Pitt and Fox had criticised in the reign of George III, what Queen Victoria had written in 1869, was more than ever true in the years following the First World War. The hatred of the British public for all things German, which was a natural aftermath of the war of 1914–1918, would have utterly precluded an alliance between any of King George V's children and a personage of royal German birth; the King had moreover specifically rejected his German origins in 1917 when he changed his family name to Windsor and requested his Teck and Battenberg relations to change their names also.* And even had there been no such popular prejudice in Great Britain the shipwreck of the princely houses of Germany after the war would have made it impossible to find a suitable *parti*. There remained Greek and Danish royalties, but it was tacitly agreed between the King and Queen that they could not object should any of their children look to members of the English or Scottish nobility. This was indeed likely enough to

---

* In 1917 Queen Mary's eldest brother, the second Duke of Teck, relinquished his German title and was created first Marquess of Cambridge, while Prince Alexander George of Teck became Earl of Athlone. Prince Louis of Battenberg became first Marquess of Milford Haven, while three of his four children took on his new English surname of Mountbatten.

happen, since, save for the Prince of Wales, the children of King George and Queen Mary had had no experience of continental life.

The first of the King and Queen's children to marry was Princess Mary who in November 1921, at the age of twenty-four, became engaged to Henry, Viscount Lascelles, eldest son of the Earl of Harewood, a Yorkshire magnate and landowner who lived at Harewood House, near Leeds. Lord Lascelles, who was fifteen years older than Princess Mary, and a famous connoisseur of pictures, was staying at York Cottage, Sandringham, that November, and it was in a room in this small house that he proposed. 'Went the usual rounds in the afternoon', we read in Queen Mary's Diary for 20 November. '—At 6.30 Mary came to my room to announce to me her engagement to Lord Lascelles! We then told G. & then gave Harry L. our blessing —We had to keep it quiet owing to G. having to pass an order in council to give his consent. Of course everybody guessed what had happened & we were very cheerful & almost uproarious at dinner— We are delighted.' 'They are both very happy & Mary is simply beaming', the Queen wrote to her eldest brother the next day. 'We like him very much & it is such a blessing to feel she will not go abroad. *I* personally feel quite excited as you can imagine.'[21] 'Mary is radiant & I am getting *so* fond of him & we get on very well', she wrote to Lady Bertha Dawkins.[22] The engagement was made public three days later, when the Royal Family had returned to Buckingham Palace. On the day after the announcement the Queen records that she took the engaged couple driving 'in an open carriage through the Park & streets & people seemed pleased to see them'.[23] Later that same afternoon Queen Alexandra and her daughters the Princess Royal and Princess Victoria came to tea at the Palace. 'Harry L. was formally presented as a relation—We had a most hilarious tea.'

The wedding of Princess Mary and Lord Lascelles took place at Westminster Abbey on 28 February 1922. As the first big state pageant since the war—since, indeed, the 1911 Coronation—the wedding aroused immense popular excitement and enthusiasm, a fact which did not surprise either King George or Queen Mary, but was found startling by younger members of the Royal Family whose memories did not carry them back to the state pageantry of the Victorian and Edwardian epochs, when every Royal wedding was the occasion for public festivities and loyal demonstrations. 'Mary's wedding', the Duke of York wrote to the Prince of Wales, who was abroad, 'is causing a great deal of work to many people, & as far as I can make out the 28th

is going to be a day of national rejoicing in every conceivable & un-
conceivable manner. . . . In fact it is now no longer Mary's wedding
but (this from the papers) it is the "Abbey Wedding" or the "Royal
Wedding" or the "National Wedding" or even the "People's Wedding"
(I have heard it called) "of our beloved Princess".' On the evening of
the wedding day, the Duke wrote an account of the ceremony to his
brother: 'The actual ceremony at the Abbey was beautiful & everything was arranged wonderfully well', he wrote. 'The streets were
overcrowded all along the route of the procession at one time it was
thought the crowd would break through merely from the pressure of
people behind. Mary looked lovely in her wedding dress & was perfectly calm all through the ceremony.'24

Upon Queen Mary the preparations for the marriage, and the
wedding ceremony itself, had had a tonic effect, though once all was
over a reaction set in:

Most darling David [she wrote to the Prince of Wales on 2 March]
—The wonderful day has come & gone & Mary is married & has flown
from her home leaving a terrible blank behind her as you can well imagine.
Papa & I are feeling very low & sad without her especially as Georgie
had to return to Malta yesterday while Harry has at last joined the
10th Hussars at Canterbury & Bertie has gone hunting for a few days—
Nothing could have gone off better than the wedding did, a fine day, a
beautiful pageant from start to finish, a fine service in the Abbey, Mary
doing her part to perfection (a very great ordeal before so many people)—
& everyone happy & pleased. . . . Grannie was wonderful & looked very
nice in violet velvet wearing the Garter & many fine jewels. Enormous
crowds everywhere & a great reception when we stepped on to the Balcony.
—We gave a large family luncheon (both families) in the state dining room
and Mary & Harry L. drove off at 3.45—Papa & all of us throwing rice
& little paper horse shoes & rose leaves after them. Papa & I felt miserable
at parting, poor Papa broke down, but I mercifully managed to keep up as
I so much feared Mary wld break down. However she was very brave &
smiled away as they drove off in triumph to the station.25

Although in the days following the wedding she distracted herself
by sorting her daughter's presents at St James's Palace, Queen Mary
succumbed before an unwonted onset of depression. When the Court
moved to Windsor for Easter, this mood darkened still further. 'I
confess', she wrote in April 1922, 'I miss Mary dreadfully here, & her
passage seems so empty & silent.' Other factors tended to make that
spring of 1922 at Windsor discouraging. 'There has been', wrote

Queen Mary, 'a perfect epidemic of deaths. Ly Farquahar's, Col: Erskine's mother Ly Horatia Erskine, Dow: Ly Derby, Bertha's Aunt, Wigram's brother in law, then Leopold* & then Ly Stamfordham who as you know has been ill since last July—It is all rather sad & depressing & this added to the most odious cold dull rainy weather makes life almost intolerable.'[26]

For Queen Mary to be depressed at Windsor was in itself curious enough. What she would call 'this dear glorious old castle so full of historical associations' always provided her with pleasant occupation 'in the armoury, library & the rooms—a never ending joy to me with all their interests & so forth'.[27] Moreover, the residence of the Court at Windsor invariably gave the Queen opportunities to discuss the serious topics of the day, or the interesting by-paths of history, with a succession of intelligent and erudite guests—for at Windsor King George's respect for the hospitable tradition set by Queen Victoria and King Edward VII overcame his inborn distaste for entertaining as such. Back in Buckingham Palace, on the other hand, Queen Mary was thrown entirely on her own resources once her day's work was over, for King George V's liking for simplicity and for seclusion had grown with the years. Only four or five times in a London season could he be persuaded to dine out in one of the great London houses of his friends. Apart from distinct state occasions, he and the Queen now entertained very little themselves. Day after day they would lunch alone together, night after night they would dine alone together. At these meals Princess Mary had, before her marriage, made what her brother the Duke of York termed 'a permanent third'. Now the Princess had left the Palace, her parents faced one another across the dining table in the unbroken privacy of the *tête-à-tête*.

IV

The comparative seclusion in which King George V and Queen Mary were living in the nineteen-twenties contrasted strangely with the contemporaneous revival of social life in London and with the wild jazzy tone of that post-war decade. An absolute quiet reigned within Buckingham Palace, which to young members of the family seemed not at all unlike that royal court of the Perrault fairy-tale under the

---

* Lord Leopold Mountbatten (b. 1889), the second son of King George V's aunt, Princess Beatrice, died on 23 April 1922 and was buried at Windsor on 1 May.

R*

spell of Carabosse. This resistance to change and rejection of gaiety puzzled the sons of the King and Queen. They became restive, and seized upon or manufactured opportunities to avoid family evenings which ended at ten or at ten-thirty, and during which the King would interrogate one or other of them as to what he had been doing latterly and why he had been doing it, showing at the same time a disturbing, uncanny knowledge of their activities. At Buckingham Palace, during these years, the element of fun was noticeably absent.

The Duke of York had hoped that Princess Mary's marriage might make his parents change their ways:

Things will be very different here, now that Mary has left & Papa & Mama will miss her too terribly, I fear, but it may have a good effect in bringing them out again into public [he had written optimistically to the Prince of Wales on the day of their sister's wedding in February 1922]. I feel that they can't possibly stay in & dine together every night of their lives & . . . I don't see what they are going to do otherwise, except ask people here or go out themselves. But we shall know more about this as days go on.[28]

Days did go on, but no alteration became visible in the staid habits of the King and Queen. As a young man King George, whose two passions in life were shooting and collecting stamps, had hated entertaining and had had little use for metropolitan or social amusements. Now that he was approaching sixty, in indifferent health, anxious and over-worked, he liked privacy more than ever. Queen Mary had never cared for 'Society', since she deprecated gossip and detested small-talk; she still liked dancing and she loved going to the theatre, but she was prepared to forgo these pleasures at the King's wish. No longer shy, she remained diffident, and she was perfectly contented with the restrained pattern of life which she and her husband had evolved during their long years of marriage. Their affection for each other had, if anything, increased with the stress of the war. 'You know how devoted I have always been to you & how much I love you', the King wrote to Queen Mary in July 1919, '. . . now I also admire you, but I won't say any more otherwise I might turn your head.' 'Everything is a blank here without you', he wrote to her from Balmoral in August 1923.[29] Queen Mary, on her side, responded: 'It is delightful to think we shall meet I hope in 3 days, 3 weeks is a long time to be parted for a Darby & Joan such as we are!' she wrote to him from Goldsborough Hall, Yorkshire, in the summer of 1926.[30] She had now achieved the supreme feminine happiness of knowing that she was indispensable, and, more than ever, her whole existence centred upon shielding her husband from needless anxiety or from anything which might annoy him. Long ago, at the time of King George V's accession, she had written in reply to an enquiry from her eldest son Prince Edward: 'I believe the right way to write to me is The Queen, & to Grannie Queen Alexandra, as she is now the Queen Mother & I am the wife of the King.'* [31]

'May makes herself happy wherever she is', the Duchess of Teck had once said of her daughter, in the old White Lodge days when it had seemed as though nothing very enthralling would ever come to disturb the placid tenor of Princess May's life. Since then how much had happened—her engagement to the Duke of Clarence, his sudden death, her engagement to the Duke of York, their marriage, the births of their children, the long journeys to India, to Canada and to Australia, King George V's accession to the Throne, their Coronation, the Delhi Durbar, the War, the Victory. Now, a Queen Consort in late middle-age, the mother of five grown-up children, she continued to 'make herself happy', filling her leisure hours with activity, or, rather, so arranging her day that she had no leisure hours at all. 'She was never idle, even if she was only stitching', a member of her Household says of her; and, in fact, while she was working at her tent-stitch embroidery, she would also be listening to some new book being read aloud. To many people besides her own children the framework of Queen Mary's life at this period might have seemed inflexible and monochrome; to herself, had she ever thought about it, her days would have appeared beautifully arranged and quivering with interest and colour. Queen Mary once jotted down in the margin of a book purporting to be her own biography, against a passage in which the author averred that the Queen was easily bored, the terse comment: 'As a matter of fact, The Queen is never bored.'

We have already noticed that Queen Mary was not by nature introspective, that she lived in the present and that she never brooded on the past—this last an enviable trait which brings a happiness all its own. She would allow herself to criticise incompetence, and to complain

* Queen Mary's letters to King George contain much evidence of her conception of this role, e.g. a letter written to the King, then at Balmoral, from Carberry Tower in August 1925, which has as postscript: 'P.S. Will you be at home Wed. to meet me & will you want me to walk with you at once, if you do please telegraph & I will dress accordingly.' [32]

about the weather, of which—like King George V—she was inordinately aware. Apart from political anxiety,* it was only the illness or death of a friend or relative, bringing with it a sense of loss and an unwelcome apprehension of mortality, which depressed Queen Mary in these years. 'Life is *not* obliging is it', she wrote on one such occasion from York Cottage, Sandringham, in 1924.[34]

It might, as a matter of fact, have seemed that, in the nineteen-twenties, life was at last being rather obliging to Queen Mary for, a universally respected figure, she now had the satisfaction of knowing that her qualities of heart and brain, and her dedicated sense of public duty, were gratefully recognised by her husband's subjects. 'Only give me the chance & I will do things as well as anybody, after all why shouldn't I?' she had written to old Hélène Bricka in 1897,[35] a period at which we may recall that, as Duchess of York, she was openly criticised by members of the Duke's own family as well as by the fashionable world of London. She had now shown that she could 'do' most things just as well as anybody else, and a certain number of things much better.

The years were guiding Queen Mary swiftly and smoothly on towards her sixtieth birthday; how could she foresee that, on the very verge of seventy, she would be called upon to face the cruellest and most wounding experience of her whole personal and public life? Meanwhile, in the deceptive lull of the early twenties, the Queen continued to lead the peaceful, dignified existence of a Consort, presiding with the King over the four Courts which regularly marked each London Season, attending with him the Opening of Parliament, helping him to entertain Cabinet Ministers and other guests at Windsor, migrating with him to Sandringham or to Balmoral at fixed moments of the year. She was also engaged in her many charities; and she was working at her 'one great hobby' of reorganising the Royal collections and the furniture in the Royal residences, and of retrieving portraits, plate, pieces of furniture, miniatures and relics which had, in earlier years, been dispersed and which she now re-integrated into the collections at Windsor Castle.

The 1914–1918 war had interfered with the 'one great hobby' but Queen Mary had been able, at snatched moments, to continue her

* She was, e.g., terribly concerned over the Chanak crisis of October 1922, which seemed to herald a new war. 'The Queen stayed in bed all day, & could not come to dinner, as she has lost her voice & she worried over the troublous times', Lady Bertha Dawkins wrote from Balmoral at this time.[33]

re-arrangements at Windsor, although naturally enough she had had very little free time to devote to this absorbing pursuit. Now, in the nineteen-twenties, she consecrated hour after hour to completing these changes at Windsor Castle and in Buckingham Palace, as well as at Balmoral and, on her rare visits there, at Holyrood. On her husband's accession to the throne in 1910, the Queen had at once set herself this task of conservation. Now, in a post-war epoch of flux and doubt and dissolution, it seemed to her more than ever imperative to garner and preserve every tangible remnant of the history of British Royalty. She was for ever matching up, cataloguing, re-organising and adding to the historical parts of the Royal collections. With her phenomenal memory there went a very shrewd eye, and the staff of the various Royal residences found that it was impossible to remove for cleaning or repair the smallest coral object from some obscure vitrine without the Queen noticing its absence and sending to enquire whither it had been taken. During these years she was, as always, constantly enlarging her own knowledge of certain aspects of European history and in certain fields of the applied arts. She had now thoroughly learned to appreciate the beautiful as well as the curious and the rare. In conversation at this time she would always attribute her love of fine objects to her father the Duke of Teck: 'only he was poor', she would add, 'and could not afford to buy.'

Parallel to such additions to the Royal collections, was the extensive collection of her own which Queen Mary was now forming. Although her taste was essentially catholic, and her artistic interests were heterogeneous, she concentrated more and more on improving her standard of knowledge by consultations with museum experts, by comparing notes with other collectors, and by paying regular visits to the showrooms of the best London dealers.

Collecting had now become a major preoccupation of Queen Mary's life. It was an interest which King George V did not share—although he did collect rich snuff-boxes—but it was one of which he did not disapprove. In her eldest brother Prince Dolly, since 1917 Lord Cambridge, the Queen found a strong sympathiser, for he, too, had inherited the first Duke of Teck's love of the arts. Lord Cambridge and his wife lived in Shropshire, but whenever he came to London his sister would hurry him off round galleries and museums. 'What do you want to go & see, the Wallace Collection, or Victoria & Albert or National Portrait Gallery', she wrote to him in a typical note in February 1925.[36] 'Should any of these smile on you wld you like me

to let the Director know as it is nice sometimes to have a knowledge-
able person with one, & one of whom one can ask questions? Have
you ever seen the Soane Museum because that is most interesting &
you wld like it? Then will you be free Sat. afternoon because Mary
will be staying with us that Sat. to Mon. & will I know be quite ready
to do a Gallery or Museum with you and me— . . . There are 2 or 3
things in the Palace I should like to show you, small alterations which
I think you will approve of, perhaps these I could show you on
Sunday.' On those afternoons in London when she had no official
duty to perform—no hospital to visit and no charitable home to open
or to inspect—the Queen would set out with an attendant Lady to
look at some gallery or museum, or to call on a dealer or an *antiquaire*.
They would leave Buckingham Palace punctually at two-forty-five.
The Queen would be back in good time to give King George V his tea.

It may be useful in the context of this brief survey of Queen Mary's
diurnal life after the First World War to take a look at the manner
in which the Queen organised her day. This ran with the precision
of a well-made clock. Each morning, Queen Mary was called at
seven-fifteen. At nine the King and the Queen had breakfast together.
At half-past nine a bell would summon the Lady currently on duty
to the Queen's sitting-room, where she would find Queen Mary seated
upright at her desk, a stack of opened letters before her. The Queen
had inherited from her mother the Duchess of Teck the habit of
herself opening every letter addressed to her personally, but unlike
the Duchess of Teck she dealt with these immediately with a quiet
efficient speed, marking up deserving cases with the initials of some
appropriate charity with which she had influence. Unlike Queen
Alexandra, who was reputed to have sent a new five-pound note to
anyone who wrote to her asking for help, Queen Mary judiciously
assessed the sincerity of the writer by studying each letter. She rejected
those which did not seem to her genuine, and, on investigation, her
instinct was usually proved to have been correct. She could also recognise on an envelope a handwriting of which she might once have seen
one specimen, many years before. 'Ah yes, I thought I knew that
hand', she would say with satisfaction—for she was proud of her
excellent memory. The Queen would next deal carefully with the
correspondence brought by her Woman-of-the-Bedchamber, and
when this was completed she would interview her Private Secretary.
The remainder of the morning Queen Mary spent alone in her room,
writing and working until luncheon which, like breakfast, was shared

with the King. At both these meals King George's parrot, Charlotte, would attend, its mood at times amiable, at times the reverse. In the afternoon, provided she had no public or charitable duty to perform, the Queen would sally forth, as we have seen, to look at some gallery or to shop. Before dinner she would rest, her Lady reading aloud to her while she herself did embroidery, and, unless some member of the family were invited, she would then dine alone with the King, who would usually have to work at his 'red boxes' again after dinner.

This daily domestic life was designed to enable the King to get through his work in peace and to relax in the quiet ways he liked. From time to time they would go out to a large dinner-party, or ask some friends to dine at Buckingham Palace; but these were exceptional breaks in the routine.

v

The spring of 1922, and the spring of 1923, provided short but delightful and unusual breaks in this routine of Queen Mary's life, for in May of the first year she accompanied the King on a state visit to the King and Queen of the Belgians in Brussels, and in May of the second year she went with him to Rome on a state visit to the King and Queen of Italy. We may remember Queen Mary's disappointment in 1913, when the Liberal Cabinet would not agree to a British state visit to the Emperor Francis Joseph in Vienna, a project which Queen Mary had confidently hoped would initiate a series of fascinating tours of all the courts of Europe. Now, in the post-war era, there were few European courts left to visit, and this plain fact, added to King George V's distaste for going abroad, tended to keep the King and Queen at home. In the years between the signature of peace and King George V's death—sixteen years in all—King George and Queen Mary spent exactly seven weeks out of Great Britain: going to Belgium for eight days in 1922, to Italy for six days in 1923, and cruising, in 1925, off the Italian coast for five weeks after the King's severe bronchial attack. The Italian cruise was the last occasion on which Queen Mary ever left the shores of England, although she lived for another twenty-eight years.

The state visit to Brussels in May 1922 had an almost war-time flavour, since part of it was spent in visiting the cemeteries of British war-dead, and in such ceremonies as laying a wreath upon Nurse Cavell's tomb. Queen Mary, who was pleased to see 'dear Albert and

Elizabeth'—the King and Queen of the Belgians—once again, found much to interest her in Brussels and its neighbourhood. She visited the field of Waterloo and the farm at Hougoumont, she looked at the 'curious remains of prehistoric animals' in the Iguardodon in Brussels, admired the church of Sainte Gudule, inspected Prince Napoleon's collection of ancestral relics and was received by Cardinal Mercier at Malines while the Cathedral *carillon* played *Rule Britannia* and the organ played *God Save the King*. 'Felt rather tired', Queen Mary noted in her Diary at the end of this packed visit. 'I enjoyed my Belgian stay very much indeed.'37

Queen Mary looked forward avidly to the Roman visit, since this was a city which she did not know. It would, too, be the first time that she had returned to Italy after leaving Florence with her parents in 1885 at the age of seventeen. 'We are looking forward to going to Rome in May, on our State visit to their Italian Majesties', she wrote to her old friend of I Cedri days, little Emily Alcock. '—How I should like to see you but fear that this will be impossible as every minute will be taken up with something or other. As for meeting at Pisa I don't know which way we shall go & as we shall travel by special train I don't suppose we shall stop at many places *en route*. I am so sorry but I feel you will realise the difficulties and understand. I have never been to Rome so I must try & see something of its beauties.'38 Even under the constricting and *protocolaire* circumstances of a state visit, Queen Mary succumbed to the irresistible spell of the Roman spring. 'How wonderful Rome is with all its treasures & we had such perfect weather, real summer & everything looked so beautiful— People were most kind in giving us a great reception. The King & Queen are awfully nice & the Pce of Piemonte a most charming & intelligent young man, full of interest in historical & artistic things— We have returned to winter here which is a great disappointment.'39 Although Lord Curzon (then Foreign Secretary) had refused to allow any political significance to be attributed to the state visit to Rome, the Italian public were pleased and impressed by their sight of the British Sovereign and of his Consort. An Italian lady still remembers how, as a small girl walking with her nurse in the Piazza of St Peter's, she caught a glimpse of the King and Queen arriving at the Vatican to call upon Pope Pius XI. Queen Mary, who would never wear black if she could avoid it, had chosen to be dressed entirely in white, with a white lace veil upon her head. She was wearing ropes of pearls and round her throat was a pearl choker. To the foreign child this irridescent figure seemed the very epitome of how a Queen should look. Neither on this visit to Italy, nor in 1925, did Queen Mary revisit Florence or 'the dear Cedri'. 'On leaving Rome', she wrote, when back in Buckingham Palace', 'we only passed thro' dear Florence about midnight when I was again in bed, rather worn out with the fatigue of our most delightful & interesting visit.'[40]

In the January preceding this May visit to Rome, the King and Queen's second son Albert, Duke of York, then twenty-seven years old, had become engaged to Lady Elizabeth Bowes-Lyon,* who had been one of his sister's bridesmaids at Westminster Abbey and who was twenty-two. Having telegraphed the news to Sandringham by a prearranged signal, the Duke of York hurried down there to tell his parents formally and to obtain their approval. 'We are delighted', Queen Mary noted in her Diary, 'and he looks beaming.'[41] 'The only reason why we cannot definitely fix date of wedding', she wrote a few days later to her brother Lord Cambridge, 'is that we may have to pay an official visit to Rome & we are finding out when the Italians really want us to go. Elizabeth is with us now, perfectly charming, so well brought up & will be a great addition to the family.'[42]

'I hope we shall be as lucky with our daughters in law as Lady Holford has been, I must say I dread the idea and always have', King George had written to Queen Mary, who was staying with the Holfords at Westonbirt, in August 1922;[43] in the event, the King's apprehensions faded away, for he was immediately disarmed by the future Duchess of York. Queen Mary was as gratified as was King George by this match; the descent of Lady Elizabeth from the old Kings of Scotland seemed to her especially appropriate and appealed to her historical sense. For some years she had been anxious for the Duke of York to marry and early in 1920 she had even taken the wholly uncharacteristic step of speaking to him directly about it, but since this was just before Prince Albert had met Lady Elizabeth Bowes-Lyon he had not responded to his mother's hints. Full of good intentions and earnest endeavour, the Duke of York had matured slowly and at this time he lacked self-confidence. He had a nervous impediment in speaking and he was given to attacks of melancholia. Together with his mother's

---

* Lady Elizabeth Bowes-Lyon, fourth daughter and ninth child of the fourteenth Earl of Strathmore, was born in 1900 at St Paul's Walden Bury in Hertfordshire. She became Queen Consort in December 1936 on the Duke of York's accession to the throne, and since King George VI's death in February 1952 has been known as Queen Elizabeth The Queen Mother.

shyness he had inherited the impatience of his grandfather the Duke
of Teck. For two years Lady Elizabeth could not make up her mind
to marry him, for she was reluctant to give up her freedom for the
pomp and constriction of a Royal life. The engagement was made
public in January and the wedding took place at Westminster Abbey
in April, evoking the same kind of public enthusiasm which had greeted
that of Princess Mary and Lord Lascelles the year before.

King George VI's biographer has shown to what degree his marriage
proved to be the Duke of York's liberation. With his elder brother
the Prince of Wales often abroad, and living in any casè at York House
when he was in London, with Prince Henry in the Army and Prince
George at sea, it was the Duke of York who had spent the most time
in these post-war years at home with his parents. His father's sudden
stormy criticisms and his mother's tactful silence had worked upon
the Duke's nerves; by contrast, the happy ease of married life came
as a revelation to him. All the same, he was afraid that his mother
might miss him: 'I do hope you will not miss me very much', he wrote
to Queen Mary on the day after his marriage, from Polesden Lacey,
'though I believe you will as I have stayed with you so much longer
really than the brothers.'44

Queen Mary felt that she and 'the Family' had gained by her son's
marriage. She became devoted to her daughter-in-law and from now on
her letters and Diaries are full of affectionate references to 'Bertie & E.'
When, in April 1926, the Duchess of York gave birth to her first
child, the present Queen Elizabeth II, Queen Mary recorded the event
with delight: 'We were awakened at 4 a.m. by Reggie Seymour who
informed us that darling Elizabeth had got a daughter at 2.40. Such a
relief and joy.'45 That afternoon she and the King went to Bruton
Street to see 'the little darling', and in the following years the child
became her grandparents' favourite.

With one son satisfactorily married, Queen Mary continued to hope
anxiously for another marriage in the family—that of 'most darling
David', the Prince of Wales.

VI

The Prince of Wales had been in England for his brother's wedding.
Except for a short visit to Canada in 1923 and another to the United
States and Canada in the autumn of 1924 he did not go abroad again
until the spring of 1925, when he paid official visits to South Africa

and to some of the South American republics. Queen Mary thus saw more of her eldest son than she had had the chance to do in the years immediately following the Peace Treaty. In April 1924 she heard him, at Wembley, formally ask the King to declare open the British Empire Exhibition of which the Prince of Wales was President. This was the first occasion on which King George V broadcast, and the first time that more than a handful of his subjects had ever heard a British Sovereign's voice.

The Wembley Exhibition, which consisted of a series of massive pavilions devoted to the products of those Dominions and Colonies which then formed part of the British Empire, was such a success that it was repeated on the same site in the year following, 1925. Queen Mary was particularly interested in it, for the Exhibition offered a blend of the instructive, the imperial and the impressive which was after her own heart. She paid a series of private visits to Wembley, as well as going round it with the King when they showed the Exhibition to the Italian and the Roumanian Sovereigns, who paid separate state visits to this country in May 1924. One feature of the Wembley Exhibition which drew admiring crowds was that fabulous tribute to Queen Mary, 'The Queen's Doll's House'.

The idea to give Queen Mary a doll's house of her own had originated in the fertile brain of Princess Aribert of Anhalt, better known as Princess Marie-Louise,* a granddaughter of Queen Victoria and called, in the Royal Family, 'Cousin Louie'. In *My Memories of Six Reigns*, Princess Marie-Louise has described how, on finding her sister Princess Helena Victoria and their mother Princess Christian of Schleswig-Holstein busy one day at their home, Cumberland Lodge, she discovered that they were collecting 'miniature *objets d'art*' for some doll's house which Queen Mary was then furnishing. Queen Mary's weakness for 'miniature *objets d'art*' was well known in the family; and indeed glass cases at Buckingham Palace and even more at Sandringham House bear witness by their contents to her love of tiny golden tea-sets, minute chairs in mother-of-pearl, infinitesimal carriages in gilt and tortoiseshell, filigree-covered *vinaigrettes* the size

* Princess Marie-Louise, fourth child and second daughter of Prince Christian of Schleswig-Holstein and Queen Victoria's third daughter Princess Helena, was born 1872, married Prince Aribert of Anhalt (from whom she afterwards separated) in 1891 and died in 1957, shortly after the publication of her book of recollections *My Memories of Six Reigns* (Evans Bros., 1956), in which she describes in detail the evolution of the Queen's doll's house.

of a child's thumb-nail. Princess Marie-Louise determined to ask Sir Edwin Lutyens, whom she knew well, to design a doll's house worthy of presentation to Queen Mary by a group of her friends and well-wishers. Lutyens was then engaged upon the rather large-scale task of building the city of New Delhi; the sense of contrast between this work and the planning of a house for dolls appealed to him. Princess Marie-Louise next enquired whether the Queen would accept the gift. Queen Mary agreed to do so.

Any hint of fantasy in the original project put forward by Princess Marie-Louise was soon drained from it, for a committee was set up to deal with the plans for the doll's house, and Princess Marie-Louise acted as what Queen Mary termed 'liaison officer' between herself and those principally concerned in the work. Lutyens had decided that the miniature house should be decorated with pictures and furniture specifically made to scale by the leading painters and craftsmen of the day so that, when finished, it 'would enable future generations to see how a King and Queen of England lived in the twentieth century and what authors, artists and craftsmen of note there were during their reign'. This revised version of the plan was approved by Queen Mary, since it raised the doll's house from the sphere of the fanciful to that of historical purpose. The doll's house would also serve, in an exact sense, as a microcosm of Queen Mary's taste. It did not, however, reflect the taste of the age, since modern paintings and objects were as rigidly excluded from the doll's house as they were from Windsor Castle itself.

The house was Georgian in design, and was built on four floors, with a mezzanine and a basement. It stood in a painted-tin and velvet garden, laid out by Miss Gertrude Jekyll. It was designed to accommodate a family of persons six inches tall. If these persons wished to entertain, they could give a dinner-party of eighteen in the dining-room, and each of their guests could eat off gold plate or off Royal Doulton. In the King's Library, dominated by portraits of the Tudor Sovereigns, bookshelves held two hundred volumes the size of postage stamps each written by a contemporary author in his own hand, while minute portfolios bulged with seven hundred water-colours and drawings of the same size. The Queen's Saloon was lined in rose-coloured silk and furnished in the style of the later eighteenth century. The bedrooms of the King and Queen faced healthily south and west, and the bed-linen had taken 'a Franco-Irish lady' fifteen hundred hours to weave. The bathrooms were particularly luxurious, with walls of ivory and shagreen, and floors of African marble and mother-of-pearl. Real water spurted from the taps; waste from the baths and from the lavatories ran into real tanks beneath the house. The cupboards were filled with china and glassware, the larder was full of food, and the wine-cellar was stocked with miniature bottles of wine. The kitchen stove was perfect in all its details, and the gramophone in the children's nursery played *God Save the King*. In the garage beneath the doll's house stood a series of extremely costly reproductions of the royal Daimlers. An elaborate mechanical device enabled the walls of the house to be raised at will when one wished to see what was going on inside.

Nothing, in fact, went on inside the Queen's doll's house, for it lacked an essential component: a family of doll royalties. Although a capacious drawer had been provided in the base of the house for storing those little persons who should have benefited by so much forethought and luxury, this drawer remained eerily empty. The only dolls to be seen were a pipe-major and the five guardsmen who stood eternally at attention in the sentry boxes, guarding the uninhabited house. By the green garden door a miniature white dog waited 'expectantly . . . till it shall please the Queen, his mistress, to walk in her garden'.

The planning of the doll's house and its contents provided Lutyens and his colleagues with much amusement; it was a test of ingenuity and it was being built to please the Queen. This aim it effectively achieved, for Queen Mary watched its progress contentedly. 'Yesterday', she wrote to the King in July 1923, 'I went to see the doll's house which is getting on very well, & is most beautiful & all the details quite perfect—Some of the little pictures by the good artists are very attractive & Mr Ranken's tiny ones of the Windsor rooms look so well hung up.'[46] In January 1924 she recorded that the doll's house was 'nearing completion', and later in that month she was able herself to take the rooms seriously in hand, making the main ones habitable and adding personal touches to her bedroom—in which was a portrait of her mother the Duchess of Teck reduced to scale—and to her boudoir. 'The Prime Minister came to see G. to tender his resignation & G. sent for Mr Ramsay MacDonald the labour leader who agreed to form a Govt.', Queen Mary recorded in her Diary for 22 January 1924. 'In the afternoon Joan and I went to see the doll's house & arranged some of the rooms.' Before the official opening of the Wembley Exhibition Queen Mary went to examine 'the small Pavilion where my doll's house is to stand'. The Queen's doll's house was ultimately installed in Windsor Castle, in a room of its own, and flanked by two dolls' orangeries also designed by Sir Edwin Lutyens. These orangeries are used to store furniture not for the moment needed in the house itself.

VII

22 January 1924, the day on which Mr Baldwin resigned from the position of Prime Minister and on which the King asked Mr Ramsay MacDonald to form the first Labour Government of Great Britain, happened to be the anniversary of Queen Victoria's death at Osborne in 1901. 'Today 23 years ago dear Grandmama died', King George noted in his Diary. 'I wonder what she would have thought of a Labour Government!' The new Labour Ministers were also aware of the historical significance of the day, as the Lord Privy Seal, Mr J. R. Clynes, has recorded in his *Memoirs*:

> As we stood waiting for His Majesty, amid the gold and crimson magnificence of the Palace, I could not help marvelling at the strange turn of Fortune's wheel, which had brought MacDonald the starveling clerk, Thomas the engine-driver, Henderson the foundry labourer and Clynes the mill-hand, to this pinnacle beside the man whose forebears had been Kings for so many splendid generations. We were making history. We were, perhaps, somewhat embarrassed, but the little, quiet man whom we addressed as 'Your Majesty' swiftly put us at our ease.[47]

King George V was in every way better equipped to work harmoniously with a Socialist administration than either his grandmother Queen Victoria or his father King Edward would have been. As he told Ramsay MacDonald that January morning he had 'served in the Navy for 14 years—and thus had opportunities of seeing more of the world and mixing with his fellow creatures than would otherwise have been the case'.[48] The King had never been class-conscious. His whole aim was to help his new Ministers, who had had no previous experience of Government. He was anxious, too, that they should not find their contacts with himself and with his Court in any degree embarrassing. It was here that the King was enormously helped by Queen Mary. The Queen already knew several of the Ministers' wives—Mrs Clynes, for example, and Mrs Snowden—through work during the war and, as we have seen, her knowledge of the ideals of the Labour Party had been greatly clarified by her talks with Mary Macarthur at that time.

Owing to the biographies of Mr John Gore and of Sir Harold Nicolson, King George V's exemplary and considerate attitude towards his first Socialist Cabinet is now an established part of British history. Queen Mary's major role in this connection is not so well known since, as usual, she acted in a quiet and self-effacing way.

Queen Mary prided herself upon judging people on their own merits and quite apart from the fact that they might, like Mary Macarthur, hold political opinions with which her specialised upbringing and outlook had not prepared her to agree. Fourteen years before, in August 1910, she had received a tribute to her tolerance from her Aunt Augusta. The Queen had written to Neu Strelitz to say what 'a pleasant man' the then Liberal Lord Chancellor seemed to be. The old Grand Duchess had replied:

I admire you for being able to see what is pleasing or clever in a man, who in other respects—political—is so different from your views; this is lucky in your position. I fear I am not up to it, and I was pitying you reading of the several Ministers in duty at Balmoral, knowing your views.[49]

Aunt Augusta would have been filled with even more admiration— or else perhaps she would merely have been very much shocked— had she lived to read in the Court Circular for August 1924 that Socialist Ministers were in attendance at Balmoral. 'The Prime Minister arrived before luncheon', one of Queen Mary's Ladies wrote in a letter that August,[50] 'so the Queen took him, Lord Stamfordham & me for a drive, as it was a lovely day for once. He is most agreeable & charming, & very easy to get on with; he talks interestingly on so many subjects, even political ones.' Queen Mary, who had been shocked by the 'rowdyism' of the General Election of December 1923, and had been as surprised as everyone else at what she called Baldwin's 'leap in the dark',* now concentrated on making the new Socialist Prime Minister feel at home at Balmoral. Both she and the King genuinely liked Ramsay MacDonald, whose legislative programme during this first short tenure of office was in any case Socialism in its mildest form. With her customary lack of bias, Queen Mary was prepared to suspend judgement on the Socialist experiment. In a letter to the King in May 1930, in answer

---

* Against the advice of many of his colleagues, Mr Baldwin had asked for a dissolution of Parliament in November 1923, since he wished to introduce tariff reform. In the resultant election the Conservatives lost 88 seats. Unemployment figures at this time were 1,300,000.

to one of his rare expressions of that sincere gratitude towards her which he felt more frequently than he admitted, Queen Mary wrote:

I am so glad you realise that I do try & help you in your difficult task which thanks to your character & determination & devotion to duty you have so successfully carried through during these extremely difficult years— The great thing is that people do see this, and understand how difficult your position often is, especially with a Labour Govt in Office—with whom one cannot always see eye to eye.[51]

The last phrase of this letter is altogether characteristic, for Queen Mary was far too intelligent and broad-minded to condemn any body of opinion, large or small, out of hand. She herself attributed the terrible social unrest of the nineteen-twenties to housing conditions: 'I don't think', she wrote to the Prince of Wales,[52] 'there wd be much discontent if only the people were housed properly.'

The first Labour Government fell in October of the year in which it had taken office. Baldwin succeeded MacDonald as Prime Minister. For the King and Queen the year, 1924, drew towards its close in its normal manner: in December the Royal Family repaired to Sandring-ham for what turned out to be Queen Alexandra's last Christmas, but in February 1925 King George's health broke down seriously. Influenza was followed by severe bronchitis and the doctors insisted upon his going for a Mediterranean cruise in March and April. The King and Queen travelled overland with their suite to Genoa, and there boarded the Royal Yacht *Victoria and Albert*. King George had invited his sister Princess Victoria to come too: 'Dear Victoria', Queen Mary noted, 'joined us from Venice, not looking well.'[53] The voyage lasted five weeks and included visits to Naples and Pompeii, and to Syracuse, Palermo and other places of renown in Sicily. It was not a success.

Apparently [wrote a member of the family] the yachting trip is a failure. The King is bored, as one would expect. The Queen angry because nobody else cares to sight-see; & Princess Victoria very restless & no sooner begins one thing than she wants to do another. It is all going exactly as one expected & does not look well for the future, because I hear Hewett* says he must go abroad every year in future. Of course King Edward & Queen Victoria had to do it too.[54]

Queen Mary's last journey to the Continent thus proved a thorough disappointment. She had been looking forward to the cruise, for she had never seen Naples or the towns of Sicily; but on learning that the

---

* Sir Stanley Hewett (1880–1954) was Surgeon-Apothecary to King George V.

King had invited his sister to come with them, she realised that the journey was foredoomed—for Princess Victoria aroused in her brother all those philistine tendencies of 'the Wales cousins' from which Queen Mary had suffered so much in the first years of her marriage. The King and his sister refused to look at the natural beauties and the monuments of the places at which the yacht called, and if they were persuaded to do so by Queen Mary they spoiled her pleasure by a cataract of chaff and jokes. Queen Mary's disappointment expressed itself in unusually forcible and insular terms:

I am *so* glad to be back because I *loathed* the sea tho' I was not ill [she wrote to a friend]. The King is much better for the cruise. We had good weather in Sicily, of course I liked seeing so many new places & some lovely—but give me England! The dirt of Italy & bad roads were indescribable but S. Italy is worse than the North.[55]

VIII

Unwelcome though it may have been to Queen Mary, the King's invitation to his sister Victoria to come on the Italian cruise had been prompted by the kindest of motives: for, her mother's daily companion at Sandringham, Princess Victoria had recently been living through a heart-breaking time.

In December 1924 Queen Alexandra had celebrated her eightieth birthday. Unlike those of Aunt Augusta Strelitz and of Queen Mary when she herself reached that age, the Queen Dowager's faculties were not unimpaired. 'My old head is coming to a breakdown soon', she had written pathetically to King George in October 1923; and in March 1925, while the King and Queen were in Italian waters, she wrote to him, simply, 'I feel *completely* collapsed—I shall soon go'.[56] Already in 1920 Queen Alexandra's eyesight had begun to fail: 'Being so deaf', Queen Mary explained to her eldest son, 'this not being able to see clearly has upset her nerves to a great extent & I fear poor Aunt Toria & Charlotte have a most difficult time . . . it is almost impossible to make her hear still she likes seeing us & knowing we are about her. All this is an extra worry for dear Papa for whom I am truly sorry. Really life is a great worry what with one thing & another.'[57]

With her sensitive dread of illness and of age, Queen Mary found her mother-in-law's decline unbearably poignant: 'it is so hard to see that beautiful woman come to this', she remarked. In the last four years of her life Queen Alexandra came up to London seldom. Month after month she remained immured in the Big House at Sandringham, attended by Princess Victoria, by Miss Charlotte Knollys and by Sir Dighton Probyn, the last two being well over eighty years of age. Queen Mary thus saw her mother-in-law only when she and the King were in residence at York Cottage. 'Went to see dear Mama whom I had not seen for 9 months', she recorded in her Diary for 17 October 1924. 'Found her fairly well. Then to the Cottage which looked very nice.' 'Went to tea with Mama whom I had not seen since Feb.,' she wrote in October of the next year, 1925, 'she looked well in the face but it is difficult to understand what she says. We were back by 6 & I unpacked my things.'58

On 19 November 1925 Queen Alexandra suffered a fatal heart attack; she lingered on for twenty-four hours and died towards evening on Friday November 20th. All day long King George and Queen Mary had been backwards and forwards from their Cottage to the House. 'Saw darling Mama who knew us & I kissed her hand & her forehead', Queen Mary noted on the 19th. On the day after Queen Alexandra's death the King and Queen, with the Prince of Wales and the Duke of York went to a short service in Queen Alexandra's bedroom: 'Motherdear looked so lovely & young with pink draperies & flowers round her.' Five days later the coffin, which had been resting in the little church at Sandringham where Queen Alexandra had worshipped for so many decades, was taken on a gun carriage to Wolferton Station, across the quiet snow.

Some snow showers then fine [Queen Mary recorded]. Lunched at 1 & at 1.45 drove to the Church where a short service was held after which Mama's coffin was carried by 10 Grenadiers of the King's Company to the gun carriage, & G. the boys & Olav, & the gentlemen walked after it down to Wolferton station, we ladies following in carriages & the people of the estate on foot & people lining the roads. All most touching.

On 27 November the funeral service of Queen Alexandra was held in Westminster Abbey: 'Most beautiful & impressive—Crowds in streets. Wonderfully nice feeling shown'; and on the day after that the Queen Dowager's body was buried in the Memorial Chapel at Windsor. 'Now darling Mama lies near dear Eddy', Queen Mary wrote in sad recollection of that other funeral, also after a winter death at Sandringham, then almost forty years ago.59

The disappearance of Queen Alexandra reduced to three the number of close relatives of King George V and Queen Mary in the older generation still living. There were left the King's uncle, the Duke of Connaught, and the King's surviving aunts, Princess Louise, Duchess of Argyll, and Princess Beatrice, both of whom were widows. Of all the children of Queen Victoria and the Prince Consort, these alone remained. It was now King George and Queen Mary who were regarded as the older generation of the Royal Family.

In 1927, two years after the death of Queen Alexandra and the year in which Queen Mary celebrated her sixtieth birthday, her elder brother Prince Dolly died suddenly of peritonitis at the age of fifty-nine; his widow, Lady Cambridge, died two years later. Already the shadows were beginning to lengthen; the menace of illness and death which Queen Mary had feared ever since those childhood vigils beside her old grandmother the Duchess of Cambridge, immobile and alarming in her invalid chair, was now never far away. Queen Mary had reached an age at which introspective persons begin to wonder how many years of life are left to them. This kind of speculation was not, as we know, in keeping with Queen Mary's character. She would have considered such a train of thought a morbid waste of time, and she had moreover a well-founded faith in what her Aunt Augusta used to call 'the Cambridge constitution': 'we are a long-lived family', Queen Mary would say of her own branch of the descendants of George III. Her health was robust and she was hardly ever tired. This was not true of the King.

IX

We may recall that under the will of King Edward VII the 'Big House' at Sandringham had been left to his widow for her lifetime, and that in consequence King George V and Queen Mary had been forced to go on living in the cramped quarters of York Cottage which, despite alterations and enlargements,* seemed hardly more comfortable or capacious than it had been when they spent their honeymoon there in July 1893.

The tenancy of Queen Alexandra at the Big House had lasted longer than King Edward had imagined that it would. The fact that the

---

* These alterations did not greatly increase the limited space available inside York Cottage. 'This house is looking very cosy & nice but it seems smaller than ever!' Queen Mary wrote to her eldest son in November 1910, after three of the bedrooms had had their window-bays enlarged.[60]

Queen Dowager, with her daughter Princess Victoria and a small suite, occupied only a few of the rooms of the house, leaving the rest to decay, had been a long-standing source of secret grievance to the inhabitants of York Cottage. Queen Alexandra's death in November 1925 meant that York Cottage could at long last be vacated and that the King and Queen of England with their family and the Court could take up their residence in a country house of reasonable size. In January 1926 the King and Queen began to take stock of the contents of the Big House: 'Such a bewildering lot of things & pictures', Queen Mary noted.[61] They retrieved those Crown Jewels which Queen Alexandra had retained for her own use, as well as dividing her personal jewellery amongst the members of the family: 'Fine', Queen Mary noted for Saturday, 9 January. 'At 11 to S. where Toria & Maud with G. & me divided dear Mama's jewels—it was interesting but sad.'

On the return of the Court to London, Queen Mary turned her attention to Marlborough House, which had of course also fallen vacant with Queen Alexandra's death. 'My time', she wrote in February 1926,[62] 'is kept fairly occupied looking over the things from Marl. Hse & helping George to place them in suitable positions. You never saw such a mass of things of all kinds as there are, a motley collection of good & bad things—A warning to one not to keep too much for nothing was ever thrown away in those 60 years!' Going through the accumulations at Marlborough House—discovering a Berlin tea service, weeding out the less valuable china, sorting and arranging—formed for Queen Mary an ideal pastime; but the real object of her activities was to persuade the Prince of Wales to move from his own agreeable lodgings in York House, St James's Palace, to the larger and more dismal building which had come to be recognised as the traditional residence of the Prince of Wales, across the way. For a young bachelor, however, Marlborough House held no attractions and to his mother's bewilderment the Prince of Wales flatly refused to conform by going to live there. 'I had a most charming dinner with David last evening,' Queen Mary wrote three years later of an evening at York House, 'everything very well done & he is an excellent host. The rooms are really very nice & in good taste & he is very much pleased with the result & that I approved of them! a pity he did not take all this interest & trouble for Marlborough House—'[63]

Queen Mary had long formed the habit of spending the weeks between the close of the London Season and the move of the whole

Court to Balmoral in paying private visits to her daughter in York-shire and to her elder brother in Shropshire, as well as to friends like Lord and Lady Shaftesbury or Lord and Lady Mount Stephen. In August 1926, however, she went down to Sandringham, where she had scarcely been in the summer since her honeymoon. Here she worked away at getting the Big House ready for herself and the King to occupy that autumn. The Prince of Wales spent a day or two with her:

You cannot think how terribly I miss you here, yr rooms seem so empty & desolate & make me feel quite sad & lonely [the Queen wrote to King George from York Cottage on 13 August].—It was a good thing for me that David came down for 2 nights & he was simply enchanted with Sandringham in the summer & with the lovely flower beds in front of the house & with the garden. I don't think he had ever been here in the summer since he was a child—All the alterations we have made met with great favour & I was so glad to see how he liked everything. . . . Really this place is too lovely just now & I am so glad to see it once in all its beauty.[64]

'I am delighted you & David were both pleased with the dear place, in summer it is lovely,' King George replied, 'we must really try & see if we could not go there for a few days in the summer, but I know it is always difficult to get away from London, especially if we go to Holyrood. Anyhow I am glad he took an interest in it, although he certainly didn't stop long, but rushed off to his tiresome golf. . . . So you are pleased with the alterations & with the decorations of the rooms at the house, yr rooms, in fact all our rooms will I am sure be most comfortable. Hope you are gradually getting the ballroom cleared, as I do not want it to become a store room or lumber room. I am sure the gardens & grounds are a dream.' 'The pictures want sorting out & arranging', he wrote a few days later, 'but you must remember that there will be marks on the walls where the paper has faded.'[65]

Queen Mary's chief aim at Sandringham House was to thin out the cloud of small objects and knick-knacks with which Queen Alexandra had loved to surround herself. 'All the rooms are more airey now and less full of those odds & ends which beloved Mama wld poke into every corner of the house which was such a pity', she wrote during this fortnight of August 1926.[66] 'HM has worked wonders already,' noted Lady Bertha Dawkins;[67] 'one would not recognise some of the rooms which used to be so overcrowded & overloaded with trifles.' 'At last I can report that everything is now as nice as I can make it at S.', Queen Mary wrote at the end of her two weeks' work, '& I hope that all will meet with yr approval—We have all worked very hard to make the rooms nice, & to match up the pictures etc. Of course some of the curtains & carpets are faded as well as wall papers but all this can be put right some day & at our leisure—I showed Annie Jones the rooms today, she was enchanted & paid me the compliment of saying "You have made alterations without altering the character of Sandringham" & I think this is true.'[68]

Constricted and inconvenient though York Cottage had been, it was with real regret that Queen Mary emptied and abandoned the strange little house by the pond. 'I fear this will be my last letter to you from our dear old home where we have been for 33 years—I am sad at leaving it with it's many memories & old associations', she wrote to the King.[69]

On 14 October 1926, King George and Queen Mary took up residence in Sandringham House, the home which the King loved beyond all others and in which, like his brother Prince Eddy and his mother Queen Alexandra, he was destined—and in the not so remote future—to die.

x

It was in late November 1928, after a week's shooting at Sandringham with a house-party, that King George V fell dangerously ill. He and the Queen had left Sandringham House on the 19th, and had returned to Buckingham Palace, the façade of which was wreathed in the blackish fog of an especially raw winter. 'George had a chill & had to go to bed—too tiresome', Queen Mary noted in her Diary for 21 November, whilst the King himself recorded on the same day: 'I was taken ill this evening. Feverish cold they call it & I retired to bed.'

On the next day, since the King's 'feverish cold' was no better, Queen Mary deputised for him at the opening of the new Spitalfields Market—which she described as 'a fine hall filled with fruit & vegetables from all parts of the Empire'—and, later the same afternoon, at that of the restored Old Hall of Lincoln's Inn Fields. That night she found that the King was 'very feverish & in some pain at 10.30 o'clock'. The following morning it was clear to the King's doctors that he was in fact suffering from an acute form of septicaemia, although they were then unable to locate the source of the poison. By the second of December Queen Mary was writing 'G. was very ill in the evening as the heart began to give out. Terribly anxious.' On 4 December six Counsellors, headed by Queen Mary and including the Prince of Wales who was still away in East Africa, were appointed to act for the King during his illness. Violent fluctuations in the King's temperature continued. 'The strain', Queen Mary noted,[70] 'is very wearing.' A warning telegram had been quickly dispatched to the Prince of Wales, who reached home on 11 December after what was then the extraordinary feat of travelling almost seven thousand miles in nine days. 'He looked well', Queen Mary recorded, 'but was of course very tired—I took him to G's room, he recognised him & spoke to him quite clearly— G. seemed more himself.' On 12 December the doctors at last located the seat of the infection and performed an operation to drain an abscess in the King's lung. 'Drs. satisfied', wrote Queen Mary, 'but it is anxious work.'

So soon as the London public understood the grave nature of the King's illness, silent crowds began drifting by day and by night past the Palace, studying through the November murk the bulletins that were posted on the gates. Even fashionable circles in London, where ordinarily the King and Queen were little mentioned, became affected by this national anxiety. Death, and consequently any illness apparently serious enough to result in it, has ever proved a phenomenon of popular appeal. We may remember that in a famous definition of the royal functions, Bagehot has declared that 'Royalty is a government in which the attention of the nation is concentrated on one person doing interesting actions';[71] and reflect that to the great majority of people the action of dying remains one of the most dramatic, certainly the most inexplicable and mysterious, action that any man can do. 'A Princely marriage is the brilliant edition of a universal fact', Bagehot wrote also; and may we not equally apply his words to a Princely death? In January 1892 the British nation had mourned for the untimely end of the Duke of Clarence, a youthful figure of few gifts and of considerable obscurity whom, as the newspaper obituaries openly admitted, most of the English public had never even seen. We have noticed earlier in this volume how suddenly King Edward VII's popularity was increased by the fact that he had undergone a dangerous operation for appendicitis just before the date fixed for his Coronation in the summer of 1902. George V had reigned twice as long as his father. He was universally respected and beloved. His face and his voice were, owing to modern inventions, more familiar to his subjects than those of any British Sovereign hitherto had been. His sudden illness of November 1928 came as a stabbing reminder to the public that this popular monarch, too, was mortal.

For some days the rumour ran through the fog-bound streets of London that the King was dead.

CHAPTER SIX

THE END OF A REIGN

T HE KING was not dead; but he had come perilously close to dying. His early convalescence was slow and filled with setbacks. Queen Mary recorded these relapses, when hope once more gave way to anxiety, and the King seemed again to be tarrying upon the brink of the grave. On Christmas Eve, 1928, King George appeared decisively better:

Dull day [the Queen noted]. Good night. G. clearer & we had a little talk but he must not talk much as it tires him. Unpacked Xmas parcels— Lots of lovely flowers arrived—At 5 all our children came to tea & sweet Lilibet, after which we went to the Throne Rm where I had arranged presents & a small Xmas tree. . . . We missed dear George dreadfully but feel so thankful he is improving at last. Small family dinner.[1]

On Christmas morning the King and Queen exchanged their own Christmas presents, Queen Mary receiving from her husband 'a beautiful pink topaz & diamond pendant'. On the last night of the old year, the King was worse again, and Queen Mary confided to her Diary: 'the last weeks have brought us much suffering—God grant the New Year may bring us peace & happiness & the restoration to health of our dear one'. On 6 January the King was well enough to have a sustained conversation with Queen Mary: 'After tea G. sent for me, he was perfectly clear & we had a talk for 20 minutes which cheered me much after not having spoken to me for practically 6 weeks. George signed his name just to show me he could do so—The Drs were much pleased at this advance but we must not let him do too much.'[2] On the following day the King was able to see his Private Secretary, Lord Stamfordham, for the first time in six weeks. The King's deafness had now become more marked.

Towards the end of January it was decided to move the invalid to the South coast of England, on the theory that the brisk sea air of the English Channel in mid-winter might do him good. A house at Bognor named Craigweil—described by Queen Mary when she inspected it as 'nice & convenient & close to the sea'—was taken on lease, and on the ninth of February 1929 the King was transported thither by motor-ambulance, the Queen travelling separately in her own motor-car so as to be ready at Bognor to receive him. The Queen was pleased to hear that he 'had the blinds up on the drive & waved to the people *en route* to their delight'.3 The King was still looking haggard and worn: 'I caught sight of His Majesty twice when he was being moved yesterday', wrote a member of the Household, '& was shocked with his appearance, such a long thin face, all eyes, but he does not seem to have got any whiter in his beard.'4

The weather at Bognor proved a disappointment. 'An awful day,' Queen Mary noted forty-eight hours after their arrival, 'arctic with N.E. wind & a very rough sea.'5 The biting cold persisted, but there were interludes of sunshine during which the King could lie or sit in the sun-room at Craigweil House, where he smoked his first cigarette since his illness. In March the King's favourite grandchild, Princess Elizabeth, then almost three years old, came to stay at Craigweil House with her nurse. 'G. delighted to see her', Queen Mary noted, and we read in her Diary for the next day: 'I played with Lilibet in the garden making sand pies! The Archbishop of Canterbury came to see us & was so kind & sympathetic.'6 As soon as the King seemed to be improving, Queen Mary made occasional short expeditions to look at neighbouring country-houses or to rummage in local antique shops. She became at this time deeply interested in a collection of tropical fish and blue budgerigars kept by a lady resident of Bognor.

On Easter Monday 1929 the King made what was virtually his first appearance in public. It was, Queen Mary recorded, a 'blustery & chilly' day: 'We sat out in a sheltered spot & listened to the Kneller Hall band which played for $1\frac{3}{4}$ hours, very enjoyable—A number of people came right up to our "sea-walk"—We went & waved to them afterwards & there was great cheering—George looked especially well.'7

Throughout the long period of desperate anxiety about the King's health, Queen Mary had astonished her family by the self-control and reserve which she had shown. It was at this time that the Duke of York made to the Prince of Wales the remark about their mother which we have already quoted: 'Through all the anxiety she has never once revealed her feelings to any of us. She is really far too reserved; she keeps too much locked up inside herself.' The whole family had, of course, rallied round Queen Mary. Her sons and her daughter-in-law paid visits to Bognor, the Prince of Wales flying there in his private aeroplane. The oldest generation of the Royal Family also did their best to help; when Queen Mary went up to London in May to hold the first of four Courts in the place of the King, she wrote to him: 'To my surprise I hear that dear At Louise* at 81 is actually coming to the Court tomorrow, too nice of her & I feel much touched.'8 Queen Mary deputised for the King at many functions that spring, but it was holding the Courts all alone that she minded the most: 'I dread the 2 Courts without you as you can imagine but for the sake of the "trade" I feel it is right to hold them—'9

The King and Queen remained at Craigweil House until the middle of May, when they left it by road for Windsor Castle. 'We left . . . by car via Bognor where we had a great reception. . . . to Windsor which we reached before 1 o'clock', Queen Mary recorded. 'The Mayor met us near Queen Victoria's statue, & the Eton boys cheered us inside the Castle gates—A very touching drive. George was not too tired— . . . Glad to be at dear Windsor again—& with George so much better.'10 The King was not, however, as well as he seemed nor as Queen Mary and the royal doctors hoped; on the 27th of May he was feeling very ill and on 31 May a new and unsuspected abscess broke through the scar left by his operation. This abscess did not drain properly, and when the King attended the National Thanksgiving Service for his total recovery, held on 7 July 1929, it was, as he pointed out to his doctors, with 'an open wound' in his back: 'Fancy', he said cheerfully, 'a Thanksgiving Service with an open wound in your back.' Two days later Lord Dawson of Penn declared that a second operation had become necessary. This was successfully performed on 15 July. Towards the end of August, the King and Queen retired to Sandringham, since the journey up to Balmoral was clearly impossible in the King's uncertain state of health. 'We left London', Queen Mary noted on 24 August, 'at last for Sandringham. . . . delighted to be at home again. Everything looked delightful.' 'Masses of people lined the streets all the way to King's Cross', wrote one of Queen Mary's Ladies who travelled with the King and Queen, '& it was very touching.—Then, again, at the station, Wolferton & all the way here, there were again crowds. The King got through the journey very well, . . . & walked about at once, so glad to be home again. It came on to rain after tea.'11

* i.e. Queen Victoria's fourth daughter, Princess Louise, Duchess of Argyll (1848–1939).

The winter of 1929, and virtually the whole of the year 1930, were for Queen Mary overshadowed by her perpetual concern for the King's health, which showed no very solid improvement. In May 1930, the Queen again presided at two Courts, this time assisted by the Prince of Wales. In June she and the King went as usual to Windsor for Ascot races, then on to Cowes, and in August north to Balmoral— which, since it had been empty for two years, was cold and damp. The King continued in intermittent pain from attacks of neuritis. He also tired more easily than before.

In May 1930 there fell the twentieth anniversary of King George V's accession to the throne. 'I can hardly realise that it is 20 years today that dear Papa died, how time flies', he wrote to Queen Mary on 6 May, 'but what years they have been & what troublous & anxious ones. I do feel grateful to God that he has enabled me to pass through them & I can never sufficiently express my deep gratitude to you, darling May, for the way you have helped & stood by me in these difficult times. This is not sentimental rubbish, but is what I really feel.'[12]

II

The years 1930 and 1931 were, politically, as 'troublous and anxious' as any that King George V had experienced during his long reign. The Labour Party, which had won the General Election of May 1929, was faced with growing tensions at home and abroad. Throughout Europe unemployment figures were rising; in this country, in the years 1929 to 1931, they were more than doubled. The 'World Depression', which had begun in 1929, did not fully affect Great Britain until two years later, when the August crisis of 1931 brought the King hastening down from Balmoral to London, where he persuaded the three political parties to form a National Administration to save the country from bankruptcy. Although, as the newspapers agreed, the King had 'done wonders' in London, and although members of his entourage felt that he returned to Scotland 'all the better for having been able to play the Sovereign for once, & give a lead to his rattled Ministers', the crisis of August 1931 severely taxed King George V's health. He had been bronchial in April 1931, and Queen Mary recorded that his doctors had advised him to 'take it very easy for a bit'; he had also in that year endured three great personal sorrows which had lowered his resistance.

In January 1931 King George's eldest sister Louise, the Princess Royal, had died; a fortnight later his oldest friend Sir Charles Cust, with whom he had been in the Navy as a boy, died too. In March came one of the heaviest blows of all—the death of Lord Stamfordham, who had been the King's Private Secretary, his adviser and his confidant for more than thirty years. 'I shall miss him terribly. His loss is irreparable', King George entered in his Diary. 'He was', he wrote to a member of the Royal Family, 'the most loyal friend I ever had.'[13] 'He taught me how to be a King', he said. Queen Mary also was distressed at Lord Stamfordham's death: 'Dear Ld Stamfordham passed away at 4.30', she wrote on Tuesday, 31 March 1931. 'A great loss to us after 30 years as well as a great grief.'

Ever since King George's accession to the throne, Queen Mary had pursued a diligent policy of non-interference in all matters which were not overtly her concern. Accordingly, Lord Stamfordham's successors were surprised to find how little Queen Mary's personality seemed to impinge upon their department. They concluded that the Queen was neither interested in nor acquainted with affairs of State. As a matter of fact the King frequently discussed such matters with her, since he respected her intelligence and her judgement and he knew that he could rely on her discretion absolutely. In her diffident way, Queen Mary never wished to intrude, and so long as Lord Stamfordham was alive she would ask him to put up to the King, as though on his own initiative, suggestions or solutions which she had thought out herself. Little notes from the Queen would appear upon the Private Secretary's desk. Like the King she was genuinely attached to 'dear Bigge', and she would end her letters to him with the words 'believe me your most sincere friend Mary R.' One note preserved among Lord Stamfordham's papers is typical of Queen Mary's consideration for those who worked for her: 'May I suggest that if you want to come up to see me', she wrote to Lord Stamfordham, who had been ill, 'you should *not* use the King's staircase which is *very* steep but walk straight along the lower passage & come up in my lift outside my room.' 'Many grateful thanks for the delicious smelling daphne you have so kindly sent me', she wrote on another occasion. '—I am much touched.'[14] The death of Lord Stamfordham, who was over eighty and had been ill for some months, was in the course of Nature; but to King George V the loss of this wise, devoted friend and counsellor gave to the ominous year of 1931 an added note of doom.

The crisis which brought the King back to London in August 1931 developed on the very day, 21 August, on which he and the Queen had arrived at Balmoral for their customary holiday. King George had suspected that a crisis would blow up suddenly, and he had proposed to the Prime Minister that it might be best to postpone the journey to Scotland and to remain at Sandringham. Mr MacDonald had replied that for the King to appear to cancel his visit to Balmoral at the last minute would give rise to 'alarming rumours and cause consternation'. No sooner had the King reached Balmoral, however, than he found that he had to return to London again: 'Too vexing & disappointing', Queen Mary entered in her Diary, while in a letter to the King[15] she expressed herself even more strongly: 'I feel desperately sorry for you in this further anxiety & worry—It was too bad your having come all the way up here, only to have to return South at once, of course we ought never to have left Sandringham with the Government in such a plight, but the Govt. always thinks of itself first & it's own position.' To her Lady-in-Waiting the Queen remarked that she was 'furious' that they had been allowed to go to Scotland at such a moment and that if the King stayed long in London she proposed joining him. 'I will not', she declared, 'be left sitting on a mountain!' Queen Mary dearly liked to know what was going on; she likewise thought that she might be of use to the King in this fresh crisis:

I felt dreadfully sad at seeing you go yesterday evening without me [she wrote to him on 23 August] as we have always been together so far in all the many crises you have had to go through since 1910—and except for the War I think this must be quite the worst one for our poor unfortunate country—God grant that some satisfactory solution may be found & agreed to, but things do look very black at present.

The King kept her fully informed by telephone: 'It was wonderful how easily I could hear your voice on the telephone last evening', Queen Mary wrote to him after one of these talks, 'just as if you were in the room—What an anxious time it is & I am miserable at not being with you—'[16] After the formation of the National Government, the King returned North, reaching Balmoral on 27 August. 'He told us', noted Queen Mary, 'all about the talks he had in London etc.'[17]

The autumn of 1931, a year which Queen Mary characterised as 'a tiresome year full of anxieties', was, for the King and Queen, uneventful. In October the National Government was returned at the polls—'Gains over 500,' Queen Mary noted, 'rather too large for

internal peace';[18] and on 5 November she and the King gave an afternoon party for the delegates to the Round Table Conference on
India: 'Mr Gandhi caused great excitement in his odd get up, loin
cloth & slippers!'[19] Mr Gandhi had indeed little enough in common
with the jewelled and glittering pageant which the name India evoked
in the mind's eye of the Queen.

III

Both of King George V's biographers have demonstrated how discouraged and perplexed he became during his last four years on the
throne. The King had disliked the social and political developments
of England in the post-war decade, during which he had been engaged
in what his eldest son has described as a 'private war with the twentieth
century'; he disliked what he saw of the decade of the nineteen-thirties
even more. King George did not take to the general speeding-up of
the tempo of daily life in that era; and, while most anxious for the
happiness of all his subjects, he failed to appreciate the new emphasis
on social welfare which had replaced the Imperial and continental
preoccupations of his father's and his grandmother's reigns. It was
the period in which whole regions of industrial England began to be
labelled, in the genteel phraseology dear to Government Departments,
'Distressed Areas'. At home there was a general atmosphere of uncertainty and disturbance, while abroad Nazi Germany was beginning
to seem a threat. The King felt ill and tired and gloomy, and there
were indeed valid reasons for his gloom. Queen Mary, who was in her
customary state of good health, and had in any case no constitutional
responsibilities, could adapt herself more easily to a changing epoch,
yet she, too, felt that the old social values in which she believed were
steadily losing currency. She had, as we know, always hated disorder,
and some of the reactions of the British working people to the living
and wage conditions produced by the depression of 1931 seemed to
her distinctly disorderly. 'We did not go out on account of the
"Hunger Marchers"—Procession to the Hse of Commons', she
recorded, for instance, on 21 October 1932. 'Apparently it was a
failure.' But, concerned though she might be, Queen Mary did not
show it. She pursued her way steadily onwards, performing her public
duties in her own serene, distinguished way, and, as necessary,
deputising for the King when the neuritis in his arm became too bad.
In September 1934 she drove to Glasgow from Balmoral to launch

the famous Cunard liner which bears her name: 'A most impressive sight', she noted in her Diary. 'Unfortunately it rained all the time.'[20]

Two months later, on 29 November 1934, Queen Mary's youngest son, Prince George, Duke of Kent, was married in Westminster Abbey to Princess Marina, a granddaughter of Queen Alexandra's brother King George I of Greece and of that Queen Olga who had, in 1893, been partially instrumental in arranging the marriage of King George V and Queen Mary. The Duke of Kent was a particular favourite of Queen Mary's, for he had inherited her passion for collecting, and he was genuinely interested in works of art. His engagement to a member of 'the Greek family' had seemed to his mother highly suitable: 'I am sure we shall like Marina & that she will be a charming addition to the family', the Queen had written to King George in August 1934.[21]

In the year following that of the Kent wedding, the year 1935, there came the Silver Jubilee, for King George V and Queen Mary had now been a quarter of a century upon the throne. In their youth the King and Queen had each taken part in the two great Jubilees of Queen Victoria's reign—the Golden Jubilee of 1887 and the Diamond Jubilee of 1897, and they both knew by experience what exertions a Royal Jubilee year was liable to demand. 'We have all been so overworked this year we are nearly dead', Princess May of Teck had written in July 1887 to a friend[22]—and we may remember that Princess May's role in the Golden Jubilee festivities was, inevitably, a very minor one. In 1897, as Duchess of York, she had been much more prominent in the Diamond Jubilee celebrations, a frantic period during which Aunt Augusta Strelitz had written from London: 'Here all are more or less off their heads, only May keeps her head on her shoulders.'[23] Now, faced in 1935 with the Jubilee of her husband's elevation to the throne, Queen Mary continued to 'keep her head on her shoulders'. Since the King had not been well in the first six weeks of what would certainly prove physically a very taxing year, Queen Mary took him down in February 1935 to stay for a month at Eastbourne, where they were lent the Duke of Devonshire's house, Compton Place.

Like Luton Hoo, Compton Place was a house which had already played a part in Queen Mary's earlier life, for it was there that King Edward and Queen Alexandra, then Prince and Princess of Wales, had retired with their remaining children after the Duke of Clarence's death in January 1892; and it was at Compton Place that Princess May herself spent with them those days of February 1892 which should have been the first ones of her marriage to Prince Eddy. On Wednesday, 27 February 1935, Queen Mary, who had reached Eastbourne with the King the day before, wrote in her Diary:

An awful night of wind & rain—Read & wrote—It cleared at 3 & we drove along the esplanade & then to Beachy Head, a nice drive—Walked in the grounds here & actually picked primroses—By a curious coincidence I again spent the 27th Feb. here where I spent it with my Parents in law in 1892 after Eddy's death—It was the day chosen for our wedding & they asked me to come here to be with them. They gave me the row of diamonds they had chosen for me as a wedding gift & they also gave me the travelling bag Eddy had ordered for me—I write these details as I think them so interesting—

From Eastbourne, the King and Queen went—by way of London where they spent a week during which Queen Mary saw her dressmakers—to Windsor. Here, in early April, they found 'the wall flowers all out on the Terrace'. The King's health did not improve with this warmer weather, and he now took to dining alone in his room. Queen Mary busied herself 'choosing wall papers & cretonnes for some of the bedrooms', visiting Hampton Court, arranging the family museum she was making at Frogmore House and looking at the new bog garden near the Obelisk in Windsor Park. On 24 April she went over with Prince Henry, who had returned from a visit to Australia that March, to see the Prince of Wales's garden at Fort Belvedere.

Fort Belvedere, or as its new tenant called it more simply 'The Fort', is a small eighteenth-century house, re-designed by Wyattville and situated near Virginia Water. The fanciful architecture of the Fort had appealed to the Prince of Wales when he had first discovered it in 1930. He had asked his father's permission to live in it, and had made it his home. 'Very cold again but fine', Queen Mary noted of this afternoon call at Fort Belvedere. ' . . . At 3 Harry & I went over to Belvedere to see David's garden, we then walked with him thro' the Cedar Walk which he has improved by cutting away laurels etc to the Ruins—David came back with us to tea & we stopped to look at the Bog Garden.'[24]

Despite the proximity of Fort Belvedere to Windsor Castle, where the Court was in residence for almost all of April 1935, Queen Mary did not, in those weeks, see very much of her eldest son. She had never possessed the knack of winning the confidence of her sons in

s*

their boyhood; it was too late to rectify this now they were grown up. Like the King, Queen Mary was fully informed of, and desperately worried by, an overpowering emotional predicament into which Fate had forced the heir-apparent to the throne. Her knowledge was based on hearsay only, for, intensely reserved and lacking the common language of intimacy, she was not likely herself to broach so awkward and private a topic with her own son, nor was she capable of creating an atmosphere of understanding which might have encouraged him to talk freely to her about it. This, we may think, was one case in which silence was not golden. The unmentioned, which was at the same time the all-important, was left floating like a submerged mine beneath the surface of the life of the Royal Family during the last months of the reign of King George V.

IV

On 28 April 1935 King George and Queen Mary came back from Windsor to London to prepare themselves for the Jubilee Procession and Thanksgiving Service scheduled to take place on 6 May, and for the many other functions implicit in the celebration of the Silver Jubilee. Queen Mary's Diary now takes on an almost hectic note: 'Saw a dressmaker—Masses of letters & parcels to deal with—London looking very festive with the decorations', she noted, for example, on the evening of 28 April; or, on 2 May: 'Lovely warm day at last— Busy morning—Missy of Roumania came to luncheon—At 3 with Joan V. to Ly Melchett's house in Lowndes Square to see the Exn of Work done by Ex-Service men, such very nice things—I spoke to the men in the garden afterwards. They gave me a lovely *couvre- pieds* emb. by them on white satin with my M. & crown—Drove thro' the Brompton Rd & along Piccadilly, the Mall & Birdcage Walk to see the decorations—Very pretty.'

Monday, 6 May, as Queen Mary noted in her Diary, was a 'lovely warm day'. The London crowds were out early that spring morning, merrily elbowing and jostling their way into good positions along the line of the processional route, down which the freshly sprinkled sand lay gritty and yellow in the sunshine, with the scarlet tunics of the guardsmen on duty adding a further note of gaiety to the scene. It was a happy and affectionate crowd, composed largely of family units, turned out all together, to cheer and to thank the King and Queen.

'Our Silver Jubilee', Queen Mary recorded. 'Crowds in the parks

& streets quite early—At 10 we went downstairs & saw all the members of our family who were to take part in the various carriage processions. We left at 5 to 11 in the big open carriage with 6 grey horses—We had a marvellous reception from the crowds of people all the way to St Pauls Cathedral & back—The thanksgiving service at 11.30 was beautiful—Back before 1 & we all went on to the Balcony where the crowds cheered us—After luncheon we had to go on to the Balcony again—Sat out in the afternoon & read letters & ansd. telegrams—Toria came to tea. At 8 Xenia* Harry & I listened to G's wonderful message to his People which was broadcasted—most moving. After dinner we had to go out on the balcony again—A wonderful day.'[25] 'The greatest number of people in the streets I have ever seen in my life. The enthusiasm was indeed most touching', the King noted.[26] 'I'd no idea they felt like that about me. I am beginning to think they must really like me for myself', he remarked, in modest amazement, after a state drive through East London later in the month.

The next weeks were ones of ceaseless activity for the King and Queen. There was the presentation of addresses by the Diplomatic Corps, by the Dominions Prime Ministers, by the House of Lords and the House of Commons; there were vociferous receptions by tens of thousands of L.C.C. schoolchildren and ex-service men; there were state drives in open carriages with a Sovereign's Escort of the Household Cavalry to more distant areas of London, and there were simpler private visits by motor-car to see the back street decorations: 'the decorations in the smaller streets . . . were very touching, many people recognised us & cheered', Queen Mary wrote of one such drive on 10 May through Battersea and Kennington. Wherever they went there were throngs of grateful roaring people. Night after night the King and Queen were summoned by their cheers to step out on to the central balcony of the Palace.

On 26 May 1935 Queen Mary celebrated her sixty-eighth birthday; the Grenadier Guards Band played at the family luncheon and in the afternoon she and the King 'took a drive round North London taking Mary & Lilibet with us—Such nice decorations still left'. 'Spent', Queen Mary summed up, 'a happy day.' On 3 June it was the King's birthday. He was seventy. Four days later the King and Queen left London for Sandringham: 'Lovely evening', Queen Mary wrote of

* King George V's first cousin, the Grand Duchess Xenia, sister to the murdered Tsar Nicholas II, was staying at the Palace.

their arrival, '& rhodos looking beautiful on way from station.'[27] Once at Sandringham, the King, who had borne all the fatigues of the last month manfully, collapsed with a cold. His doctors declared that he should stay at Sandringham for the present, which meant that Queen Mary must preside alone at the second Court Ball, on 13 June, and also entertain at Windsor Castle for Ascot races without the aid of the King. At the beginning of August the King was well enough to go to Cowes, and towards the end of the month the Court was, as usual, settled at Balmoral, there to remain until late September. On 20 September there was a Ghillies' Ball at Balmoral: 'great fun', Queen Mary noted. '—I danced 12 dances running from 9.30 till 11.30—It was a great success.'

During this August of 1935, Prince Henry, Duke of Gloucester, third son of the King and Queen, had become engaged to Lady Alice Montagu-Douglas-Scott, a daughter of King George V's old friend the seventh Duke of Buccleuch. It was arranged that the Duke of Gloucester's wedding should, like that of his brother the Duke of Kent in the previous year, take place in November.

v

Since the Duke of Buccleuch died suddenly that October, the Duke of Gloucester's wedding to Lady Alice Scott was celebrated very quietly in the Chapel of Buckingham Palace instead of in Westminster Abbey. 'A lovely day for the wedding of Harry & Alice in the Chapel here', Queen Mary recorded on 6 November. 'We went down to the Bow Room at 11. Met various members of our family, & saw the bridesmaids who looked charming—Lilibet & Margaret looked too sweet. Alice arrived before 11.30 looking lovely in her wedding dress. We had a beautiful service & the Archbishop of Canterbury gave such a nice address. . . . We had luncheon in the supper room, about 120 guests, all our family & many of the Scott family—They left after 3. . . . May God bless the dear Couple.' On the 11th of November, after the annual Armistice Service at the Cenotaph which King George was not able to attend, the Court moved to Sandringham for a week. On the return of the King and Queen to London they motored down to call on the King's sister Princess Victoria, in her house, Coppins, at Iver in Buckinghamshire: 'we had not seen her for ages', wrote Queen Mary, 'as she has been so unwell but is getting better.'[28] Princess Victoria was not getting better; on the 2nd of

December the King and Queen had 'very bad news of poor darling Toria . . . we kept on getting serious news all day long'. Towards evening of that day they were informed that Princess Victoria 'could not last thro' the night—Too too sad';[29] and on Tuesday, 3 December, they learned that Princess Victoria had died.

King George V's family and entourage believed that the loss of his favourite sister sounded his own death knell. They had already noticed that the King's health had worsened since his return that autumn from Balmoral. He had not been well enough to lay his wreath on the Cenotaph on 11 November, and he had not been able to go out shooting at Sandringham. Such was the mortal shock of Princess Victoria's death that for the first and the last time in his life King George V felt that he could not carry through a public duty; he cancelled the State Opening of Parliament, which was billed to take place on the afternoon of the day on which his sister died. The King did not appear in public again.

Four days before Christmas the King and Queen proceeded as usual to Sandringham by train. 'Awfully cold here', Queen Mary noted on their arrival. Christmas Eve and Christmas Day were observed with the traditional Sandringham ceremonies: on Christmas Eve the family presents were distributed round the great tree in the ballroom of Sandringham House, while on Christmas Day the staff were given their presents, and everyone listened to the King's Christmas message which he broadcast from a small room on the ground floor formerly occupied by Sir Francis Knollys. On 31 December the film of *Monte Cristo*, which Queen Mary judged 'excellent', was shown in the house. 'The last day of the old year', she added, 'which has been a most wonderful one.'[30]

'Once the house is completed, Death enters in', runs a Turkish proverb quoted by Théophile Gautier. The Silver Jubilee celebrations of 1935—so triumphant in their warmth and spontaneity—can be regarded as the apotheosis of the life and reign of King George the Fifth. After such positive, public and unchallengeable proof of his success in that role of King-Emperor for which he was neither born nor trained, there was nothing left for the King to do but die.

King George entered upon the New Year of 1936 feeling weak and wretched. In the first few days of January he still went out on his white pony, Jock. With Queen Mary walking beside him he looked his last upon the gardens and the grounds of Sandringham, the place which he preferred above all others in the world. Light snow drifted

over the bare garden beds and powdered the dark evergreens; the
pond, scene of so many jovial skating parties in the long ago, was
thinly coated with ice. On some mornings the east wind brought
bitter rain. In this garden in another January, forty-four years ago, he
had paced the paths in bleak misery, Princess May of Teck at his side,
while his brother Prince Eddy lay in an upstairs bedroom, delirious
and dying.

On 14 January, the anniversary as it happened of Prince Eddy's
death, the King went out of doors for the last time. In the house he
had been helping Queen Mary to arrange the fine collection of Fabergé
objects which had belonged to his mother Queen Alexandra, and which
he had now inherited upon his sister's death; carefully they replaced
them in the vitrines in which they had originally been displayed in
Sandringham House. On 15 January he had dinner in his bedroom,
which he never left alive again: 'Poor George,' Queen Mary noted,
'who had not been feeling well for some days, felt worse & had to go
to bed before dinner.' The next day she wrote that he 'had a cold &
stayed in his room all day, not in bed all the time—Most worrying'.
On 17 January she realised that the King was 'very ill' and sent for
his chief physician Lord Dawson of Penn at the same time summoning
the Prince of Wales, who was shooting at Windsor. The note which
she sent her eldest son was carefully worded, so as not to cause him
alarm; Queen Mary was also naturally anxious that his sudden arrival
should not arouse the suspicions of the King about his own danger:
'I think you ought to know that Papa is not very well', she wrote to
the Prince of Wales, adding that Lord Dawson was 'not too pleased
with Papa's state at the present moment'.[31] The Prince of Wales
arrived at Sandringham by aeroplane.

King George spent his last days sitting in front of a crackling fire
in his bedroom, clad in an old Tibetan dressing-gown that was a relic
of one of the visits to India, and gazing through the bay-window at
the square tower of Sandringham church jutting up above the leafless
winter trees. The guests who had been at Sandringham for Christmas
now left; the missing members of King George's family began to
arrive. On Sunday, 19 January, the Prince of Wales drove up to
London to inform Mr Baldwin, then Prime Minister, that the King
was dying. 'G. about the same,' Queen Mary recorded of this Sunday,
'sat with him from time to time—Did not go to church as the place
was surrounded by reporters & photographers, too heartless—Walked
with Mary morning & afternoon—Wigram came with us—Georgie

[the Duke of Kent] arrived at 7—also Archbishop of Canterbury—David & Bertie left but will return tomorrow.'[32]

The reporters and photographers encamped outside the confines of the Sandringham estate formed the essential link between this long gaunt red-brick house within which an elderly bearded man was dying, and the outer world of the many millions of the King's subjects to whom he was both a symbol and a friend. Meanwhile, Counsellors of State were appointed to transact the King's business at Sandringham, for the 'red boxes' were piling up demandingly and would not wait even for death. The death-beds of Kings are as inevitably organised as their lives must be; regular bulletins were issued at intervals, the most famous of which was the penultimate message: 'The King's life is moving peacefully towards its close.' On Monday, 20 January—a mild day after rain in the night—King George V died in the presence of Queen Mary and his children. '*Am brokenhearted*', Queen Mary wrote at the beginning of her account of the King's death. ' . . . at 5 to 12 my darling husband passed peacefully away—my children were angelic.' 'Words commemorating King George V death', she wrote on another page of her Diary. ' "The sunset of his death tinged the whole world's sky"—'[33]

No sooner was King George V dead, than Queen Mary, in a gesture of historic import, took the hand of her eldest son in hers and, stooping, kissed it. The King who had been Queen Mary's husband was dead. The King who was her son lived on—His Most Excellent Majesty Edward the Eighth, by the Grace of God, of Great Britain, Ireland, and the British Dominions beyond the Seas, King, Defender of the Faith, Emperor of India.

VI

On the morning after his father's death, the King flew in his aeroplane to London with his brother the Duke of York to hold his Accession Council. 'David & Bertie', noted Queen Mary, 'went to London for the Proclamation. David very brave & helpful for he has a difficult task before him—Answered endless telegrams—The doctors & the Archbishop left.' At five o'clock that afternoon the lid of the late King's coffin was screwed down. The coffin was then carried out of the main door of the house, and was placed upon a small bier which, flanked by towering Grenadiers from the King's Company, and followed by Queen Mary, her family and a few members of the

Household—some twelve persons in all—was taken through the garden (which was dark and windy, with flurries of rain) to the little church of Sandringham. The King's Piper played a lament as the bier was wheeled along the paths. The only light came from a small electric torch in someone's hand. 'As we came round the corner of the shrubbery that screens the Church', one of the mourners wrote next day, 'we saw the lych-gate brilliantly lit, with Fuller, the San-dringham Rector, standing beneath it in his surplice and hood. There was nobody else in sight. The Guardsmen, with scarcely a sound, slung the coffin on their shoulders and laid it before the Altar; and there, after a very brief service, we left it to be watched for thirty-six hours by the men of the Sandringham estate.'34 'We had a very comforting short service', wrote Queen Mary, '—the church full of our own kind people—Such a sad sad day—It is curious my having been present in this house at the death beds of 2 brothers Eddy & George.'

With her memories of the long interval allowed to elapse between the death of her father-in-law King Edward VII and the committal of his corpse to the Royal Vault at Windsor, Queen Mary had par-ticularly asked that her husband's body should not remain unburied for more than a week. In accordance with her wish, the coffin rested in Sandringham Church for thirty-six hours only: 'Went to the Church after luncheon', Queen Mary recorded on 22 January. 'It all looked very peaceful—but so sad—My sons returned also Harry & Alice & Elizabeth. Did business with David who was most helpful and kind.'

On Thursday, 23 January, the body of King George V was taken on a gun-carriage to Wolferton Station. It was a clear morning of frost and sun as the simple little procession wound its way through the sandy pinewoods of Norfolk to Wolferton, the late King's old piper Forsyth playing *The Flowers of the Forest*. The King, his brothers and his brother-in-law walked behind the bier, while Queen Mary and the other ladies of the family rode in carriages. King George V's white pony, Jock, led by a groom, and many hundreds of neighbours, tenants and gamekeepers completed the procession. At Wolferton the coffin was placed aboard a special funeral train, London-bound. At King's Cross Station another gun-carriage was waiting, as well as the Imperial Crown which was then fixed on the top of the draped coffin.

With the King and the rest of her family, Queen Mary travelled to London on the funeral train; on arrival at King's Cross she went by car to Buckingham Palace and thence to Westminster Hall 'to meet the coffin—We all walked behind it into the Hall', she recorded, '& then we had a short service—It looked so beautiful & peaceful— Returned home by 4. Read letters & papers.' The coffin was placed upon a great catafalque in the centre of Westminster Hall, where officers of the Household Troops kept vigil over it day and night while nearly one million mourning Londoners filed slowly past. Late one evening the King and his three brothers, incognito, took part in the vigil by the catafalque: 'At midnight', wrote Queen Mary on 27 January, 'my 4 sons stood guard over their father's coffin for 20 minutes, a very touching thought.' Queen Mary afterwards commissioned Mr F. E. Beresford to paint a picture of this episode; known as *The Vigil of the Princes* it was given to the King as a birthday present by his relations on 23 June.

The Duke of Windsor has described the odd and, as it were, portentous incident which happened while his father's coffin was being taken from King's Cross to Westminster Hall:

That simple family procession through London [he writes] was, perhaps more impressive than the State *cortège* on the day of the funeral and I especially remember a curious incident that happened on the way and was seen by very few. The Imperial Crown, heavily encrusted with precious stones, had been removed from its glass case in the Tower and secured to the lid of the coffin over the folds of the Royal Standard. In spite of the rubber-tyred wheels, the jolting of the heavy vehicle must have caused the Maltese cross on the top of the Crown—set with a square sapphire, eight medium-sized diamonds, and one hundred and ninety-two smaller diamonds —to fall. For suddenly, out of the corner of my eye, I caught a flash of light dancing along the pavement.

The cross was deftly retrieved from the gutter by the Company Sergeant Major who brought up the rear of the two files of Grenadiers. This incident impressed itself upon the King's mind: 'It seemed a strange thing to happen', he wrote, 'and, although not superstitious, I wondered whether it was a bad omen.'[35]

After lying in state in Westminster Hall for four days, the dead King's body was taken to Windsor on the morning of Tuesday, 28 January. Four crowned heads and the President of the French Republic were amongst the host of foreign representatives who had converged on London for the funeral. The day was misty and damp;

the London crowds in the streets were so dense that the *cortège* reached Windsor, where the Archbishop of Canterbury was waiting, two hours late. 'A terrible day of sadness for us', Queen Mary wrote. ' . . . First we fetched him from Westminster Hall, he was drawn by bluejackets on the gun carriage, then a long drive, the men walking, to Paddington through wonderful crowds of sorrowing people mourning their dead King. . . . Another drive, the men walking, thro' Windsor & the gates into the grounds, to St George's Chapel, & we left him sadly, lying for the present with his ancestors in the Vault.'[36]

Apart from the slight, fair-haired figure of the new King, public attention on this solemn day was focused upon Queen Mary, who, wearing the peaked coif and thick *crêpe* veils of German royal mourning, stood alone, just ahead of her family, at the foot of King George V's coffin in St George's Chapel at Windsor. The tributes paid to the late King in the House of Lords and in the House of Commons contained warm and loyal references to Queen Mary: 'We are thankful indeed', said the Prime Minister, Mr Baldwin, in his eulogy of King George V, 'to think that even in her sorrow Queen Mary is spared to the people who love her, and I am sure that we, all of us, all our people, will show her in whatever way they can how close she is to their hearts and how they will treasure her not only for the King's sake, but for her own. . . . Do I need to say a word in this House of how his power and influence were enhanced in a million ways by that rich companionship he shared with the Queen?'[37] Seven members of the Commons were selected to tender to Queen Mary the 'condolence, reverence and affection' of the House. In the Lords an address was also moved to convey to the Queen their Lordships' appreciation of 'the royal partnership, perfect in the intimacy of the home as in the full light of public life, which death has so suddenly dissolved'.

All those who saw Queen Mary privately at this time were profoundly moved by her intrepidity and calm, qualities she had shown from the very moment of King George's death. 'I was told afterwards', wrote the Archbishop of Canterbury, Dr Lang, 'that the sons . . . were painfully upset—I suppose they had seldom if ever seen death—and that it was the Queen, still marvellously self-controlled, who supported and strengthened them.'[38] On the day after the funeral at Windsor the Archbishop went to Buckingham Palace to see Queen Mary: 'I had a long talk with her and dear Princess

Mary', he noted, '—her [the Queen's] fortitude still unbroken. Let it not be supposed that this unfailing self-control was due to any sort of hardness. On the contrary her emotions were always ready to break through; only her courage restrained them.'39 Dr Lang's friendship with King George and Queen Mary went back nearly forty years, when, as Vicar of Portsea in the Isle of Wight, he had in 1898 been brought to the attention of Queen Victoria and of her son the Prince of Wales. He had even at this period stayed at Sandringham, when King George V, then Duke of York, had walked him over to York Cottage 'to see the Duchess (who would not come out, as she was expecting another Royal babe). She was,' Lang noted, 'as usual, very pleasant, in spite of a certain shyness. I like her personality very much, very sincere and genuine. They showed me over their little house with a quite charming and almost naïve keenness. It might have been a curate and his wife in their new house.'40

Because of this old friendship, King George V had formed the habit of discussing family affairs with the Archbishop; amongst other topics he had discussed the life of his eldest son, now King Edward VIII. Dr Lang suspected that the new King was aware of these discussions and might, somewhat naturally, have resented them, so, after his talk with Queen Mary at Buckingham Palace on 29 January 1936, he asked if he might have an audience of King Edward. Both the Archbishop and the Duke of Windsor have written detailed accounts of this not very satisfactory interview. Although 'impressed by his alertness and obvious eagerness to know and to learn', the Archbishop left the King's presence with the uneasy conviction that 'a chapter . . . is closed. There is not only a new reign', he wrote in a memorandum of the interview, 'but a new régime. I can only be most thankful for what has been, and for what is to be, hope for the best. God guide the King!'41

VII

That prospect of change which filled the Archbishop of Canterbury with foreboding seemed to many other of the King's subjects timely and interesting: 'signs were not wanting', as the Duke of Windsor has himself written in his Memoirs, 'that many welcomed the advent of my reign as an event of happy augury.'42 The chief newspapers, the Prime Minister, the Archbishop of Canterbury himself, all combined to welcome publicly and to encourage the new occupant of the throne, who has recalled that in his first weeks as King he had 'the uneasy sensation of being left alone on a vast stage, a stage that was the British Empire, to play a part not yet written', and that 'it was some time before I became accustomed to identifying the term "King" with myself'.43 'He has', Mr Baldwin declared of the new King, 'the secret of youth in the prime of age'; and indeed King Edward VIII seemed to have inherited not merely the beguiling charm of his grandmother Queen Alexandra, but also her gift of almost perennial youth. He was forty-one when he succeeded to the throne of the British Empire, but he looked ten or fifteen years younger than his age.

We have already noticed how, as Prince of Wales, the new King had come to symbolise for millions of his contemporaries—and not only amongst his compatriots—the hopes and aspirations of the young. Now that he had ascended the throne these contemporaries took it for granted that he would wish to make changes and, to some degree, to modernise the Monarchy. He has himself denied that he had any 'notion of tinkering with the fundamental rules of Monarchy, nor of upsetting the proud traditions of the Court. In truth, all that I ever had in mind was to throw open the windows a little and to let into the venerable institution some of the fresh air that I had become accustomed to breathe as Prince of Wales.' 'I had', the Duke writes further, 'no desire to go down in history as Edward the Reformer. Edward the Innovator—that might have been to the point.'44 It requires no very vigorous stretch of the imagination to suppose that these aims and projects of the new King aroused little enthusiasm in his mother. After Queen Victoria's death in 1901 Queen Mary, then Duchess of Cornwall and York, had disapproved of the speed and scope of the changes her parents-in-law initiated at their Court: 'it is always best to do such things very piano & with much reflection', she had written to her Aunt Augusta. If, as a young woman in 1901, she had regretted the innovations made by King Edward the Seventh, it was improbable that she would now welcome those proposed by King Edward the Eighth in 1936. Characteristically, the Queen suspended judgement and tried to help her son in his new role of King-Emperor in every way she could.

The first months of the new reign and of her own widowhood made little outward change in the circumstances or the order of Queen Mary's daily life. She was no longer Queen Consort, but, since the King was a bachelor, she was not Queen Dowager either. She continued living in Buckingham Palace, where the King set up a small office for transacting business, retaining York House as his temporary home. Aided by the Princess Royal* and intermittently by the King himself Queen Mary occupied herself in the sad task of sorting her late husband's papers and possessions, and dividing some of the latter amongst members of the family. She also embarked on the re-decoration of Marlborough House, where she was henceforth going to live. After twenty-six years in Buckingham Palace Queen Mary prepared to leave it slowly and sorrowfully; the moving of all her possessions to Marlborough House formed, in her eldest son's words, 'a melancholy task of no mean magnitude, for in the course of her active life she had assembled an immense collection of *objets d'art* and historical souvenirs of the Royal Family'.[45] In 1910 Queen Mary had been irritated at the length of time it took her mother-in-law Queen Alexandra to move from Buckingham Palace to Marlborough House, but now that she had in her turn to make a similar transition she found that it was not really possible to hurry the process. Queen Mary did not settle at Marlborough House until the 1st of October, nearly ten months after King George V's death.

One of the new King's first innovations was to cut the period of Court mourning from one year to six months. This was a change which Queen Mary, with her inborn dislike of wearing black, wholeheartedly approved. In July, so soon as the mourning period was over, the King gave two afternoon receptions for débutantes in Buckingham Palace Garden, to replace the more formal Courts of the previous reign, and he also invited to another garden party eight thousand Canadians who had attended the unveiling of the Canadian War Memorial at Vimy Ridge and were returning home by way of England. Queen Mary had a glimpse of these entertainments from a window of the Palace. On 23 June, the King's birthday, she drove to the Horse Guards Parade to see the Trooping of the Colour: 'David held the parade of course which was a lovely sight as usual', she wrote, '—but tears were often in my eyes thinking of the past & of him we so sorely miss.' On 16 July she watched the King present new Colours to various Battalions of the Brigade of Guards—'David did it beautifully', she noted. It was during the King's return from this last ceremony that the lunatic McMahon tossed a loaded revolver at the King's horse over the heads of the crowd.

* Princess Mary, Countess of Harewood, had been declared Princess Royal after the death of her eldest aunt, Princess Louise, in 1931.

During all this part of the summer Queen Mary continued busily sorting out her own possessions from those which had belonged to King George V and were now her son's. On 13 July she divested herself of the Crown Jewels, 'which', she wrote, 'have been in my care since 1910—Felt very sad at parting'.[46] She was seeing the King frequently, and she recorded in her Diary her gratitude to him for the consideration which he showed her; if it happened that she had not seen him for an interval of some days at a time she would write to tell him what she had been doing, much as she used to write to her husband during their brief separations. 'My walk in Hampton Court today was most successful,' she informed King Edward, for instance, on 15 May, 'the lilacs were a sight & the tulips lovely, & Bushy Park & the chestnuts lovely too—it was a beautiful afternoon & so warm— & I was even able to sit out in the little house here on my return.' 'I was at Windsor yesterday to arrange some more things in the "lace Rm"* where the family souvenirs are', she wrote to him on another day, '& I asked March about the German sword with Papa's seal on the top which the Emp. William gave Papa when he became Col. in Chief of the 8th Cuirassiers somewhere about the year 1905— March did not know which it was so I went & looked at the swords & found it so all is well & March marked it for you to see. I then

---

* The importance which Queen Mary attached to the collections she placed in the Lace Room at Windsor Castle, and in Frogmore House, is explained in the following memorandum which she wrote out on a piece of Sandringham writing-paper, and headed: *Notes made by Queen Mary in 1946*. The memorandum runs as follows:

In the lace room at Windsor Castle I placed lace, souvenirs, & so forth which had belonged to King Edward VII, King George V, Queen Victoria, Queen Alexandra, and to myself, as well as to Queen Charlotte, Queen Adelaide, Princess Charlotte of Wales, the Duke of Connaught & Princess Louise, Duchess of Argyll etc. There are a few more modern souvenirs as well, and King George VI placed a few things of interest in this room.

In Frogmore House I arranged souvenirs of King George III, Queen Charlotte & their children in a room upstairs, in another room souvenirs of Queen Victoria & the Prince Consort, in another room things of King Edward VII, Queen Alexandra, King George V & things of my own—& a few souvenirs in a small room next door, and in a room opposite—Downstairs I placed a collection of *papier mâché* boxes, pieces of furniture etc., work boxes, pictures, and odds & ends picked up in antique shops or given me by friends. There are also books, albums of our travels, and my collection of Christmas and New Year cards from 1874 till this year—as well as various things belonging to our children—some of them upstairs, some downstairs—.

went down to Frogmore where the Russian children* were having great bicycle rides & making a good deal of noise, of course the poor things did not know I was in the house, but all the same it is a decided bore.'47 Sometimes she would send him little requests—could he not lend the Infanta Beatrice the King's Cottage at Kew, or the Duke of Kent some of the surplus silver? Could he allow Dr Borenius to see the Winterhalter drawings at Windsor for his book? What should be done about a bust of King George V for the Jockey Club? There is a distinct pathos about these notes—the fresh loneliness of someone accustomed to reporting her daily doings to a lifelong companion who is suddenly no longer there; they show, too, Queen Mary's strong sense that on every subject she must, as always, consult the King.

On 30 July 1936 Queen Mary left Buckingham Palace, where her own rooms were about to be dismantled, and drove to Sandringham by car. 'I took leave of my lovely rooms with a sad heart', she told her Diary. 'David kindly came to see me off. . . . I am glad to be here but miss my G. too dreadfully, his rooms look so empty & deserted.' On arriving at Sandringham she wrote a letter to the King, for she felt—as she had so often felt with her own husband—that she had not been very successful in expressing her thanks to him by the spoken word.

I fear I was very quiet today when you came to see me but I feel sure you realised that I felt very very sad at leaving those lovely comfortable rooms which have been my happy Home for 25 years, & that I was terribly afraid of breaking down—It was dear of you to come & see me off & I thank you with all my heart. . . . It is very nice here & peaceful & I am sure I shall like it, but I miss dearest Papa quite dreadfully, even more than in London & his rooms look so empty and deserted without him; I forced myself to go in & look round but felt very sad. Papa adored this place & I love it, it is full of so many happy memories of my whole married life, tho' of course Papa & I went through sad times too—especially when poor Grannie became so frail those last two years.48

That summer, breaking with his father's tradition of spending August on the grouse moors, King Edward VIII had chartered a yacht, the *Nahlin*, in which, escorted by two destroyers, he proposed

* Frogmore Cottage had been lent by King George V to the Grand Duchess Xenia, sister of the murdered Tsar Nicholas II, and her family.

to cruise with a small staff and a few of his personal friends off the Adriatic coast. The King had at first hoped to board the yacht at Venice, but, in view of the anti-British feeling then current in Italy over the imposition of sanctions, the Foreign Office did not deem this wise. The King and his guests therefore joined the *Nahlin* at Sibenic, a small port on the Dalmatian coast. 'I am glad you have chartered a yacht', wrote Queen Mary from Sandringham, '& I hope you will find sunshine & good weather abroad & be able to get out to Venice or wherever you join the yacht in comfort, I hope too that this autumn may be free from complications of which we have had more than our share for years. It was a nice day today & less cold & no rain for a wonder.'[49] In Queen Mary's usage, 'complications' was a capacious word; like the adjectives 'tiresome' and 'worrying' it could be made to cover any number of awkward or critical situations, from an international crisis like that caused by the Italian attack on Abyssinia to a matter of the most private family or domestic concern.

To the world at large, and most specifically to the public of the United States of America, the short cruise of the *Nahlin* was the subject of violent curiosity and loud conjecture, for it was known that amongst the guests aboard the yacht was a married lady from Baltimore, Mrs Wallis Warfield Simpson; and to everyone but the readers of the discreet and loyal British press it was equally known that the bachelor King Edward VIII and Mrs Simpson were in love. Dogged by reporters, photographers and tourists wherever they landed, the party found their only true privacy on board the yacht.

On 14 September King Edward got back to London. He went that same night to dine with his mother at Buckingham Palace, where Queen Mary was for the moment occupying the late King's rooms. 'Greeting her', he writes, 'I wondered how much she knew about the stories appearing in the American press. But her conversation told me nothing.' Queen Mary asked him whether he had enjoyed the cruise of the *Nahlin*: 'Didn't you find it terribly warm in the Adriatic?' she enquired. 'Her curiosity about the simple details of the voyage', the Duke of Windsor recalls, 'reminded me of how she used to talk to us when we returned from school.'[50] Queen Mary, who had spent most of the day arranging furniture at Marlborough House, was feeling tired: 'David got back from abroad looking very well', she noted in her Diary, '—and came to dine with me & we had a nice talk.' The Queen asked her son about King George II of Greece, whom he had seen at Corfu, and who had only returned to Greece in 1935 after an exile of eleven years. 'Poor George', she said, on hearing that he seemed thin and homesick for London. 'I don't envy the rulers of those Balkan countries.'

VIII

The Coronation, in Westminster Abbey, of King Edward VIII had been fixed for the 12th of May 1937. Preparations for this ceremony were already well advanced in the autumn of 1936. It was a quarter of a century since there had been any Coronation in the Abbey, and there had been none in living memory of a British monarch without a Consort. To find a precedent you would have had to look back to the Coronation of Queen Victoria in 1838, two years before her marriage, or to that of George IV—after his legal separation from his wife, Queen Caroline—in 1821. Thus, to the generation which had grown up during the First World War, and even to a good many of their parents, the prospect of the crowning of the bachelor King Edward seemed less that of the performance of an immemorial rite than the expectation of an interesting novelty. Even Queen Mary went to examine the model of a Peeress's Coronation robe on view that autumn at Norfolk House, the home of the hereditary Earl Marshal of the Realm.

All this time Queen Mary was steadily and actively pursuing her own plans for moving from Buckingham Palace to Marlborough House. 'Things are getting on very slowly', she complained to her Diary, after one of her daily visits of inspection at Marlborough House in early September.[51] She now hoped to achieve the final move in the last fourteen days of that month, while the King was entertaining at Balmoral. 'The news that I intended to spend the last two weeks of September at Balmoral pleased her', writes the Duke of Windsor of his mother at that time. 'To my mother the habits and customs of the family meant almost as much as the official obligations devolving upon us: she hoped now that I had become the head of the family that I would return more to the ways of my father.'[52] For Queen Mary this particular hope proved a forlorn one, since the King's September house-party at Balmoral seemed inspired more by the carefree spirit of the *Nahlin* cruise than by any conscious imitation of the staid, traditional hospitality which King George V and Queen Mary had dispensed year after year to certain chosen statesmen, to the Archbishop of Canterbury and to King George's old friends Sister Agnes

Keyser and Canon Dalton.* Upon the courtiers of the last reign, the very names officially announced in the newspapers as those of some of King Edward VIII's guests at Balmoral Castle that September of 1936 had a rather jarring effect—giving them the same sort of jolt which a lifelong devotee of Henry James might feel on finding a few pages by Hemingway or Faulkner bound up in a copy of *The Wings of The Dove*. The names of individuals, as history has repeatedly shown us, can suddenly and without warning assume an importance unexplained by any theory of semantics. For some time past the plain and unpretentious surname, Simpson, had taken on for Queen Mary and for her family an ominous ring.

Up at Balmoral some of the King's brothers began to feel that they no longer enjoyed the King's confidence. In especial, the heir-presumptive to the throne, the Duke of York, found himself, in his official biographer's words, 'shut off from his brother, neglected, ignored, unwanted. . . . He felt that he had lost a friend and was rapidly losing a brother';54 for King Edward VIII's emotions, strong and exclusive, were characteristically concentrated upon the person whom he loved. In the United States of America and in continental Europe the newspapers were now frankly predicting that when Mrs Simpson, who had applied for a divorce that summer, should have become free, she would marry the King and mount the British throne as Queen Consort and Empress of India. In this country the London and provincial press still maintained, although with increasing difficulty, its voluntary silence on the subject, but the number of letters of shock and protest from British residents abroad which now poured into Buckingham Palace and 10 Downing Street, Lambeth Palace and *The Times* office in Printing House Square, grew daily in volume. Many such letters were addressed to Queen Mary, at Marlborough House, urging her to act before it was too late. The letter-writers did not, however, indicate what action Queen Mary could take over a situation which was ambiguous and which, since it concerned her King, she would not discuss or acknowledge. Queen Mary read the letters, put

---

* Canon J. N. Dalton (1841–1931) had been Tutor to King George V and to his brother and had accompanied them on the cruise of the *Bacchante*, 1879–1882. Miss Agnes Keyser, known as 'Sister Agnes', was founder and Matron of King Edward VII's Hospital for officers in Grosvenor Crescent. 'She specialised in patients from the Household Cavalry and the Brigade of Guards, and enjoyed repeating to the King, not always with useful results, the talk of the town', writes Sir Harold Nicolson.53

them by, and tried to seek distraction from her agony of doubt in superintending the placing of furniture, of pictures and of *objets d'art* in her new home, Marlborough House.

Deeply worried and unhappy, Queen Mary nevertheless threw all her customary energy into the move. 'To Marl. H. at 10.25 & stayed there till after 1—supervising various things & arranging furniture— Went there again at 3 & stayed till 7.30!!! I took my tea there & had it with Mrs Moore our housekeeper, picnic fashion in one of the rooms—Felt dead tired on my return', reads a typical Diary entry for these weeks.55 'We went to Marl. Hse morning & afternoon & arranged books & hung pictures with the aid of 2 men from Walker's Bond St—I wish the move was not so fatiguing!!!' she wrote on 21 September. Queen Mary supervised every detail of the large house, taking characteristic trouble to see that the rooms of 'my people' (as she always called her staff) were well arranged: 'Lovely warm day', she wrote on 25 September. 'To M. Hse both morning and afternoon —Went to see all the servants quarters. My housekeeper Mrs Moore has worked very hard to make the rooms comfortable for them.' A few days later she recorded that the house was 'beginning to look more liveable'. At last it was ready and the Queen decided to leave the Palace on the 1st of October. 'Sad to think this is my last day in my old Home of 25 years', she wrote. '—*Tout passe, tout casse, tout lasse*, such is life—but one must be content with the happy memories which remain—.'

Thursday, 1 October, was a fine day: 'My last day in dear Buckingham Palace.' Three luggage brakes filled with the residue of Queen Mary's personal belongings left Buckingham Palace for Marlborough House that morning, together with the remaining members of her household and a cairn terrier which had belonged to King George V. Queen Mary also went to Marlborough House that morning 'for a short time to finish off'. She then returned to Buckingham Palace to have luncheon with the King, just back from Balmoral. At three o'clock the King and the Princess Royal drove with their mother out from the garden entrance of the Palace, along the Mall and by way of Clarence Gate and Cleveland Row up to the portico of Marlborough House. 'David was delighted with the rooms', she noted with satisfaction. 'He left after 4. After tea we wandered from one room to another altering small things—I think I shall be quite contented here tho' there must always be the fearful blank.'56

Queen Mary had hardly been established at Marlborough House

a fortnight, when it became known that Mrs Simpson's petition for divorce from her second husband would be heard towards the end of the month in the county court of Ipswich, in Suffolk. Like the three mallet-blows which precede the raising of the curtain in a French theatre, this brief announcement of the date for hearing the divorce petition—Tuesday, 27 October—declenched a drama which galvanised the literate world, and simultaneously revealed the elasticity and the inborn strength of the Constitution of the British Empire and of the British Monarchy.

The crisis of the autumn and winter of 1936 was, in fact, a triumphant proof that the life-work of King George the Fifth and of Queen Mary had not been in vain: 'in any other country', Queen Mary wrote when all was over, 'there wld have been riots, thank God people did not lose their heads.'57

CHAPTER SEVEN

MOTHER TO THE KING

M UCH HAS BEEN WRITTEN about the abdication of King Edward VIII from the Imperial throne in December 1936; more will no doubt be written in the future. The Duke and the Duchess of Windsor have each of them published their narratives of the events which led up to the crisis. They have explained their motives and have indicated the emotional climate in which their parts in this drama were enacted. The official biographer of King George VI has now published that King's precise and careful chronicle of the days which preceded the abdication of his elder brother and his own accession to the throne. Two lives of Lord Baldwin have already appeared, as well as biographical studies of such ancillary figures as Archbishop Lang. The chronology and the interplay of character in this startling episode in English history are, therefore, well established and, indeed, the documentation now available to students may be thought to be reasonably complete. In this chapter we are solely concerned with one aspect of the abdication of 1936: its effect upon the mother of two King-Emperors, Queen Mary.

It can be simply stated that Queen Mary greeted her son's decision to give up the throne with consternation, with anger and with pain. To other members of the Family she declared both at that time and subsequently that no single event in the whole of her life—which, we may recall, had not been an invariably happy one—had caused her so much real distress or left her with so deep a feeling of 'humiliation'. Even the pride she felt in watching the development as King and Queen of her second son and of his wife failed to obliterate for her the memory of the shock which King Edward VIII's abdication had caused.

We have seen that although, for many, many months, Queen Mary had been subterraneously aware of King Edward VIII's love for Mrs Simpson she had never discussed the matter with him, hoping that with time the strength of the emotion might evaporate. She had, however, consulted one or two extraneous persons in her anxiety and she had even urged the Cabinet to take some sort of 'action' before Mrs Simpson's divorce case came up for hearing. Queen Mary's anxiety arose, as is well known, from the fact that Mrs Simpson, who was born of a good family in Maryland, had already divorced one husband and was on the verge of divorcing the second: Mrs Simpson had, in fact, in Queen Mary's own phrase, 'two husbands living', and she had, in Queen Mary's opinion, captivated the King. Queen Mary's views on divorce were clear and strict: one divorce could seldom or never be justified, and to divorce twice, on any grounds whatever, was to her unthinkable. As for the possibility of a lady 'with two husbands living' marrying her eldest son and becoming Queen Consort this was out of all question.

The sequence of events of the winter of 1936 showed that Queen Mary's standpoint was one that was shared by the British Cabinet, and by the administrations of the Dominions, as well as by large sections of British and Imperial public opinion. The British public were prepared to accept innovations in kingship from King Edward VIII; they were not prepared for, nor did they want, a total break with the traditions of the past or the paradox evidently offered by the prospect of their King, who was at the same time Defender of the Faith, married to what was at that epoch called 'a divorcee'. Moreover, our political relations with the United States of America during the post-war years had been notably inharmonious, and the majority of the King's subjects did not relish the idea of a transatlantic successor to Queen Mary on the throne.

The daily developments of those weeks during which Mrs Simpson's divorce suit was pending at Ipswich do not concern us here; we may, briefly, recall that the Prime Minister, Mr Stanley Baldwin, first discussed the matter with King Edward VIII at Fort Belvedere on 20 October, that a week later the King saw Mr Mackenzie King of Canada on the same subject, and that, on 13 November, the King's Private Secretary, Major Alexander Hardinge, wrote the King a letter apprising him that the British press was about to break the long silence it had hitherto preserved about himself and Mrs Simpson, whose decree *nisi* had been granted to her on 27 October. On 16 November King Edward VIII again saw Mr Baldwin, declaring that he intended to marry Mrs Simpson and to do so, would, if necessary, abdicate the throne. It was on the evening of this day that the King dined with his mother at Marlborough House. The King's sister the Princess

Royal was also present at this meeting, and, like Queen Mary, listened carefully to what the King had to say.

When, sitting in Queen Mary's boudoir after dinner, the King broached the subject of his feeling for Mrs Simpson, he found his mother and his sister sympathetic; but when they learned that he was prepared to give up the throne in order to marry her, they were astounded and shocked: 'To my Mother', writes the Duke of Windsor, 'the Monarchy was something sacred and the Sovereign a personage apart. The word "duty" fell between us. But there could be no question of my shirking my duty.'[1] The longer they talked, the more apparent became the divergence of their views. To Queen Mary her son had two alternatives, two choices which he could make: to give up marrying Mrs Simpson or to give up the throne. To the King these choices did not seem to exist: he was convinced that he could not endure his present life unless he were married to Mrs Simpson, that he could no longer carry on as King without her 'help and support', and that therefore, in the last resort, he must go. In this sense it seemed to the King that his duty was to leave the throne, while to Queen Mary it seemed equally plain that it was his duty to stay upon it. This was, in essence, a conflict of realities. Not surprisingly the discussion resulted in a deadlock, since neither party to it could give way. Queen Mary's arguments, which are of historical interest and which have not hitherto been published, were enumerated by her very clearly in a letter which she wrote to the Duke of Windsor eighteen months subsequently, that is to say in July 1938:

You ask me in your letter of the 23rd of June to write to you frankly about my true feelings with regard to you and the present position and this I will do now. You will remember how miserable I was when you informed me of your intended marriage and abdication and how I implored you not to do so for our sake and for the sake of the country. You did not seem able to take in any point of view but your own. . . . I do not think you have ever realised the shock, which the attitude you took up caused your family and the whole Nation. It seemed inconceivable to those who had made such sacrifices during the war that you, as their King, refused a lesser sacrifice. . . . My feelings for you as your Mother remain the same, and our being parted and the cause of it, grieve me beyond words. After all, all my life I have put my Country before everything else, and I simply cannot change now.[2]

In his own book the Duke of Windsor has explained that in his final and irrevocable decision to abdicate he also was inspired by a purely patriotic motive—the wish to avoid splitting the country on the issue of his marriage, and thus endangering the Empire and the throne.

On the morning after this harrowing talk at Marlborough House —which had ended with Queen Mary's refusal of her son's suggestion that she should herself see Mrs Simpson—Queen Mary sent the King a sorrowful, maternal little note: 'As your mother', she wrote, 'I must send you a line of true sympathy in the difficult position in which you are placed—I have been thinking of you all day, hoping you are making a wise decision for your future—I fear your visit to Wales will be trying in more ways than one, with this momentous action hanging over your head.'3

That same day Queen Mary received the Prime Minister, Mr Stanley Baldwin. During the night the Queen's bewilderment and shock had crystallised into a positive exasperation. To give vent to her feelings she reverted, suddenly and unexpectedly, to a Cockney slang expression of her youth, picked up from her brothers in the distant, gay, Victorian days of life at White Lodge. 'Well, Mr Baldwin!' Queen Mary exclaimed, stepping briskly into the room, her hands held out before her in a gesture of despair, '*this* is a pretty kettle of fish!'

II

For Queen Mary these anxious winter days of 1936 were terrible and bleak. In common with a great many other people in positions of responsibility, the Queen had very natural fears of what damaging effect an abdication might not have upon the position of the Monarchy and its influence throughout the British Empire. All that she valued and admired in life seemed threatened, all that for which she and King George V had patiently and steadfastly worked. With that overriding passion for the British throne which had illuminated her whole life since her girlhood, the idea that one Monarch should step down from his high position and another take his place appalled Queen Mary, for in her mind the very concept of 'abdication' implied ceasing to do your duty.*

The history of the British Royal Family, as well as that of Queen Mary's paternal forebears in Württemberg, showed various instances of royal persons marrying for love outside their sphere. We may

---

* When Queen Mary heard, in 1948, that Queen Wilhelmina of the Netherlands had abdicated in favour of her daughter, she remarked: 'Wilhelmina is only sixty-eight and that is *no* age to give up your job.'

likewise recall that in 1890 Queen Victoria herself was prepared to consider the Duke of Clarence abdicating his rights as heir-pre-sumptive to her throne in order to marry the Roman Catholic Princess Hélène of Orleans. But that a King of England should resign the Crown for an overpowering emotion was not a situation for which there had been either precedent or parallel. Queen Mary, who but a few short weeks before had said that she 'did not envy' King George of Greece and other Balkan Monarchs the uncertainty of their fate, was now heard to remark bitterly: 'Really! this might be Roumania!'

All through these days, Queen Mary did her utmost to help her two elder sons—the actual King, Edward VIII, and the King of the future, who was still the Duke of York. King Edward came to tea at Marlborough House on 24 November; after this further talk which, like the first one, made no headway, Queen Mary did not see the King for another ten days, since, anxious to avoid public demon-strations, he withdrew quietly to Fort Belvedere. Queen Mary did, however, have news of the King from the Duke of York, whom she was seeing regularly, and who, like the Duchess of York, was dreading his possible accession to the throne. Determined to maintain at least an outward appearance of calm, Queen Mary spent the last week of November in doing Christmas shopping, visiting exhibitions and going to look at the London Museum. On Monday, 30 November, the Crystal Palace on Sydenham Hill was burned down: 'After dinner', Queen Mary noted, 'Mary and I were horrified to hear the Crystal Palace was on fire with no hope of saving it. We saw the smoke from my window—What a pity, a great landmark gone.'

It was on 3 December that the news of the constitutional crisis over the King's wish to marry Mrs Simpson appeared in all the London papers. The Duke of York, who had been to Edinburgh for two days to be installed as Grand Master Mason of Scotland, has recorded the shock he experienced on reaching Euston Station that morning: 'At Euston', he wrote, 'I was both surprised & horrified to see that the posters of the Daily Press had the following as their headlines in block letters "The King's Marriage".'[4] Down at Fort Belvedere, where Mrs Simpson, with her aunt Mrs Merriman as chaperone, had taken refuge from a curious public, King Edward and his future bride were, as they have told us in their memoirs, equally astounded that morning by the tone of the press. At Marlborough House Queen Mary likewise was aghast; it was the first time that national newspapers had openly

T

criticised or attacked a British Monarch since the jubilant obituary notices of George the Fourth in 1832 and the outcry raised in 1864 against Queen Victoria's seclusion in her widowhood. 'Darling David,' Queen Mary wrote at two-thirty p.m. to King Edward, 'This news in the papers is very upsetting, especially as I have not seen you for 10 days—I would much like to see you, won't you look in some time today? I shall only be out from 3 to 5—Ever yr loving Mama, Mary.'[5]

Queen Mary was out that afternoon because she wished to see the smoking ruins of the Crystal Palace. She was accompanied by her brother Lord Athlone and her sister-in-law Princess Alice (who were staying with the Queen to give her support in this crisis), as well as by the Princess Royal: 'went to see what was left of the poor Crystal Palace—a very sad sight', she recorded. This deliberate visit to the burned-out shell on Sydenham Hill had, as Queen Mary intended it to have, a very salutary effect upon public morale and was an altogether typical gesture: 'Since the crisis Queen Mary has paid two visits south of the river', recorded, for example, *The Yorkshire Post* on 8 December. 'On Thursday she motored to Sydenham, to view the ruins of the Crystal Palace; and this excursion, so peculiarly irrelevant in the circumstances, was widely appreciated for its sedative effect upon an excited country. Today Her Majesty has been occupied in a fashion even more placid. She has been to Dulwich Park where she spent some time watching the birds in the aviary.' But behind this façade of dignity and valour, Queen Mary was awaiting with flayed nerves and a ghastly apprehension for the decision of her eldest son.

On receiving Queen Mary's note that afternoon of 3 December, King Edward, exhausted as he was, drove late at night to Marlborough House, where he found the Duke and Duchess of York, who had been dining there. The King explained to his mother that he had refrained from seeing her during the preceding days as he had been anxious to avoid giving her pain. 'As simply as I could', he writes,[6] 'I explained the reasons for my apparent aloofness. "I have no desire to bring you and the family into all this. This is something I must handle alone." If she had hoped to learn from me that I had changed my mind, she gave no sign. I left Marlborough House sorry to disappoint her.' 'David said to Queen Mary', the Duke of York recorded, 'that he could not live alone as King & must marry Mrs - - - - -. When David left after making this dreadful announcement to his mother he told me to come & see him at the Fort next morning.'[7]

The King did not in fact receive the Duke of York until three days later, the 7th of December. On the morning of the 8th the Duke called at Marlborough House, and on the following day, Wednesday, 9 December, the Queen drove down with her daughter to the Royal Lodge at Windsor, the home of the Duke and Duchess of York. 'I met my brother at Royal Lodge & he & his mother were together some time', the Duke of York noted in his Memorandum. There, in the drawing-room of Royal Lodge, as the winter afternoon shortened to twilight and the fog closed in over the garden beyond the window-panes, Queen Mary heard of her eldest son's irrevocable decision to leave the throne:

She was already waiting in the drawing-room when I arrived [writes the Duke of Windsor]. I gave her a full account of all that had passed between Mr Baldwin and myself during the six days since our last meeting on the Thursday before. She still disapproved of and was bewildered by my action, but now that it was all over her heart went out to her hard-pressed son, prompting her to say with tenderness: 'And to me, the worst thing is that you won't be able to see her for so long.'[8]

Queen Mary's own Diary account of this momentous interview is laconic: 'Rather foggy day', she wrote. 'At 1.30 with Mary to meet David (on business) at the Royal Lodge—Back before 5—Georgie & Marina dined.' After dinner, the Duke of York arrived at Marlborough House and with Queen Mary looked over the draft Instrument of Abdication, a document which he himself regarded with revulsion and his mother read with incredulity. 'I went to see Queen Mary', the Duke recorded, '& when I told her what had happened I broke down & sobbed like a child.'[9] Unlike her mother the Duchess of Teck, and unlike her mother-in-law Queen Alexandra, Queen Mary had never been given to an excessive use of exclamation marks. Seldom does this useful form of punctuation interrupt or emphasise passages in the calm narrative of her Diary. In her account of the Duke of York's visit that night the Queen did, however, have recourse to the exclamation mark:

Bertie arrived very late from Fort Belvedere and Mr W. Monckton brought him & me the paper drawn up for David's abdication of the Throne of this Empire because he wishes to marry Mrs Simpson!!!!! The whole affair has lasted since Novr. 16th and has been very painful—It is a terrible blow to us all & particularly to poor Bertie.

On the following day, 10 December 1936, King Edward VIII signed the Instrument of Abdication in the presence of his brothers. King

George VI succeeded to the throne. 'Dark gloomy day', Queen Mary recorded. 'I saw Ld Salisbury & the PM—At 3 to Piccadilly to see Elizabeth* who was in bed with a cold, too unlucky. The PM made his announcement in the house about David's final decision—which was received in silence & with real regret—The more one thinks of this affair the more regrettable it becomes.'

III

On surrendering the Crown, King Edward VIII automatically reverted to the status of a Prince of the Blood Royal and became H R H Prince Edward of Windsor. He had arranged to leave England on the night following the public announcement that he was no longer King. Prince Edward therefore asked some of his family to meet him for dinner at Royal Lodge, before he made a farewell broadcast to his former subjects from nearby Windsor Castle. Sending the Prince a note to say how much her thoughts had been constantly with him, Queen Mary commented also upon the 'wonderfully dignified manner' in which the Prime Minister had made the abdication announcement in the House of Commons that afternoon: 'the Country', she wrote, 'has taken the sad news calmly.' The Queen went on to try to dissuade Prince Edward from making his broadcast: 'Don't you think that as he [the Prime Minister] has said everything that could be said', she wrote, '. . . it will now not be necessary for *you* to broadcast this evening, you are very tired after all the strain you have been & are going through, and surely you might spare yourself this extra strain and emotion—Do please take my advice—Bertie tells me you wish us to meet you at dinner at Royal Lodge this evening, I hope there will not be any fog.'[11]

Prince Edward attached the highest importance to this broadcast, which would give him his first opportunity since the crisis began to speak out candidly to the nation and to explain personally and publicly the reasons for his action: 'I have made this, the most serious decision of my life', ran one part of his text, 'upon a single thought of what would in the end be best for all.' He thus kept to his plan, and leaving

---

* 'An additional anxiety for the Duke of York', writes Sir John Wheeler-Bennett in his biography, 'was that the Duchess had contracted influenza and was lying ill at 145 Piccadilly. He was therefore deprived of her comforting presence and was compelled to suffer his ordeal alone.'[10] We may here recall that as from 10 December 1936 the Duchess of York became Queen Consort and Empress of India.

the new King, his mother, his sister and his two other brothers, as
well as his uncle Lord Athlone and his aunt Princess Alice at Royal
Lodge after dinner, he drove up to Windsor Castle where he delivered
the broadcast from a room in the Augusta Tower, returning to Royal
Lodge again when it was finished. 'After dinner', Queen Mary recorded,
'David made his private broadcast to the Nation which was good &
dignified, he did it at the Castle, we listened to it at Royal Lodge.'
In his broadcast, which concluded with the words: 'God bless you all.
God Save the King!' Prince Edward had paid a tribute to the comfort
he had received 'during these hard days' from his mother and his
family. When he got back to these at Royal Lodge the Prince relates
that he 'had the feeling that what I had said had to some extent eased
the tension between us'.[12] It was by then getting late, and fog still
shrouded the Thames valley. Queen Mary and the Marlborough House
party began to think of their drive back to London: 'and then', wrote
Queen Mary, 'came the dreadful good bye as he was leaving that
evening for Austria. The whole thing was too pathetic for words.'[13]

Prince Edward of Windsor took leave of his younger brother the
King of England at midnight, on 11 December 1936, and drove through
the murk to Portsmouth across the Hartford Bridge Flats. At Portsmouth he found the destroyer *Fury* waiting to carry him over the
dark Channel to happiness and to what he has himself described as
'life in the real world—the world which by my own free will I had
chosen'.[14] After one of the most dramatic renunciations in history he
thus left the shores of the country over which he had ruled for a
period of just over three hundred days.

At his Accession Council next morning, King George VI announced
that the first act of his reign would be to confer upon his brother a
dukedom, and that he proposed the novel title Windsor, which,
although it had, since 1917, been the family name of the Reigning
House of Great Britain had never been a Royal dukedom. The Duke
of Windsor, who now changed his name for the seventh time in his
life* settled upon the shores of an Austrian lake, there to await the

* Born Prince Edward of York, he had become successively Prince Edward of
Cornwall and York, Prince Edward of Wales, Duke of Cornwall, Prince of Wales,
King Edward VIII, Prince Edward of Windsor and Duke of Windsor. The
dukedom of Windsor was gazetted on 28 May 1937, with a special provision
made 'on the advice of Ministers' that the Duke's future wife should not make
use of the title of Royal Highness. Made also at the insistence of Queen Mary,
this provision did nothing to improve her current relations with her eldest son,
then living abroad.

declaration of the decree absolute of Mrs Simpson's divorce, which would give them liberty to marry one another.

For many months after his departure from England, Queen Mary's relations with her eldest son were not harmonious; for although it was he who had won in that great conflict of realities which we have noted earlier, his mother could never conclude that he had been right. They kept up a somewhat sporadic correspondence; she would write to say she supposed he must be very lonely in Austria and to assure him 'that we are all out to help you in every way we can'.[15] That the abdication was now an accomplished fact was, to Queen Mary, in itself a reason for not discussing it on paper any more. She would send her son small items of personal news such as:

I went to 2 premières last week in aid of charities & have also been to 2 plays—It was rather an effort at first as you can imagine not having been out for a year, but I had such a charming welcome from the crowds that I felt quite encouraged.[16]

Or she would make some non-committal comment on his activities: 'I was interested in reading you drove through Gmunden, where in 1884 my parents Alge & I spent 2 months with the Cumberlands who later built a big Schloss there. . . . The country all round is pretty as far as I remember & I did go to Ischl once.'[17]

'We all felt miserable,' Queen Mary noted in her Diary on the day of her second son's Proclamation at St James's Palace, which she, the King and his two daughters watched from the Wardrobe Room at Marlborough House, 'at the same time there was a sense of relief that all was settled.'[18] The plain fact was that, as well as feeling miserable, Queen Mary was likewise feeling angry. 'H M is still angry with the Duke, & I really think that helps her to bear what she called "the humiliation" of it all', wrote an old friend with whom the Queen Dowager 'talked hard about the Duke of Windsor and all her troubles' in March 1937.[19] But, sorrowful and indignant, Queen Mary had risen magnificently to meet this crisis; the new King and Queen, and indeed the whole of the Royal Family, recognised how much the smooth transition from one Monarch to another owed to Queen Mary's wisdom and popularity. 'Thank God we have all got you as a central point, because without it [the Family] might easily disintegrate', one of the Family wrote to her at this time.[20]

The abdication had indeed passed off far better than Queen Mary could have hoped. King Edward VIII had scrupulously avoided any appeal to public opinion, which might have divided the country; already the London crowds, who had acclaimed King Edward VIII outside Buckingham Palace, were cheering outside 145 Piccadilly, still the home of the new King and Queen. The very title chosen by Prince Albert, Duke of York, when he became King—George VI—in itself suggested a reassuring return to his father's traditional ways. Christmas 1936 was, as usual, spent at Sandringham: 'Fine day', Queen Mary recorded on 22 December. 'Left London with Bertie, E. & their children for dear Sandringham to spend Christmas there, my staff running it this year. . . . Happy to be back in the old Home.'

As might have been expected, now that the intense strain of the abdication crisis was over, Queen Mary suffered a physical reaction. She became so unwell that she spent Christmas Day and most of that week in her room, although not in bed. On Thursday, 31 December, she was able to dine downstairs again and later saw 'an amusing Film. Thank God', she wrote on the last day of 1936, 'this sad year is over.'

IV

It was still hard, in the first months of the year 1937, to assess just how severely the structure of the Monarchy had, in fact, been damaged by the abdication of King Edward VIII. 'I will do my best to clear up the inevitable mess', the new Sovereign, then Duke of York, had written to Sir Godfrey Thomas on 25 November 1936, 'if the whole fabric does not crumble under the shock and strain of it all.'[21] Both the Duke and the Duchess of York were well known to the public, and the fact that the new Queen Elizabeth was the first Consort to come of British stock since the sixteenth century was in itself popular. Any fears King George or Queen Elizabeth may have felt about their new roles were, as Sir John Wheeler-Bennett has shown, dispelled at their Coronation on 12 May 1937.

In December 1936 the preparations for the Coronation of the bachelor King Edward VIII were, as we have seen, well under way, and accordingly the date fixed for this ceremony was kept for the Coronation of the new King and Queen. 'The whole of London is full of stands for the Coronation,' Queen Mary wrote to the Duke of Windsor,[22] whose diamond Garter Star she wished to borrow so that she might wear it at his brother's Crowning, 'too ugly and the poor daffodils are squashed & hidden underneath.'

By a tradition said to date back to the days of the Plantagenet

Sovereigns, no British Queen Dowager had ever attended the Coronation of her husband's successor on the throne. Queen Adelaide had remained shut up in Marlborough House when her niece Victoria was crowned in 1838, and, as we may recall, Queen Alexandra had withdrawn to Sandringham in 1911, merely taking part in a simple form of Coronation prayers in the little church there, attended by Princess Victoria, by Sir Dighton Probyn and by Miss Charlotte Knollys. The origin of this tradition is obscure, but it is no doubt connected with another tradition of apparently equivalent antiquity: that no crowned head attends the Coronation of a European Sovereign. It was in accord with this theory that King George and Queen Mary had, when Prince and Princess of Wales, attended as representatives of the King and Queen of England the Coronation of King Haakon VII of Norway and of Queen Maud at Trondheim in 1906. Torn between her inborn respect for historical tradition and by her inevitable wish to watch a son of hers being crowned as King of England, Queen Mary decided that she would for once herself make a constitutional innovation, and ask the King if she might not witness the Abbey ceremony and take her own part in the Coronation procession through London. This decision of Queen Mary's added to the sense of solidarity with which the whole Royal Family was facing the new reign. It was amply rewarded by wild demonstrations of affection from the crowd: as the procession wound past Marble Arch, for instance, 'the cheering redoubled, took on a deeper note, and after the splendid figure of the Blues came a glass coach bearing Queen Mary who never looked happier or more regal. Obviously deeply touched by the warm affection of the crowd's greeting, she smiled and waved her acknowledgements again and again.' At Piccadilly 'a sudden storm of exclamation, "Queen Mary!" heralded the approach of the coach bearing Queen Mary'.[23]

Queen Mary entered into the Coronation plans that January of 1937 with characteristic vigour. She brought to bear upon them a wealth of memories and of past experience; here, and in many other ways as well, her advice and help proved invaluable and reassuring to the new King and Queen, who were bravely shouldering the unexpected and unwanted burden of Sovereignty. 'Bertie, E. & I, Cromer & Wig*

* i.e. the second Earl of Cromer (1877–1953), Lord Chamberlain, 1922–1938, and Sir Clive (later Baron) Wigram (b. 1873), Private Secretary to King George V after Lord Stamfordham's death in 1931. He served King George VI as Permanent Lord-in-Waiting throughout his reign.

had a long confabulation about Coronation arrangements', Queen
Mary noted on 24 January 1937. 'A good many points were decided
on—.' 'At 12 to Westminster Abbey to see some of the preparations
for the Coronation, the Royal box, Annexe etc. A marvellous sight',
she wrote again some weeks later.[24] Queen Mary drove about London
in early May 'to see the pretty decorations, there were crowds in the
streets',[25] and at Marlborough House she held rehearsals with the four
pages who were to carry her train, as well as other rehearsals inside
the Abbey. She also went 'to Garrard's to see the jewellers working
on the resetting of Bertie's & Elizabeth's crowns—Most interesting'.[26]
Foreign royal representatives were soon gathering in London in the
first week of the month of May. Two days before the Coronation Day
itself Queen Mary recorded a 'family lunch' at Buckingham Palace,
'after which we gave our gift of a gold tea set which had belonged to
the Duke of Cumbd. to Bertie & E. I also gave E. a tortoiseshell &
Diamond fan with ostrich feathers which had belonged to Mama Alix,
& to Bertie a dark blue enamel snuff box with *our* miniatures. Bertie
then gave us his family order, his miniature on a pink ribbon, lovely,
he also gave me the Victorian Chain, & to others various orders. . . .
Maud & I dined at the Palace, State Banquet to 450 people in Ball
Rm & Supper Rm, Bertie in Ball Rm, E. in Supper Rm. I sat opposite
Bertie with Gustaf of Sweden & Rico of Denmark as neighbours. . . .
Went off very well.'[27] This was the known, accepted world of Queen
Mary's reality. Taking part in such a gathering of related royalties,
assembled to witness the solemnity of the Coronation, Queen Mary
momentarily forgot her sufferings during the abdication six months
before.

Coronation Day, 1937, proved dull and rainy. Accompanied by
Queen Maud of Norway, Queen Mary left Marlborough House in a
glass coach escorted by a troop of mounted Horse Guards, at ten
minutes past ten in the morning. Robed in purple and ermine, wearing
many fine jewels and with an open crown of diamonds upon her curled
white hair, the regal figure of Queen Mary aroused, as we have seen,
immense enthusiasm among the crowds. Together with her sister-in-
law Queen Mary proceeded up the nave of Westminster Abbey:

Maud and I processed up the Abbey to the Royal Box. I sat between Maud
& Lilibet, & Margaret came next, they looked too sweet in their lace dresses
& robes, especially when they put on their coronets. Bertie & E. looked so
well when they came in & did it all too beautifully. The Service was wonderful & impressive—we were all much moved. . . . A wonderful day.[28]

T*

Fourteen days after the Coronation Queen Mary celebrated her seventieth birthday with a luncheon party at Marlborough House, where the table was 'pretty with silver and pink carnations'. The third of June was for Queen Mary another, but sad, anniversary, for it had been the birthday of her dead husband King George V. It was also, that Coronation Year of 1937, the day on which the Duke of Windsor attained his heart's desire: for on that morning at the Château de Candé, near Monts in France, he was married to Mrs Wallis Warfield.* Queen Mary had not reconciled herself to her eldest son's marriage to a divorced lady: 'Alas! the wedding day in France of David & Mrs Warfield. . . . We all telegraphed to him', she noted in her Diary.

v

Altogether it may be said that Queen Mary thoroughly enjoyed the glorious summer of King George VI's Coronation. She attended every Court function and festivity, went to the Derby, saw the Aldershot Tattoo, took her part as a Dame of the Garter in the Garter Service at Windsor that June and, later in the same month, wearing academic robes, laid the foundation stone of the new Bodleian Library Annexe at Oxford. Queen Mary also resumed her long-standing custom of going to watch the International Lawn Tennis Championships at Wimbledon, as well as visiting London theatres and galleries. It was at this time, too, that she initiated a system of taking the new heir-apparent to the Throne, Princess Elizabeth, and her sister Princess Margaret Rose, on educational expeditions to the Tower of London, to Hampton Court, to Greenwich Palace and to other places of historical interest.

In August of Coronation Year Queen Mary retired to Sandringham, and in September she stayed for varying lengths of time in four different country houses. While at Sandringham that August she went to a ball —described in her Diary as 'a most enjoyable entertainment'—given by Lord and Lady Cholmondeley at Houghton Hall: 'I actually took 2 or 3 turns in valses', wrote Queen Mary with legitimate satisfaction, for she was now seventy years of age. While at Sandringham the Queen had her mother's *Life* by Kinloch Cooke re-read to her: this was the official biography of the Duchess of Teck 'which came out about 1900',

---

* On obtaining her decree absolute, Mrs Ernest Simpson had reverted to her maiden name of Warfield.

noted Queen Mary, '—& which is most interesting & brings back to my mind many people & incidents.'[29]

All these activities, together with the unique brand of help and advice that she alone could give the King and Queen during their first months upon the throne, contributed to Queen Mary's own life a fresh sense of purpose. Once more she was conscious of supporting and serving the Crown. All the same, Queen Mary, now in the second year of her widowhood (and no longer wearing the mourning she disliked although it became her so well), was feeling the loss of her husband King George V more than ever. She had spent the first anniversary of his death—20 January 1937—at Sandringham: 'received', she recorded, 'many kind letters & flowers & was glad to be surrounded by the family—Went into his room.' In April 1937 Queen Mary attended two ceremonies in commemoration of the dead King. The first of these was the unveiling of the Brigade of Guards Memorial in the Guards Chapel, Wellington Barracks; the second was the unveiling, at Windsor, of the townspeople's Memorial to King George V designed by Lutyens and erected at the bottom of the Castle Hill. Both these ceremonies were performed by King George the Sixth.

During the three years 1937, 1938 and 1939, other monuments to the memory of the dead King were in the course of preparation. These included the statue destined to stand at Westminster, another statue which showed King George V in the robes which he had worn at the Delhi Durbar in 1912 and which was to be shipped to Calcutta, a plaque of the King's profile for Sandringham church and the fine recumbent effigy now in St George's Chapel, Windsor. Queen Mary was consulted about all these Memorials, and took a strong interest in them, particularly in the effigy for St George's Chapel, the commission for which had been given to Sir William Reid Dick by King Edward VIII and Queen Mary who shared the cost equally between them. During the progress of this work Queen Mary paid a whole series of visits to Sir William Reid Dick's studio. She also at this time gave him sittings to enable him to make an effigy of herself to be placed, after her death, beside that of King George V on what was to be their joint tomb. This project was dictated by Queen Mary's feeling for the chronologically appropriate, as well as by her common sense. 'I come of a long-lived family', she remarked—reflecting that her grandmother the Duchess of Cambridge had lived until the age of ninety-one, her Aunt Augusta Strelitz until ninety-four, her Uncle George Cambridge until ninety-three. Queen Mary's conclusion was that she herself might reasonably expect to live on into her tenth decade, and she was anxious that, should she do so, there should be no noticeable discrepancy in age between the appearance of King George V and of herself in their two effigies.

Sir William Reid Dick's work upon the monument of King George V was completed in February 1939, and the dead King's effigy was placed upon the new table-tomb prepared for it in the nave of St George's Chapel. In March the tomb was dedicated by Canon Deane of Windsor in the presence of Queen Mary, the King and Queen, the Duke and Duchess of Gloucester and the Duke and Duchess of Kent. A simple public announcement stated that the body of King George V had been removed from the Royal Vault at St George's and placed within the new tomb. Today the effigy of Queen Mary lies beside that of her husband, just as her coffin lies beside his coffin within the tomb.

Queen Mary had also commissioned, in February 1937, the gravestone of her sister-in-law Princess Victoria, who was buried in the new Family Burial Ground by the Mausoleum at Frogmore. Of King George V's three sisters, the whispering 'Wales cousins' of Queen Mary's youth, only her favourite sister-in-law, Queen Maud of Norway, was living. As we have seen, Queen Maud had shared Queen Mary's procession up the Abbey at the 1937 Coronation; she still came often to England to stay at her house in Norfolk, Appleton near Sandringham. Two years younger than Queen Mary, there was no reason to suppose that Queen Maud had not many more years of life before her, although like her sisters Princess Louise and Princess Victoria, and her brothers the Duke of Clarence and King George V, she had never shared Queen Mary's exceptional strength of constitution. In November 1938, however, Queen Maud of Norway died suddenly after an operation in a London nursing home. So soon as she heard that Queen Maud was ill, Queen Mary had hurried to Claridge's Hotel to see her, and had sat with her for several hours on the day before the operation. The operation, like all operations, was reported to have gone off well, but, three days after it, Queen Maud of Norway was dead:

Wet day [Queen Mary noted for Sunday, 20 November 1938]. At 9 to my consternation I received the news that darling Maud had died at 12.25 a.m. of heart failure, after the serious operation on Wed. last—I felt stunned at the tragic news as we had hoped she was improving.

Queen Maud had been christened in the Chapel at Marlborough House when her parents lived there as Prince and Princess of Wales, and so her body was brought back to the same Chapel after her death. Queen Mary received a telegram that day from the old Duke of Connaught, one of the three surviving children of Queen Victoria: 'My thoughts are with you today when dear Maud will be brought back to her old home to rest in the Chapel in which she was christened previous to her crossing the seas to the land of her adoption.' The next morning Queen Mary and other members of the Family followed Queen Maud's coffin to Victoria Station, whence it was taken by train to Portsmouth to be placed aboard a battle-cruiser for Oslo.

Queen Mary had now outlived her husband, his brother and their three sisters. She had seen two of her own three brothers die. In this rather isolated position within her own generation she leaned upon her brother Lord Athlone—the former Prince Alexander George of Teck—and on his wife Princess Alice, who had so much helped her during the abdication crisis; but Queen Mary was soon deprived of this support also, for Lord Athlone was appointed Governor-General of Canada some months after the outbreak of the Second World War of 1939–1945. The outbreak of this conflict, in early September 1939, had been preceded in this country by a long period of horrible anxiety, across which had flashed that illusory moment of hope known loosely to contemporaries as 'the time of Munich'.

VI

On 31 December 1937, Queen Mary looked back upon the past year with pleasure and forward to the new year with considerable zest. 'The last day of a very wonderful and interesting year', she had written in her Diary. 'We saw the interesting film "Marie Walewska" after dinner & at midnight sang *Auld Lang Syne* & had a snap dragon— Very nice being altogether.' Superficially Queen Mary had every reason to look forward to 1938, the year in which, as it turned out, the threat of immediate European war was temporarily averted at Munich. In 1936 she had been in mourning, and engaged in moving house; in 1937 she had been caught up in a whirl of Coronation excitements and festivities; 1938 would be the first full year of a new freedom which she had not known for decades. Marlborough House was now in perfect running order and filled with her collections as well as with what she lovingly called her 'little treasures'; she happily recorded that she gave five dinner-parties there in the spring of 1938. Queen

Mary was, as always, busy with her charities—first and foremost the London Hospital (which she termed 'my Hospital'). She also visited the Princess Mary Village Homes at Addlestone, the Governesses' Home she had founded long ago at Petersham, the Royal Cambridge Home for Soldiers' Widows and many other institutions. In the spring she paid several visits to Kew Gardens to admire the crocuses and the almond blossom, and later in the year she went, as usual, to Wimbledon. All this time she kept an intelligent eye upon events in Europe: 'We heard', she noted on 11 March 1938, 'that the Germans had made Austria's Chancellor resign (Schuschnigg) & that the Nazis had seized hold of the government—A pleasant state of affairs!'

Instead of going up to Balmoral, which she had never much enjoyed, Queen Mary had planned a whole series of country visits for herself that summer. She went to stay with the Duke and Duchess of Buccleuch at Boughton, she went to stay at Flete in the West Country, she stayed with Lady Byng at Thorpe Hall in Essex, and in September as well as going to Harewood she spent ten days, with her brother Lord Athlone and Princess Alice as her guests, at Holyrood in Edinburgh: 'I looked out of a window', she noted in her Diary of her arrival at Holyrood '& saw my Standard flying on the Palace of Holyrood House & felt very proud.'[30] 'I travelled 1687 miles in my car during this month', Queen Mary noted on 29 September, after her return to London from Badminton House.

Queen Mary's visit to her niece the Duchess of Beaufort* and her husband at Badminton in Gloucestershire—a house which the Queen had known since her girlhood, but with which she was shortly to become very much more closely acquainted—was curtailed by the international crisis over Czechoslovakia. 'The news from Germany disquieting', she noted on 24 September, 'so I determined to return to London on Monday.' On her arrival Queen Mary went to see the King and Queen and found them 'sad at turn of events in spite of PM's gallant attempts at peace—'.[31] The next day Queen Mary was fitted for her gas-mask, and listened on the wireless to her daughter-in-law the Queen launching the great Cunarder *Queen Elizabeth* at Glasgow: 'she made her speech admirably, Bertie's really', Queen Mary recorded, 'as owing to the crisis he was unable to accompany her. . . . Listened in to the PM's excellent but gloomy statement about the Crisis.'[32]

* Elder daughter of Queen Mary's eldest brother Lord Cambridge (previously second Duke of Teck and familiar in this narrative as 'Prince Dolly').

On 28 September Queen Mary went with the Duchess of Kent to the Ladies' Gallery at the House of Commons to hear Mr Chamberlain's further statement on the crisis. In common with everyone else in England, Queen Mary was horror-struck at the possibility of a new war, and she was moreover secretly convinced that, however victorious this country might be, a Second World War would spell the decline of the British Empire. She was, in consequence, as delighted as the majority of those in the House of Commons that day when Mr Chamberlain's speech was interrupted by Sir John Simon handing him a message from Hitler. This dramatic episode caught Queen Mary's imagination, and inspired her to a longer and more descriptive Diary entry than any she habitually made:

The P M's speech was clear & explained everything. As he was finishing Sir John Simon touched his arm & gave him a paper which he read & then he made the astonishing announcement that Hitler would see him again at Munich tomorrow & that Daladier & Mussolini wld also join them in order to find a way out of this dreadful *impasse*—It was a most dramatic & wonderful ending to the speech & the relief felt all round the house was remarkable & all the members of the Conservative & National Govt cheered wildly—I was myself so much moved I could not speak to any of the ladies in the Gallery, several of them, even those unknown to me seized my hand, it was very touching. Let us pray now that a lasting Peace may follow—I went to see Bertie—A most wonderful day—God be praised.33

During the next day of suspense, Queen Mary went to tea with the King 'but he had had no news from Munich so far'. Queen Mary also went to Hyde Park, where she had heard that trenches were being dug, for at that time it was still supposed that primitive earthworks such as these would protect the population of London from aerial attack: 'Went to Hyde Pk to see trenches being dug', Queen Mary noted, 'also the Dahlias in the usual border,* what a contrast! ditto in Regent's Pk.' The strain of these late autumn days proved too much for Queen Mary, Mr Chamberlain's triumphant return with Hitler's signature from Munich found her in bed with laryngitis: 'I heard the cheers', she wrote, '& then I listened to his arrival in Downing St. Very exciting.'34

* i.e. the border near Lancaster Gate, which at Queen Mary's suggestion had for some years been devoted to dahlias. This border forms but one example of the many innovations and improvements made in London's parks at the suggestion of Queen Mary.

It was at this moment that Queen Mary received a letter of congratulation on the Munich settlement from a most unexpected quarter; for, as we have already noticed earlier in this volume,* ex-Kaiser Wilhelm II picked up his indelible pencil at Doorn in Holland and wrote his cousin the British Queen Dowager a little heartfelt letter, dated 1 October 1938:

May I [wrote the ex-Kaiser] with a grateful heart relieved from a sickening anxiety by the intercession of Heaven unite my warmest sincerest thanks to the Lord with yours & those of the German & British People that He saved us from a most fearful catastrophe by helping the responsible statesmen to preserve Peace! I have not the slightest doubt that Mr N. Chamberlain was inspired by Heaven & guided by God who took pity on his children on Earth by crowning his mission with such relieving success. God bless him. I kiss your hand in respectful devotion as ever.

This was the first communication which any member of the British Royal Family had yet had with their exiled cousin. Queen Mary sent it on to King George VI, suggesting that he should show it to the Prime Minister and then consign it to the Archives at Windsor Castle. 'Poor William', she wrote, 'he must have been horrified at the thought of another war between our 2 countries. . . . I am sure you feel as angry as I do at people croaking as they do at the PM's action, for once I agree with Ly Oxford who is said to have exclaimed when she left the H. of Commons yesterday "He brought home Peace, why cant they be grateful"—It is always so easy for people to criticise when they do not know the ins & outs of the question.'35

Queen Mary and the former Kaiser were not alone in welcoming the Munich Agreement with relief and enthusiasm. Events proved this optimism unjustified; but for Queen Mary and for most of the peoples of the Empire, it seemed, that October of 1938, that the threat of general war was over.

VII

The opening days of 1939, a year destined to ruin finally all that the First World War had left of the Europe of Queen Mary's youth, found the Royal Family as usual at Sandringham. It was a snowy January, but the weeks passed happily enough for Queen Mary, who made an expedition to Lynn to buy snow-boots for her brother, visited one or two neighbours, and went to help Miss von Hanno, the devoted

* See page 289.

lady-in-waiting of the late Queen Maud of Norway, who was packing up Queen Maud's house, Appleton. Films were now shown regularly after dinner at Sandringham House; Queen Mary, who had the most positive views upon what she liked in the cinema, enjoyed, for instance, the film of Dr Cronin's novel *The Citadel*, but found *Alexander's Ragtime Band* 'very vulgar . . . horrid music or not what I call music'. On other evenings charades were acted, in all of which Queen Mary took part, and on one occasion she wrote that 'We ladies put on funny hats for dinner which was amusing'.[36] This holiday atmosphere was a last respite from the sombre anxiety which the international situation was once more causing, but even so the Royal Family were not allowed to forget the probable dangers that lay ahead: 'We watched ARP Exercise near York Cottage', Queen Mary noted on Saturday, 28 January. 'Most interesting.' On the first of February Queen Mary returned to Marlborough House: 'Took leave of dear Bertie & the family with much regret after spending 5 pleasant weeks at dear S.'

On 15 March Hitler seized Czechoslovakia. Two days later Mr Chamberlain denounced him as a perjurer in a famous speech at Birmingham. This was the signal for the commencement of that Diplomatic Revolution by which Great Britain abandoned 'splendid isolation' for a system of guarantees offered to threatened European nations. Queen Mary did not record the seizure of Czechoslovakia in her Diary, but she was greatly disturbed by the fate of King Zog and Queen Geraldine of Albania, when Mussolini snatched that small country in April 1939: 'We were horrified', she wrote, 'to hear that the Italians had kicked out Zog, King of Albania, & taken Albania with very little resistance. The poor Queen had to leave with her baby son of 2 days old.'[37] A fortnight before the collapse of Albania, Queen Mary had helped the King and Queen to entertain the President of the French Republic, Monsieur Lebrun, who, with his wife, was paying a state visit to this country. The President and Madame Lebrun went to tea at Marlborough House. Queen Mary attended the Buckingham Palace banquet for one hundred and ninety-six guests in their honour, as well as a dinner-party at the French Embassy which was followed by a performance of the ballet of the *Sleeping Beauty* at Covent Garden. The Covent Garden programme, Queen Mary noted with humour, was completed by the playing of 'a very dull piece by Debussy . . . & nearly everybody went to sleep!'[38]

A visit to Canada and to the United States had been arranged for King George VI and Queen Elizabeth for that May of 1939. In spite of the now self-evident fact that there was likely to be a European War, the King felt in duty bound to fulfil this obligation: 'I feel we must start for Canada on Saturday unless there is any really good reason as to why we should not', he wrote to Queen Mary.39 'I hate leaving here with the situation as it is, but one must carry on with one's plans as they are all settled, & Canada will be so disappointed.' Queen Mary and other members of the Family, including the two little Princesses, went down to Portsmouth to see the King and Queen off on what proved to be, owing to icebergs and fog, an adventurous and indeed a perilous transatlantic crossing. Queen Mary went on board the *Empress of Australia* and examined the Royal cabins with her careful eye for the details of comfort; she judged the cabins 'very nice'. 'We then took a tender farewell of them both & landed—The ship left punctually at 3—it was a fine sight from the jetty—& we waved handkerchiefs. Margaret said "I have my handkerchief" & Lilibet ansd. "To wave, not to cry"—which I thought charming. We all returned to London by train arriving at 5—'40 While they were in Canada, the King and Queen heard to their horror of Queen Mary's grave motor-car accident, which might well have converted the farewell at Portsmouth into a final one.

By an odd coincidence—of which she was herself aware—the very serious accident in which Queen Mary was involved in May 1939 occurred seventy years almost to the day after that in which her grand-mother Augusta, Duchess of Cambridge, had been nearly killed in her brougham upon the Kew Road in May 1869. In each case these ladies were seventy-one, and in each the Royal vehicle was overturned; but whereas the Duchess of Cambridge's brougham was hit by a hansom cab darting out from behind a market cart, modern progress had provided that Queen Mary's maroon-coloured Daimler limousine should be hit by a heavy lorry carrying a load of steel tubing. In the case of the Duchess of Cambridge's accident Her Royal Highness had been badly bruised, but her companion, Colonel Purves, died later, as we may recall, from the effects of lock-jaw from a wound in his leg. In the accident to Queen Mary's car, no one was killed. Travelling with her were Lord Claud Hamilton, her Comptroller, and Lady Constance Milnes Gaskell, her Woman of the Bedchamber; the Queen was just pointing out to Lord Claud that he had a caterpillar upon his trouser leg, when there was a thunderous crash of crunching metal, and the Queen, Lord Claud and Lady Constance found themselves lying in a heap against the broken windows of the overturned

Daimler: 'it was a wonder we 5 occupants* were not killed', wrote Queen Mary. 'We three were in a heap at the bottom of the car & we got out by the help of two ladders. We went for a short time to a Dr Revell's house in Wimbledon Pk Rd & then drove home in my big car which had been sent down—I was much bruised & suffered from shock, Claud had a bruised shoulder & Constance a black eye.'[41]

Queen Mary's behaviour on this occasion won the whole-hearted admiration of the London public, as well as of her fellow-victims in the motor-car. 'Nothing, perhaps, that Queen Mary has done on occasions of State or at private ceremonies, has ever become her so well as ... the manner of her leaving the wrecked car', Mr Louis Wulff has written in his 'authoritative portrait' of Queen Mary.[42] 'She joked with one of the workmen who helped her, and bent to adjust her dress before she was taken into a nearby house while doctors were informed by telephone.' 'She climbed up and down these ladders', wrote a witness, 'as if She might have been walking down the steps at the Coronation. She had not Her hat or one curl out of place. . . . The only outward sign of disorder was a broken hat pin and Her umbrella broken in half.'[43]

On her return to Marlborough House, Queen Mary was found to be not only very severely bruised and shaken, but to have an injury to her left eye from a piece of glass which had, in her own words, 'brushed off the film of the eye, a lucky escape'. To her Diary she admitted that her back 'hurt abominably', but she refused to remain in bed longer than ten days—one of which was her seventy-second birthday—and although she had always been 'rather an apprehensive passenger' in a car she absolutely refused to make any change in her motoring habits, or to allow the world to know how very close she had been to death.

VIII

The outbreak of war on 3 September 1939 found Queen Mary at Sandringham. She listened to Mr Neville Chamberlain's solemn statement that Sunday morning in the little Norfolk church of St Mary Magdalene, for the rector Mr Fuller had installed his wireless in the nave. 'Everyone was silent but it was a tense moment & one could only pray & hope.'[44] Like many other worshippers on that fell Sunday, Queen Mary was interrupted at her devotions by the test air-raid alarm which was sounded throughout England at about eleven-thirty.

* Five occupants with Queen Mary's chauffeur and her detective.

On 4 September she noted that 'an air raid signal at 2.45 drove us from our beds. I dressed hurriedly & descended with the help of Green (detective) to basement. The children* were there & behaved beauti- fully. At 3.30 we heard "All clear" so I returned to bed but not to sleep!' Later that morning Queen Mary left Sandringham, which she did not see again until 1945, for Badminton House, Gloucestershire, her home for the next five years.

The plan for Queen Mary to withdraw into the West Country in the event of war was one which had been prepared some time before, and which she had greeted with no enthusiasm. For her to leave London in war-time was not, she declared, 'at all the thing', for she looked upon it as a dereliction of duty. It was, however, explained to her by the King that in remaining at Marlborough House she would be causing needless trouble and anxiety, and so she agreed to accept the hospitality of her niece's husband, the Duke of Beaufort. Accordingly the Queen set off from Sandringham at twenty to ten on the morning of Monday 4 September, driving across country to Badminton which she reached at six o'clock that evening. 'My servants & luggage followed my cars—quite a fleet', she noted; for Queen Mary was taking with her the majority of her Marlborough House staff of sixty-three persons, together with their dependants. In the absence of the Duke of Beaufort, who had already joined his Regiment, Queen Mary was received by her devoted niece the Duchess who, while feeling it a privilege to house the Queen in this emergency, watched the arrival of her aunt's massive convoy with a certain apprehension.

Queen Mary, who had travelled via Peterborough, Oundle and Northampton to Althorp where Lord and Lady Spencer had given her luncheon, had then sped on, followed by her cavalcade of motor-cars, through Oxford, Swindon and Chippenham—'a lovely drive'. Not at all tired by eight hours and a half upon the road, Queen Mary began at once to settle down, and to arrange and organise the entirely new kind of life she would now be leading at Badminton House—life in the country.

* The two children of the late Duke and of the Duchess of Kent were staying at Sandringham House.

CHAPTER EIGHT

LIFE IN THE COUNTRY

FOR QUEEN MARY, at the age of seventy-two, life in the country was a totally new experience, for, as those who have followed the Queen's career thus far may have deduced, her interests, like her character, were not merely urban but of their very essence metropolitan. Queen Mary was, in fact, utterly innocent of country ways and country lore. White Lodge in Richmond Park had not been truly rustic, nor, for all its leafy lanes, was Kensington. At Sandringham, where the property was primarily organised for the shooting, Queen Mary had confined herself to the lawns and flower-gardens, save for the routine tour of the Home Farm on Sunday afternoons, and for shooting luncheons in a tent pitched at a point of vantage in some windswept ploughed field. As a girl she had never learned to ride as her cousins the Wales Princesses had done. She had sometimes owned a puppy when a child; a dog, Heather, given to her as a wedding present had soon been handed over to her husband. Abroad, we may recall, her youthful experience had been of stiff German court-life in cold and draughty *Schlösser* set amid gravel walks and formal beds of geranium and heartsease.

When Queen Mary had stayed with friends or relations in the country her hosts had been at pains to show her other historical houses, abbeys, ruins or gardens worthy of her notice and they would naturally never have bothered her with the details of their estate management nor of their farms. Thus, when she settled at Badminton House in September 1939 and remained resident there for six long years, Queen Mary was exposed to a novel atmosphere and offered a new range of experience which, after a certain bewildered hesitation, she accepted with her customary thoroughness and zest. Initially she felt at a loss in a *milieu* in which the paramount topics of conversation were crops, livestock, or the hunting-field. But Queen Mary was, as ever, anxious to learn. In those first September days she startled the Duchess of Beaufort, who was pointing out to her aunt a remarkable field of hay, by enquiring: 'So *that's* what hay looks like?' and closely examining the mysterious crop with her lively and alert blue eye.

Badminton is one of the finest among the great country-houses of the West of England. It is built of yellowish Cotswold stone and stands upon three sides of a square. The estate, which includes a park nine miles in circumference, was purchased by Lord Somerset of Cashel in 1600, passed from him to his kinsman the first Duke of Beaufort and has remained in the possession of the same family ever since. In the early eighteenth century the house was re-faced by the architect William Kent, who also altered the outline of its roofs. Twice painted by Canaletto, Badminton House contains these two pictures, as well as famous portraits by Allan Ramsay and Thomas Hudson, and many pictures and objects formerly belonging to Cardinal Alberoni. There is much good furniture and many thousand choice books housed in a lofty library whose shelves are topped by a parade of classical busts. There is a vast saloon designed by Wyatt, a smaller 'yellow drawing-room', a big dining-room and, on the first floor, two handsome 'State bedrooms' in the Chinese style. These Chinese rooms had been occupied by the Duchess of Teck and her daughter Princess May when they went to stay at Badminton in the later eighteen-eighties.

On adopting Badminton House for her own war-time use in September 1939, Queen Mary selected one of the many other bed-rooms on the first floor, with an adjacent sitting-room and bathroom and a splendid outlook across the park. As a dining-room she used the so-called 'Oak Room', lined with heavy, black diamond-shaped panelling of the Jacobean period removed from Raglan Castle when this was demolished in the nineteenth century. As a drawing-room for receiving those guests whom she did not invite up to her sitting-room, the Queen made use of the large former dining-room. The state drawing-rooms and bedrooms were closed for the duration of the war.

At first Queen Mary was frankly restless at Badminton. For this there were several obvious reasons. Firstly, she felt isolated from her immediate family—from the King and Queen, from her other children and from her grandchildren. She would ruefully compare her lot to that of the Birmingham evacuees in Badminton village, or to the soldiers torn from their home surroundings by the demands of war. Next, she felt cut off from London and from news of what was afoot; King George VI, who suspected that his mother might be feeling out of touch with events, gave instructions that Foreign Office news summaries should be sent down to Queen Mary in an official red leather despatch box of which she kept the key.* Thirdly, as we have seen, country life seemed strange to Queen Mary. Fourthly, she felt that for one of the first times in her life she was not being of use—and this at a moment of grave crisis for her country. 'I long to be at "Home",' Queen Mary wrote to a friend on 20 September, from Badminton.¹ 'I feel rather useless here but I can visit Evacuees & Work depots, they seem to like to see one which is a mercy!'

During the autumn and winter of 1939, and indeed right up until the moment when the air-raids of September 1940 made rail-travel awkward,† Queen Mary went to London almost weekly—to look in at Marlborough House, to see her dentist, to go to bookshops, art-dealers and exhibitions, and to lunch at Buckingham Palace where she often found the King and Queen. No exertion was too strenuous to achieve these expeditions: 'Up at 6.15 & drove to Chippenham to catch the 8.28 to London for the day—Arrived Paddington 10.30 . . . got back here by 6.25', she noted in her Diary of the first such sortie on 12 September 1939, when she had been installed and, as her Family had assumed, settled, at Badminton for just over a week: '. . . London looks very warlike, sandbags, ARP men with tin helmets & gas masks, Police ditto—windows boarded up etc.' 'It was curious to see all the precautions on the railway for the blackout', she observed of another journey to London, from which she had returned by a late train. 'From 7 till 8.15 we could not read as we only had a faint blue light—The moon was bright though—'³

As we know, it was not Queen Mary's habit to be idle. Within the shortest possible time of her arrival at Badminton she was hard at work—visiting evacuee children, neighbouring factories and work-shops, canteens and hospitals. In this period of what was rather optimistically called 'the phoney war'—'What a dreadful mysterious war', Queen Mary wrote in November 1939⁴—the Queen also em-barked upon an activity which engrossed more and more of her time and attention and which ended by greatly improving whole tracts of

* It was characteristic of Queen Mary's discretion that she neither mentioned these summaries to her entourage nor commented on them when returning the despatch boxes to London. The only intimation that the King's Private Secretary ever received that Queen Mary was reading the summaries was a note placed in an empty box in July 1943: 'From Mary R. The lock of this box is very stiff.'

† 'Here, we have constant air raid warnings, & much flying by night & day, but it is the same everywhere so we must not grumble', Queen Mary wrote on 18 October 1940.² '—I do not go to London now, as there & back takes 5 hours by train & one cannot make any appointments, it is simply waste of time.'

the Badminton estate. The first modest references in her Diary to this activity are dated 25 and 26 September 1939, and read:

Lovely morning which we spent clearing ivy off the trees in the grounds while Jack Coke* hacked off branches off 2 chestnut trees & an elm not far from the house & the gardeners began to clear a wall of ivy near Mary B's bedroom.

and:

Lovely morning which we spent clearing ivy off trees—We watched a whole wall of ivy of 50 years standing at the back of Mary B's bedroom being removed—most of it came down like a blanket—

Queen Mary's enmity towards ivy had long been proverbial at Sandringham, and she had never missed an opportunity to attack it wherever it appeared within the grounds. Badminton offered a wider field for this private battle against ivy—there was more of it to be attacked, it was older and stronger, and consequently, in Queen Mary's view, more destructive to stonework, brickwork and trees. She was soon busily engaged in the garden, from which her hosts tactfully diverted her farther afield to the long, low stone wall surrounding the estate. Her equerry, her current lady-in-waiting, her Private Secretary and anyone who was staying in the house were swiftly enrolled in the 'Ivy Squad'. Besides being useful and providing healthy exercise, this fight against ivy satisfied that urge to tidy up and to put in order which was, as we know, basic to Queen Mary's nature.

By September 1940, the Ivy Squad had so extended its range that it became a 'Wooding Squad'. Into this the Queen had incorporated first her own four despatch riders attached to her for the duration of the war, and then the men of the company of fighting troops which stood guard at Badminton to defend Queen Mary in the event of an invasion of this country by the Germans, or an enemy attempt to kidnap her by aeroplane. Amongst the Queen's immediate entourage the Wooding Squad, whose work was arduous in the extreme, aroused small enthusiasm; but, indefatigable and thorough, Queen Mary exacted from her Household the same effort which she threw into the work herself. Her Diaries contain many entries recording the progress of the squad's work, as well as notes of future projects: 'After luncheon

---

* Major the Hon. Sir John Coke, K C V O (1880–1958), served as equerry to Queen Mary from 1938 until her death.

walked with C., J.C. & Major Rooke* to look at an overgrown plan-tation opposite Watson's house, which they want our wood "Squad" to clear out—It may be an interesting job—we picked up chestnuts later', for example; or 'Went for a walk to see the spinney near the Allan Grove which Master† wants us to thin out for him—I think it will be amusing to do.':

At first, to save petrol, Queen Mary insisted on proceeding to the more distant working sites in a farm-cart, drawn by two horses and con-taining a couple of basket chairs for herself and her Lady. 'Aunt May', remarked her niece, 'you look as if you were in a tumbril!' 'Well, it may come to that yet, one never knows', Queen Mary answered happily as the cart jolted off. Subsequently the Queen made use of her old green Daimler car, in which she would set off after luncheon each day, hack-saws and other equipment tied on to the back. Among the durable results of this portion of Queen Mary's war-time presence at Badminton is 'Queen Mary's Plantation' of young firs, no less than sixteen and a half acres in extent and occupying ground cleared solely by the Queen and her Wooding Squad.

Another aspect of local war-work in which Queen Mary became strongly interested was the salvage campaign. Already in the First World War she had inspired the schoolchildren round Sandringham to collect empty bottles. Now that the need was urgent, and the call for salvage was being made upon a national scale, she set to with a will. 'Very cold dull day', Queen Mary noted in her Diary for 19 December 1939. 'We began the Salvage, namely we searched round the walls of the Vicarage Walk & Kennel Drive, for old bottles, old tins, & scrap iron, we were most successful & filled over a wheel-barrow full—We are doing this at the request of the Ministry of Supply—& I hope to start it in all the villages in the neighbourhood.' 'Some of the [Birmingham evacuee] children came to help', she recorded of another salvage operation, '& we salvaged old bones, tins etc., evidently an old rubbish heap—while others cut down elders—I raked away a lot of rubbish.'[6] 'Went to see Mr Lewis's splendid dump of scrap iron in the timber yard', she wrote in March 1940; and, a few days later, 'to see . . . the Slaites Quarry where the Salvage dump is—to the Vicarage to see the paper dump, to the Portcullis to see the

* i.e. Lady Cynthia Colville, Sir John Coke, and the officer commanding the troops at Badminton.

† Queen Mary's niece's husband, the tenth Duke of Beaufort, known to his family and friends as 'Master'.

bottle dump.'⁷ Her enthusiasm for salvaging scrap iron, combined with her ignorance of country habits, occasionally carried Queen Mary away: and several times the green Daimler would return loaded with field harrows and other implements which farmers usually leave out in their fields in all weathers, and which Queen Mary espying had concluded to be discards ready for the scrap dump. In these cases the objects were quietly returned to their owners without the Queen's knowledge.

In the time not absorbed by wooding and by salvage, by visiting factories and hospitals, by helping sell at 'bring-and-buy' sales or serving tea in the troops' canteen, by taking part in sing-songs and attending Ensa performances in the recreation hut of her guard company, by calling on villagers and their evacuee guests, Queen Mary occupied herself at Badminton in many ways. She sorted her parents' papers, as well as those of the Somerset family; she named old photographs and took them out of their frames to place in portfolios; she read certain books and listened while many others were read to her; she worked at her tent-stitch embroidery; she put in order her own series of box-files containing miscellaneous historical information which she labelled 'Interesting Notes'; she re-read and annotated her old Diaries. In addition to all this Queen Mary delved into the Somerset archives and checked through eighteenth-century Badminton inventories, searching the house to identify pictures and *objets d'art* recorded in them. Friends like the Archbishop of Canterbury, Sir George Arthur or the Spanish Representative in London, the Duke of San Lucar, would come to spend the night at Badminton, while members of Queen Mary's family visited her whenever their war-time duties allowed. The most frequent, and perhaps the most welcome of these family visitors, was Queen Mary's youngest son Prince George, Duke of Kent. His mother found the Duke of Kent increasingly congenial. They had in common a passion for collecting, and they would together make expeditions to the antique shops of Bath. The Duke of Kent was able to go to Badminton more often than other members of his family, for, as an Air Commodore in charge of the welfare of Royal Air Force units, he made several tours of inspection in the West Country. To Queen Mary his visits to Badminton were a source of sparkling joy.

II

Such, then, was the busy, useful life which Queen Mary contrived for herself at Badminton House, and upon which she entered with courage and with high spirits reminiscent of her girlhood at White Lodge. Her interest in all local happenings, her patent enjoyment of the simplest country pastimes, her consideration for others, the energy and humour with which she dragooned her Wooding Squad endeared her to all upon the Badminton estate. Her four despatch riders, who had begun by being scary of responsibility for so famous a Royal personage, quickly came to regard the Queen with personal affection; they recall the wiles Queen Mary would employ to discover the dates of their birthdays so as to give them surprise birthday presents, or the way in which she handed round cigarettes during the short break in a 'wooding' afternoon, chatting to them about her family or theirs as she stood amongst them, herself smoking a cigarette. The devotion which Queen Mary inspired at Badminton was a sheer triumph of personality, and it compensated for much that she had lost by leaving London.

Admirable, too, and vigorous, was Queen Mary's attitude to air-raids: 'We were all furious', she wrote after one particularly bad night of broken sleep, and she soon ceased 'descending' as she called it to a reinforced room on the ground floor used as a shelter, where, in the earlier period of night air-raid alarms, Queen Mary might be found at three a.m.—perfectly dressed and sitting bolt upright solving a crossword puzzle—by other members of the household who arrived dishevelled in their dressing-gowns and half-asleep. Owing to its proximity to Bristol, and to the Admiralty organisations at Bath, Badminton received a constant series of alerts by day and night in 1940, when enemy bombers were heading for those cities. 'Went for a short walk', Queen Mary recorded in July 1940,[8] '& were pursued by one of the sentries who told us there was a Red warning so we hurried indoors—What times we are living in!' In August of the same year Queen Mary was caught at Marlborough House by a day-time air-raid warning: 'Another red warning but I paid no attention & went on doing the various things which I had to do.'[9] In 1940 Marlborough House suffered severely from blast on more than one occasion: 'Marl. Hse', wrote Queen Mary in October 1940, 'has every window broken & doors bashed in—The dear old House cannot stand much more of this, & I tremble each day for news of it's having succumbed! not a cheerful outlook—'[10] It was on 16 October 1940 that Marlborough

House had suffered in 'very bad bombing': a week later more of Queen Mary's collections were moved down to the comparative safety of Badminton: 'A van arrived late in the afternoon with some of my pictures and china from Marl. Hse.', the Queen noted on 25 October. 'When packing things into the van bombs went off, & the men had to take shelter—I am thankful I have the things here—.' Queen Mary's jewels, and some of her most valuable possessions, had been placed in strong boxes in the Sally Port at Windsor Castle. 'What a lot of trouble & expense that hateful fiend has put us to!' Queen Mary wrote when asking that this arrangement should be made, 'how I hate the Germans!'[11] 'We are all miserable at the destruction of the Guildhall, of so many lovely Wren churches & of so many interesting buildings, what a horrible enemy we are fighting against', she wrote, from Badminton, in January 1941. 'I did not realise that I could really *hate* people as I do the Germans, tho' I never liked them.'[12]

With the spring of 1940 Queen Mary's hatred of Hitler and the Nazis, like that of many millions of other people in Europe and in Great Britain, was increasing hour by hour. 'I was horrified to hear that the Germans had occupied Copenhagen & that Norway had declared war on Germany in consequence of their having landed troops in various Norwegian ports—', the Queen wrote on 9 April 1940. 'What a vile enemy, I feel very bitter—Poor Christian of Denmark and poor Charles of Norway.' 'Lovely day', she noted on 10 May. 'Heard that Belgium & Holland had been invaded! What a dreadful enemy . . . we heard later that Lille, Brussels, The Hague & Calais had been bombed & that incendiary bombs had been dropped on Canterbury. . . .'[13] A week later there arrived at Badminton a telegram announcing that the Duchess of Beaufort's brother, Queen Mary's nephew the popular Lord Frederick Cambridge, was a battle casualty; Lord Frederick's death was confirmed on 28 May, the day that King Leopold of the Belgians surrendered his country to the Germans.

During the next few weeks Queen Mary drove about the military camps of the neighbourhood, inspecting contingents of men back from Dunkirk, buying for them shirts and socks wholesale in Bath, and doing all she could to help. On 10 June the Queen recorded Italy's declaration of war, and on 17 June the fact that the French had capitulated. On this latter day Queen Mary was in London and, after lunching at Buckingham Palace, went to look at the Women Artists' Exhibition in the Piccadilly Galleries and to Bumpus's bookshop to see the Agnes Strickland relics then on display there. Throughout this desperate period in the fortunes of her country, Queen Mary remained perfectly confident: 'a terrible blow but we must not be disheartened' was her comment on King Leopold's behaviour—and 'disheartened' Queen Mary never once allowed herself to be.

Soon after the fall of France it had been decided that in the case of invasion Queen Mary would be safer at Windsor Castle. On 19 June she wrote sadly that she was 'very sorry to abandon Badminton & its kind inmates—Packed & put things together'; but the following morning the Queen determined not to move. 'Decided on my own responsibility to remain here, anyhow for the present as Windsor being defended sounded so depressing.'14 'The Raids are tiresome', she told a friend in mid-July, 'but in a way I am more independent here, than I shld be at Windsor which is an armed Camp!'*15. Her decision once taken Queen Mary stayed on at Badminton, watching with lively interest the progress of the local anti-invasion precautions: 'At 3.15 by car to the Slaites', she noted, for example, on 20 July 1940, 'where about 40 men & boys from the village were digging holes in 2 large fields to place poles in to prevent enemy aeroplanes from landing—the holes had to be dug 5 feet deep & as there was a good deal of stone in the fields it made digging difficult—I visited many of the holes & talked to the men who were digging.' Queen Mary was also interested in a clutch of unexploded bombs which fell in a potato patch behind the post office in Badminton Village, and which was disposed of by a bomb unit from Bristol. She examined the craters left by the explosion, gave the officers and men an audience and 'complimented them on having done their job'. That summer of the Battle of Britain found Queen Mary, in fact, unperturbed and game for any contingency.

It was at this period, when one hundred and twenty men of the Gloucestershire Regiment had been billeted in the Badminton stables as a guard for the Queen in the event of German invasion, that, as mother of the Regiment's Colonel-in-Chief, the Duke of Gloucester, Queen Mary began to wear the Regiment's famous 'fore and aft' cap-badge in her hat. Typically, she wished to verify the origin of this double cap-badge, which was said to date from the battle of Alexandria in 1801: 'can you verify this for me?' Queen Mary wrote to the Librarian at Windsor Castle. 'It was then the french attacked them in the flank & the rear rank turned their caps to the back to show they were not running away since when they wear their badge both front & back "fore & aft", a sphinx with laurel leaves. I am allowed to wear

* The King and Queen were living at Windsor Castle at this time.

the badge, so the aft is pinned at the back of my hat!'[16] Not even the threat of an enemy invasion could deflect Queen Mary's mind from a subject for her historical curiosity. It was not that the Queen discounted or belittled the danger of invasion: 'in case of invasion', she wrote, 'I do *not* wish to become a prisoner of Hitler as you can imagine—.'[17]

The threat of invasion receded with the British air victory known to history as the Battle of Britain; and Queen Mary was able to celebrate her second Christmas at Badminton by going to the Canteen Hut to give 'small presents in a bran tub to the Detachment here after which some of the men regaled us with a "Sing Song" which was great fun'.

'Goodbye to the old Year which has not been a pleasant one', Queen Mary wrote, in an access of understatement, on the last page of her Diary for the year 1940. 'We pray this new year may bring us Peace—'

III

The pattern of Queen Mary's daily life at Badminton was now set. It was altered only by bad weather or by her hay-fever and occasional colds in the head. Even bad weather was not permitted to deprive the Queen of exercise, in which she firmly believed: 'Rained all day on top of slushy snow', she recorded in January 1941. 'Dick* & I walked on a sanded path I had had made between the 2 conservatories, we walked like 2 caged lions or bears for nearly an hour! The air was good & it was not very cold—.'[18] Although, as the many photographs of Queen Mary at Badminton demonstrate, she never really managed to look countrified, the Queen's knowledge of country things was increasing steadily: her Diaries are now sprinkled with words like 'withybed' and by the harvest-time of 1941 she even went so far as to comment on the state of various crops which she had examined in their respective fields. The work of the Wooding Squad continued: New Year's Day 1941 was occupied in working 'in Stride's coppice ... many of the children coming with us—we liked the new place which is well worth clearing out'. Later in the same year the tangled undergrowth in front of Worcester Lodge—a charming Kent gatehouse containing a small banqueting chamber in stucco—attracted Queen Mary's notice: 'Worked at W.L. in afternoon in a new place which is

---

* Major the Hon. Sir Richard Molyneux, KCVO (1873–1954), was Groom-in-Waiting to King George V from 1919 to 1936 and served as Extra Equerry to Queen Mary from 1936 until her death.

in a great muddle—dead thorns & elderberries—I hope we shall be able to manage it.'[19] The Queen continued her visits to factories and hospitals, and to the bombed areas of Bristol and Bath. She recorded bleakly in her Diary the swift succession of calamities which overtook the British and the Americans in the Far East.

In the year 1942, that of her seventy-fifth birthday, Queen Mary had arranged to pay a couple of visits to Windsor Castle—the first, in March, for the confirmation of Princess Elizabeth (whom her grandmother thought 'looked so nice in white with a small veil & was quite composed'[20]) the second for the christening on 4 August of the Duke and Duchess of Kent's third child and second son, Prince Michael, who had been born that July. The christening Queen Mary voted 'a successful day', on which she had seen 'lots of old friends, servants etc.', as well as many of her royal relations driven from their own countries by the Nazi invaders.[21] Nine days after the christening, Queen Mary motored to Coppins, the former home of her sister-in-law, Princess Victoria, who had left the house to the Duke of Kent in her will. This was a particularly satisfactory visit: 'The baby is sweet— Had luncheon & tea there—Walked in the garden—Georgie showed me some of his interesting things.'[22] The happy, cultivated family life of the Duke and Duchess of Kent, each of them in their own way so vital and good-looking, gave Queen Mary especial pleasure: 'he looked so happy with his lovely wife & the dear baby', she wrote of that day with her youngest son.[23]

On the morning of 25 August, a Tuesday of heavy and continuous rain, Queen Mary went over to Lord Methuen's house, Corsham Court, to listen to a lecture given in the great picture-gallery there in connection with the National Association of Girls' Training Corps. The Queen afterwards looked at the pictures in the gallery, and at some of the other rooms, returning to Badminton for luncheon. The long, wet afternoon was spent arranging photographs with Lady Cynthia Colville in Queen Mary's huge scarlet folio albums. After tea Lady Cynthia read aloud to the Queen, who did her needlework. After dinner a telephone message came through from Balmoral to tell Queen Mary that the Duke of Kent was dead.

The Duke of Kent, who was thirty-nine, had been killed instantaneously when the aeroplane in which he was travelling to inspect RAF establishments in Iceland had smashed into a hillside at Morven, on the Duke of Portland's Langwell estate in North-West Scotland, and burst into flames. Once Queen Mary had recovered from the first shock—'I felt so stunned by the shock I could not believe it', she wrote[24]—her immediate thought was for her daughter-in-law, and so she set off the next morning for Coppins to try to comfort the Duchess of Kent. The Duke's funeral took place in St George's Chapel on 29 August; to attend this Queen Mary spent her first night away from Badminton since the beginning of the war. The Duke's coffin, covered by his Standard, lay during the night of the twenty-eighth to the twenty-ninth of August in the Memorial Chapel, which contains the monuments of two other English Princes who had endured early death —Queen Victoria's son Prince Leopold, Duke of Albany, and her grandson, Prince Albert Victor, Duke of Clarence.

Never, perhaps, in her whole life, did Queen Mary display more Christian fortitude or a greater power of self-control than over the death of the Duke of Kent. All her thoughts were concentrated upon her son's widow and his children. The stoicism which early sorrows had taught Queen Mary she now once more summoned to her aid. On the way back to Badminton from the funeral—a journey accomplished in a fearful thunderstorm—the Queen gave a lift in her limousine to 'a charming young American parachutist, most friendly', and to 'a nice Sergeant Observer (Air Force) who had taken part in the raid on Dieppe last week',[25] and succeeded in talking to both of them in her natural, amiable way. The next few days were spent in opening and answering letters and telegrams. On 2 September, with the courage of despair, Queen Mary resumed her wooding activities, aided this time by the Princess Royal who had come to stay with her mother for some days. 'We worked very well & it did us both good—I am so glad I can take up my occupations again—Georgie wld have wished me to do so', wrote Queen Mary with heartbroken simplicity.[26]

IV

The lift in her motor-car which Queen Mary had given to the American parachutist and the English Sergeant Observer during her drive back from Windsor to Badminton on the day of the Duke of Kent's funeral was not a solitary occurrence. As soon as she had grasped the idea that she could thus help members of the Forces whom her motor passed trudging along the roads, Queen Mary had given orders to her despatch riders and to her chauffeur that they should stop and invite any pedestrian soldier, sailor or airman into her car. She felt that she was in this way being of practical use; but these chance encounters had another, unexpected, result—they taught Queen Mary much that she had never had an opportunity of learning about the average life of the average young. Members of her Household agree that during the Badminton period Queen Mary became more democratic than ever before, and that she benefited enormously by her glimpses of the ordinary, everyday life of England from which, ever since her marriage, she had been shut off by the screen of Royal protocol.

Queen Mary stayed on at Badminton until the Allied victory in Europe was complete, returning to Marlborough House on 11 June 1945. She followed the fortunes of war with avid interest and a buoyant optimism: 'Dull day', she noted, for instance, of 5 June 1944. 'Heard that the Allies have entered Rome—Hooray!—To the wood.' On 'VE Day', the 8th of May 1945, Queen Mary listened to broadcasts by the King and by the Prime Minister, Mr Churchill, and also to the full-throated crowds cheering the King and Queen outside Buckingham Palace. Her day ended with an evening visit to the Portcullis Club in the local public house, 'where the Village was celebrating. We sang songs, a friendly affair and amusing.'[27]

When the time came for Queen Mary to leave Badminton House for London—a day to which theoretically she had been looking forward for years—the Queen had tears in her eyes. She had come to love the life of Gloucestershire, and she had been loved in return. Never since her youth as Princess May of Teck had she enjoyed such freedom as at Badminton. Before leaving, Queen Mary gave separate audiences to the nine Heads of Departments on the Duke of Beaufort's estate. Tears streaming down her face, she handed to each a valuable and carefully chosen present. 'Oh, I *have* been happy here!' she said to one of them. 'Here I've been anybody to everybody, and back in London I shall have to begin being Queen Mary all over again.'

U

CHAPTER NINE

A LONDON SUNSET

———————

T WO MONTHS before the actual day of her return to London—11 June 1945—Queen Mary had begun systematically preparing for it. At Badminton that April she was already looking out 'a number of pictures etc sent here from Marl. Hse in 1940 & 1941 which are to go back now'.[1] On 3 May she noted: 'Heard that Rangoon had fallen, also Hamburg. Began packing up my things.'

In the great ground-floor reception rooms at Marlborough House, which had been damaged by blast, ceilings were down, doors blown from their hinges and most of the windows were boarded up and had no glass. None the less Queen Mary had made a series of expeditions to her house that spring to assess which parts of it could most swiftly be made habitable, and by 31 May she found that her own suite of rooms on the first floor was 'beginning to look quite nice' again. Mahogany, satinwood and lacquered furniture, Chinese and European porcelains, 'treasures' of agate and lapis and gold were now emerging from what Queen Mary termed their 'hide-outs', and were welcomed by their proud owner with affectionate excitement and with the pleasurable shock of recognition. 'It is such a joy to be at "home" again at last', Queen Mary wrote to Sir Owen Morshead when she had been settled back at Marlborough House a week.[2] 'I am gradually unpacking all my things, but cannot arrange them, as all the windows in my drawing rooms library and dining room are still out with little hope of their being mended yet.* I am writing in the garden, so nice.' 'Unpacked lots of things' is now a daily entry in Queen Mary's Diaries; 'arranged books in my boudoir, so the room looks more furnished' she also notes, or 'Mr Sparks came in the evening to help me to rearrange the Chinese cabinet'.[3] The garden at Marlborough House benefited at this time from Queen Mary's Badminton activities.

---

* In the period immediately after the war, window-glass, like all other building materials, fuel, food and clothing, was so hard to obtain that, for Londoners, only the cessation of bombardment gave convincing proof that the war was over.

'Jack Coke & I did some gardening in my garden here & tidied some of the shrubs', Queen Mary recorded in October.4 Queen Mary's jewels also returned to Marlborough House, whence they had been taken to the Sally Port at Windsor Castle in 1940: 'interesting', Queen Mary wrote, 'to see them again.'5 Distinguished foreign visitors began to call at Marlborough House almost as soon as the Queen Dowager's personal Standard was broken from the rooftop; the first of these was General Eisenhower, who was received in audience on the very day following that of Queen Mary's return: 'such a nice man, he came over here to receive the Freedom of the City'.6

Although it was not until more than a year later, in October 1946, that the famous Saloon at Marlborough House was ready to receive its furniture, this will be a convenient moment to consider more fully than we have yet been able to do the nature and the quality of Queen Mary's collections, some part of which were shown to the public after her death in a memorial exhibition opened at the Victoria and Albert Museum on 26 May 1954.7

Under Queen Mary's auspices, the Victorian alterations made at Marlborough House by her parents-in-law during their long tenancy as Prince and Princess of Wales had in the main been abolished, until the Saloon, the large Red and smaller Green Drawing-Rooms and the State Dining-Room looked much as they must have done when Sir Christopher Wren handed over the completed house to its first owners, the Duke and Duchess of Marlborough in 1710. In Queen Mary's day the central Saloon was hung with fine Brussels tapestries of the mid-eighteenth century, work of the brothers van der Borcht and Peter van den Heck from designs of rustic life by David Teniers the Younger. The Saloon provided a setting for the five imposing pieces of mahogany furniture with carved and gilt enrichments and lion-headed consoles formerly at Rokeby Hall in Yorkshire, and of which at least three pieces are attributable with certainty to the eighteenth-century English cabinet-maker Vile. The room also contained two black lacquer cabinets with Chinese scenes upon the doors and sides, and a pair of cabinets of English or Dutch nineteenth-century origin inlaid with various woods illustrating household objects. A tortoiseshell and gilt brass French eighteenth-century clock, two powder-blue Chinese vases with ormolu mounts, and a pair of bronze statuettes after the Marly horses by Coustout the Elder were among the lesser ornaments of the Saloon.

Passing from the Saloon to the two drawing-rooms, you found gilt side-tables, more lacquer cabinets, a French eighteenth-century cabinet of tortoiseshell inlaid with over four hundred pieces of engraved mother-of-pearl, as well as vitrines filled with a quantity of English and continental porcelain of the eighteenth and nineteenth centuries, with Queen Mary's unrivalled collection of objects in piqué-work, with such bibelots as gold musical-boxes and jewelled watches, with snuff-boxes of crystal or agate or tortoiseshell or glass or lacquer mounted in gold, with *étuis*, with patch-boxes, with scent-bottles of porcelain, rock crystal and agate, with enamels made in Battersea or in Berlin. The general effect was fastidious, rich and, in the main, eighteenth century. The pictures and miniatures were almost exclusively Family portraits: two Allan Ramsays of George III, another of Augusta, Princess of Wales, a picture of Queen Charlotte with the castle of Strelitz in the background, enamels of William IV and of George IV as Prince of Wales. The rooms, like all Queen Mary's rooms, were always filled with flowers in and out of season—white and mauve lilac, roses, delphiniums, sweet-pea, and Queen Mary's favourite flower, lily-of-the-valley.

In the midst of this shimmering Georgian enclave in bedraggled post-war London, visitors found Queen Mary herself, upright, distinguished, dressed perhaps in blue velvet or in pale grey, around her neck her ropes of matchless pearls. Awed strangers spoke of Queen Mary at Marlborough House as representative of another epoch, but this was a misjudgement, for the Queen Dowager was in no way isolated, a magnificent relic, in these eighteenth-century surroundings. She would sally forth from Marlborough House to listen to the proceedings at a court for juvenile delinquents—'It was most interesting but I have never heard so many lies told in my life'[8]—or to enjoy *Oklahoma* or *Annie Get Your Gun*.

From the downstair reception rooms, a small comfortable lift upholstered in rose-red brocade carried the Queen up to her own private suite of rooms, situated on the first floor. The windows of her large bedroom looked west over St James's Palace and south over the Mall. Her sitting-room, which led out of it, was, comparatively, small, its walls hung with blue-grey silk, upon which Queen Mary had placed portraits of her husband King George V, an oil-sketch by Frith of her mother-in-law, Queen Alexandra, and a Gainsborough picture of Queen Charlotte, as well as the oval Winterhalter portrait of the Duchess of Teck, and the portrait of her Aunt Augusta which the old Grand Duchess had sent to her niece as a birthday present in the year of King George V's Coronation, 1911. On the mantelpiece were cassolettes of Blue John with ormolu mounts by Matthew Boulton, and vases of blue quartz with ormolu mounts. A late eighteenth-century French bracket-clock surmounted by a trophy of arms, and a large satinwood book-case holding some of Queen Mary's best books were also against the walls. The furniture consisted of two settees and of painted satinwood chairs, the seats embroidered by Queen Mary, a gilt armchair, the seat, back and arms of which were also embroidered by the Queen, and, in the very centre of the room, facing the doors into the bedroom, a large rosewood writing table with gilt brass mounts. This writing table was constantly used by Queen Mary, and it was estimated by a housemaid, one of whose duties it was to dust this desk, that there were upwards of ninety single objects upon it, including two candlesticks and an ink-stand in jasper-ware in the manner of Wedgwood. A small work-table held ivory utensils, while other tables were laden with Royal seals cut in topaz mounted in gold, memorial rings of members of the Royal Family, miniatures and photographs of the Queen's children, cameos and Fabergé animals of platinum, diamonds and gold. In a show-case against one of the walls were the superb series of gold boxes which had belonged to King George V, as well as a part of Queen Mary's own collection of these boxes, which, often misnamed snuff-boxes, have a framework of gold into which lapis, bloodstone, chalcedony and other precious materials have been fitted. The most magnificent box in Queen Mary's possession was of bloodstone with gold mounts encrusted with diamonds, and made at Potsdam in the reign of Frederick the Great, probably as a present from that Monarch to the Empress Catherine of Russia. Amongst the numerous other items in this sitting-room were a rose-quartz Buddha with jewelled head and hands which could be set in motion, a miniature piano in Siberian jade, and a crystal swan, dated 1911, on a lapis-lazuli base.

Queen Mary's private dining-room was decorated with water-colour paintings of flower-gardens, a needlework picture of George III and Queen Charlotte with their children after Zoffany, a mahogany book-case dated 1755 with pediment top and mirror panels, more Blue John, and a portion of her excellent collection of Chelsea, as well as a remarkably complete travelling service of Ludwigsburg porcelain in its original case, given by the Queen's ancestor Duke Karl Eugen of Württemberg to the French Ambassador to his court in 1772.

Except for short summer-time and Christmas visits to Norfolk, it

was in this atmosphere of taste and comfort that Queen Mary passed
the seven years that now remained to her of life on earth.

II

Starved of picture galleries, exhibitions and theatres, Queen Mary
took up the London round once more with vigour and with relish.
Hardly a day passed that she did not visit some gallery or dealer, or
go to see how the staff of the Wallace Collection or the Victoria and
Albert Museum were getting on with their 'unpacking'. London welcomed Queen Mary back with enthusiasm: 'on seeing me the people
gave many cheers!'9 she would record, with her diffident satisfaction.
As usual, everything that happened aroused her interest, and when a
huge unexploded bomb—christened 'Annie' by its disposal squad—
was finally blown up in St James's Park in April 1946, the Queen
walked across with Princess Alice to study the crater and to discuss
the strength of the explosion with the bomb-disposal men. She watched
the Victory Parades and peace celebrations with sympathetic attention,
although she felt disillusioned when she realised that peace had not
brought security.

In this final phase of her life at Marlborough House, Queen Mary
entertained seldom. She began to find that she could no longer stay
up late at night. Princess Alice and Lord Athlone stayed with her on
their visits from Canada, and she also gave hospitality to her daughter
the Princess Royal and to the Duke of Windsor. It was on Friday,
5 October 1945 that Queen Mary at length saw her eldest son again:
'Lovely day', she recorded. 'Lunched with Bertie who arrived this
morning from Balmoral. At 4 *David* arrived by plane from Paris on
a visit to me—I had not seen him for nearly 9 years! it was a great
joy meeting again, he looked very well—Bertie came to dinner to
meet him.' With her customary unswerving consistency of mind,
Queen Mary would never go so far as to meet her eldest son's wife,
but when the Duchess was ill in New York in February 1951, the
Queen wrote to the Duke: 'I feel so sorry for your great anxiety about
your wife, and am thankful that so far you are able to send a fair
account so we must hope the improvement will continue. Do write
me a short account of what has really happened.'10

On 31 January 1947, Queen Mary accompanied to Portsmouth the
King and Queen, who, with the two Princesses, were embarking for
their visit to South Africa. After examining the cabins in HMS

Vanguard, which she found were partly furnished with fittings from the old Royal Yacht *Victoria and Albert*, Queen Mary 'took a sad farewell' and returned to London by train. During the King's absence in South Africa there occurred the gravest fuel crisis since the war; although Queen Mary was not one of the three Counsellors of State appointed to take over the Monarch's duties during his absence abroad* she saw the Prime Minister weekly during the crisis, and was of great assistance to her third son the Duke of Gloucester† as well as to Mr Attlee. After three months the King and his Family returned to England from their successful tour, and Queen Mary went to welcome them at the Palace on the 12th of May. On 26 May, Queen Mary realised with something of a shock that she was eighty years old. The eulogies of herself in the newspapers, a special film of her career, a programme devoted to her favourite airs on the BBC all pleased her but combined to bring home to Queen Mary that her expectation of life was on the wane. She stoutly resented the onset of old age: 'so tiresome getting old!!!' she wrote, and 'It is a great bore getting old!!!'[11] Among a number of festivities arranged to celebrate this birthday was a small party which Queen Mary herself gave to old friends at Marlborough House. At this entertainment, for which she wore a pink dress embroidered with thousands of beads, the Queen was presented with a dark blue enamel and gold *étui*. Thanking her friends for this communal gift, Queen Mary shyly made one of the rare speeches of her life.

The engagement, in July 1947, of Princess Elizabeth to Prince Philip of Greece pleased Queen Mary: 'Heard with great pleasure of darling Lilibet's engagement to Philip Mountbatten', she wrote on 10 July. 'They both came to see me after luncheon looking radiant.' She gave her granddaughter the jewellery which had comprised her own chief wedding-present in July 1893. The fifty-fourth anniversary of this distant day had just gone by: 'Nearly all the members of our family, who were present on that occasion are no more', Queen Mary noted sadly.[12] Queen Mary thoroughly enjoyed her granddaughter's wedding. On 18 November she went to an evening party at Bucking-

---

* Under the then existing Regency Act, Queen Mary was not, as Queen Mother, eligible as a Counsellor of State, although she had been so while Queen Consort. By the new Regency Act of 1953, Her Majesty Queen Elizabeth the Queen Mother became eligible as a Counsellor.

† Who, with the Princess Royal and her son Lord Lascelles, had been appointed Counsellors of State.

ham Palace: 'Saw many old friends, I stood from 9.30 till 12.15 a.m.!!! not bad for 80.'

The birth of Prince Charles in November 1948 gave Queen Mary a fresh interest: 'I am delighted at being a great grandmother!' On 15 December she attended the child's christening in the Music Room at Buckingham Palace. 'I gave the baby a silver gilt cup & cover which George III had given to a godson in 1780', she recorded, '—so that I gave a present from my gt grandfather, to my great grandson 168 years later—'¹³

Excitement over the birth and christening of Prince Charles was, however, modified by anxiety about the health of his grandfather, King George VI, who was suffering from a thrombosis in the leg, in consequence of which the Family's Christmas could not be celebrated at Sandringham. The Court remained in London. In March of the New Year, 1949, an operation on the King's leg was performed, with seeming success.

Queen Mary herself had now begun to find, to her deep chagrin, that walking tired her, and she reluctantly resigned herself to the intermittent use of a wheel-chair. In the winter of 1949 to 1950 she was attacked by sciatica, which did not relinquish its grip until the summer. 'You will be glad to hear I am better at last & that the rather better weather has put an end (touchwood) to that dreadful sciatica', she wrote to the Duke of Windsor,¹⁴ '& I am able at long last to take up my ordinary activities to a certain extent in spite of my *age* which is hampering and a great nuisance!!!' The old Queen's vitality was unimpaired, but she could no longer take part in many public functions, and when the President of the French Republic, Monsieur Vincent Auriol, and his wife came to London on a state visit in March 1950, Queen Mary confined herself to waving to them from the little balcony outside her sitting-room, as they passed by in procession up the Mall. In June 1950 the sale of the carpet which she had worked, and which had been sent on a dollar-raising tour to the United States and Canada, delighted Queen Mary: 'Saw Dow. Ly Reading who told me my Carpet had been bought for Canada by the "Im. Daughters of the Empire" for £35,000 to which may be added more money by degrees —This is my gift towards the National Debt—!!'¹⁵

Neither exhaustion, nor a public appearance in a wheel-chair, could deflect Queen Mary from her determination to attend the service at St Paul's Cathedral in May 1951 at which King George VI initiated the Festival of Britain, held to commemorate the Centenary of the

Great Exhibition which Queen Victoria had opened in May 1851. 'A hundred years ago today', Queen Mary reflected, 'my mother was present at the Opening of the 1851—when she was 17—& now I her daughter was present at this opening at the age of nearly 84—Lovely service—most impressive, Bertie's speech on the steps of St Paul's was very good—At 4 o'clock I went for a drive to see the decorations in the streets which were pretty.'[16] The next day Queen Mary toured the Exhibition on the South Bank* and judged it 'really extraordinary & very ugly'. That this verdict expressed no mere idle prejudice against modernity is proved by a subsequent entry in the Queen's Diary, after she had been, later that same month, to see, at the Victoria and Albert Museum, a display of some of the original objects shown at the Great Exhibition in 1851: 'Most of them were simply frightful', she recorded, 'but I was much interested in seeing them.'[17]

For Queen Mary, in her eighty-fifth year, life still held anguish in store. In September, whilst he was at Balmoral, the King developed what seemed to be a heavy cold on the chest. Returning south to London, he underwent a bronchoscopy which showed, although His Majesty did not himself know it, that he had developed cancer of the left lung. On Sunday, 23 September, an operation, made all the more hazardous by the probability that it might give rise to a coronary thrombosis, was performed. Queen Mary spent 'a dreadful morning of anxiety' at Marlborough House, whilst reports were telephoned to her from the Palace. The reports were only 'fairly satisfactory': 'there must be *great anxiety* for several days', Queen Mary wrote.[18] She had been to see the King three days before the operation and had found him 'very thin but very plucky & reasonable',[19] but when she finally saw him after the operation she thought him 'looking wonderful after his dreadful ordeal—he was sitting in the room beyond his writing room—we had a nice talk'.[20]

The King was well enough to go with his family to Sandringham for Christmas, where Queen Mary busied herself, as usual, arranging Christmas presents in the ball-room, and was able, each evening, to dine downstairs.

---

* During the year of the Festival of Britain, exhibitions were organised throughout the country. The main exhibition in London was arranged on a site on the South Bank of the River Thames.

III

Norfolk in mid-winter did not provide an ideal climate for an octogenarian lady suffering from rheumatism, and Queen Mary accordingly left Sandringham House on the 15th of January: 'very sorry to leave them all', she noted, 'but my rheumatism was so bad there owing to the changeable weather. Arrived London before 3. Did some work ... & unpacked my things.' She had left the King in an optimistic mood about his health: 'I am seeing all my doctors next Tuesday morning, & I hope they will be pleased with my progress,' he wrote to his mother on 23 January. At this examination, on 29 January, the doctors expressed themselves delighted with King George VI's condition.

The next day, 30 January, Princess Elizabeth and the Duke of Edinburgh went to Marlborough House, to take leave of Queen Mary before their departure for a five months' tour of Africa, Ceylon, Australia and New Zealand. 'I felt', Queen Mary wrote, 'very sad at having to take leave for such a long time.' The following morning Queen Mary watched her granddaughter's Standard being hauled down from the roof of Clarence House, and listened on the wireless to the account of the farewell scenes at London Airport, where the King, hatless and in a high wind, was waving his daughter good-bye. In the afternoon the Queen went to an exhibition of 'French drawings from Fouquet to Gauguin' at the Arts Council's premises in St James's Square—'some lovely things'—and on to tea with the King and Queen at Buckingham Palace. On the 1st of February the King and Queen, together with Princess Margaret, returned to Sandringham.

Although Queen Mary was now, perforce, cutting down her activities and seeing fewer people—'I wish', wrote her brother Lord Athlone to the Duke of Windsor, 'she would see her friends a little more instead of one or two at a time. She is afraid of tiring herself talking to a number of people'[21]—the days following Princess Elizabeth's departure for Nairobi were busy ones at Marlborough House. Queen Mary received Prince Xavier of Bourbon-Parme, who told her the result of his researches into the Windsor Archives for material on Louis XVIII and Charles X—'not very successful, I fear'—as well as his nephew Prince André of Bourbon-Parme. She went to tea with the Princess Royal, drove in Richmond Park, did some tidying-up in the Family museum at Frogmore, and visited the Royal School of

Needlework to arrange about the finishing of a new carpet she had started to work the year before.

At 9.30 a.m. on Wednesday, 6 February, Queen Mary, as was usual at that hour, was working in her sitting-room when her Woman-of-the-Bedchamber, Lady Cynthia Colville, asked to see her. Looking steadily at Lady Cynthia as she came through the door, Queen Mary asked: 'Is it the King?' Lady Cynthia answered that a telephone message had just come from Sandringham to say that King George VI had been found dead by the valet who had gone to call him that morning.

From this, the last great emotional shock of her life, Queen Mary did not recover. Her Household noticed that from now on the old Queen aged rapidly. Even so she did not give in. To a lifelong friend, Lady Shaftesbury, who came to visit her about this time, Queen Mary made one of her rare references to the likelihood of her own death. 'I suppose', she said suddenly, 'one must force oneself to go on until the end?' 'I am sure', replied Lady Shaftesbury, 'that Your Majesty will.'

King George VI was the fourth English Monarch to die during Queen Mary's lifetime; and now, as in her childhood and youth, Great Britain was once more ruled by a Queen. The new Monarch, who succeeded to the throne with the style and title of Queen Elizabeth II, reached London from Nairobi the next day, at four o'clock in the afternoon. At 4.30 Queen Mary drove out of the gates of Marlborough House to do homage to her Sovereign: 'Her old Grannie and subject', she said, 'must be the first to kiss Her hand.' At Clarence House Queen Mary was received by her eldest granddaughter, who at the early age of twenty-five was thus suddenly invested with the mystic aura of the British Crown.

The coffin of King George VI, like that of his father before him, was brought from Sandringham to London, where it lay in state in Westminster Hall. This was a day of relentless rain. In the downpour Queen Mary, heavily veiled, with the new Queen, her mother, and the rest of her family, followed the late King's coffin to its place of rest upon a catafalque in the centre of the Hall. On 15 February she watched the funeral procession from her window, as it wound slowly into the Mall. She then followed its further progress, as well as the interment in the vault at Windsor Castle, on her television set.

Many foreign relatives had come over for the funeral, and Queen Mary saw several of these in the days that followed. With characteristic vigour she also set about making a new Will, and going through the catalogues of her possessions and what she called 'my interesting things' which, previously bequeathed to King George VI, were now destined to go to Queen Elizabeth II. With this end in view, Queen Mary spent many days in March and April at work on her catalogues and 'tracing' objects in her extensive collections. There was no morbidity in these proceedings, which were merely sensible measures based on the recognition of the hard and simple fact that she could not live for ever. Severely practical and orderly in life, Queen Mary was determined that her death should leave behind it no vestige of ambiguity nor confusion.

All through this, the last year of her long life, Queen Mary continued to find solace and encouragement in works of art. She visited the Quincentenary Exhibition of Leonardo da Vinci at Burlington House, examined the Hanover Family silver which was shown at the Victoria and Albert Museum, and continued to call at the shops and galleries of her favourite dealers to look at their 'tempting things'. At the beginning of April 1952 she fell ill. She remained in bed for five weeks. During this period, and for almost the first time in Queen Mary's life, the pages of her Diary are blank.

In the first week of May, Queen Mary began to feel better. She resumed her daily record of her activities, and she was soon able to make an expedition to Kensington Palace to study the details of Queen Victoria's Coronation robes, which she felt should form a precedent for those of the new Queen Regnant. Monday, 26 May 1952, was Queen Mary's eighty-fifth birthday:

Nice fine day, not so hot [she noted]—my 85th birthday! spent a hectic morning with endless presents arriving & lots of flowers—Mary kindly came at 12 & helped me, we had lunch & tea together—Between 2.30 & 4.30 a number of my family came to see me, very nice of them—hundreds of letters, cards etc. arrived—we tried to deal with them—I felt very much spoilt & had a nice day in spite of my great age—

In the summer, Queen Mary went down to stay at Sandringham for a few weeks. Back in London that autumn she carried on with her usual activities, though in a diminished form. Christmas at Sandringham found her too tired to do much more than get up in the late afternoon and stay in her own rooms. The New Year, 1953, was that of the Coronation of Queen Elizabeth II. Queen Mary, who drove out in Hyde Park in February to look at the stands being erected along the processional route, let it be known at Buckingham Palace that, should she no longer be there to attend the Coronation, this solemnity must on no account of mourning be postponed. This, we may think, was the final self-effacing gesture of one whose lifetime's single aim, as Princess and as Queen, had been to serve the British Throne.

On 9 February, a 'horrid & cold' day, Queen Mary drove for the last time through the London in which she had been born and which she loved. She did not go out again. As an icy February gave way to an overcast and windswept March, it was clear to those around her that Queen Mary was dying. Yet, on the very threshold of the tomb, the Queen retained her interest in all that she had most liked in life. On the night before she died, she asked to have a book about India read aloud to her, and the last letter Queen Mary ever wrote concerned a work of art. Dated 18 March and addressed to a friend who had sent her a catalogue of the Goya Exhibition at Basle, which contained amongst its illustrations one of Goya's portrait of his small grandson, this letter reads:

My dear Friend,
   I feel weary and unwell but your charming catalogue of the Goya pictures has given me great pleasure. I particularly like the portrait of Marianito Goya with the silk hat—as one sees it was painted with great love.[22]

During the evening of the 24th March 1953, Queen Mary died.

IV

On a lowering wintry day, to the roll of funeral drums and the military sound of marching feet, the body of Queen Mary was borne slowly and majestically through the London streets, held empty of traffic by lofty barriers painted, in mourning, royal purple.

On the thronged pavements Londoners stood silent and bareheaded as, for the last time, Queen Mary passed, on her way to Westminster and Windsor, through their midst. Most of those in that crowd could scarcely recall a period in which Queen Mary had not seemed an essential part of life in London, personifying for them all that was noblest in their country's tradition. They were conscious—some sharply, others dimly—that on that chilling afternoon they were mourning the unique.

For it was Queen Mary's crowning reward, as it is the fundamental lesson to be drawn from any contemplation of her life, that, by undeviating service to her own highest ideals, she had ended by becoming, for millions, an ideal in herself.

REFERENCE NOTES

The initials 'R.A.' stand for Royal Archives, and designate the correspondence and diaries preserved in the Archives at Windsor Castle.

Unless otherwise stated, all references to 'Kronberg Archives' signify letters from Queen Victoria to her daughter the Empress Frederick.

BOOK ONE

CHAPTER ONE

A MAY CHILD AND HER PARENTS

1 R.A., Pce. Teck to his sister Amélie, 4 Dec. 1867
2 R.A., Z 19 26
3 R.A., Pss. Mary Adelaide to her sisters-in-law, 5 June 1867
4 Kronberg Archives, 2 June 1867
5 R.A., Q. Victoria to Dss. of York, 25 May 1896
6 R.A., Q. Victoria to Pss. Mary Adelaide, 4 June 1867
7 R.A., Z 152 4
8 Kronberg Archives, 3 May 1865
9 R.A., Q. Victoria's Journal, 21 June 1867; Kronberg Archives,
22 June 1867; 4 Apr. 1868
10 R.A., Q. Victoria's Journal, 21 June 1867
11 R.A., Q. Victoria to Pss. Mary Adelaide, 27 July 1867
12 Ld. Redesdale, *Memories*, Vol. II, p. 702
13 R.A., Pss. of Wales to Gd. Dss. of Mecklenburg-Strelitz, 10 Apr.
1909
14 R.A., Gd. Dss. of Mecklenburg-Strelitz to Pss. of Wales, 14 Apr.
1909
15 *ibid.*, 18 Feb. 1909; 19 Feb. 1903
16 Ly. Burghclere, *A Great Lady's Friendships*, p. 134
17 R.A., Pss. Mary Adelaide to Gd. Dss. of Mecklenburg-Strelitz,
2 May 1851
18 Ld. Redesdale, *op. cit.*, Vol. II, p. 702
19 Ld. Clarendon, *My Dear Duchess*, p. 201
20 R.A., M 22 115 and 117
21 Kronberg Archives, 23 Nov. 1867; 7 Dec. 1867
22 R.A., A.M. A/8 378
23 *The Journal of Benjamin Moran, 1857–1865*, Vol. I, p. 93
24 Ross, *The Fourth Generation*, p. 62
25 Kinloch Cooke, *Pss. Mary Adelaide, Dss. of Teck*, Vol. I, p. 308
26 R.A., I 77 11
27 R.A., Q. Victoria to Pss. Mary Adelaide, 25 Nov. 1853
28 R.A., Y 77 46
29 R.A., Z 52 7

30 R.A., I 77 10
31 R.A., J 12 61
32 R.A., Z 7 11
33 Kronberg Archives, 27 Sept. 1858
34 Ld. Clarendon, *My Dear Duchess*, p. 116
35 R.A., Z 7 11
36 *Letters of Q. Victoria*, 2nd Series, Vol. I, p. 633
37 R.A., J 12 61
38 R.A., G 49 29
39 Kronberg Archives, 10 Mar. 1866; 14 Feb. 1866
40 R.A., Q. Victoria to Dss. of Teck, 30 Aug. 1892
41 Kronberg Archives, 21 Apr. 1866
42 R.A., A.M. A/12 895 and 896
43 R.A., Gd. Dss. of Mecklenburg-Strelitz to Duke of Cambridge, 13 Mar. 1866
44 *ibid.*, 29 Jan. 1866; 13 Feb. 1866; 1 Feb. 1866
45 *ibid.*, 13 Feb. 1866
46 *ibid.*, 12 Apr. 1866
47 R.A., Q. Victoria to Pss. Mary Adelaide, 18 May 1866
48 R.A., Gd. Dss. of Mecklenburg-Strelitz to Duke of Cambridge, 12 Apr. 1866
49 Ponsonby Papers, 28 Feb. 1878
50 R.A., A.M. A/8 390
51 R.A., Gd. Dss. of Mecklenburg-Strelitz to Dss. of Teck, 12 June 1891
52 Kronberg Archives, 13 June 1866
53 R.A., A.M. A/17 144
54 Kronberg Archives, 12 May 1866
55 Kinloch Cooke, *op. cit.*, Vol. I, p. 424
56 R.A., A.M. A/8 400

CHAPTER TWO

KENSINGTON PALACE AND MARLBOROUGH HOUSE

1 R.A., Gd. Dss. of Mecklenburg-Strelitz to Pss. Mary Adelaide, 14 Jan. 1870
2 Kronberg Archives, 15 Apr. 1874
3 R.A., Pss. May to Gd. Dss. of Mecklenburg-Strelitz, 5 Nov. 1890
4 R.A., Z 22 34

5 R.A., Pss. of Wales to Pss. Mary Adelaide, 7 Dec. 1867
6 R.A., Q. Mary to Ly. Mount Stephen, 16 Mar. 1914
7 Kinloch Cooke, *Pss. Mary Adelaide, Dss. of Teck*, Vol. II, p. 8
8 R.A., L 1 31 and 32
9 R.A., A.M. A/12 626 and 627
10 R.A., Q. Mary to Sir O. Morshead, 26 Oct. 1948
11 Kronberg Archives, 18 Feb. 1887
12 R.A., A.M. A/8 390
13 R.A., Pce. Teck to Pss. May, 21 Jan. 1871
14 R.A., Q. Victoria to Dss. of Teck, 6 May 1872; 1 July 1874
15 R.A., S 22 21
16 R.A., A.M. A/8 118
17 *Empress Frederick Writes to Sophie*, p. 263
18 R.A., Dss. of Teck to Gd. Dss. of Mecklenburg-Strelitz, 24 Feb. 1875
19 R.A., Pce. of Wales to Pss. Mary Adelaide, 12 Feb. 1858
20 Q. Marie of Roumania, *Story of my Life*, Vol. I, p. 43
21 Ld. Granville, *My Dear Duchess*, p. 210
22 Kinloch Cooke, *op. cit.*, Vol. II, p. 74
23 R.A., Pss. of Wales to Pss. Mary Adelaide, undated [? 1870]
24 R.A., Pss. of Wales to Dss. of Teck, 27 Dec. 1878
25 R.A., Dss. of Teck to her children, 14 Apr. 1882
26 R.A., Duke of Teck to his sons, 5 Apr. 1883
27 R.A., Dss. of Teck to her children, 2 Feb. 1873
28 R.A., Pss. of Wales to Pss. Mary Adelaide, 3 June 1870
29 Kronberg Archives, 2 May 1868; 7 Mar. 1868
30 Q. Marie of Roumania, *op. cit.*, Vol. I, p. 43
31 R.A., Pss. May to Gd. Dss. of Mecklenburg-Strelitz, 26 Feb. 1886

CHAPTER THREE

CHILDHOOD INFLUENCES

1 A. Ponsonby, *Henry Ponsonby*, p. 50
2 R.A., Q. Victoria to Pss. Mary Adelaide, 22 Mar. 1869
3 R.A., A.M. A/22 306
4 R.A., A.M. A/15 3682
5 R.A., Q. Victoria to Sir H. Ponsonby, 15 Oct. 1882
6 R.A., O 14 118

7 Mrs Hunt's Papers

8 Kinloch Cooke, *Pss. Mary Adelaide, Dss. of Teck*, Vol. II, p. 40

9 R.A., Dss. of Teck to Gd. Dss. of Mecklenburg-Strelitz, 26 Jan. [1875]

10 *ibid.*, 9 Feb. 1875; 26 Jan. [1875]

11 *ibid.*, 27 Jan. 1875

12 Kinloch Cooke, *op. cit.*, Vol. II, p. 91

13 Kronberg Archives, 27 Mar. 1874

14 Kinloch Cooke, *op. cit.*, Vol. II, p. 73

15 *ibid.*, Vol. II, p. 111 and p. 108

16 R.A., Pce. Teck to his sister Amélie, 6 Oct. 1867

17 Kinloch Cooke, *op. cit.*, Vol. II, p. 91

18 R.A., Pss. May to Dss. of Teck, 15 Apr. 1882

19 Athlone Papers, Dss. of Teck to Pce. Alexander George, 28 Sept. 1887

20 Kinloch Cooke, *op. cit.*, Vol. II, pp. 33–34

21 *ibid.*, p. 34 n.

22 R.A., Gd. Dss. of Mecklenburg-Strelitz to Dss. of York, 4 June 1901

23 R.A., Z 152 9

24 R.A., Duke of Teck to his sister Amélie, 10 Apr. 1889

25 R.A., Z 152 11

26 R.A., Dss. of Teck to Gd. Dss. of Mecklenburg-Strelitz, 10 Feb. 1875

27 R.A., Duke of Teck to his sister Amélie, 10 Apr. 1889

28 R.A., Dss. of Teck to Gd. Dss. of Mecklenburg-Strelitz, 9 Feb. 1875

29 R.A., Q. Victoria to Dss. of Teck, 7 Aug. 1875

30 Kronberg Archives, 3 Mar. 1875

31 Pss. Marie zu Erbach-Schönberg, *Reminiscences*, p. 181

32 Kinloch Cooke, *op. cit.*, Vol. II, p. 77

33 R.A. Pss. of Wales to Gd. Dss. of Mecklenburg-Strelitz, 10 Apr. 1909

34 R.A., A.M. A/8 49

35 R.A., Dss. of Teck to her sons, 6 May 1882

36 R.A., Gd. Dss. of Mecklenburg-Strelitz to Dss. of Teck 22 Aug. 1877

CHAPTER FOUR

RUMPENHEIM, NEU STRELITZ AND REINTHAL

1 Kinloch Cooke, *Pss. Mary Adelaide, Dss. of Teck*, Vol. I, p. 421
2 *ibid.*, Vol. II, p. 157
3 R.A., Pss. May to Dss. of Cambridge, 1876
4 R.A., Pss. May to Mlle Bricka, 12 May 1892
5 Crewe, *Lord Rosebery*, Vol. I, p. 348
6 *Autobiography of Miss Knight*, Vol. II, p. 143
7 R.A., Ly. G. Somerset's Journal, Aug.–Sept. 1863
8 R.A., Gd. Dss. of Mecklenburg-Strelitz to Duke of Cambridge, 13 Oct. 1871
9 Kinloch Cooke, *op. cit.*, Vol. II, p. 47; p. 50; pp. 50–1
10 R.A., Q. Mary to Sir O. Morshead, 4 Sept. 1940
11 R.A., Pss. May to her brothers, undated [1876]
12 R.A., Dss. of Teck to her sons, 27 Sept. 1876
13 R.A., Pss. May to her brothers, 9 Sept. [1878]
14 R.A., Q. Mary to Sir O. Morshead, 29 May 1948
15 R.A., Z 152 20
16 R.A., *ibid.*
17 Kronberg Archives, 22 Sept. 1867
18 R.A., Gd. Dss. of Mecklenburg-Strelitz to Duke of Cambridge, 28 June 1866
19 R.A., Gd. Dss. of Mecklenburg-Strelitz to Pss. of Wales, 19 Jan. 1905
20 R.A., Ly. G. Somerset's Journal, 19 Oct. 1865
21 *ibid.*, 6 Oct. 1865
22 R.A., A.M. A/8 114
23 R.A., Gd. Dss. of Mecklenburg-Strelitz to Q. Mary, 17 Feb. 1912
24 *ibid.*, 26 Jan. 1910
25 R.A., Gd. Dss. of Mecklenburg-Strelitz to Duke of Cambridge, 4 Dec. 1878
26 R.A., Dss. of Teck to Duke of Cambridge, 1 Jan. 1872
27 R.A., Gd. Dss. of Mecklenburg-Strelitz to Duke of Cambridge, 25 Dec. 1873
28 Kinloch Cooke, *op. cit.*, Vol. II, p. 54
29 R.A., Geo. V, CC 8 38
30 R.A., Gd. Dss. of Mecklenburg-Strelitz to Pss. of Wales, 19 Jan. 1909; 25 Apr. 1910

31 R.A., Gd. Dss. of Mecklenburg-Strelitz to Pce. Adolphus of Teck, 14 Nov. 1893

32 R.A., Gd. Dss. of Mecklenburg-Strelitz to Q. Mary, 23 May 1911

33 R.A., Dss. of Teck to Gd. Dss. of Mecklenburg-Strelitz, 22 Jan. 1875

34 R.A., Gd. Dss. of Mecklenburg-Strelitz to Pce. Adolphus of Teck, 26 Apr. 1885; 11 Aug. 1887

35 R.A., Gd. Dss. of Mecklenburg-Strelitz to Q. Mary, 19 Apr. 1911

36 *ibid.*, 14 Mar. 1911

37 *ibid.*, 13 Dec. 1884

38 R.A., Q. Mary to Gd. Dss. of Mecklenburg-Strelitz, 21 June 1912

39 R.A., Gd. Dss. of Mecklenburg-Strelitz to Q. Mary, 26 June 1912

40 *ibid.*, 26 Jan. 1910

41 R.A., Q. Victoria to Dss. of Teck, 30 Aug. 1892

42 R.A., Z 152 39

43 R.A., Pce. Francis of Teck to Duke of Teck, 11 July 1885

44 R.A., Dss. of Teck to Dss. of York, 20 July 1893

45 R.A., Mrs Girdlestone to Dss. of Cambridge, 30 Oct. 1873

46 Kinloch Cooke, *op. cit.*, Vol. II, p. 65

47 R.A., Mrs Girdlestone to Dss. of Cambridge, 30 Oct. 1873

48 R.A., Q. Mary's Diary, 12 Nov. 1884

49 R.A., Dss. of Teck to Pce. Adolphus of Teck, 7 Dec. 1884

50 R.A., Geo. V, CC 6 18

51 R.A., Dss. of Teck to Pce. Adolphus of Teck, 7 Dec. 1884

CHAPTER FIVE

EXILE TO FLORENCE

1 R.A., Pss. May to Mlle Bricka, 24 Mar. 1892; 20 Feb. 1910

2 R.A., Dss. of Teck to her sons, 19 Mar. 1883

3 R.A., Duke of Teck to Sir H. Ponsonby, 31 May 1883

4 R.A., Duke of Cambridge to Dss. of Teck, 25 May 1883

5 Kinloch Cooke, *Pss. Mary Adelaide, Dss. of Teck*, Vol. II, p. 125

6 R.A., G. T. Gould to Sir H. Ponsonby, 19 May 1883

7 R.A., Z 209 55

8 R.A., Ly. G. Somerset's Journal, 15 Sept. 1883

9 R.A., Q. Victoria to Dss. of Teck, 27 Nov. 1883

10 Kinloch Cooke, *op. cit.*, Vol. II, p. 128

11 *ibid.*, p. 130

12 R.A., Dss. of Teck to Pce. Francis of Teck, 12 Dec. 1883; 14 Dec. 1883

13 Kinloch Cooke, *op. cit.*, Vol. II, p. 131

14 *ibid.*, pp. 133–4

15 *ibid.*, p. 131

16 R.A., Dss. of Teck to Pce. Francis of Teck, 12 Dec. 1883

17 R.A., Pce. Edward of Saxe-Weimar to Sir H. Ponsonby, 4 Jan. 1884

18 R.A , Pss. May to Pce. Adolphus of Teck, 1 Dec. 1883

19 R.A., Dss. of Teck to Pce. Francis of Teck, 12 Dec. 1883

20 R.A., Pss. May to Pce. Adolphus of Teck, 1 Dec. 1883

21 R.A., Dss. of Teck to her children, 4 Jan. 1880

22 R.A., Geo. V, CC 5 120

23 Kinloch Cooke, *op. cit.*, Vol. II, p. 136

24 R.A., Ly. G. Somerset's Journal, 1 Jan. 1884

25 H. T. Jones, *Recollections of a Court Painter*, p. 94

26 R.A., Pss. May to Pce. Adolphus of Teck, ?th Mar. 1884

27 R.A., Pss. May to Gd. Dss. of Mecklenburg-Strelitz, 3 Mar. 1884

28 R.A., Ly. G. Somerset's Journal, 22 Nov. 1883

29 H. T. Jones, *op. cit.*, p. 70

30 Ross, *The Fourth Generation*, pp. 212–13

31 H. T. Jones, *op. cit.*, pp. 59–60

32 R.A., Pss. May to Pce. Adolphus of Teck, ?th Mar. 1884

33 Kinloch Cooke, *op. cit.*, Vol. II, p. 142 [20 Mar. 1884]

34 R.A., Gd. Dss. of Mecklenburg-Strelitz to Dss. of Teck, 9 Apr. 1884

35 R.A., Ly. G. Somerset's Journal, 6, 9 and 15 July 1884

36 *ibid.*, 28 Nov. 1884

37 Kinloch Cooke, *op. cit.*, Vol. II, p. 143

38 R.A., Pss. May to Gd. Dss. of Mecklenburg-Strelitz, 10 Mar. 1885

39 Kinloch Cooke, *op. cit.*, Vol. II, pp. 145–6

40 H. T. Jones, *op. cit.*, p. 67

41 Kinloch Cooke, *op. cit.*, Vol. II, pp. 149, 150 and 153

42 R.A., Pss. May to Pce. Adolphus of Teck, 11 May 1884

43 Kinloch Cooke, *op. cit.*, Vol. II, p. 151

44 R.A., Pss. May to Pce. Adolphus of Teck, 31 May 1884

45 Kronberg Archives, 27 Oct. 1885; 20 Jan. 1874

46 Kronberg Archives, Empress Frederick to Pss. F-K. of Hesse, 3 Feb. 1897

47 R.A., Gd. Dss. of Mecklenburg-Strelitz to Pss. of Wales, 26 May 1903; 4 June 1908

48 R.A., Pss. May to Pce. Adolphus of Teck, 31 May 1884
49 *ibid.*, 11 May 1884
50 R.A., Pss. of Wales to Dss. of Teck, 22 Dec. 1884
51 R.A., Pss. May to Pce. Adolphus of Teck, 1 Dec. 1883; ?th Mar.
    1884, and 5 Dec. 1884
52 R.A., Geo. V, CC 1 7
53 R.A., Q. Victoria to Dss. of Teck, 14 Apr. 1884
54 *ibid.*, 30 Aug. 1884
55 R.A., Ly. G. Somerset's Journal, Dec. 1884
56 *ibid.*, 28 Sept. 1884
57 *ibid.*, 12 Jan. 1885; 17 Nov. 1884; and 12 Oct. 1884
58 R.A., Q. Mary to Miss Emily Alcock, 29 May 1917
59 R.A., Pss. May to Gd. Dss. of Mecklenburg-Strelitz, 8 July 1884

CHAPTER SIX

SOME SUMMER HOLIDAYS

1 R.A., Gd. Dss. of Mecklenburg-Strelitz to Dss. of Teck, 9 May
    1884
2 R.A., Pss. May to Gd. Dss. of Mecklenburg-Strelitz (enc.), 22
    June 1884
3 R.A., Q. Mary's Diary, 7 July 1884
4 Kinloch Cooke, *Pss. Mary Adelaide, Dss. of Teck*, Vol. II, pp.
    158–9
5 R.A., Q. Mary's Diary, 2 Aug. 1884
6 R.A., Pss. May to Gd. Dss. of Mecklenburg-Strelitz, 10 Aug. 1884
7 R.A., Dss. of Teck to Pces. Adolphus and Francis of Teck, 7 Oct.
    1884
8 H. T. Jones, *Recollections of a Court Painter*, p. 78
9 R.A., Gd. Dss. of Mecklenburg-Strelitz to Pss. May, 16 May 1892
10 R.A., Pss. May to Gd. Dss. of Mecklenburg-Strelitz, 5 Nov. 1890
11 R.A., Dss. of Teck to Dss. of York, 9 Sept. 1894
12 R.A., Duke of Teck to his children, 16 Sept. 1877
13 R.A., Q. Mary's Diary, 23 Aug. 1884
14 *ibid.*, 31 Aug. 1884
15 H. T. Jones, *op. cit.*, p. 79
16 *ibid.*, p. 87
17 R.A., Dss. of Teck to Dss. of York, 21 Sept. 1894; 9 Sept. 1894
18 H. T. Jones, *op. cit.*, p. 85

19 R.A., Z 51 34
20 H. T. Jones, *op. cit.*, pp. 86–7
21 R.A., Pss. May to Mlle Bricka, 27 Apr. 1892; 4 Mar. 1898
22 R.A., Dss. of York to Dss. of Teck, 12 Aug. 1893
23 R.A., Geo. V, AA 32 22
24 Athlone Papers, Dss. of York to Pce. Alexander George of Teck, 16 Mar. 1898
25 Kronberg Archives, 28 Mar. 1887
26 *ibid.*, 24 Sept. 1889; 4 Oct. 1889
27 R.A., Geo. V, AA 31 9
28 R.A., Q. Mary's Diary, 22 Oct.; 27 Sept.; 15 Oct.; 18 Oct.; 23 Sept. 1884
29 R.A., Pss. May to Gd. Dss. of Mecklenburg-Strelitz, 30 Sept. 1884
30 R.A., Geo. V, AA 46 66
31 Kronberg Archives, 26 Sept. 1882
32 R.A., Geo. V, AA 46 66
33 R.A., Q. Mary's Diary, 24 Nov. 1884
34 R.A., Ly. G. Somerset's Journal, 18 May 1885
35 R.A., Duke of Teck to Pce. Adolphus of Teck, 30 Apr. 1885
36 R.A., Pss. May to Pce. Adolphus of Teck, 22 May 1885
37 R.A., Pss. May to Miss Emily Alcock, 2 Apr. 1888

CHAPTER SEVEN

BACK AT HOME

1 Kinloch Cooke, *Pss. Mary Adelaide, Dss. of Teck*, Vol. II, p. 164
2 Colnaghi Papers, Pss. May to Mr Dominic Colnaghi, 6 June 1885
3 R.A., Ly. G. Somerset's Journal, 3 June 1885
4 Kinloch Cooke, *op. cit.*, Vol. II, p. 165
5 *ibid.*, p. 166
6 R.A., Ly. G. Somerset's Journal, 3 June 1885
7 R.A., Pss. May to Gd. Dss. of Mecklenburg-Strelitz, 7 Dec. 1884
8 R.A., Ly. G. Somerset's Journal, 2 June 1885
9 R.A. Gd. Dss. of Mecklenburg-Strelitz to Ly. E. Dugdale, 28 May 1910
10 R.A., Q. Victoria to Dss. of Teck, 30 July 1885
11 R.A., Pss. May to Gd. Dss. of Mecklenburg-Strelitz, 4 Aug. 1885
12 *ibid.*, 11 May 1886
13 R.A., A.M. A/8 395

14 R.A., Pss. May to Miss Emily Alcock, 25 July 1887

15 R.A., Ly. G. Somerset's Journal, 4 Mar. 1886

16 R.A., Dss. of Teck to her sons, 26 July 1885

17 R.A., Ly. G. Somerset's Journal 23 July 1886; 7 Jan. 1888

18 *ibid.*, 6 June 1886

19 R.A., Pss. May to Pce. Adolphus of Teck, 9 Oct. 1885

20 R.A., Pss. May to Gd. Dss. of Mecklenburg-Strelitz, 28 Dec. 1886

21 R.A., Pss. May to Pce. Adolphus of Teck, 9 Oct. 1885

22 R.A., Pss. May to Gd. Dss. of Mecklenburg-Strelitz, 28 Dec. 1885

23 Mrs Hunt's Papers, Dss. of Teck to Mrs Master, 24 Feb. 1888

24 R.A., Ly. G. Somerset's Journal, 12 Jan. 1886

25 R.A., Gd. Dss. of Mecklenburg-Strelitz to Dss. of Teck, 15 June 1894

26 R.A., Pss. May to Gd. Dss. of Mecklenburg-Strelitz, 11 Sept. 1890

27 *ibid.*, 2 Dec. 1890; 26 Feb. 1886

28 Kinloch Cooke, *op. cit.*, Vol. II, p. 203

29 Mrs Hunt's Papers, letter of 1899

30 R.A., Dss. of York to Mlle Bricka, 9 July 1893

31 R.A., Duke of Teck to Dss. of York, 4 Jan. 1896

32 R.A., Pss. May to Mlle Bricka, 18 Dec. [? 1886]; 29 Aug. 1902

33 Athlone Papers, Mlle Bricka to Pce. Alexander George of Teck, 5 July [1895]

34 R.A., Q. Mary to Gd. Dss. of Mecklenburg-Strelitz, 4 Oct. 1914

35 Kinloch Cooke, *op. cit.*, Vol. II, p. 329

36 Colnaghi Papers, Dss. of Teck to Mr Colnaghi, 18 Feb. 1886

37 R.A., Z 152 23

38 Kinloch Cooke, *op. cit.*, Vol. II, p. 322

39 *ibid.*, p. 386

40 Mrs Hunt's Papers, Dss. of York to Mrs Master, 14 Nov. 1894

41 R.A., Pss. May to Gd. Dss. of Mecklenburg-Strelitz, 11 May 1886

42 Kinloch Cooke, *op. cit.*, Vol. II, p. 387; R.A., Dss. of Teck to Pss. May, 10 Nov. 1891

43 R.A., Dss. of Teck to Pss. May, 6 Nov. 1891

44 Kinloch Cooke, *op. cit.*, Vol. II, p. 387

45 R.A., Geo. V, CC 1 192

46 R.A., Pss. May to Pce. Adolphus of Teck, 13 Jan. 1886

47 R.A., Pss. May to Gd. Dss. of Mecklenburg-Strelitz, 1 May 1886

48 R.A., Geo. V, CC 5 1

49 Kronberg Archives, 20 Dec. 1889

50 R.A., Ly. G. Somerset's Journal, 31 July 1887

51 R.A., Pss. May to Gd. Dss. of Mecklenburg-Strelitz, 12 Sept. 1887

52 R.A., Pss. May to Miss Emily Alcock, 25 July 1887

53 R.A., Ly. G. Somerset's Journal, 3 Oct. 1887

54 R.A., Pss. May to Gd. Dss. of Mecklenburg-Strelitz, 9 July 1889

55 Kronberg Archives, 30 June 1889; 29 July 1889

56 R.A., Pss. May to Gd. Dss. of Mecklenburg-Strelitz, 14 Aug. 1889

57 R.A., A.M. A/8 397

58 R.A., Pss. May to Miss Emily Alcock, 2 Apr. 1888

59 R.A., Pss. May to Gd. Dss. of Mecklenburg-Strelitz, 14 Mar. 1888

60 R.A., Pss. May to Pce. Adolphus of Teck, 28 May 1888

61 R.A., Pss. of Wales to Gd. Dss. of Mecklenburg-Strelitz, 10 Apr.
   1909

62 Kronberg Archives, 8 Apr. 1889

63 *ibid.*, 13 Apr. 1889

64 R.A., A.M. A/8 396

65 R.A., Pss. May to Gd. Dss. of Mecklenburg-Strelitz, 6 Aug. 1891

66 R.A., Gd. Dss. of Mecklenburg-Strelitz to Pss. May, 8 Aug. 1891

67 R.A., Z 51 49

68 Kronberg Archives, 2 Dec. 1891

69 *ibid.*, 5 May 1894

70 R.A., A.M. A/8 397

CHAPTER EIGHT

THE DUKE OF CLARENCE AND AVONDALE

1 R.A., A.M. A/12 1797

2 Kronberg Archives, 3 May 1890

3 Private Papers of Q. Sophie of Greece, Dss. of Sparta to Empress
   Frederick, 25 Apr. 1890

4 R.A., Gd. Dss. of Mecklenburg-Strelitz to Duke of Cambridge,
   16 Dec. 1891

5 *The Journal of Benjamin Moran, 1857–1865*, Vol. II, p. 1255

6 Westmorland Papers, Duke of Clarence to Ly. S. St Clair Erskine,
   21 June 1891

7 R.A., Z 475 244

8 R.A., Z 475 20

9 R.A., Z 475 18

10 R.A., Geo. V, AA 36 20

11 R.A., Z 475 18

12 R.A., Geo. V, AA 36 29

13 Kronberg Archives, 3 June 1890

14 R.A., Z 475 17

15 R.A., Z 475 18

16 Kronberg Archives, 7 May 1890

17 R.A., Z 475 3

18 R.A., Geo. V, AA 39 62

19 *ibid.*

20 R.A., Geo. V, AA 39 63

21 R.A., A.M. A/12 1879

22 Kronberg Archives, 19 Nov. 1892

23 Westmorland Papers, Duke of Clarence to Ly. S. St Clair Erskine, 21 June 1891; 28 June 1891; 29 Nov. 1891

24 R.A., Gd. Dss. of Mecklenburg-Strelitz to Dss. of Teck, 2 June 1891

25 R.A., Z 52 1

26 R.A., Pss. May to Gd. Dss. of Mecklenburg-Strelitz, 8 Nov. 1891

27 R.A., Z 152 32

28 R.A., Q. Victoria to Pss. Mary Adelaide, 26 Nov. 1870

29 A. Ponsonby, *Henry Ponsonby*, p. 115

30 Kronberg Archives, 20 July 1865

31 R.A., Geo. V, AA 39 64

32 Kronberg Archives, 5 Mar. 1880

33 R.A., Pss. May to Dss. of Teck, 5 Nov. 1891

34 R.A., Dss. of Teck to Pss. May, 6 Nov. 1891

35 R.A., Pss. May to Dss. of Teck, 8 Nov. 1891

36 Kronberg Archives, 12 Nov. 1891

37 R.A., Z 51 47

38 Kronberg Archives, 19 Nov. 1891

39 R.A., A.M. A/8 140

40 R.A., Z 152 33

41 R.A., Ly. G. Somerset's Journal, 12 Nov. 1891; 15 Nov. 1891

42 R.A., Z 475 23

43 R.A., Pss. May to Gd. Dss. of Mecklenburg-Strelitz, 16 Nov. 1886

44 Kinloch Cooke, *Pss. Mary Adelaide, Dss. of Teck*, Vol. II, p. 180

45 R.A., Q. Mary's Diary, 4 and 5 Dec. 1891

CHAPTER NINE

THE FIRST ENGAGEMENT

1 R.A., Ly. G. Somerset's Journal, 7 Dec. 1891
2 *ibid.*, 24 Dec. 1891
3 R.A., Q. Victoria to Pss. May, 13 Dec. 1891
4 R.A., Q. Mary's Diary, 22 Dec. 1891
5 Kronberg Archives, 16 Dec. 1891
6 R.A., Q. Victoria to Dss. of Teck, 30 Dec. 1891
7 R.A., Z 52 3
8 R.A., Gd. Dss. of Mecklenburg-Strelitz to Dss. of Teck, 7 Dec. 1891
9 Kronberg Archives, 2 Dec. 1891
10 R.A., Gd. Dss. of Mecklenburg-Strelitz to Q. Victoria, 17 Dec. 1891
11 R.A., Gd. Dss. of Mecklenburg-Strelitz to Duke of Cambridge, 16 Dec. 1891
12 Kronberg Archives, 22 Mar. 1880; 16 May 1887
13 R.A., Pss. May to Gd. Dss. of Mecklenburg-Strelitz, 26 Dec. 1891
14 R.A., Gd. Dss. of Mecklenburg-Strelitz to Duke of Cambridge, 25 Dec. 1891
15 R.A., Q. Victoria to Dss. of Teck, 8 Jan. 1892
16 R.A., Pss. May to Gd. Dss. of Mecklenburg-Strelitz, 26 Dec. 1891
17 R.A., K. George V's Diary, 5 Jan. 1892
18 R.A., Creswell, *Eighteen Years on the Sandringham Estate*, p. 180
19 R.A., K. George V's Diary, 8 Jan. 1892
20 R.A., Z 475 137
21 *The St. James's Gazette*, 14 Jan. 1892
22 R.A., A.M. A/12 1833
23 R.A., Z 95 6
24 R.A., Z 95 9
25 R.A., Pss. May to Miss Emily Alcock, 13 Feb. 1892
26 Kronberg Archives, Empress Frederick to Pss. F-K. of Hesse, 8 Mar. 1893
27 R.A., Gd. Dss. of Mecklenburg-Strelitz to Duke of Cambridge, 20 Jan. 1892; 24 Jan. 1892
28 Ld. Ronald S. Gower, *Old Diaries*, p. 168
29 R.A., Q. Mary's Diary, 22 Jan. 1892
30 R.A., Pss. May to Miss Emily Alcock, 13 Feb. 1892

CHAPTER TEN

THE CYPRESS SPRAY

1 R.A., Pss. May to Mlle Bricka, 24 Jan. 1892
2 Kronberg Archives, 13 Feb. 1892
3 Kronberg Archives, Dss. of Teck to Empress Frederick, 24 Feb. 1892
4 R.A., Z 52 35
5 Ld. Clarendon, *My Dear Duchess*, 26 Apr. 1865
6 R.A., Ly. G. Somerset's Journal, 26 Feb. 1892
7 *ibid.*, 9 Feb. 1892
8 R.A., Duke of Teck to his sisters, 29 Feb. 1892
9 R.A., Q. Mary's Diary, 27 Feb. 1892
10 Mrs Hunt's Papers, Dss. of Teck to Mrs Master, 24 Feb. 1888
11 R.A., Z 95 20
12 Kronberg Archives, Dss. of Teck to Empress Frederick, 24 Feb. 1892
13 R.A., Duke of Teck to his sisters, 16 Mar. 1892; 17 Mar. 1892
14 R.A., Z 152 35
15 R.A., Pss. May to Mlle Bricka, 11 Mar. 1892
16 R.A., Z 152 35
17 R.A., Pss. May to Mlle Bricka, 24 Mar. 1892
18 *ibid.*, 27 Apr. 1892
19 R.A., Geo. V, CC 1 2
20 Mrs Hunt's Papers, letter of Apr. 1892
21 *ibid.*
22 R.A., Duke of Teck to his sister Amélie, 6 Mar. 1892 [? 6 April]
23 R.A., Pss. May to Mlle Bricka, 27 Apr. 1892
24 R.A., Duke of Teck to his sister Amélie, 5 May 1892 [? 15 May]
25 Kronberg Archives, Empress Frederick to Pss. F-K. of Hesse, 8 Nov. 1898; 16 Nov. 1898
26 R.A., Gd. Dss. of Mecklenburg-Strelitz to Dss. of York, 26 Nov. 1898; 3 Aug. 1900
27 R.A., Geo. V, CC 1 226
28 R.A., Pss. May to Gd. Dss. of Mecklenburg-Strelitz, 5 Nov. 1890
29 R.A., Gd. Dss. of Mecklenburg-Strelitz to Pss. May, 16 May 1892
30 R.A., Z 152 36
31 R.A., Duke of Teck to his sister Amélie, 4 May 1892 [? 14 May]
32 R.A., Geo. V, CC 1 3

33 R.A., Z 152 36
34 R.A., A.M. A/15 5814
35 R.A., Ly. G. Somerset's Journal, 2 Mar. 1892
36 *ibid.*, 3 June 1892
37 R.A., Duke of Teck to his sister Amélie, 10 Nov. 1892
38 R.A., Q. Mary's Diary, 1 Dec. 1892
39 R.A., Geo. V, CC 5 3
40 R.A., Geo. V, CC 5 4

CHAPTER ELEVEN

THE DUKE OF YORK

1 Kronberg Archives, Pss. A. of Schaumburg-Lippe to Empress Frederick, 8 June 1892
2 Private Papers of Q. Sophie of Greece, Dss. of Sparta to Empress Frederick, 18 Mar. 1890
3 R.A., Geo. V, AA 31 33
4 R.A., Geo. V, AA 31 3
5 R.A., Geo. V, AA 31 12
6 R.A., Geo. V, AA 31 22; AA 31 30
7 R.A., Geo. V, AA 36 19
8 R.A., Geo. V, AA 31 16; AA 31 17
9 Kronberg Archives, 5 June; 7 June; 13 June; 14 June 1892
10 R.A., Geo. V, AA 31 23
11 R.A., Ly. G. Somerset's Journal, 16 May 1892; 11 July 1892
12 R.A., Geo. V, AA 31 29
13 R.A., A.M. A/12 2016–7–8
14 R.A., A.M. A/12 2041
15 Private Papers of Q. Sophie of Greece, Dss. of Sparta to Empress Frederick, 9 Sept. 1892
16 R.A., Geo. V, AA 31 27
17 R.A., Geo. V, CC 1 8
18 Private Papers of Q. Sophie of Greece, Dss. of Sparta to Empress Frederick, 13 Apr. and 28 Apr. 1893
19 Kronberg Archives, Empress Frederick to Pss. F-K. of Hesse, 9 Mar. 1893
20 *ibid.*, 18 Nov. 1898
21 *ibid.*, 23 Feb. 1893
22 Kronberg Archives, 31 July 1880

23 Kronberg Archives, Empress Frederick to Pss. F-K. of Hesse,
    2 Feb. 1897
24 *ibid.*, 24 Feb.; 1 Mar.; 26 Mar. 1893
25 R.A., Q. Mary's Diary, 3 May 1893
26 *Empress Frederick Writes to Sophie*, p. 147
27 R.A., Geo. V, CC 4 86

CHAPTER TWELVE

PRINCESS MAY'S WEDDING

1 Kronberg Archives, 13 May 1893
2 R.A., Pss. of Wales to Pss. May, 12 May 1893
3 R.A., Geo. V, CC 1 10
4 Kronberg Archives, 17 May 1893
5 R.A., Geo. V, CC 5 15
6 R.A., Geo. V, CC 1 20
7 R.A., Geo. V, CC 1 16
8 R.A., Geo. V, CC 5 20
9 R.A., Geo. V, CC 1 10
10 R.A., Geo. V, CC 5 9
11 R.A., Ly. G. Somerset's Journal, 14 May 1893
12 R.A., Geo. V, CC 1 26
13 R.A., Ly. G. Somerset's Journal, 6 Mar. 1892
14 R.A., Gd. Dss. of Mecklenburg-Strelitz to Pss. May, 19 May 1893
15 *The Lady's Pictorial*, Royal Wedding Number, 8 July 1893
16 R.A., Geo. V, CC 5 21
17 Kronberg Archives, 8 July 1893
18 Kinloch Cooke, *Pss. Mary Adelaide, Dss. of Teck*, Vol. II, p. 247
19 Kronberg Archives, 8 July 1893
20 R.A., Q. Victoria's Journal, 6 July 1893
21 R.A., Ly. G. Somerset's Journal, 6 July 1893
22 Kronberg Archives, 8 July 1893
23 R.A., Dss. of Teck to Dss. of York, 9 July 1893
24 Kronberg Archives, 6 Dec. 1891
25 *ibid.*, 3 July 1893

BOOK TWO

CHAPTER ONE

LOVE IN A COTTAGE

1 Westminster Papers, Sir F. Ponsonby to his wife, 11 Dec. 1913
2 R.A., A.M. A/8 397
3 Private Papers of Q. Sophie of Greece, Dss. of Sparta to Empress Frederick, July 1896
4 *ibid.*, 9 Aug. 1895
5 R.A., Gd. Dss. of Mecklenburg-Strelitz to Duke of Cambridge, 10 Nov. 1893
6 R.A., Q. Victoria to Pss. May, 13 Dec. 1891
7 R.A., Geo. V, CC 5 57
8 R.A., Geo. V, CC 1 60
9 R.A., Dss. of York to Mlle Bricka, 9 July 1893
10 R.A., Gd. Dss. of Mecklenburg-Strelitz to Dss. of York, 11 July 1893
11 Athlone Papers, Dss. of Teck to Pce. Alexander George of Teck, 27 Nov. 1893
12 R.A., Dss. of Teck to Dss. of York, 11 Feb. 1894
13 R.A., Geo. V, CC 1 43
14 R.A., Geo. V, CC 1 76
15 R.A., Geo. V, CC 5 76
16 R.A., Z 152 61
17 R.A., Dss. of York to Dss. of Teck, 21 July 1893

CHAPTER TWO

THE POWER AND THE GLORY

1 Kronberg Archives, 5 Aug. 1893
2 R.A., Dss. of York to Dss. of Teck, 3 Aug. 1893
3 Q. Marie of Roumania, *Story of my Life*, Vol. I, p. 23
4 Kronberg Archives, Empress Frederick to Pss. F-K. of Hesse, 13 Feb. 1893
5 *ibid.*, 4 Feb. 1894; 2 Feb. 1893; 16 Feb. 1893
6 R.A., Dss. of York to Dss. of Teck, 12 Aug. 1893

7 Kronberg Archives, 5 Aug. 1893

8 Kronberg Archives, Empress Frederick to Pss. F-K. of Hesse, 2 Feb. 1893

9 R.A., Dss. of York to Dss. of Teck, 3 Aug. 1893

10 R.A., *ibid.*, 13 Aug. 1893

11 R.A., *ibid.*, 3 Aug. 1893

12 R.A., *ibid.*

13 R.A., Gd. Dss. of Mecklenburg-Strelitz to Dss. of York, 10 Aug. 1893

14 R.A., Dss. of York to Dss. of Teck, 3 Aug. 1893

15 Kronberg Archives, 5 Aug. 1893

16 *Journal & Letters of Reginald Viscount Esher*, Vol. II, p. 255

17 R.A., Gd. Dss. of Mecklenburg-Strelitz to Duke of Cambridge, 28 Oct. 1892

18 R.A., *ibid.*, 25 Feb. 1893

19 R.A., Geo. V, CC 3 13

20 R.A., Geo. V, AA 32 21

21 Athlone Papers, Dss. of York to Pce. Alexander George of Teck, 23 Dec. 1897

22 R.A., Q. Mary to K. George VI, 4 Oct. 1938

23 R.A., Dss. of Teck to Dss. of York, 20 Oct. 1893

24 Augustus Hare, *The Story of my Life*, Vol. VI, p. 399 [Nov. 1895]

25 R.A., Q. Victoria to Dss. of Teck, 30 Dec. 1891

26 Athlone Papers, Dss. of Teck to Pce. Alexander George of Teck, 5 Apr. 1895

27 R.A., Dss. of Teck to Dss. of York, 7 May 1896

28 Wheeler Papers, Q. Mary to Ly. B. Dawkins, 13 July 1940

29 R.A., Gd. Dss. of Mecklenburg-Strelitz to Dss. of York, 28 July 1893

30 R.A., Gd. Dss. of Mecklenburg-Strelitz to Pce. Adolphus of Teck, 18 Mar. 1895

31 R.A., Dss. of Teck to Gd. Dss. of Mecklenburg-Strelitz, 16 Feb. 1875

32 R.A., Geo. V, CC 1 162

33 R.A., Geo. V, CC 2 92

34 Kronberg Archives, Empress Frederick to Pss. F-K. of Hesse, 14 Mar. 1894

35 R.A., Dss. of Teck to Dss. of York, 25 Oct. 1894

36 R.A., Geo. V, CC 5 76

37 R.A., Geo. V, CC 1 78

38 R.A., Dss. of Teck to Dss. of York, 26 Feb. 1894

39 R.A., Ly. G. Somerset's Journal, 30 Apr. 1893

40 R.A., Dss. of Teck to Dss. of York, 11 Feb. 1894

41 R.A., Dss. of York to Mlle Bricka, 25 Mar. 1897

42 Kronberg Archives, Empress Frederick to Pss. F-K. of Hesse, 11 Mar. 1897

43 R.A., Geo. V, CC 5 202

44 Athlone Papers, Dss. of York to Pce. Alexander George of Teck, 30 Aug. 1895

45 *The Times*, 25 June 1894

46 Kronberg Archives, 19 June 1894

47 R.A., Gd. Dss. of Mecklenburg-Strelitz to Dss. of Teck, 18 June 1894

48 R.A., Z 56 19

49 Kronberg Archives, 14 May 1894

50 *ibid.*, 21 April 1893

51 Kronberg Archives, Empress Frederick to Pss. F-K. of Hesse, 2 Feb. 1897

52 R.A., Gd. Dss. of Mecklenburg-Strelitz to Dss. of Teck, 25 June 1894

53 *The Times*, 25 June 1894

54 Kronberg Archives, 27 June 1894

55 R.A., Z 477, Vol. II, 156

56 R.A., Z 477, Vol. II, 183

57 R.A., Z 477, Vol. II, 184

58 R.A., Geo. V, AA 31 37

59 R.A., Geo. V, CC 1 67

60 R.A., Geo. V, CC 5 64

61 R.A., Geo. V, CC 1 73

62 R.A., Geo. V, CC 1 67

63 R.A., Geo. V, CC 1 60

64 Kronberg Archives, 1 Aug. 1894

65 R.A., Dss. of York to Gd. Dss. of Mecklenburg-Strelitz, 16 Aug. 1894

66 R.A., Geo. V, CC 1 34

67 R.A., Z 55 73

68 Athlone Papers, Mlle Bricka to Pce. Alexander George of Teck, 26 July [? 1895]

69 R.A., Dss. of York to Ly. M. Grosvenor, 28 July 1894

70 R.A., Dss. of York to Q. Victoria, 13 Aug. 1894

71 R.A., Dss. of York to Pce. Adolphus of Teck, 10 Aug. 1894

72 R.A., Gd. Dss. of Mecklenburg-Strelitz to Dss. of Teck, 25 Apr. 1894

73 R.A., Dss. of Teck's Journal, 7 Aug. 1894

74 R.A., Geo. V, CC 5 52

75 R.A., Geo. V, CC 5 70

76 R.A., Dss. of Teck's Journal, 16 Aug. 1894

77 R.A., *ibid.*, 19 Aug. 1894

78 R.A., Geo. V, CC 5 78

79 R.A., Geo. V, CC 1 93

80 R.A., Geo. V, CC 5 78

81 R.A., Dss. of Teck to Ly. M. Grosvenor, 3 Nov. 1894

82 R.A., Gd. Dss. of Mecklenburg-Strelitz to Dss. of York, 17 Nov. 1894

83 R.A., Geo. V, CC 5 79

84 R.A., Geo. V, CC 1 83

85 R.A., Geo. V, CC 1 86

86 R.A., Geo. V, CC 5 90

87 R.A., Geo. V, CC 1 88

88 R.A., Z 152 52

89 R.A., Geo. V, CC 5 103

90 R.A., Geo. V, CC 5 104

91 R.A., Z 152 53

92 R.A., *ibid.*

93 HRH Duke of Windsor, *A King's Story*, p. 51

CHAPTER THREE

IN THE SHADOW

1 *The St James's Gazette*, 14 Jan. 1892

2 Gore, *King George V*, pp. 128–9

3 Kronberg Archives, Empress Frederick to Pss. F-K. of Hesse, 7 Mar. 1894

4 *ibid.*, 28 Feb. 1894

5 Athlone Papers, Dss. of York to Pce. Alexander George of Teck, 13 July 1895

6 Athlone Papers, Dss. of Teck to Pce. Alexander George of Teck, 21 June 1895

7 R.A., Pss. of Wales to Mlle Bricka, 30 Aug. 1906

8 R.A., Z 477, Vol. II, 272

9 Augustus Hare, *The Story of my Life*, Vol. VI, p. 516. [Journal dated 31 [*sic*] Sept. 1899]

10 Athlone Papers, Dss. of Teck to Pce. Alexander George of Teck, 20 Dec. 1895

11 R.A., Dss. of York to Mlle Bricka, 9 Jan. 1896

12 Athlone Papers, Dss. of Teck to Pce. Alexander George of Teck, 17 Jan. 1896

13 Athlone Papers, Ly. E. Dugdale to Dss. of Teck, 17 Dec. 1895 (Copy)

14 R.A., Z 477, Vol. II, 236

15 R.A., Z 477, Vol. II, 235

16 R.A., *ibid.*

17 Kronberg Archives, 22 Dec. 1895

18 Athlone Papers, Dss. of Teck to Pce. Alexander George of Teck, 17 Jan. 1896

19 R.A., Gd. Dss. of Mecklenburg-Strelitz to Pce. Adolphus of Teck, 1 Feb. 1896

20 R.A., Dss. of York to Pce. Adolphus of Teck, 28 Jan. 1896

21 R.A., Dss. of Teck to Dss. of York, 21 Jan. 1896

22 R.A., *ibid.*, 9 Feb. 1896

23 R.A., Pce. Francis of Teck to Dss. of Teck, 21 Dec. 1895

24 R.A., Q. Victoria to Dss. of Teck, 4 Dec. 1895

25 R.A., Pce. Francis of Teck to Dss. of Teck, 10 June 1896; 4 Apr. 1897

26 R.A., Dss. of York to Dss. of Teck, 30 Apr. 1896

27 R.A., Pce. Francis of Teck to Dss. of Teck, 25 Sept. 1896; 21 Oct. 1896

28 R.A., *ibid.*, 8 Feb. 1897

29 R.A., *ibid.*, 21 Aug. 1896

30 Athlone Papers, Dss. of Teck to Pce. Alexander George of Teck, 29 Aug. 1895

31 R.A., Gd. Dss. of Mecklenburg-Strelitz to Pce. Adolphus of Teck, 22 Aug. 1895

32 Athlone Papers, Dss. of Teck to Pce. Alexander George of Teck, 5 July 1895

33 R.A., Pce. Francis of Teck to Dss. of Teck, 2 July 1896; 22 July 1896

34 Kronberg Archives, Empress Frederick to Pss. F-K. of Hesse, 20 Feb. 1895

35 Kronberg Archives, 5 June 1894

36 *ibid.*, 23 June 1894

37 Athlone Papers, Mlle Bricka to Pce. Alexander George of Teck, 1 Nov. 1895

38 R.A., Geo. V, CC 5 135

39 Athlone Papers, Dss. of Teck to Pce. Alexander George of Teck, 12 Mar. 1896

40 R.A., Pce. Francis of Teck to Dss. of Teck, 3 April [? 1896]

41 R.A., Geo. V, AA 31 42

42 R.A., Geo. V, CC 5 192

43 R.A., Dss. of York to Dss. of Teck, 9 Sept. 1896

44 R.A., Prince of Wales to Pce. Adolphus of Teck, 26 Dec. 1906

45 R.A., Ly. M. Lygon to Dss. of Teck, 22 Apr. 1896

46 R.A., Dss. of York to Dss. of Teck, 15 Apr. 1896

47 R.A., *ibid.*, 18 Apr. 1896

48 R.A., Dss. of York to Q. Victoria, 27 Apr. 1896

49 R.A., Dss. of York to Dss. of Teck, 30 Apr. 1896

50 R.A., Ly. M. Lygon to Dss. of Teck, 6 May 1896

51 R.A., *ibid.*

52 R.A., Dss. of York to Dss. of Teck, 3 May 1896

53 R.A., Ly. M. Lygon to Dss. of Teck, 6 May 1896

54 R.A., Geo. V, CC 2 67

55 Athlone Papers, Dss. of York to Pce. Alexander George of Teck, 6 Sept. 1898

56 R.A., Pss. of Wales to Gd. Dss. of Mecklenburg-Strelitz, 6 Apr. 1902

57 Westminster Papers, Sir F. Ponsonby to his Mother, 20 Apr. 1904

58 *Journals & Letters of Reginald Viscount Esher*, Vol. II, p. 140

59 R.A., Geo. V, AA 32 22

60 R.A., Geo. V, CC 3 88

61 R.A., Dss. of York to Dss. of Teck, 30 Apr. 1896

62 Kronberg Archives, 11 Aug. 1866

63 R.A., Pss. of Wales to Gd. Dss. of Mecklenburg-Strelitz, 14 Mar. 1909

64 R.A., Q. Alexandra to Pss. of Wales, 21 Jan. 1908

65 R.A., Geo. V, CC 4 3

66 R.A., Dss. of York to Gd. Dss. of Mecklenburg-Strelitz, 27 Aug. 1898

67 R.A., Gd. Dss. of Mecklenburg-Strelitz to Duke of Cambridge, 29 Sept. 1898; to Dss. of York, 1 Oct. 1898

68 R.A., Geo. V, CC 5 155

69 R.A., Geo. V, CC 5 170

70 R.A., Q. Mary's Diary, 3 Sept. 1896

71 R.A. Geo. V, CC 5 181

72 R.A., Pce. Francis of Teck to Dss. of Teck, 3 Oct. 1896

73 R.A., Geo. V, CC 5 182

74 R.A., Z 53 21

75 Kronberg Archives, 30 May 1893

76 R.A., Dss. of York to Gd. Dss. of Mecklenburg-Strelitz, 25 Sept. 1896

77 *Empress Frederick Writes to Sophie*, pp. 230–1

78 Private Papers of Q. Sophie of Greece, Dss. of Sparta to Empress Frederick, 17 Sept. 1896

79 Athlone Papers, Dss. of Teck to Pce. Alexander George of Teck, 19 Sept. 1895

80 *Empress Frederick Writes to Sophie*, p. 229

81 *ibid.*, p. 287

82 R.A., Dss. of York to Dss. of Teck, 9 Sept. 1896

83 R.A., *ibid.*

84 Kronberg Archives, 5 May 1897

85 Mrs Hunt's Papers, Mlle Bricka to Mrs Master, Dec. 1896

86 Kronberg Archives, Empress Frederick to Pss. F-K. of Hesse, 4 Mar. 1897

87 R.A., Pce. Francis of Teck to Dss. of Teck, 27 Apr. 1897

88 R.A., Geo. V, CC 5 186

89 Kinloch Cooke, *Pss. Mary Adelaide, Dss. of Teck*, Vol. II, p. 298

90 R.A., Duke of York to Dss. of Teck, 6 May 1897

91 R.A., Dss. of Teck to Dss. of York, 8 May 1897; 15 May 1897

92 Kinloch Cooke, *op. cit.*, Vol. II, p. 301

93 R.A., Gd. Dss. of Mecklenburg-Strelitz to Dss. of Teck, 27 Apr. 1897

94 *Empress Frederick Writes to Sophie*, p. 253

95 R.A., Gd. Dss. of Mecklenburg-Strelitz to Pce. Adolphus of Teck, 19 June 1897

96 R.A., Dss. of Teck to Dss. of York, 22 Sept. 1897

97 Athlone Papers, Gd. Dss. of Mecklenburg-Strelitz to Pce. Alexander George of Teck, 7 Oct. 1897

98 R.A., Pce. Francis of Teck to Dss. of Teck, 9 Oct. 1897

99 R.A., Q. Mary's Diary, 26 Oct. 1897

100 R.A., Geo. V, CC 5 226
101 R.A., K. George V's Diary, 27 Oct. 1897
102 R.A., A.M. A/8 55
103 R.A., Ly. E. Dugdale to Dss. of York, [? 30th Oct. 1897]
104 R.A., Dss. of York to Q. Victoria, 27 Oct. 1897
105 R.A., Dss. of York to Gd. Dss. of Mecklenburg-Strelitz, 3 Nov. 1897
106 R.A., Gd. Dss. of Mecklenburg-Strelitz to Dss. of York, 28 Oct. 1897
107 Athlone Papers, Pce. Alexander George of Teck to Gd. Dss. of Mecklenburg-Strelitz, 15 Dec. 1897
108 R.A., A.M. A/17 952
109 R.A., A.M. A/4 144
110 Kronberg Archives, 9 Oct. 1897; 15 Oct. 1897

CHAPTER FOUR

'GOOD BYE TO THE OLD CENTURY'

1 R.A., Gd. Dss. of Mecklenburg-Strelitz to Dss. of York, 17 Feb. 1898
2 Athlone Papers, Dss. of York to Pce. Alexander George of Teck, 10 Mar. 1898
3 R.A., Dss. of York to Dss. of Teck, 15 Apr. 1896
4 R.A., Gd. Dss. of Mecklenburg-Strelitz to Dss. of Teck, 25 June 1894
5 R.A., Gd. Dss. of Mecklenburg-Strelitz to Dss. of York, 6 Apr. 1898
6 Kronberg Archives, 21 Dec. 1897; 9 Jan. 1898
7 R.A., Geo. V, CC 6 18
8 R.A., Geo. V, CC 2 25
9 R.A., Geo. V, CC 6 6
10 R.A., Q. Victoria to Dss. of York, 9 Oct. 1897
11 R.A., Dss. of York to Gd. Dss. of Mecklenburg-Strelitz, 27 Jan. 1901
12 R.A., Geo. V, CC 5 126
13 R.A., Geo. V, AA 31 21
14 R.A., Q. Victoria to Dss. of York, 6 Nov. 1893
15 R.A., Geo. V, CC 6 75
16 R.A., Geo. V, CC 2 27

17 Westminster Papers, Sir F. Ponsonby to his Mother, 26 Aug. 1898; 2 Sept. 1898

18 R.A., Geo. V, CC 6 95

19 R.A., Geo. V, CC 6 76 and 85

20 Ld. Ronald S. Gower, *Old Diaries*, p. 373

21 R.A., Geo. V, CC 6 168

22 *Our King and Queen*, Vol. I, p. 221

23 Gore, *King George V*, p. 137

24 R.A., Gd. Dss. of Mecklenburg-Strelitz to Dss. of York, 14 Apr. 1900; 6 Apr. 1900

25 R.A., Geo. V, AA 32 21

26 R.A., Geo. V, AA 36 47

27 R.A., Geo. V, CC 2 186

28 R.A., Geo. V, CC 3 77

29 R.A., Dss. of York to Miss E. Alcock, 30 Dec. 1900

30 R.A., Gd. Dss. of Mecklenburg-Strelitz to Dss. of York, 26 Dec. 1899

BOOK THREE

CHAPTER ONE

THE NEW CENTURY

1 R.A., Q. Mary's Diary, 22 Jan. 1901
2 R.A., Dss. of York to Gd. Dss. of Mecklenburg-Strelitz, 27 Jan. 1901
3 R.A., Dss. of York to Mlle Bricka, 26 Jan. 1901
4 Gore, *K. George V*, p. 148
5 R.A., Dss. of York to Gd. Dss. of Mecklenburg-Strelitz, 3 Feb. 1901
6 R.A., Gd. Dss. of Mecklenburg-Strelitz to Dss. of York, 6 Feb. 1901
7 R.A., *ibid.*, 27 Dec. 1900
8 R.A., Gd. Dss. of Mecklenburg-Strelitz to Duke of Cambridge, 19 Feb. 1901
9 R.A., Gd. Dss. of Mecklenburg-Strelitz to Dss. of York, 20 Mar. 1901
10 R.A., Geo. V, CC 7 3
11 R.A., Geo. V, CC 7 11
12 R.A., Geo. V, AA 32 30
13 R.A., Q. Mary to Gd. Dss. of Mecklenburg-Strelitz, 29 Oct. 1915
14 R.A., *ibid.*, 28 May 1901
15 R.A., Geo. V, CC 3 3
16 R.A., Dss. of York to Mlle Bricka, 17 May 1901; 27 Nov. 1906; and 16 Sept. 1897
17 R.A., Q. Mary to Gd. Dss. of Mecklenburg-Strelitz, 12 June 1910
18 R.A., Pss. of Wales to Gd. Dss. of Mecklenburg-Strelitz, 24 Jan. 1909
19 R.A., Gd. Dss. of Mecklenburg-Strelitz to Duke of Teck, 20 Aug. 1910
20 Kronberg Archives, 30 Dec. 1865; 6 Jan. 1866; and 15 Nov. 1866
21 R.A., Gd. Dss. of Mecklenburg-Strelitz to Dss. of York, 15 June 1901
22 R.A., Dss. of York to Gd. Dss. of Mecklenburg-Strelitz, 17 June 1901
23 R.A., *ibid.*, 4 Dec. 1904
24 R.A., *ibid.*, 16 Feb. 1901
25 R.A., *ibid.*, 27 Jan. 1901

26 Ly. M. Lygon to Ly. Ampthill, 22 Feb. 1901

27 R.A., Dss. of York to Gd. Dss. of Mecklenburg-Strelitz, 16 Sept. 1900

28 R.A., Gd. Dss. of Mecklenburg-Strelitz to Dss. of York, 20 Sept. 1900

29 R.A., Gd. Dss. of Mecklenburg-Strelitz to Duke of Cambridge, 24 Sept. 1900

30 R.A., Geo. V, CC 2 238

31 R.A., Gd. Dss. of Mecklenburg-Strelitz to Duke of Cambridge, 14 Mar. 1901

32 R.A., Geo. V, AA 36 48

33 R.A., Gd. Dss. of Mecklenburg-Strelitz to Duke of Cambridge, 18 Mar. 1901

34 R.A., Dss. of York to Mlle Bricka, 16 Apr. 1901

35 R.A., Q. Mary's Diary, 30 Mar. 1901

36 Ly. M. Lygon to Ly. Ampthill, 14 May 1901; 28 May 1901; and 20 July 1901

37 R.A., Pce. Alexander George of Teck to Duke of Teck, 17 May 1901

38 R.A., Geo. V, AA 36 55; and AA 36 53

39 R.A., Pss. of Wales to Mlle Bricka, 27 Nov. 1906

40 R.A., Geo. V, CC 3 3

41 R.A., Geo. V, CC 7 4

42 R.A., Gd. Dss. of Mecklenburg-Strelitz to Pss. of Wales, 16 Jan. 1902

43 R.A., Pss. of Wales to Gd. Dss. of Mecklenburg-Strelitz, 24 Jan. 1902

44 R.A., Gd. Dss. of Mecklenburg-Strelitz to Dss. of York, 1 July 1901; and 26 May 1901

45 R.A., Q. Mary's Diary, 24 June 1902

46 Ly. M. Lygon to Ly. Ampthill, 27 June 1902

47 Mrs Hunt's Papers

48 Lee, *King Edward VII*, Vol. II, p. 106

49 R.A., Q. Mary's Diary, 9 Aug. 1902

50 Ly. M. Lygon to Ly. Ampthill, 14 Aug. 1902; and 16 May 1902

51 *Journals & Letters of Reginald Viscount Esher*, Vol. III, p. 17

52 R.A., Geo. V, CC 3 30

53 R.A., Geo. V, CC 7 36

54 R.A., Pss. of Wales to Mlle Bricka, 1 Aug. 1902

55 R.A., Geo. V, AA 32 39

56 R.A., Geo. V, CC 7 37

57 R.A., Geo. V, CC 7 39

58 Ly. M. Lygon to Ly. Ampthill, 4 Sept. 1902

59 R.A., Geo. V, CC 7 42

60 R.A., Geo. V, CC 7 167

61 R.A., Pss. of Wales to Mlle Bricka, 3 July 1905

62 R.A., Geo. V, CC 7 166

63 R.A., Pss. of Wales to Gd. Dss. of Mecklenburg-Strelitz, 11 Sept. 1909

64 R.A., Geo. V, AA 32 31

65 R.A., Geo. V, AA 37 3

66 R.A., Q. Mary's Diary, 20 Apr. 1902

67 R.A., Pss. of Wales to Miss E. Alcock, 22 Aug. 1902

68 R.A., Gd. Dss. of Mecklenburg-Strelitz to Pss. of Wales, 12 Mar. 1903

69 Sir G. Arthur, *Queen Mary*, p. 100

70 R.A., Gd. Dss. of Mecklenburg-Strelitz to Pss. of Wales, 8 Apr. 1903

71 R.A., Geo. V, CC 3 18

72 R.A., Geo. V, CC 7 25

73 R.A., Geo. V, CC 7 52

74 R.A., Pss. of Wales to Gd. Dss. of Mecklenburg-Strelitz, 5 Apr. 1903

75 R.A., *ibid.*, 8 Nov. 1903; 14 Feb. 1904

76 R.A., Q. Mary's Diary, 10 May 1903

77 Ly. M. Lygon to Ly. Ampthill, 17 July 1903

78 R.A., Pss. of Wales to Gd. Dss. of Mecklenburg-Strelitz, 12 May 1907

79 R.A., Geo. V, CC 3 114

CHAPTER TWO

TRAVEL AND TRANSITION

1 R.A., Pss. of Wales to Gd. Dss. of Mecklenburg-Strelitz, 21 June 1903

2 R.A., Gd. Dss. of Mecklenburg-Strelitz to Pss. of Wales, 25 June 1903

3 Kronberg Archives, 10 July 1867

4 R.A., Geo. V, CC 8 6

5 R.A., Pss. of Wales to Gd. Dss. of Mecklenburg-Strelitz, 31 May 1903

6 R.A., Geo. V, CC 7 63

7 R.A., *ibid.*

8 R.A., Geo. V, CC 7 67

9 R.A., Geo. V, CC 6 15

10 R.A., Gd. Dss. of Mecklenburg-Strelitz to Dss. of York, 27 June 1901

11 R.A., Pss. of Wales to Gd. Dss. of Mecklenburg-Strelitz, 5 Apr. 1903

12 R.A., Gd. Dss. of Mecklenburg-Strelitz to Pss. of Wales, 8 Apr. 1903

13 R.A., Geo. V, AA 32 30

14 R.A., Geo. V, CC 5 214; and Q. Mary's Diary, 21 July 1896

15 R.A., Gd. Dss. of Mecklenburg-Strelitz to Q. Mary, 16 June 1913; and 12 Nov. 1912

16 R.A., *ibid.*, 8 Sept. 1909; and 15 Sept. 1909

17 R.A., *ibid.*, 12 Sept. 1911

18 R.A., Q. Mary to Gd. Dss. of Mecklenburg-Strelitz, 15 Sept. 1911

19 R.A., *ibid.*, 26 Apr. 1904

20 R.A., Gd. Dss. of Mecklenburg-Strelitz to Pss. of Wales, 21 Apr. 1904

21 R.A., Pss. of Wales to Gd. Dss. of Mecklenburg-Strelitz, 26 Apr. 1904

22 Ly. M. Lygon to Ly. Ampthill, 26 Apr. 1904

23 R.A., Pss. of Wales to Gd. Dss. of Mecklenburg-Strelitz, 11 Apr. 1908

24 R.A., *ibid.*, 26 Apr. 1904

25 R.A., *ibid.*, 18 Mar. 1904

26 R.A., *ibid.*, 27 Mar. 1904

27 R.A., Gd. Dss. of Mecklenburg-Strelitz to Pss. of Wales, 22 Mar. 1904

28 R.A., Pss. of Wales to Gd. Dss. of Mecklenburg-Strelitz, 27 Mar. 1904

29 R.A., Gd. Dss. of Mecklenburg-Strelitz to Pss. of Wales, 3 Mar. 1904

30 R.A., *ibid.*, 12 Feb. 1903

31 R.A., *ibid.*, 3 June 1904

32 R.A., Pss. of Wales to Gd. Dss. of Mecklenburg-Strelitz, 10 July 1904

33 R.A., Gd. Dss. of Mecklenburg-Strelitz to Pss. of Wales, 23 June 1904

34 R.A., Pss. of Wales to Gd. Dss. of Mecklenburg-Strelitz, 26 June 1904

35 R.A., Geo. V, CC 7 100

36 R.A., Gd. Dss. of Mecklenburg-Strelitz to Pss. of Wales, 12 Jan. 1905

37 R.A., Geo. V, CC 5 139

38 H R H Duke of Windsor, *A King's Story*, pp. 27–8

39 *ibid.*, pp. 24–5

40 R.A., Geo. V, CC 5 187

41 R.A., Geo. V, CC 5 145

42 R.A., Q. Mary's Diary, 16 Feb. 1907

43 R.A., Pss. of Wales to Gd. Dss. of Mecklenburg-Strelitz, 3 Sept. 1905

44 R.A., Gd. Dss. of Mecklenburg-Strelitz to Pss. of Wales, 6 Feb. 1907

45 R.A., Pss. of Wales to Gd. Dss. of Mecklenburg-Strelitz, 10 Feb. 1907

46 R.A., Q. Alexandra to Dss. of York, 19 July 1901

47 R.A., Pss. of Wales to Mlle Bricka, 13 Sept. 1904

48 R.A., *ibid.*, 19 Dec. 1905

49 R.A., Geo. V, CC 3 191

50 R.A., Gd. Dss. of Mecklenburg-Strelitz to Pss. of Wales, 5 Oct. 1905

51 R.A., Pss. of Wales to Gd. Dss. of Mecklenburg-Strelitz, 30 Jan. 1906

52 R.A., *ibid.*, 24 Oct. 1905

53 R.A., Q. Alexandra to Pss. of Wales, 29 Dec. 1905

54 R.A., Geo. V, CC 7 180

55 R.A., Pss. of Wales to Gd. Dss. of Mecklenburg-Strelitz, 31 Oct. 1905

56 R.A., *ibid.*, 8 Jan. 1906

57 R.A., *ibid.*, 20 Nov. 1905; 26 Nov. 1905; 2 Dec. 1905; 11 Dec. 1905; and 27 Dec. 1905

58 R.A., *ibid.*, 6 Mar. 1906

59 R.A., *ibid.*, 2 Dec. 1905; 3 Feb. 1906; 6 Mar. 1906; and 7 Apr. 1906

60 R.A., Q. Mary's Diary, 17 Mar. 1906

61 R.A., Pss. of Wales to Gd. Dss. of Mecklenburg-Strelitz, 26 Mar. 1906

62 R.A., Q. Mary's Diary, 19 Mar. 1906
63 R.A., Pss. of Wales to Gd. Dss. of Mecklenburg-Strelitz, 26 Mar. 1906

CHAPTER THREE

THE LARGER SCALE

1 R.A., Pss. of Wales to Gd. Dss. of Mecklenburg-Strelitz, 7 Apr. 1906
2 R.A., *ibid.*, 14 Apr. 1906
3 R.A., Q. Mary's Diary, 17 Apr. 1906
4 R.A., *ibid.*, 18 Apr. 1906
5 R.A., *ibid.*, 19 Apr. 1906
6 R.A., Geo. V, CC 3 198
7 R.A., Gd. Dss. of Mecklenburg-Strelitz to Pss. of Wales, 29 Jan. 1906
8 R.A., *ibid.*, 5 Mar. 1906
9 R.A., *ibid.*, 12 Feb. 1906
10 R.A., Geo. V, CC 8 3
11 R.A., Geo. V, CC 3 196
12 R.A., Pss. of Wales to Gd. Dss. of Mecklenburg-Strelitz, 10 June 1906
13 R.A., *ibid.*, 20 Apr. 1906
14 R.A., *ibid.*, 24 May 1906
15 R.A., Gd. Dss. of Mecklenburg-Strelitz to Pss. of Wales, 28 May 1906
16 Pss. Marie zu Erbach-Schönberg, *Reminiscences*, pp. 305–29
17 R.A., Gd. Dss. of Mecklenburg-Strelitz to Q. Mary, 20 June 1910
18 R.A., *ibid.*, 3 June 1906
19 R.A., Pss. of Wales to Gd. Dss. of Mecklenburg-Strelitz, 10 June 1906
20 R.A., *ibid.*, 24 June 1906
21 R.A., *ibid.*
22 R.A., Gd. Dss. of Mecklenburg-Strelitz to Pss. of Wales, 10 Aug. 1905; 28 Nov. 1905; and 24 Oct. 1905
23 R.A., *ibid.*, 30 Apr. 1906; and ? 16th May 1906
24 R.A., Pss. of Wales to Gd. Dss. of Mecklenburg-Strelitz, 25 Jan. 1906
25 R.A., *ibid.*, 24 June 1906
26 R.A., *ibid.*, 1 July 1906; and 24 June 1906

27 R.A., *ibid.*, 24 June 1906

28 R.A., *ibid.*

29 R.A., Pss. of Wales to Ly. Mount Stephen, 10 Feb. 1910

30 R.A., *ibid.*, 14 Mar. 1921

31 R.A., *ibid.*, 26 May 1927; 30 May 1932; and 29 Sept. 1920

32 R.A., *ibid.*, 12 Mar. 1914

33 R.A., *ibid.*

34 R.A., Pss. of Wales to Gd. Dss. of Mecklenburg-Strelitz, 14 Mar. 1909

35 R.A., *ibid.*

36 R.A., Gd. Dss. of Mecklenburg-Strelitz to Pss. of Wales, 18 Mar. 1909

37 R.A., Pss. of Wales to Gd. Dss. of Mecklenburg-Strelitz, 19 Apr. 1908

38 R.A., *ibid.*, 16 Feb. 1908

39 R.A., Pss. of Wales to Mlle Bricka, 13 Mar. 1910

40 R.A., Q. Mary's Diary, 6 May 1910

41 R.A., K. George V's Diary, 6 May 1910

42 R.A., Gd. Dss. of Mecklenburg-Strelitz to Duke of Teck, 2 June 1910

BOOK FOUR

CHAPTER ONE

NO BED OF ROSES

1 R.A., Gd. Dss. of Mecklenburg-Strelitz to Q. Mary, 24 May 1910
2 R.A., Q. Mary to Gd. Dss. of Mecklenburg-Strelitz, 29 May 1910
3 R.A., Gd. Dss. of Mecklenburg-Strelitz to Q. Mary, 20 June 1910
4 R.A., Q. Mary to Gd. Dss. of Mecklenburg-Strelitz, 18 June 1910
5 R.A., *ibid.*, 10 July 1910
6 R.A., *ibid.*, 7 Aug. 1910
7 R.A., Gd. Dss. of Mecklenburg-Strelitz to Ly. E. Dugdale, 28 May 1910
8 R.A., Geo. V, CC 4 62
9 R.A., Geo. V, CC 8 118
10 R.A., Geo. V, CC 4 63
11 R.A., Geo. V, CC 4 71
12 R.A., Geo. V, CC 8 134 and 146
13 R.A., Geo. V, CC 8 166
14 R.A., Q. Mary to Mlle Bricka, 11 Dec. 1910
15 R.A., Geo. V, CC 8 118
16 R.A., Q. Mary to Gd. Dss. of Mecklenburg-Strelitz, 2 Dec. 1910
17 *Private Diaries of Daisy, Princess of Pless*, p. 243
18 Pss. of Pless, *What I Left Unsaid*, p. 35
19 R.A., Q. Mary's Dress Books, 10 May 1911; 25 May 1911
20 Wheeler Papers, Ly. B. Dawkins to her daughter, 3 Apr. 1930
21 R.A., Q. Mary to Gd. Dss. of Mecklenburg-Strelitz, 7 May 1911
22 R.A., Geo. V, CC 3 169
23 R.A., Gd. Dss. of Mecklenburg-Strelitz to Q. Mary, 15 Dec. 1910
24 R.A., Geo. V, CC 8 121
25 R.A., Geo. V, CC 4 66
26 R.A., Pss. of Wales to Gd. Dss. of Mecklenburg-Strelitz, 20 Dec. 1903
27 R.A., Q. Mary's Diary, 22 Apr. 1902
28 R.A., Q. Mary to Gd. Dss. of Mecklenburg-Strelitz, 26 Feb. 1911
29 R.A., *ibid.*, 5 Mar. 1911
30 R.A., Geo. V, AA 37 26
31 R.A., Q. Alexandra to Q. Mary, 27 Feb. 1911

32 R.A., Geo. V, CC 8 143

33 R.A., Gd. Dss. of Mecklenburg-Strelitz to Pss. of Wales, 25 Apr. 1910

34 R.A., Pss. of Wales to Gd. Dss. of Mecklenburg-Strelitz, 6 June 1909

35 R.A., Q. Mary to Duke of Teck, 21 June 1911

36 R.A., Gd. Dss. of Mecklenburg-Strelitz to Q. Mary, 14 Mar. 1911

37 R.A., Q. Alexandra to Q. Mary, 3 July 1911

38 R.A., Q. Mary to Gd. Dss. of Mecklenburg-Strelitz, 1 Jan. 1911

39 R.A., Q. Alexandra to Q. Mary, 27 Feb. 1911

40 R.A., Geo. V, AA 37 22

41 R.A., Q. Mary to Gd. Dss. of Mecklenburg-Strelitz, 11 Feb. 1911

42 R.A., Q. Alexandra to Q. Mary, 6 Feb. 1911

43 R.A., Q. Mary's Diary, 31 May 1911; 2 June 1911

44 R.A., Q. Mary to Gd. Dss. of Mecklenburg-Strelitz, 2 Apr. 1911

45 R.A., *ibid.*, 14 May 1911

46 R.A., Gd. Dss. of Mecklenburg-Strelitz to Q. Mary, 7 Aug. 1911

47 R.A., Q. Mary to Gd. Dss. of Mecklenburg-Strelitz, 12 June 1910

48 R.A., Gd. Dss. of Mecklenburg-Strelitz to Q. Mary, 8 June 1910

49 R.A., Q. Mary to Gd. Dss. of Mecklenburg-Strelitz, 26 Mar. 1911

50 R.A., Gd. Dss. of Mecklenburg-Strelitz to Q. Mary, 21 Mar. 1911

51 R.A., Q. Mary to Gd. Dss. of Mecklenburg-Strelitz, 26 Mar. 1911

52 R.A., Geo. V, CC 8 123

53 R.A., Geo. V, CC 4 69

54 R.A., Gd. Dss. of Mecklenburg-Strelitz to Q. Mary, 22 June 1911

55 R.A., Q. Mary to Gd. Dss. of Mecklenburg-Strelitz, 21 May 1911

56 R.A., K. George V's Diary, 22 June 1911

57 R.A., Q. Mary to Gd. Dss. of Mecklenburg-Strelitz, 25 June 1911

58 R.A., Geo. V, CC 7 118

59 R.A., Geo. V, CC 5 166

CHAPTER TWO

HER IMPERIAL MAJESTY

1 R.A., Q. Mary to Gd. Dss. of Mecklenburg-Strelitz, 25 June 1910

2 HRH Duke of Windsor, *A King's Story*, p. 78

3 R.A., Q. Mary's Diary, 13 July 1911

4 HRH Duke of Windsor, *op. cit.*, p. 79

5 R.A., Gd. Dss. of Mecklenburg-Strelitz to Q. Mary, 15 Oct. 1912

6 R.A., *ibid.*, 17 Feb. 1913

7 R.A., Q. Mary to Gd. Dss. of Mecklenburg-Strelitz, 21 Feb. 1913

8 R.A., Geo. V, CC 4 230

9 H R H Duke of Windsor, *op. cit.*, p. 99

10 R.A., Q. Mary to Gd. Dss. of Mecklenburg-Strelitz, 12 Dec. 1912

11 R.A., *ibid.*, 17 Dec. 1912

12 *Journals & Letters of Reginald Viscount Esher*, Vol. III, p. 107 [17 Sept. 1912]

13 Gore, *King George V*, pp. 263–4

14 R.A., Q. Mary to Gd. Dss. of Mecklenburg-Strelitz, 13 Dec. 1911

15 Pope-Hennessy, *Lord Crewe*, p. 104

16 R.A., K. George V's Diary, 11 Jan. 1912

17 Pope-Hennessy, *op. cit.*, p. 94

18 *ibid.*, p. 96

19 *ibid.*, p. 88

20 *ibid.*, p. 95

21 R.A., Geo. V, CC 8 134

22 R.A., Q. Mary to Gd. Dss. of Mecklenburg-Strelitz, 8 Sept. 1911

23 R.A., Geo. V, CC 8 136

24 Fortescue, *Narrative of the Voyage to India*, p. 81

25 R.A., Geo. V, AA 37 34

26 R.A., Geo. V, AA 37 32

27 R.A., Geo. V, AA 37 33

28 R.A., Q. Mary to Gd. Dss. of Mecklenburg-Strelitz, 16 Nov. 1911

29 P. Jacomb Hood, *With Brush and Pencil*, p. 240

30 *ibid.*, pp. 241–2

31 *ibid.*, p. 246

32 R.A., Q. Mary to Gd. Dss. of Mecklenburg-Strelitz, 1 Dec. 1911

33 *The Diary of A. C. Benson*, p. 311

34 R.A., Q. Mary to Gd. Dss. of Mecklenburg-Strelitz, 6 Dec. 1911

35 R.A., *ibid.*

36 R.A., *ibid.*

37 R.A., *ibid.*, 13 Dec. 1911

38 *Our King and Queen*, Vol. II, p. 504

39 *ibid.*, p. 505

40 P. Jacomb Hood, *op. cit.*, p. 252

41 R.A., Geo. V, AA 37 36

42 R.A., Gd. Dss. of Mecklenburg-Strelitz to Q. Mary, 1 Jan. 1912

43 R.A., Q. Mary's Diary, 25 Dec. 1911; 26 Dec. 1911; and 27 Dec. 1911

44 R.A., *ibid.*, 20 Dec. 1911; 28 Dec. 1911

45 R.A., Geo. V, CC 4 86

46 R.A., Q. Mary to Gd. Dss. of Mecklenburg-Strelitz, 1 Jan. 1912

47 R.A., Geo. V, AA 37 40

48 Pope-Hennessy, *op. cit.*, p. 104

49 R.A., Q. Mary's Diary, 10 Jan. 1912

50 R.A., Geo. V, AA 40 13

51 R.A., Geo. V, AA 37 40

52 HRH Pss. Arthur of Connaught, Dss. of Fife, *Egypt and Khartoum*, pp. 48–9

53 R.A., Q. Mary to Gd. Dss. of Mecklenburg-Strelitz, 30 Jan. 1912

54 R.A., *ibid.*, 11 Feb. 1912

CHAPTER THREE

A LINE OF THEIR OWN

1 Wheeler Papers, Ly. B. Dawkins to her daughter, 28 Apr. 1912

2 R.A., Q. Mary to Gd. Dss. of Mecklenburg-Strelitz, 2 June 1912

3 R.A., Geo. V, CC 4 114

4 R.A., Geo. V, CC 8 166

5 R.A., Q. Mary's Diary, 24 Feb. 1912

6 R.A., Q. Alexandra to Q. Mary, 'Tuesday evening'. [? 26 Feb. 1912]

7 R.A., Q. Mary to Gd. Dss. of Mecklenburg-Strelitz, 18 May 1912

8 R.A., Gd. Dss. of Mecklenburg-Strelitz to Q. Mary, 11 June 1912

9 Nicolson, *King George V*, p. 159

10 R.A., Geo. V, CC 8 128

11 R.A., Q. Mary to Gd. Dss. of Mecklenburg-Strelitz, 20 Mar. 1912

12 R.A., *ibid.*, 25 May 1912

13 R.A., *ibid.*, 17 Mar. 1912

14 R.A., Q. Mary's Diary, 4 June 1913

15 R.A., Q. Mary to Gd. Dss. of Mecklenburg-Strelitz, 21 Feb. 1913; 13 Mar. 1913

16 R.A., Gd. Dss. of Mecklenburg-Strelitz to Q. Mary, 11 June 1913

17 R.A., Q. Mary's Diary, newspaper cutting enclosure, 4 June 1914

18 R.A., Geo. V, CC 8 128

19 R.A., Q. Alexandra to Q. Mary, 11 Aug. 1911

20 R.A., Geo. V, CC 4 73

21 R.A., Geo. V, CC 8 129

22 R.A., Geo. V, CC 4 74

23 D. C. Somervell, *The Reign of King George the Fifth*, p. 43

24 R.A., Q. Mary to Gd. Dss. of Mecklenburg-Strelitz, 29 June 1912

25 R.A., Gd. Dss. of Mecklenburg-Strelitz to Q. Mary, 2 July 1912

26 R.A., Q. Mary to Gd. Dss. of Mecklenburg-Strelitz, 7 July 1912

27 R.A., *ibid.*, 14 July 1912

28 Pope-Hennessy, *Lord Crewe*, p. 141

29 *The Diary of Arthur C. Benson*, p. 312

30 *Journals & Letters of Reginald Viscount Esher*, Vol. III, p. 84

31 R.A., Dss. of York to Mlle Bricka, 16 Sept. 1897

32 R.A., Q. Mary to Gd. Dss. of Mecklenburg-Strelitz, 7 May 1911

33 R.A., *ibid.*, 20 Apr. 1912

34 R.A., Q. Alexandra to Q. Mary, 12 June 1913; 15 June 1918

35 R.A., Gd. Dss. of Mecklenburg-Strelitz to Q. Mary, 22 July 1912

36 R.A., Q. Mary to Gd. Dss. of Mecklenburg-Strelitz, 27 May 1911

37 R.A., Gd. Dss. of Mecklenburg-Strelitz to Q. Mary, 5 Sept. 1911

38 R.A., Q. Mary to Gd. Dss. of Mecklenburg-Strelitz, 6 Oct. 1911

39 R.A., *ibid.*, 7 July 1912

40 R.A., Gd. Dss. of Mecklenburg-Strelitz to Q. Mary, 10 July 1912

41 R.A., *ibid.*, 12 Nov. 1912

42 R.A., Geo. V, CC 8 151 and 152

43 R.A., Geo. V, CC 8 154

44 R.A., Q. Mary to Gd. Dss. of Mecklenburg-Strelitz, 28 Aug. 1912

45 R.A., Gd. Dss. of Mecklenburg-Strelitz to Q. Mary, 25 Sept. 1912
   [25 Aug. 1912]

46 R.A., Gd. Dss. of Mecklenburg-Strelitz to Duke of Teck, undated
   [1912]

47 R.A., Q. Mary's Diary, 18 Mar. 1913

48 Wheeler Papers, Ly. B. Dawkins to her daughter, 19 Mar. 1913

49 R.A., Q. Mary to Gd. Dss. of Mecklenburg-Strelitz, 28 Sept. 1912

50 R.A., Geo. V, AA 37 52

51 R.A., Q. Mary to Gd. Dss. of Mecklenburg-Strelitz, 23 Nov. 1912

52 R.A., Gd. Dss. of Mecklenburg-Strelitz to Q. Mary, 17 Feb. 1913

53 R.A., Q. Mary to Gd. Dss. of Mecklenburg-Strelitz, 4 Apr. 1913

54 R.A., Q. Mary's Diary, 21 May 1913

55 R.A., *ibid.*, 27 May 1913

56 R.A., Q. Mary to Gd. Dss. of Mecklenburg-Strelitz, 1 June 1913

57 R.A., Gd. Dss. of Mecklenburg-Strelitz to Q. Mary, 29 May 1913

58 R.A., Q. Mary to Gd. Dss. of Mecklenburg-Strelitz, 1 June 1913
59 R.A., Gd. Dss. of Mecklenburg-Strelitz to Q. Mary, 29 May 1913
60 R.A., *ibid.*, 3 June 1913
61 R.A., Q. Mary to Gd. Dss. of Mecklenburg-Strelitz, 2 Jan. 1914
62 R.A., Q. Mary's Diary, 24 June 1913
63 R.A., Q. Mary to Gd. Dss. of Mecklenburg-Strelitz, 9 Jan. 1914
64 R.A., *ibid.*, 8 Apr. 1914; 20 Apr. 1914
65 R.A., Geo. V, CC 2 20
66 R.A., Geo. V, CC 6 20
67 R.A., Gd. Dss. of Mecklenburg-Strelitz to Q. Mary, 23 Apr. 1914
68 R.A., Q. Mary's Diary, 21–23 Apr. 1914
69 R.A., Q. Mary to Gd. Dss. of Mecklenburg-Strelitz, 26 Apr. 1914
70 Gore, *King George V*, p. 287
71 R.A., K. George V's Diary, 28 June 1914
72 R.A., Q. Mary to Gd. Dss. of Mecklenburg-Strelitz, 5 July 1914
73 R.A., *ibid.*, 28 July 1914
74 R.A., Q. Mary to Ly. Mount Stephen, 5 Aug. 1914

CHAPTER FOUR

A WAR-TIME QUEEN

1 R.A., Pss. of Wales to Gd. Dss. of Mecklenburg-Strelitz, 22 Mar. 1908
2 HRH Duke of Windsor, *A King's Story*, p. 107
3 V. Markham, *Return Passage*, p. 142
4 *Journals & Letters of Reginald Viscount Esher*, Vol. III, p. 180
5 M. A. Hamilton, *Mary Macarthur*, p. 197
6 Wheeler Papers, Ly. B. Dawkins to her daughter, 15 Aug.; 17 Aug.; 22 Aug. 1914
7 Wheeler Papers, Q. Mary to Ly. B. Dawkins, 17 Feb. 1915
8 R.A., Q. Mary to Gd. Dss. of Mecklenburg-Strelitz, 25 Oct. 1914
9 R.A., Geo. V, CC 8 172
10 R.A., Geo. V, CC 8 175
11 Winston Churchill, *The World Crisis*, Vol. II, p. 17
12 R.A., Q. Mary to Gd. Dss. of Mecklenburg-Strelitz, 10 May 1915
13 R.A., Q. Mary to Pce. Henry, 18 Nov. 1916
14 R.A., Q. Mary's Diary, 16 Sept. 1915
15 R.A., Q. Mary to Gd. Dss. of Mecklenburg-Strelitz, 21 June 1915

16 R.A., Q. Mary's Diary, 27 Jan. 1915
17 Wheeler Papers, Ly. B. Dawkins to her daughter, 1 Feb. 1916
18 R.A., Q. Mary's Diary, 13 Oct. 1915
19 R.A., *ibid.*, 16 Oct. 1915
20 R.A., Geo. V, CC 8 184
21 R.A., Geo. V, CC 8 186; 187; 188; and 190
22 R.A., Geo. V, CC 8 185
23 R.A., Geo. V, CC 8 188
24 R.A., Q. Mary to Gd. Dss. of Mecklenburg-Strelitz, 6 Nov. 1915
25 R.A., Geo. V, CC 8 194
26 R.A., Geo. V, CC 8 195
27 Wheeler Papers, Ly. B. Dawkins to her daughter, 17 Jan. 1916
28 *ibid.*, 16 Jan., 1916
29 R.A., Q. Mary to Gd. Dss. of Mecklenburg-Strelitz, 24 Mar. 1916
30 R.A., *ibid.*, 9 June 1916
31 R.A., Q. Mary's Diary, 7 Dec. 1916
32 R.A., Q. Mary to Ly. Mount Stephen, 10 Nov. 1916
33 R.A., Geo. V, CC 4 163
34 R.A., Geo. V, CC 8 210
35 R.A., Q. Mary to Pce. Henry, 29 July 1917
36 R.A., Q. Mary's Diary, 14 Mar. 1919
37 R.A., *ibid.*, 30 July 1918
38 R.A., *ibid.*, 9 Aug. 1918
39 R.A., *ibid.*, 8 July 1917
40 R.A., *ibid.*, 7 July 1917
41 R.A., *ibid.*, 24 Apr. 1917
42 R.A., Geo. V, CC 8 213
43 R.A., Q. Mary's Diary, 11 Nov. 1918

CHAPTER FIVE

THE NINETEEN-TWENTIES

1 R.A., Q. Mary to Miss E. Alcock, 2 Feb. 1919
2 R.A., Q. Mary's Diary, 28 June 1919
3 R.A., *ibid.*, 17 June 1919
4 HRH Duke of Windsor, *A King's Story*, p. 130
5 R.A., Geo. V, CC 8 193
6 R.A., Q. Mary's Diary, 6 July 1918

7 R.A., Geo. V, CC 8 256

8 R.A., Gd. Dss. of Mecklenburg-Strelitz to Ly. Eva Dugdale, 28 May 1910

9 HRH Duke of Windsor, *op. cit.*, p. 224

10 *Journals & Letters of Reginald Viscount Esher*, Vol. III, p. 266

11 R.A., Q. Mary to Pce. Henry, 24 Nov. 1918

12 Wheeler-Bennett, *King George VI*, p. 159

13 R.A., Geo. V, CC 8 229

14 R.A., Q. Mary to Ly. Mount Stephen, 29 Sept. 1920

15 R.A., Geo. V, CC 8 236

16 R.A., Geo. V, CC 8 246

17 Duke of Windsor's Papers, Q. Mary to Pce. of Wales, 24 May 1922

18 R.A., Geo. V, CC 4 250

19 R.A., Pss. May to Gd. Dss. of Mecklenburg-Strelitz, 6 Aug. 1891; 24 Feb. 1891

20 *Letters of Q. Victoria*, 2nd Series, Vol. I, Q. Victoria to Pce. of Wales, 29 Nov. 1869

21 R.A., Q. Mary to Marquess of Cambridge, 21 Nov. 1921

22 Wheeler Papers, Q. Mary to Ly. B. Dawkins, 28 Nov. 1921

23 R.A., Q. Mary's Diary, 24 Nov. 1921

24 Duke of Windsor's Papers, Duke of York to Pce. of Wales, 15 Feb. 1922; 28 Feb. 1922

25 Duke of Windsor's Papers, Q. Mary to Pce. of Wales, 2 Mar. 1922

26 *ibid.*, 3 Apr. 1922; 26 Apr. 1922

27 *ibid.*, 26 Nov. 1910; 7 Apr. 1920

28 Duke of Windsor's Papers, Duke of York to Pce. of Wales, 28 Feb. 1922

29 R.A., Geo. V, CC 4 206; Geo. V, CC 4 228

30 R.A., Geo. V, CC 8 304

31 Duke of Windsor's Papers, Q. Mary to Pce. Edward of Wales, 11 June 1910

32 R.A., Geo. V, CC 8 291

33 Wheeler Papers, Ly. B. Dawkins to her daughter, 1 Oct. 1922

34 Wheeler Papers, Q. Mary to Ly. B. Dawkins, 18 Oct. 1924

35 R.A., Dss. of York to Mlle Bricka, 16 Sept. 1897

36 R.A., Q. Mary to Marquess of Cambridge, 15 Feb. 1925

37 R.A., Q. Mary's Diary, 13 May 1922

38 R.A., Q. Mary to Miss E. Alcock, 21 Feb. 1923

39 R.A., *ibid.*, 30 May 1923

40 *ibid.*

41 R.A., Q. Mary's Diary, 15 Jan. 1923

42 R.A., Q. Mary to Marquess of Cambridge, 3 Feb. 1923

43 R.A., Geo. V, CC 4 224

44 R.A., Duke of York to Q. Mary, 27 Apr. 1923

45 R.A., Q. Mary's Diary, 21 Apr. 1926

46 R.A., Geo. V, CC 8 265

47 J. R. Clynes, *Memoirs*, pp. 343-4

48 R.A., K. 1918 164

49 R.A., Gd. Dss. of Mecklenburg-Strelitz to Q. Mary, 30 Aug. 1910

50 Wheeler Papers, Ly. B. Dawkins to her daughter, 31 Aug. 1924

51 R.A., Geo. V, CC 8 337

52 Duke of Windsor's Papers, Q. Mary to Pce. of Wales, 19 Mar. 1930

53 R.A., Q. Mary's Diary, 20 Mar. 1925

54 Duke of Windsor's Papers, Ld. Lascelles to Pce. of Wales, Mar. 1925

55 Wheeler Papers, Q. Mary to Ly. B. Dawkins, 30 Apr. 1925

56 R.A., Geo. V, AA 35 56 and 61

57 Duke of Windsor's Papers, Q. Mary to Pce. of Wales, 16 May 1920

58 R.A., Q. Mary's Diary, 12 Oct. 1925

59 R.A., *ibid.*, 19 Nov.; 21 Nov.; 26 Nov.; 27 Nov.; 28 Nov. 1925

60 Duke of Windsor's Papers, Q. Mary to Pce. of Wales, 26 Nov. 1910

61 R.A., Q. Mary's Diary, 30 Jan. 1925

62 R.A., Q. Mary to Marquess of Cambridge, 10 Feb. 1926

63 R.A., Geo. V, CC 8 335

64 R.A., Geo. V, CC 8 298

65 R.A., Geo. V, CC 4 255; and Geo. V, CC 4 258

66 R.A., Geo. V, CC 8 302

67 Wheeler Papers, Ly. B. Dawkins to her daughter, 5 Dec. 1926

68 R.A., Geo. V, CC 8 302

69 R.A., *ibid.*

70 R.A., Q. Mary's Diary, 5 Dec. 1928

71 W. Bagehot, *The English Constitution*, p. 35

CHAPTER SIX

THE END OF A REIGN

1 R.A., Q. Mary's Diary, 24 Dec. 1928

2 R.A., *ibid.*, 6 Jan. 1929

3 R.A., *ibid.*, 9 Feb. 1929

4 Wheeler Papers, Ly. B. Dawkins to her daughter, 10 Feb. 1929

5 R.A., Q. Mary's Diary, 11 Feb. 1929

6 R.A., *ibid.*, 14 Mar. 1929

7 R.A., *ibid.*, 1 Apr. 1929

8 R.A., Geo. V, CC 8 335

9 R.A., *ibid.*

10 R.A., Q. Mary's Diary, 15 May 1929

11 Wheeler Papers, Ly. B. Dawkins to her daughter, 25 Aug. 1929

12 R.A., Geo. V, CC 4 293

13 R.A., K. George V's Diary, 31 Mar. 1931; and Nicolson, *King George V*, p. 452

14 Bigge Papers, Q. Mary to Ld. Stamfordham, memo. of 5 Dec. 1928, and undated memo.

15 R.A., Geo. V, CC 8 342

16 R.A., Geo. V, CC 8 343

17 R.A., Q. Mary's Diary, 27 Aug. 1931

18 R.A., *ibid.*, 27 Oct. 1931

19 R.A., *ibid.*, 5 Nov. 1931

20 R.A., *ibid.*, 26 Sept. 1934

21 R.A., Geo. V, CC 8 351

22 R.A., Pss. May to Miss E. Alcock, 25 July 1887

23 R.A., Gd. Dss. of Mecklenburg-Strelitz to Pce. Adolphus of Teck, 19 June 1897

24 R.A., Q. Mary's Diary, 24 Apr. 1935

25 R.A., *ibid.*, 6 May 1935

26 R.A., K. George V's Diary, 6 May 1935

27 R.A., Q. Mary's Diary, 8 June 1935

28 R.A., *ibid.*, 24 Nov. 1935

29 R.A., *ibid.*, 2 Dec. 1935

30 R.A., *ibid.*, 31 Dec. 1935

31 HRH Duke of Windsor, *A King's Story*, p. 261

32 R.A., Q. Mary's Diary, 19 Jan. 1936

33 R.A., *ibid.*, 20 Jan. 1936 and addition

34 Sir A. Lascelles, 21 Jan. 1936

35 HRH Duke of Windsor, *op. cit.*, p. 267

36 R.A., Q. Mary's Diary, 28 Jan. 1936

37 Hansard, 5th Series, Vol. 308, column 14, 21 Jan. 1936

38 J. G. Lockhart, *Cosmo Gordon Lang*, p. 392

39 *ibid.*, p. 395

40 *ibid.*, p. 143

41 *ibid.*, p. 395

42 H R H Duke of Windsor, *op. cit.*, p. 271
43 *ibid.*, p. 270
44 *ibid.*, p. 280
45 *ibid.*, p. 311
46 R.A., Q. Mary's Diary, 13 July 1936
47 Duke of Windsor's Papers, Q. Mary to K. Edward VIII, 15 May 1936; 15 June 1936
48 *ibid.*, 30 July 1936
49 *ibid.*
50 H R H Duke of Windsor, *op. cit.*, p. 311
51 R.A., Q. Mary's Diary, 7 Sept. 1936
52 H R H Duke of Windsor, *op. cit.*, p. 311
53 Nicolson, *King George V*, p. 515
54 Wheeler-Bennett, *King George VI*, p. 276
55 R.A., Q. Mary's Diary, 8 Sept. 1936
56 R.A., *ibid.*, 1 Oct. 1936
57 Duke of Windsor's Papers, Q. Mary to Duke of Windsor, 16 Dec. 1936

CHAPTER SEVEN

MOTHER TO THE KING

1 H R H Duke of Windsor, *A King's Story*, p. 334
2 Duke of Windsor's Papers, Q. Mary to Duke of Windsor, 5 July 1938
3 *ibid.*, 17 Nov. 1936
4 R.A., Duke of York's Chronicle, 3 Dec. 1936
5 Duke of Windsor's Papers, Q. Mary to K. Edward VIII, 3 Dec. 1936
6 H R H Duke of Windsor, *op. cit.*, p. 365
7 R.A., Duke of York's Chronicle, 3 Dec. 1936
8 H R H Duke of Windsor, *op. cit.*, p. 404
9 R.A., Duke of York's Chronicle, 9 Dec. 1936
10 Wheeler-Bennett, *King George VI*, p. 287 footnote
11 Duke of Windsor's Papers, Q. Mary to Pce. Edward of Windsor, 11 Dec. 1936
12 H R H Duke of Windsor, *op. cit.*, p. 414
13 R.A., Q. Mary's Diary, 11 Dec. 1936
14 H R H Duke of Windsor, *op. cit.*, p. 415

15 Duke of Windsor's Papers, Q. Mary to Duke of Windsor, 25 Jan. 1937

16 *ibid.*, 16 Feb. 1937

17 *ibid.*, 3 Apr. 1937

18 R.A., Q. Mary's Diary, 12 Dec. 1936

19 Wheeler Papers, Ly. B. Dawkins to her daughter, 27 Mar. 1937

20 Wheeler-Bennett, *op. cit.*, p. 283

21 *ibid.*

22 Duke of Windsor's Papers, Q. Mary to Duke of Windsor, 3 Apr 1937

23 Woodward, *The Lady of Marlborough House*, p. 185

24 R.A., Q. Mary's Diary, 5 Apr. 1937

25 R.A., *ibid.*, 3 May 1937

26 R.A., *ibid.*, 9 Apr. 1937

27 R.A., *ibid.*, 10 May 1937

28 R.A., *ibid.*, 12 May 1937

29 R.A., *ibid.*, 23 Aug. 1937

30 R.A., *ibid.*, 1 Sept. 1938

31 R.A., *ibid.*, 26 Sept. 1938

32 R.A., *ibid.*, 27 Sept. 1938

33 R.A., *ibid.*, 28 Sept. 1938

34 R.A., *ibid.*, 1 Oct. 1938

35 R.A., Q. Mary to K. George VI, 4 Oct. 1938

36 R.A., Q. Mary's Diary, 7 Jan. 1939

37 R.A., *ibid.*, 7 Apr. 1939

38 R.A., *ibid.*, 22 Mar. 1939

39 R.A., K. George VI to Q. Mary, 1 May 1939

40 R.A., Q. Mary's Diary, 6 May 1939

41 R.A., *ibid.*, 23 May 1939

42 L. Wulff, *Her Majesty Queen Mary*, p. 40

43 R.A., Ld. C. Hamilton to Sir A. Lascelles, 25 May 1939

44 R.A., Q. Mary's Diary, 3 Sept. 1939

CHAPTER EIGHT

LIFE IN THE COUNTRY

1 Wheeler Papers, Q. Mary to Ly. B. Dawkins, 20 Sept. 1939

2 *ibid.*, 18 Oct. 1940

3 R.A., Q. Mary's Diary, 28 Sept. 1939

4 Wheeler Papers, Q. Mary to Ly. B. Dawkins, 30 Nov. 1939

5 R.A., Q. Mary's Diary, 22 Sept. and 31 Dec. 1940

6 *ibid.*, 25 Sept. 1940

7 *ibid.*, 12 Mar. and 20 Mar. 1940

8 *ibid.*, 12 July 1940

9 *ibid.*, 30 Aug. 1940

10 Wheeler Papers, Q. Mary to Ly. B. Dawkins, 18 Oct. 1940

11 R.A., Q. Mary to Sir. O. Morshead, 9 Jan. 1941

12 *ibid.*, 5 Jan. 1941

13 R.A., Q. Mary's Diary, 9 Apr. and 10 May 1940

14 *ibid.*, 19 and 20 June 1940

15 Wheeler Papers, Q. Mary to Ly. B. Dawkins, 13 July 1940

16 R.A., Q. Mary to Sir O. Morshead, 21 Sept. 1940

17 Wheeler Papers, Q. Mary to Ly. B. Dawkins, 18 Oct. 1940

18 R.A., Q. Mary's Diary, 21 Jan. 1941

19 *ibid.*, 13 Oct. 1941

20 *ibid.*, 28 Mar. 1942

21 *ibid.*, 4 Aug. 1942

22 *ibid.*, 13 Aug. 1942

23 *ibid.*, added on 31 Aug. to Diary entry for 13 Aug.

24 *ibid.*, 25 Aug. 1942

25 *ibid.*, 29 Aug. 1942

26 *ibid.*, 2 Sept. 1942

27 *ibid.*, 8 May 1945

CHAPTER NINE

A LONDON SUNSET

1 R.A., Q. Mary's Diary, 24 Apr. 1945

2 R.A., Q. Mary to Sir O. Morshead, 18 June 1945

3 R.A., Q. Mary's Diary, 15 and 27 June 1945

4 *ibid.*, 27 Oct. 1945

5 *ibid.*, 20 June 1945

6 *ibid.*, 12 June 1945

7 See *Guide to the Exhibition of Q. Mary's Art Treasures*, H.M. Stationery Office

8 R.A., Q. Mary's Diary, 14 Feb. 1949

9 *ibid.*, 9 June 1946

10 Duke of Windsor's Papers, Q. Mary to Duke of Windsor, 27 Feb. 1951

11 R.A., Q. Mary's Diary, 16 Sept. 1947 and 20 Sept. 1950

12 *ibid.*, 6 July 1947

13 *ibid.*, 14 Nov. and 15 Dec. 1948

14 Duke of Windsor's Papers, Q. Mary to Duke of Windsor, 2 June 1950

15 R.A., Q. Mary's Diary, 27 June 1950

16 *ibid.*, 3 May 1951

17 *ibid.*, 20 May 1951

18 *ibid.*, 23 Sept. 1951

19 Duke of Windsor's Papers, Q. Mary to Duke of Windsor, 20 Sept. 1951

20 R.A., Q. Mary's Diary, 17 Oct. 1951

21 Duke of Windsor's Papers, Ld. Athlone to Duke of Windsor, 5 Jan. 1952

22 Q. Mary to Duke of Baena, 18 Mar. 1953

INDEX

Abergeldie, 204, 372 ff., 391, 393, 396 f.

Ada Hohenlohe, Duchess of Augustenberg, 80

Adeane, Lady Elizabeth, 23

Adelaide, Queen, 28 n., 46, 49, 363, 370, 371, 423, 437, 441, 566 n., 584

Adelheid, Duchess of Nassau (formerly Princess of Anhalt-Dessau), 81, 121 n., 143, 327

Adolphus, Prince of Schaumburg-Lippe, 246 n.

Adolphus, Prince of Teck, later Marquess of Cambridge ('Dolly'), 45 f., 76, 78, 87, 95, 96, 103, 105, 111, 118, 137, 144, 161, 163, 180, 182, 203, 206, 207, 208, 211, 214, 267, 270, 286, 303, 304, 309, 310 f., 318, 319 n., 347, 349, 360, 378, 380, 385, 403, 410, 417, 438, 441, 475, 486, 518 n., 525 f., 539, 590 n.; et passim

Adolphus, Duke of Cambridge, 28, 69, 94, 97

Adolphus, Duke of Nassau, 81, 93, 121 n.

Adolphus Frederick V, Grand Duke of Mecklenburg-Strelitz, 91, 92, 98, 101 n., 288, 339, 340 ff., 389 f., 398, 437, 476 f., 503

Adolphus Frederick VI, Grand Duke of Mecklenburg-Strelitz, 98 n., 340, 503, 514

'Affie.' See Pauline, Princess, and also Alfred, Prince, Duke of Edinburgh

Albert, King of the Belgians, 527 f.

Albert, Prince Consort, 69, 204, 215, 220, 258, 311, 316, 353, 432, 566 n.

Albert Edward, Prince of Wales. See Edward VII, King

Albert Victor, Prince, Duke of Clarence and Avondale ('Eddy'), 55, 56 f., 82, 180, 187 f., 189 ff., 195, 202, 206, 208 f., 247, 259, 301, 353, 375, 421, 423, 441, 523, 553, 558, 577, 588, 608; visits India, 190; in Navy, 192; at Cambridge, 192; in Army, 192; ill-health, 190, 191, 193; created Duke of Clarence and Avondale, 194; love affairs, 195 ff., 209; question of his marriage, 188, 189, 195 ff., 207; engagement, 210 ff.; catches cold, 219; twenty-eighth birthday, 221; influenza, 222; death, 223; subject of East Anglian ballad, 224; funeral 226; constitutional effects of death, 229; photographs of him destroyed at Stuttgart, 240; anniversary of his death, 245; et passim

Alcock, Emily, 136, 141, 157, 165, 182, 227, 349, 375, 511, 528

Alençon, Duchesse d', 333

Alexander II, Tsar, 51, 307, 308

Alexander, Tsarewitch (later Tsar Alexander III), 30, 230, 242, 307

Alexander, Prince of Battenberg, 206

Alexander, Prince of Hesse and by the Rhine, 160 n., 316

Alexander, Duke of Württemberg (Grosspapa), 36, 101 ff., 118, 146, 160

Alexander George, Prince of Teck, later Earl of Athlone ('Alge'), 45, 57, 76, 106, 109, 118, 123, 124, 130, 137, 140, 141, 144 f., 166, 180, 235, 297, 301, 304, 307, 310, 318, 336, 338, 347, 349, 367, 378, 438, 441, 475, 486, 518 n., 578, 581, 589, 590, 614, 618; et passim

Alexandra, Queen (formerly Princess of Denmark, then Princess of Wales), 24, 38, 47, 52 ff., 63, 85, 89, 90, 110, 124, 134, 137, 143, 153, 154, 164 n., 183, 204, 209, 230, 231, 246, 247, 253, 254 f., 256 f., 261, 278, 287 ff., 308, 313, 321 f., 337, 348, 355, 360, 361 f., 375 f., 394, 400, 417, 422, 430, 441, 473 f.; marriage, 31 n., 53; Silver Wedding, 181 ff.; problem of Prince

Y